Next in the *ON RECORD* book series

Vol.12 1996

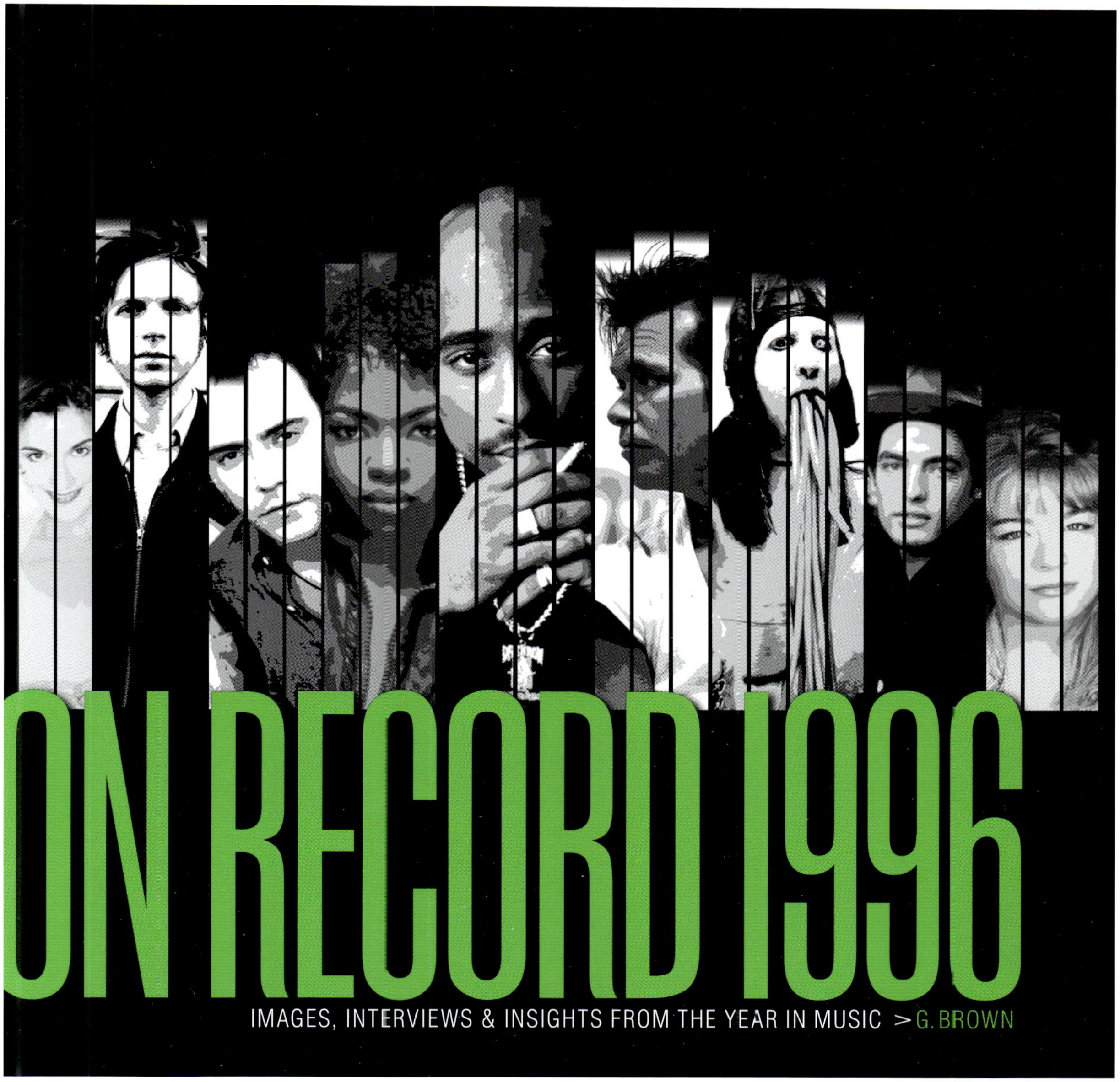

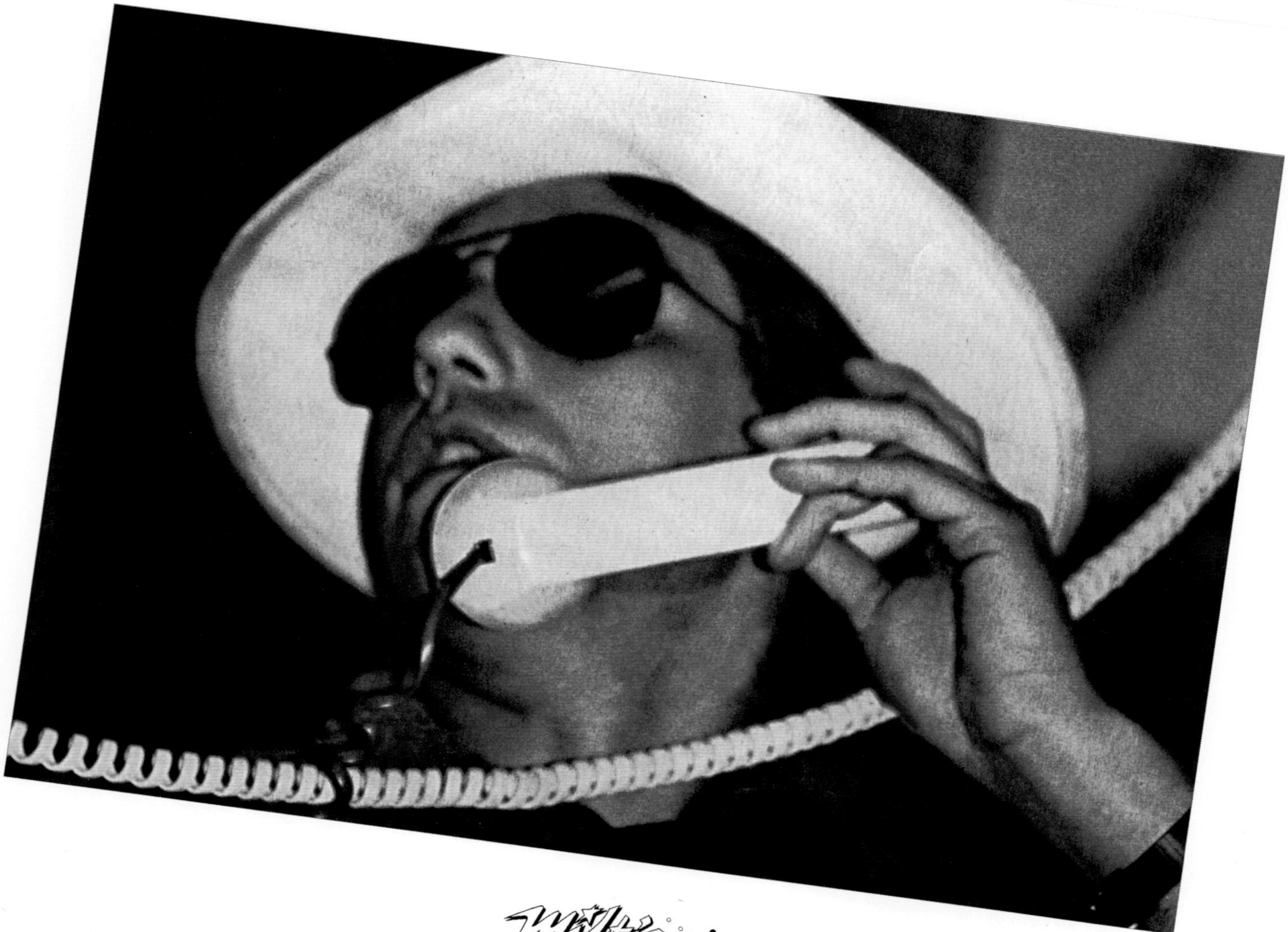

Milt's VooDoo Lounge

Laetrile Records
"it's the pits"

{ IN MEMORY OF JIM MARSHALL }

ACKNOWLEDGMENTS

Many people were essential to the creation of this book. My first thanks go to my amazing publishing team—Jon Rizzi for bringing his special brand of editorial wit and intelligence, and Kate Glassner Brainerd for her design artistry and unflagging pursuit of excellence. Special appreciation goes to the Michael & Patricia Matthews Fund, as well as John Cerullo, Annette Hobbs Magier and our colleagues at Publishers Group West.

Mike Dickson, Chip Garofalo, Jennifer Soulé, Mark Zaremba, Peter Marcus, Matt Rue, Jay Elowsky, Dave Zobl, Mark Lewis and Alexander Hau contributed expertise and resources. I am especially indebted to my dear friend Michael Jensen, as well as Sue Satriano, Janice Azrak, Bryn Bridenthal, Byron Hontas, Kathy Acquaviva, Shelly Selover, Sue Sawyer, Glen Brunman, Rick Ambrose, Bob Merlis, Bill Bentley, Heidi Ellen Robinson, Les Schwartz, Rick Gershon, Jim Merlis, Judi Kerr and Susan Blond—all of whom supported my efforts.

I specifically treasure the beneficence of Dave Rothstein, Greg Phifer, John Tope, Kevin Knee, Dick Merkle, Jeff Cook, Michael Brannen, Zak Phillips, Rich Garcia, Jason Minkler, Burt Baumgartner, Mitch Kampf, Don Zucker, Carl Walters, Charlie Reardon, Robin Wren, Jimmy Smith, Sharona White, John Ryland, Geina Horton, Michael Linehan, Mike Prince and Jeffrey Naumann, who all graciously furnished information and assistance.

I gratefully acknowledge the editing and reviewing skills of Dick Kreck, Tom Walker, Diane Carman, Mike Rudeen, Ed Smith, Jay Whearley, Mark Sims, Jeff Bradley and Peggy McKay.

I also salute David Gans, Leland Rucker, Steve Knopper, David Menconi, Jon Iverson, Gil Asakawa, Mark Bliesener, Butch Hause, Ricardo Baca, John Moore, Justin Mitchell, Michael Mehle and Harvey Kubernik, whose writings formed a vital index for the music-obsessed.

Finally, I would like to acknowledge with gratitude my beloved wife, Bridget, for her constant devotion and kindness. I cherish her—the love of my life.

EDITOR | **JON RIZZI**
ART DIRECTOR | **KATE GLASSNER BRAINERD**

ISBN 979-8-9885329-4-1   PRINTED IN CHINA | Asia Pacific Offset

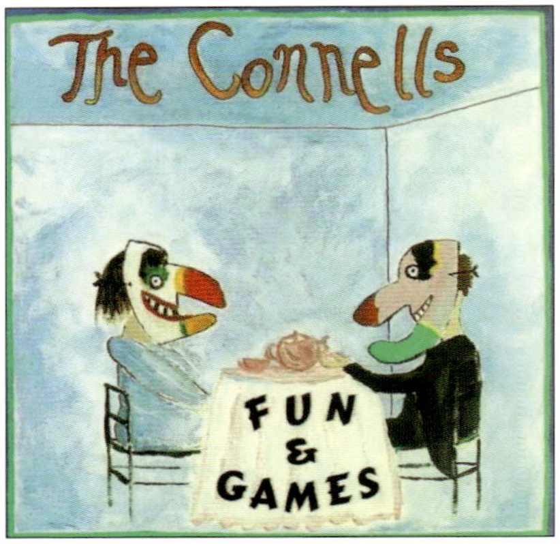

The Connells, a jangly pop act from North Carolina, released a heavier third album, *Fun & Games*, and "Something to Say" made the modern-rock charts.

Billboard 200: *Fun & Games* (#163)

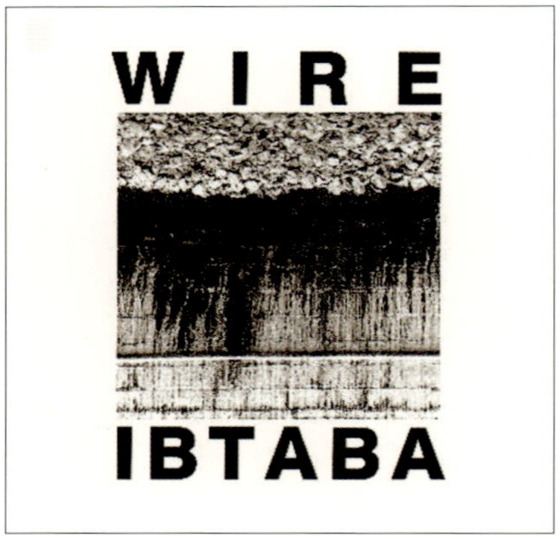

British art-punk band **Wire** issued *It's Beginning To and Back Again*, a studio reset of live tracks highlighted by the modern-rock hit "Eardrum Buzz."

Billboard 200: *It's Beginning To and Back Again* (#135)

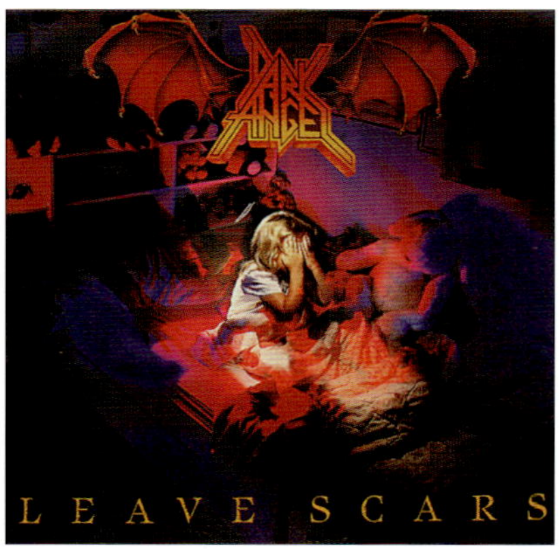

Dark Angel's *Leave Scars*, the first album to feature new singer Ron Reinhart and a progressive take, was the thrash-metal band's most successful release.

Billboard 200: *Leave Scars* (#159)

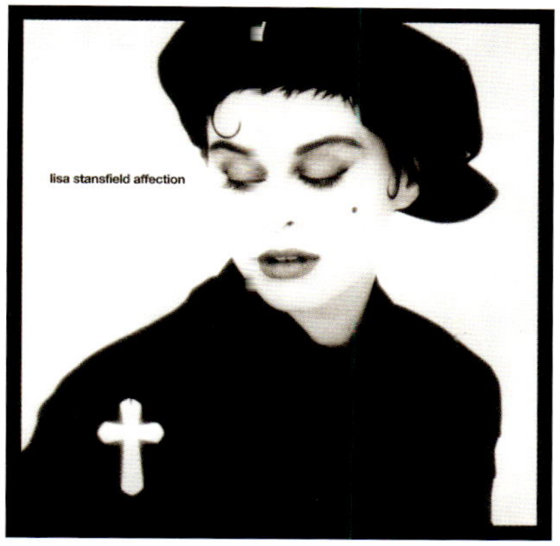

From *Affection*, her debut recording, English soul singer **Lisa Stansfield** topped the charts globally with the Barry White-inspired "All Around the World."

Billboard 200: *Affection* (#9)
Billboard Hot 100: "This Is the Right Time" (#21); "All Around the World" (#3); "You Can't Deny It" (#14)

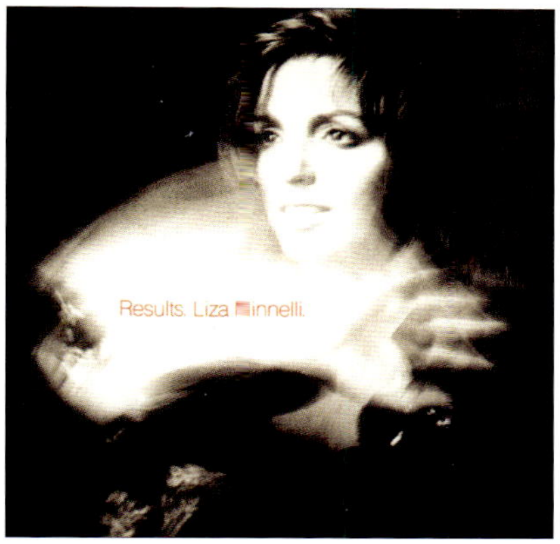

Actress and singer **Liza Minnelli** bemused her fans by taking a gamble on electronic dance-pop, collaborating with Pet Shop Boys for the album *Results*.

Billboard 200: *Results* (#128)

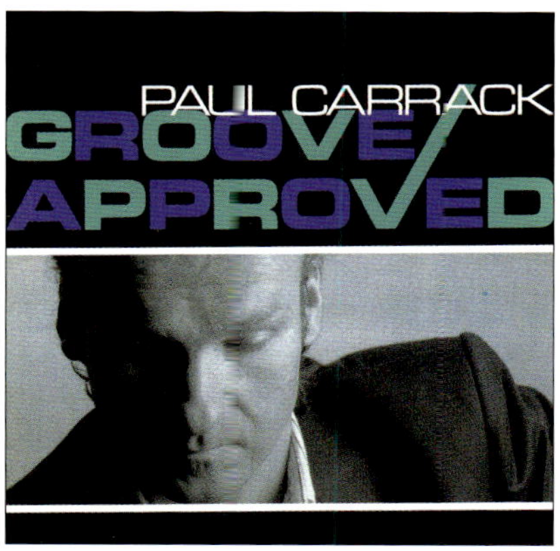

Keeping his career with Mike + the Mechanics, soulful Brit vocalist and keyboardist **Paul Carrack** released his fourth solo collection, *Groove Approved*.

Billboard 200: *Groove Approved* (#120)
Billboard Hot 100: "I Live by the Groove" (#31)

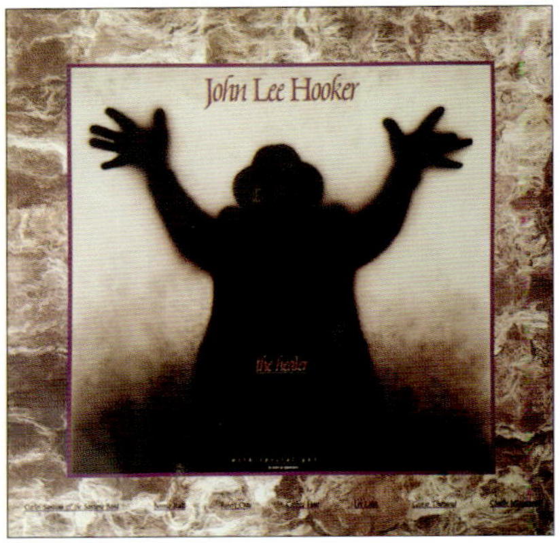

"I'm in the Mood," a 1951 classic re-recorded as a duet with guest Bonnie Raitt, earned septuagenarian bluesman **John Lee Hooker** a Grammy win.

Billboard 200: *The Healer* (#62)

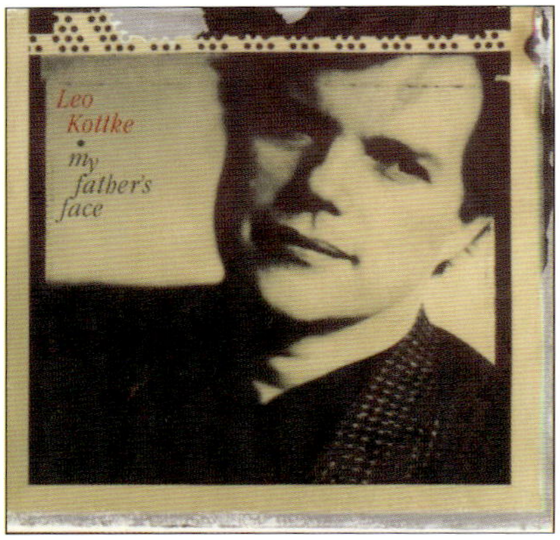

My Father's Face, acoustic guitarist **Leo Kottke**'s first vocal recording following an eight-year gap, held the sapient "Everybody Lies" and "Jack Gets Up."

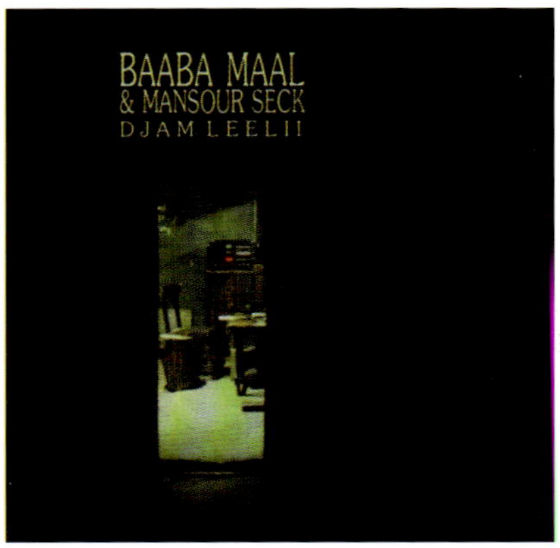

Recorded in Paris in 1984, the album *Diam Leelii* by **Baaba Maal & Mansour Seck**, a Senegalese pop singer and his guitarist crony, was widely distributed.

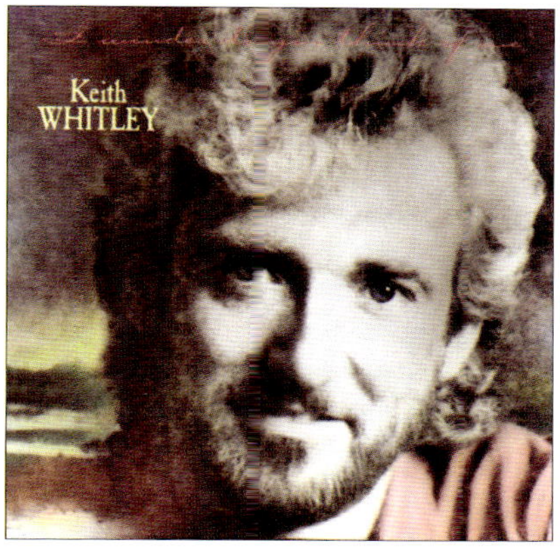

Released shortly after **Keith Whitley**'s death, *I Wonder Do You Think of Me* yielded a pair of No. 1 country singles, "I Ain't Nothin'" and the title track.

Billboard 200: *I Wonder Do You Think of Me* (#115)

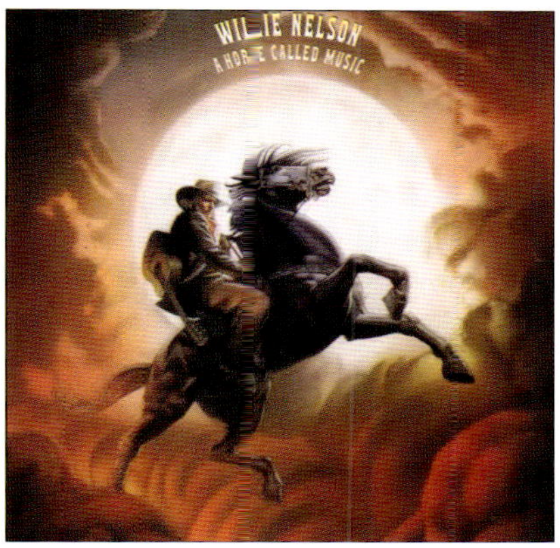

A Horse Called Music contained **Willie Nelson**'s 14th and final No. 1 country single, "Nothing I Can Do About It Now," written by Beth Nielsen Chapman.

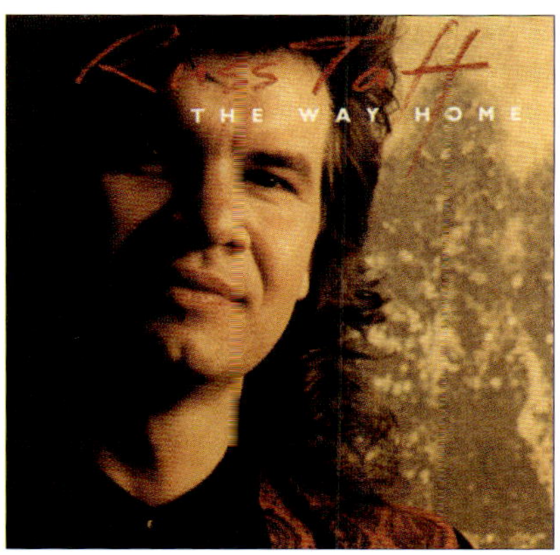

After a tenure with the gospel-bred Imperials, singer **Russ Taff** made an impact in contemporary Christian music with a fourth solo album, *The Way Home*.

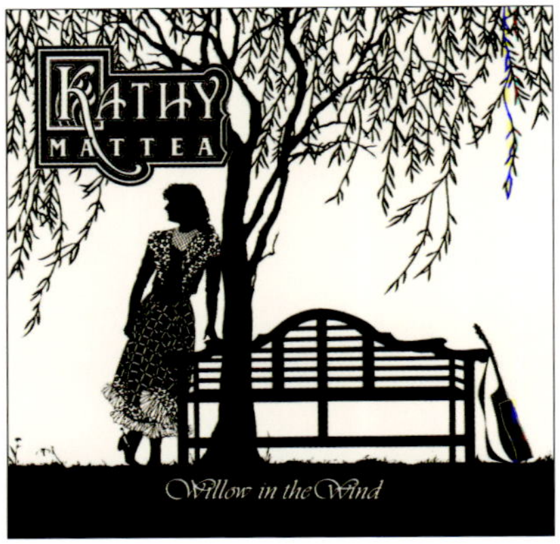

Kathy Mattea's *Willow in the Wind* chalked up back-to-back No. 1 country hits plus "Where've You Been," which earned a Grammy for Best Country Song.

Billboard 200: *Willow in the Wind* (#82)

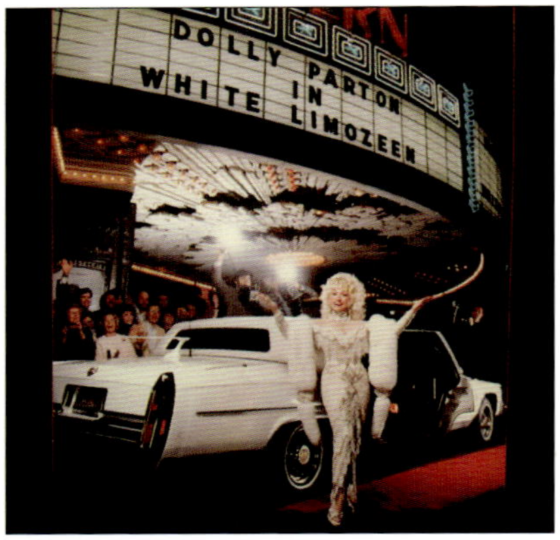

Returning to country material, Dolly Parton rolled out *White Limozeen* and the hits "Why'd You Come in Here Lookin' Like That" and "Yellow Roses."

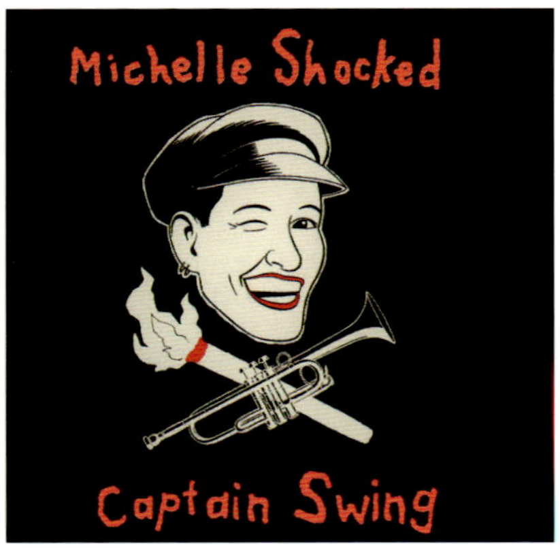

Folkish singer-songwriter Michelle Shocked adopted a western swing and big band course for *Captain Swing*, her second album in a self-described trilogy.

Billboard 200: *Captain Swing* (#95)

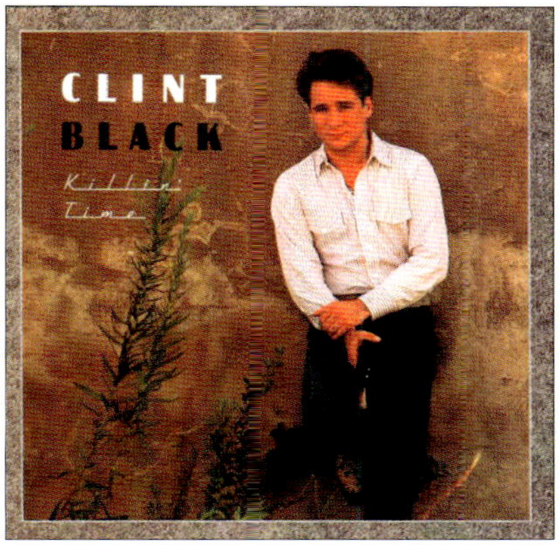

The first four singles from *Killin' Time*, Texas-based country artist **Clint Black**'s debut album, reached No. 1, including "A Better Man" and the title track.

Billboard 200: *Killin' Time* (#31)

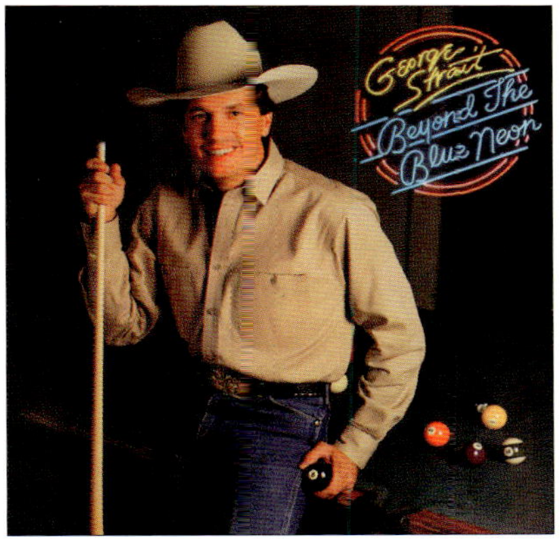

Traditional country music great **George Strait** reached the top of the charts with *Beyond the Blue Neon*, serving up a trio of tracks that peaked at No. 1.

Billboard 200: *Beyond the Blue Neon* (#92)

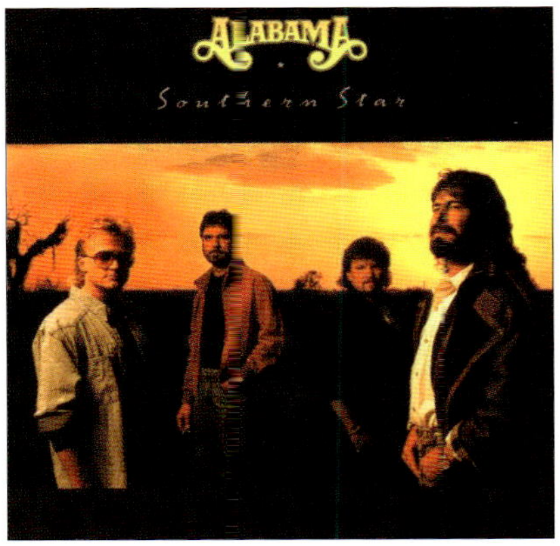

After breaking with longtime producer Harold Shedd, who'd overseen 21 No. 1 hits, **Alabama** delivered *Southern Star* and four more major country singles.

Billboard 200: *Southern Star* (#62)

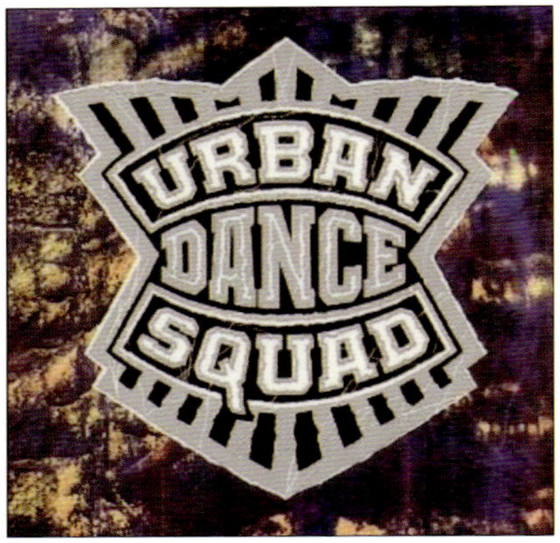

Urban Dance Squad recorded *Mental Floss for the Globe* in Belgium, and the single "Deeper Shade of Soul" gained the Dutch rap-rock act US recognition.

Billboard 200: *Mental Floss for the Globe* (#54)
Billboard Hot 100: "Deeper Shade of Soul" (#21)

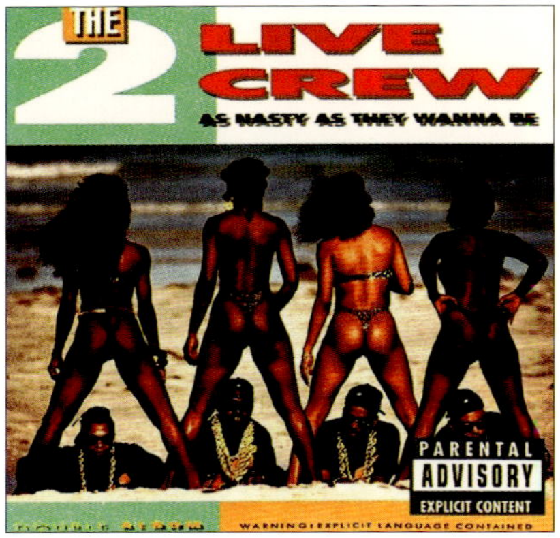

The 2 Live Crew, a controversial rap group, was taken to court for the sexually explicit and misogynistic nature of the lyrics on *As Nasty as They Wanna Be*.

Billboard 200: *As Nasty as They Wanna Be* (#29)
Billboard Hot 100: "Me So Horny" (#26)

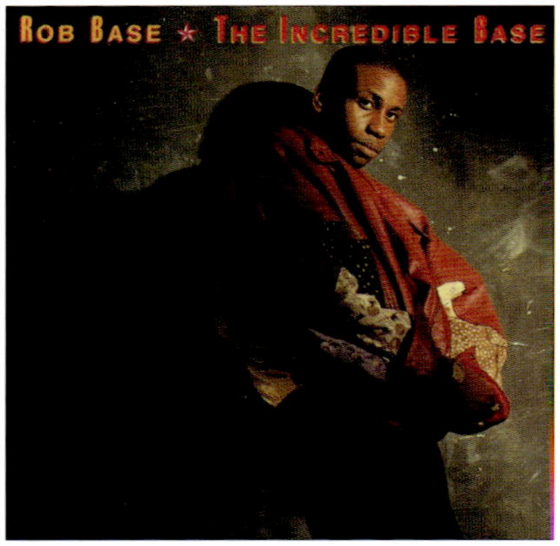

After thriving with "It Takes Two," a smash with cohort DJ E-Z Rock, Harlem rapper **Rob Base** lit out and recorded a solo album, *The Incredible Base*.

Billboard 200: *The Incredible Base* (#50)

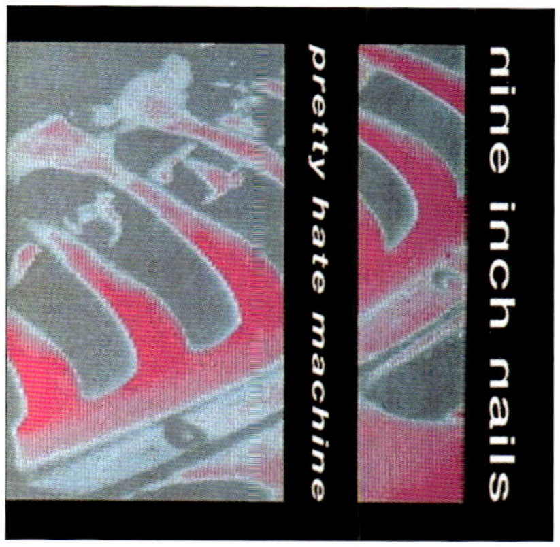

Driven by Trent Reznor, **Nine Inch Nails** issued *Pretty Hate Machine*, a debut album featuring his synth-dominated version of danceable industrial rock.

Billboard 200: *Pretty Hate Machine* (#75)

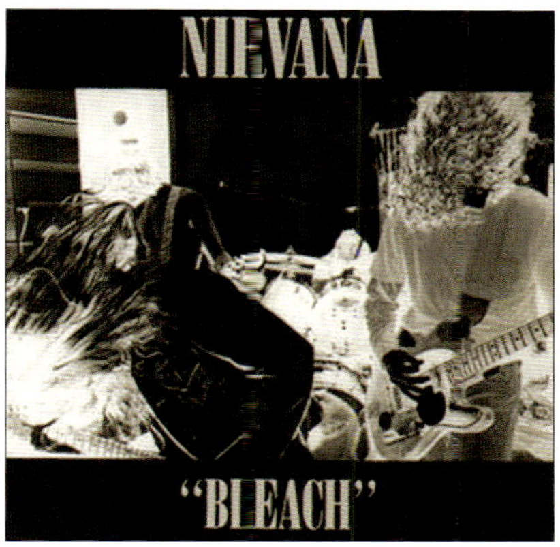

Entrenched as part of the Seattle grunge scene, **Nirvana** recorded its first album, *Bleach*, for just over $600 through the independent Sub Pop label.

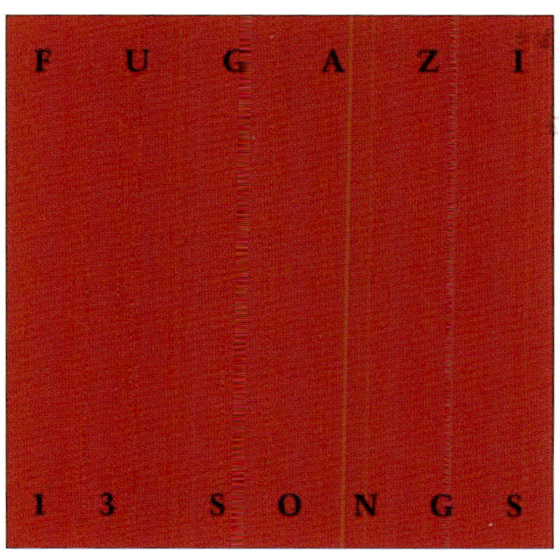

Fugazi's first two EPs were assembled as *13 Songs*, the Washington, D.C. outfit's debut full-length release and a touchstone of the post-hardcore scene.

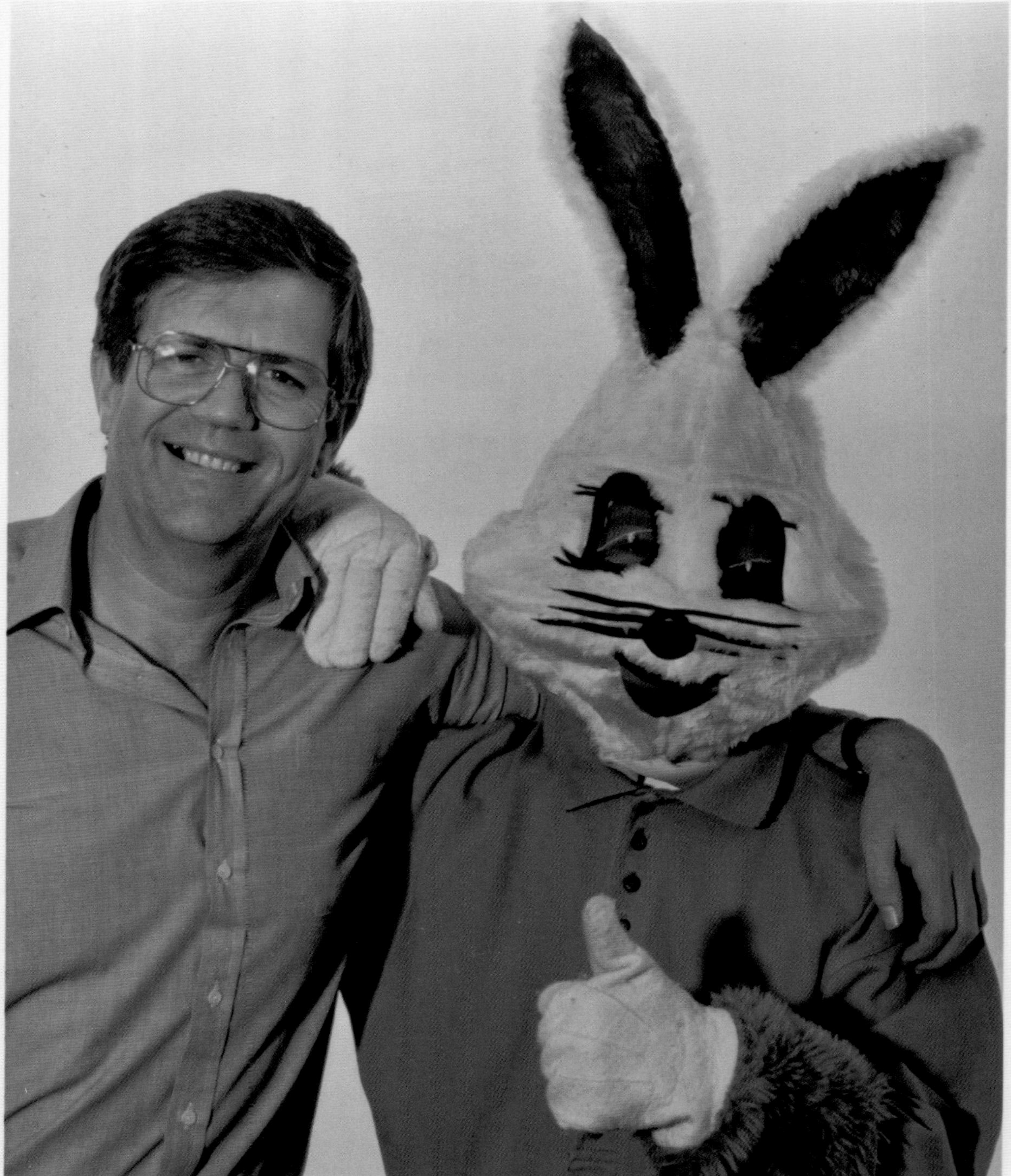

Jive Bunny and the Mastermixers

JOHN PICKLES and JIVE BUNNY

ATCO

Music Factory DANCE

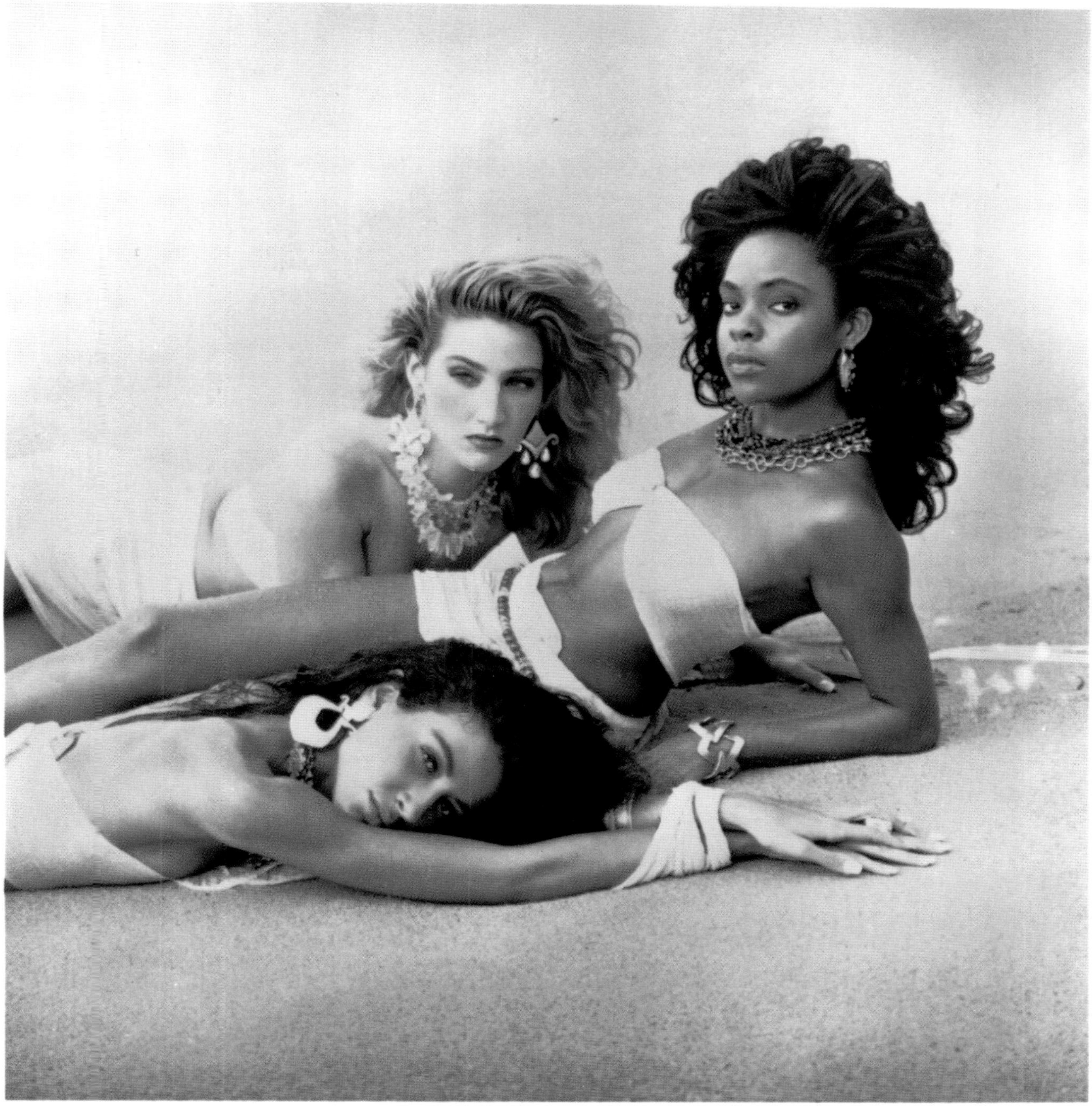

MICHELLE VISAGE
IDALIS LEON

APRIL HARRIS

SEDUCTION

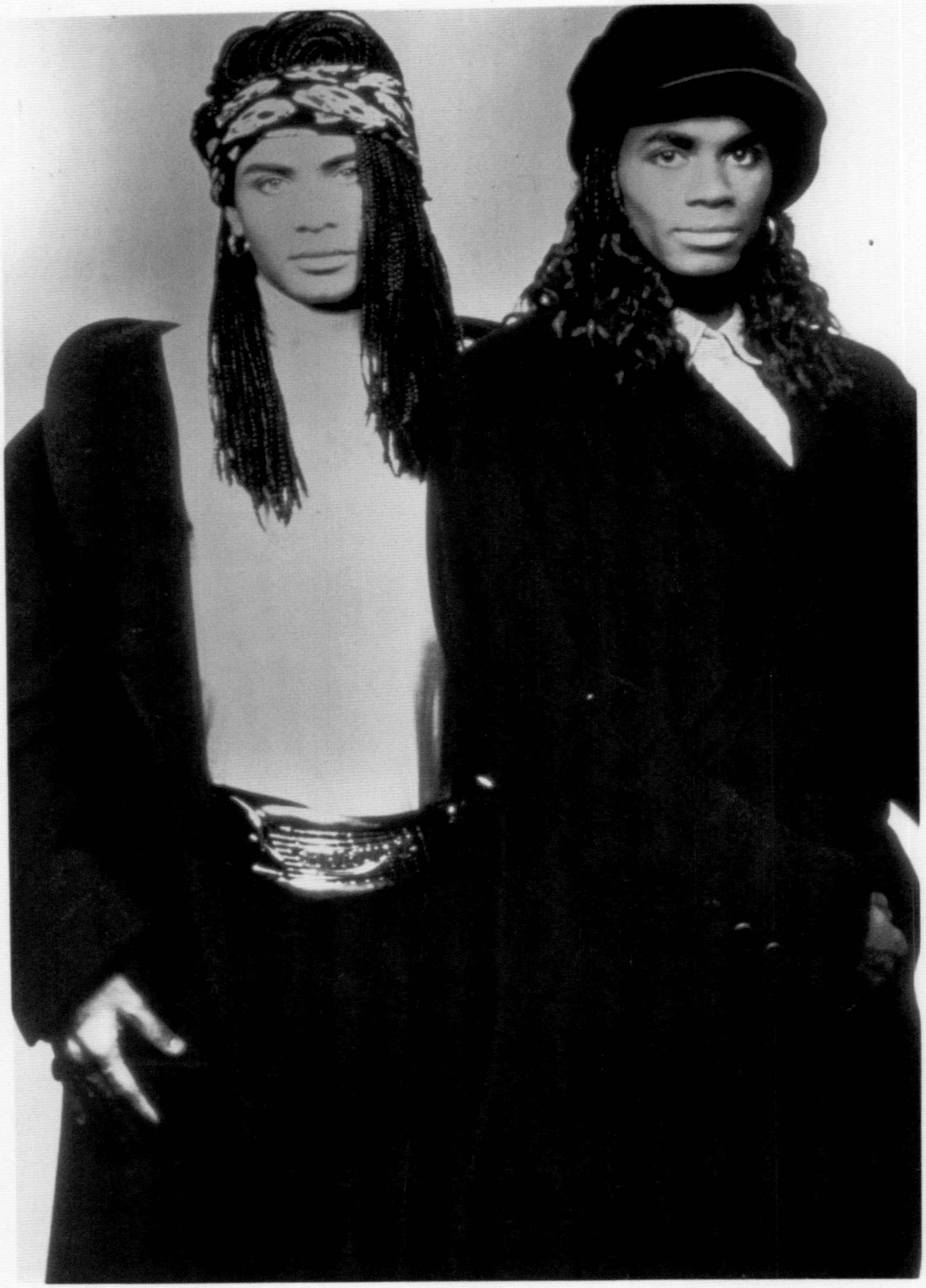

MILLI
VANILLI

ARISTA™

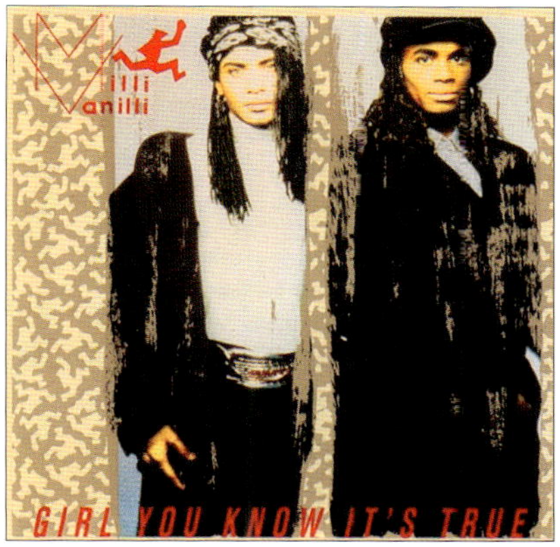

Milli Vanilli won the Grammy Award for Best New Artist, which was revoked when reports revealed the frontmen were models who didn't actually sing.

Billboard 200: *Girl You Know It's True* (No. 1)
Billboard Hot 100: "Girl You Know It's True" (#2);
"Baby Don't Forget My Number" (No. 1); "Blame It on the Rain" (No. 1);
"Girl I'm Gonna Miss You" (No. 1); "All or Nothing" (#4)

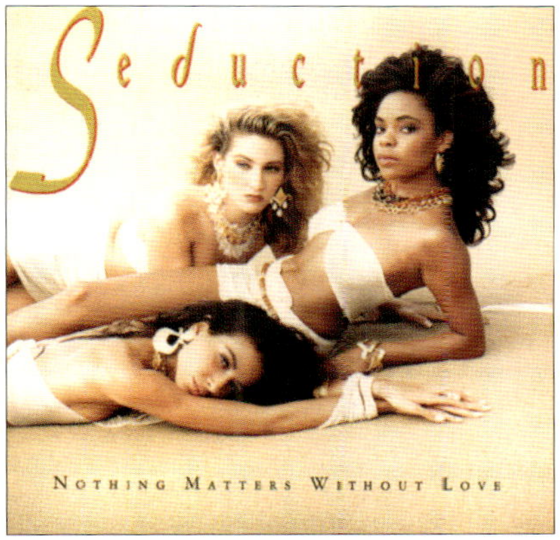

Planned as a studio initiative, producers contrived **Seduction**, a videogenic trio, and dance-pop singles such as "Two to Make It Right" emerged as hits.

Billboard 200: *Nothing Matters Without Love* (#36)
Billboard Hot 100: "(You're My One and Only) True Love" (#23);
"Two to Make It Right" (#2); "Heartbeat" (#13);
"Could This Be Love" (#11); "Breakdown" (#82)

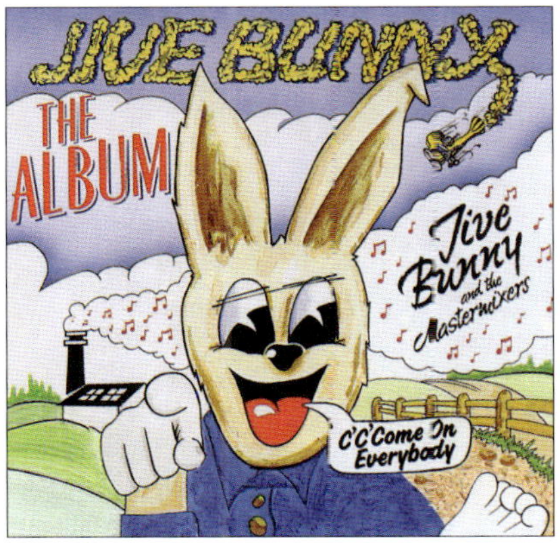

The work of British producers, **Jive Bunny & the Mastermixers**' "Swing the Mood," a medley of old songs tied together by samples, caught on in the US.

Billboard 200: *Jive Bunny: The Album* (#26)
Billboard Hot 100: "Swing the Mood" (#11); "That's What I Like" (#69)

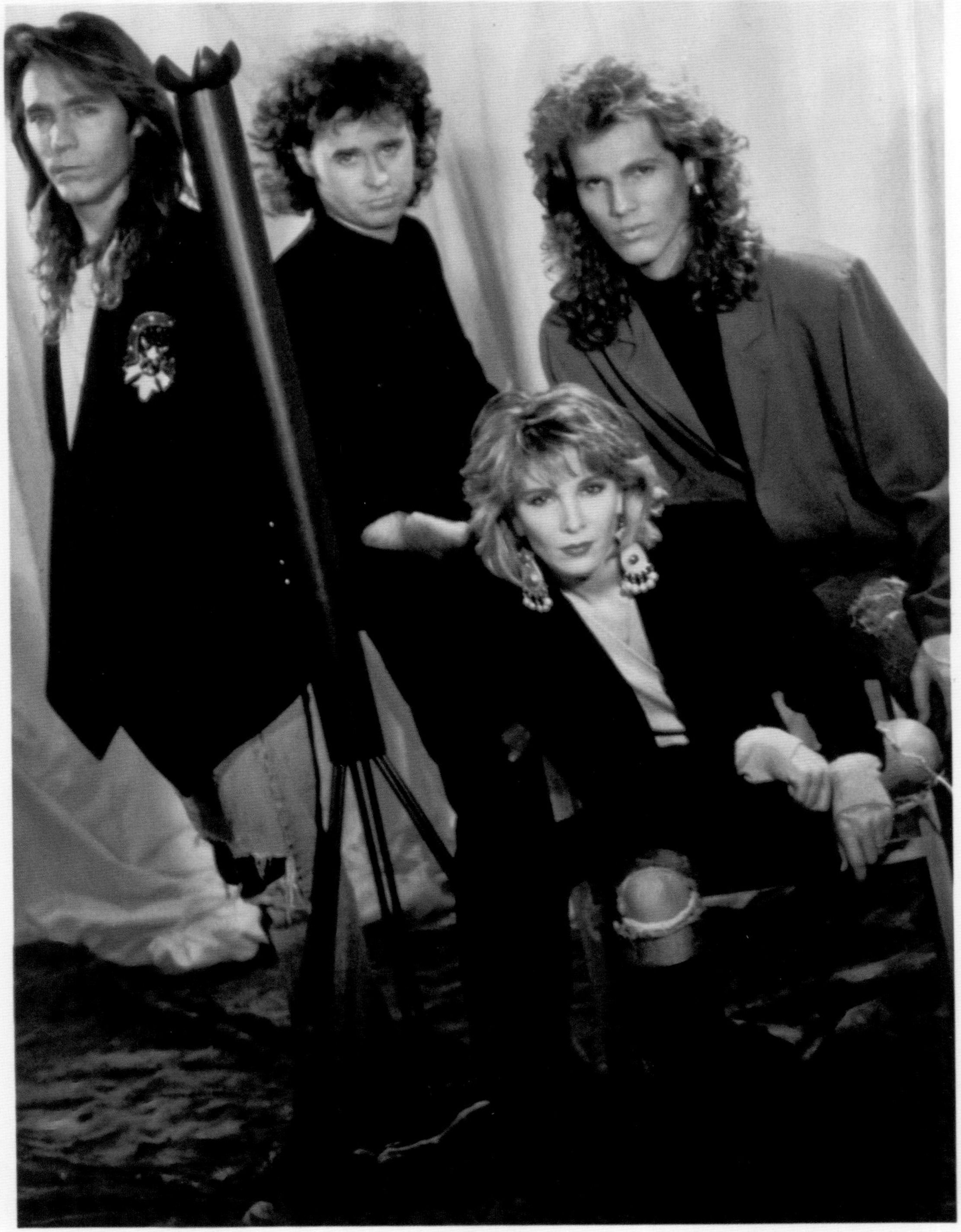

polydor

ANIMOTION

PolyGram™

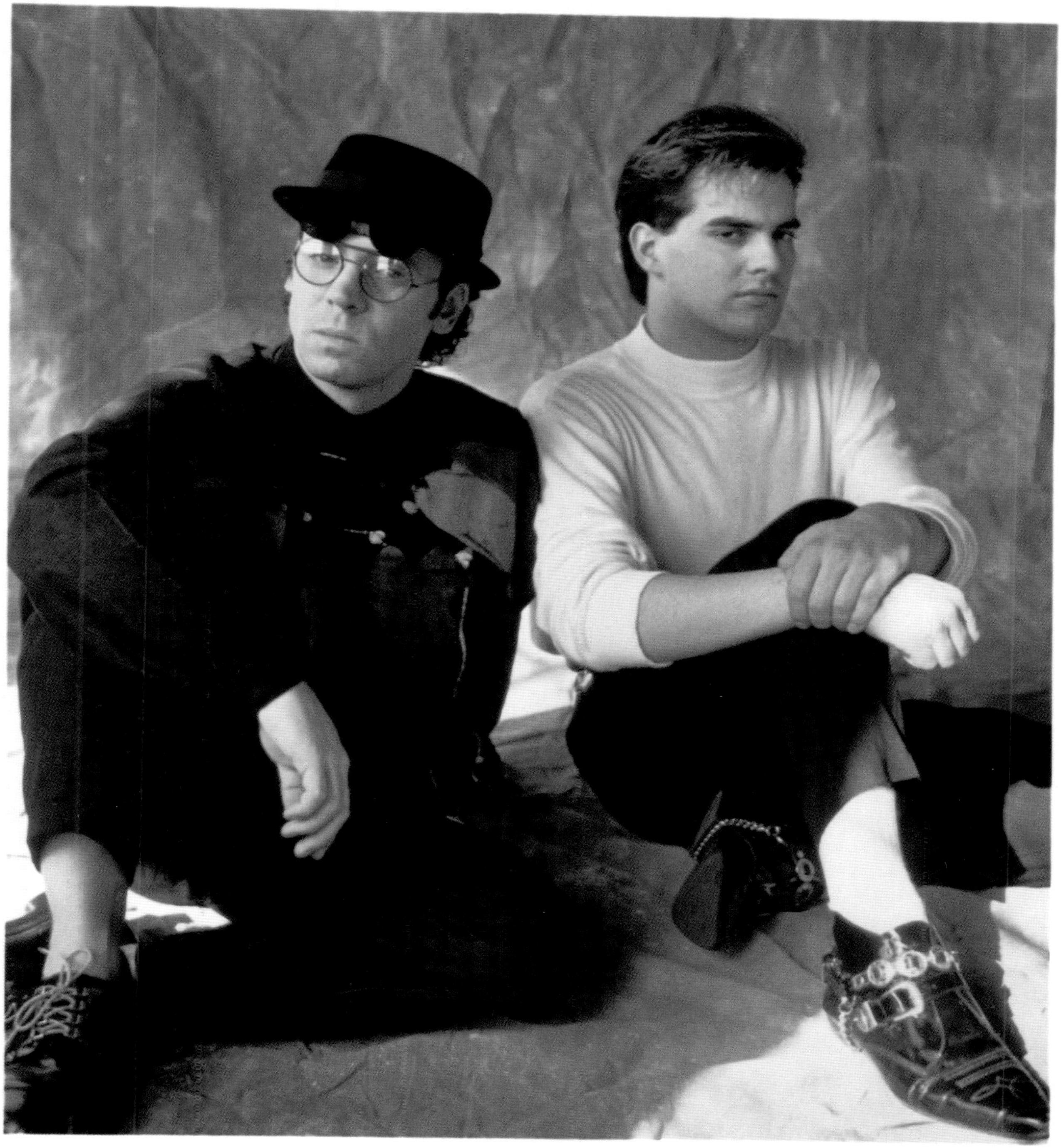

BARRY HARRIS KEVIN WYNNE

KON KAN

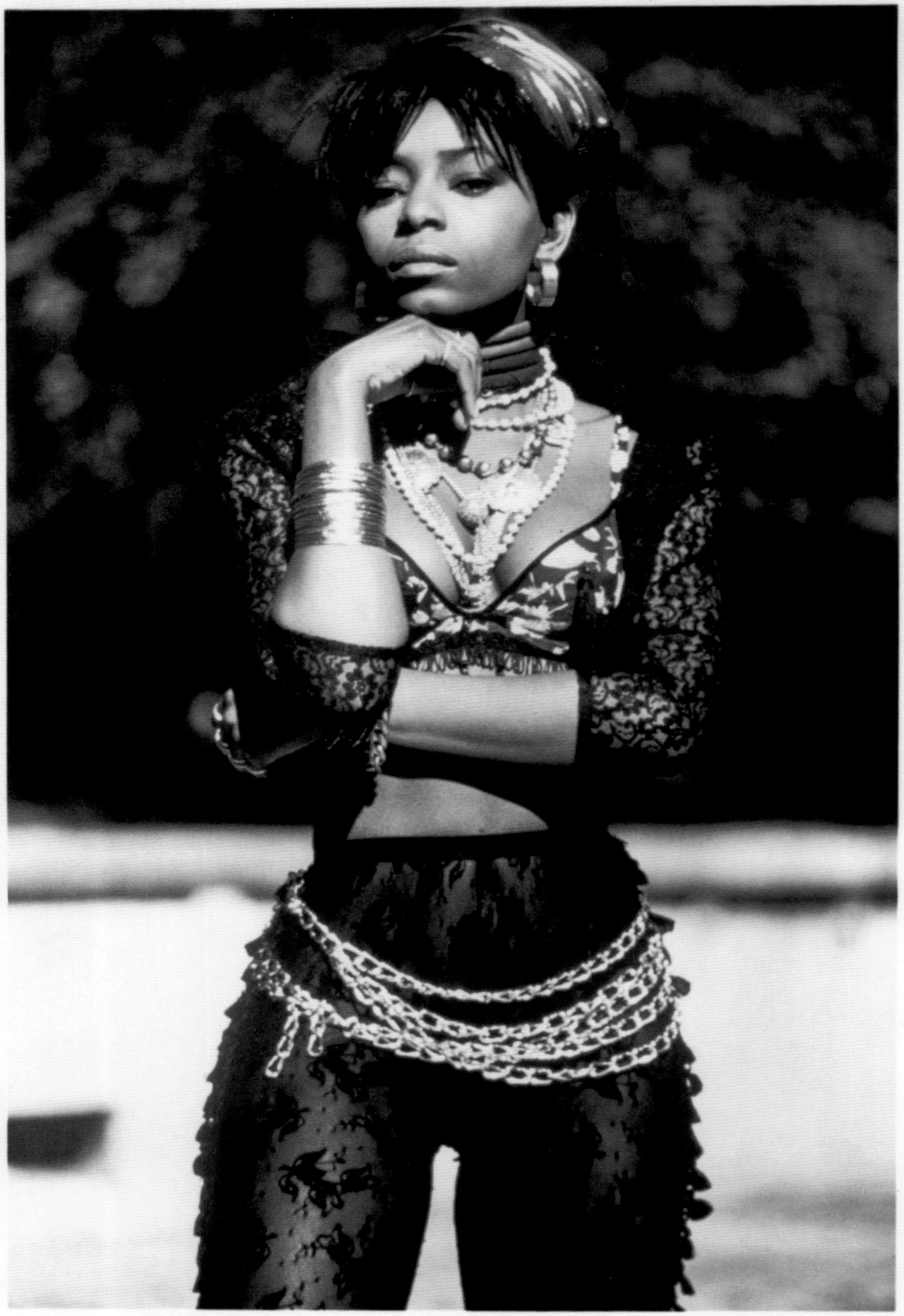

PHOTO CREDIT: MICHEL POELS

FELLY

(OF *TECHNOTRONIC*)

SBK Records

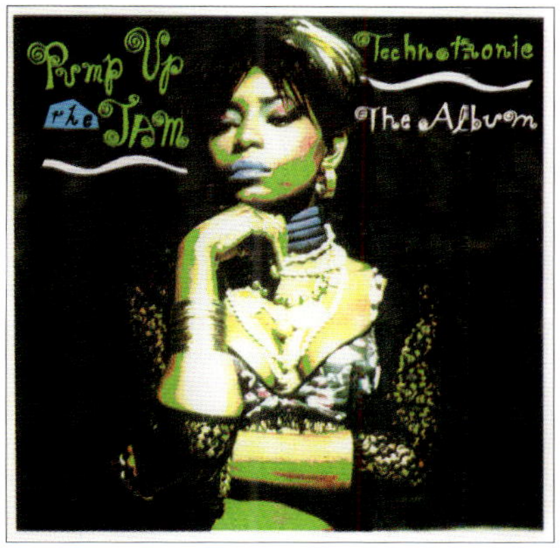

A Belgian studio-based project commixing house music with hip-hop, **Technotronic** generated the club banger "Pump Up the Jam," a worldwide smash.

Billboard 200: *Pump Up the Jam: The Album* (#10)
Billboard Hot 100: "Pump Up the Jam" (#2); "Get Up! (Before the Night Is Over)" (#7); "Rockin' Over the Beat" (#95)

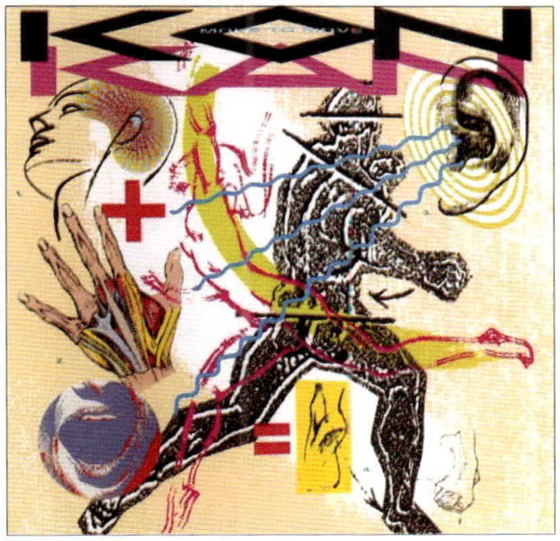

The Canadian synth-pop duo **Kon Kan** crafted the off-the-wall "I Beg Your Pardon," a global hit that sampled Lynn Anderson's "Rose Garden" from 1970.

Billboard Hot 100: "I Beg Your Pardon" (#15); "Puss N' Boots/These Boots (Are Made for Walkin')" (#58)

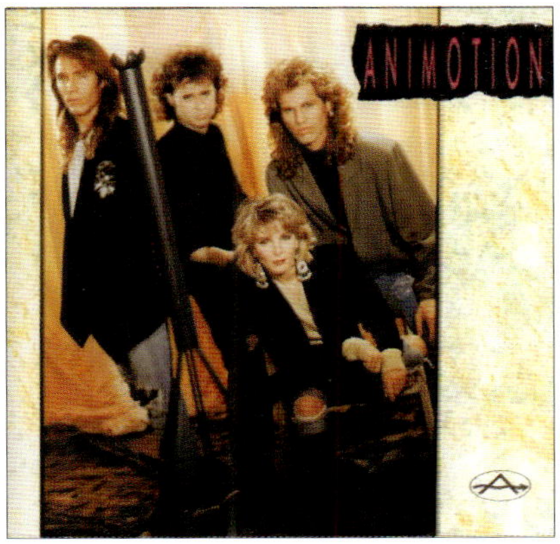

After the exodus of the original lead singers, L.A. new wavers **Animotion** managed a second Top 10 hit, "Room to Move," a remake of a Climie Fisher song.

Billboard 200: *Animotion* (#110)
Billboard Hot 100: "Room to Move" (#9); "Calling It Love" (#53)

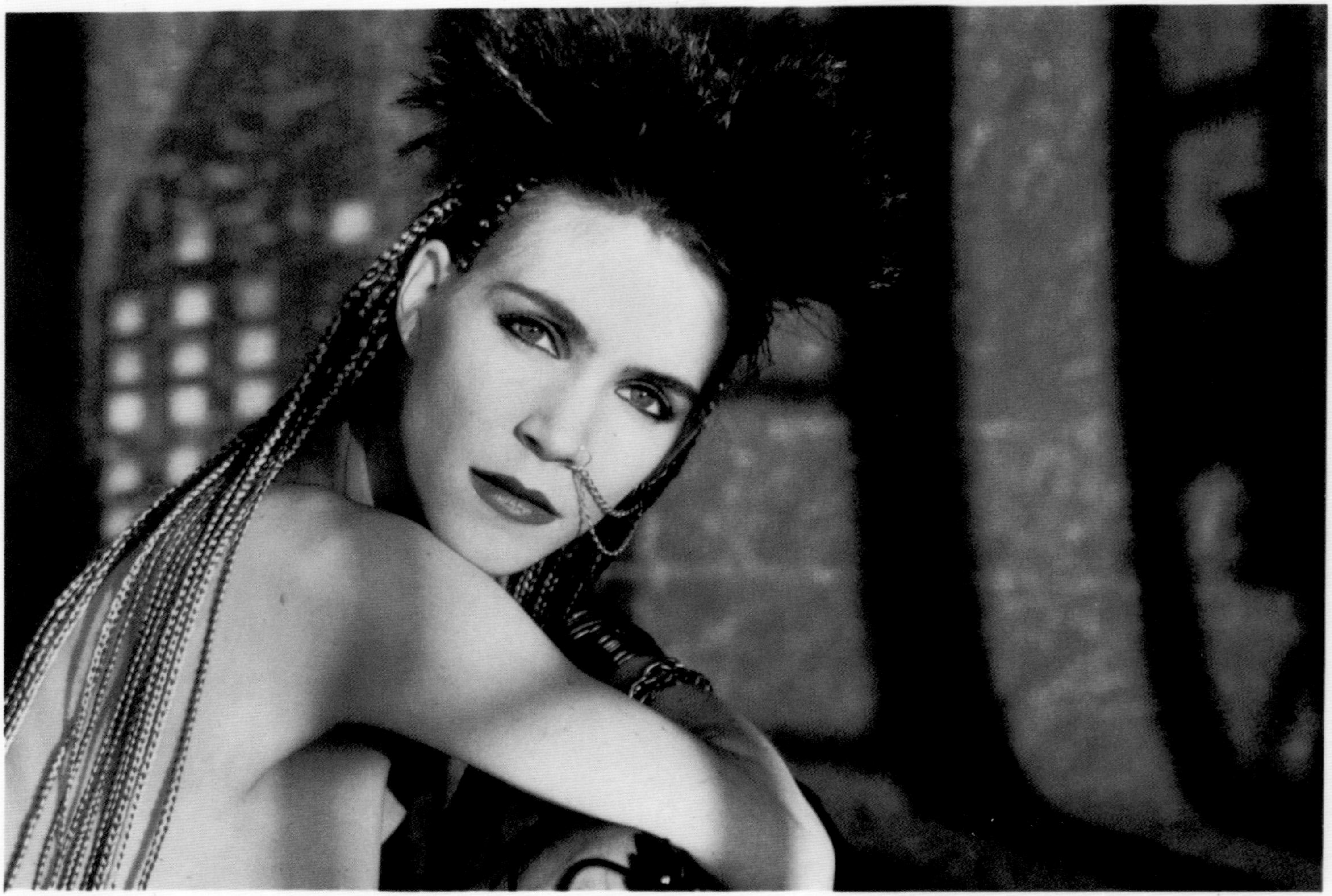

Photo Credit: Randee St. Nicholas

Jane Child

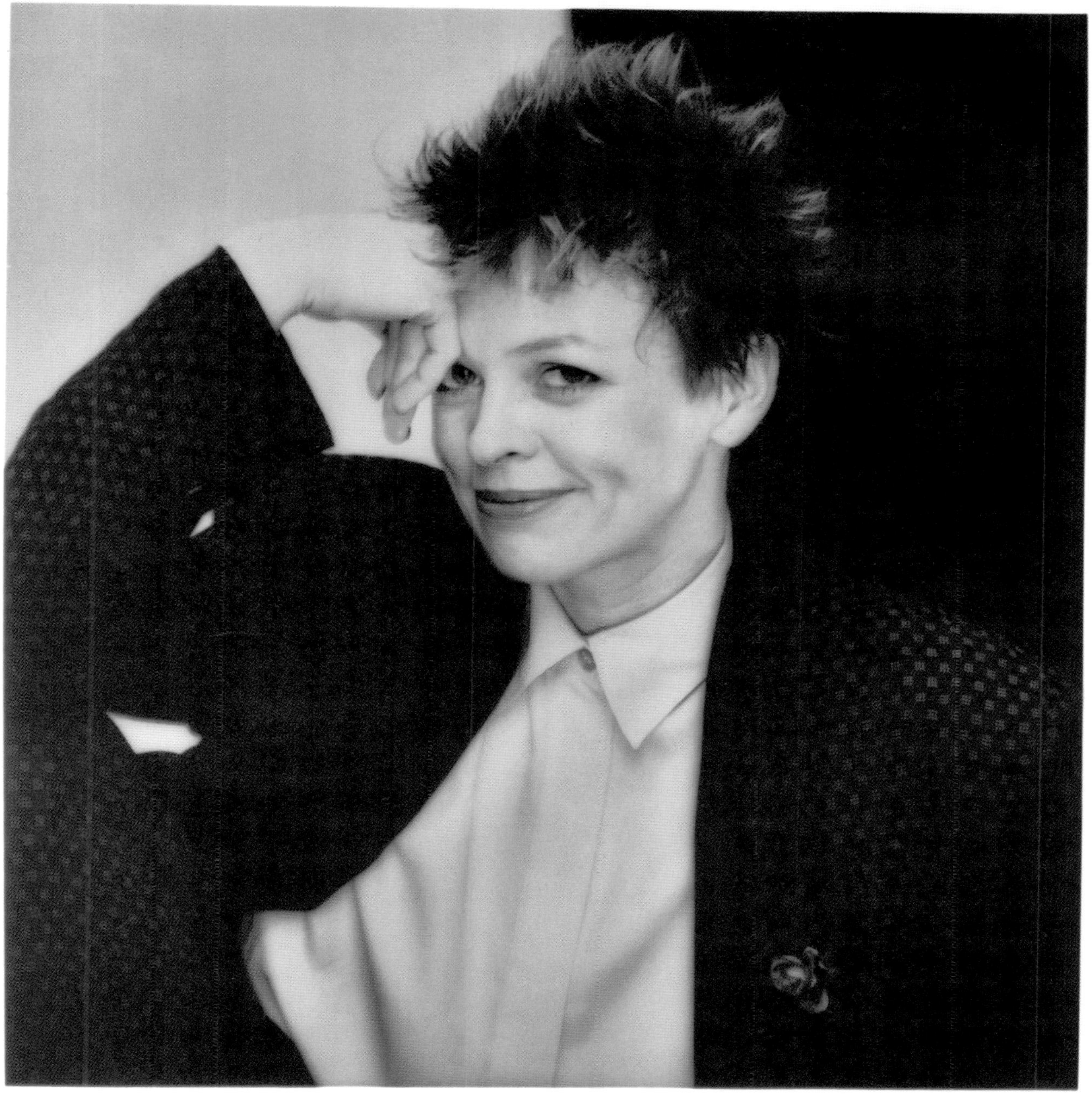

Photo Credit: Gilles Larrain

LAURIE ANDERSON

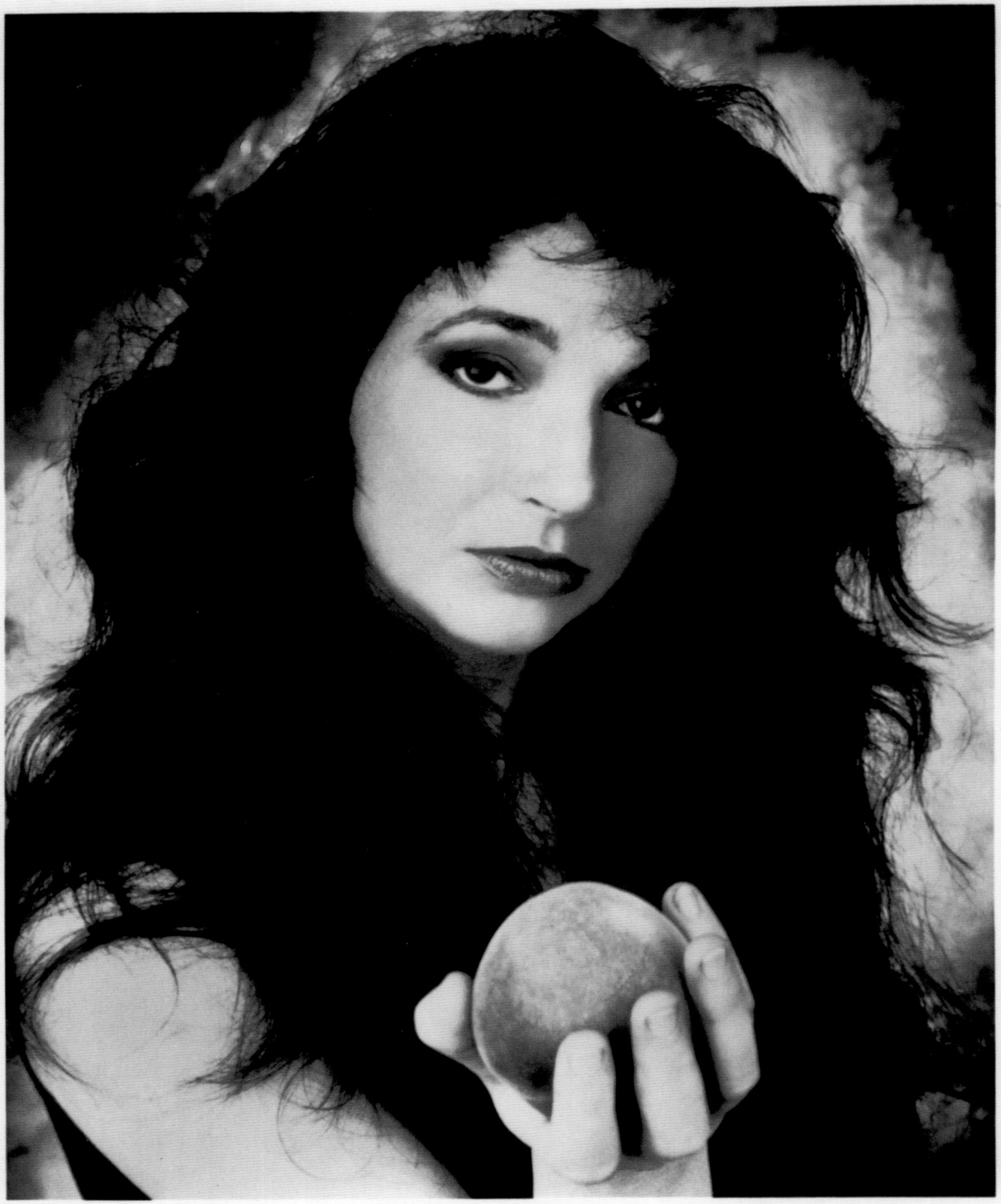

PHOTOGRAPH: JOHN CARDER BUSH

KATE BUSH

Columbia
8909

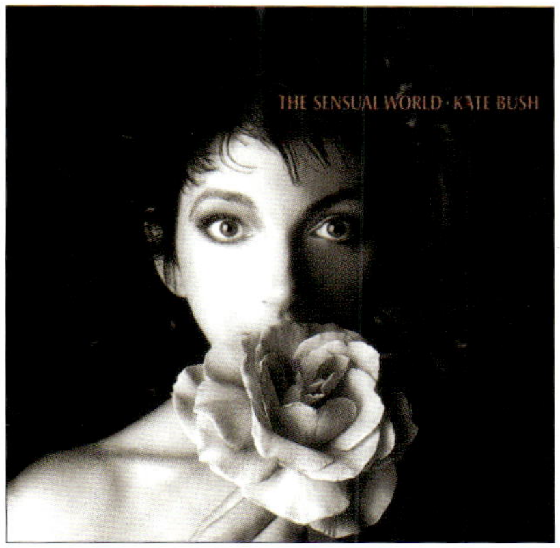

The Sensual World became English singer **Kate Bush**'s best-selling album in the US, with a title track inspired by *Ulysses*, James Joyce's landmark novel.

Billboard 200: *The Sensual World* (#43)

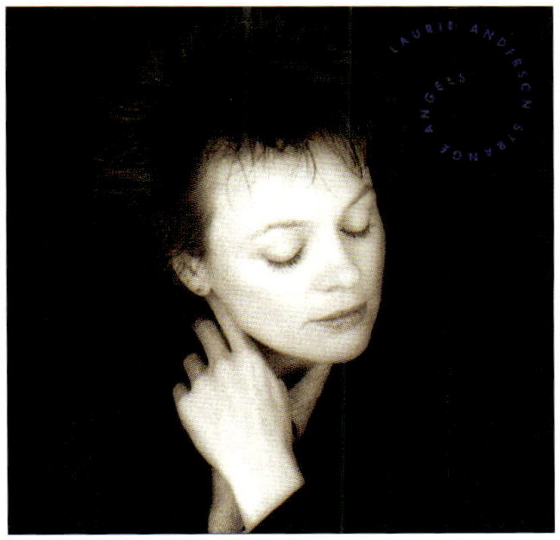

Singing more than on previous works, performance artist **Laurie Anderson** released *Strange Angels*, with "Babydoll" emerging as a modern-rock hit.

Billboard 200: *Strange Angels* (#171)

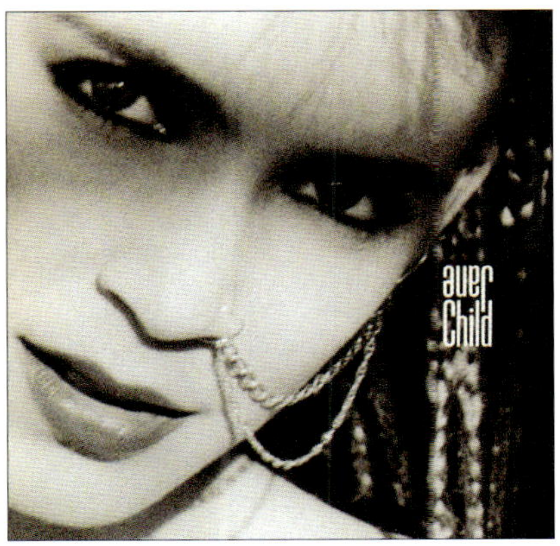

Toronto-born singer **Jane Child** wrote and produced all the music on her self-titled album, distinguished by the disarming "Don't Wanna Fall in Love."

Billboard 200: *Jane Child* (#49)
Billboard Hot 100: "Welcome to the Real World" (#49); "Don't Wanna Fall in Love" (#2)

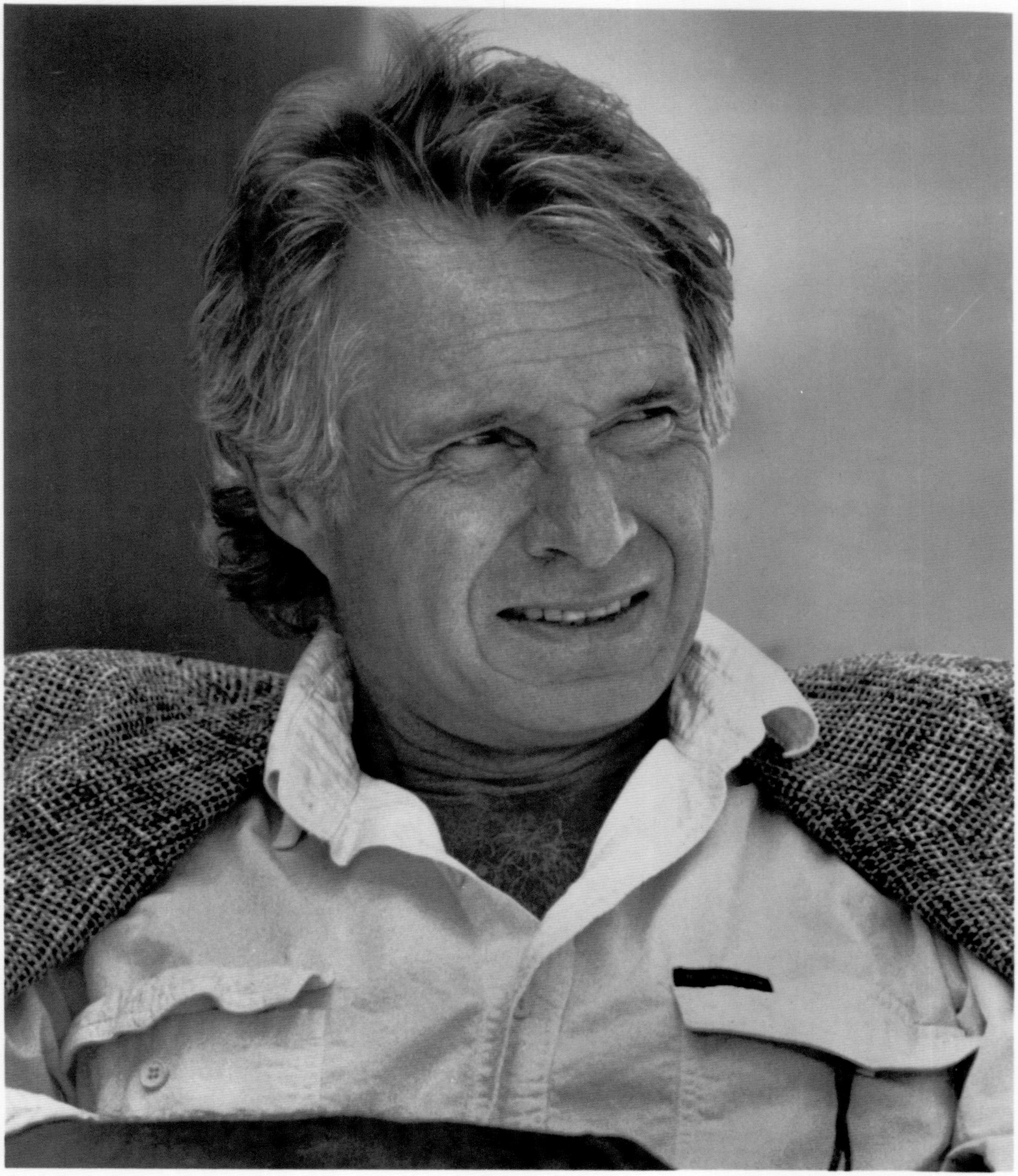

DAVE GRUSIN

GRP Records

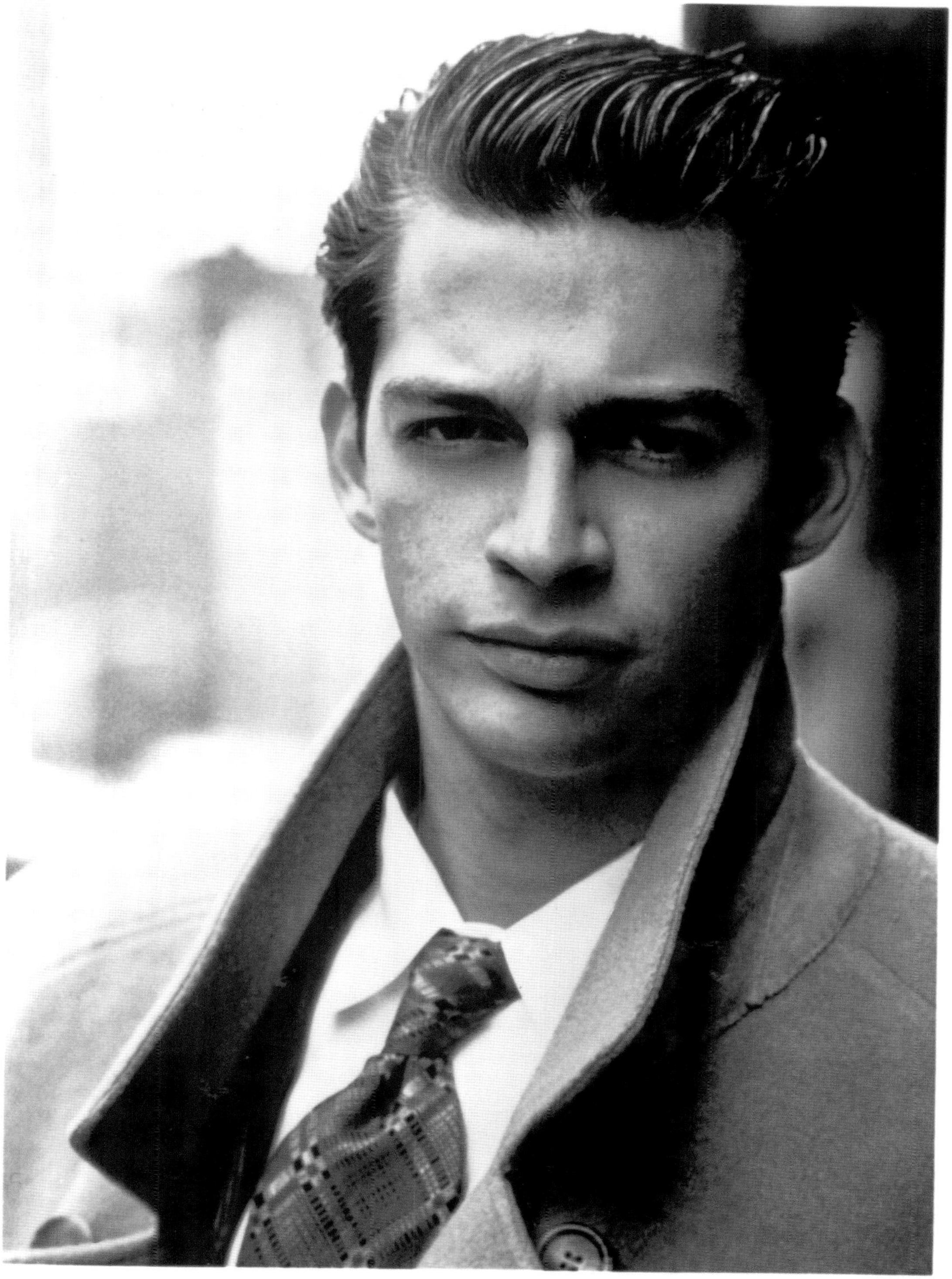

HARRY CONNICK, JR.

Columbia

8907

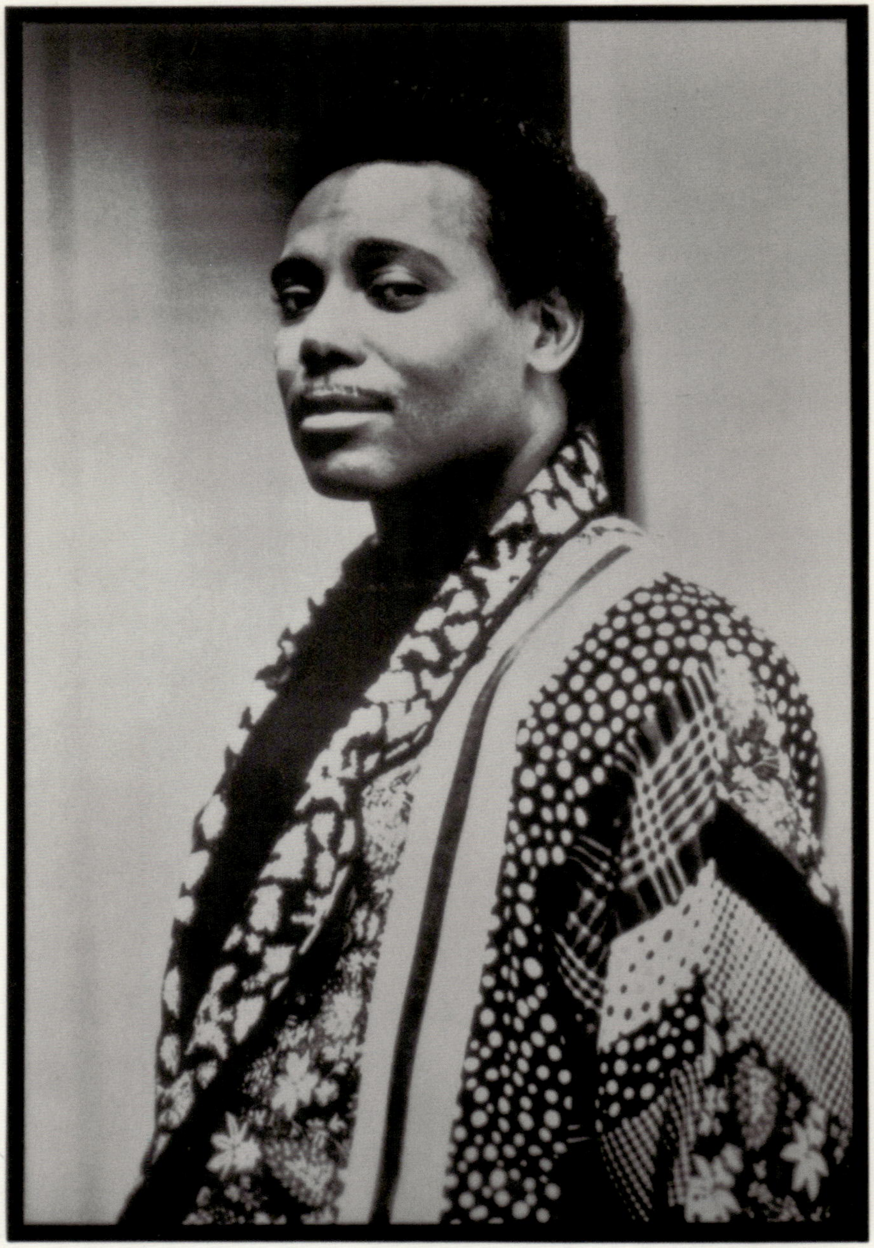

Photo Credit: Harris Savides

GEORGE BENSON

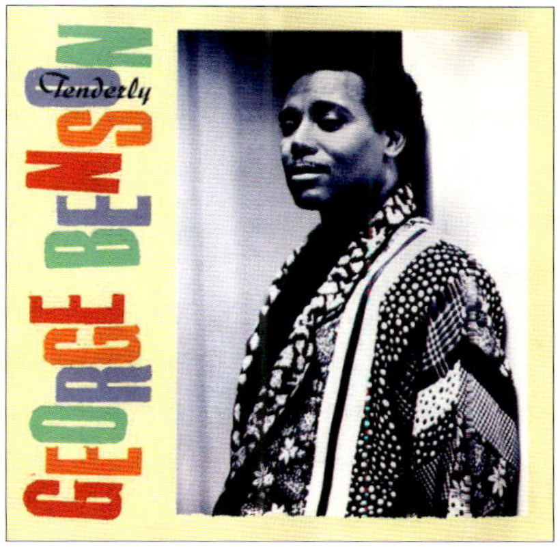

Guitarist **George Benson** topped the jazz album charts with *Tenderly*, highlighted by an affecting rendition of the Beatles' "Here, There and Everywhere."

Billboard 200: *Tenderly* (#140)

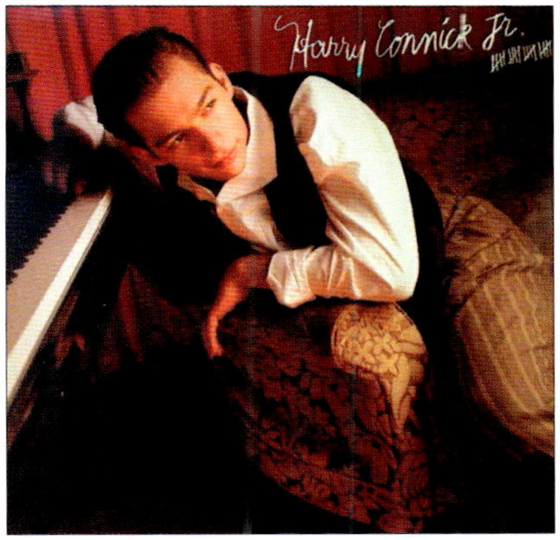

After cultivating an impeccable reputation in jazz circles, **Harry Connick Jr.** recorded *20*, titled for his age, the first album to feature his warm vocals.

Billboard 200: *20* (#133)

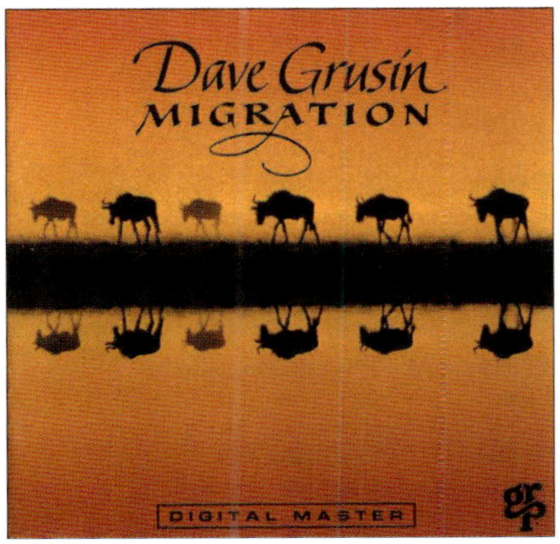

Pianist **Dave Grusin**'s *Migration* rose to No. 1 on the contemporary jazz charts, and his soundtrack suite to *The Milagro Beanfield War* won a Grammy.

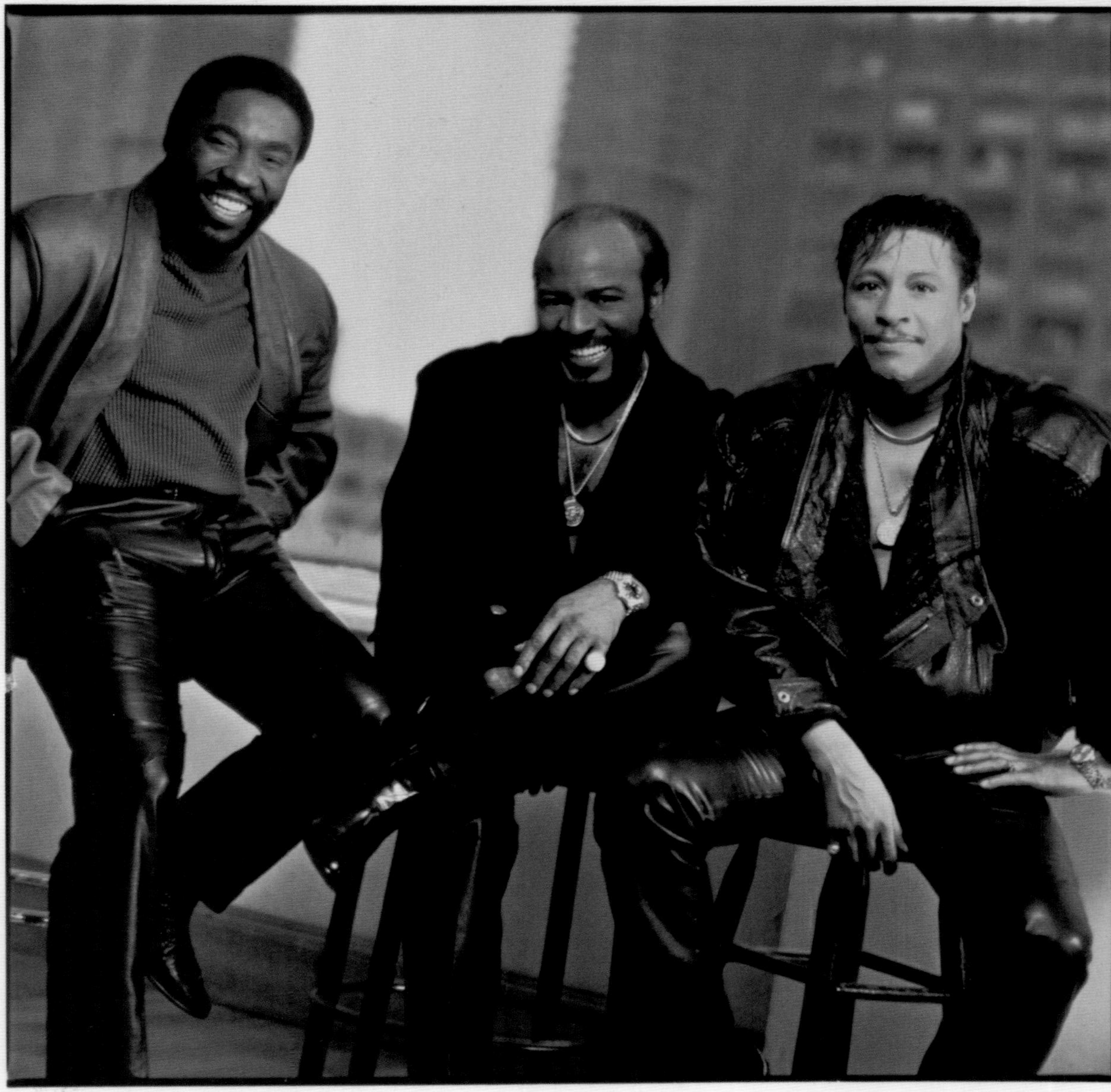

The O JAYS

EMI

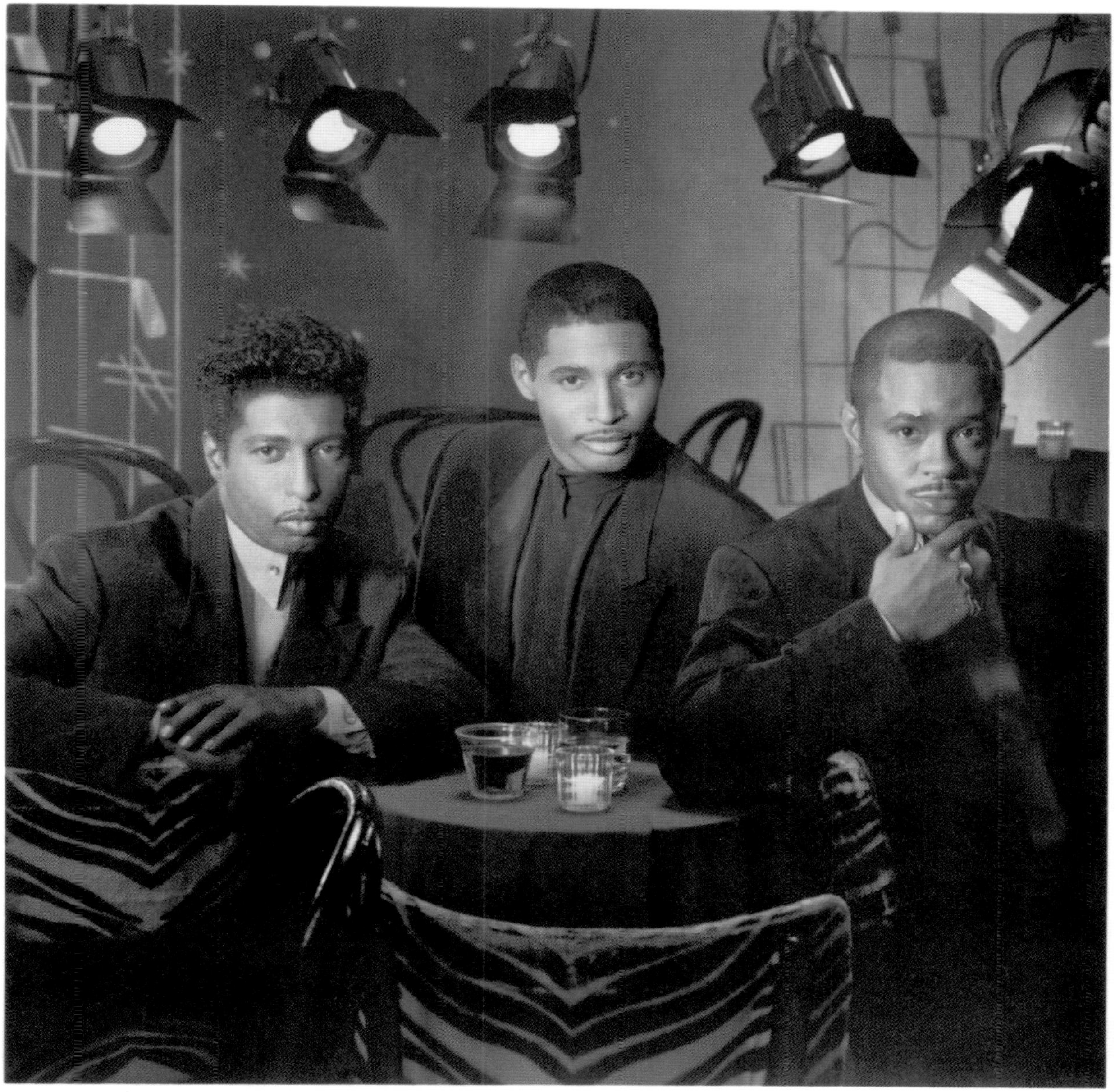

Photo Credit: Randee St. Nicholas

after 7

Virgin

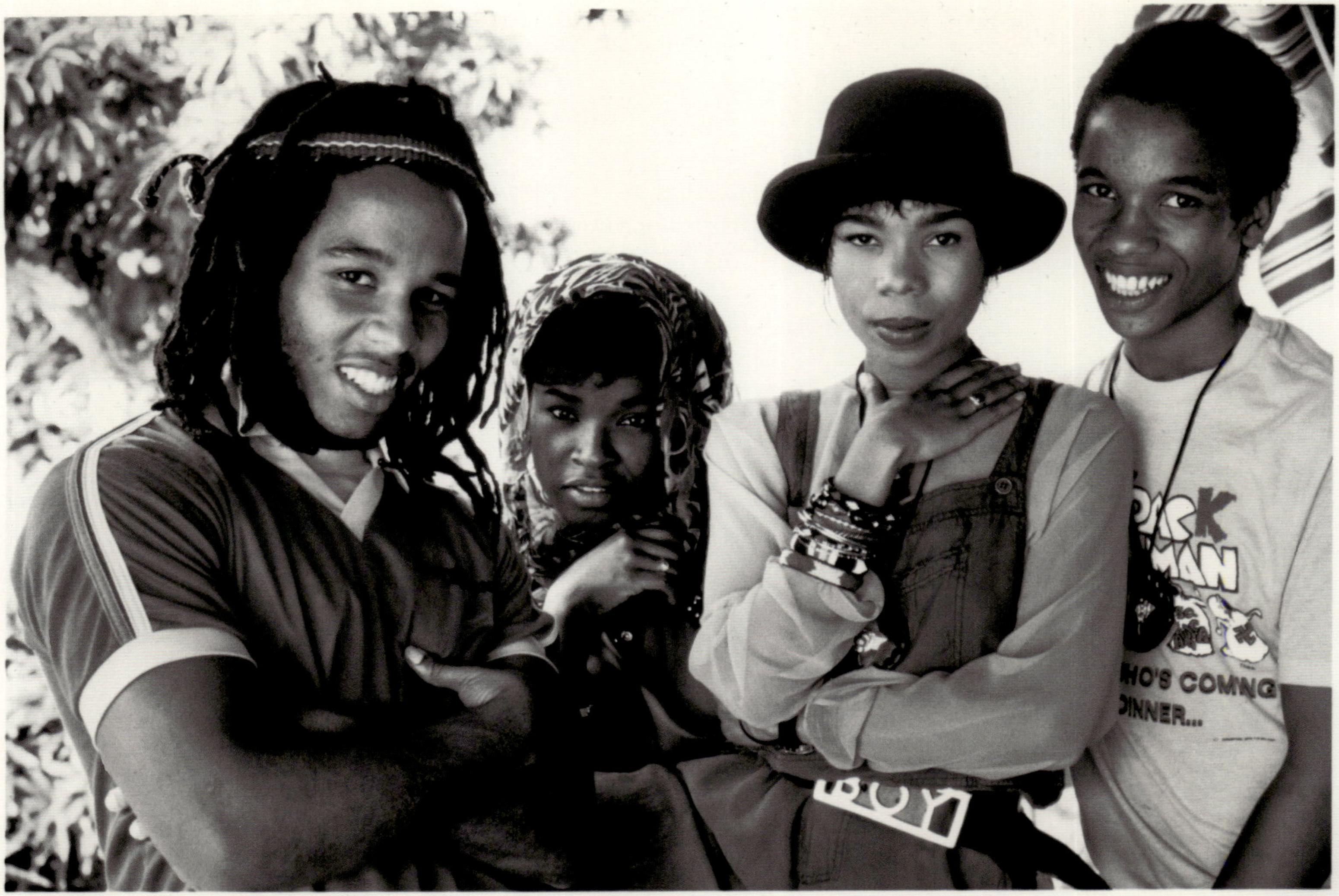

Photo Credit: Ruedi Hofmann

ZIGGY MARLEY
and
THE MELODY MAKERS

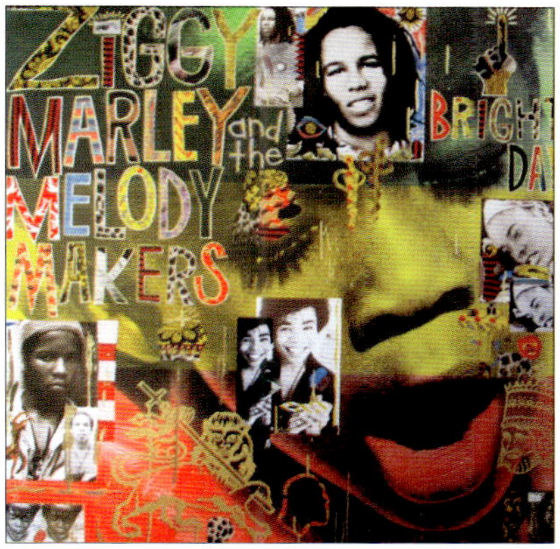

For *One Bright Day*, **Ziggy Marley & the Melody Makers**, led by the oldest son of the iconic Bob Marley, earned their second Grammy for Best Reggae Album.

Billboard 200: *One Bright Day* (#26)

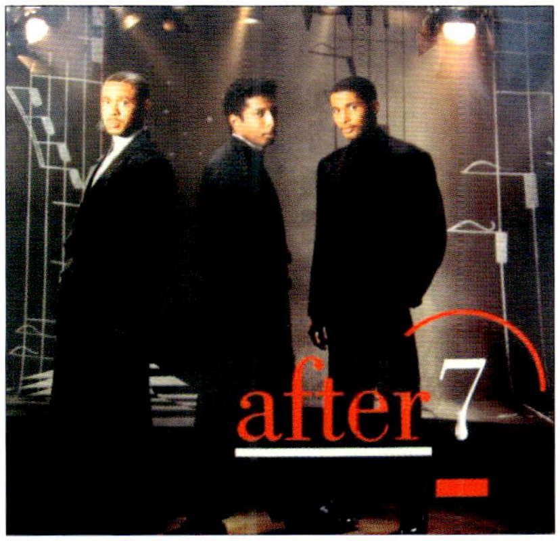

With a hand from production cohorts Babyface and L.A. Reid, **After 7**'s self-titled debut led to a pair of No. 1 R&B hits, "Ready or Not" and "Can't Stop."

Billboard 200: *After 7* (#35)
Billboard Hot 100: "Ready or Not" (#7); "Can't Stop" (#6);
"Heat of the Moment" (#19)

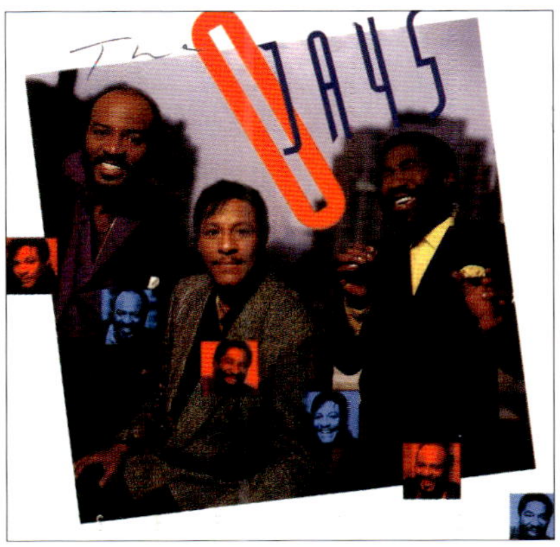

The O'Jays, at the vanguard of Philly soul in the Seventies, blended new jack swing facets into their final No. 1 R&B track, "Have You Had Your Love Today."

Billboard 200: *Serious* (#114)

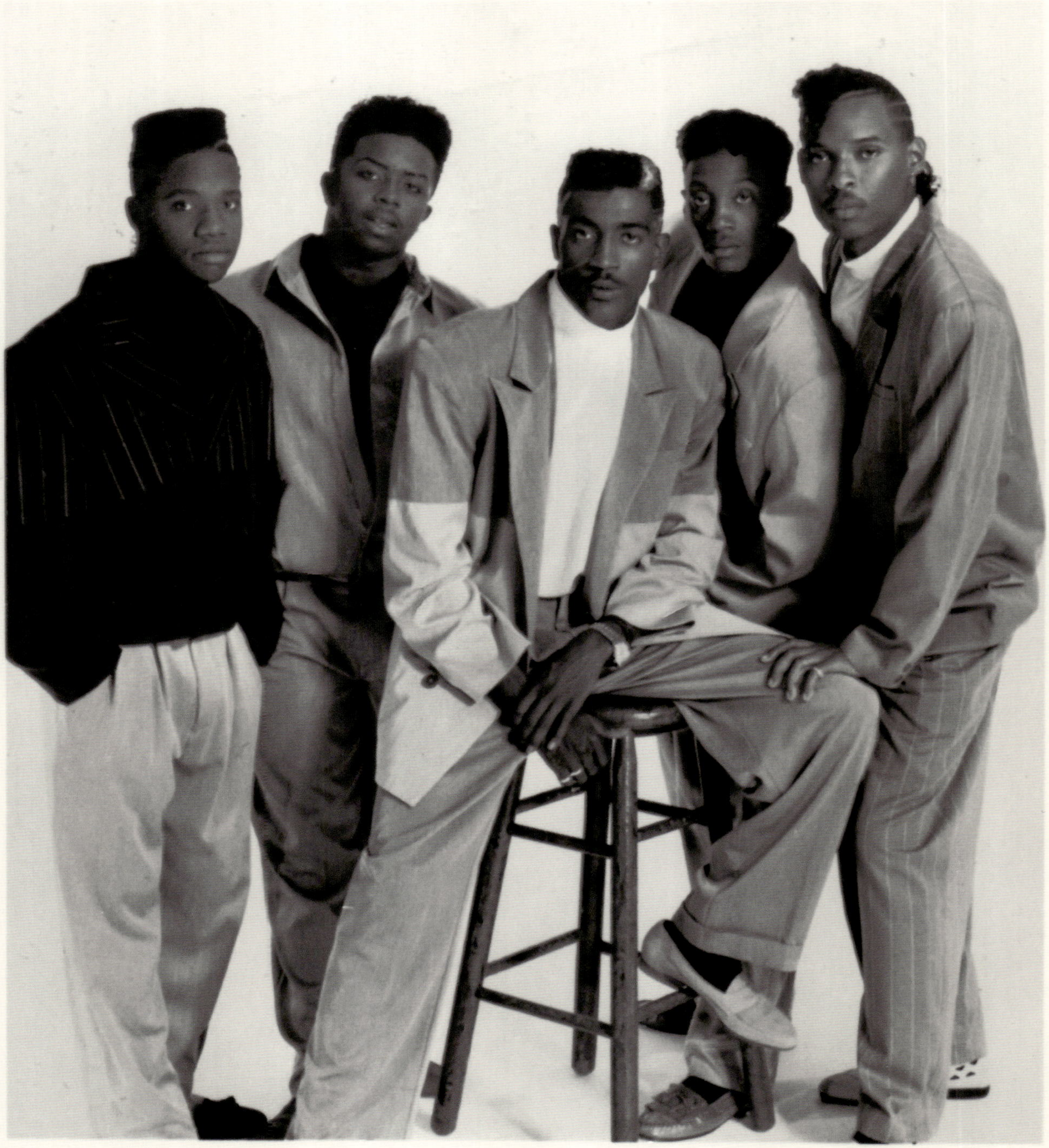

JOHN HARRELD STEVE RUSSELL REGGIE WARREN ALLEN McNEIL RODNEY BENFORD

TROOP

ATLANTIC

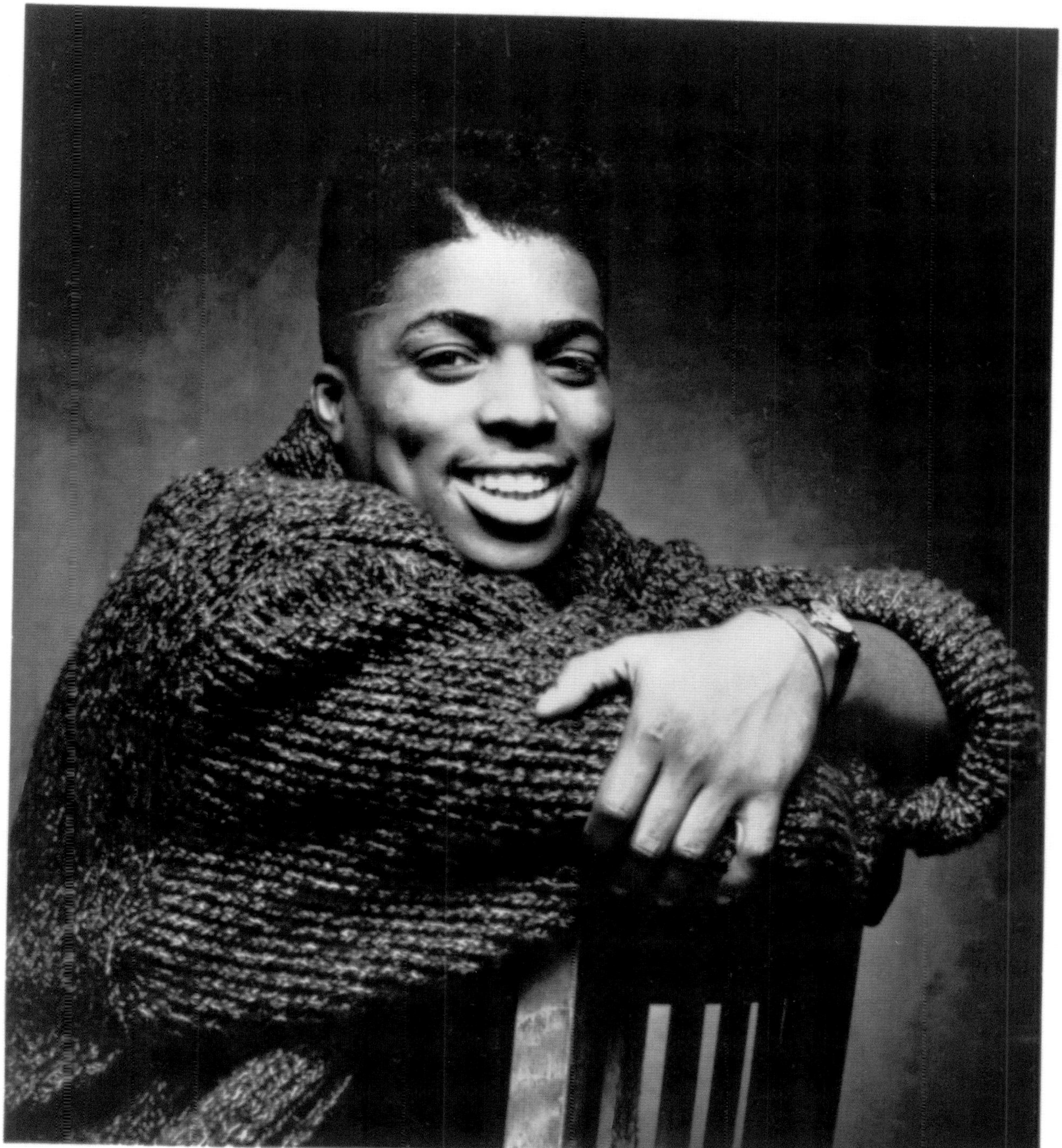

CHUCKii BOOKER

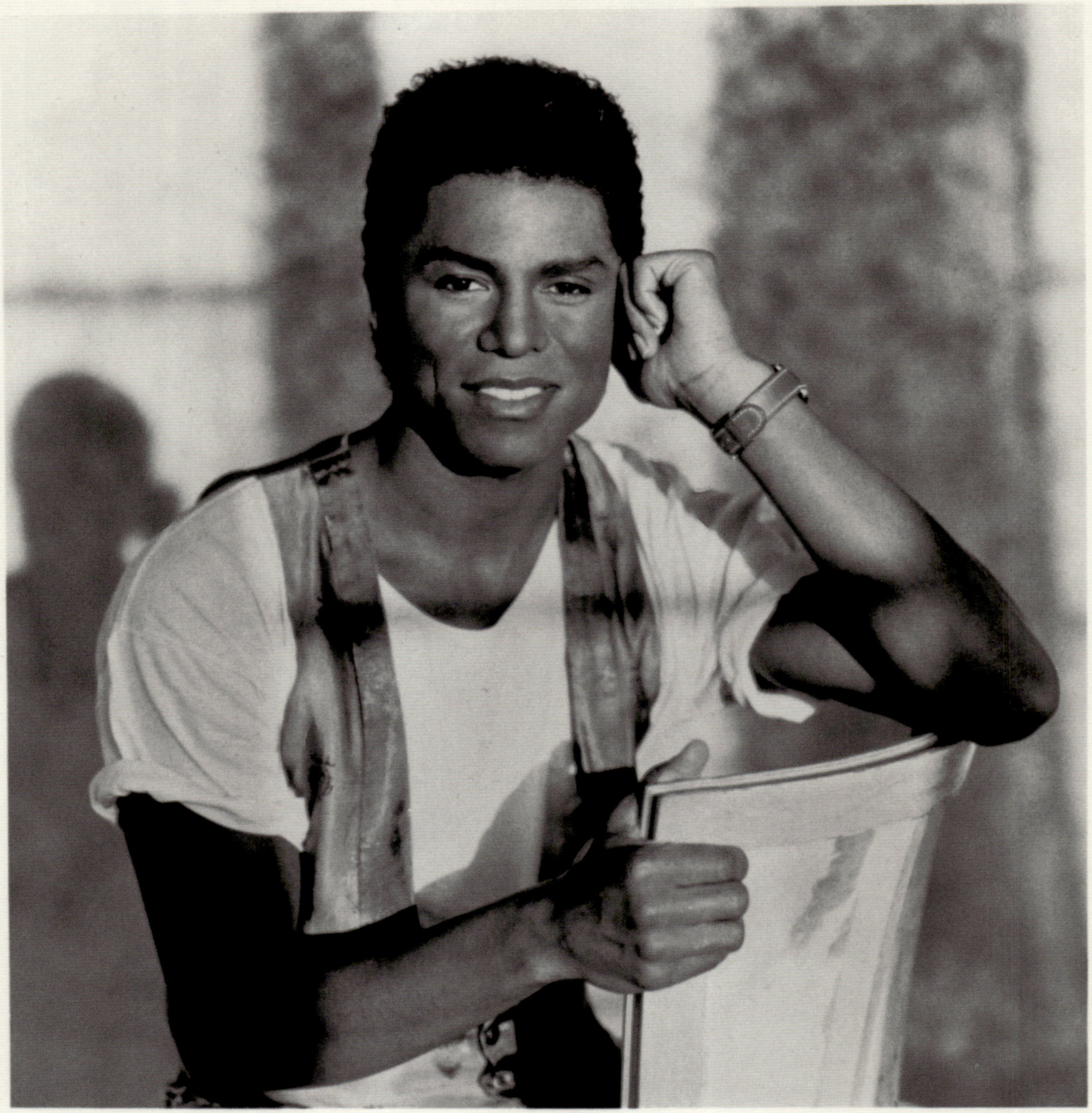

Jermaine Jackson

ARISTA

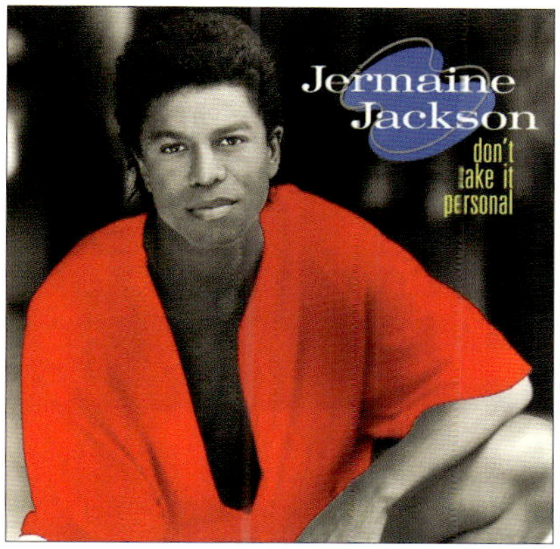

Jermaine Jackson ended the decade on a high note, making it to the top of the R&B charts with the title song from *Don't Take It Personal*, his second No. 1.

Billboard 200: *Don't Take It Personal* (#115)
Billboard Hot 100: "Don't Take It Personal" (#64)

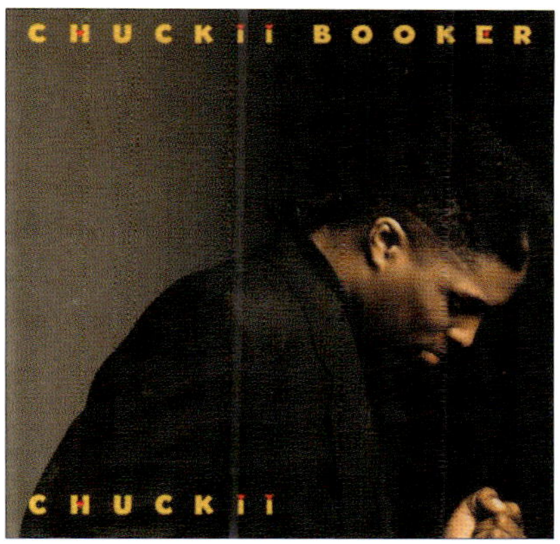

Flaunting his musical skills, **Chuckii Booker** played all the instruments and performed vocals on his debut album, featuring the No. 1 R&B hit "Turned Away."

Billboard 200: *Chuckii* (#116)
Billboard Hot 100: "Turned Away" (#42)

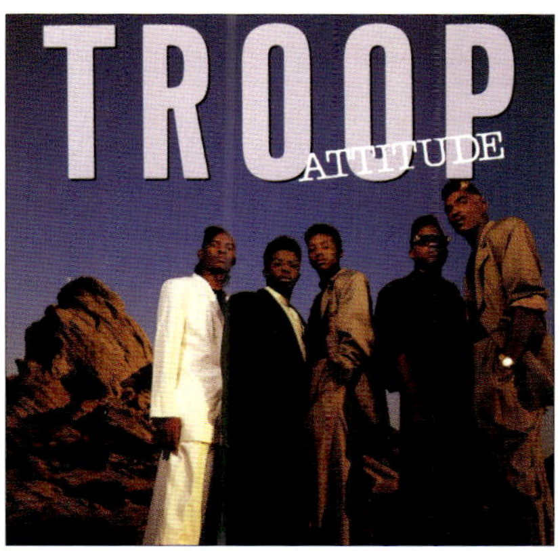

Troop had two leading R&B hits produced by Chuckii Booker—"Spread My Wings," an original song, and "All I Do Is Think of You," a Jackson 5 cover.

Billboard 200: *Attitude* (#75)
Billboard Hot 100: "All I Do Is Think of You" (#47)

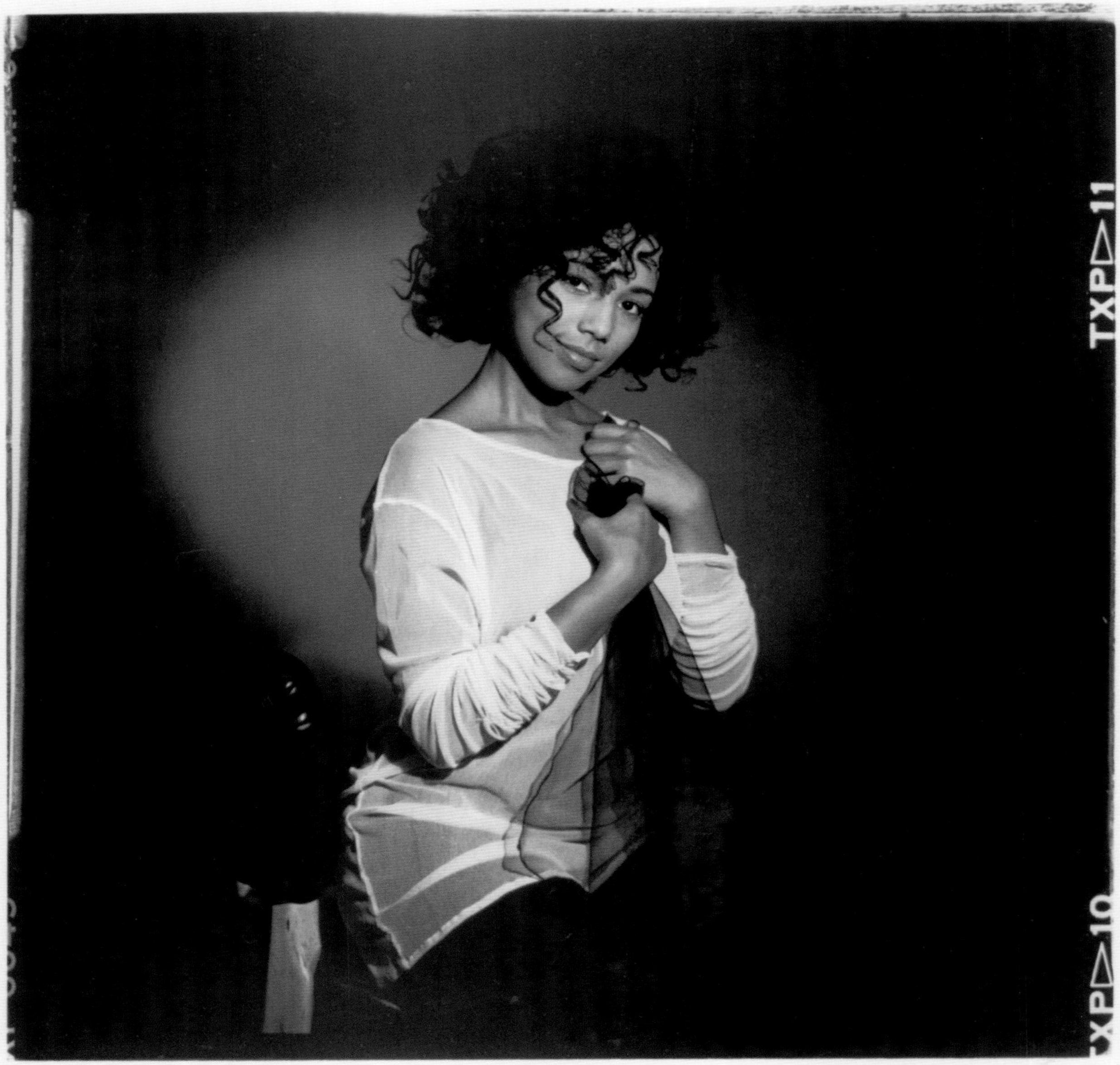

TYLER COLLINS

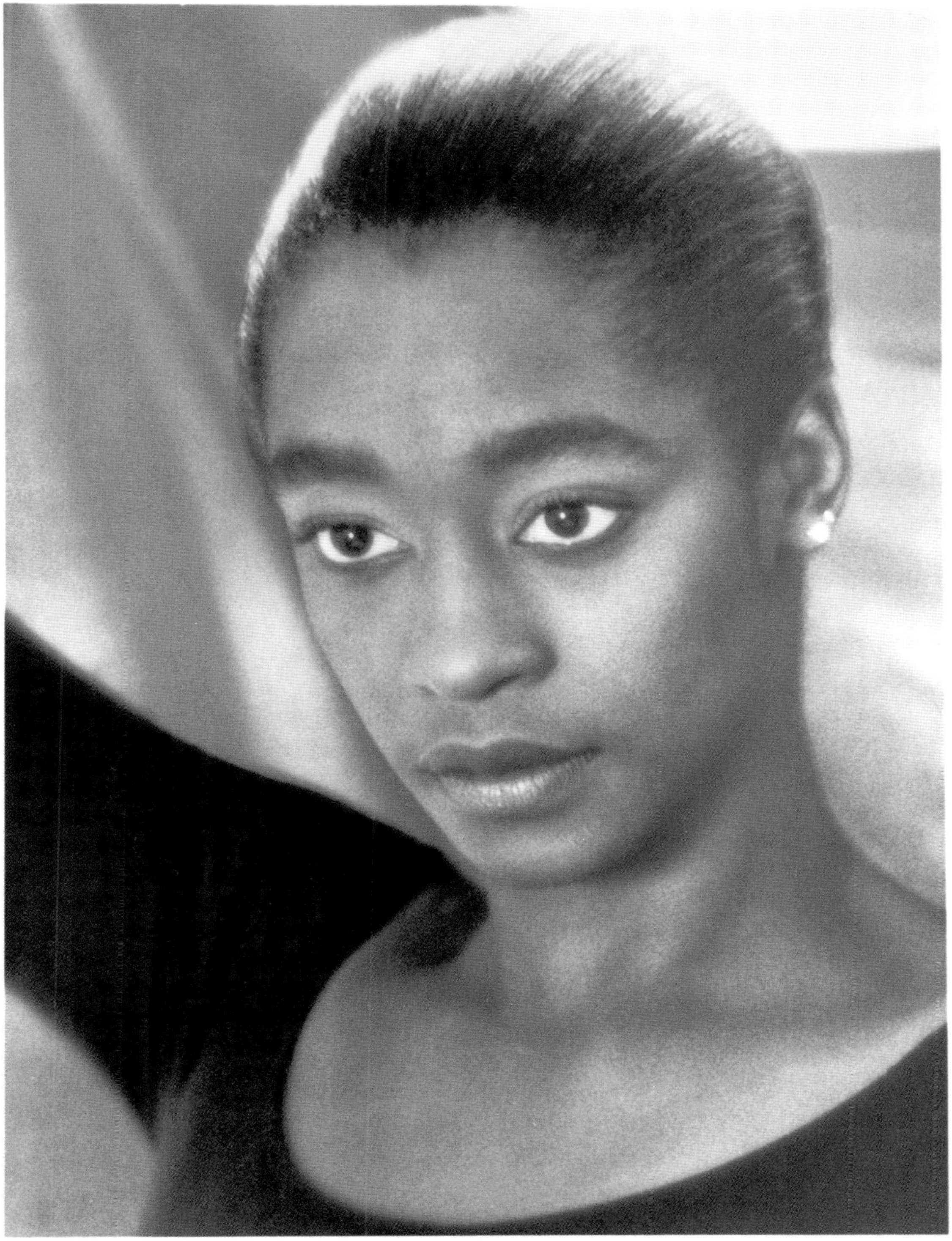

REGINA BELLE

Management:
Mervyn Dash for
Worldwide Entertainment Complex
641 Lexington Avenue
New York, New York 10022
212.421.6249

Columbia

8908

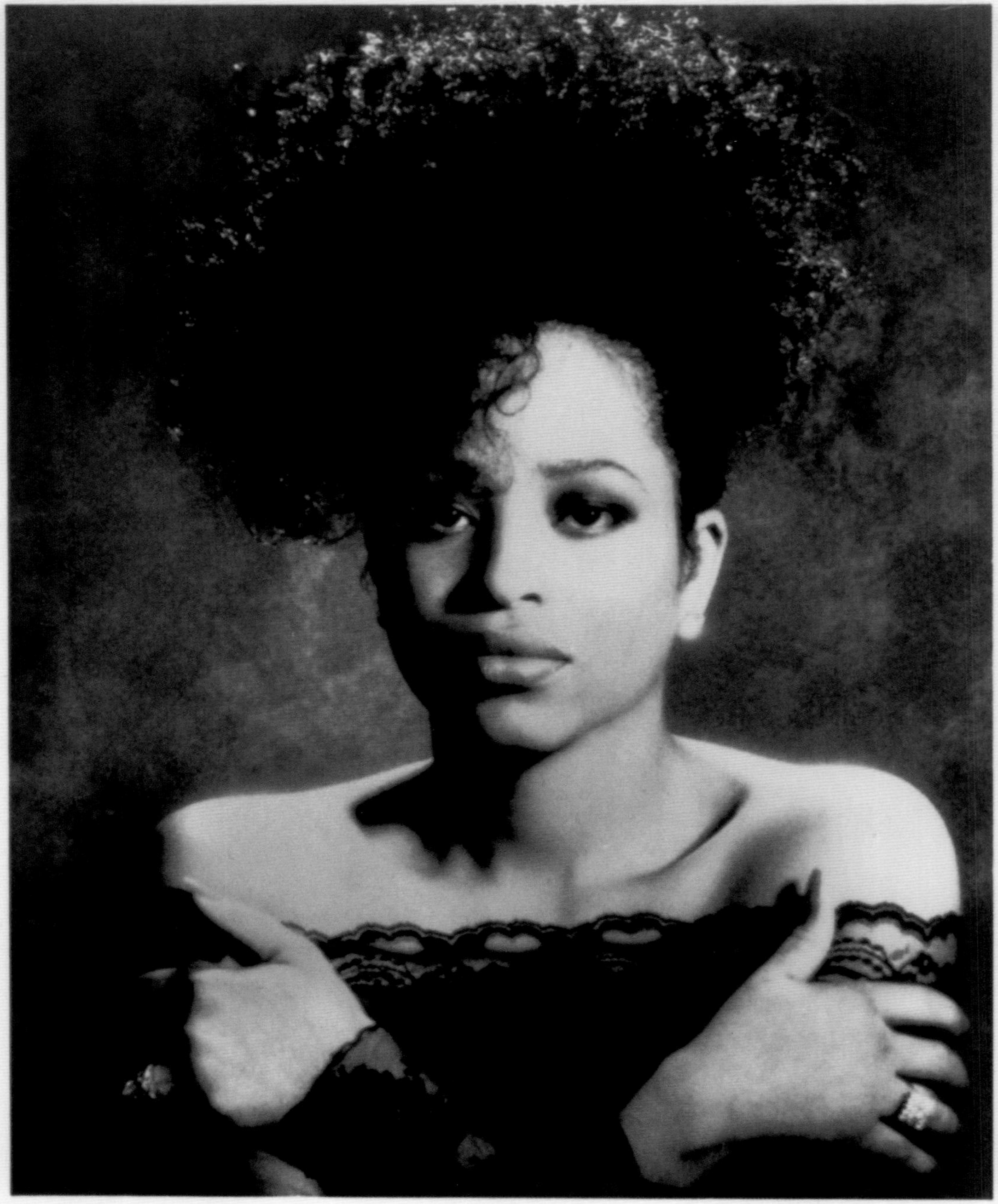

MIKI
HOWARD

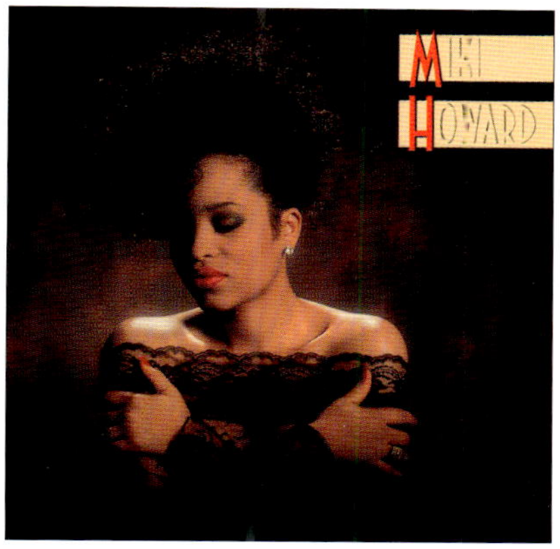

Miki Howard secured an R&B chart-topper, "Ain't Nuthin' in the World," followed by "Love Under New Management," penned amid a fling with Gerald Levert.

Billboard 200: *Miki Howard* (#112)

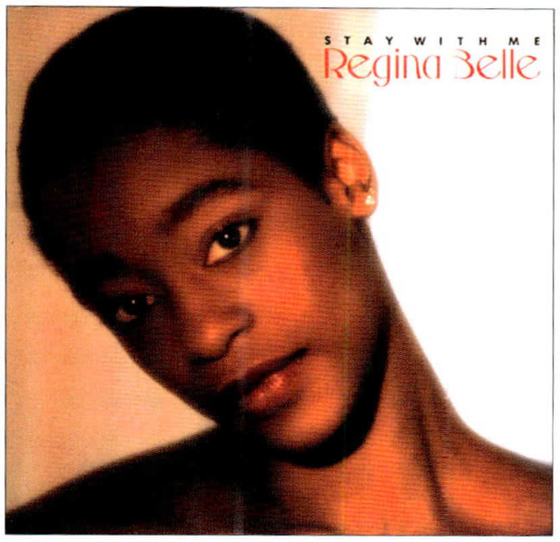

The No. 1 R&B hits "Baby Come to Me" and "Make It Like It Was," from **Regina Belle**'s second album, *Stay with Me*, secured the smooth soul singer's success.

Billboard 200: *Stay with Me* (#63)
Billboard Hot 100: "Baby Come to Me" (#60);
"Make It Like It Was" (#43)

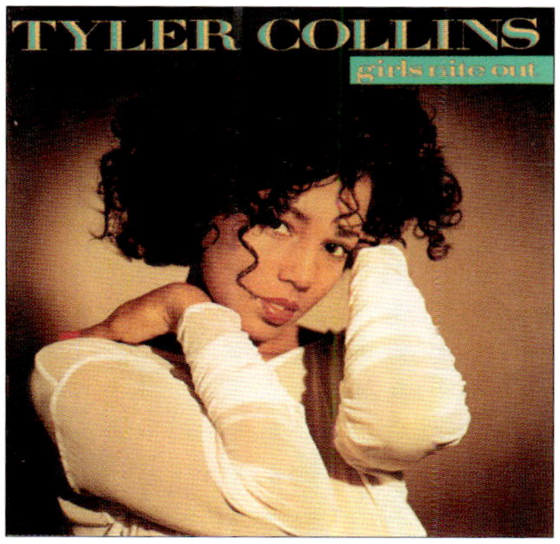

Tyler Collins scored a pair of hits, reaching the pop charts with the witty title track from *Girls Nite Out* and the R&B charts with "Whatcha Gonna Do."

Billboard 200: *Girls Nite Out* (#85)
Billboard Hot 100: "Girls Nite Out" (#6); "Second Chance" (#53)

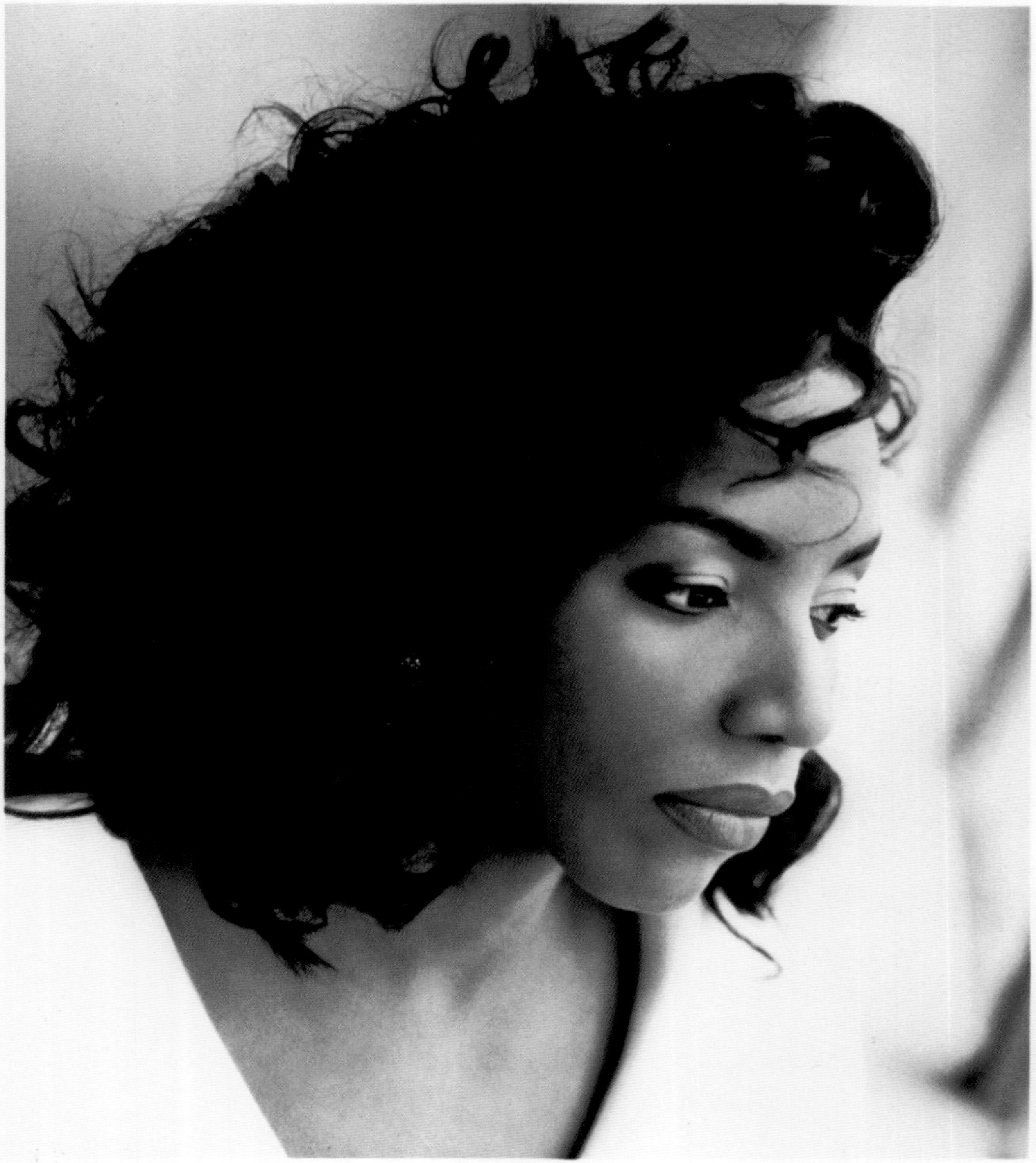

Photo Credit: Alberto Tolot

STEPHANIE MILLS

6/89

MCA RECORDS

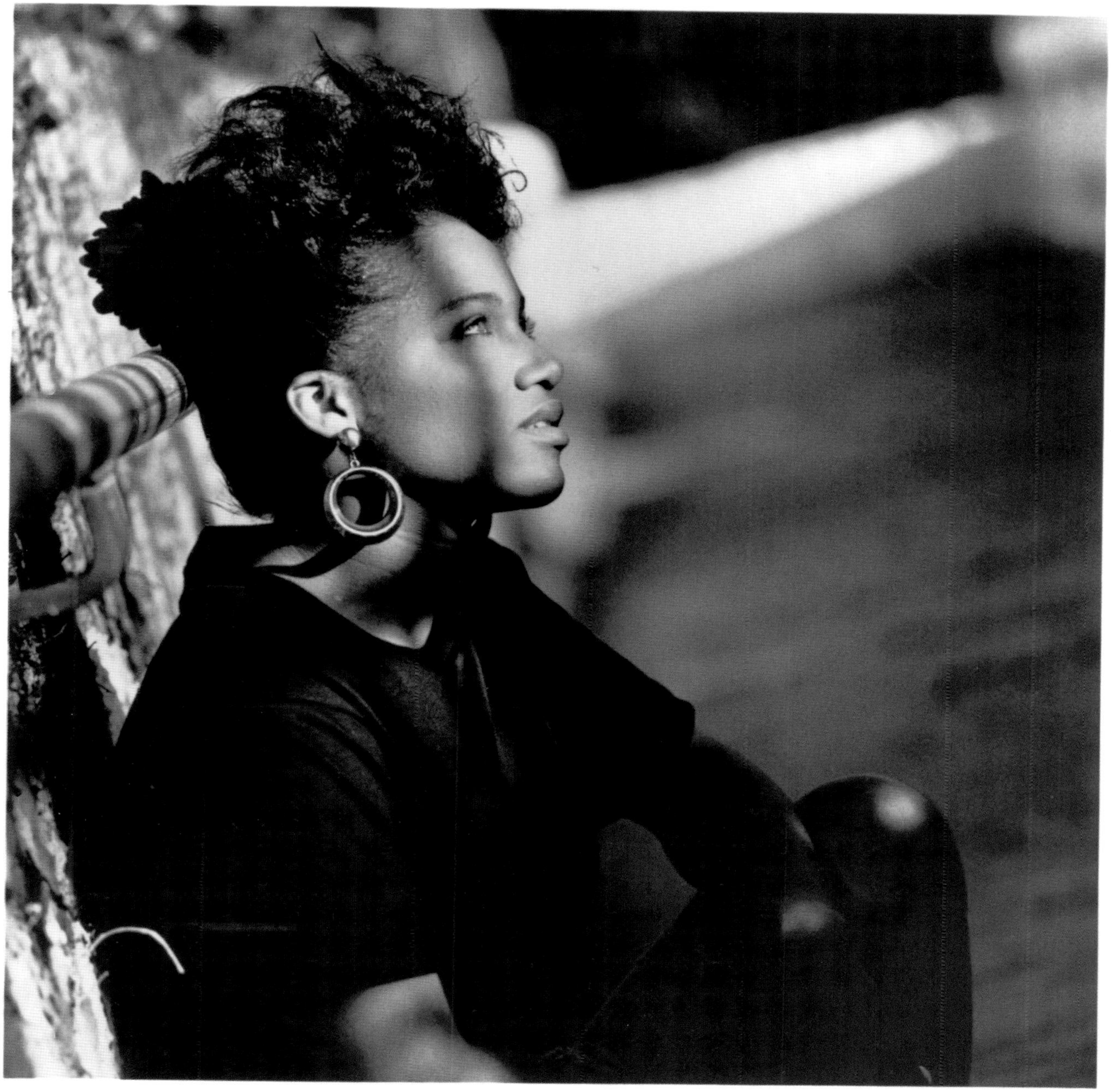

MICHEL'LE

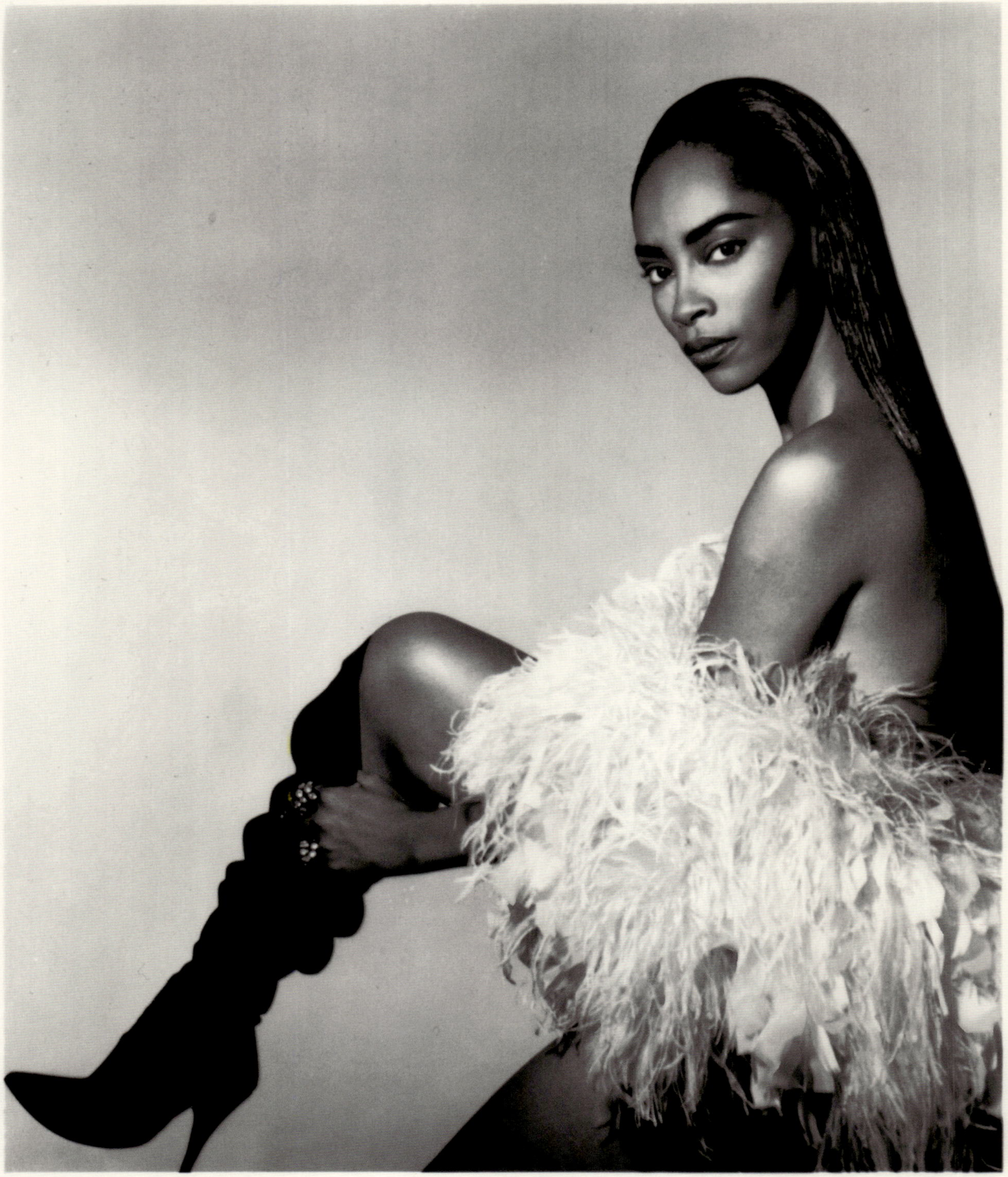

JW

3/89

MCA RECORDS

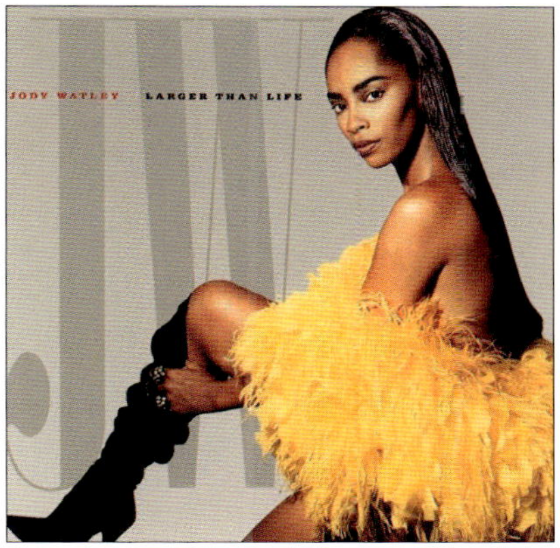

Singer **Jody Watley** chased her Grammy Award for Best New Artist with "Real Love" and "Friends," the latter song featuring raps from Eric B. & Rakim.

Billboard 200: *Larger Than Life* (#16)
Billboard Hot 100: "Real Love" (#2); "Friends" (#9); "Everything" (#4); "Precious Love" (#87)

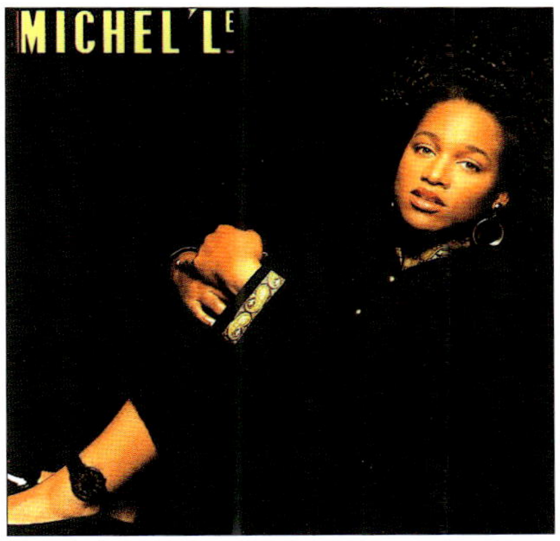

Produced by Dr. Dre but not echoing his signature gangsta-rap sound, **Michel'le**'s self-titled debut album claimed "No More Lies," a hot R&B and pop hit.

Billboard 200: *Michel'le* (#35)
Billboard Hot 100: "No More Lies" (#7); "Nicety" (#29); "Something in My Heart" (#31)

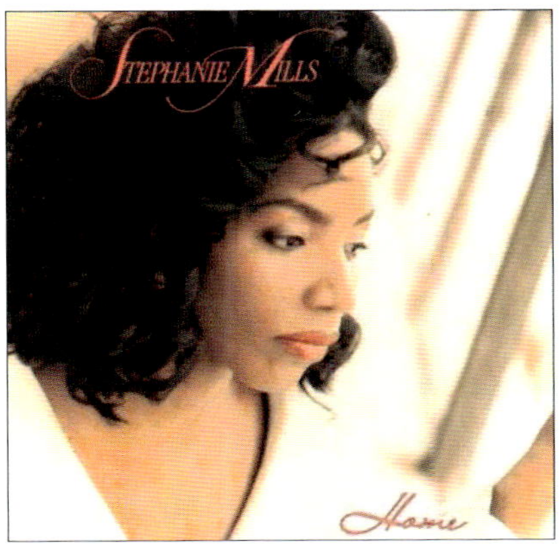

From *Home*, Broadway's **Stephanie Mills** fashioned her fourth and fifth No. 1 R&B tracks, "Something in the Way (You Make Me Feel)" and the title song.

Billboard 200: *Home* #82)

TOMMY McCONNELL
BONNE DUNNING BARRINO
WAYNE WILENTZ
DOLORES DUNNING-MILLIGAN
DENISE DUNNING CRAWFORD
ANIBAL BOOCHIE SIERRA
SOLOMON ROBERTS JR.
GERALD LEBON

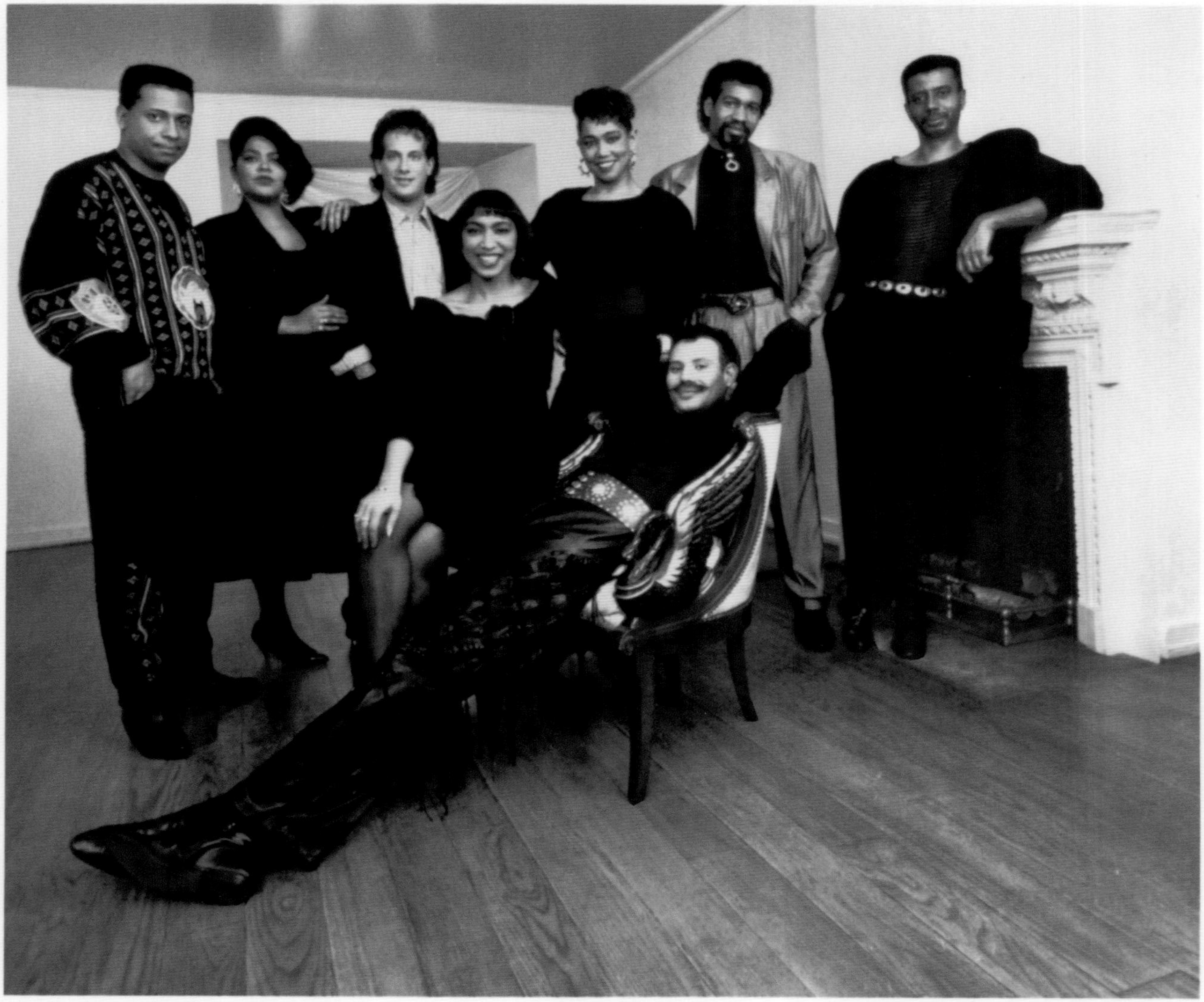

SKYY

ATLANTIC

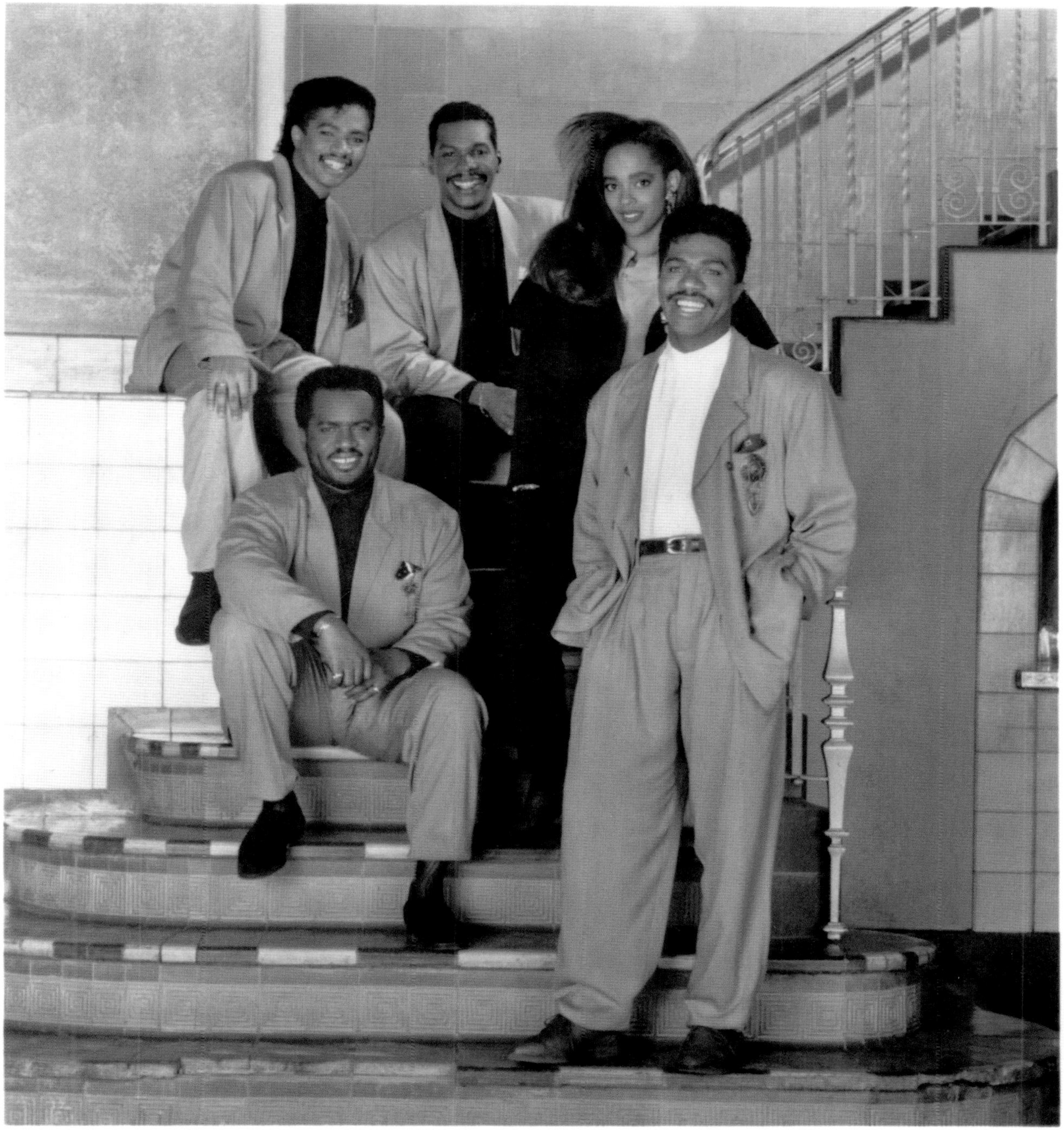

Photo Credit: Alan Dockery

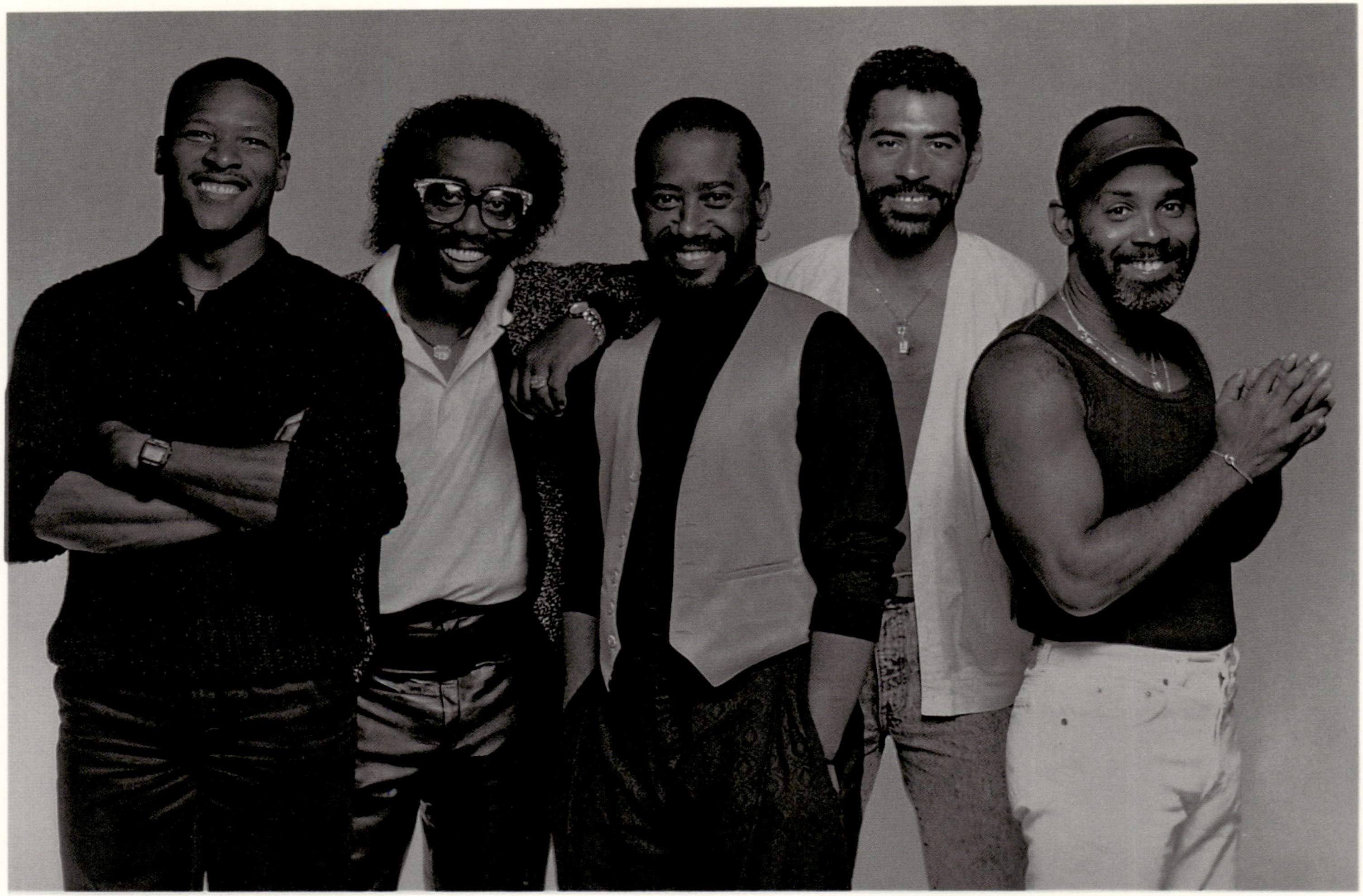

MAZE

FEATURING FRANKIE BEVERLY

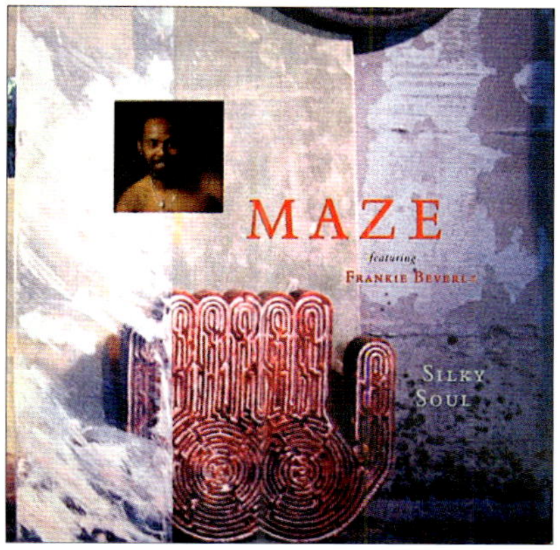

The abiding **Maze** featuring Frankie Beverly earned another gold record with *Silky Soul* and one more No. 1 R&B hit with the forlorn "Can't Get Over You."

Billboard 200: *Silky Soul* (#37)

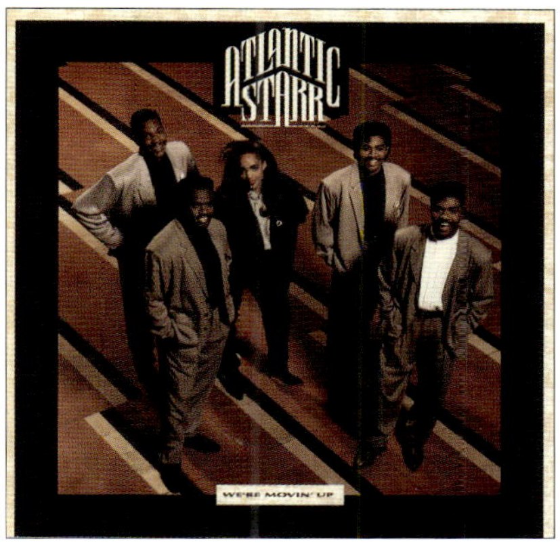

Bringing in another new female vocalist, Porscha Martin, **Atlantic Starr** produced its second No. 1 single on the R&B charts with the dreamy "My First Love."

Billboard 200: *We're Movin' Up* (#125)

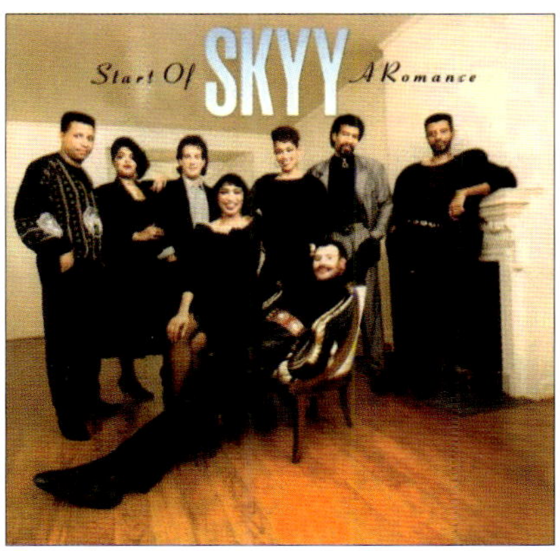

Mounting a comeback with the *Start of a Romance* album, funky disco band **Skyy** secured two No. 1 R&B hits, the title track and the smooth "Real Love."

Billboard 200: *Start of a Romance* (#115)
Billboard Hot 100: "Real Love" (#47)

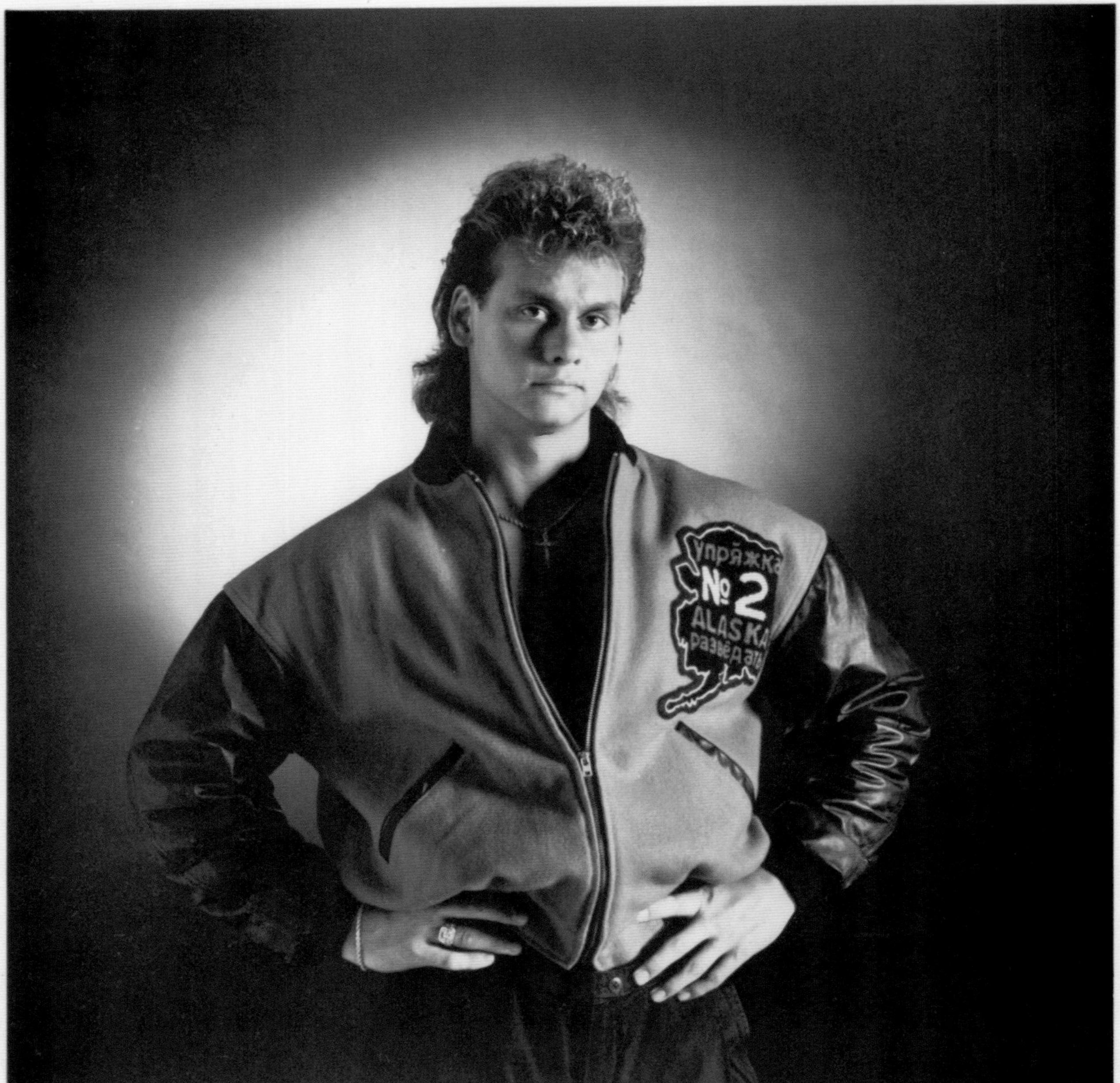

Photo Credit: George Dubose

4TH B'WAY™

DINO

DISTRIBUTED BY THE ISLAND TRADING CO. ISLAND

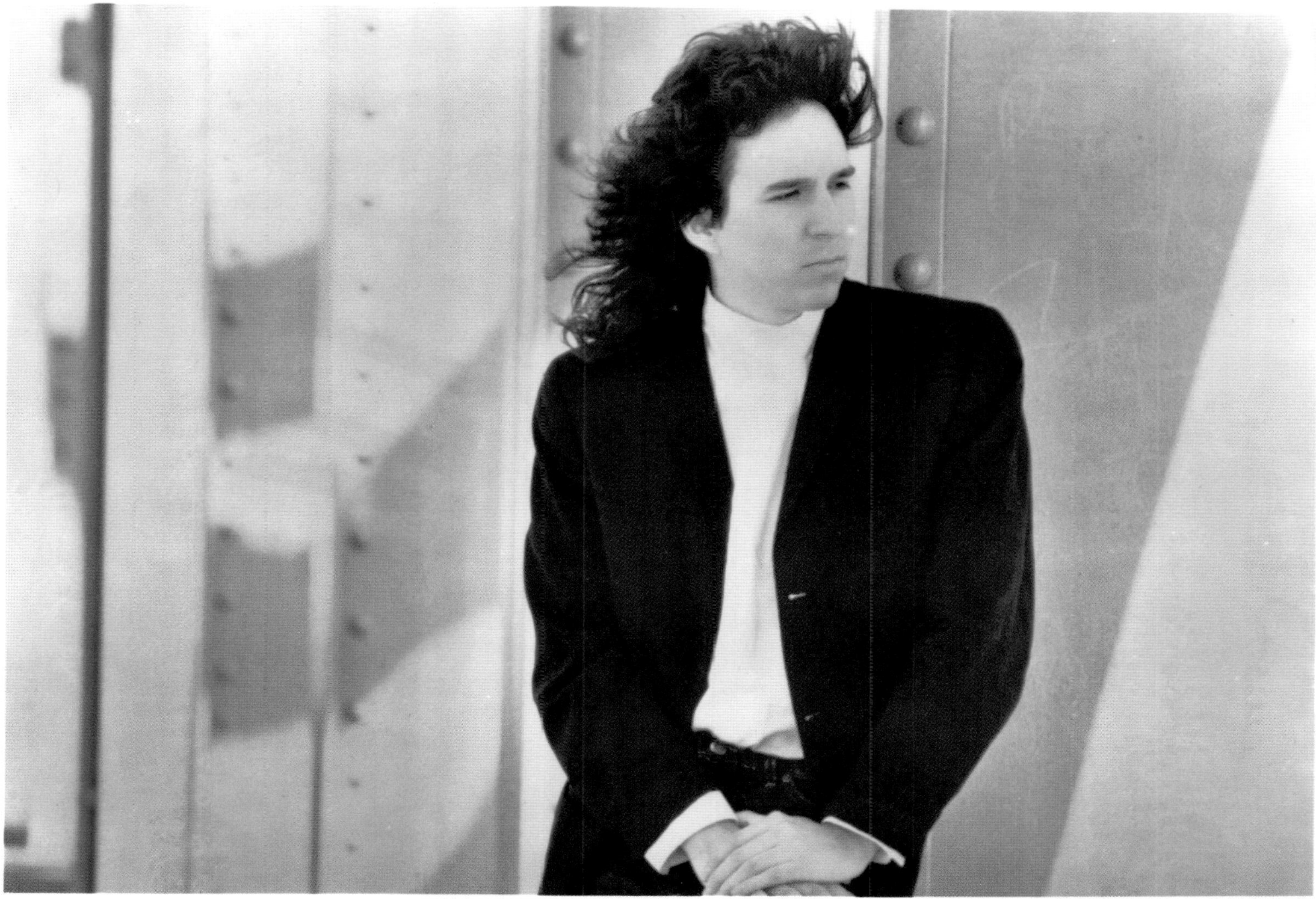

© PolyGram 1989

MICHAEL MORALES

WING RECORDS

PolyGram™

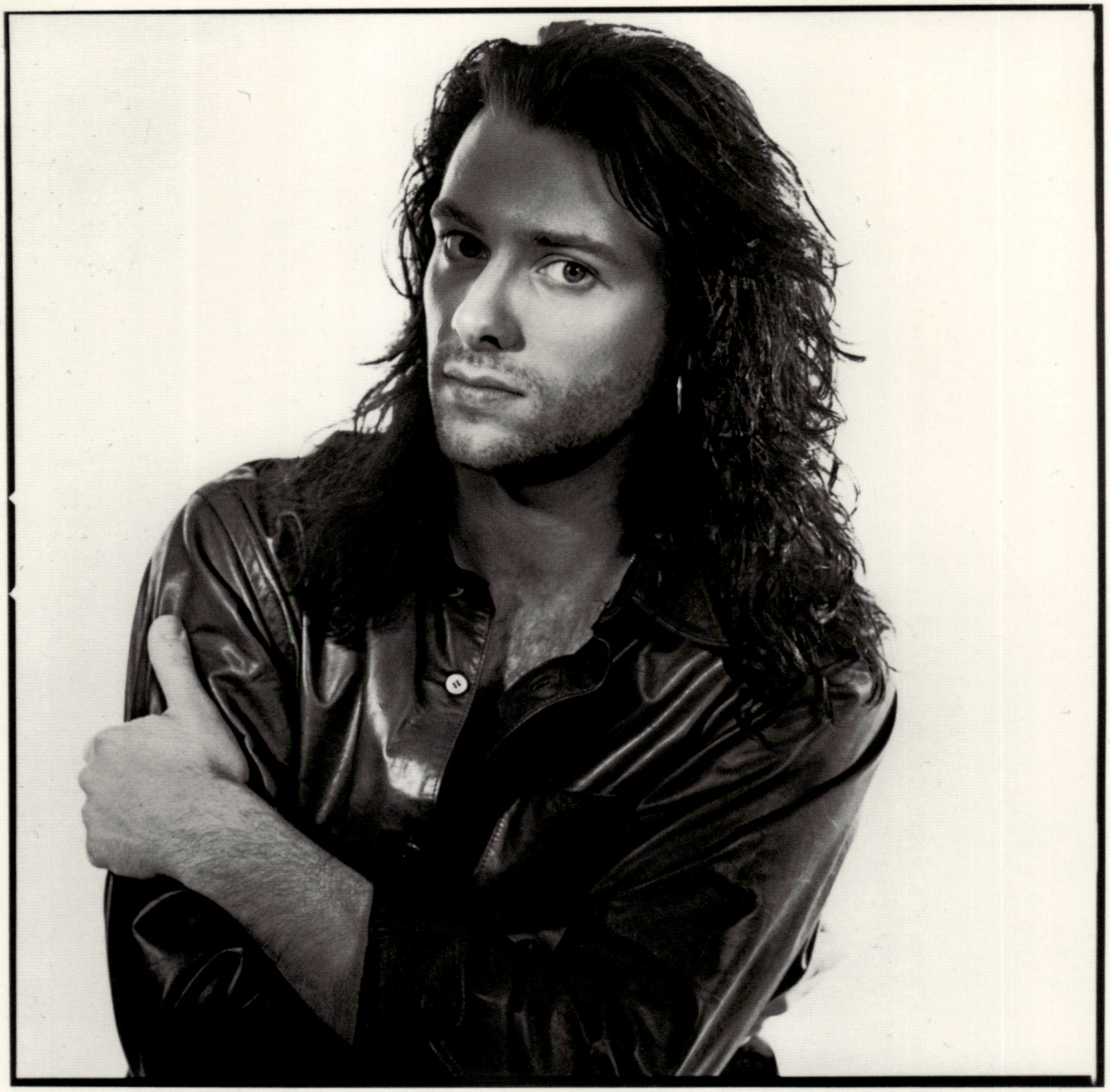

Photo credit: Brian Hagiwara 7/89

KEVIN
PAIGE

Chrysalis.

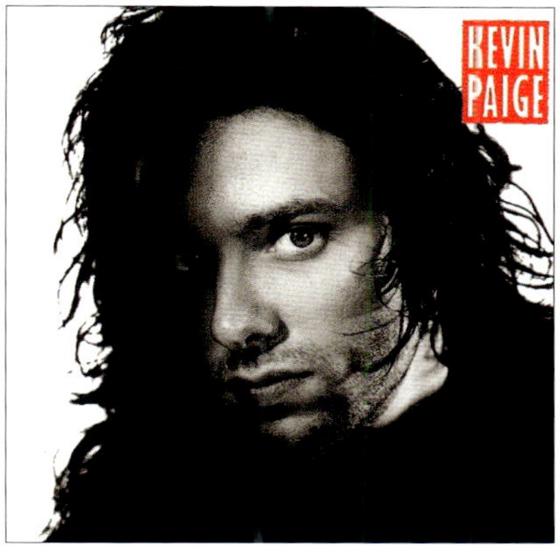

From his self-titled debut album, Memphis-based pop singer **Kevin Paige** launched a pair of Top 40 hits, "Don't Shut Me Out" and "Anything I Want."

Billboard 200: *Kevin Paige* (#107)
Billboard Hot 100: "Don't Shut Me Out" (#18);
"Anything I Want" (#29)

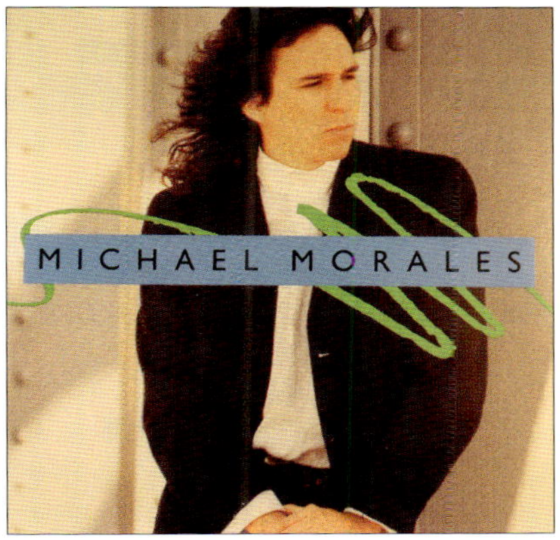

Michael Morales' first record landed three singles on the pop charts, including the sprightly "Who Do You Give Your Love To?" and a Romantics cover.

Billboard 200: *Michael Morales* (#113)
Billboard Hot 100: "Who Do You Give Your Love To?" (#15);
"What I Like About You" (#28); "I Don't Know" (#81)

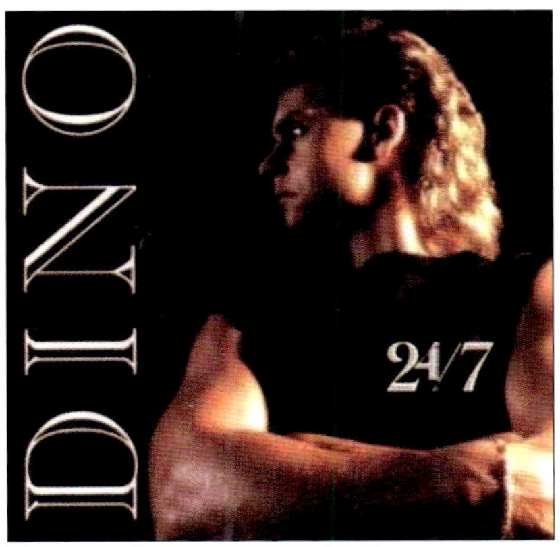

A former Las Vegas DJ, singer-songwriter **Dino** produced his first album, *24/7*, with the hit "I Like It" reaching the Top 10 on the pop and dance charts.

Billboard 200: *24/7* (#34)
Billboard Hot 100: "Summergirls" (#50); "24/7" (#42);
"I Like It" (#7); "Sunshine" (#23); "Never 2 Much of U" (#61)

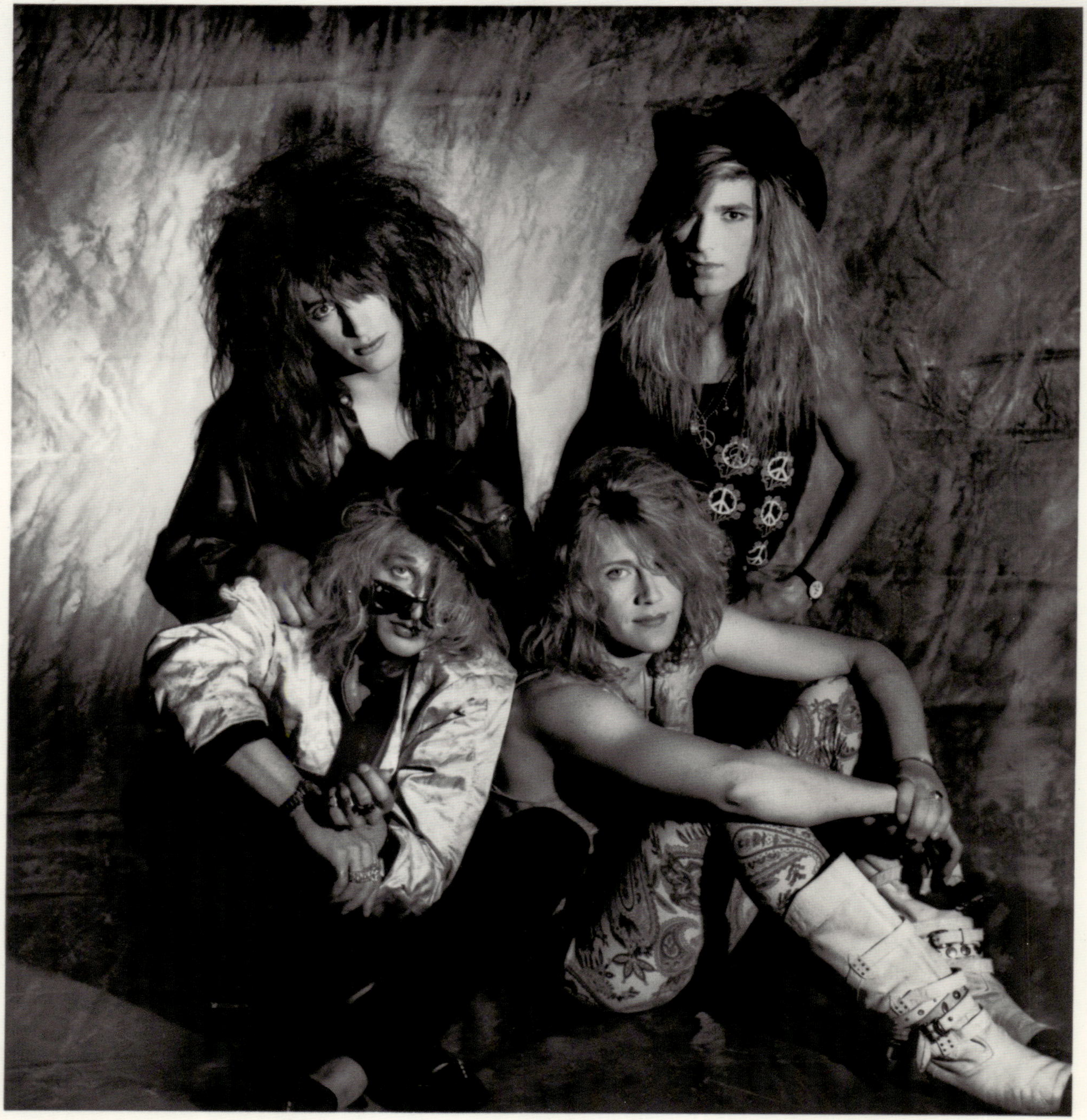

DEREK FRIGO VIKKI FOXX
CHIP Z'NUFF DONNIE VIE

ENUFF Z'NUFF

ATCO

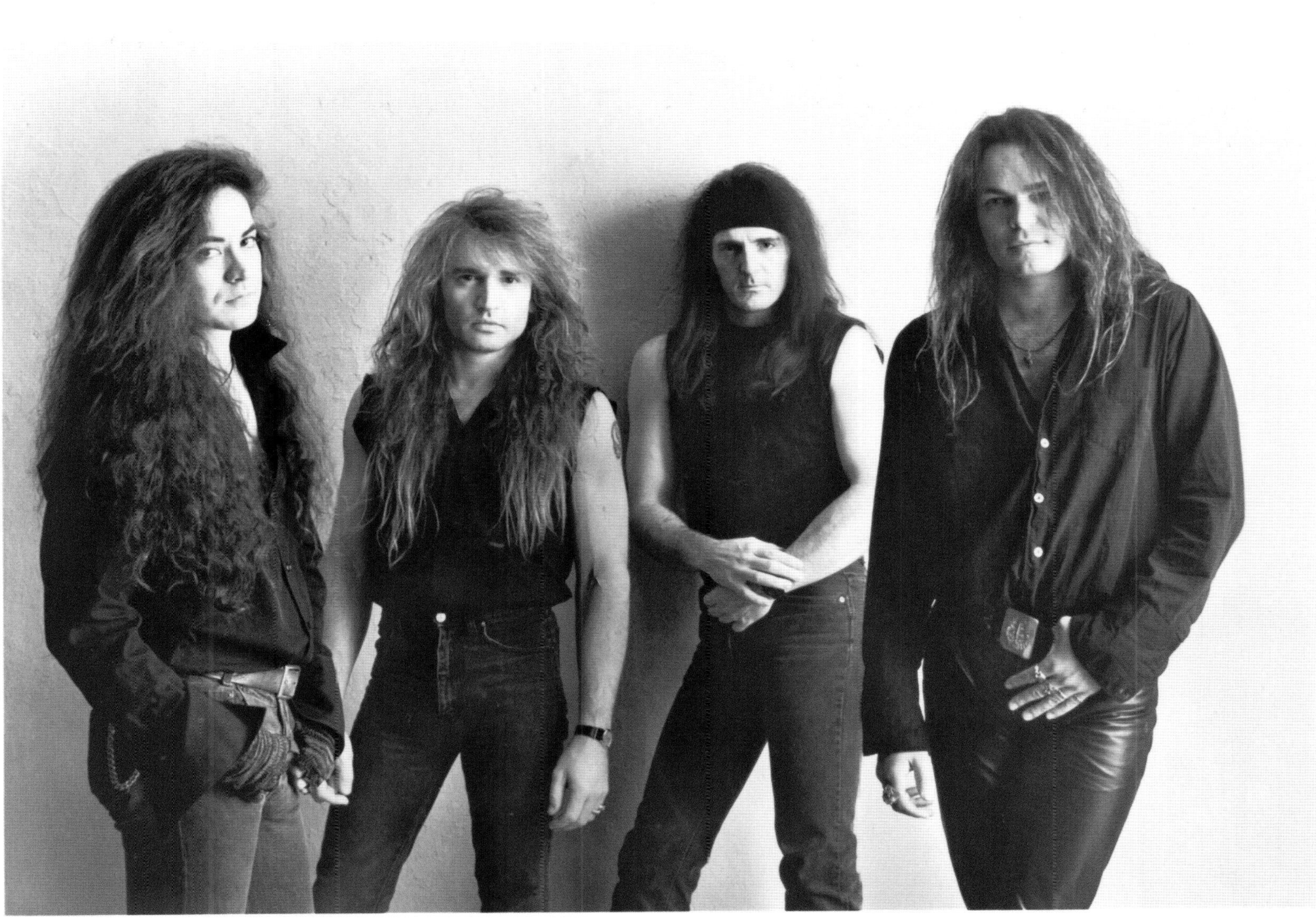

JAKE E. LEE ERIC SINGER GREG CHAISSON RAY GILLEN

BADLANDS

ATLANTIC TITANIUM

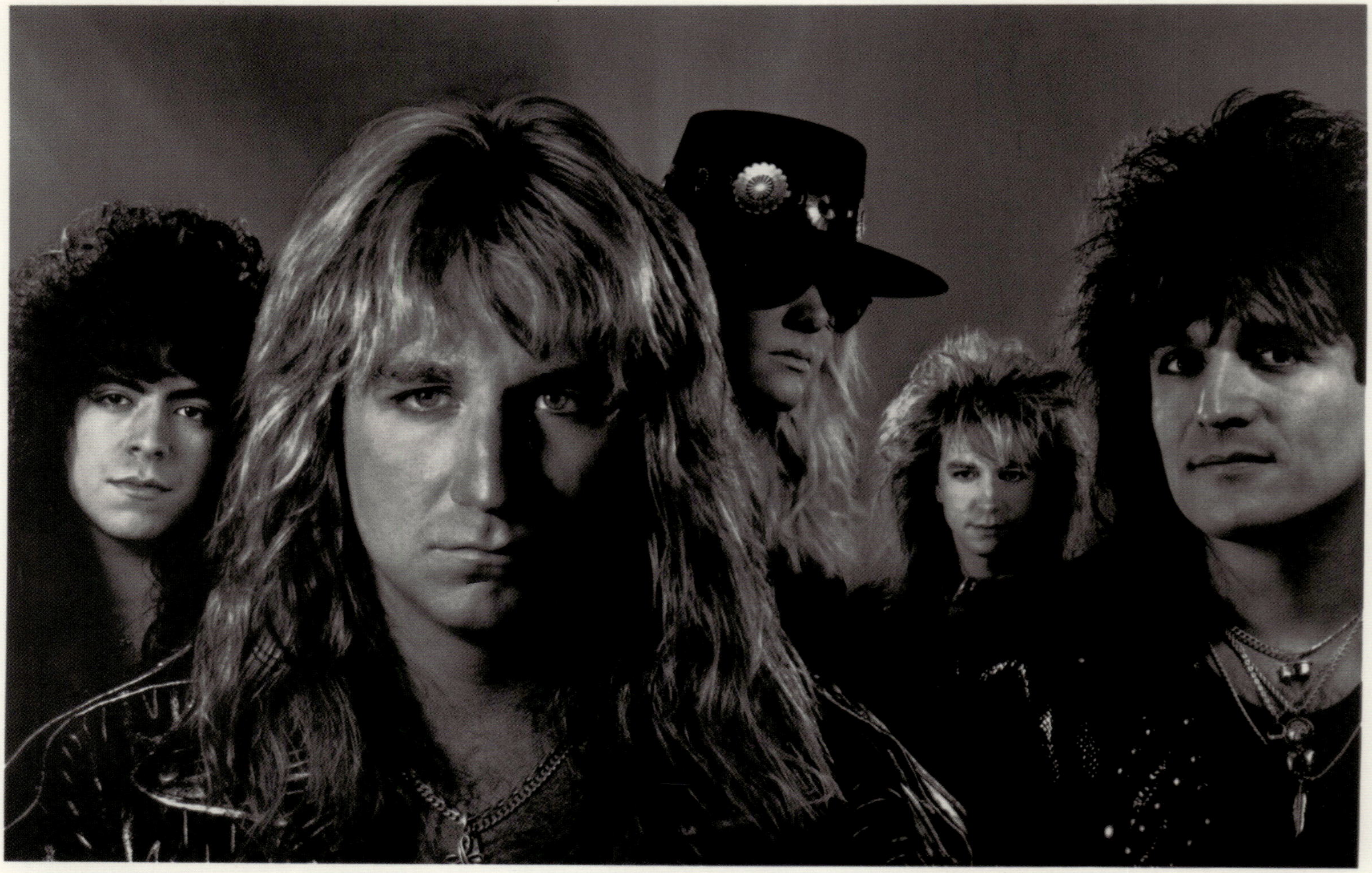

Photo: Doug Hyun / 1989

Tony Montana | Jack Russell | Mark Kendall | Michael Lardie | Audie Desbrow

Great White

Capitol Records

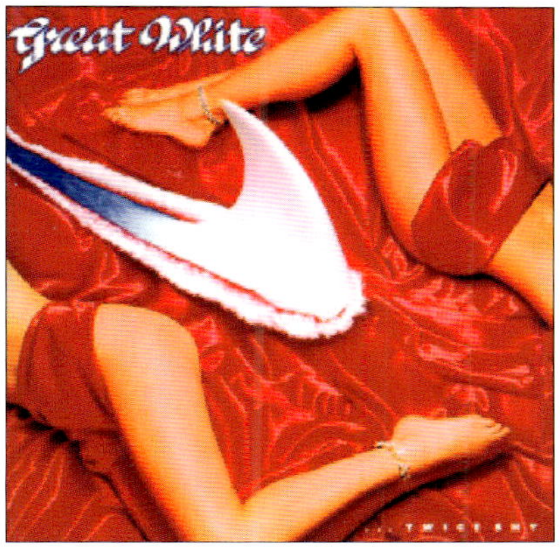

Hard-rock band **Great White** reaped massive airplay on MTV with the music video for "Once Bitten, Twice Shy," a cover of Ian Hunter's hit single in the UK.

Billboard 200: *...Twice Shy* (#9)
Billboard Hot 100: "Once Bitten, Twice Shy" (#5); "The Angel Song" (#30); "House of Broken Love" (#83)

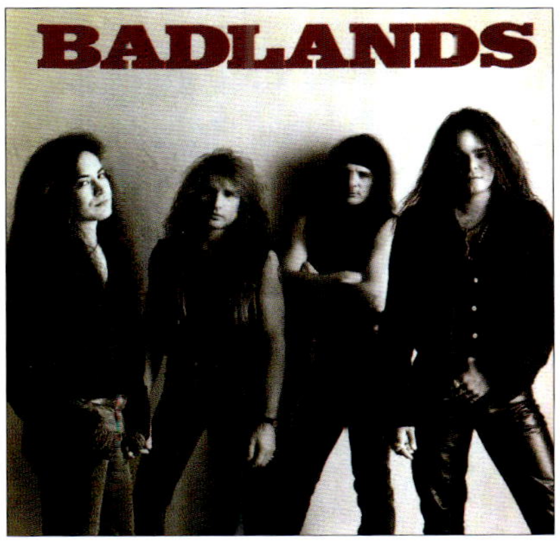

Founded by former Ozzy Osbourne guitarist Jake E. Lee and Black Sabbath singer Ray Gillen, **Badlands** served up an album of stripped-down blues-rock.

Billboard 200: *Badlands* (#57)

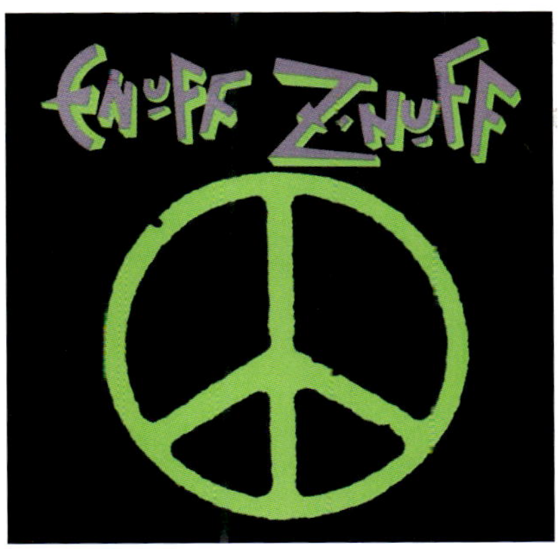

Chicago-area pop-metal band **Enuff Z'Nuff** issued a self-titled debut, scoring a pair of charting singles, "New Thing" and the ballad "Fly High Michelle."

Billboard 200: *Enuff Z'Nuff* (#74)
Billboard Hot 100: "New Thing" (#67); "Fly High Michelle" (#47)

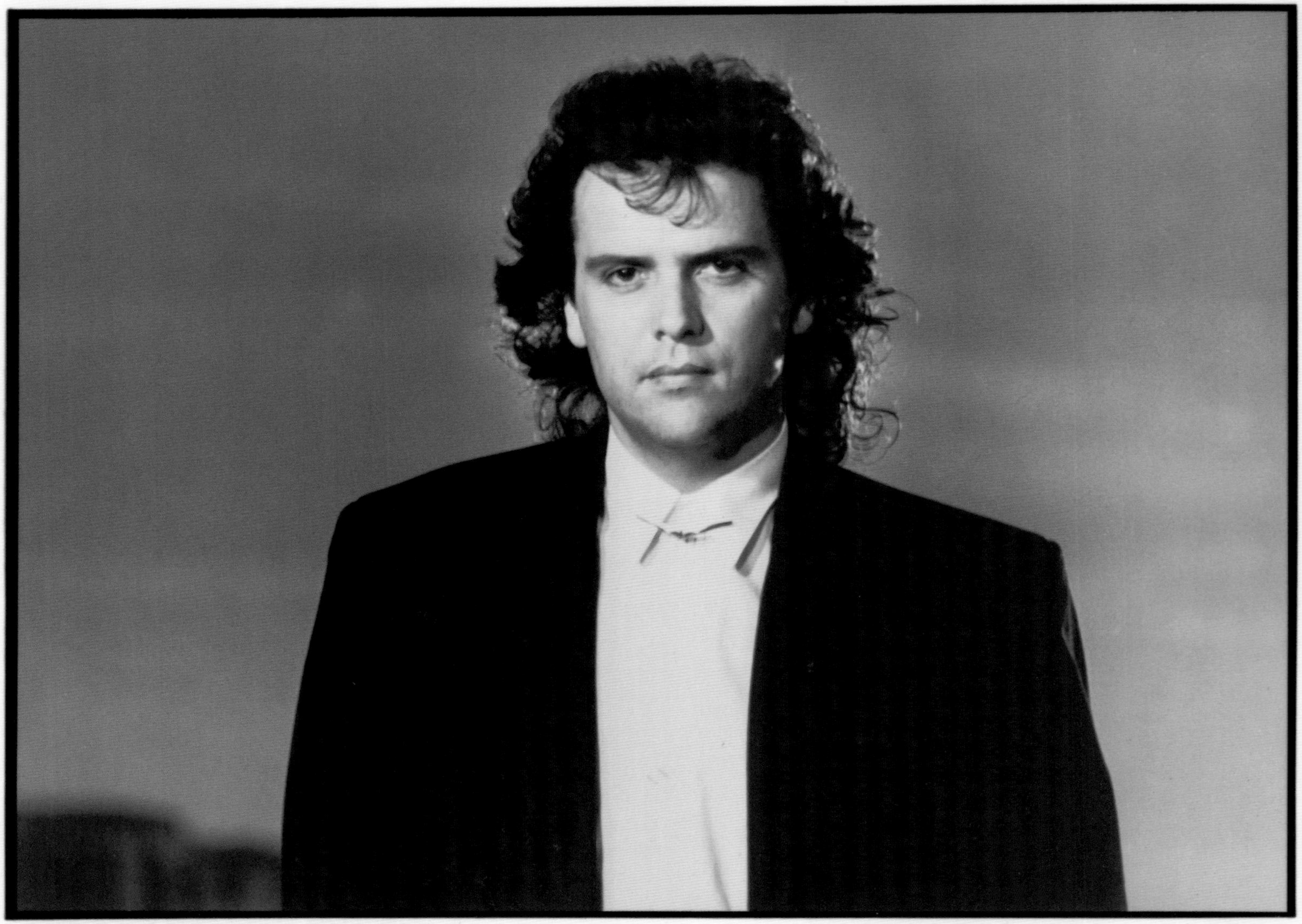

PHOTO CREDIT: LISA POWERS / 1989

TREVOR RABIN

ELEKTRA

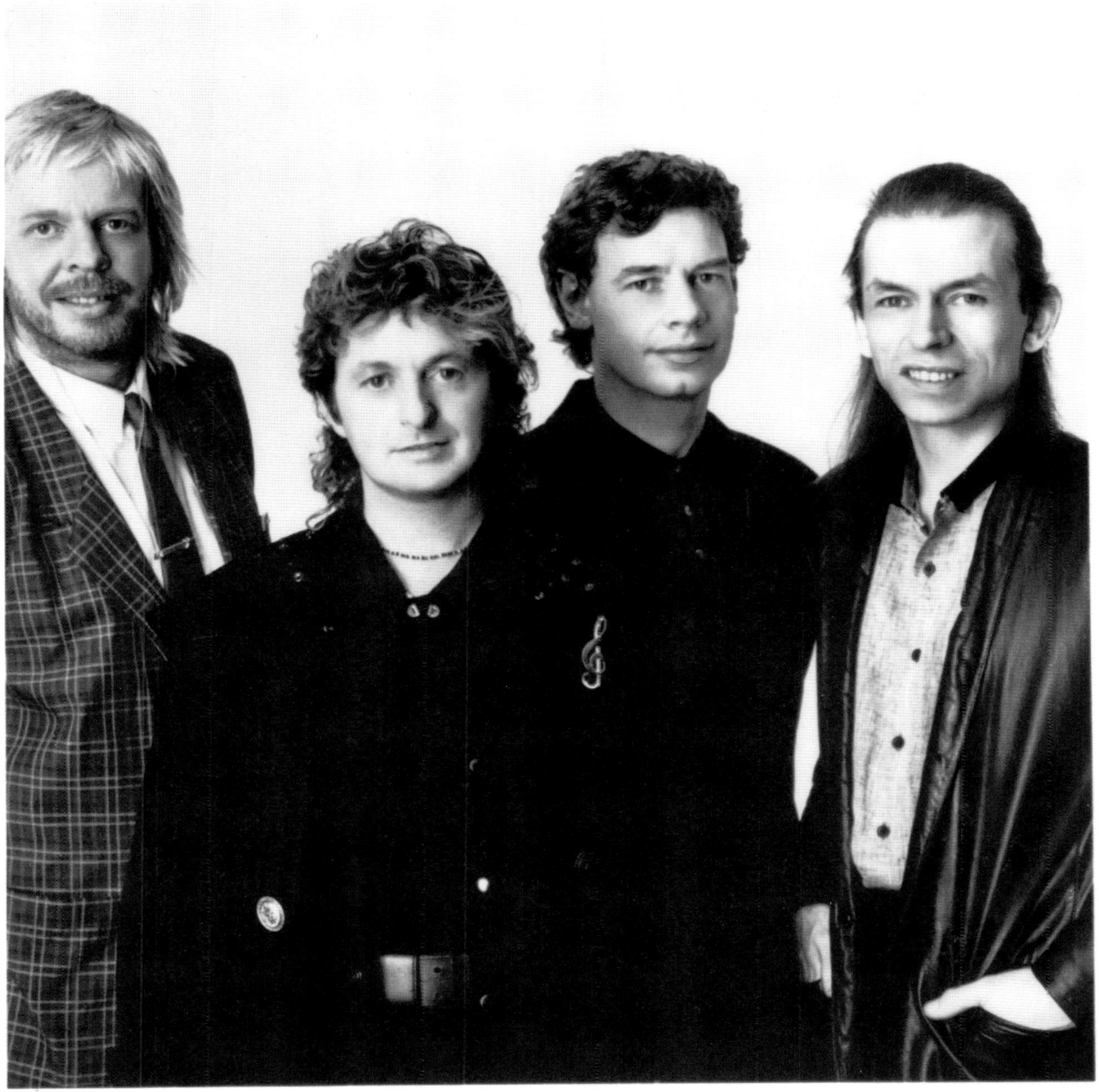

Management:

Sunarts Music Ltd.
Brian Lane
9 Hillgate Street
London W8 7SP
England

(011) (441) 727-2791

ANDERSON BRUFORD WAKEMAN HOWE

ARISTA™

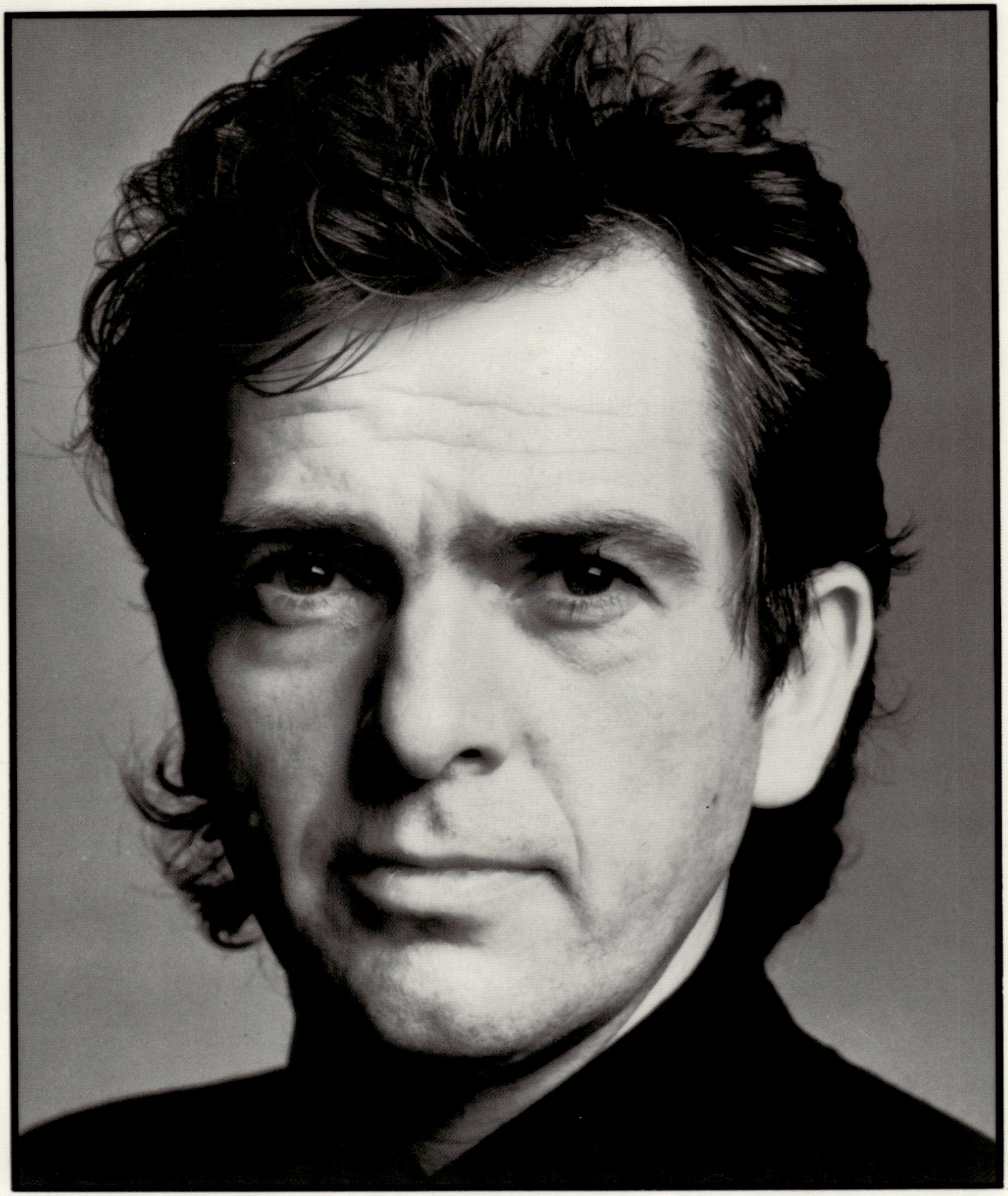

Photo Credit: Annie Leibovitz

PETER GABRIEL

GEFFEN RECORDS

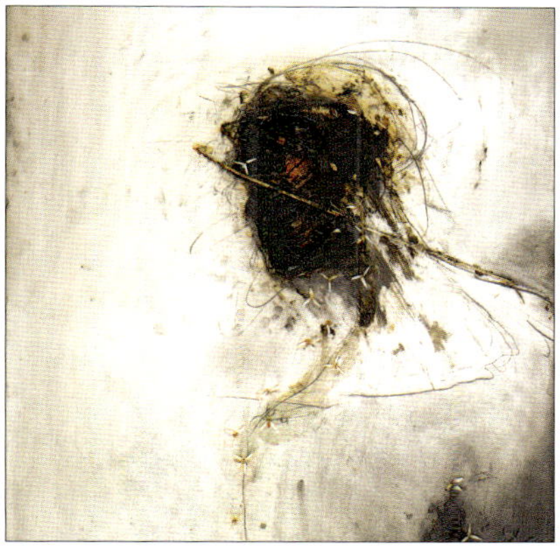

A soundtrack developed for Martin Scorsese's film *The Last Temptation of Christ*, **Peter Gabriel**'s *Passion* won a Grammy for Best New Age Performance.

Billboard 200: *Passion* (#60)

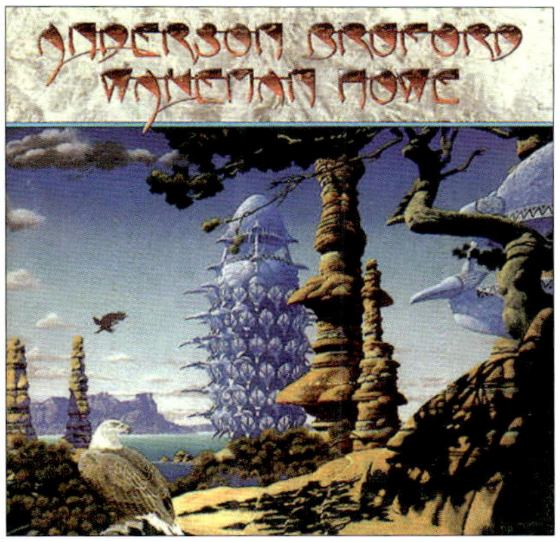

Anderson Bruford Wakeman Howe, made up of four alumni of the British progressive rock band Yes, released its lone studio album and embarked on a tour.

Billboard 200: *Anderson Bruford Wakeman Howe* (#30)

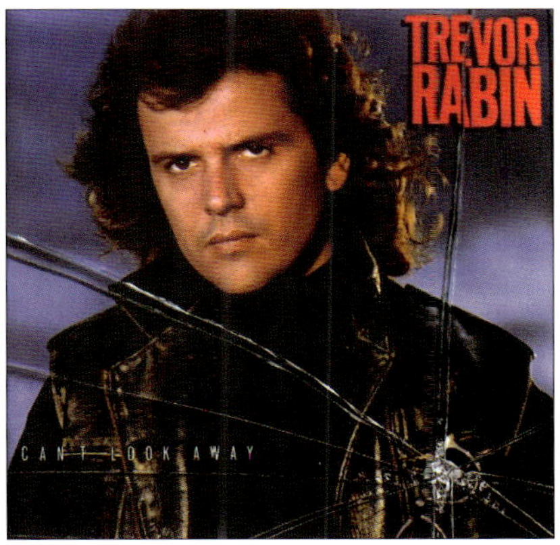

Having gained prominence during his tenure in Yes, guitarist **Trevor Rabin** used a period of inactivity to prepare his fourth solo album, *Can't Look Away*.

Billboard 200: *Can't Look Away* (#111)

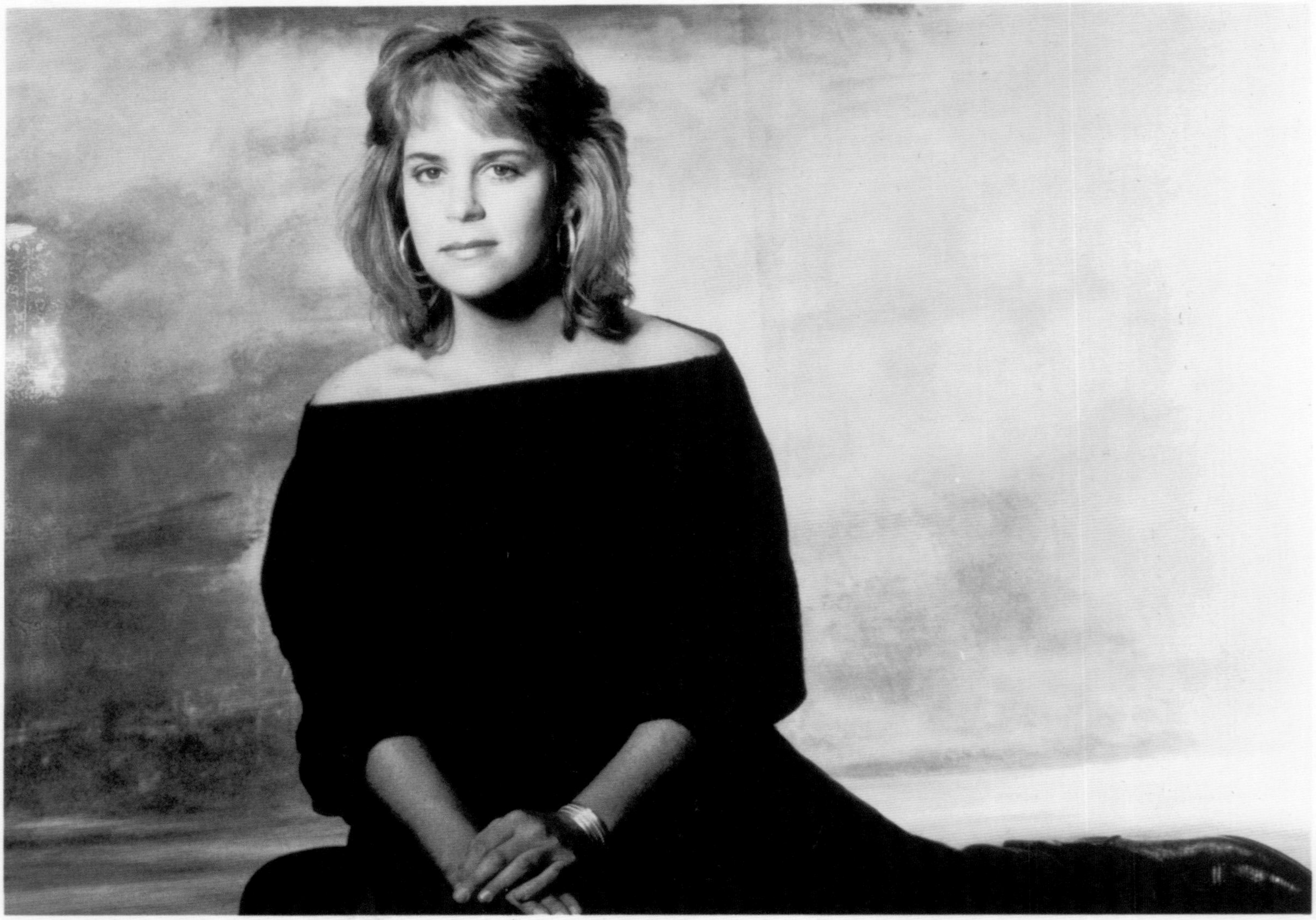
credit: Randee St. Nicholas

MARY CHAPIN CARPENTER

Columbia

8905

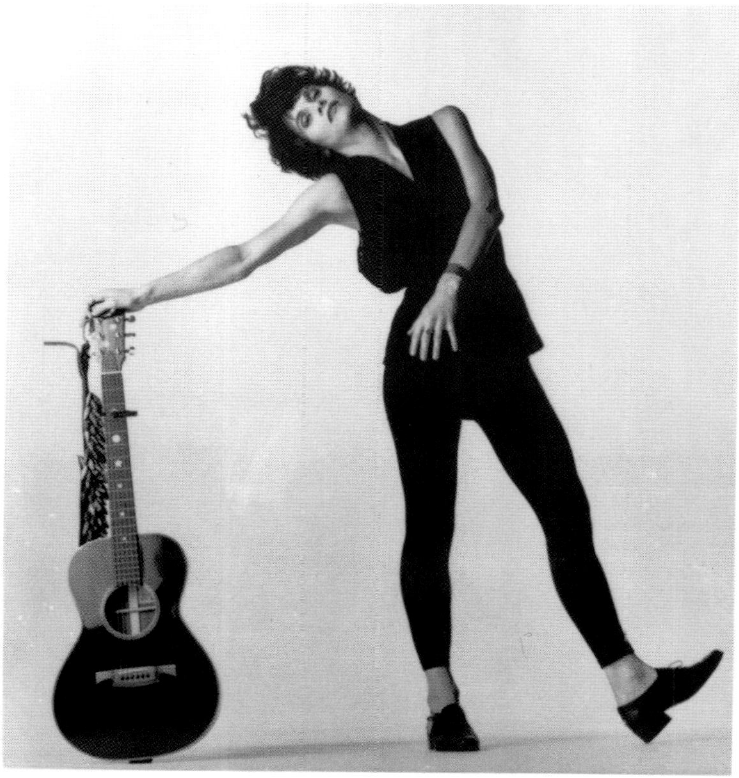

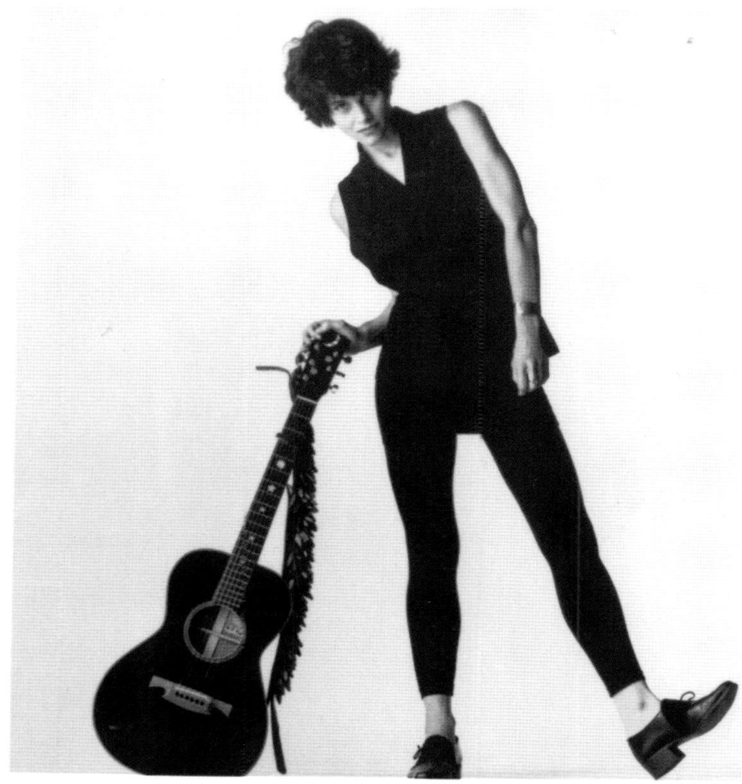

PHOTOGRAPH: FRANK OCKENFELS 3

AGF ENTERTAINMENT LTD.
1500 Broadway, Suite 1703, New York, N.Y. 10036-4015
Telephone: (212) 921-3332 Fax: (212) 302-1293
Telex: 4900009067 AGF UI, E Mail: AGF-US IMC 2952

SHAWN COLVIN

Columbia
8909

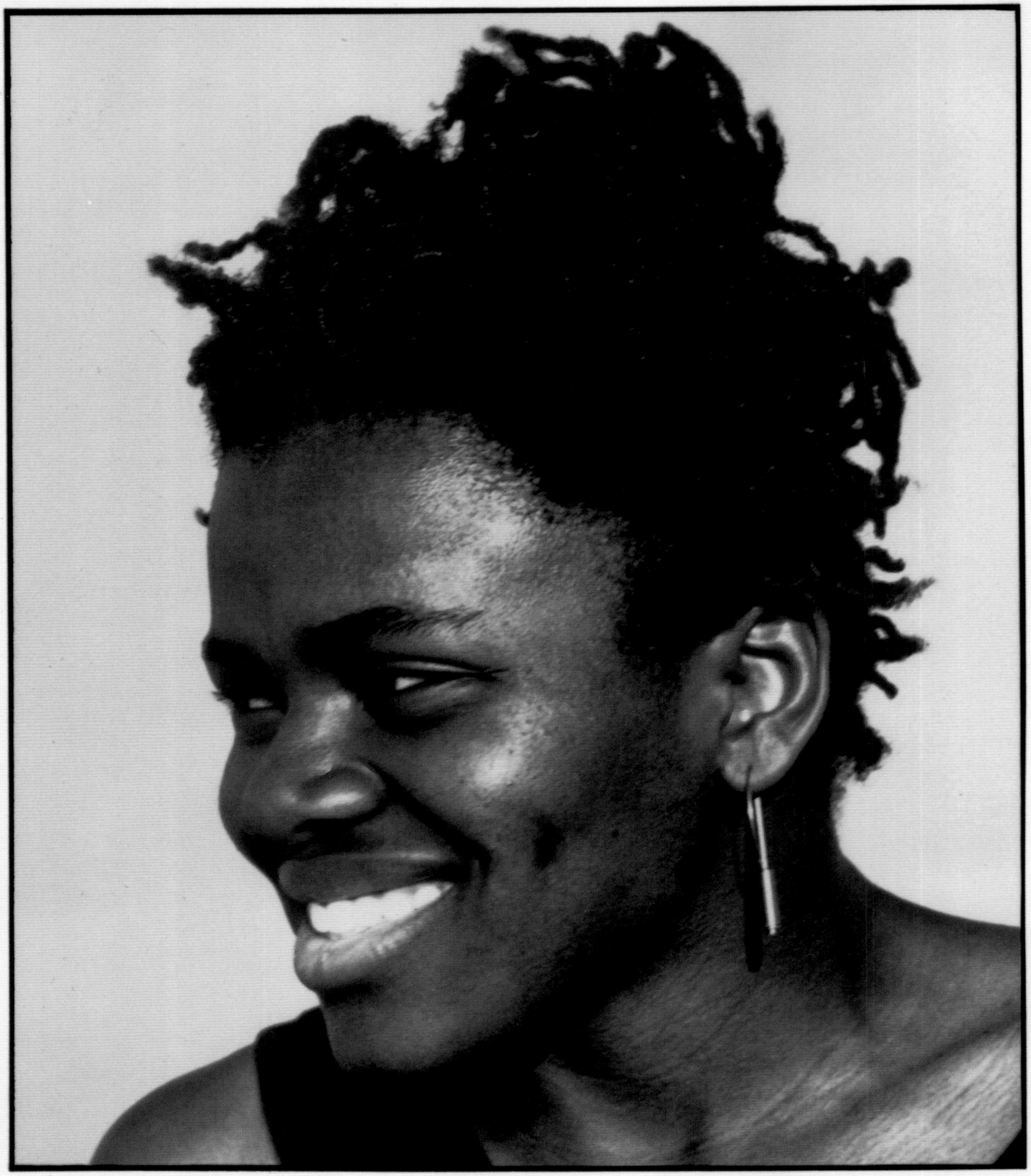

PHOTO CREDIT: HERB RITTS/1989

TRACY CHAPMAN

Elektra Entertainment

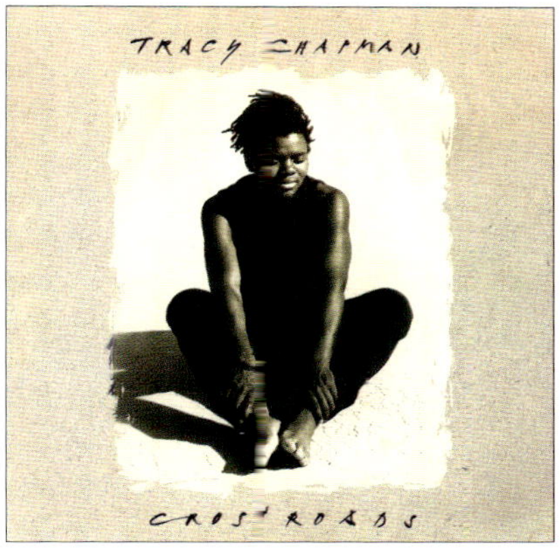

Folk-based singer-songwriter **Tracy Chapman** followed the success of her multi-platinum, Grammy-winning first album with the bleak *Crossroads*.

Billboard 200: *Crossroads* (#9)
Billboard Hot 100: "Crossroads" (#90)

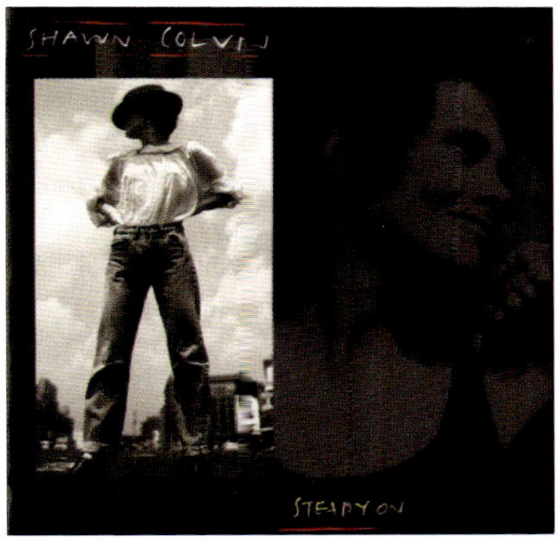

Featuring the terrific title track and "Diamond in the Rough," **Shawn Colvin**'s debut, *Steady On*, gained a Grammy Award for Best Contemporary Folk Album.

Billboard 200: *Steady On* (#111)

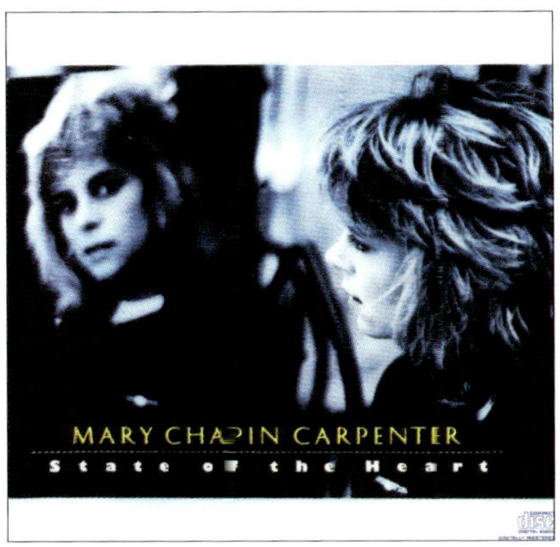

Mary Chapin Carpenter's second album, *State of the Heart*, bore her breakout country hit, "Never Had It So Good," marking a shift from folk-leaning material.

Billboard 200: *State of the Heart* (#183)

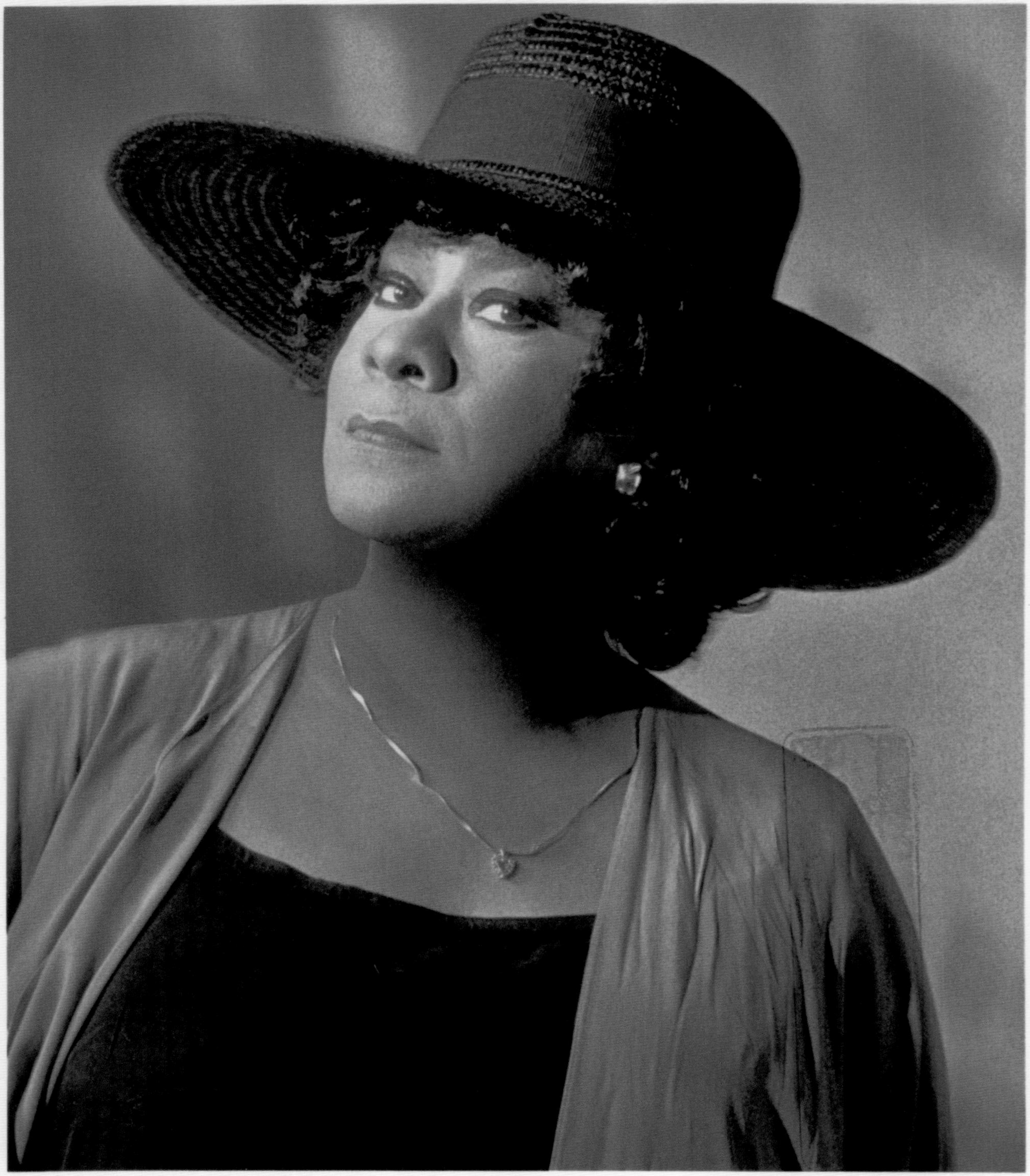

Photo: Frank Lindner

RUTH BROWN

Fantasy

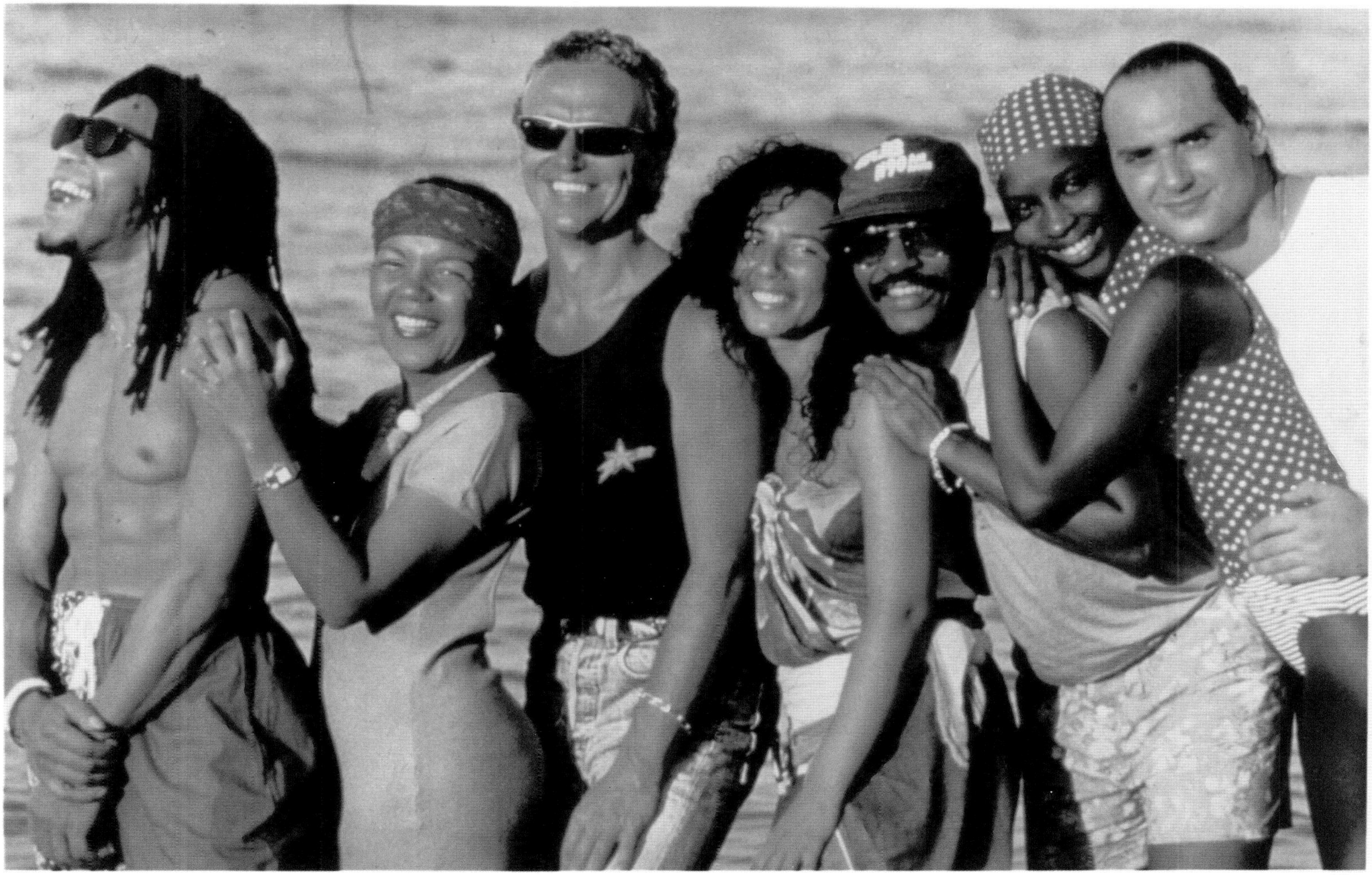

KAOMA

89 11

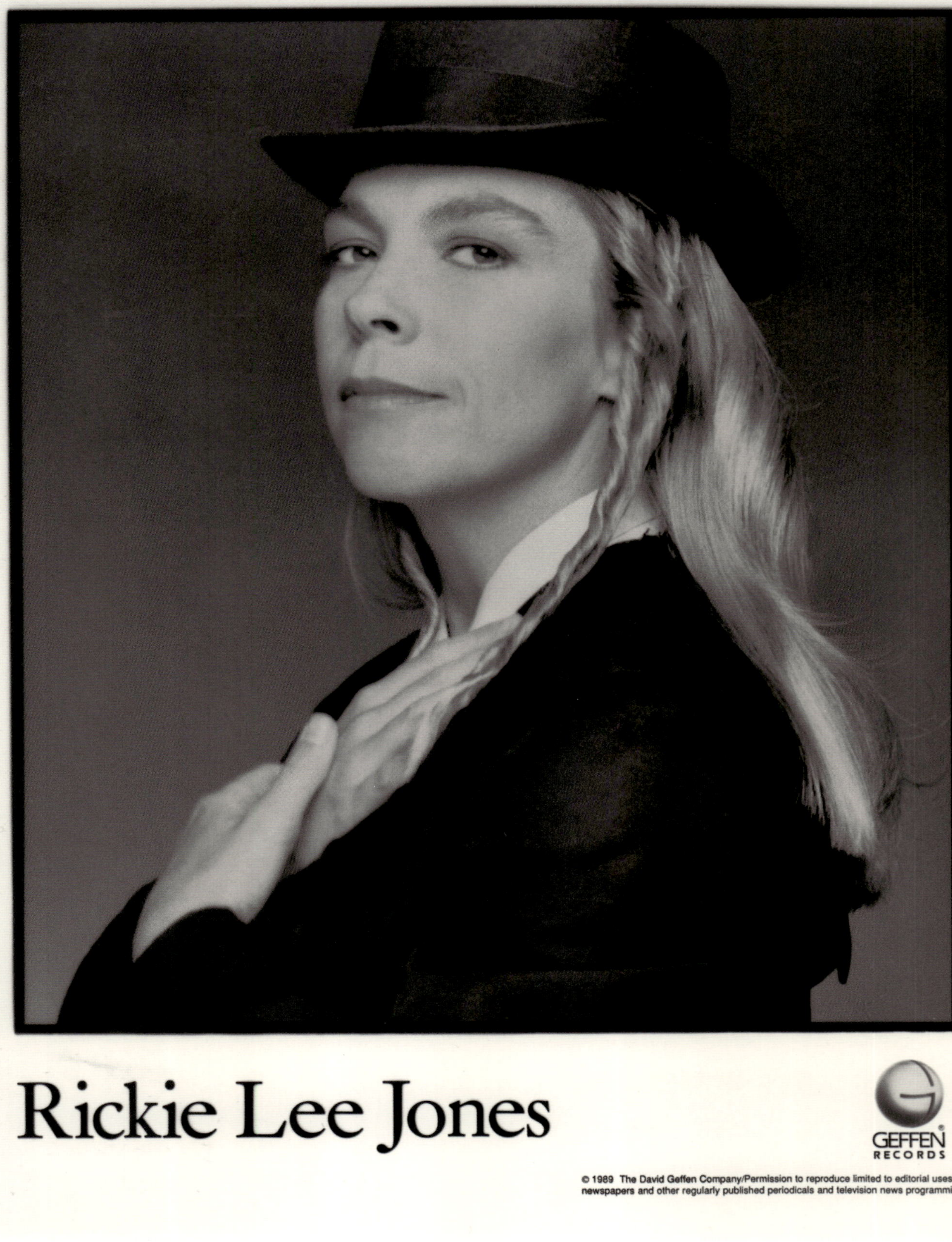

Photo Credit: Deborah Feingold

Rickie Lee Jones

GEFFEN RECORDS

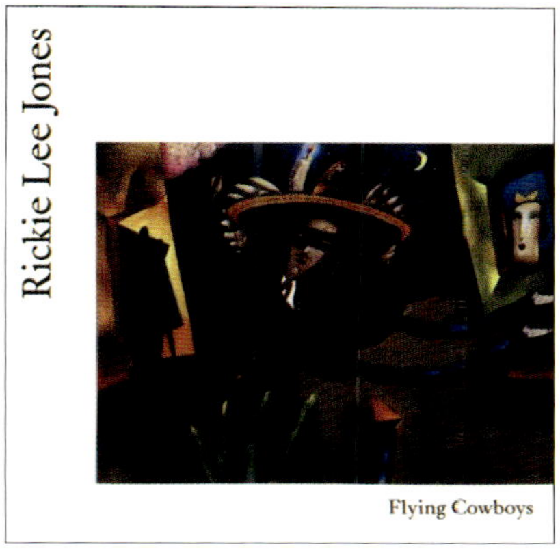

With Steely Dan's Walter Becker in the producer's chair, **Rickie Lee Jones** reemerged with *Flying Cowboys* and the sterling college radio hit "Satellites."

Billboard 200: *Flying Cowboys* (#39)

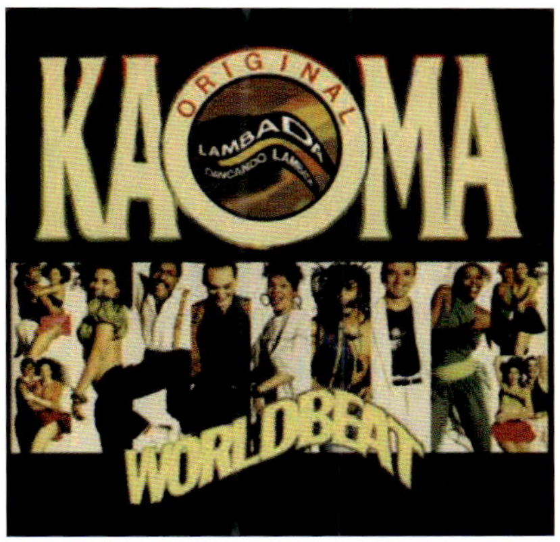

With "Lambada," an international chart-topping hit, the Paris-based band **Kaoma** exploited the interest in a fast-paced, sensual Brazilian dance form.

Billboard 200: *Worldbeat* (#40)
Billboard Hot 100: "Lambada" (#46)

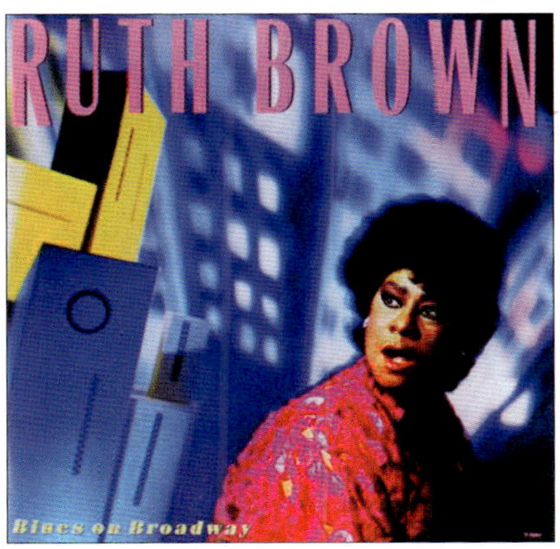

Famed for classic R&B hits in the Fifties, **Ruth Brown** took home a Grammy Award for Best Jazz Vocal Performance, Female with *Blues on Broadway*.

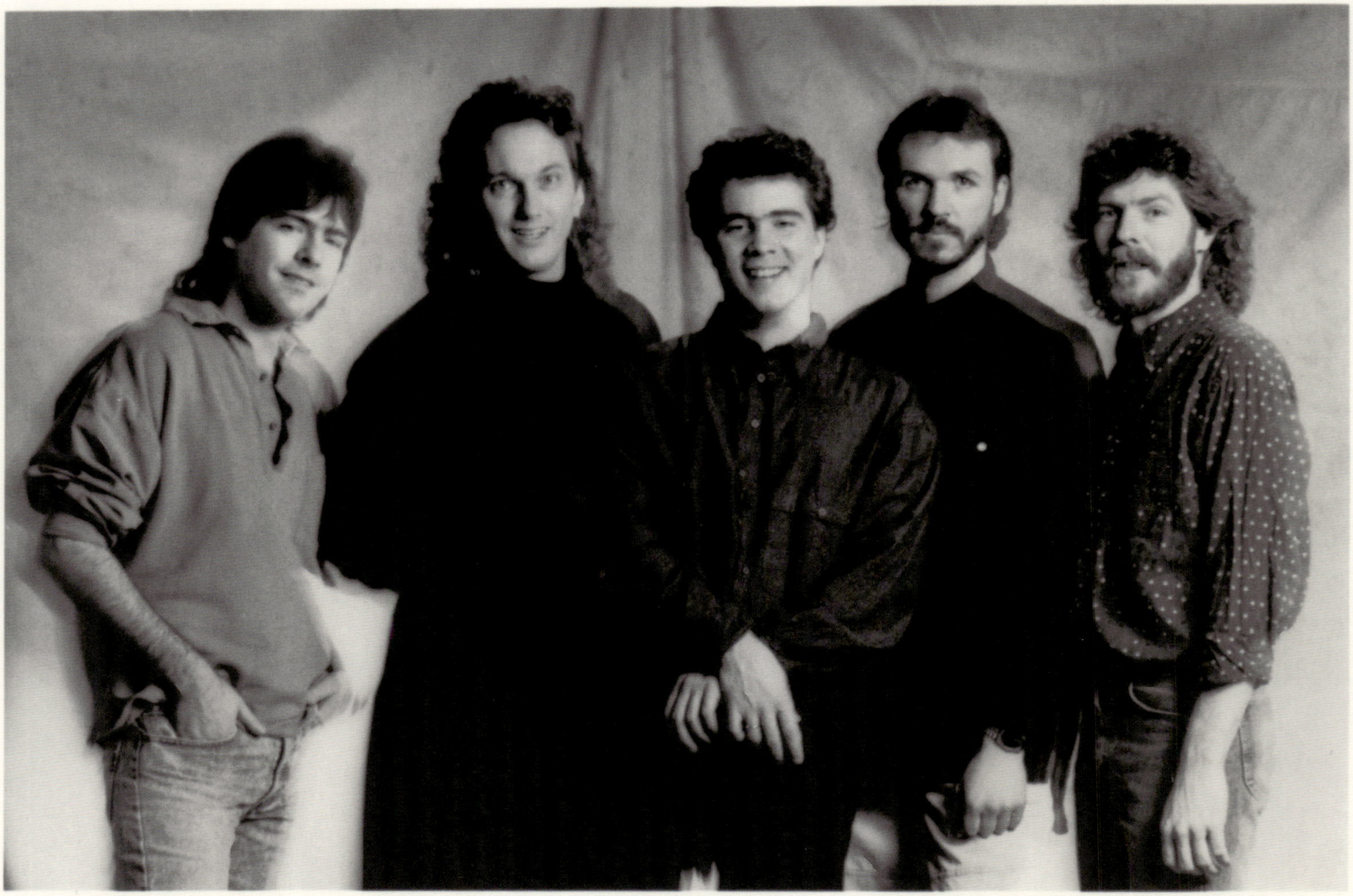

photo: Empire Studio 0489

Bela Fleck Jerry Douglas Edgar Meyer Mark O'Connor Sam Bush

STRENGTH IN NUMBERS

MCA MASTER SERIES

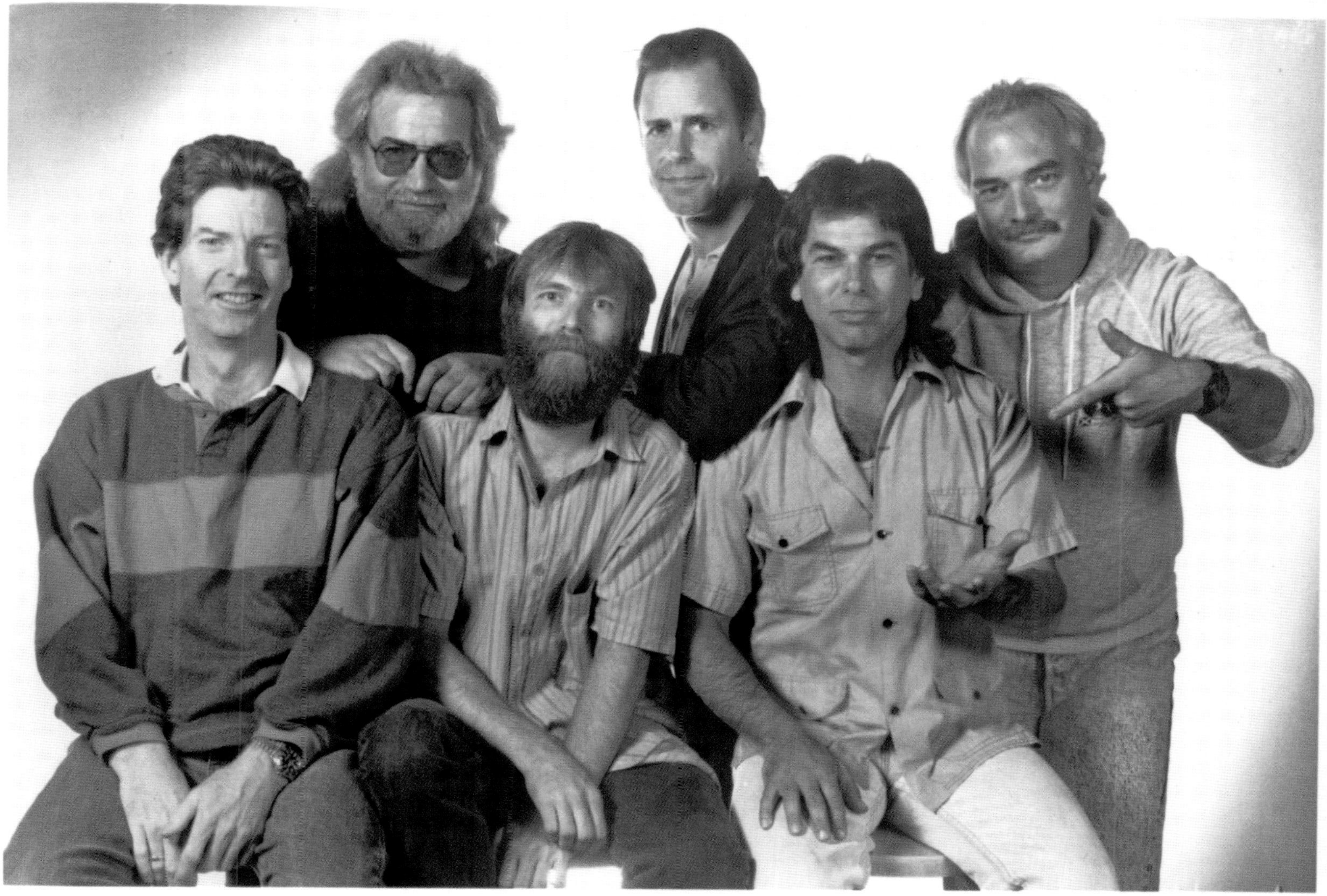

Press: D. McNally
(415) 648-4832

ARISTA

GRATEFUL DEAD
1989

Grateful Dead Productions
Box 1073
San Rafael, CA 94915

Photo: Ken Friedman

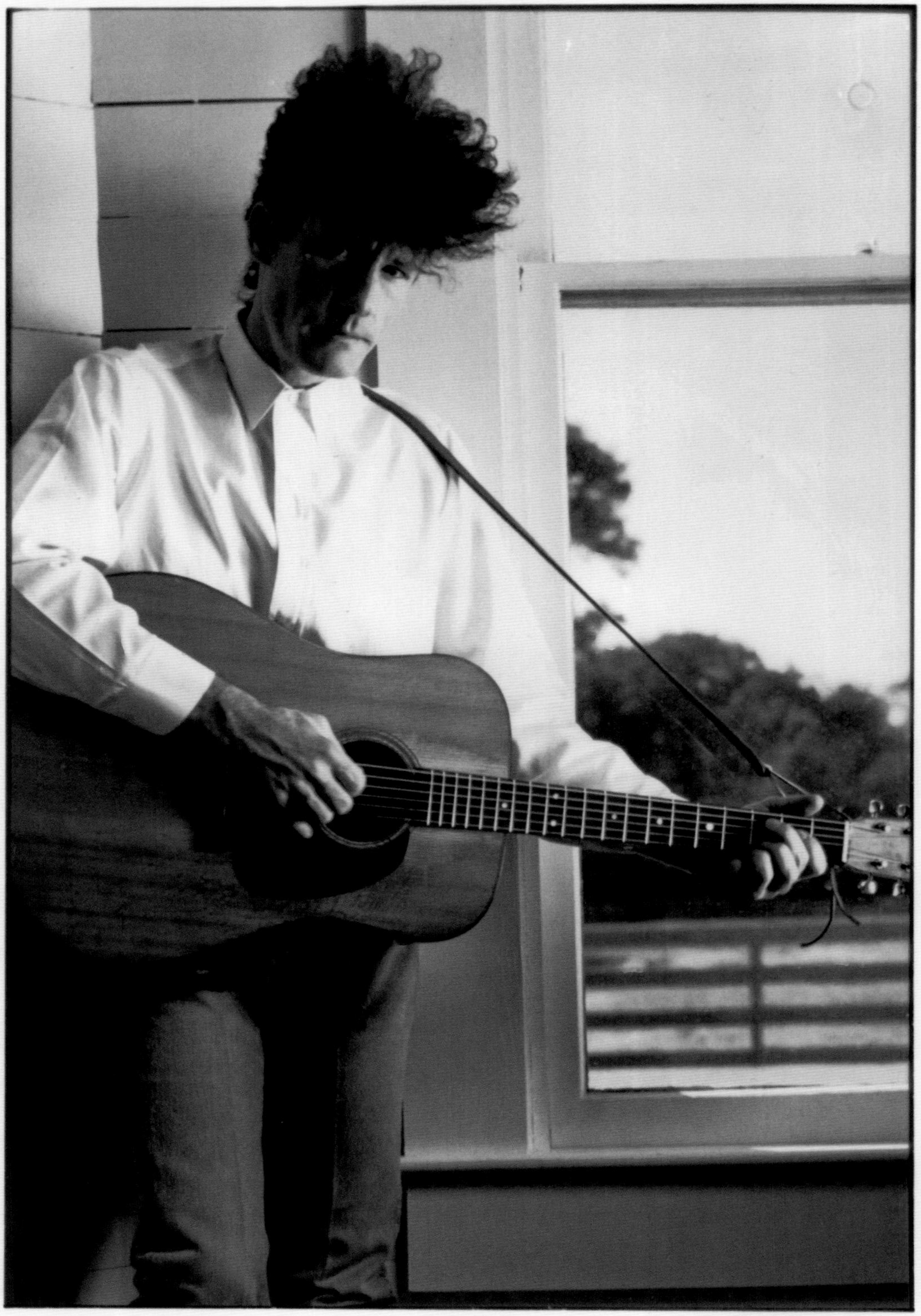

Photo Credit: Peter Nash

LYLE LOVETT

MCA RECORDS
CURB RECORDS

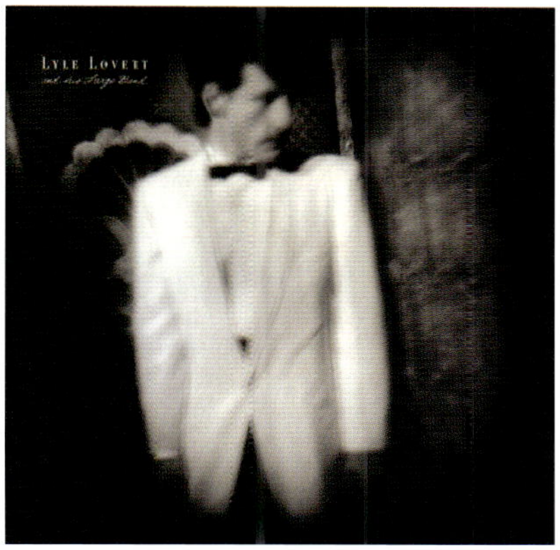

The reliably wry **Lyle Lovett** won a Grammy for *Lyle Lovett & His Large Band*, marked by a tale of delusion, "I Married Her Just Because She Looks Like You."

Billboard 200: *Lyle Lovett & His Large Band* (#62)

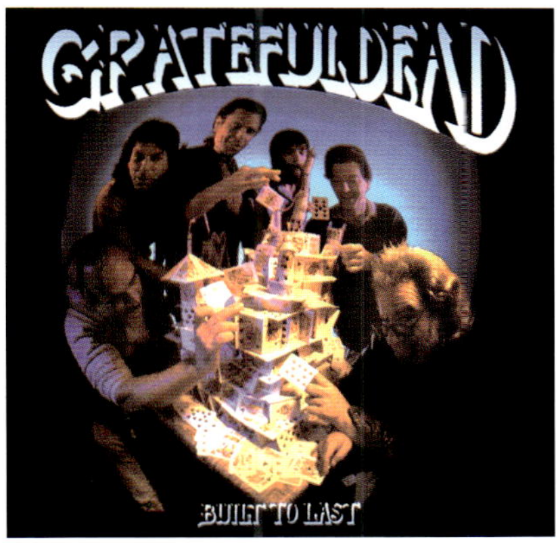

The last **Grateful Dead** studio album, *Built to Last* included songs written principally by keyboardist and vocalist Brent Mydland, who died the ensuing year.

Billboard 200: *Built to Last* (#27)

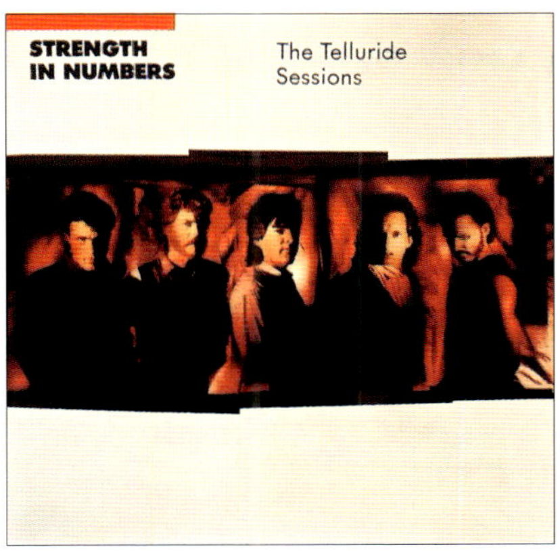

Strength in Numbers—progressive bluegrass all-stars Jerry Douglas, Mark O'Connor, Béla Fleck, Sam Bush and Edgar Meyer—issued *The Telluride Sessions*.

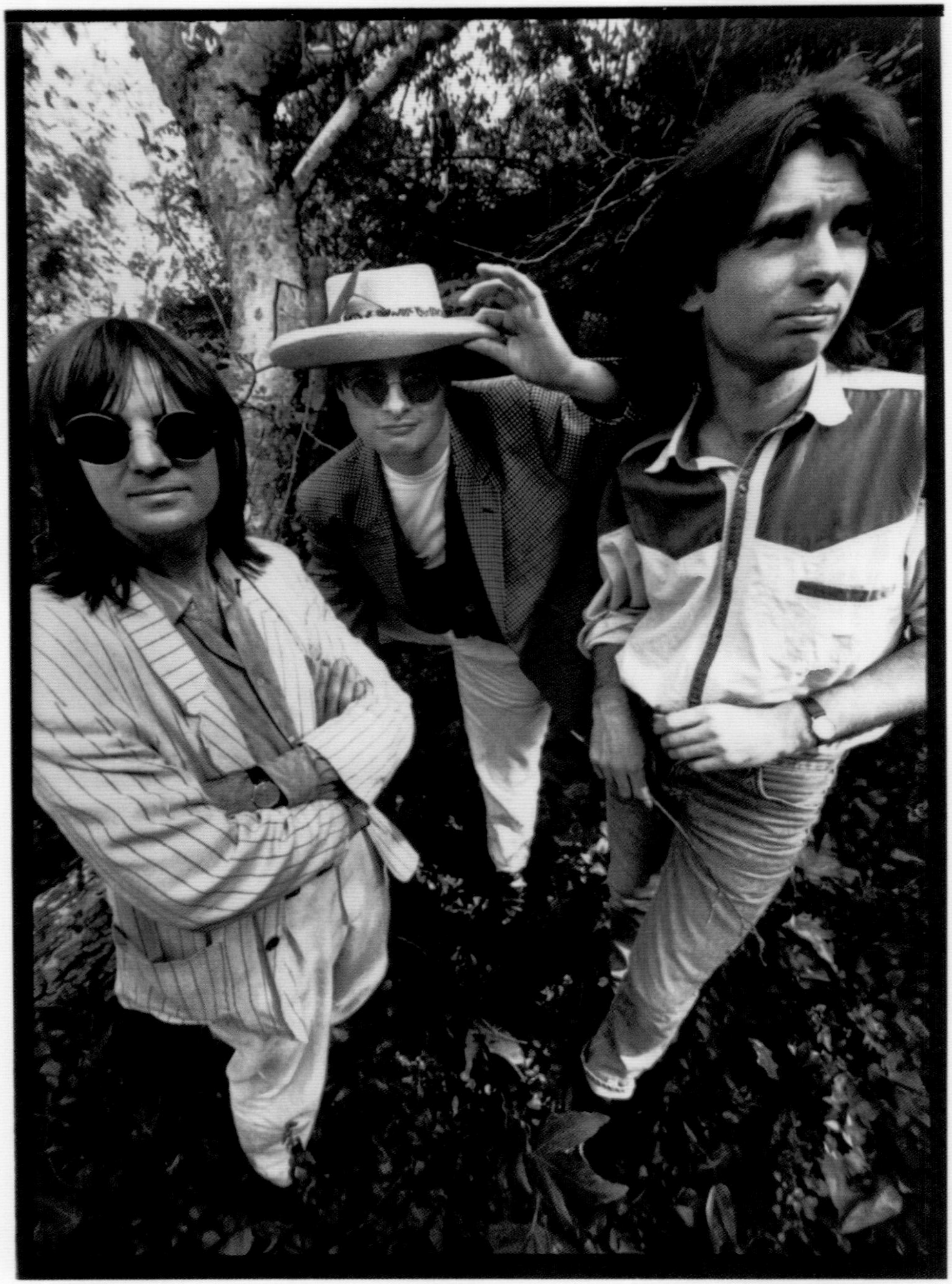

Photo Credit: Greg Allen

Dave Gregory Andy Partridge Colin Moulding

XTC

GEFFEN RECORDS

THE ALARM

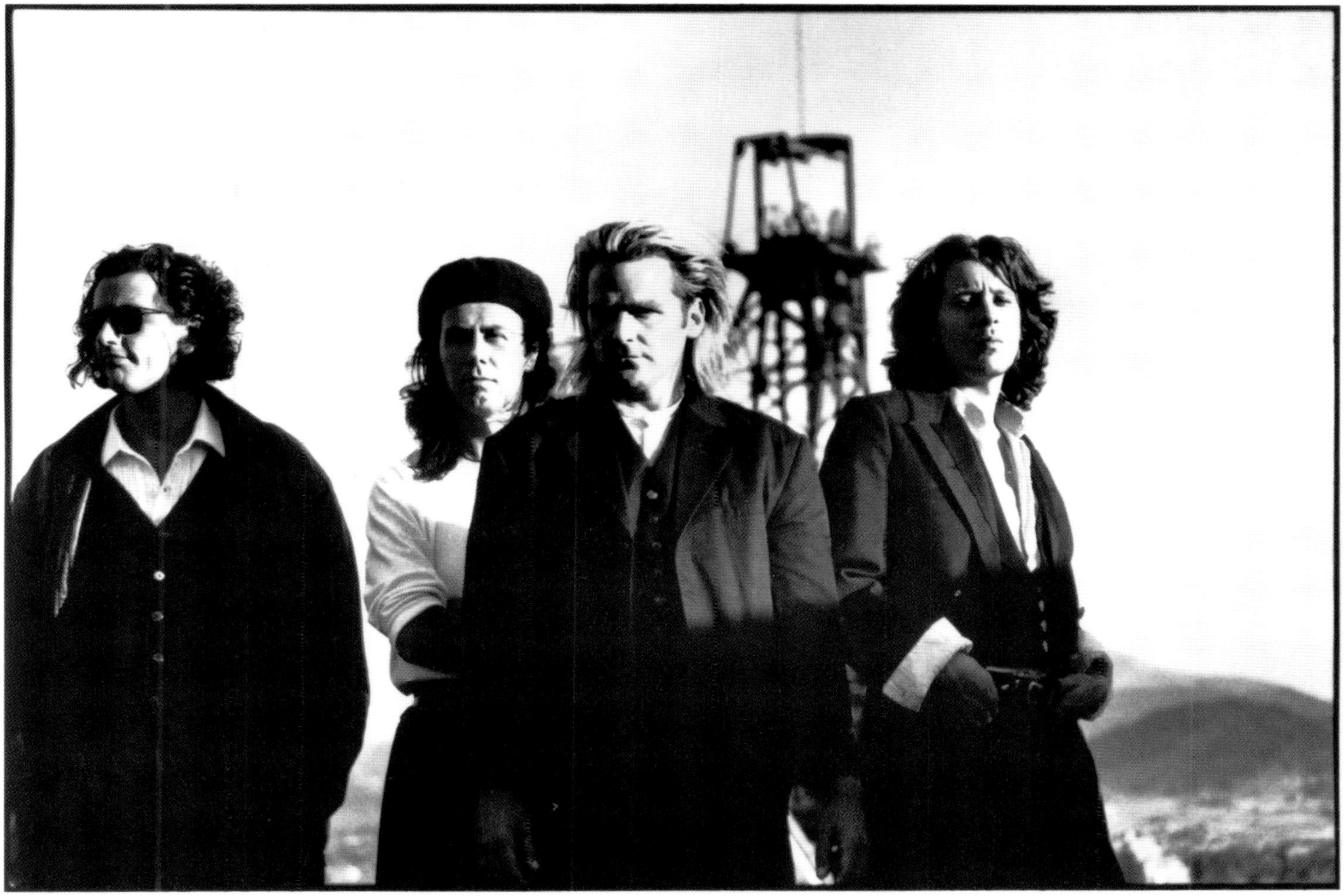

Photo: Julie Peters

L-R: TWIST, EDDIE MACDONALD, MIKE PETERS, DAVE SHARP

I.R.S.

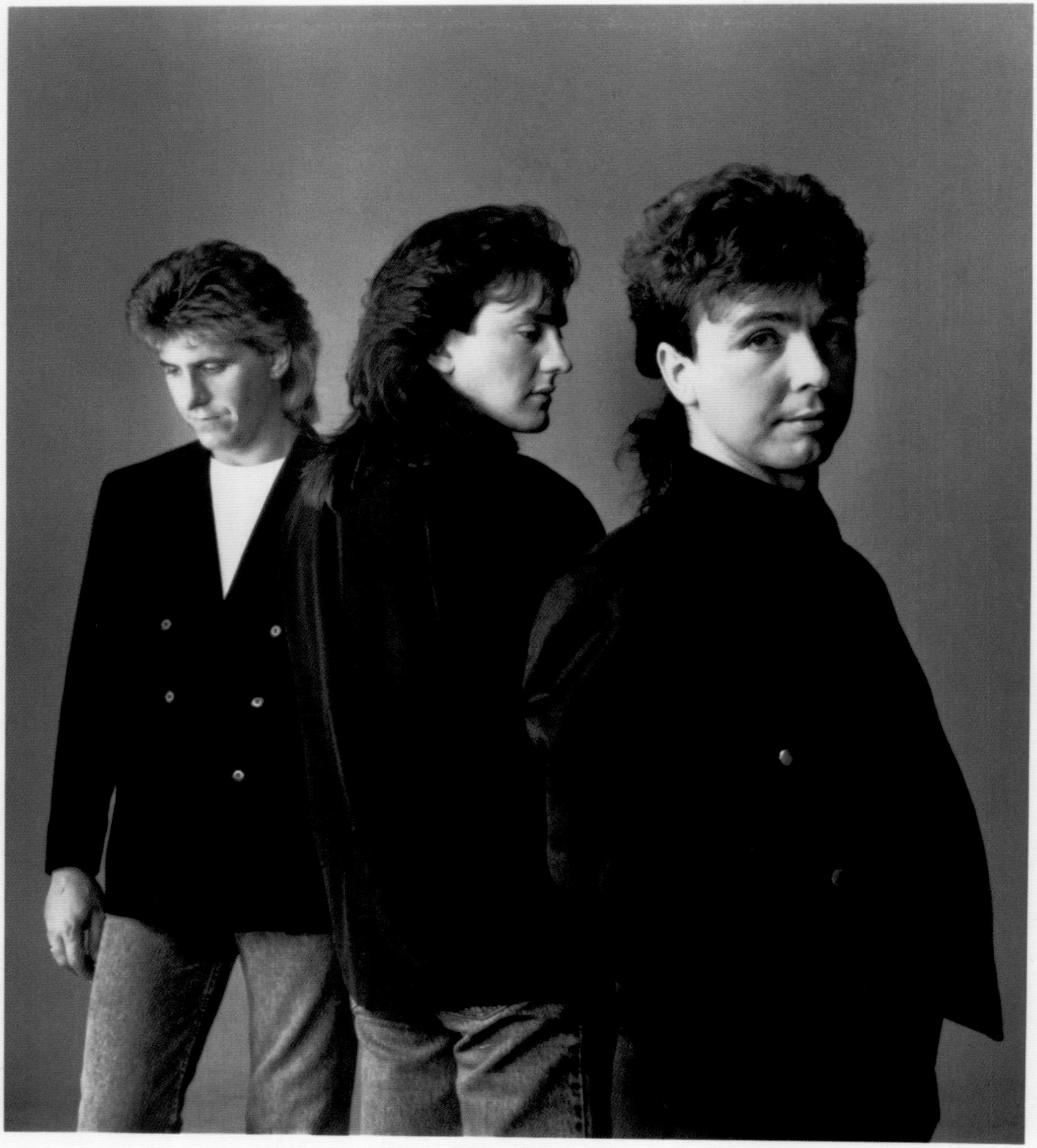

PHOTOGRAPH: MIKE PRIOR

From left: JOHN SPINKS, PAUL READ, TONY LEWIS.

THE OUTFIELD

Columbia 8907

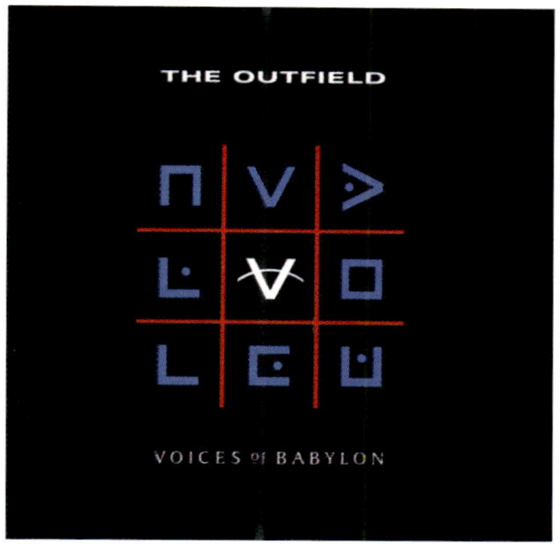

The Outfield's third album, *Voices of Babylon*, fared better in the US than the act's native Britain, hatching a mainstream-rock hit with the title song.

Billboard 200: *Voices of Babylon* (#53)
Billboard Hot 100: "Voices of Babylon" (#25); "My Paradise" (#72)

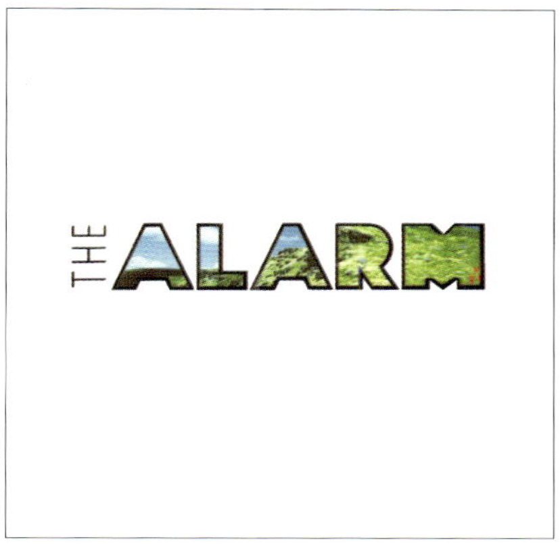

The Alarm focused on the fragmentation of culture in its native Wales, and *Change* delivered the band's biggest US hit, "Sold Me Down the River."

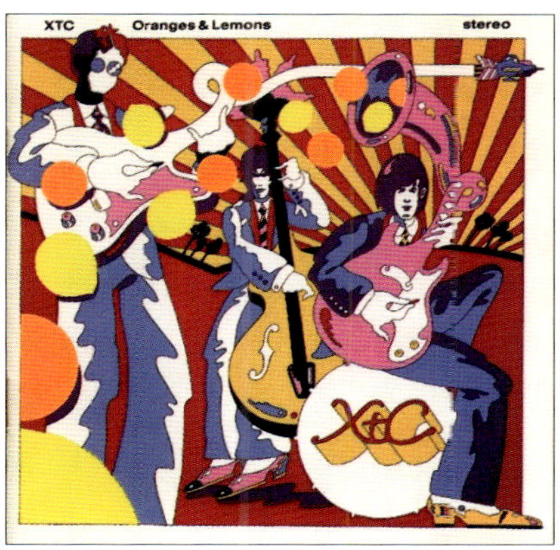

A rooted cult favorite, British band **XTC** made the US singles charts for the first time with the smart, playful pop songcraft of "The Mayor of Simpleton."

Billboard 200: *Oranges & Lemons* (#44)
Billboard Hot 100: "The Mayor of Simpleton" (#72)

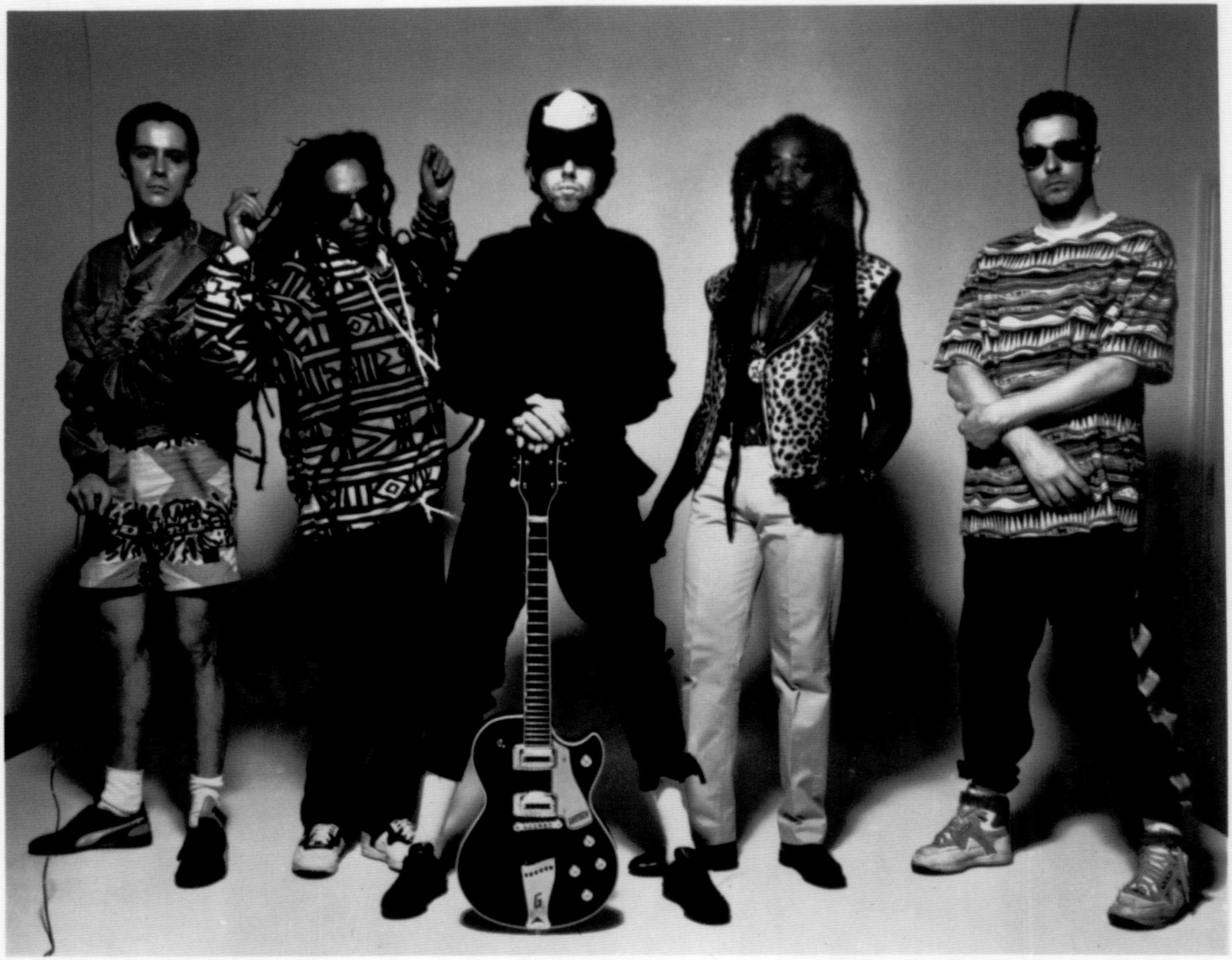

BIG AUDIO DYNAMITE

Columbia

8908

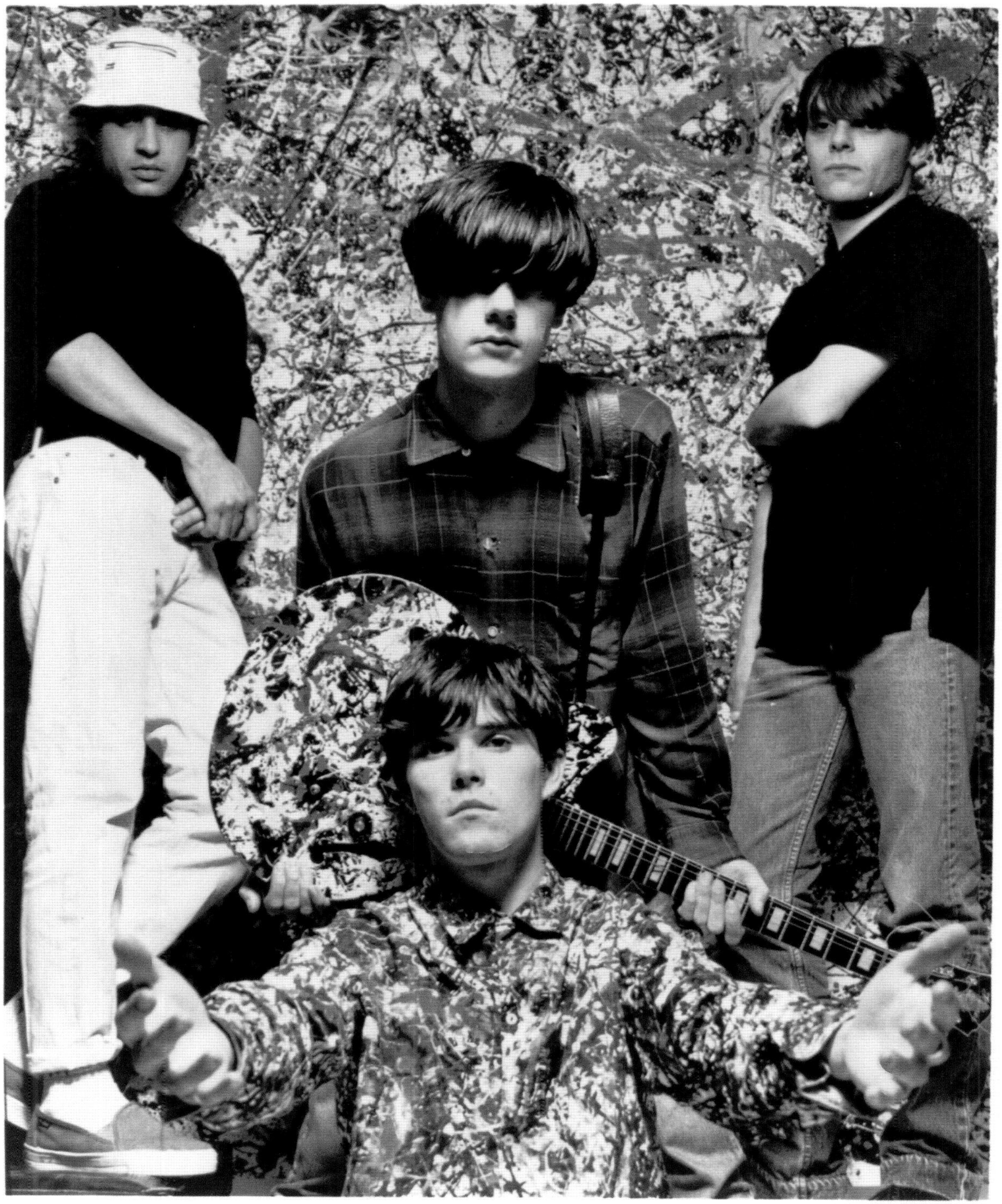

THE STONE ROSES

SILVERTONE RECORDS

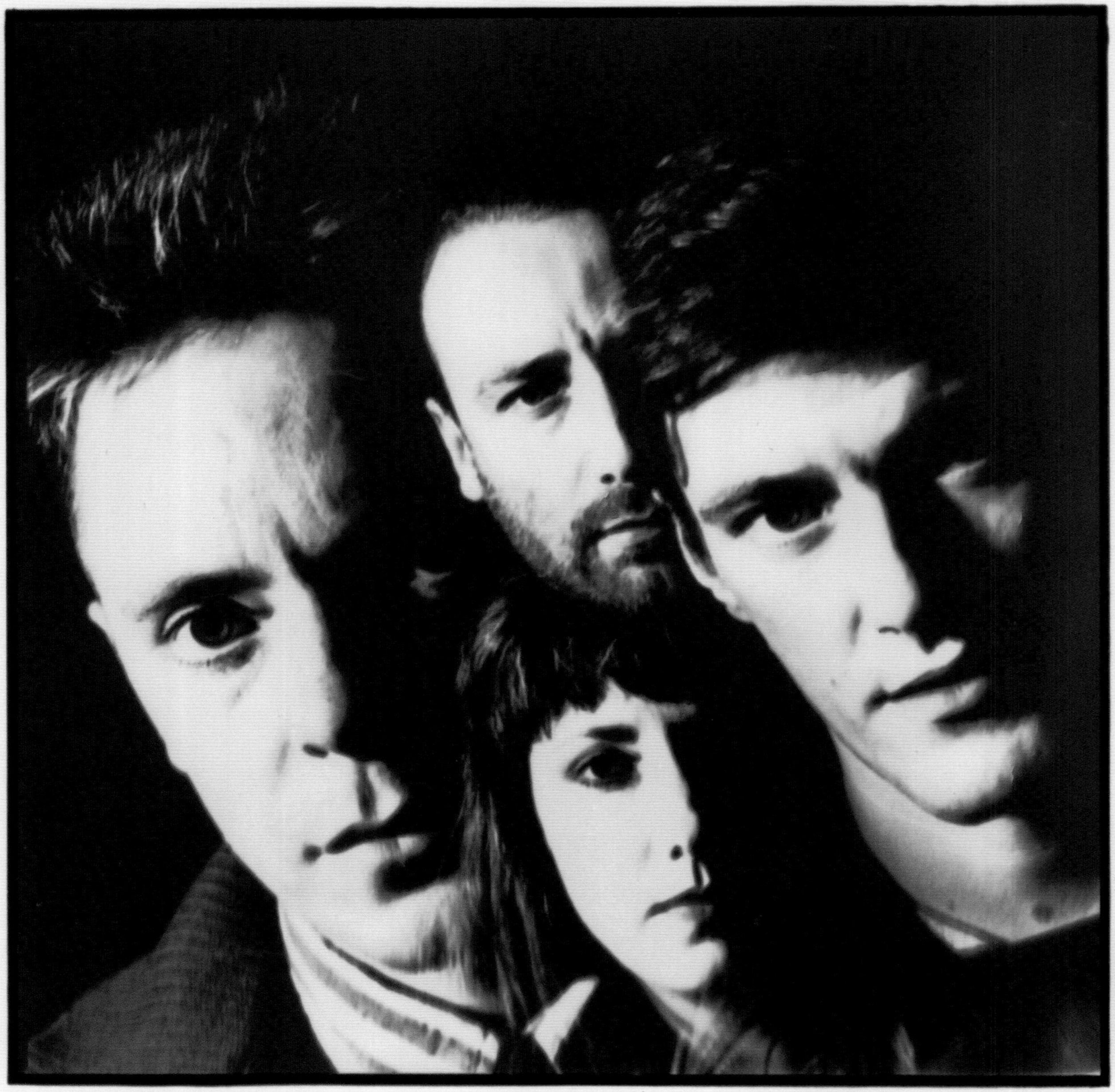

PHOTO CREDIT: ANDREW CATLIN

NEW ORDER

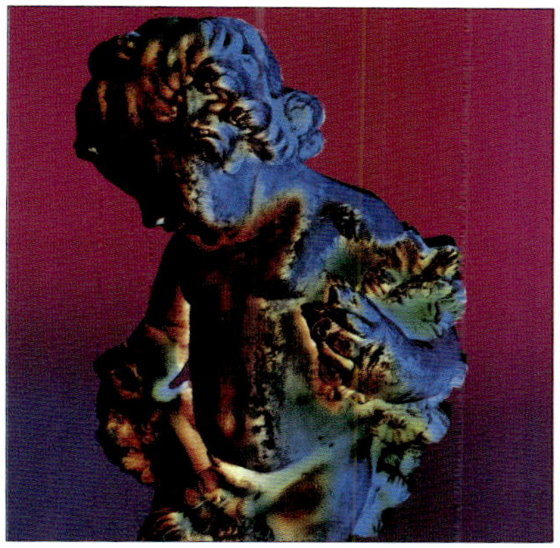

Recording *Technique* on the disco-centric island of Ibiza, the British electronic outfit **New Order** commingled dance music with heartrending compositions.

Billboard 200: *Technique* (#32)
Billboard Hot 100: "Round & Round" (#64)

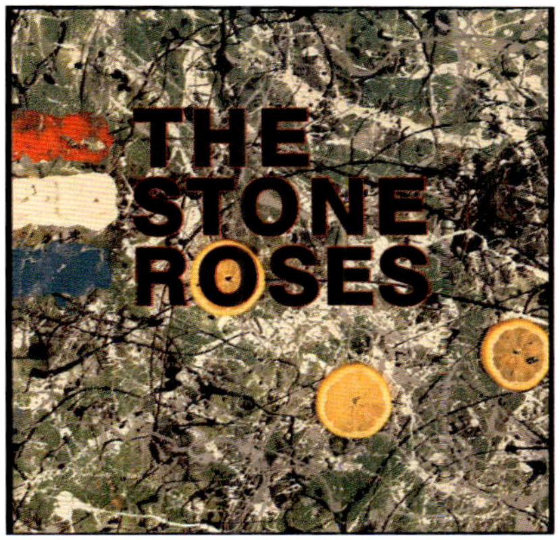

The Stone Roses, a seminal group from Manchester's club culture, were hailed by the UK music press for making one of the all-time best debut albums.

Billboard 200: *The Stone Roses* (#86)

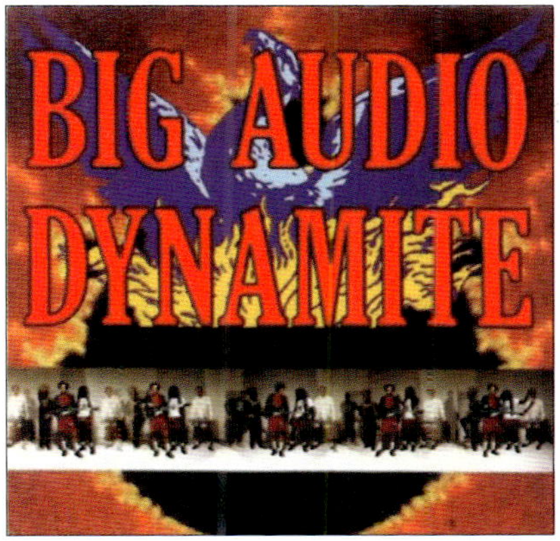

Owing to the modern-rock hits "James Brown" and "Contact," *Megatop Phoenix* had a chart run for **Big Audio Dynamite**, Mick Jones' post-Clash group.

Billboard 200: *Megatop Phoenix* (#85)

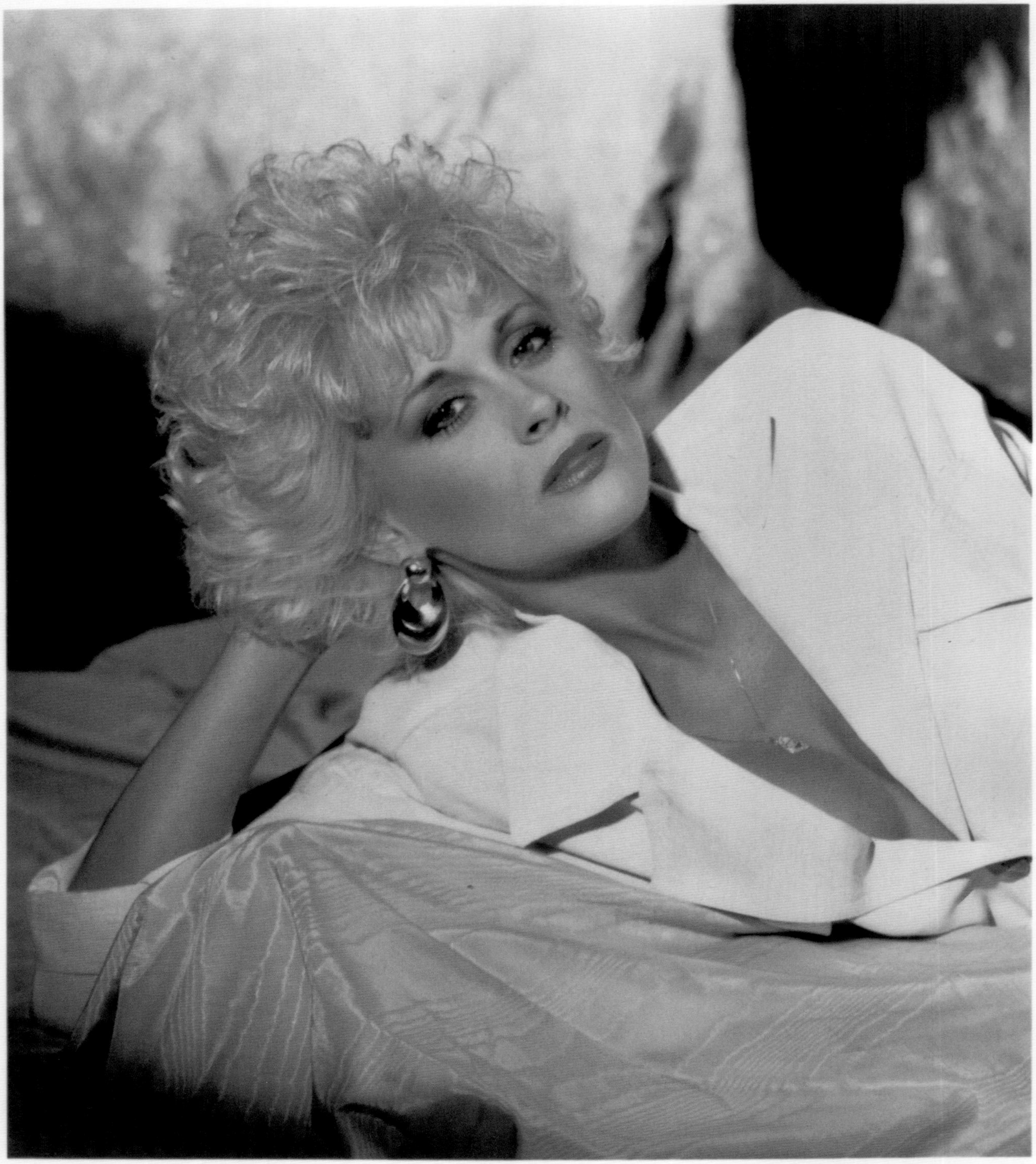

LORRIE MORGAN

Personal Management
JACK McFADDEN
818 Eighteenth Avenue South
Nashville, TN 37203
615/242-1500

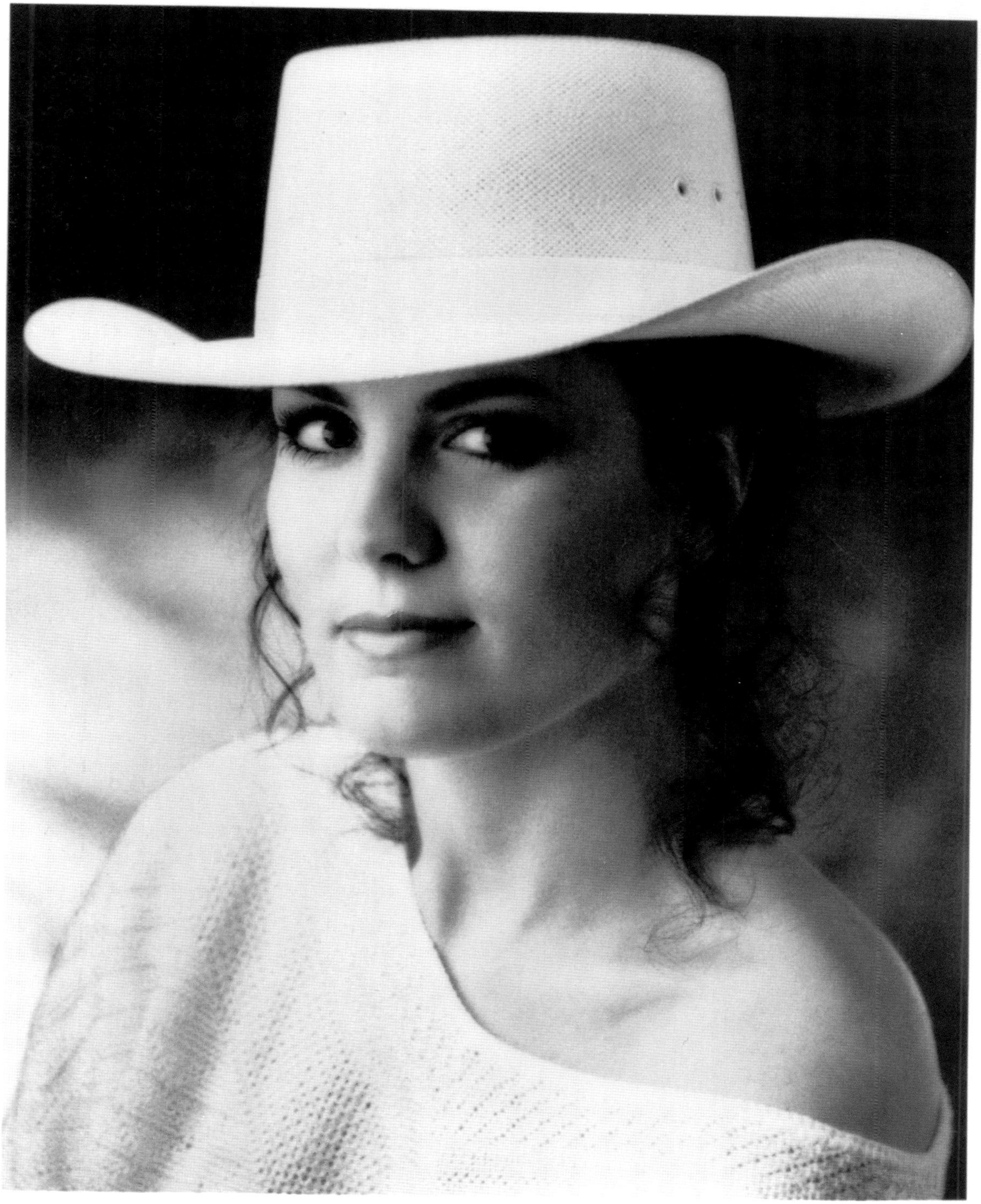

credit: Empire Studio 4/89

Holly DUNN

WARNER BROS.

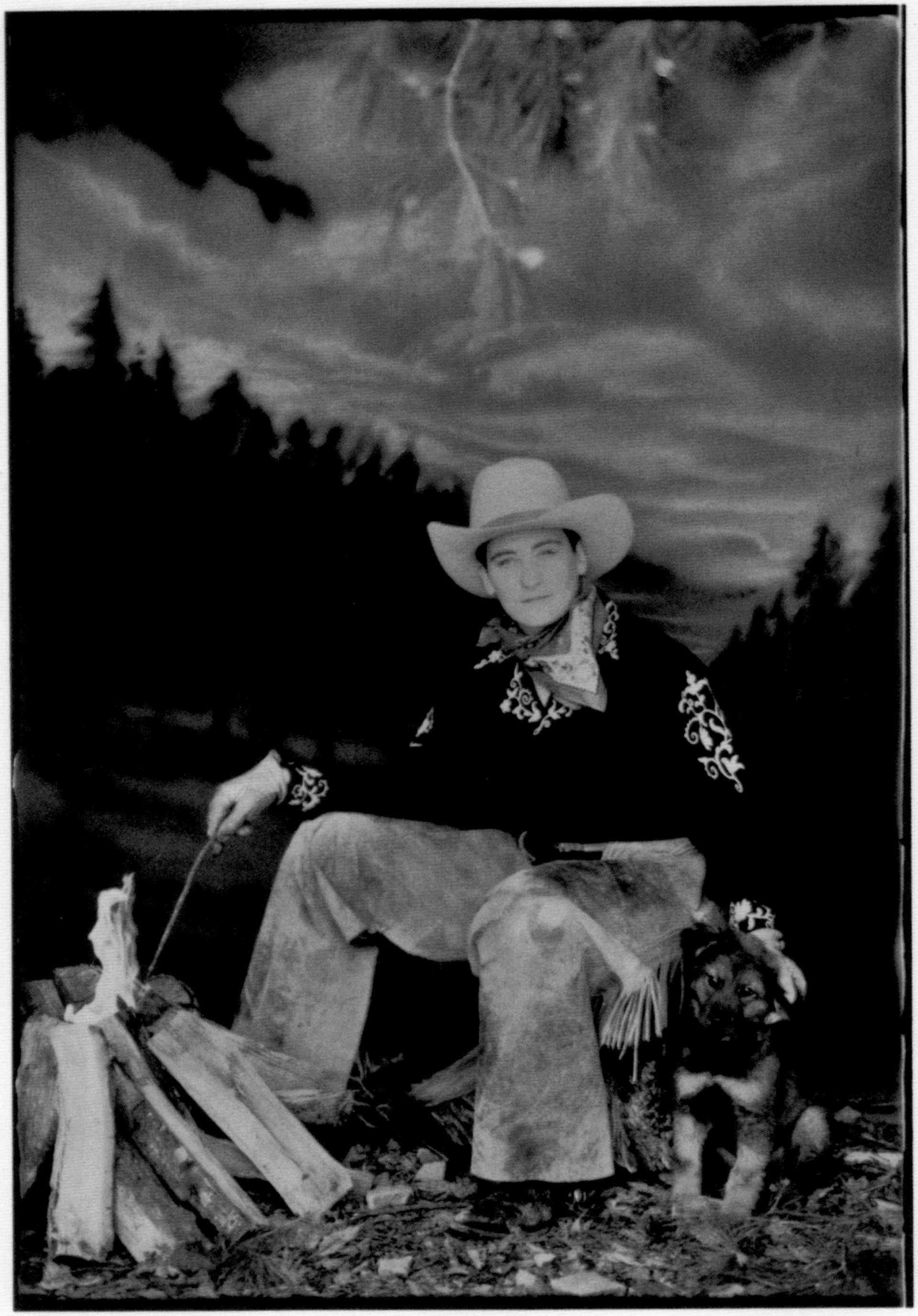

Photo Credit: Victoria Pearson

k.d. lang

SIRE®

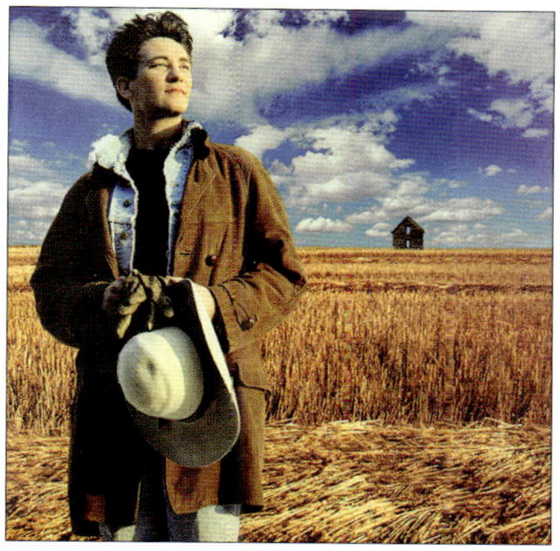

"Full Moon Full of Love" became a modest hit, and **k.d. lang** won a country music Grammy for her album with the Reclines, *Absolute Torch and Twang*.

Billboard 200: *Absolute Torch and Twang* (#60)

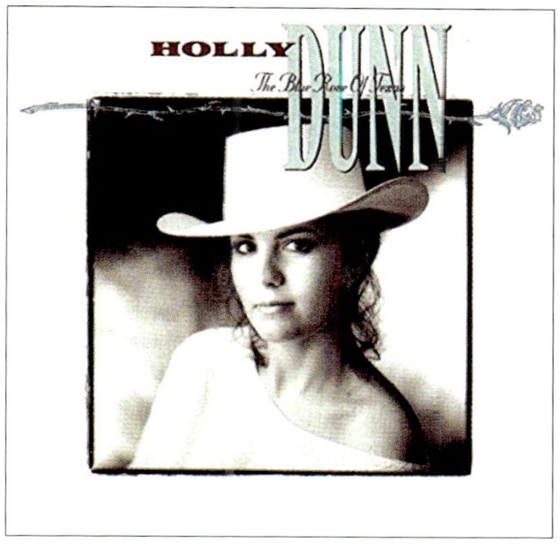

The Blue Rose of Texas generated "Are You Ever Gonna Love Me," **Holly Dunn**'s first No. 1 country single, a song co-written with her brother, Chris Waters.

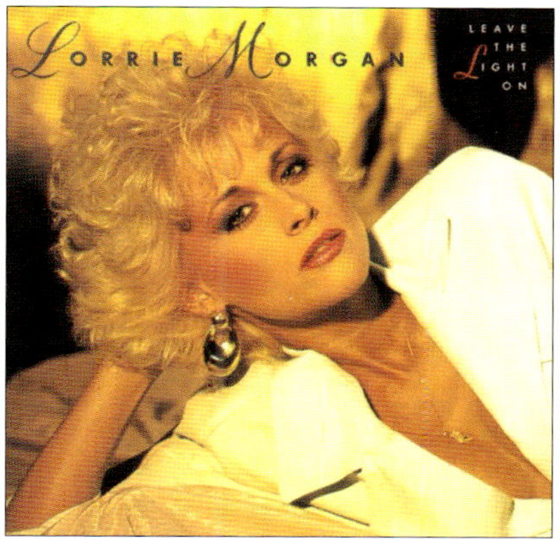

Singer **Lorrie Morgan** debuted with *Leave the Light On*, boasting the country music hits "Trainwreck of Emotion," "Dear Me" and the No. 1 "Five Minutes."

Billboard 200: *Leave the Light On* (#117)

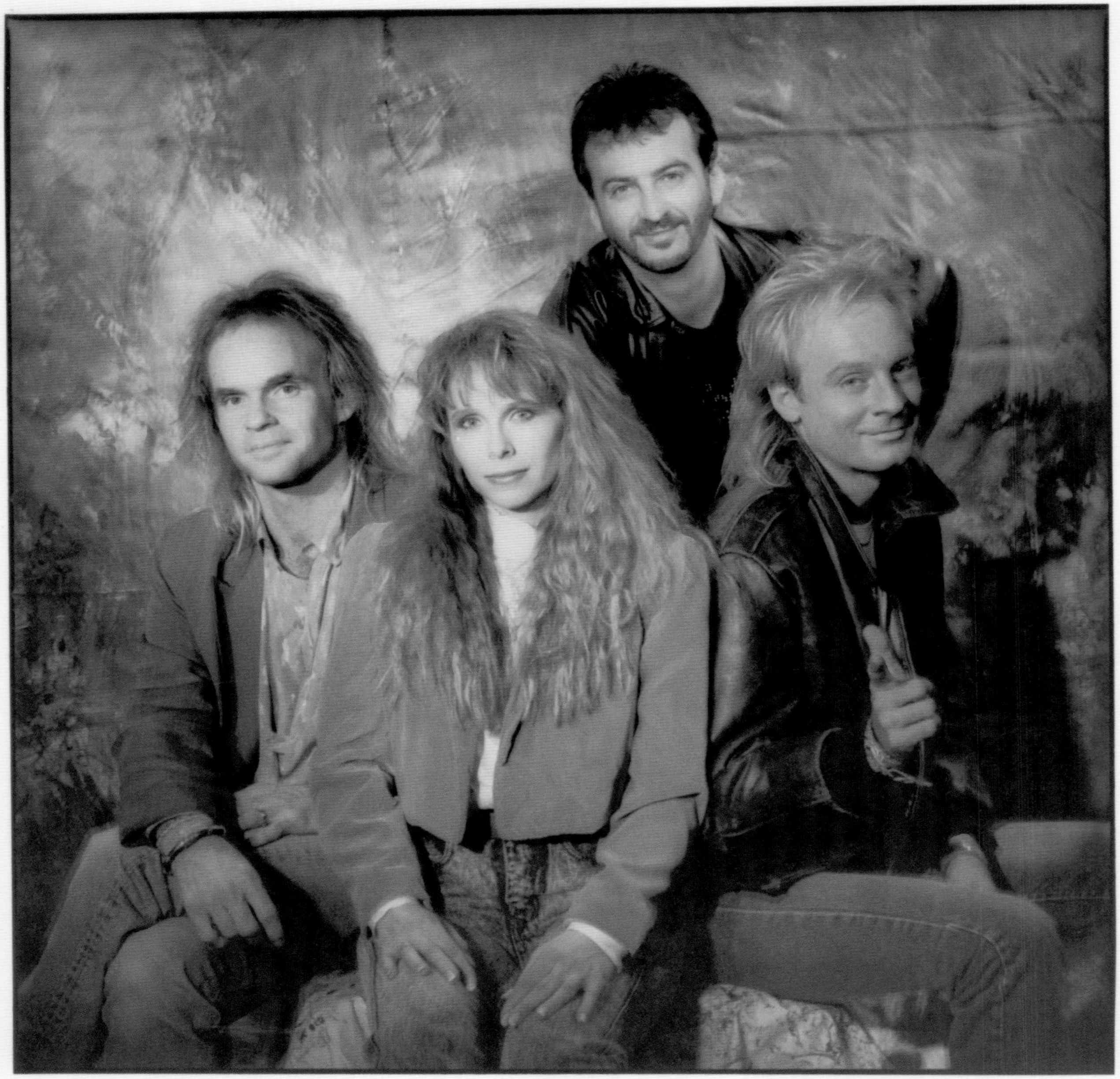

photo: Jeff Katz 3/89

Curtis Stone Paulette Carlson Jack Daniels Cactus Moser

Highway 101

WARNER BROS.

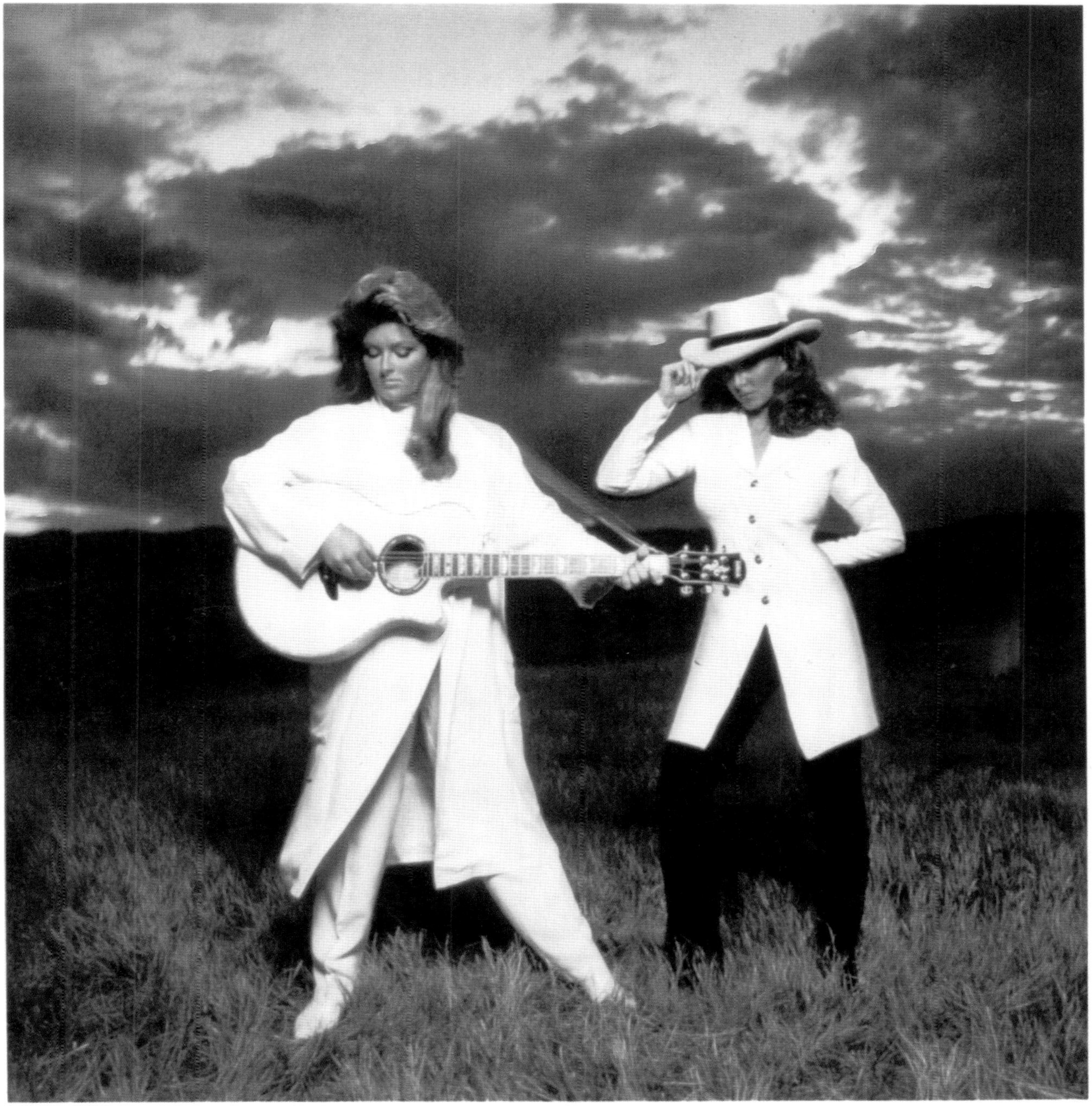

THE JUDDS

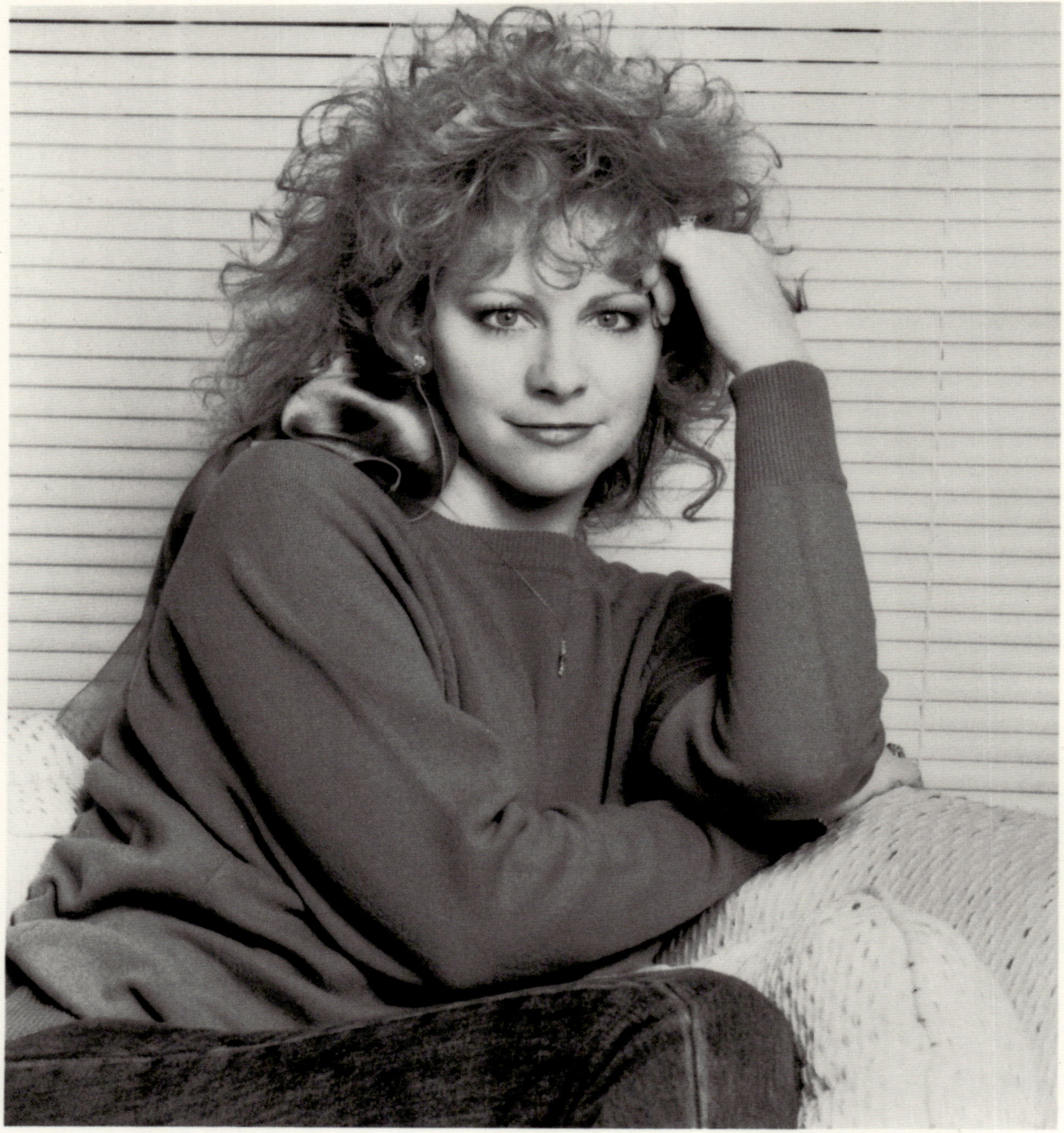

photo: McGuire 0489A

REBA McENTIRE

MCA RECORDS NASHVILLE

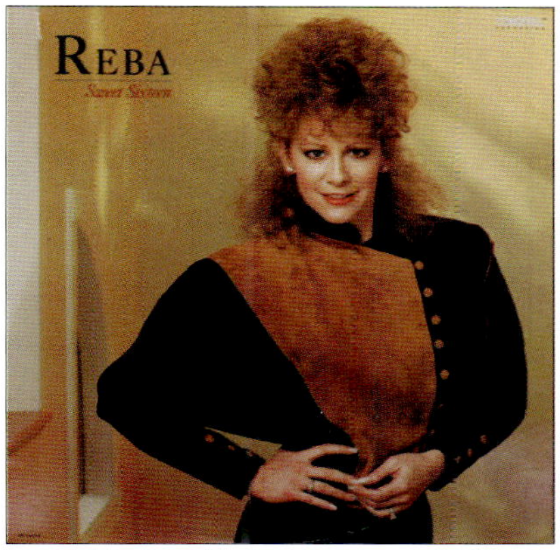

Returning to her country sound on *Sweet Sixteen*, **Reba McEntire** saw her cover of the Everly Brothers' "Cathy's Clown" climb to No. 1 on the charts.

Billboard 200: *Sweet Sixteen* (#78)

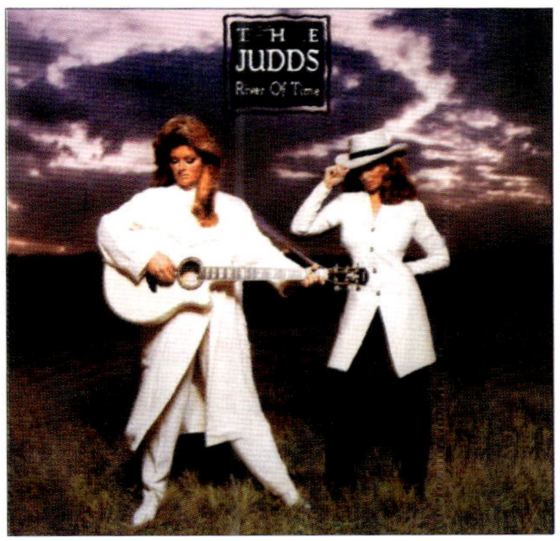

The Judds' *River of Time* contained the famed mother-daughter duo's No. 1 country hits "Young Love (Strong Love)" and "Let Me Tell You About Love."

Billboard 200: *River of Time* (#51)

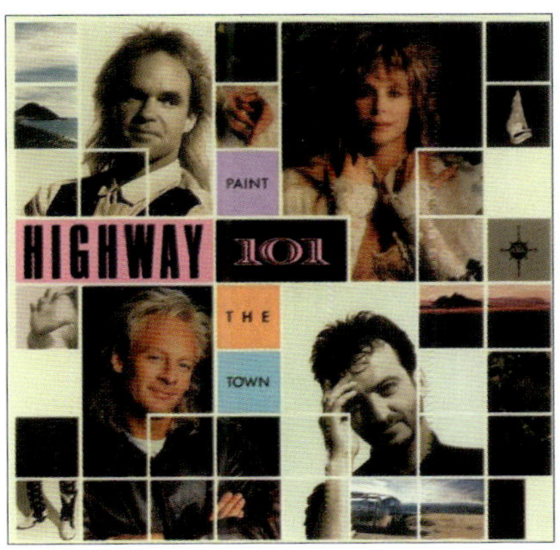

The last of **Highway 101**'s albums with lead singer Paulette Carlson, *Paint the Town* contained "Who's Lonely Now," the band's fourth No. 1 country song.

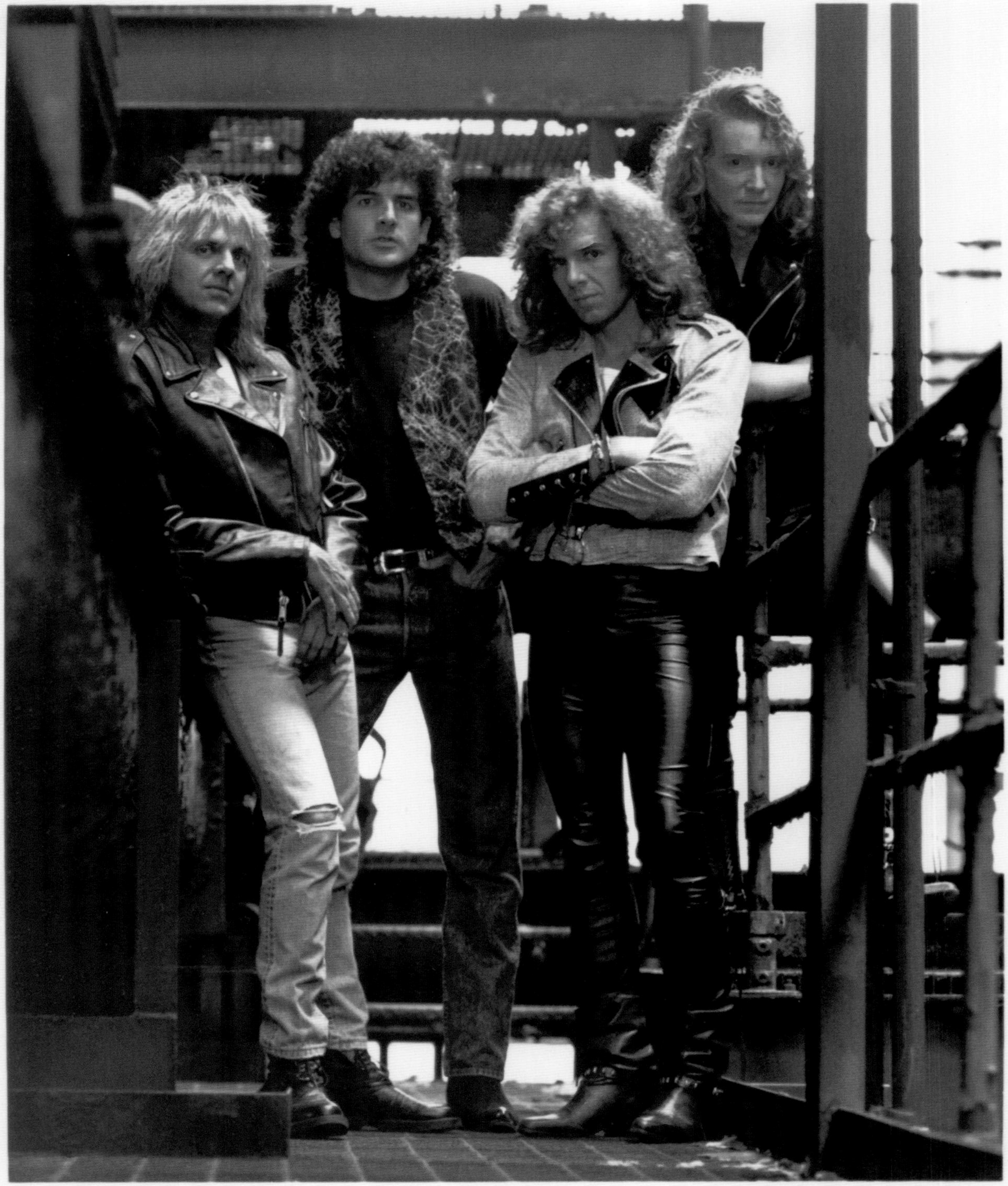

ALAN PASQUA DAVID HUFF DANN HUFF MIKE BRIGNARDELLO

E.S.P Management

GIANT

A&M RECORDS

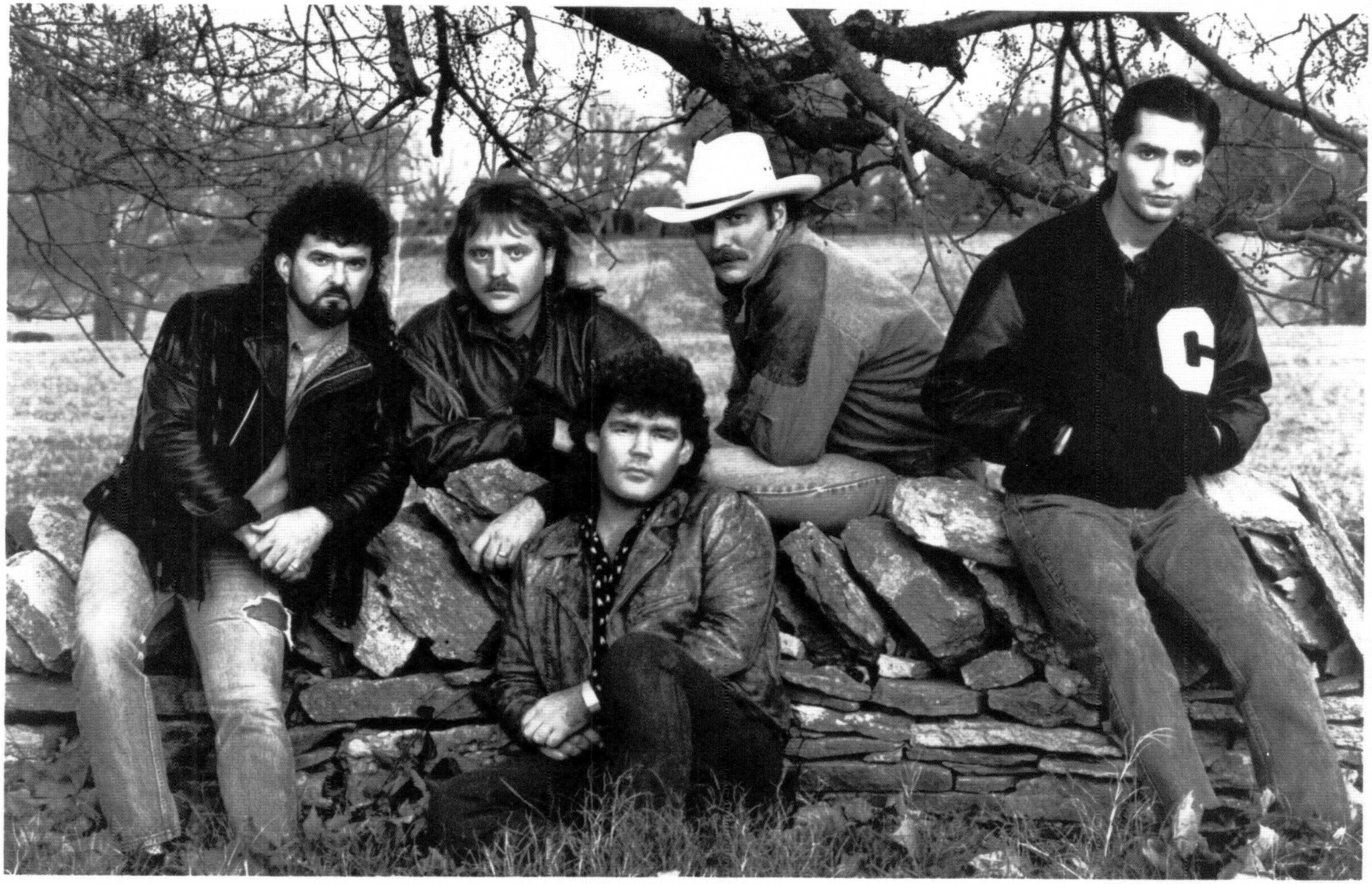

credit: Randee St. Nicholas

Mike McGuire Ralph Ezell Marty Raybon Jim Seales Stan Thorn

Shenandoah

Columbia

8901

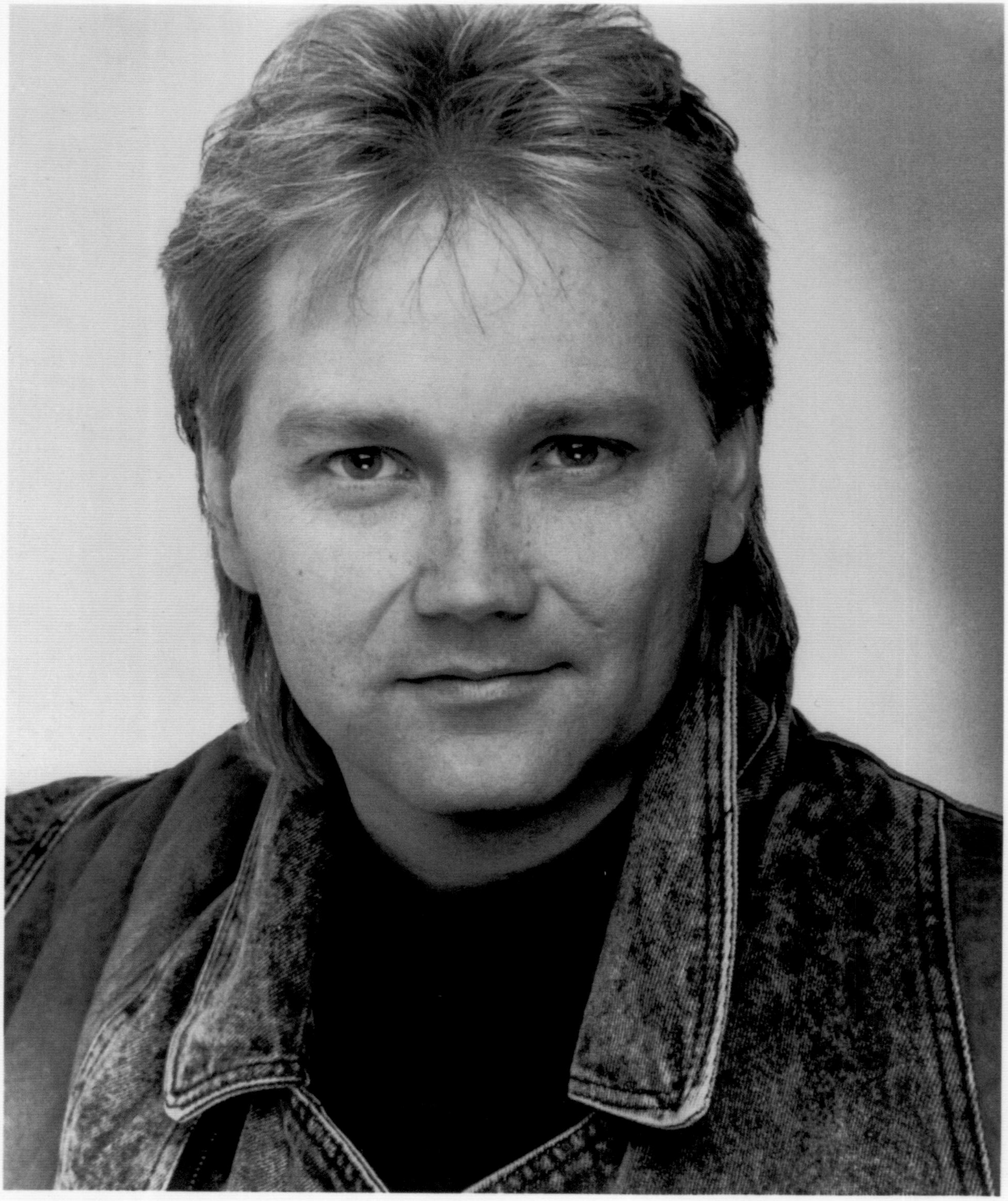

photo: Peter Nash 0389

STEVE WARINER

MCA RECORDS NASHVILLE

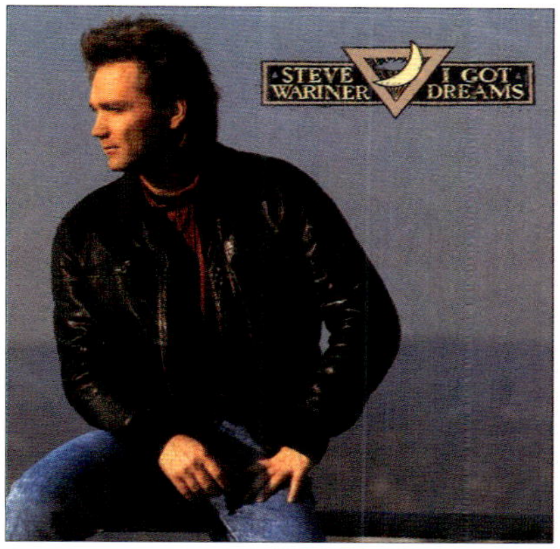

Country singer, songwriter and guitarist **Steve Wariner** sent his own compositions "Where Did I Go Wrong" and "I Got Dreams" to No. 1 on the charts.

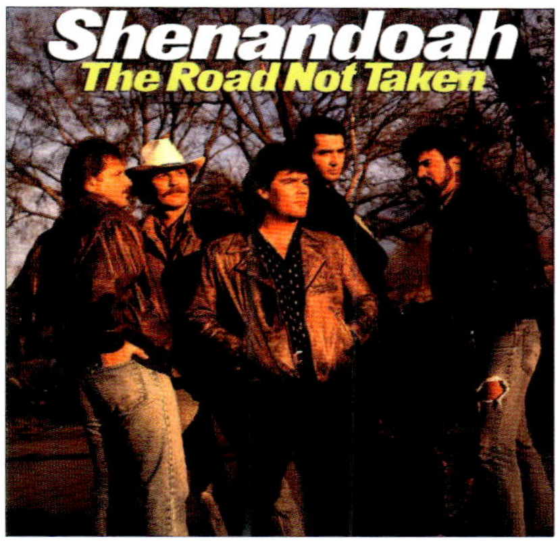

The Road Not Taken by **Shenandoah** was led by "The Church on Cumberland Road," "Two Dozen Roses" and "Sunday in the South"—all country No. 1s.

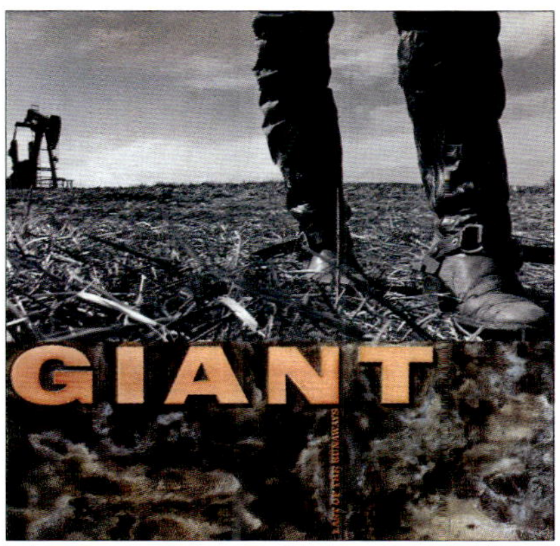

Founded by Dann Huff of the Christian-rock band White Heart, **Giant** had its only Top 20 hit with "I'll See You in My Dreams," a grandiose power ballad.

Billboard 200: *Last of the Runaways* (#80)
Billboard Hot 100: "I'm a Believer" (#56);
"I'll See You in My Dreams" (#20)

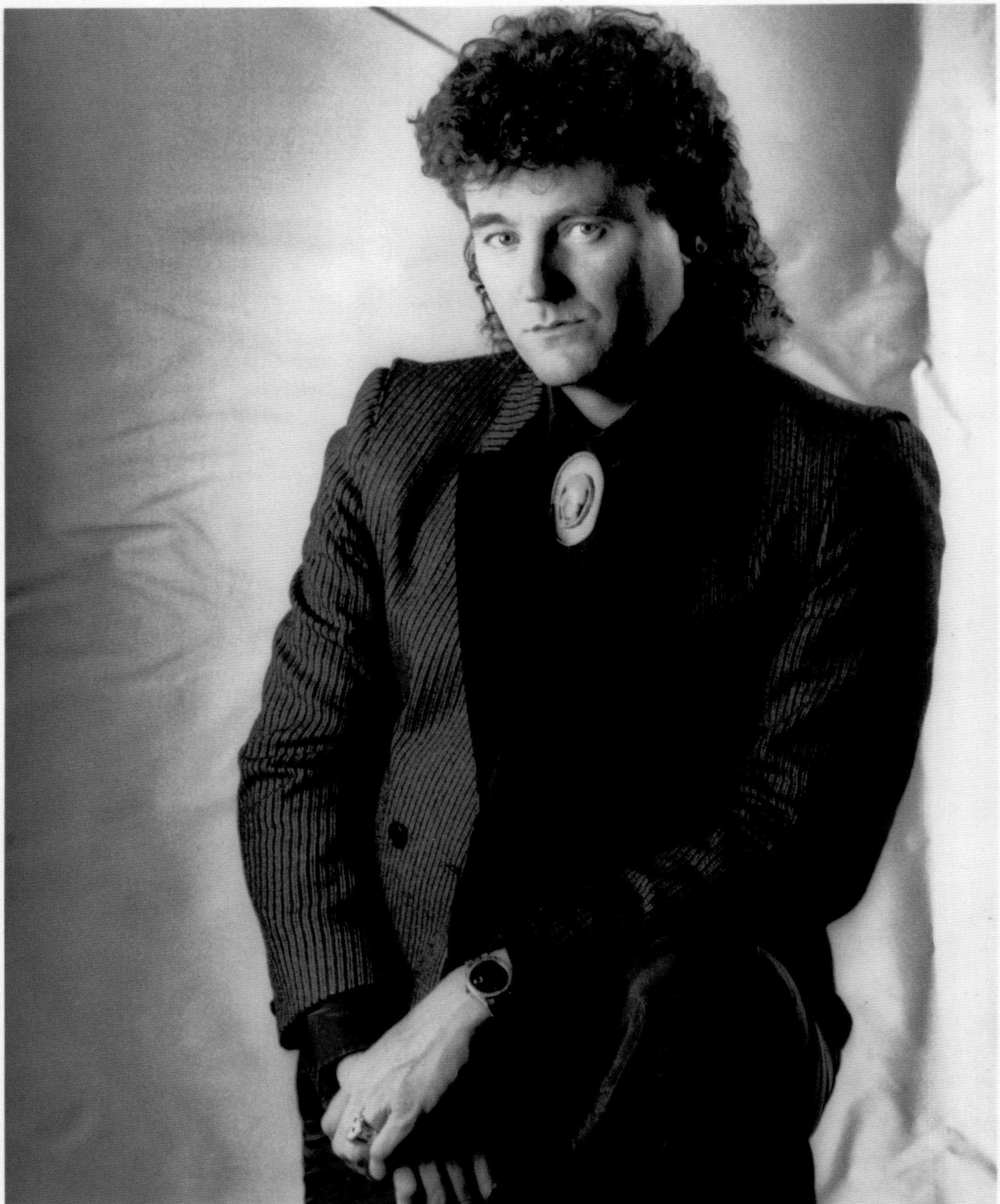

credit: Peter Nash 0389 A

EDDY RAVEN

UNIVERSAL RECORDS

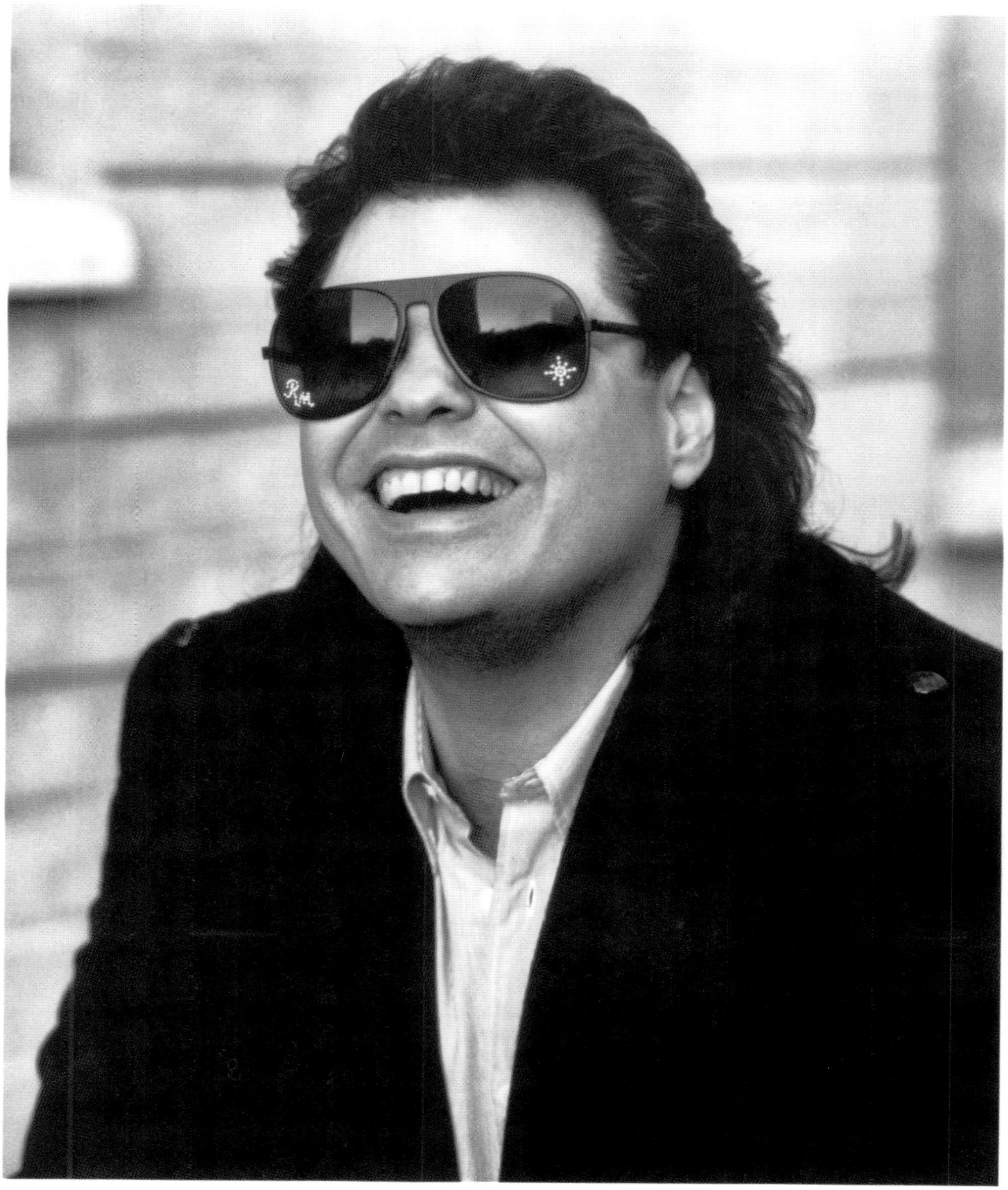

RONNIE MILSAP

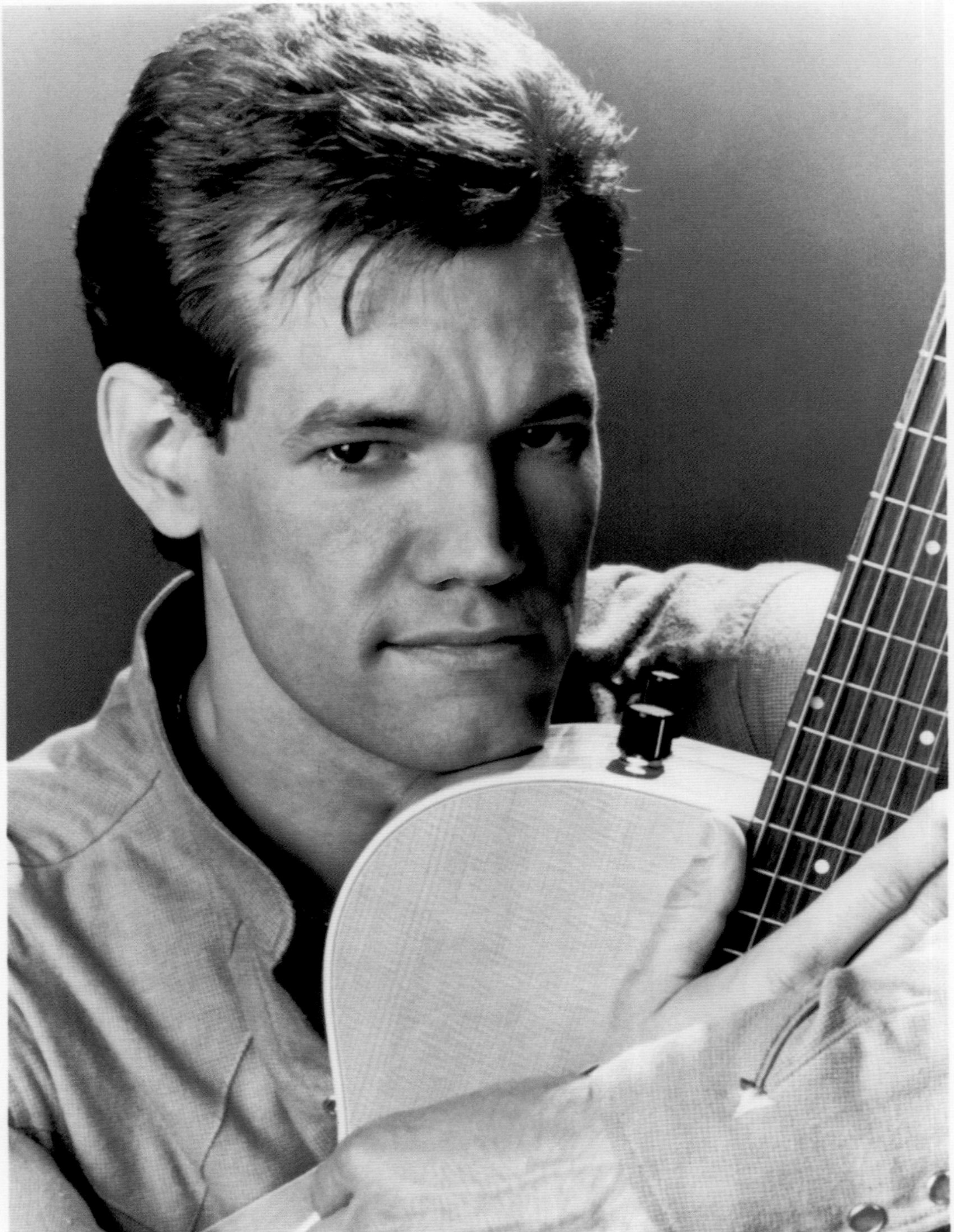

credit: Ken Regan 9/89

RANDY TRAVIS

WARNER BROS.

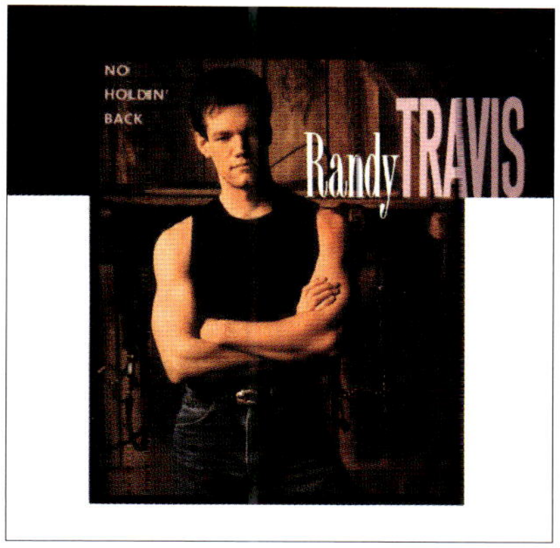

Randy Travis covered "It's Just a Matter of Time," originally recorded as a soul song by Brook Benton in 1959, and his rendition topped the country charts.

Billboard 200: *No Holdin Back* (#33)

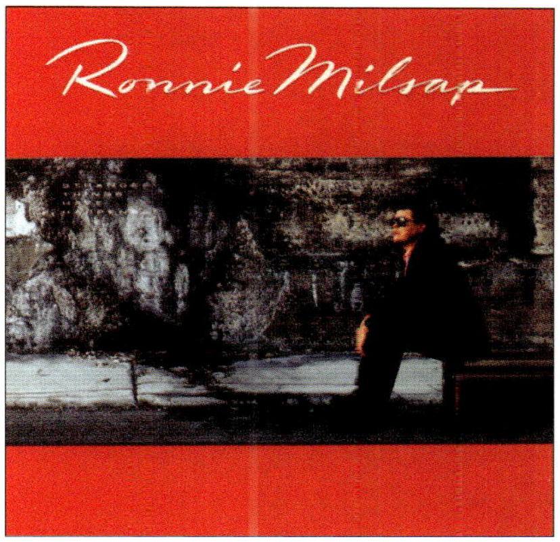

"Don't You Ever Get Tired (Of Hurting Me)" and "A Woman in Love" were the last of 35 No. 1 country hits tallied by singer and pianist **Ronnie Milsap**.

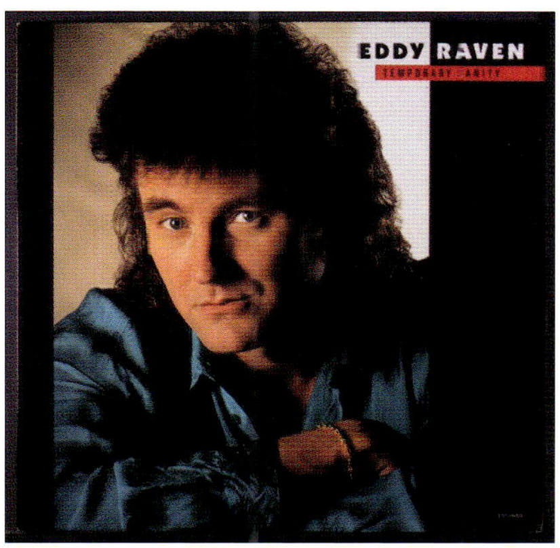

Country music singer and songwriter **Eddy Raven** racked up his fifth and sixth No. 1 singles, "In a Letter to You" and the Cajun-influenced "Bayou Boys."

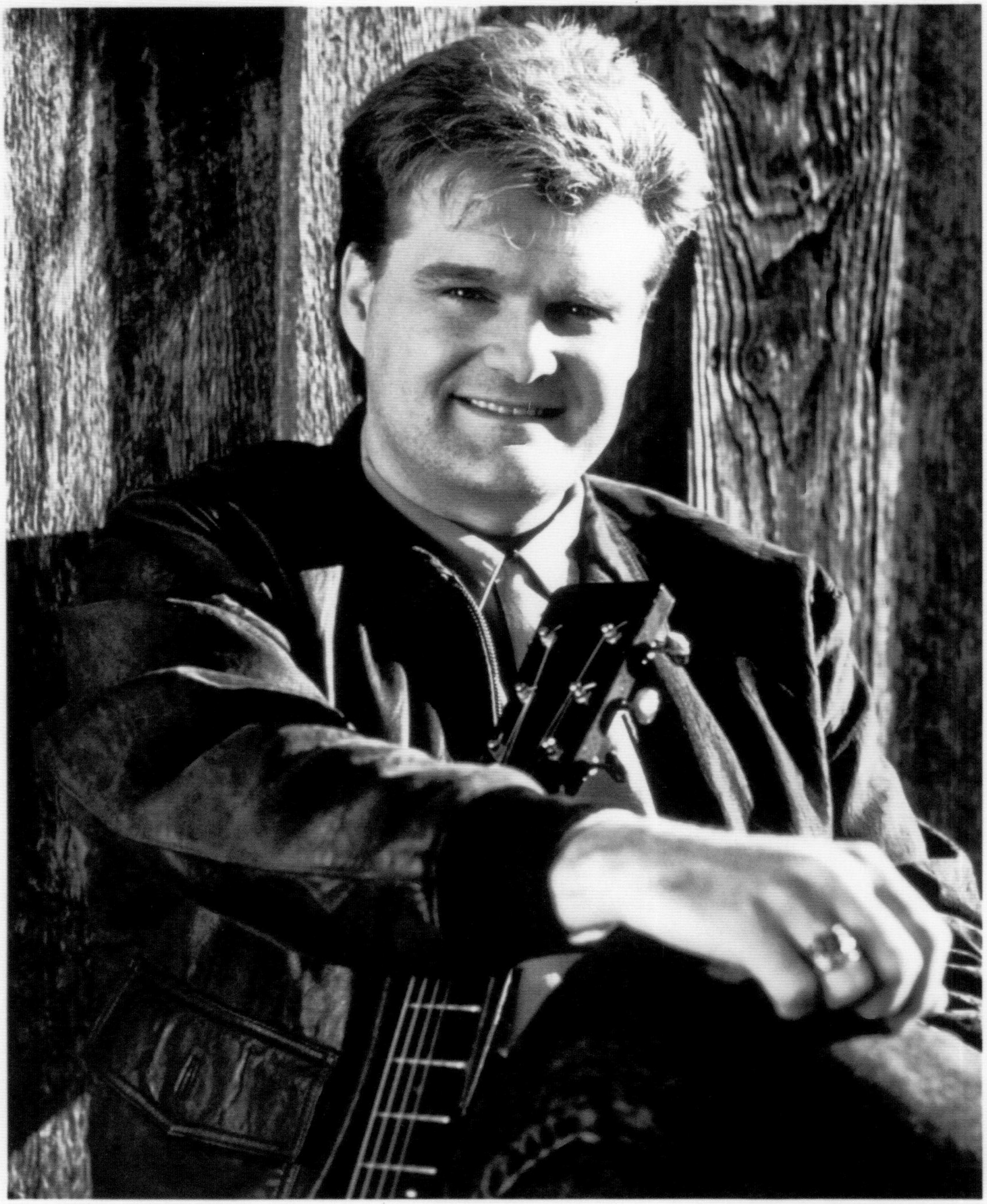

credit: Mike Rutherford

RICKY SKAGGS

Epic

8905

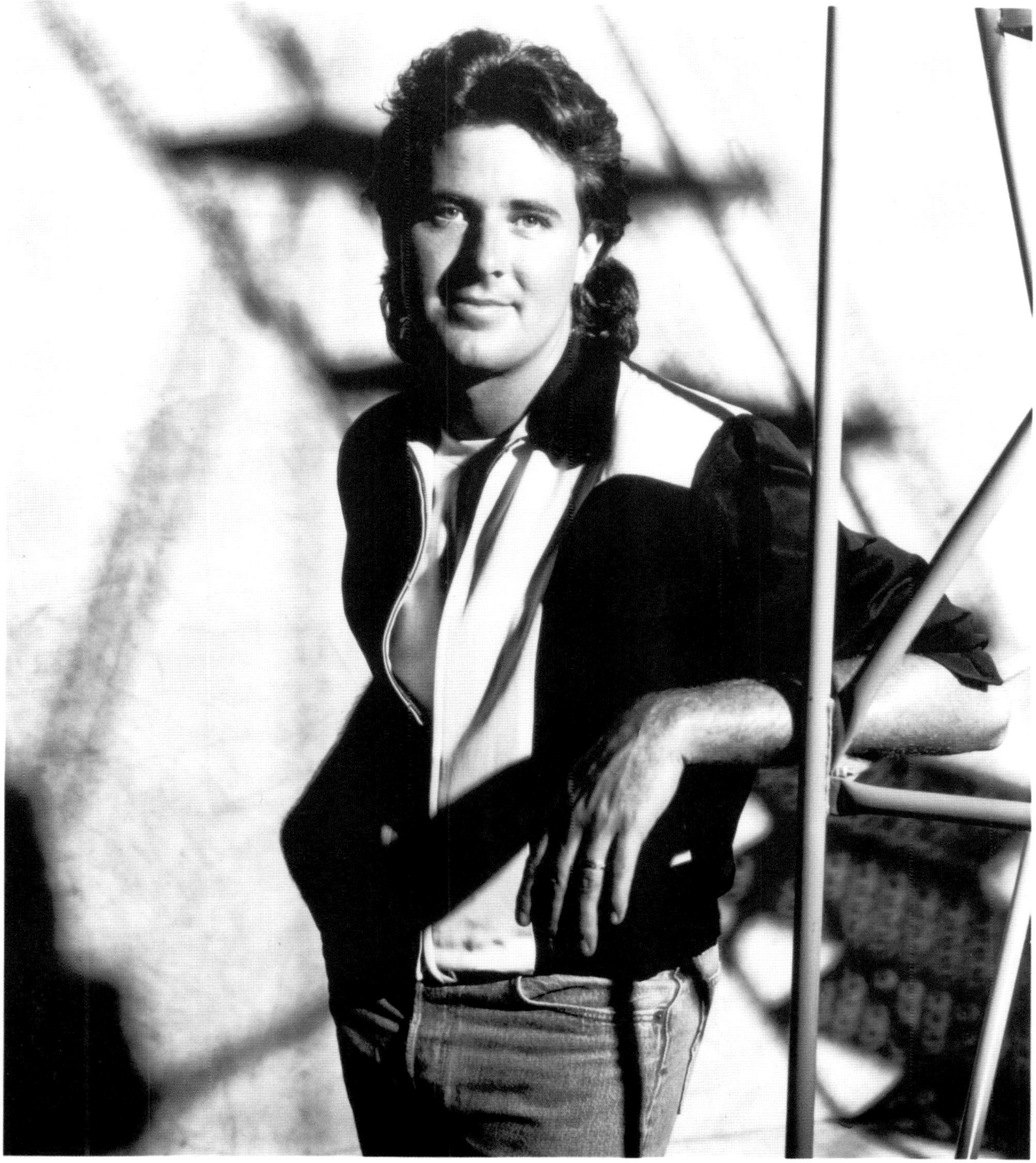

photo: Beverly Parker 1089

VINCE GILL

MCA RECORDS NASHVILLE

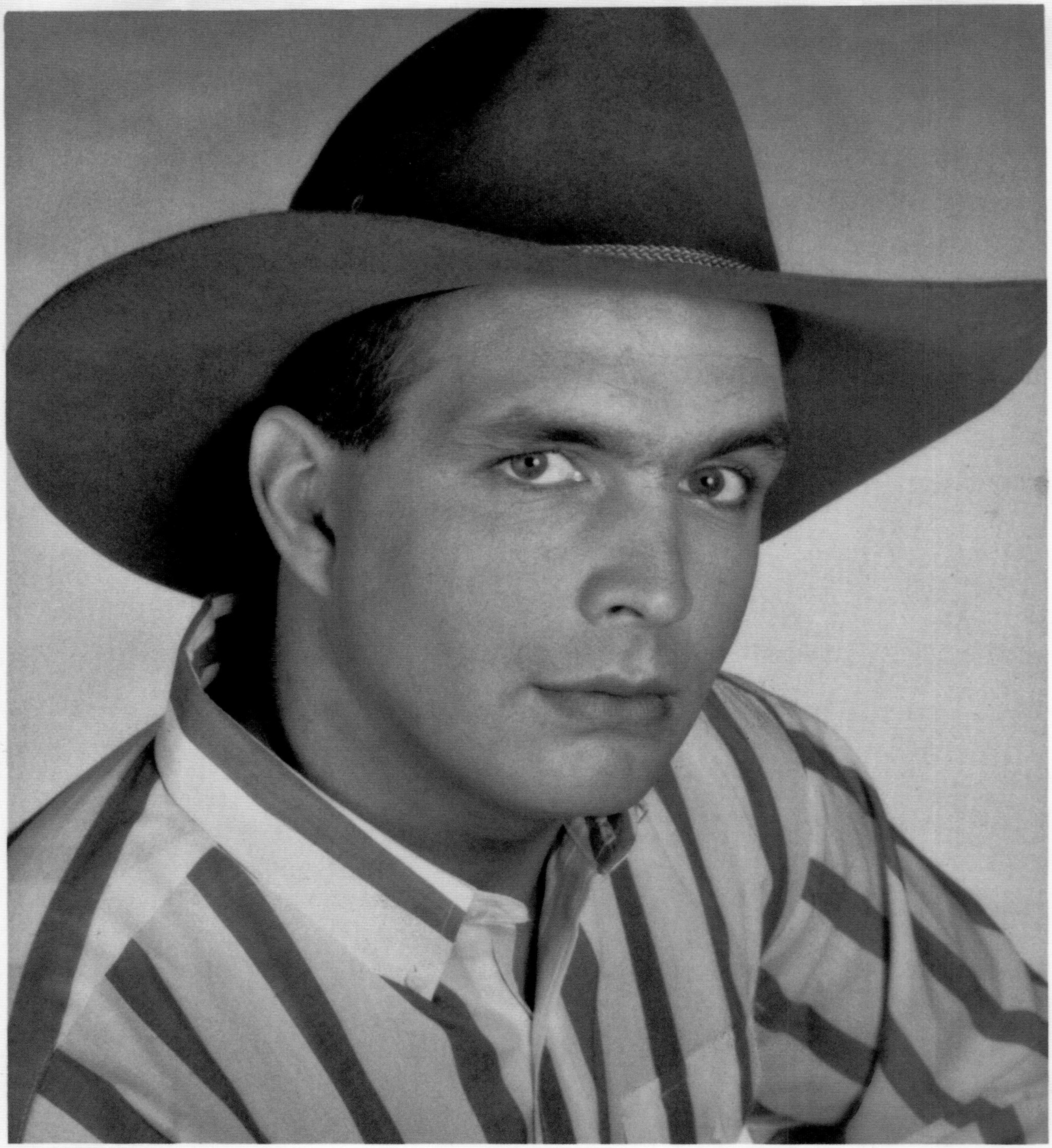

EXCLUSIVE REPRESENTATION
Buddy Lee Attractions Inc.
38 MUSIC SQUARE EAST : SUITE 300
NASHVILLE, TENNESSEE 37203 : 615/244-4336

GARTH BROOKS

Capitol Records

Garth Brooks Fan Club Int'l
27 Music Square East, Suite 172
Nashville, TN 37203

Doyle/Lewis Management
(615) 329-9447

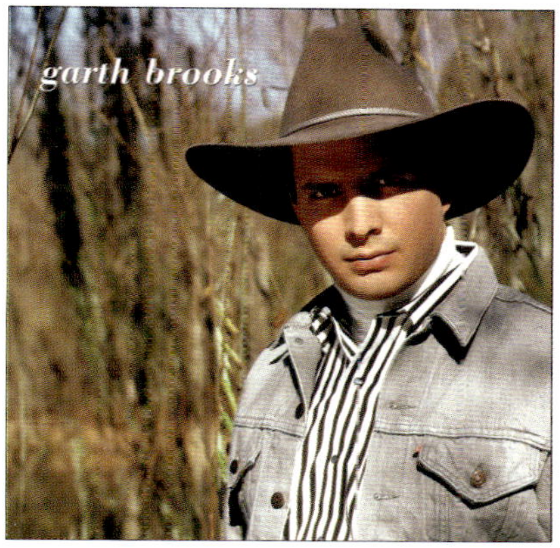

Garth Brooks mixed traditionalist country and rock genres on his debut, beginning his push toward a wider audience with "The Dance," his signature song.

Billboard 200: *Garth Brooks* (#13)

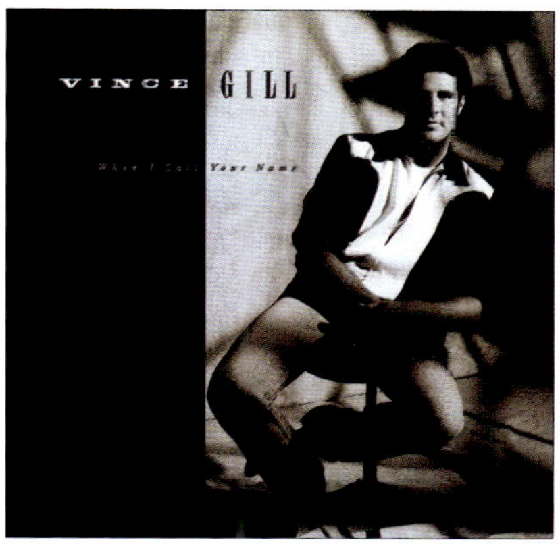

Reuniting with producer Tony Brown, country vocalist and musician **Vince Gill** sold more than a million copies of his breakthrough, *When I Call Your Name*.

Billboard 200: *When I Call Your Name* (#67)

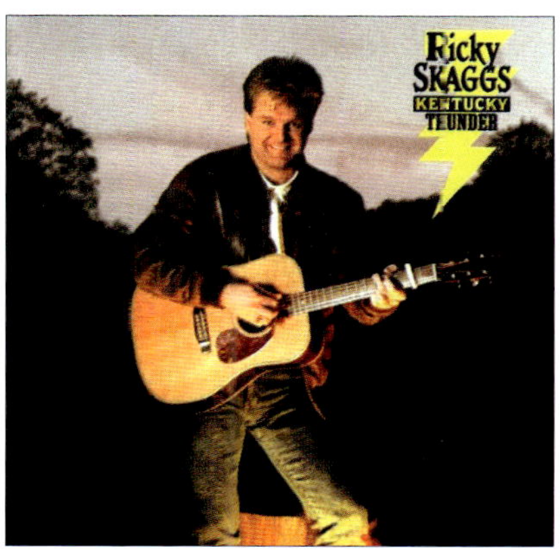

Ricky Skaggs, a traditional country and bluegrass icon in the Eighties, reaped his eleventh No. 1 hit of the decade with the uptempo "Lovin' Only Me."

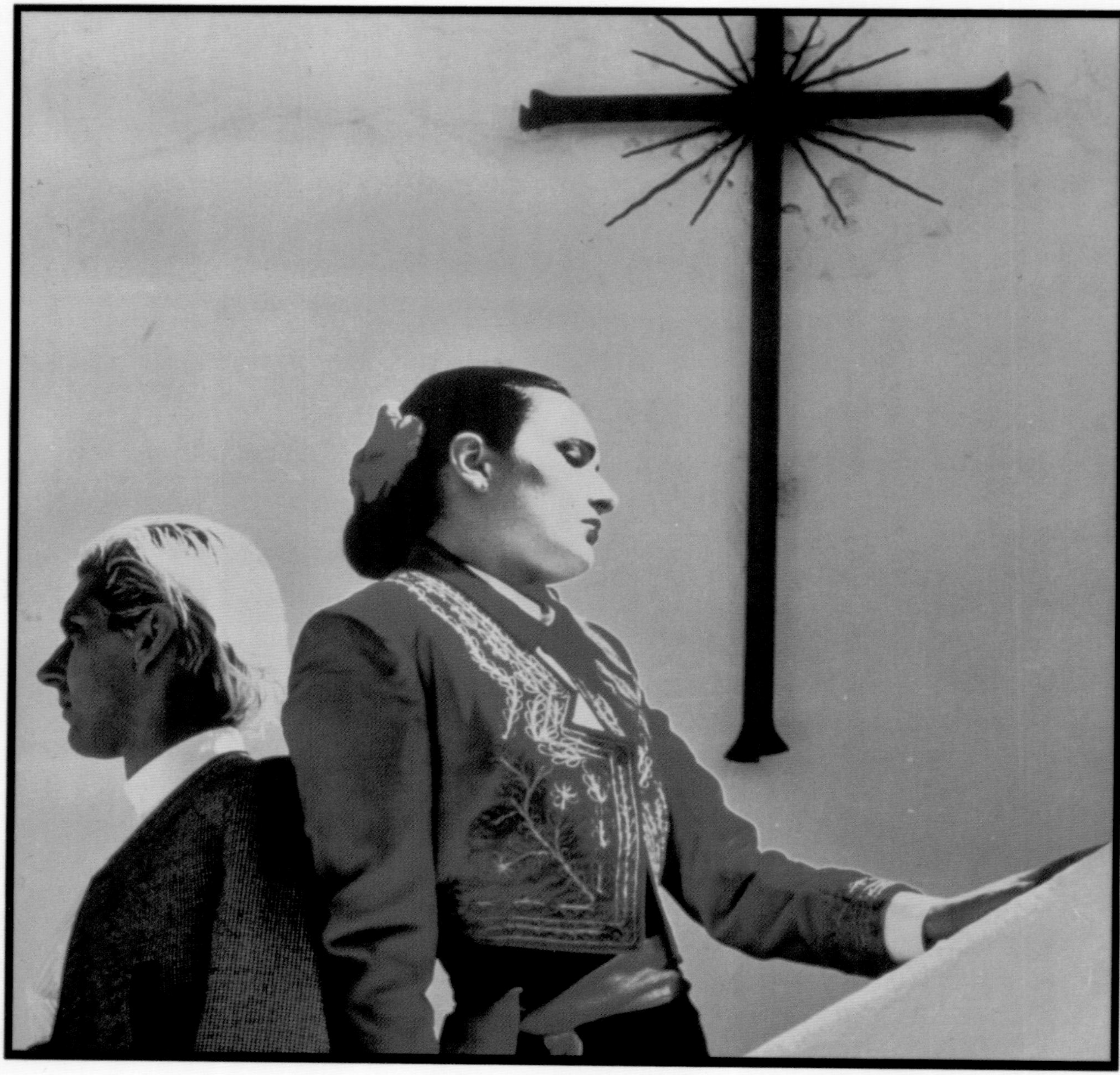

Photo Credit: Anton Corbin

Budgie Siouxsie

the creatures

GEFFEN® RECORDS

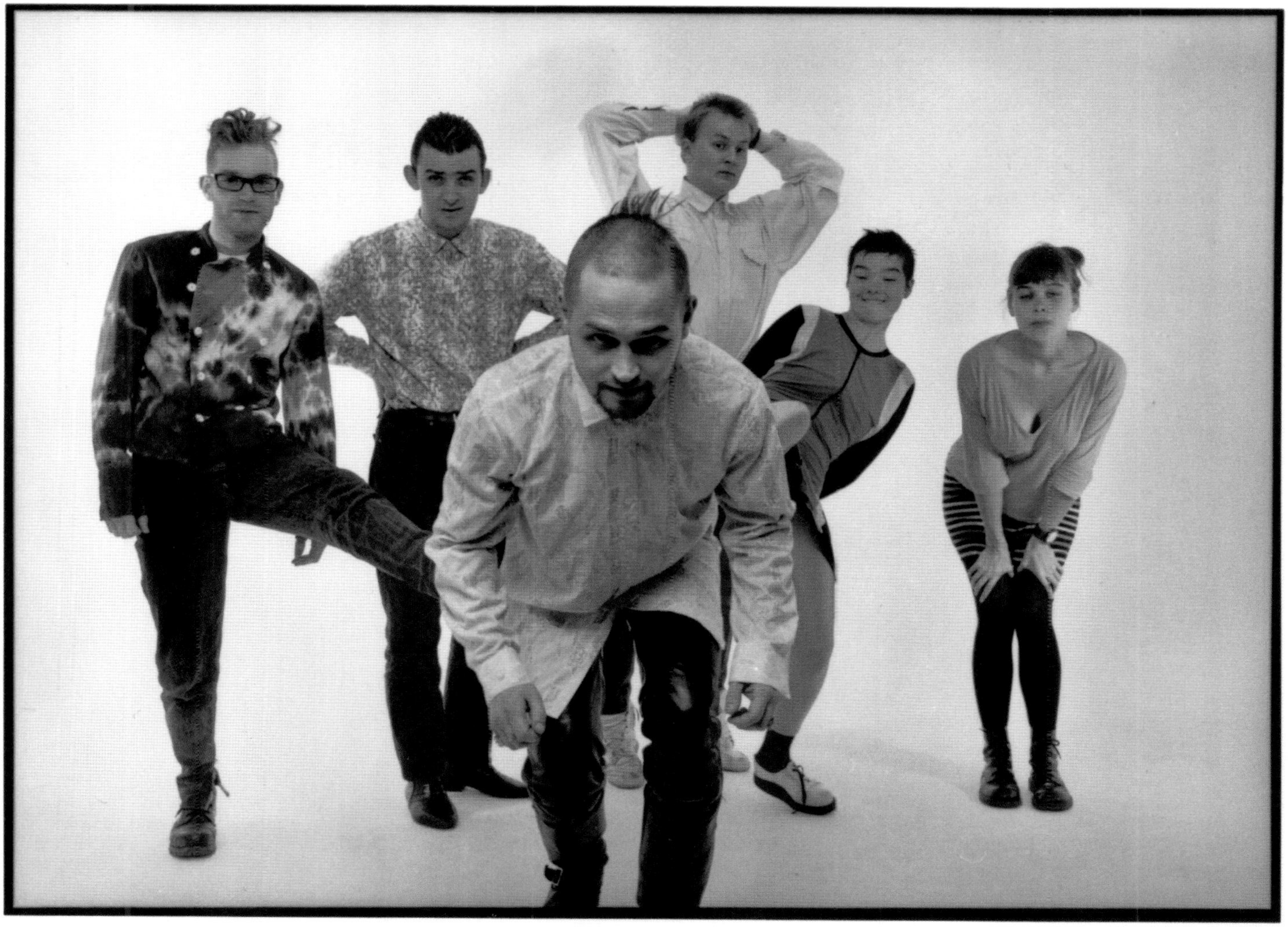

PHOTO CREDIT: SIGURGEIR

THOR BRAGI SIGGI BJORK MAGGA

EINAR

the sugar cubes

Elektra Entertainment

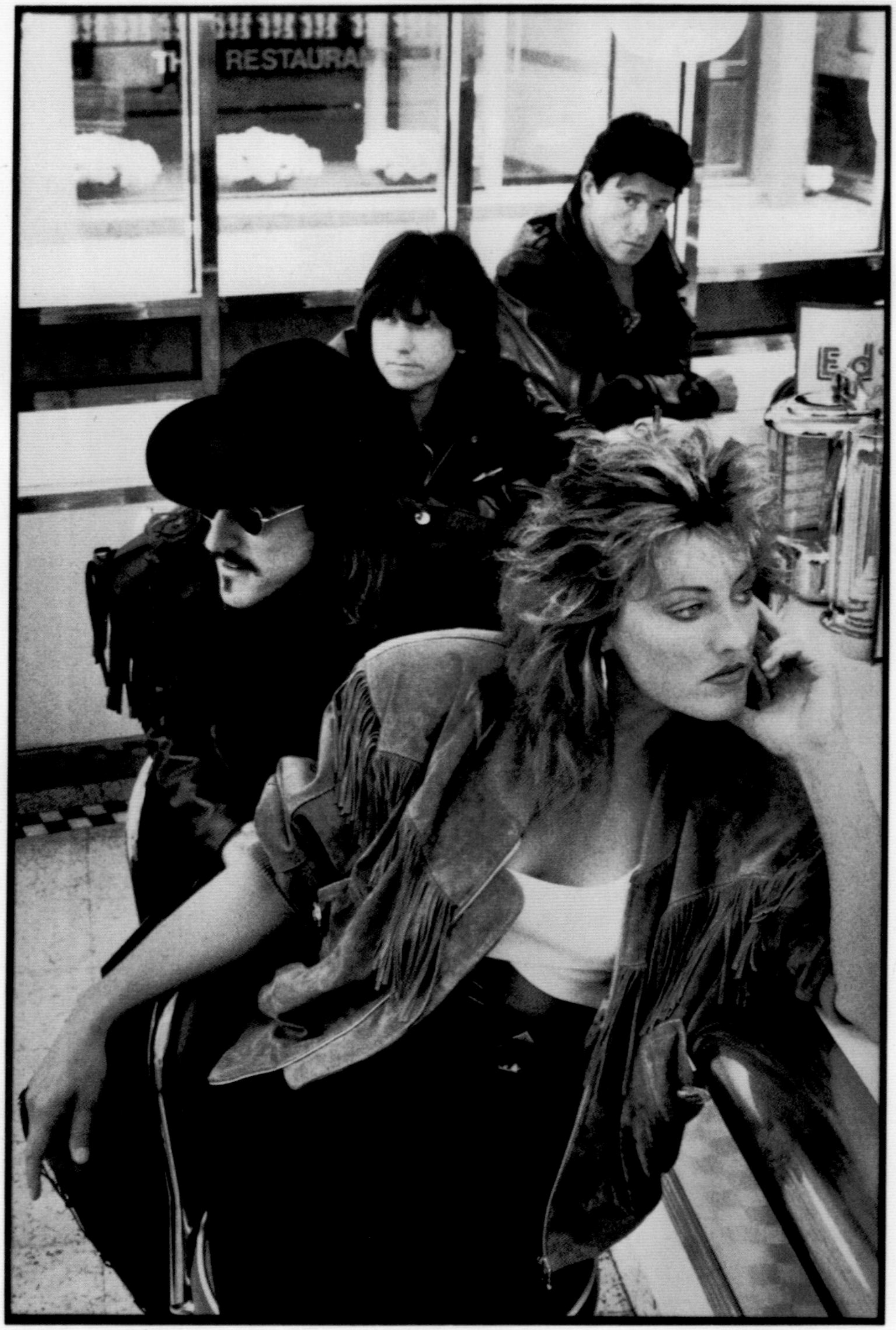

PHOTO CREDIT: SIMON FOWLER

FRONT TO BACK: KATRINA LESKANICH (VOCALS, GUITAR), VINCE DE LA CRUZ (BASS, VOCALS, GUITAR, KEYBOARDS), KIMBERLEY REW (GUITAR, VOCALS, KEYBOARDS), ALEX COOPER (DRUMS, VOCALS, KEYBOARDS)

KATRINA & THE WAVES

SBK Records

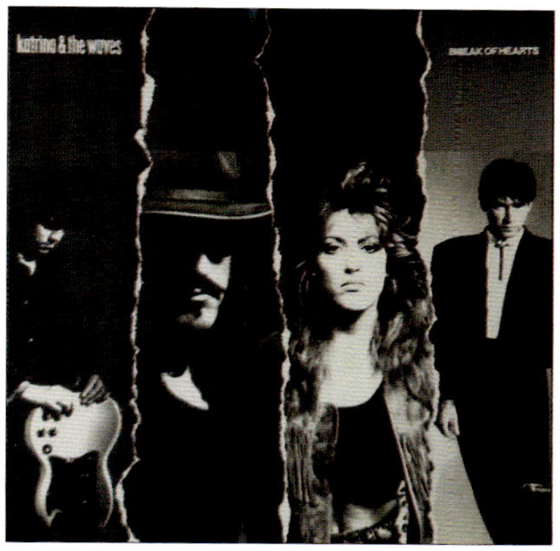

Signed to a new label, **Katrina & the Waves** produced *Break of Hearts* and worked up a Top 20 hit, "That's the Way," and the spirited "Rock N' Roll Girl."

Billboard 200: *Break of Hearts* (#122)
Billboard Hot 100: "That's the Way" (#16)

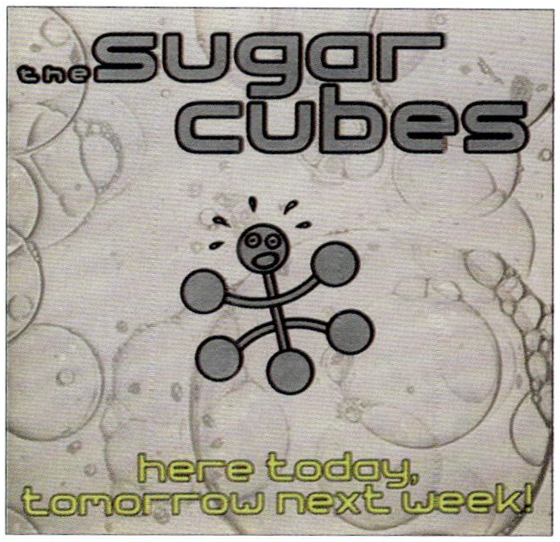

The Sugarcubes, an alternative rock band emerging from Iceland, watched "Regina" top the UK indie charts and come off well on US alternative radio.

Billboard 200: *Here Today, Tomorrow Next Week!* (#70)

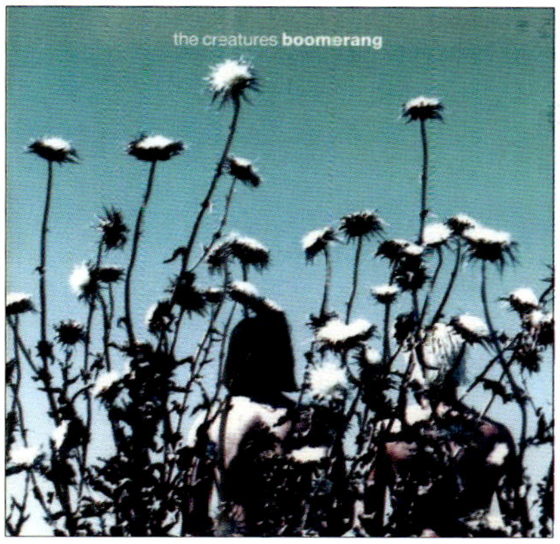

The Creatures, led by Siouxsie & the Banshees members Siouxsie Sioux and Budgie, proffered *Boomerang* and the modern-rock track "Standing There."

Billboard 200: *Boomerang* (#197)

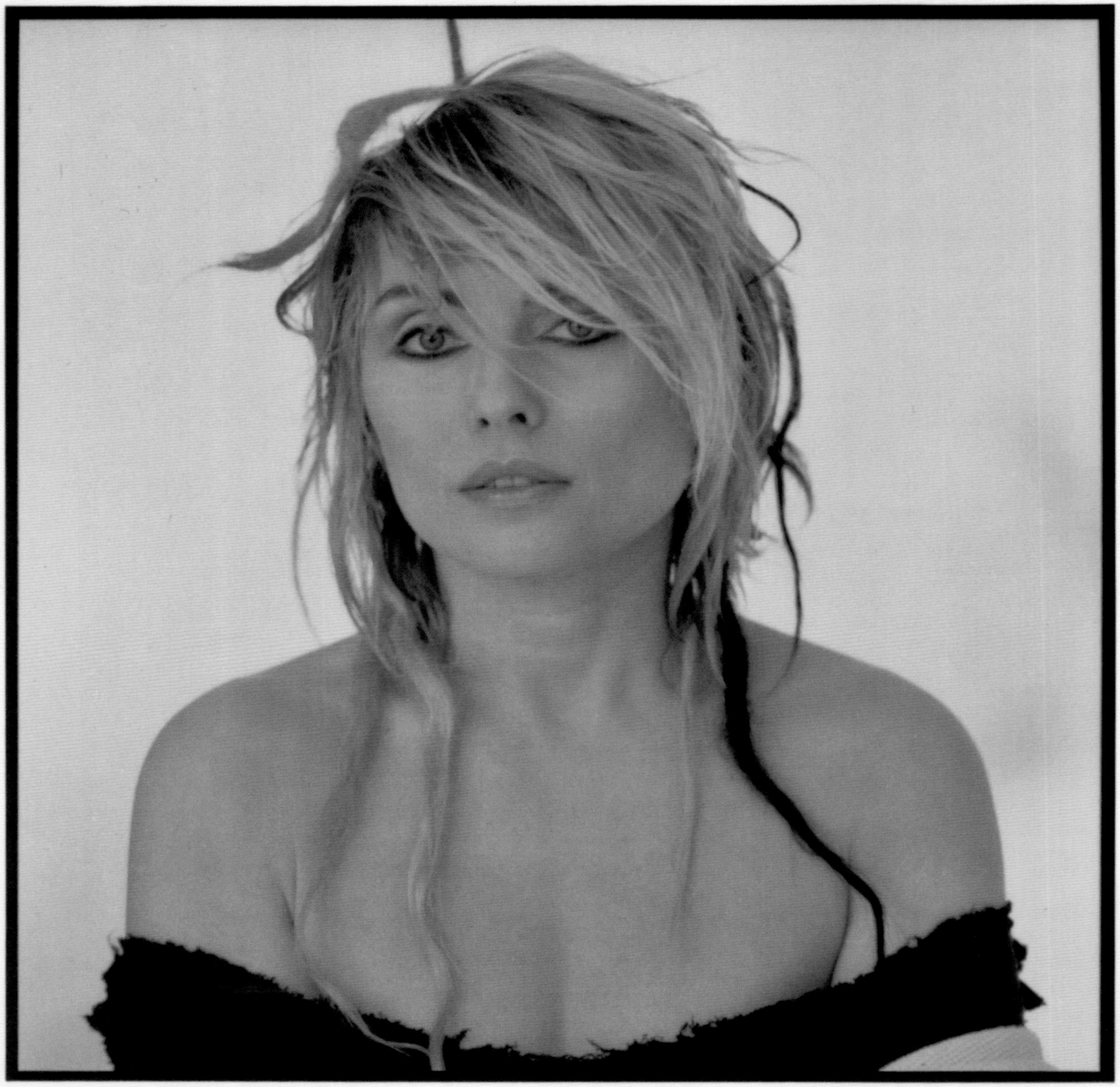

Photo Credit: Arthur Elgort

DEBORAH HARRY

SIRE® reprise®

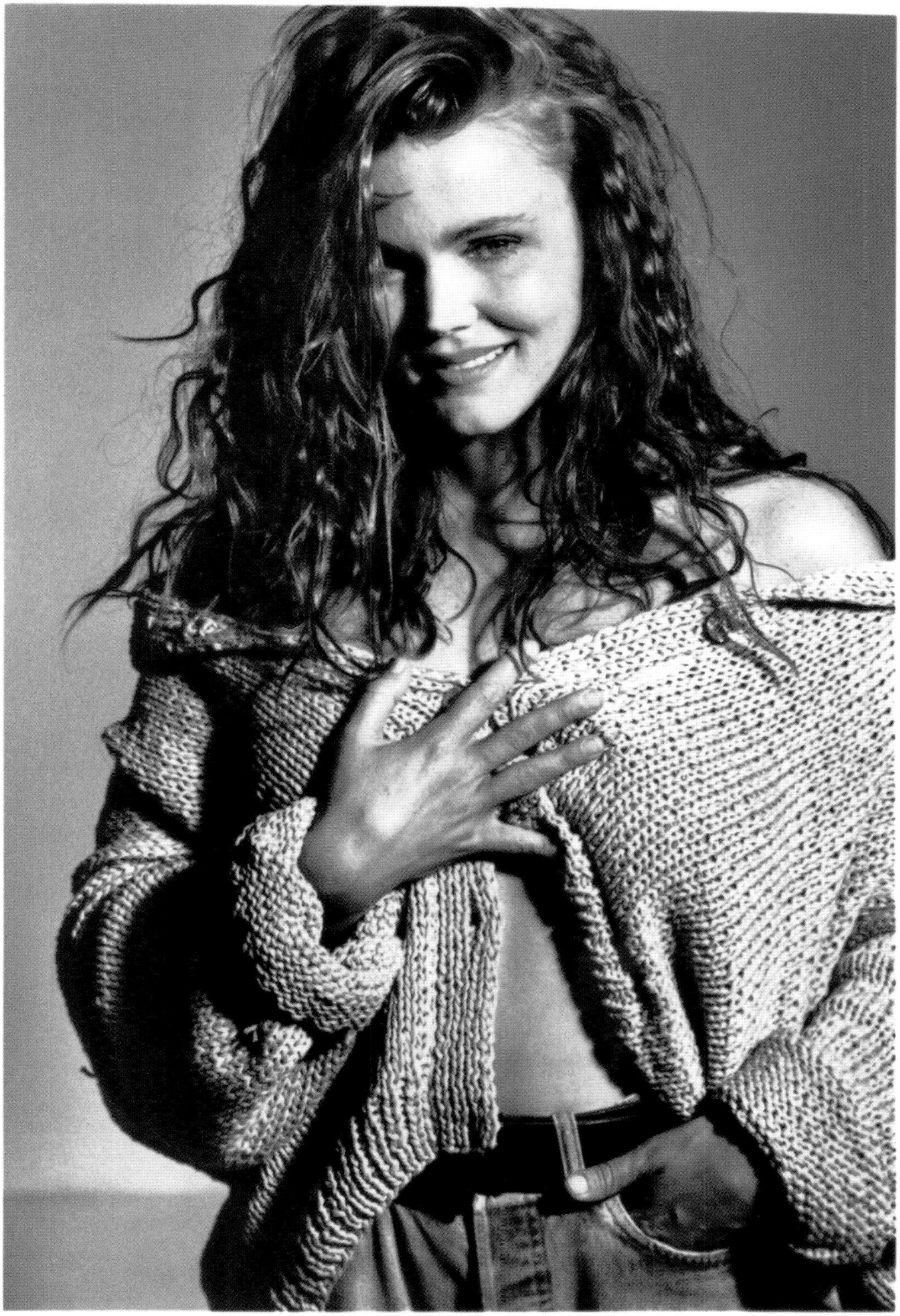

Photo Credit: Herb Ritts

Belinda Carlisle

9/89

MCA RECORDS

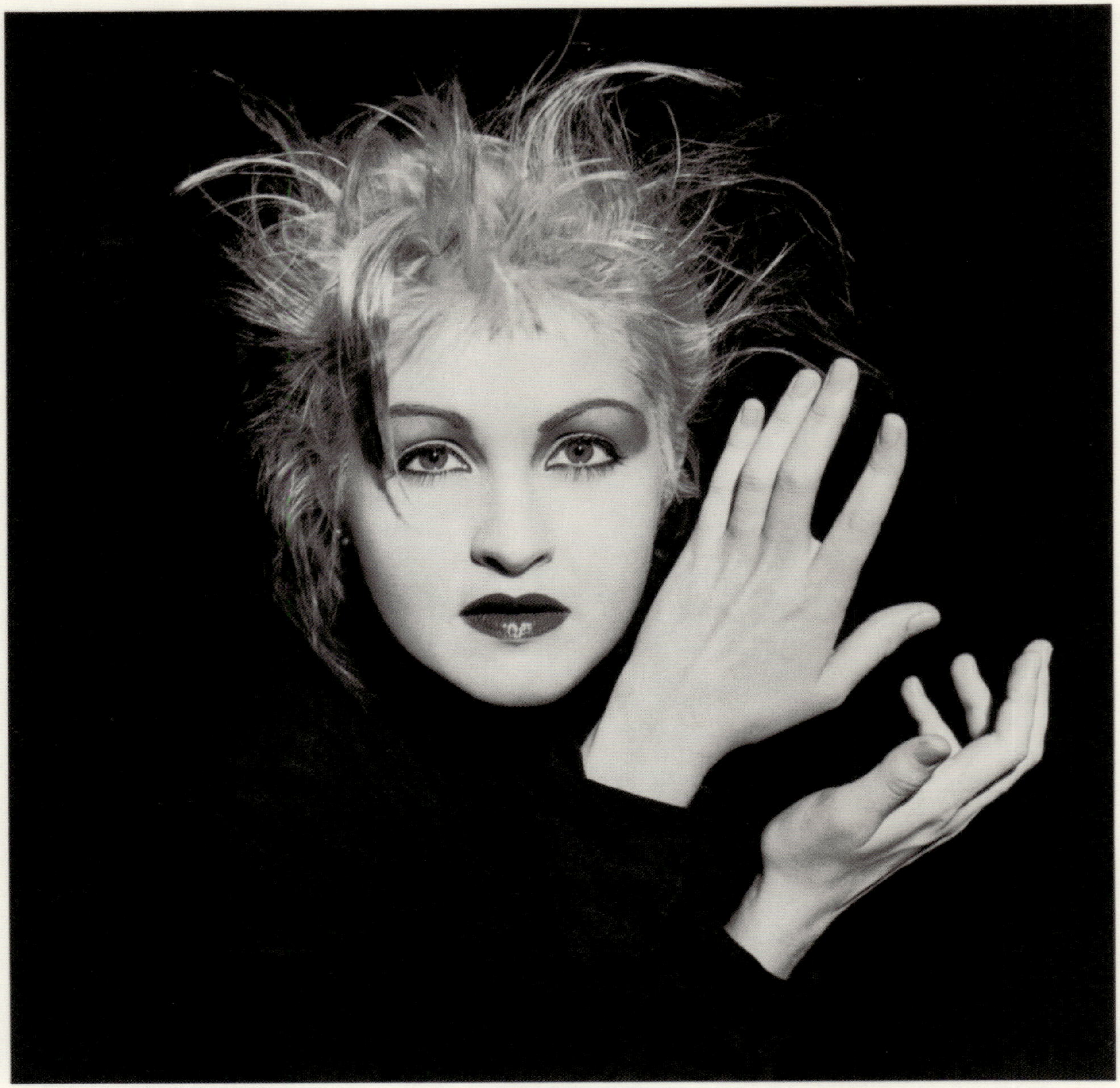

CYNDI LAUPER

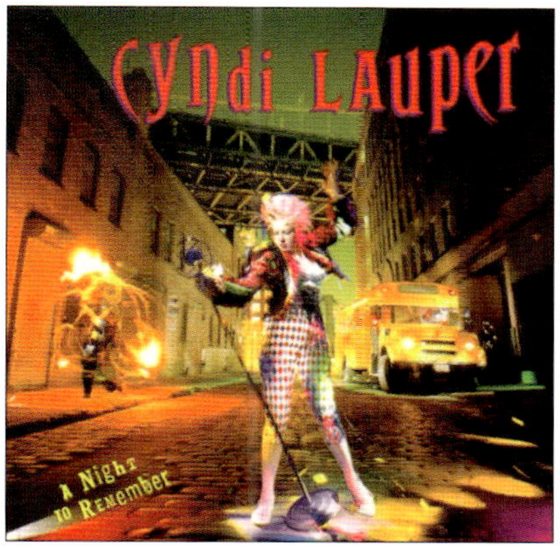

Originally penned for Roy Orbison, **Cyndi Lauper**'s rendition of "I Drove All Night" appeared as a Top 10 hit from her third album, *A Night to Remember*.

Billboard 200: *A Night to Remember* (#37)
Billboard Hot 100: "I Drove All Night" (#6); "My First Night Without You" (#62)

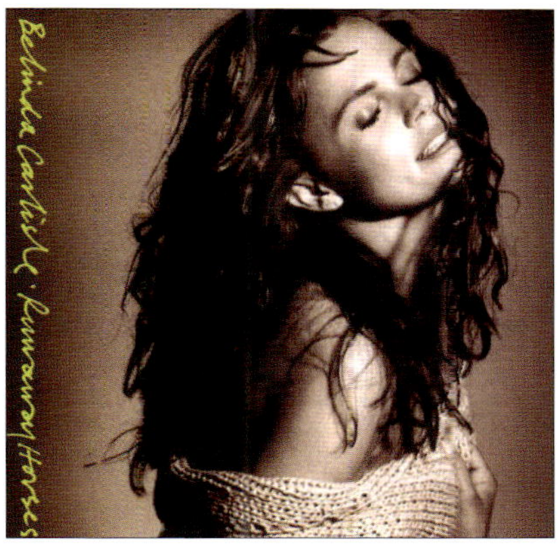

The former lead singer of the Go-Go's, **Belinda Carlisle** achieved more solo success with two singles, "Leave a Light On" and the dramatic "Summer Rain."

Billboard 200: *Runaway Horses* (#37)
Billboard Hot 100: "Leave a Light On" (#11); "Summer Rain" (#30)

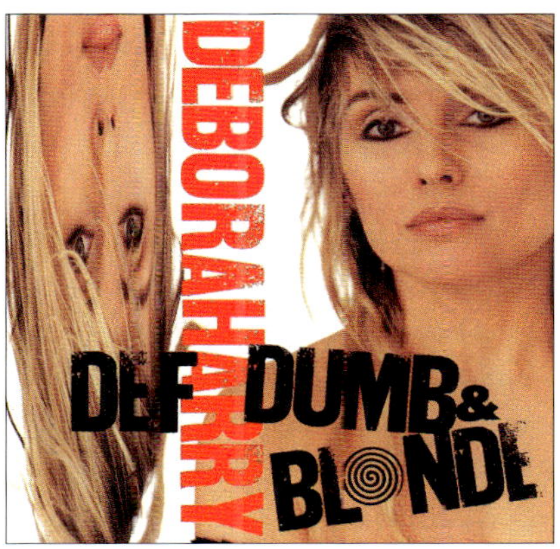

Known as Blondie's titular frontwoman, **Deborah Harry** ventured a third solo album, *Def, Dumb & Blonde*, and "I Want That Man" wowed in many countries.

Billboard 200: *Def, Dumb & Blonde* (#123)

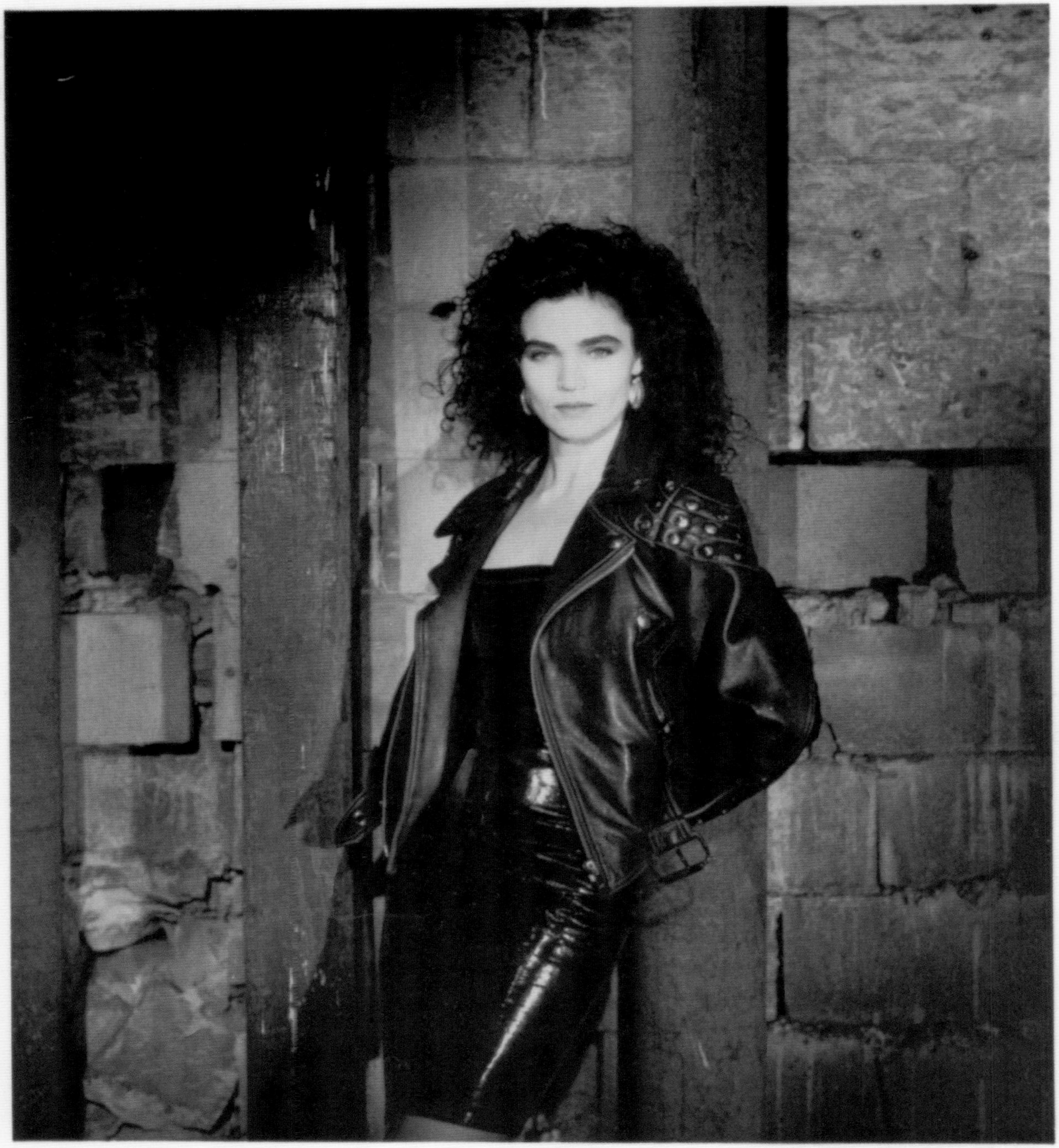

ALANNAH MYLES

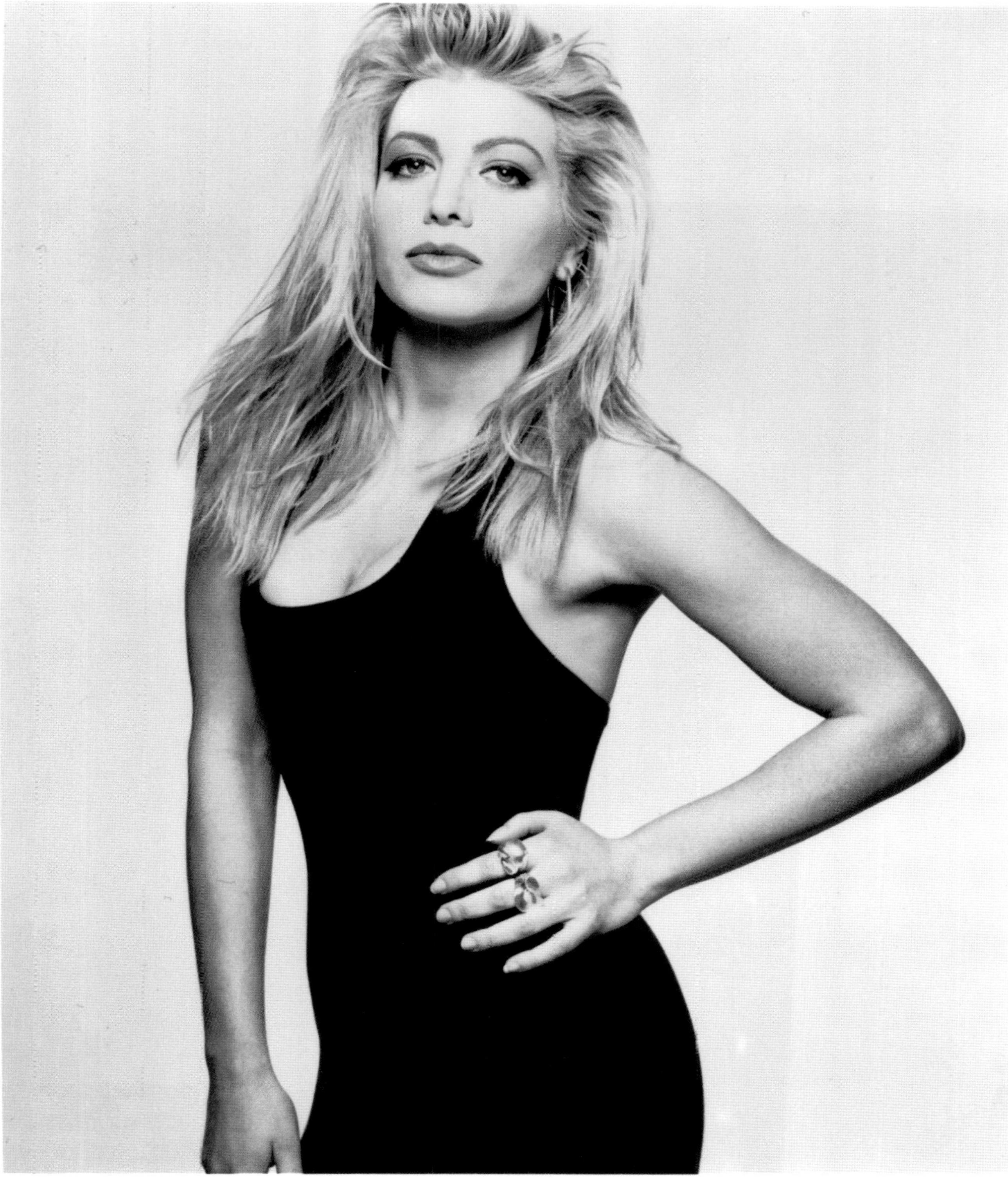

TAYLOR DAYNE

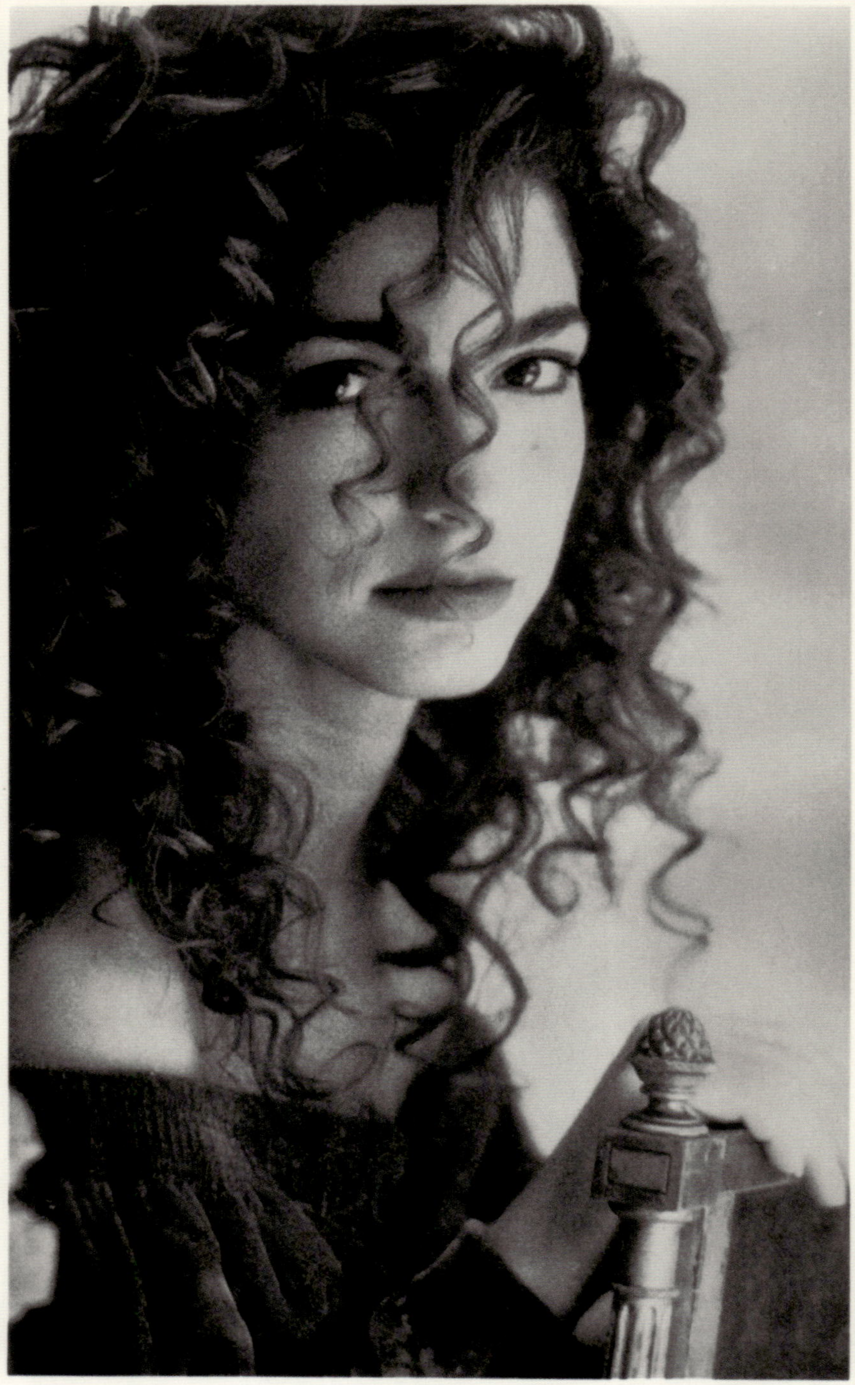

gloria estefan

Epic
8907

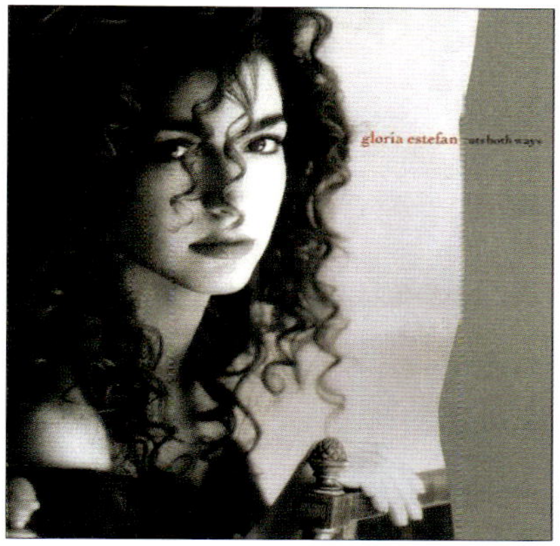

Billed as a solo artist rather than with Miami Sound Machine, **Gloria Estefan** issued *Cuts Both Ways*, firing off the No. 1 smash "Don't Wanna Lose You."

Billboard 200: *Cuts Both Ways* (#8)
Billboard Hot 100: "Don't Wanna Lose You" (No. 1);
"Get on Your Feet" (#11); "Here We Are" (#6);
"Oye Mi Canto (Hear My Voice)" (#48); "Cuts Both Ways" (#44)

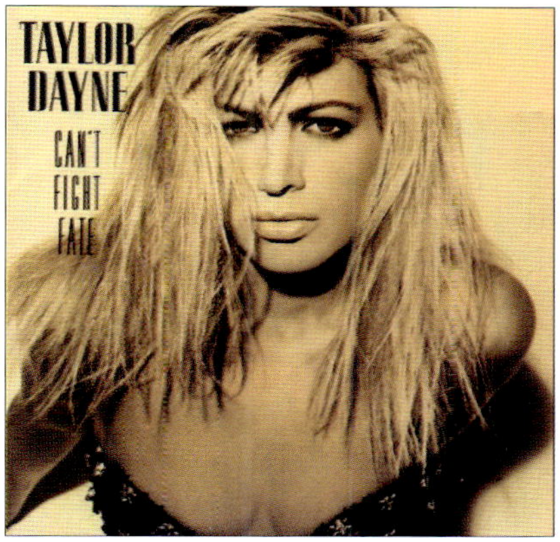

Can't Fight Fate extended dance-pop artist **Taylor Dayne**'s string of hit songs with the No. 1 "Love Will Lead You Back," two Top 10s and one Top 20.

Billboard 200: *Can't Fight Fate* (#25)
Billboard Hot 100: "With Every Beat of My Heart" (#5);
"Love Will Lead You Back" (No. 1); "I'll Be Your Shelter" (#4);
"Heart of Stone" (#12)

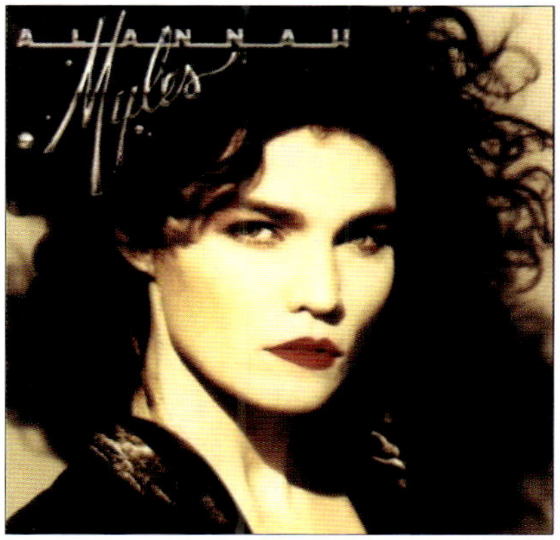

Alannah Myles' sultry rendering of "Black Velvet" became an international hit that won the Canadian singer-songwriter both a Grammy and Juno Award.

Billboard 200: *Alannah Myles* (#5)
Billboard Hot 100: "Love Is" (#36); "Black Velvet" (No. 1)

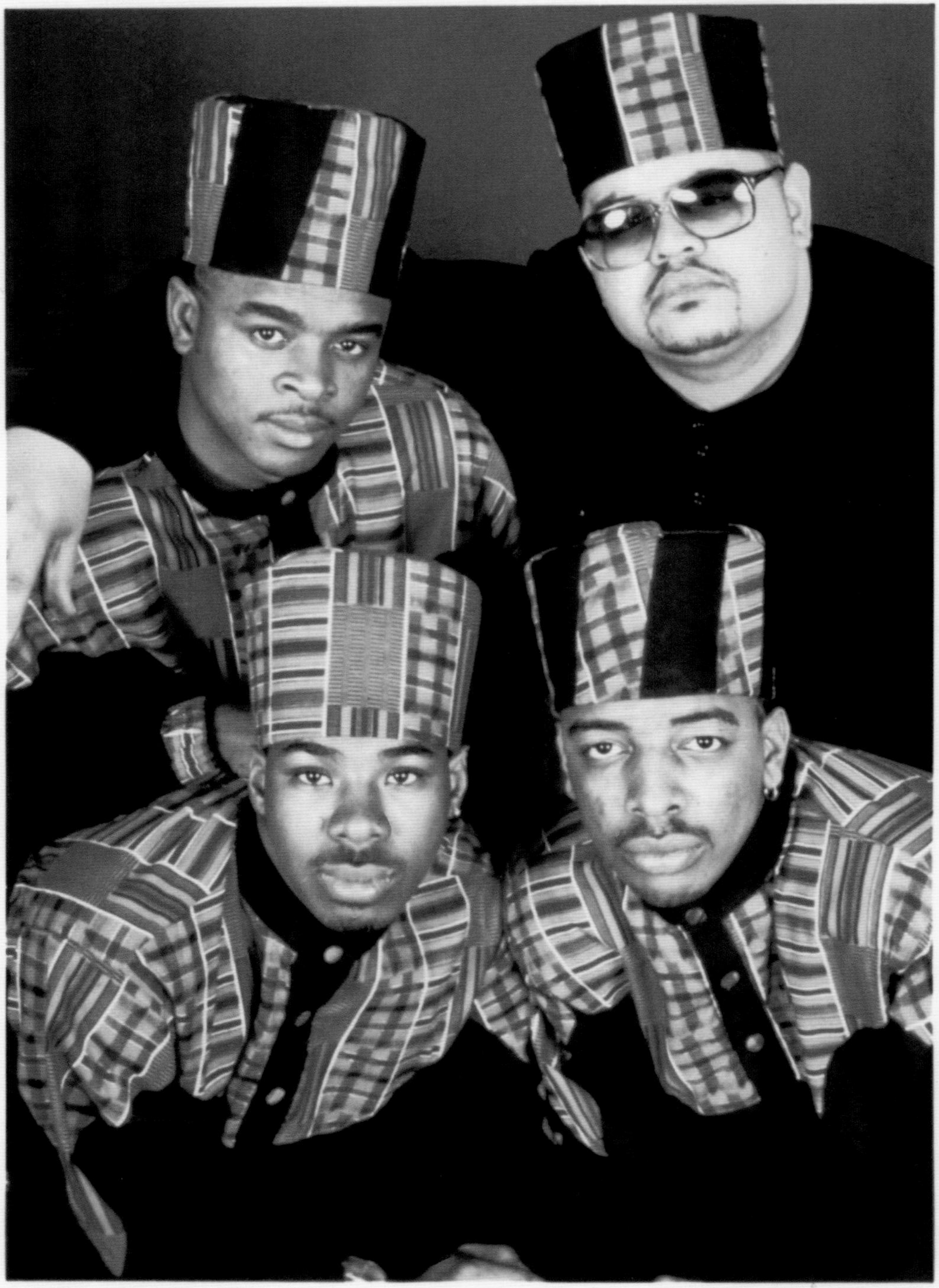

Photo Credit: Brian Perry

(L—R): Back — D.J. Eddie F, Heavy D   Front — G Whiz, Trouble T—Roy

UPTOWN
IS KICKIN' IT

HEAVY D AND THE BOYZ

5/89

MCA RECORDS

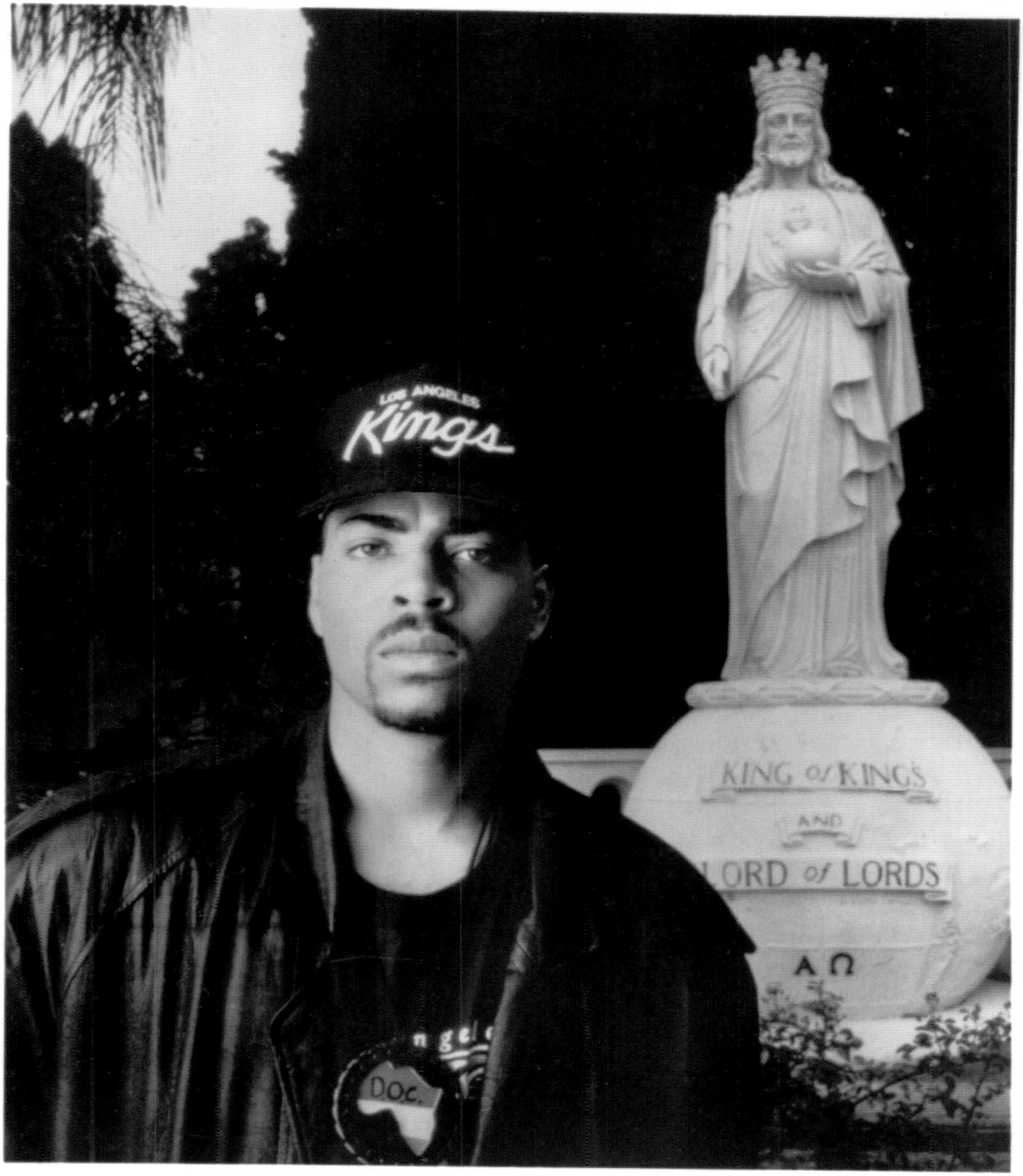

THE DOC

ATLANTIC

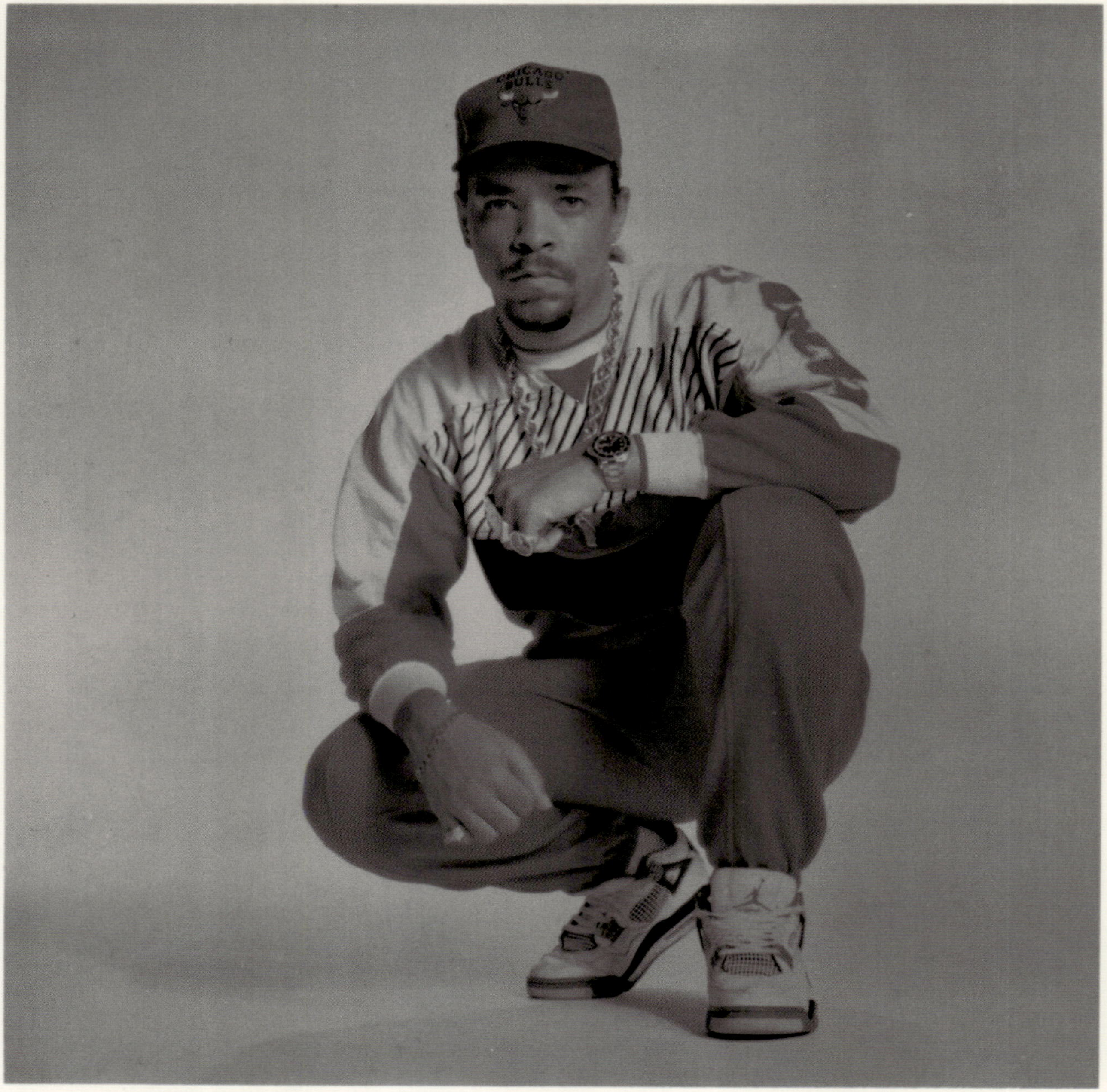

Photo Credit: Aaron Rapoport

ICE-T

SIRE®

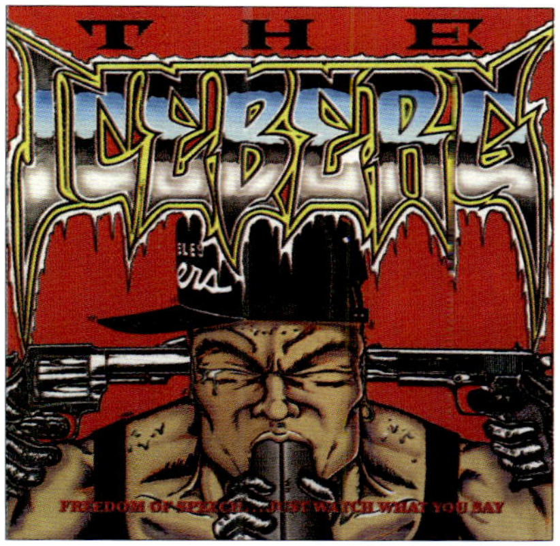

The Iceberg/Freedom of Speech...Just Watch What You Say! made West Coast rapper **Ice-T** a star, coupling harsh backdrops with rhymes against censorship.

Billboard 200: *The Iceberg/Freedom of Speech... Just Watch What You Say!* (#37)

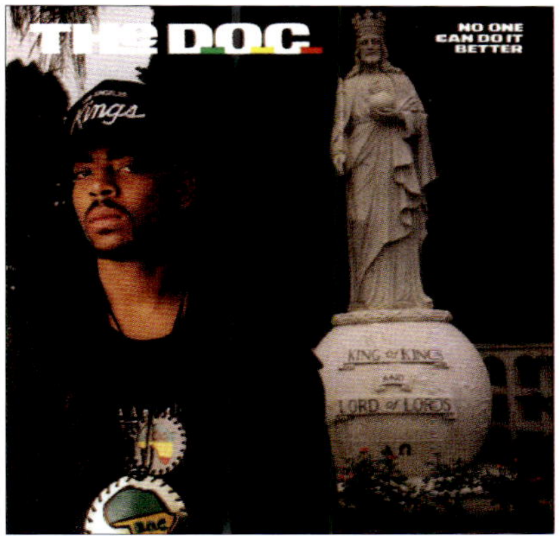

The D.O.C. delivered *No One Can Do It Better*, a No. 1 R&B/hip-hop debut album produced by Dr. Dre, before a car crash destroyed the rapper's voice.

Billboard 200: *No One Can Do It Better* (#20)

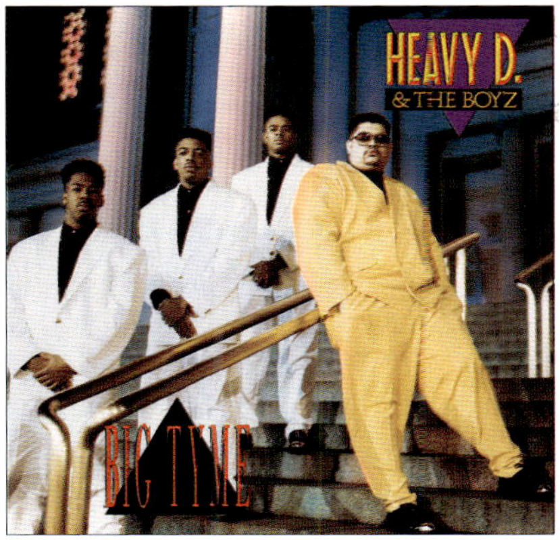

Heavy D & the Boyz took a major step forward with *Big Tyme*, topping the hip-hop album charts and achieving a No. 1 rap single, "Somebody for Me."

Billboard 200: *Big Tyme* (#19)

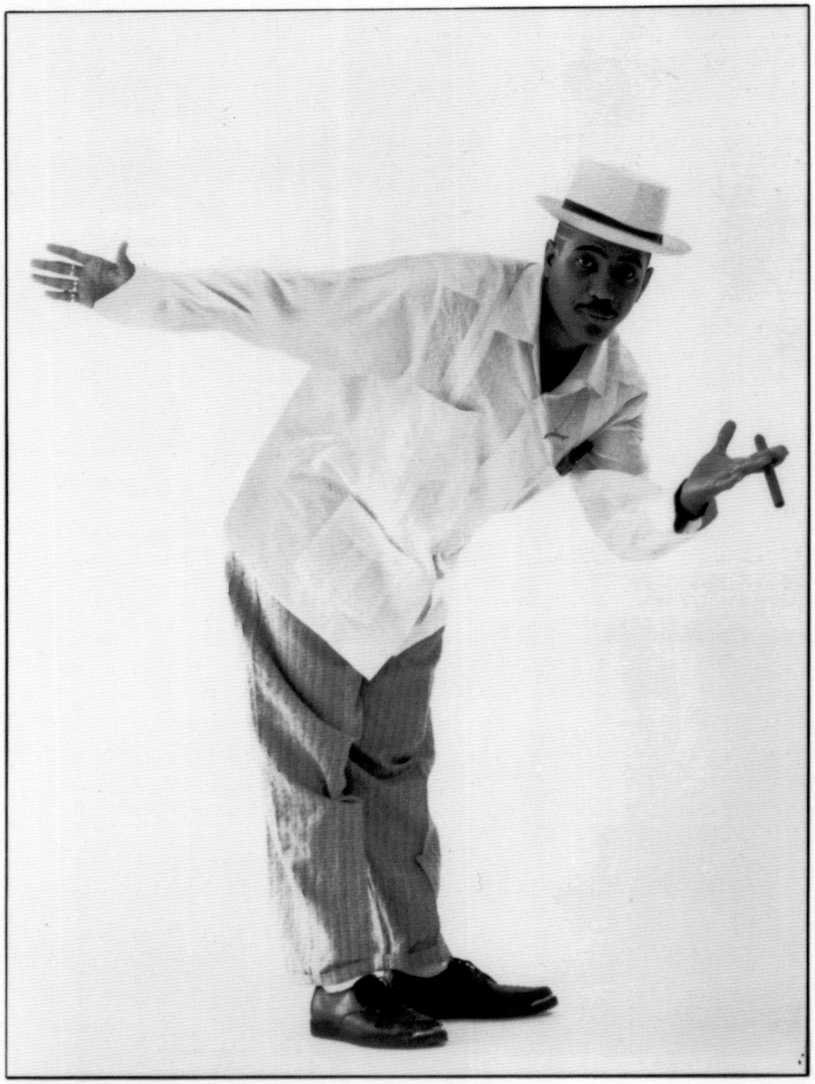

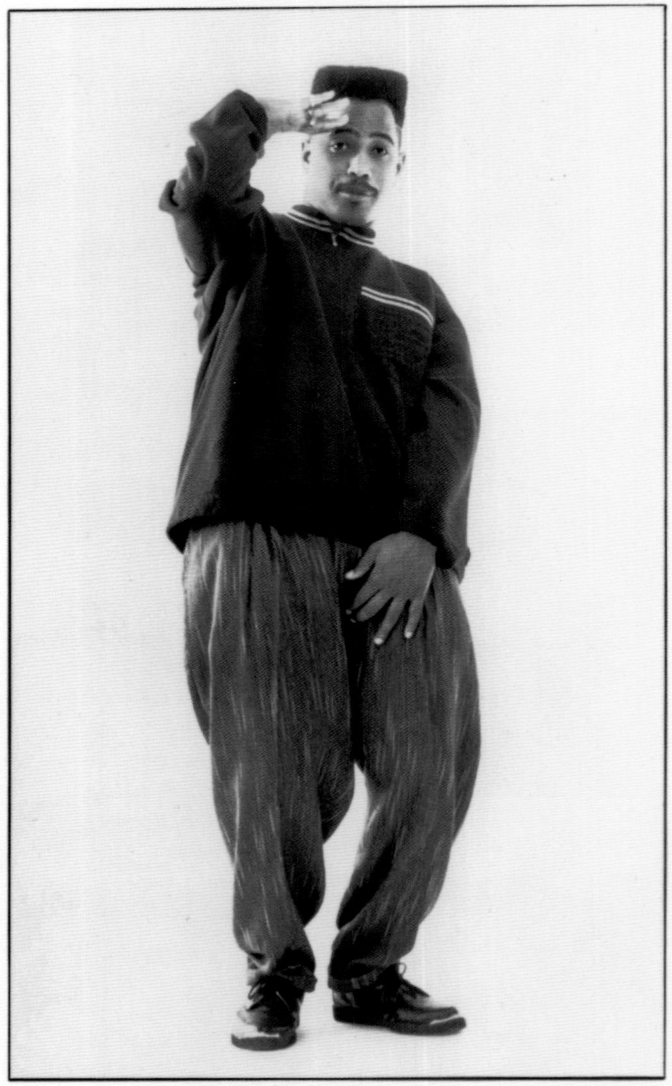

Photographer: Salomon / 1989

MELLOW MAN ACE

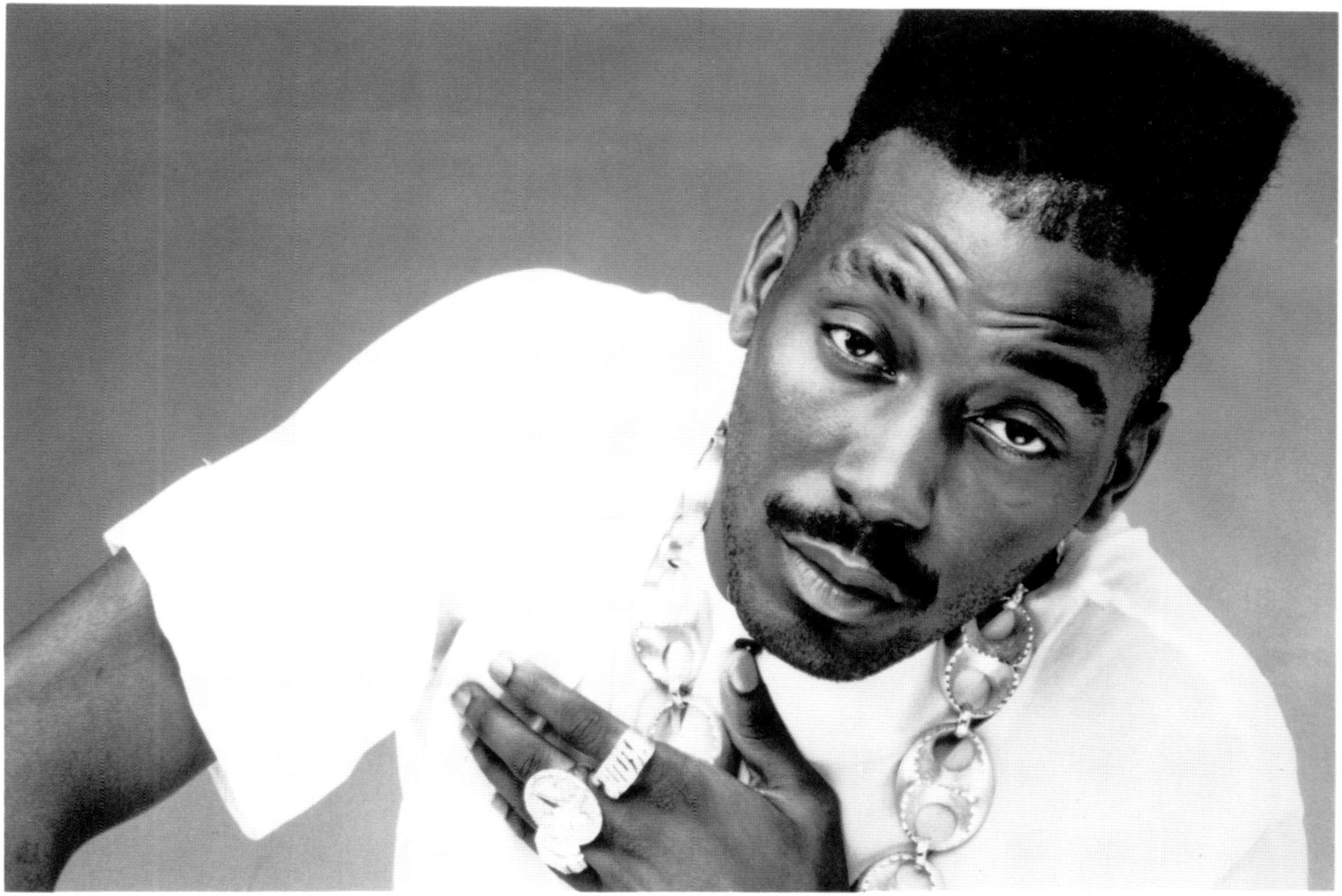

Photo Credit: Mike Jones

BIG DADDY KANE

Cold Chillin'

reprise

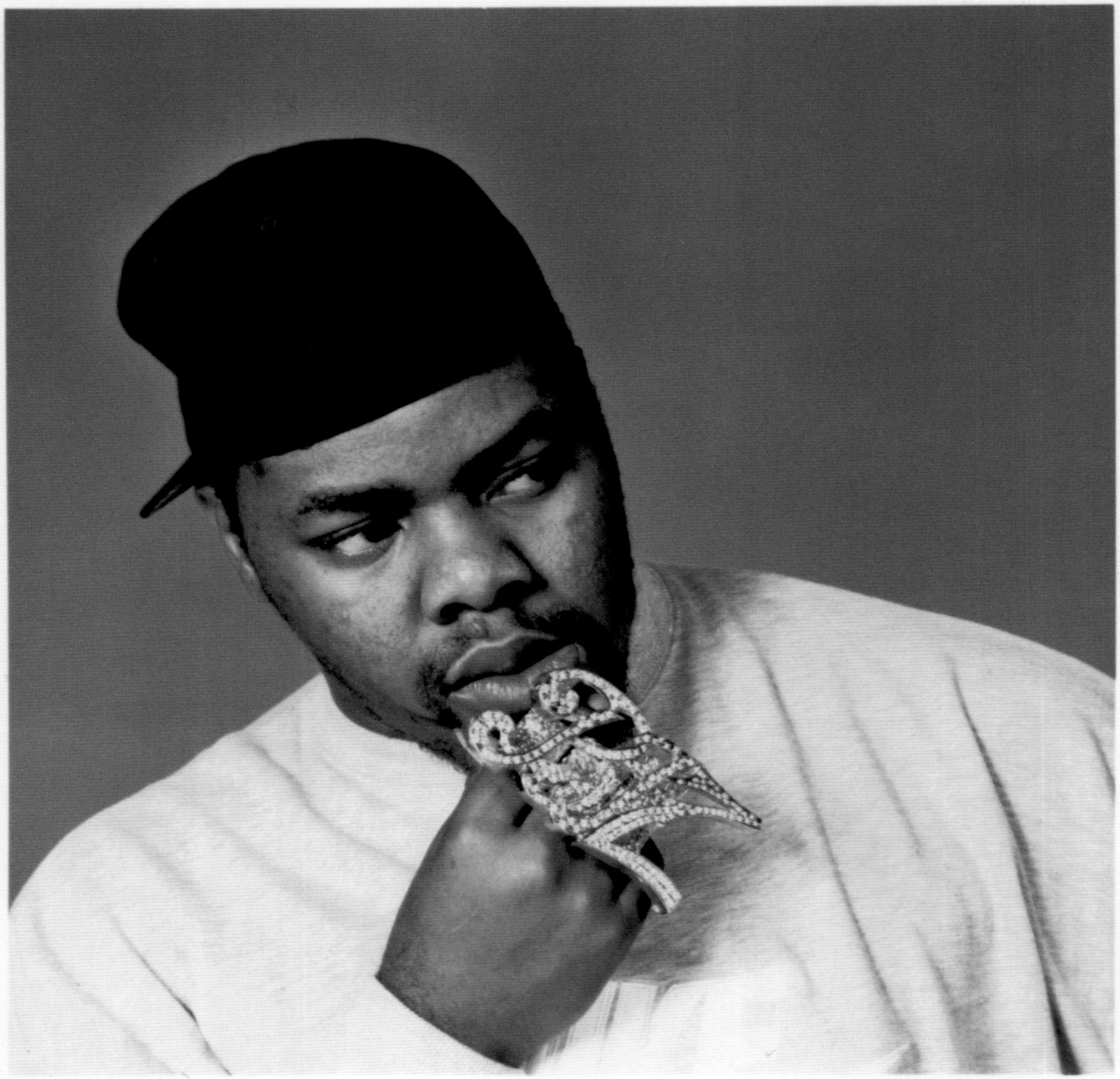

Photo Credit: George DuBose

THE DIABOLICAL
BIZ MARKIE
THE BIZ NEVER SLEEPS

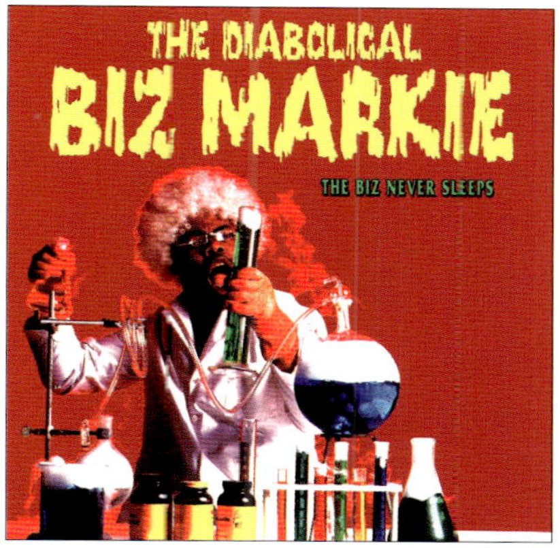

Hip-hop fans with a sense of humor were beguiled by **Biz Markie**'s "Just a Friend," a storytelling rap smash featuring a weird binge of tuneless crooning.

Billboard 200: *The Biz Never Sleeps* (#66)
Billboard Hot 100: "Just a Friend" (#9)

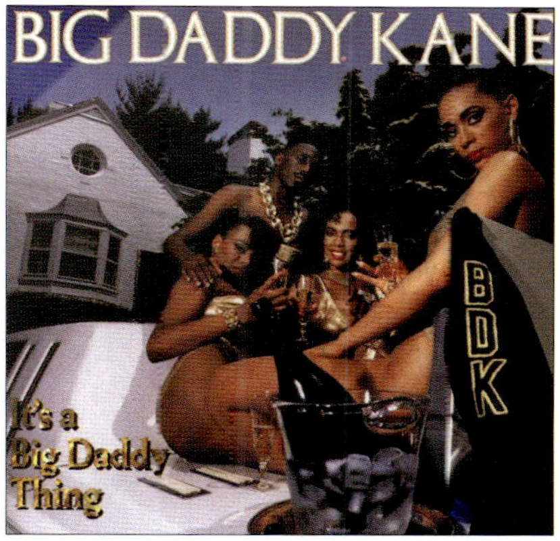

"Smooth Operator" and "I Get the Job Done," culled from **Big Daddy Kane**'s second album, *It's a Big Daddy Thing*, cited the rapper's loverman posturing.

Billboard 200: *It's a Big Daddy Thing* (#33)

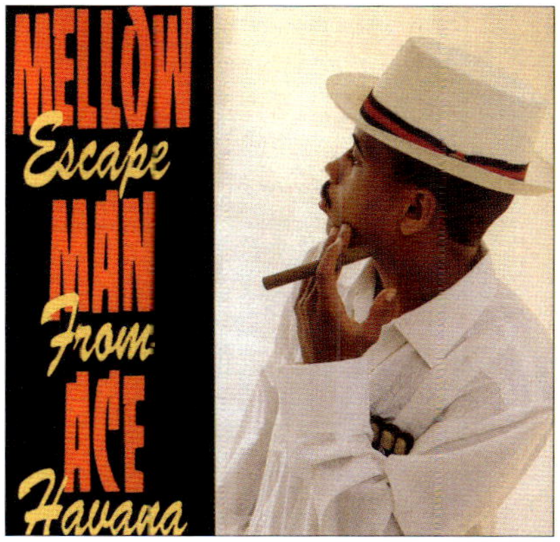

Performing in Spanglish, Latino rapper **Mellow Man Ace** fashioned the hooks of his "Mentirosa" from two Santana songs and came up with a Top 20 hit.

Billboard 200: *Escape from Havana* (#69)
Billboard Hot 100: "Mentirosa" (#14)

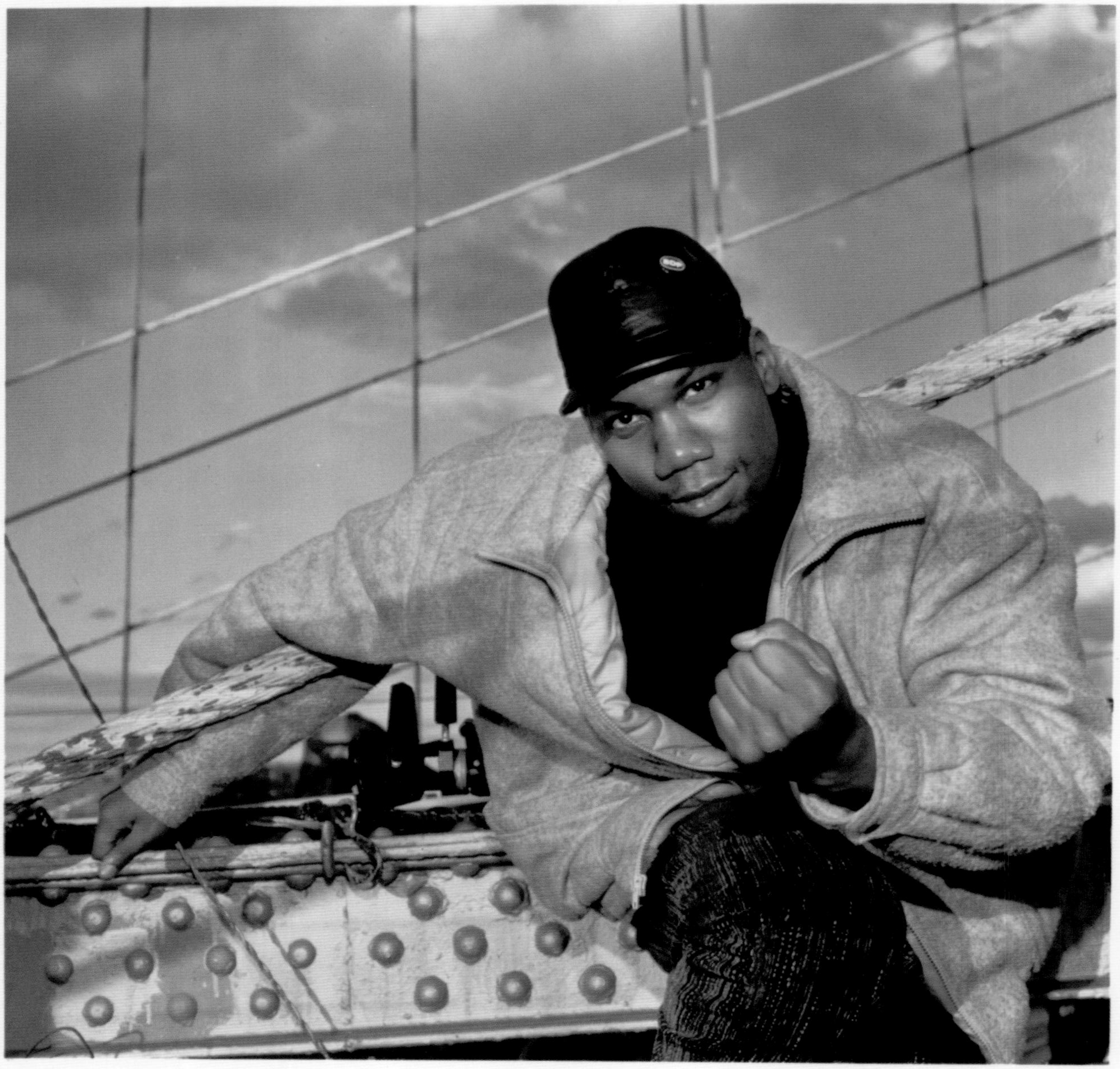

BOOGIE DOWN PRODUCTIONS

JIVE

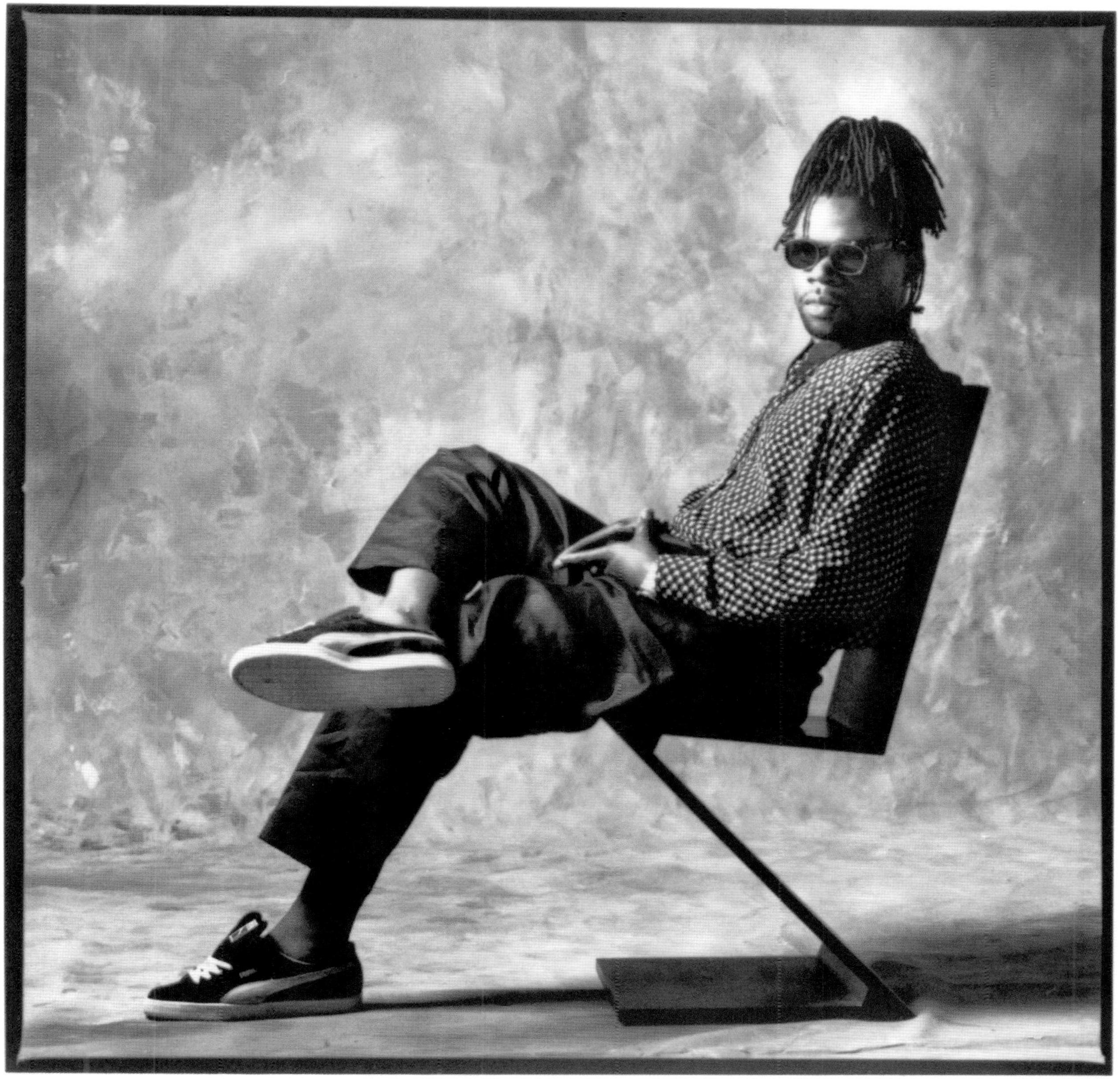

Photo Credit: Jeffrey Scales

**JAZZIE B
of
SOUL II SOUL**

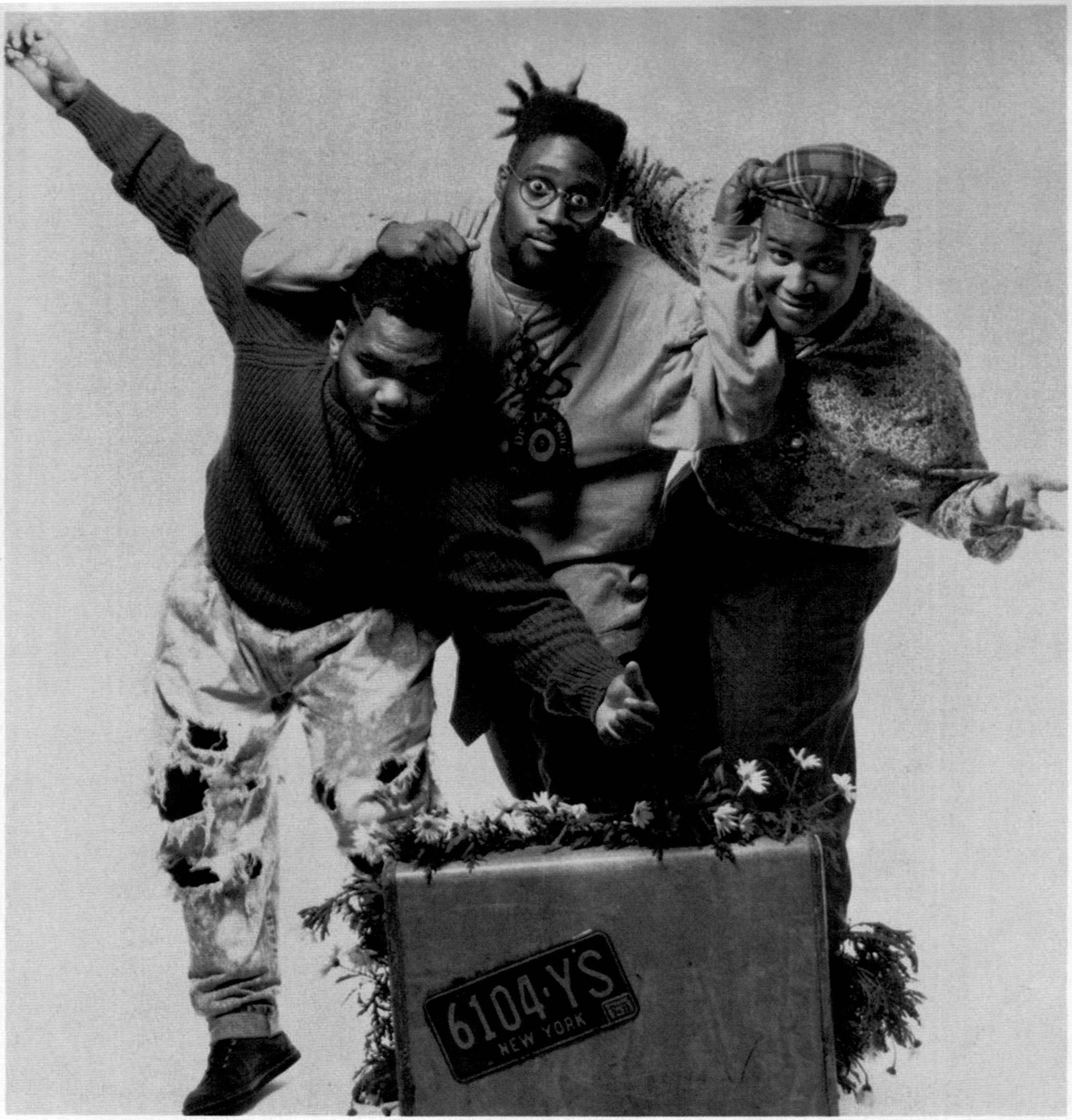

MASE POSDNUOS DOVE

BIG LIFE

DE LA SOUL

Tommy Boy

walkerprint
London 01-580 7021

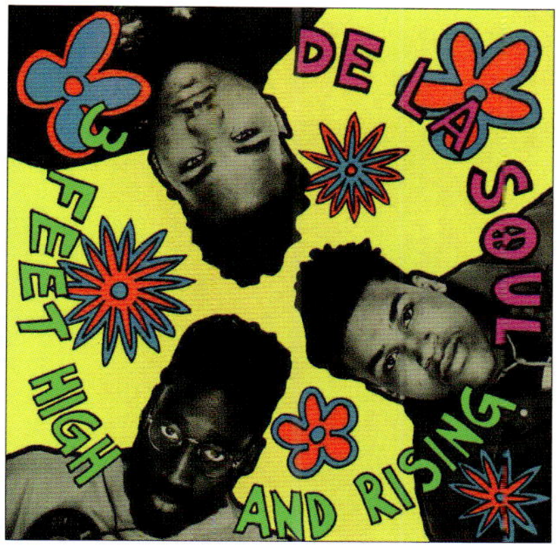

For its sprightly wordplay, ingenious sampling and clever skits, **De La Soul**'s debut album *3 Feet High and Rising* was acclaimed as a hip-hop masterpiece.

Billboard 200: *Six Feet High and Rising* (#24)
Billboard Hot 100: "Me Myself and I" (#34)

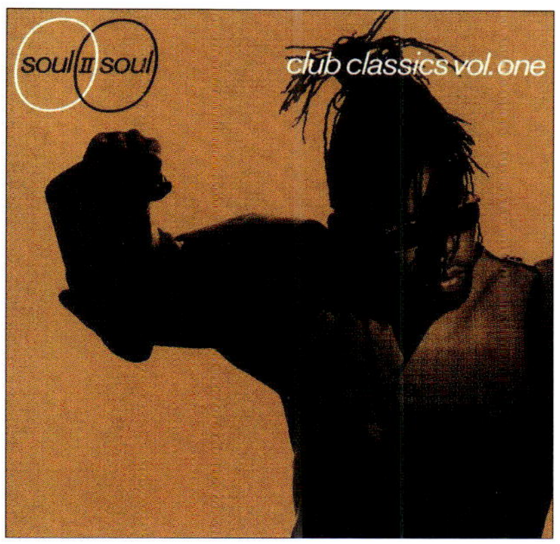

Led by Jazzie B, British act **Soul II Soul** topped the US R&B charts with two creative hits, "Back to Life (However Do You Want Me)" and "Keep on Movin'."

Billboard 200: *Club Classics Vol. One* (#14)
Billboard Hot 100: "Keep on Movin'" (#11);
"Back to Life (However Do You Want Me)" (#4)

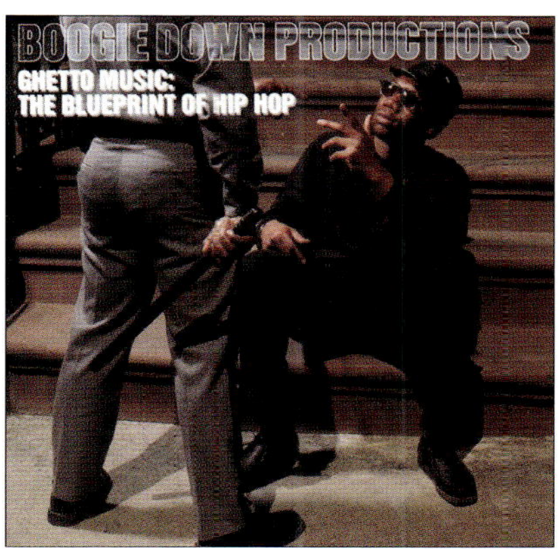

KRS-One broached life on the South Bronx streets with **Boogie Down Productions**' politicized, intellectual *Ghetto Music: The Blueprint of Hip Hop* album.

Billboard 200: *Ghetto Music: The Blueprint of Hip Hop* (#36)

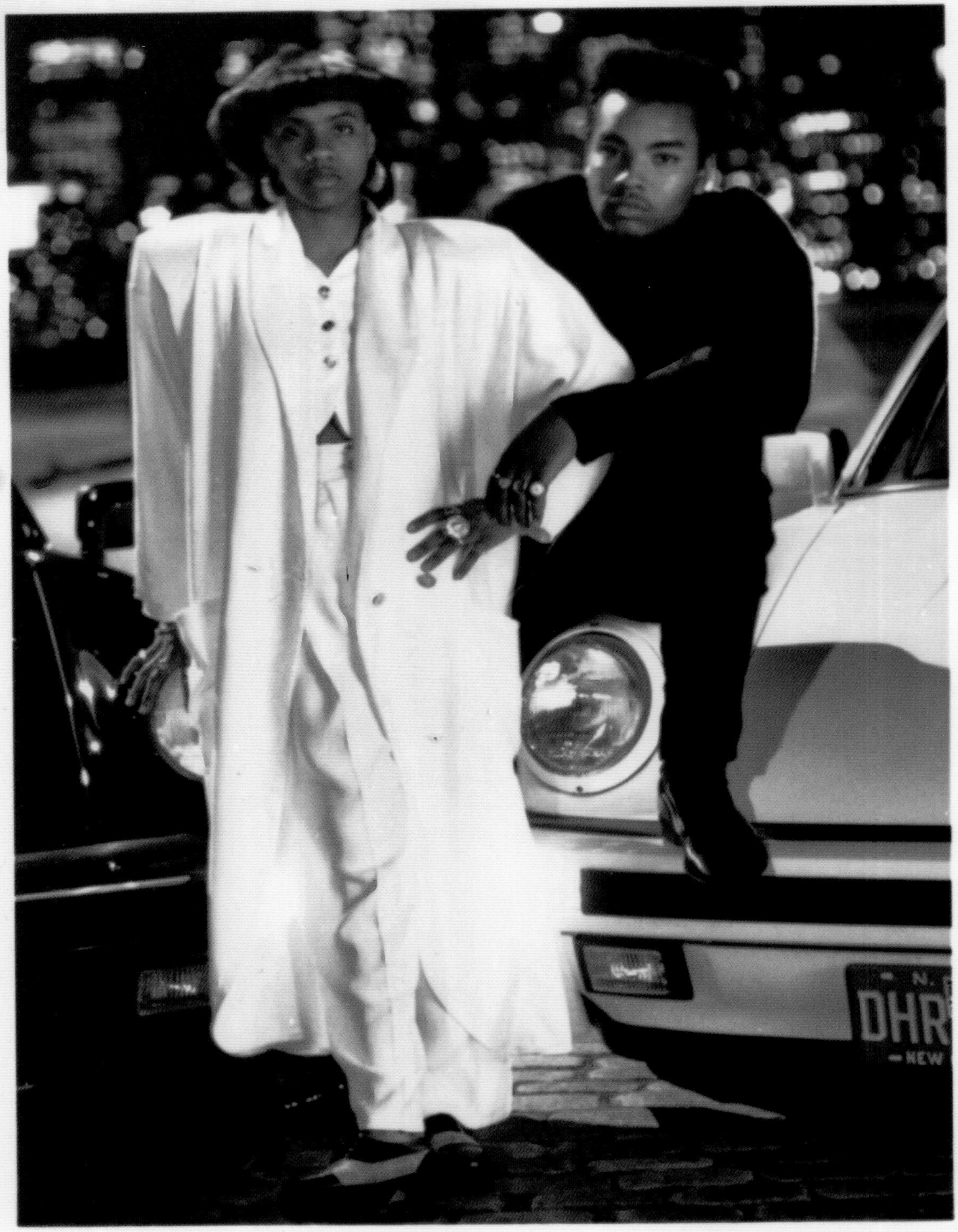

MC LYTE
& D.J. K-ROCK

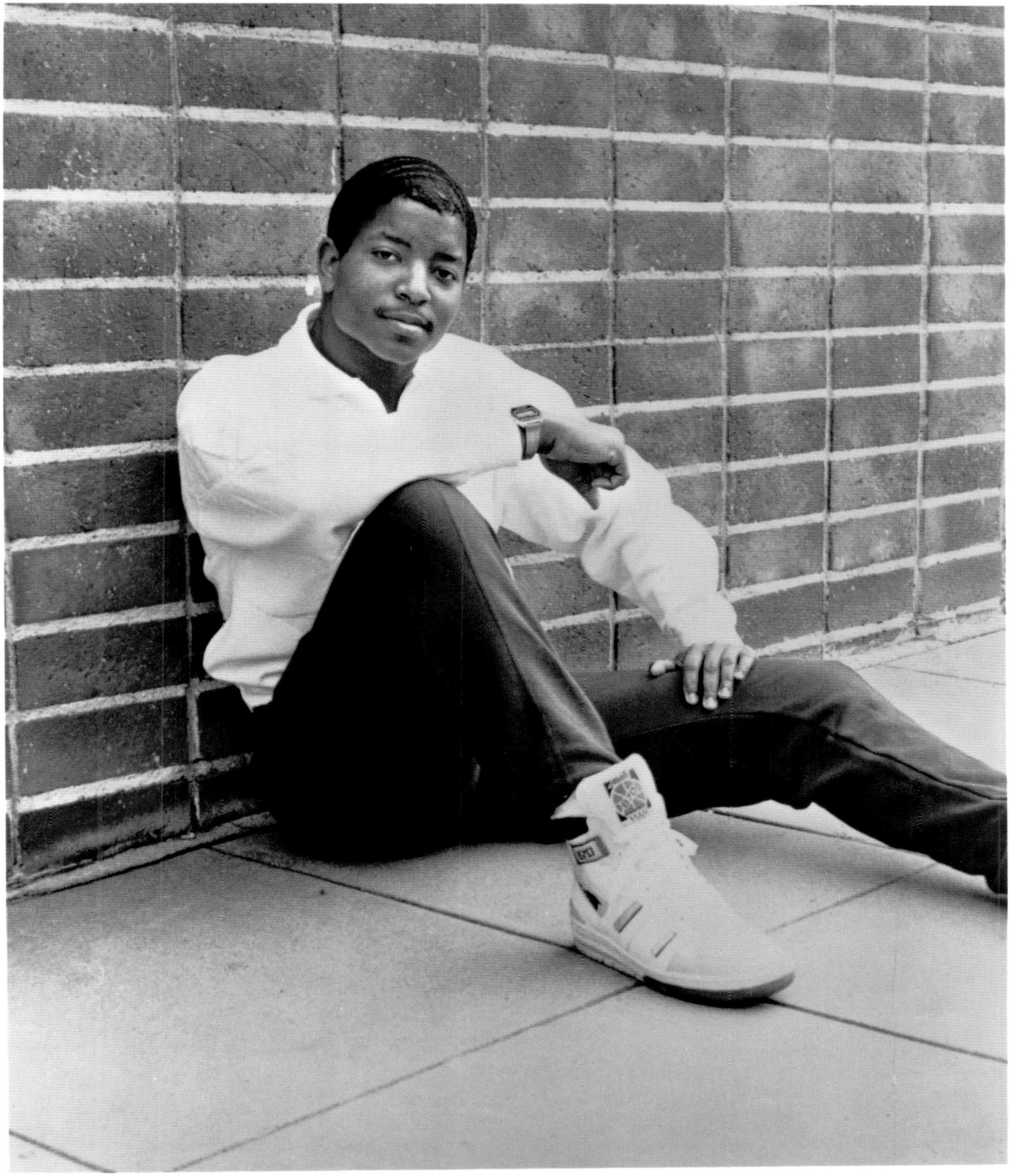

DISTRIBUTED BY THE ISLAND TRADING CO.

YOUNG MC

MICHAEL GARDNER COMPANY

Delicious VINYL

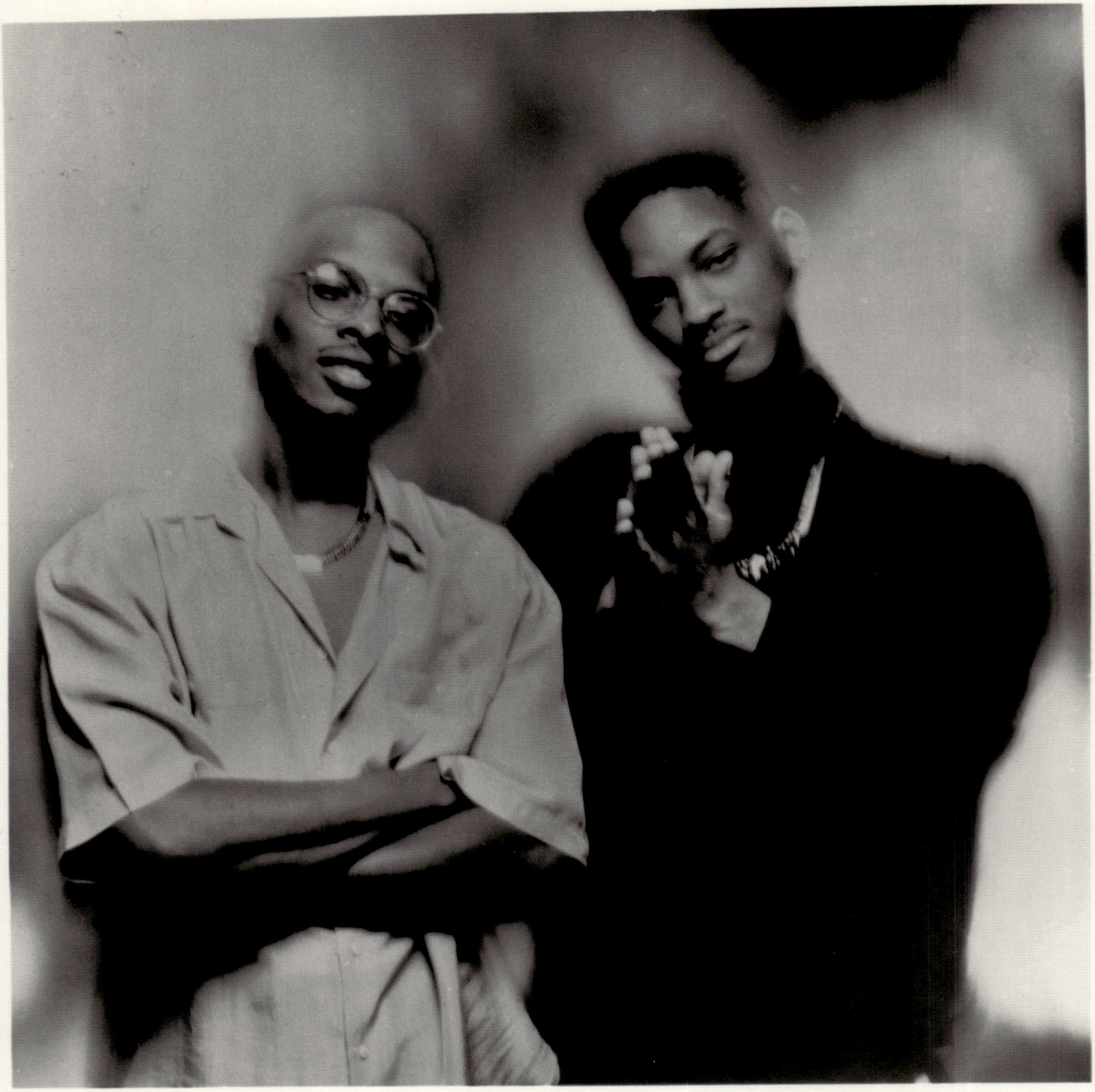

D.J. Jazzy Jeff & THE FRESH PRINCE

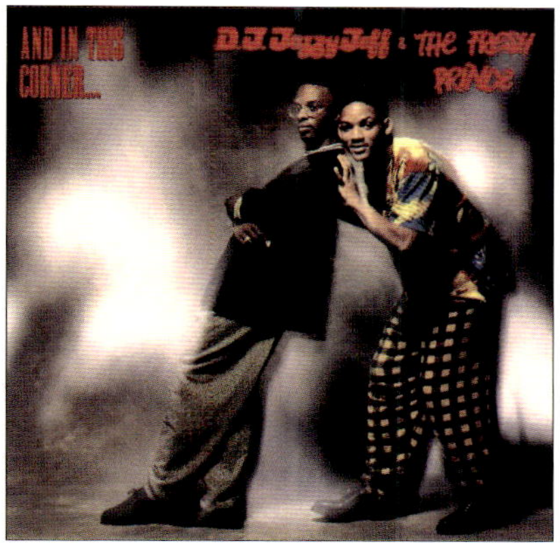

"I Think I Can Beat Mike Tyson" was another in a streak of inoffensive, congenial hit singles released by hip-hop duo **D.J. Jazzy Jeff & the Fresh Prince**.

Billboard 200: *And in This Corner...* (#39)
Billboard Hot 100: "I Think I Can Beat Mike Tyson" (#58)

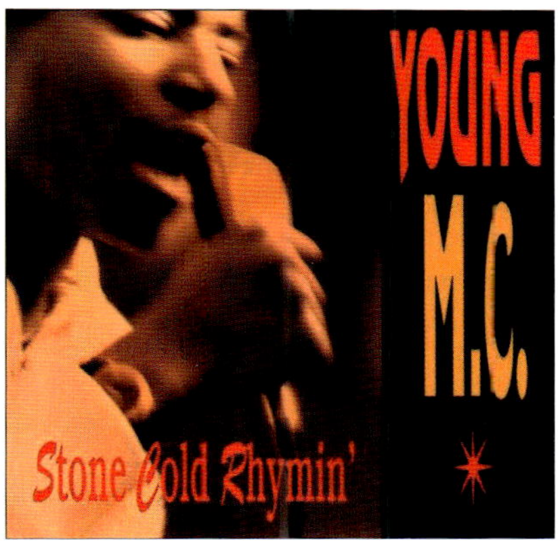

After co-writing hits for Tone Lōc, **Young MC** was singled out for his good-humored "Bust a Move," taking home the Grammy for Best Rap Performance.

Billboard 200: *Stone Cold Rhymin'* (#9)
Billboard Hot 100: "Bust a Move" (#7);
"Principal's Office" (#33); "I Come Off" (#75)

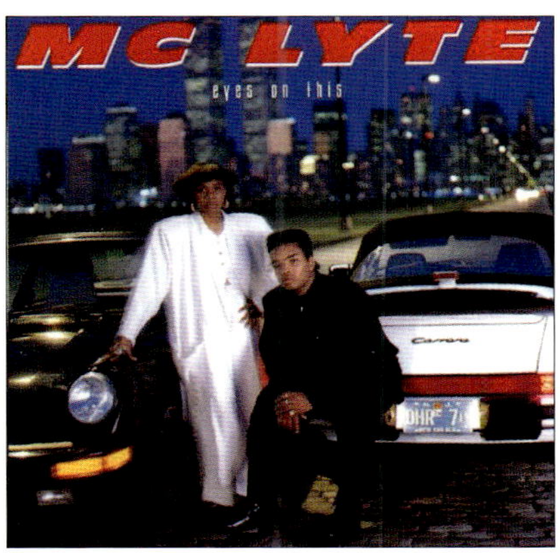

Approbation accompanied female rapper **MC Lyte**'s *Eyes on This*, characterized by "Cha Cha Cha," a pithy No. 1 rap hit, and the canny "Cappuccino."

Billboard 200: *Eyes on This* (#86)

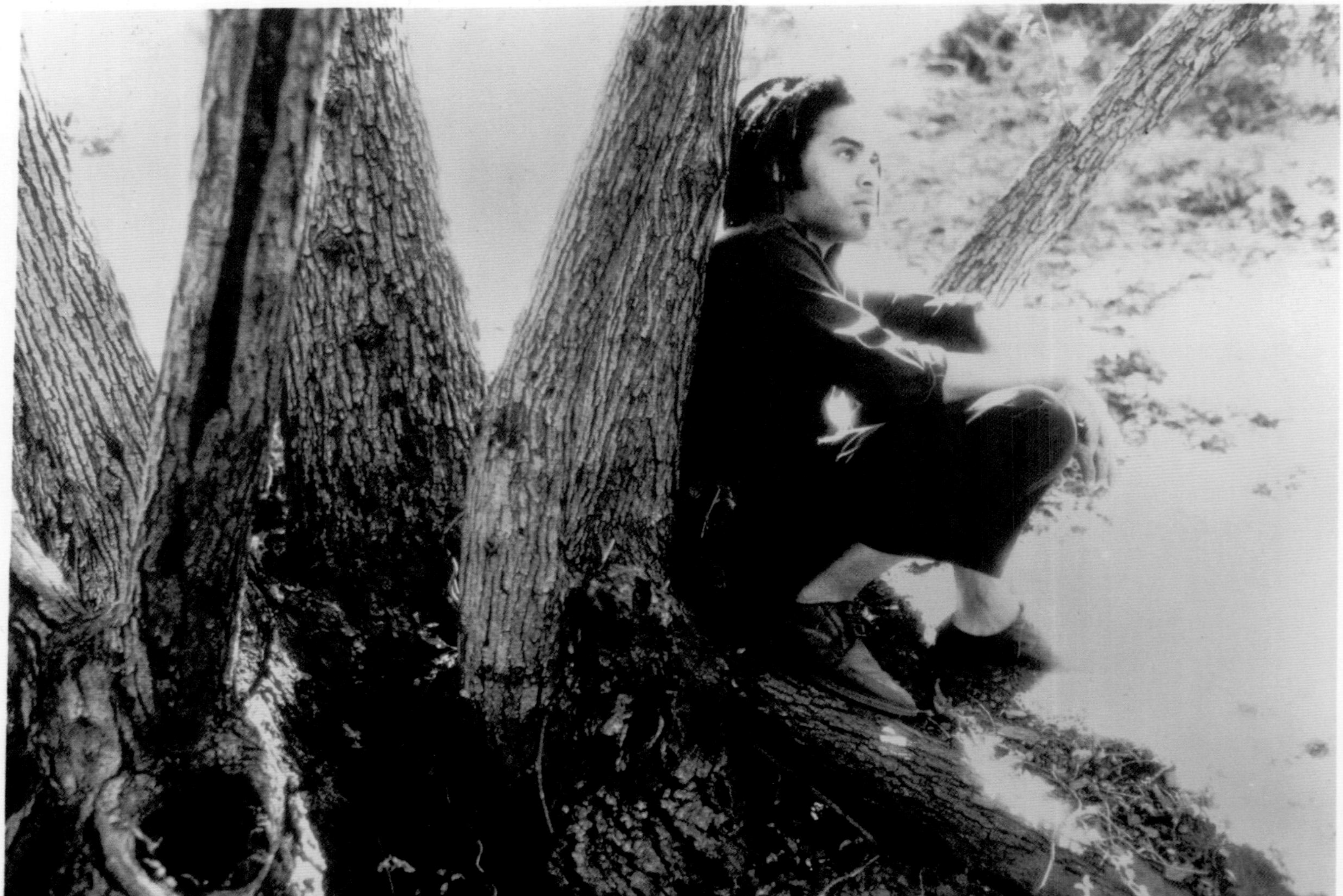

Photo Credit: Melanie Nissen

LENNY KRAVITZ

Virgin

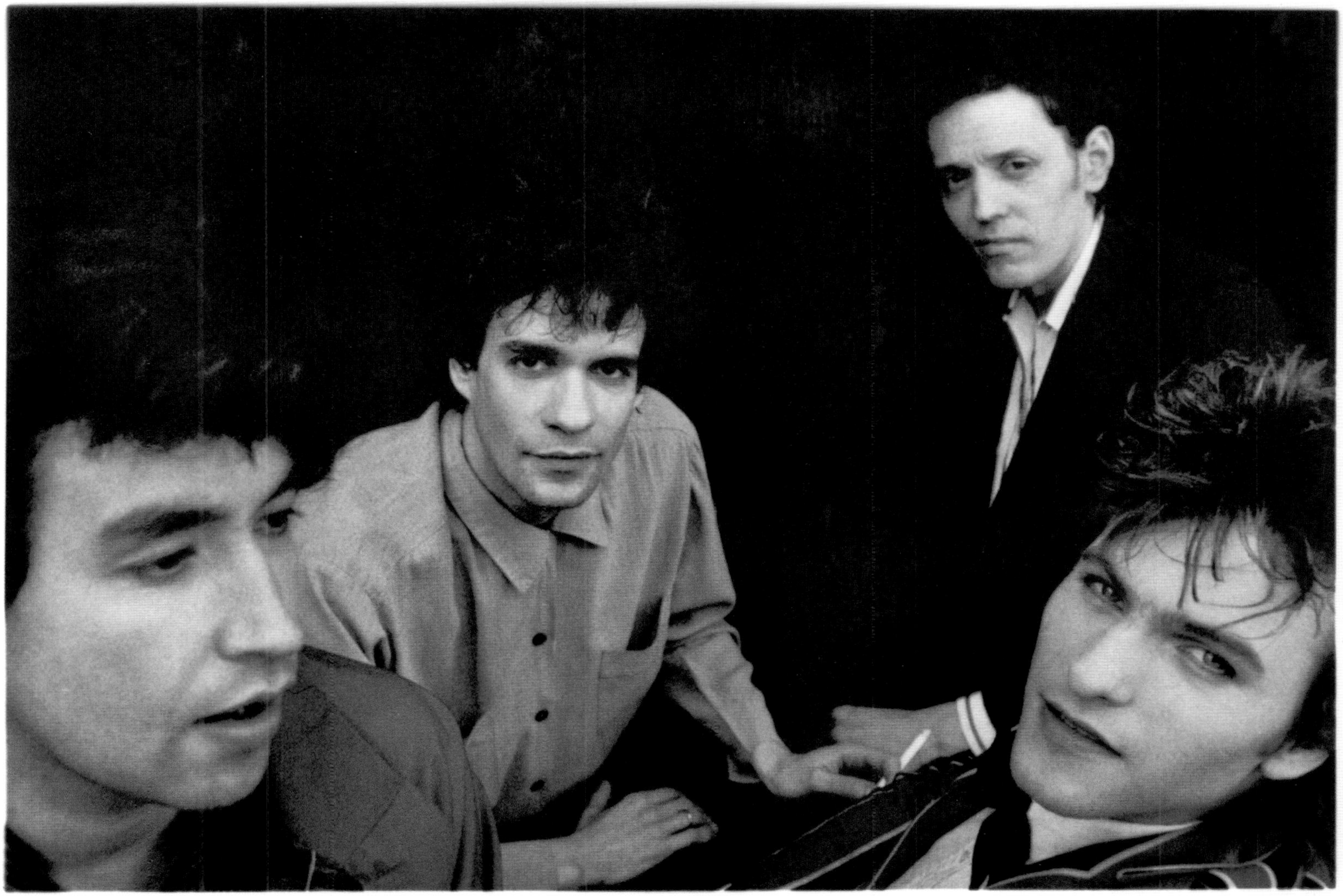

Photo Credit: Bonnie Schiffman

THE REPLACEMENTS

reprise SIRE

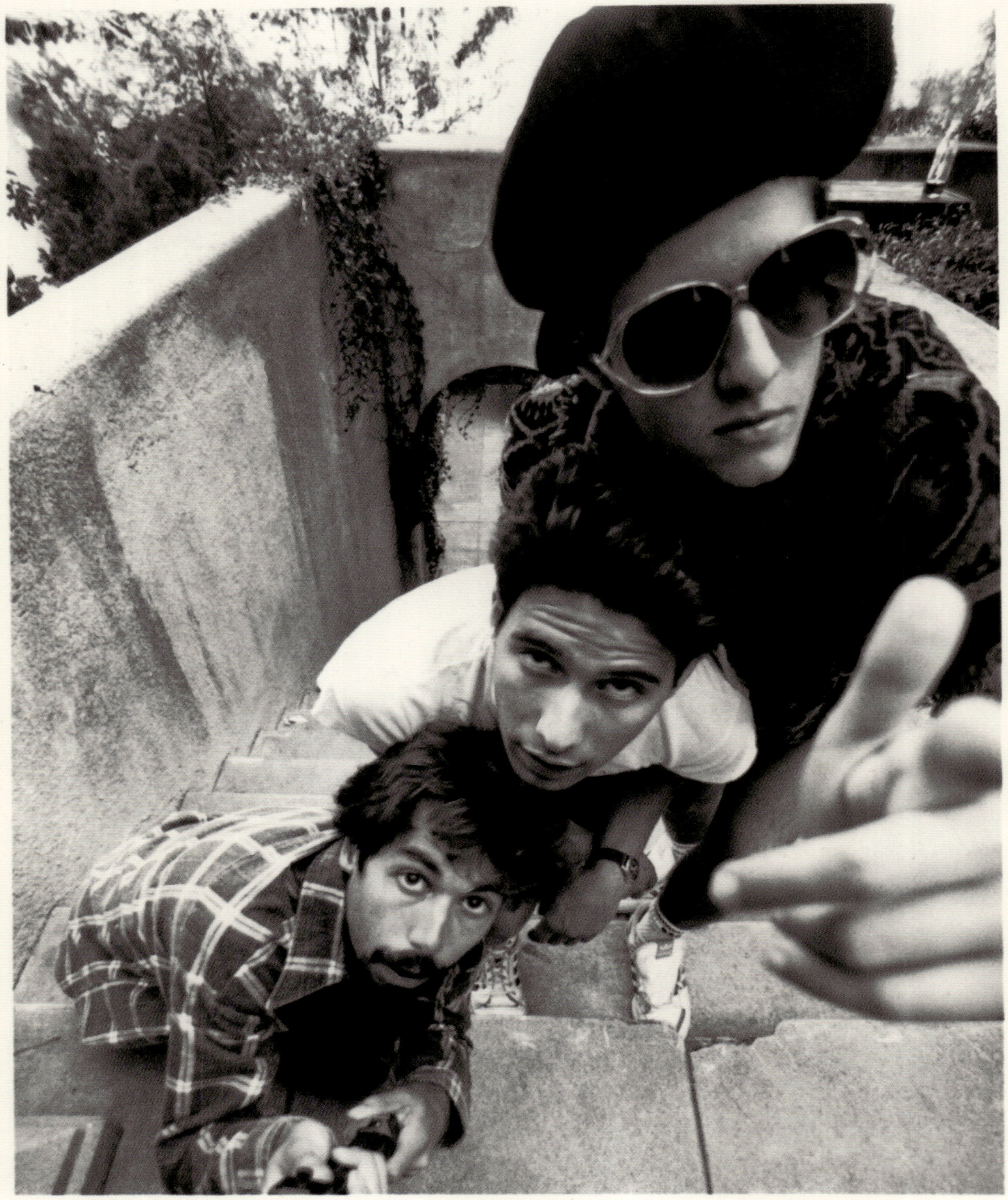

MCA King Ad-Rock Mike D

BEASTIE BOYS

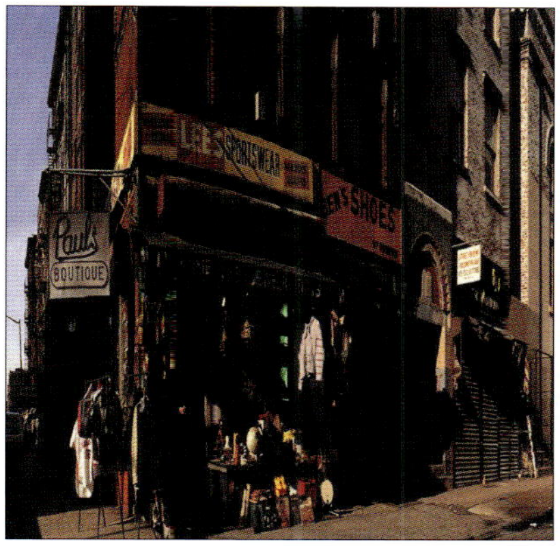

Paul's Boutique, **Beastie Boys**' sophomore album, was rated highly for fashioning dense, interwound layers almost exclusively from diverse samples.

Billboard 200: *Paul's Boutique* (#15)
Billboard Hot 100: "Hey Ladies" (#36)

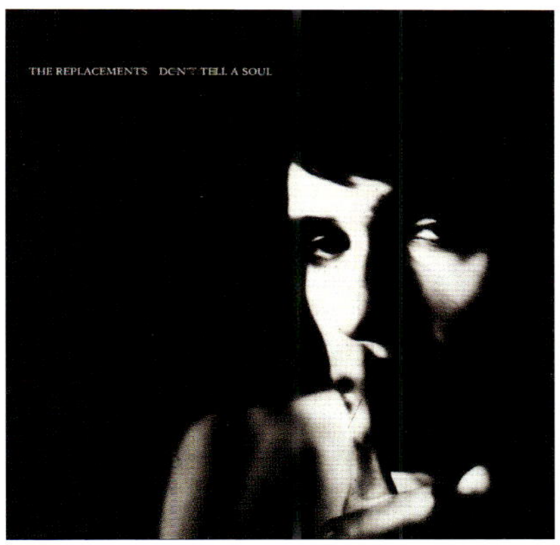

The Replacements leavened their punk roots with studio polish on *Don't Tell a Soul*, resulting in "I'll Be You," their first pop hit and a modern-rock No. 1.

Billboard 200: *Don't Tell a Soul* (#57)
Billboard Hot 100" "I'll Be You" (#51)

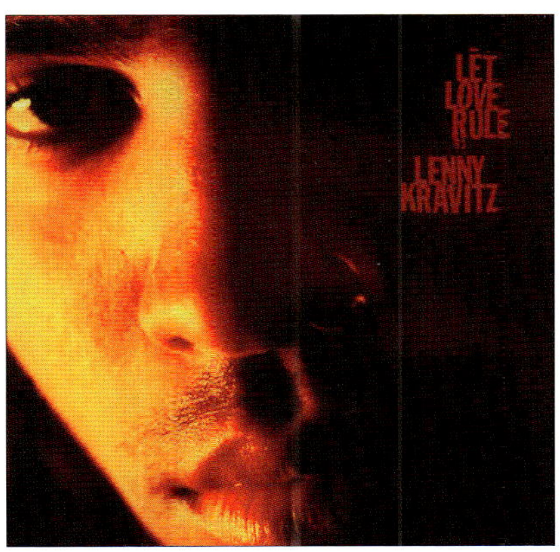

Writing and producing the songs and playing multiple instruments, **Lenny Kravitz** birthed *Let Love Rule*, a debut mixing rock and soul with a boho vibe.

Billboard 200: *Let Love Rule* (#61)
Billboard Hot 100: "Let Love Rule" (#89)

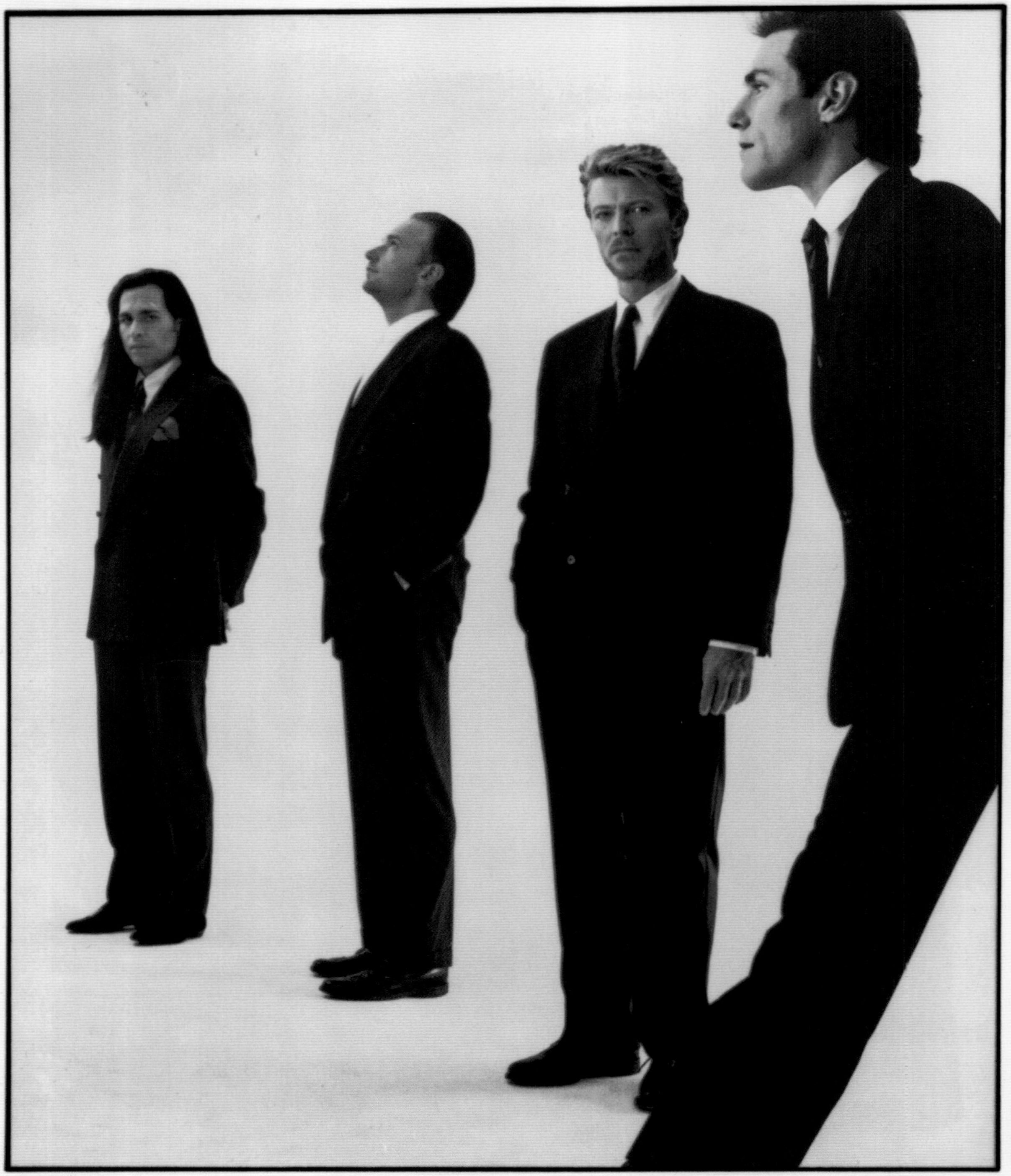

Photography: Sukita

tin machine

EMI®

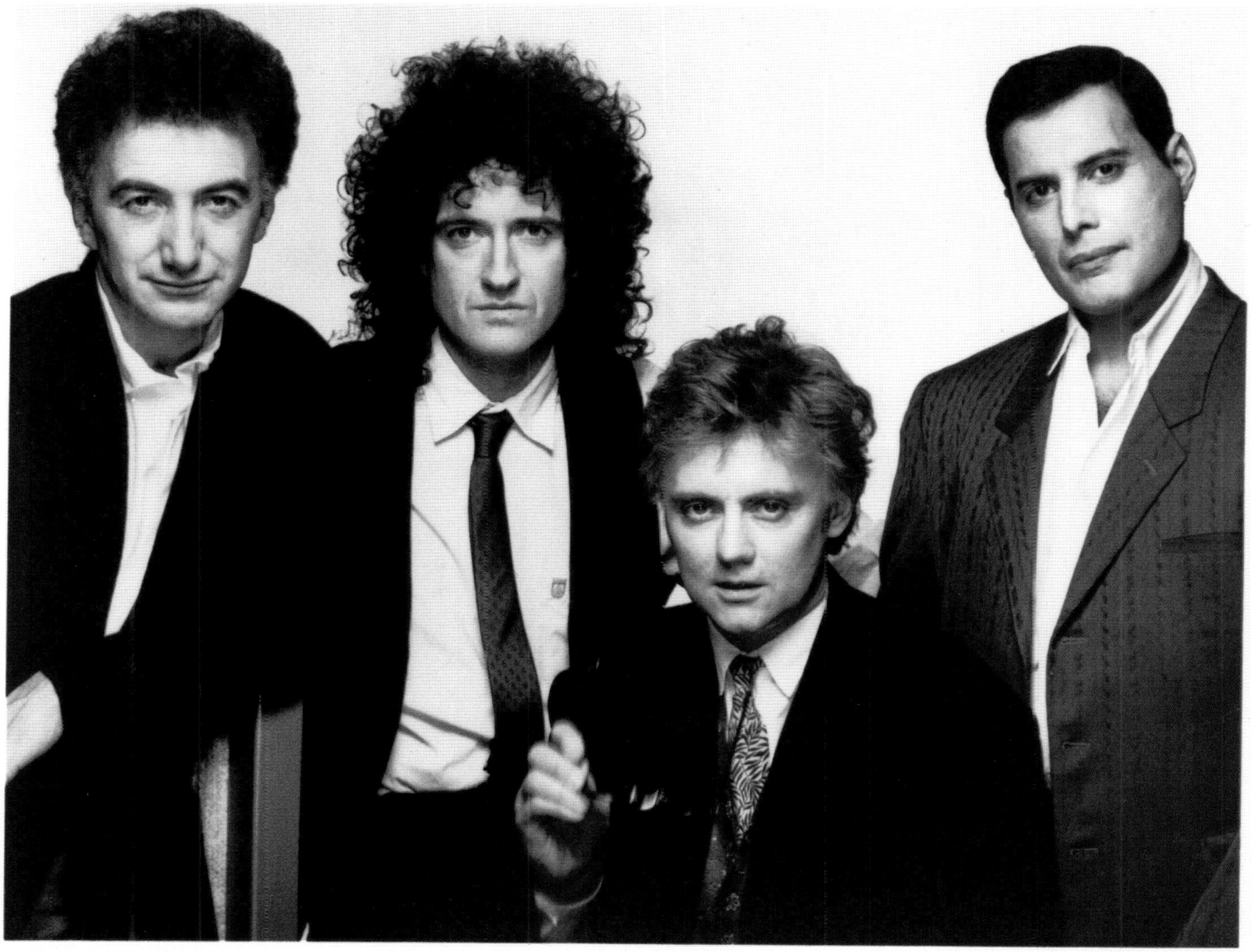

John Deacon Brian May Roger Taylor Freddie Mercury

QUEEN

Capitol Records

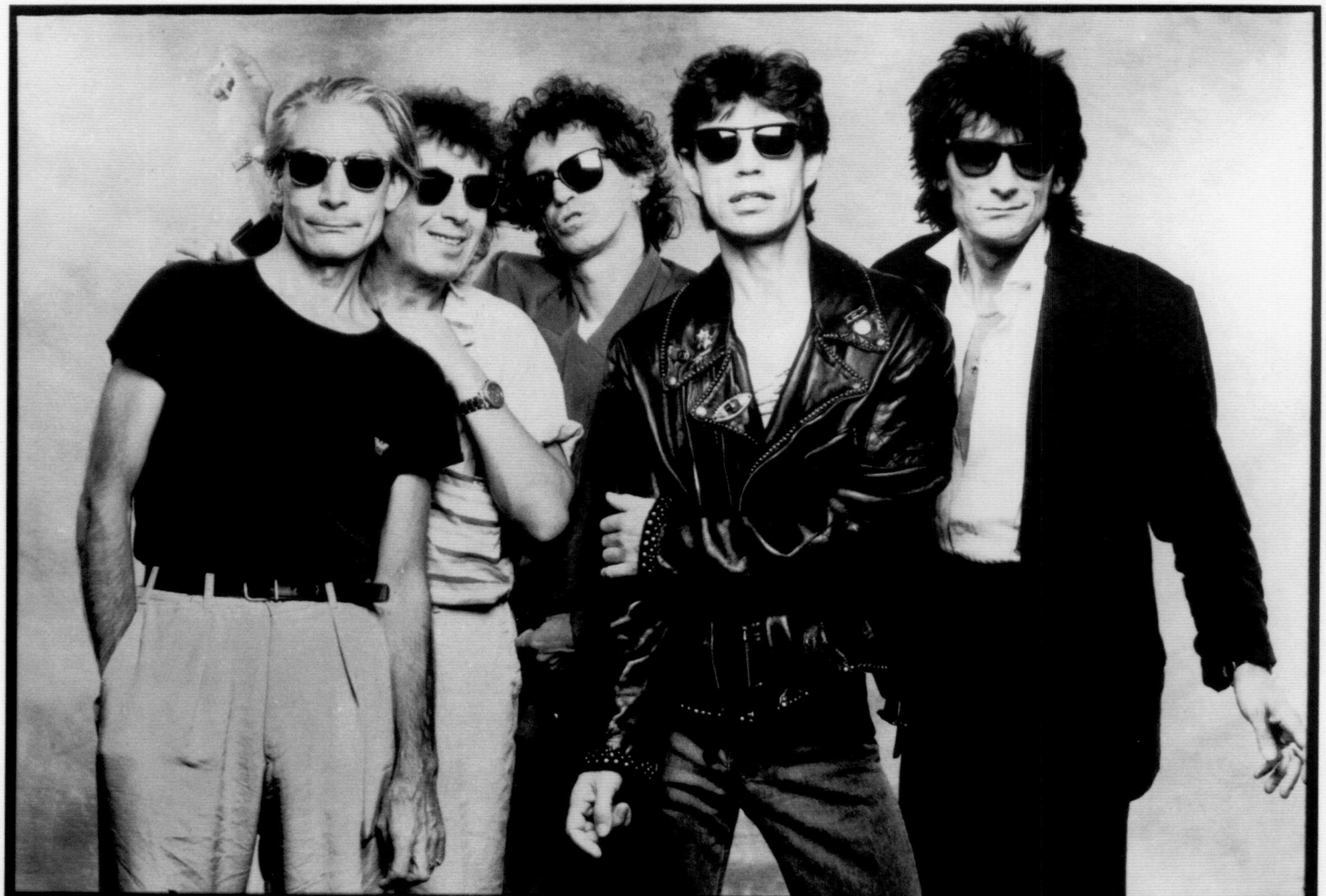

THE ROLLING STONES

TM

8908

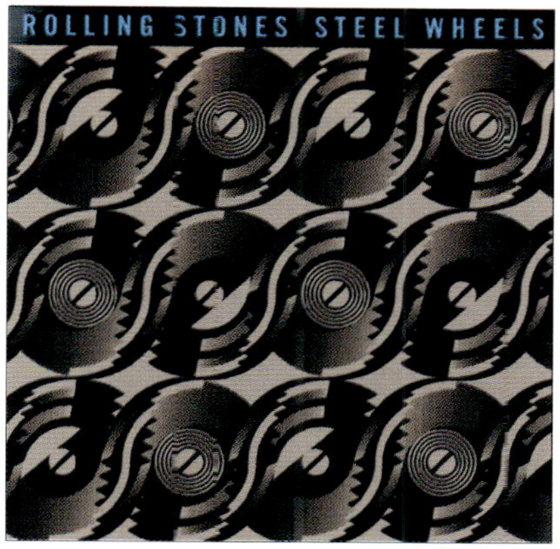

The Rolling Stones mended the rift between Mick Jagger and Keith Richards, issuing *Steel Wheels* and launching their first world tour in seven years.

Billboard 200: *Steel Wheels* (#3)
Billboard Hot 100: "Mixed Emotions" (#5);
"Rock and a Hard Place" (#23) "Almost Hear You Sigh" (#50)

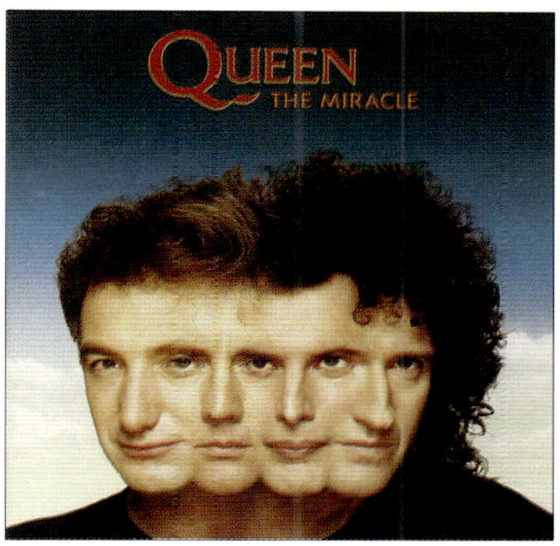

Having nursed a far-reaching, devoted fan base playing in foreign markets, **Queen** enjoyed a global smash with *The Miracle* and the single "I Want It All."

Billboard 200: *The Miracle* (#24)
Billboard Hot 100: "I Want It All" (#50)

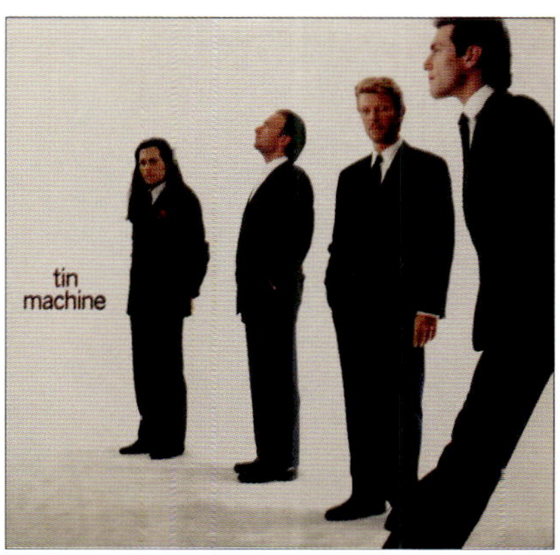

Rock star David Bowie presented as a member of a band, fronting **Tin Machine** with guitarist Reeves Gabrels and the rhythm section of Tony and Hunt Sales.

Billboard 200: *Tin Machine* (#28)

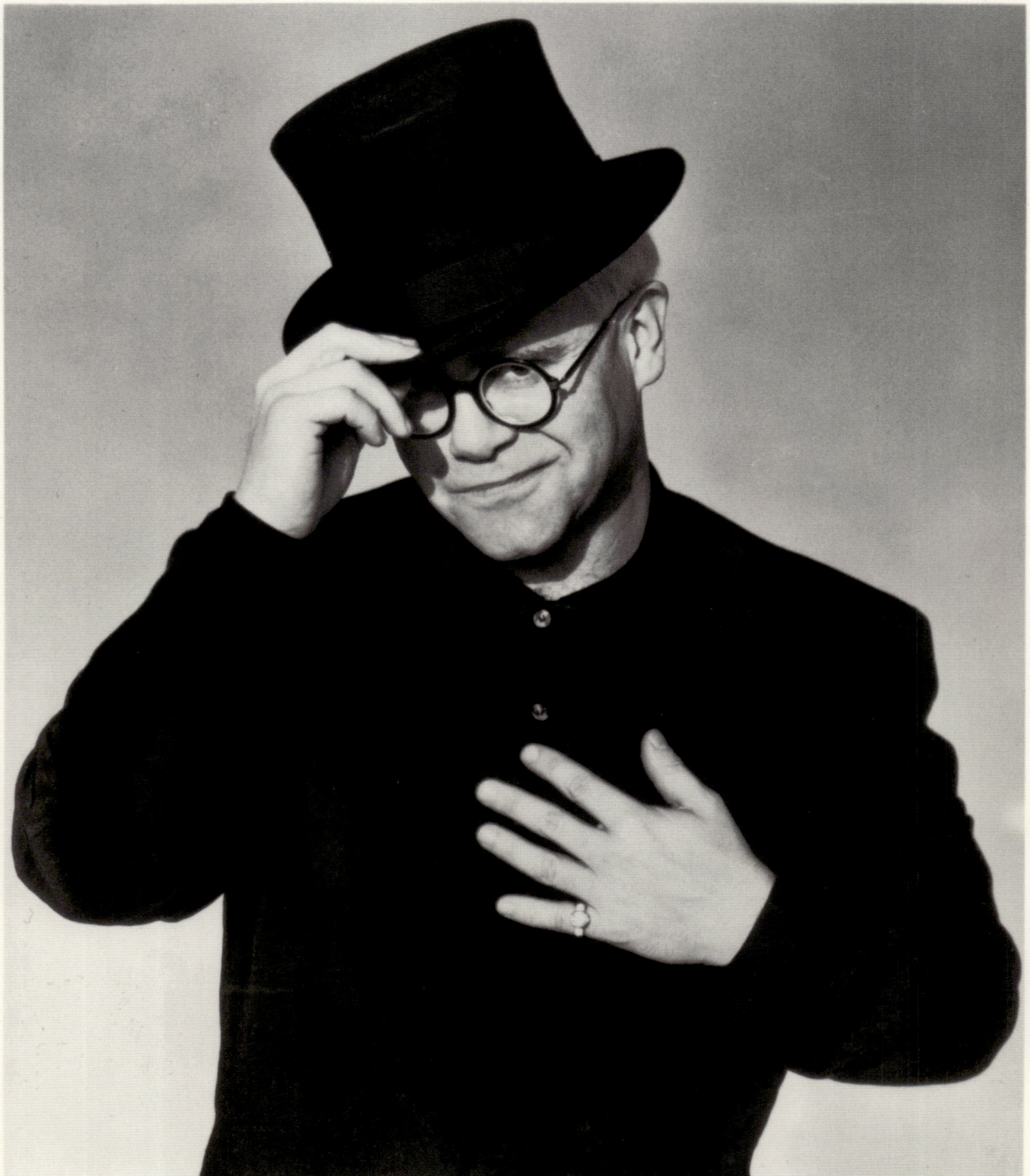

Photo Credit: Herb Ritts

elton *john*

8/89

MCA RECORDS

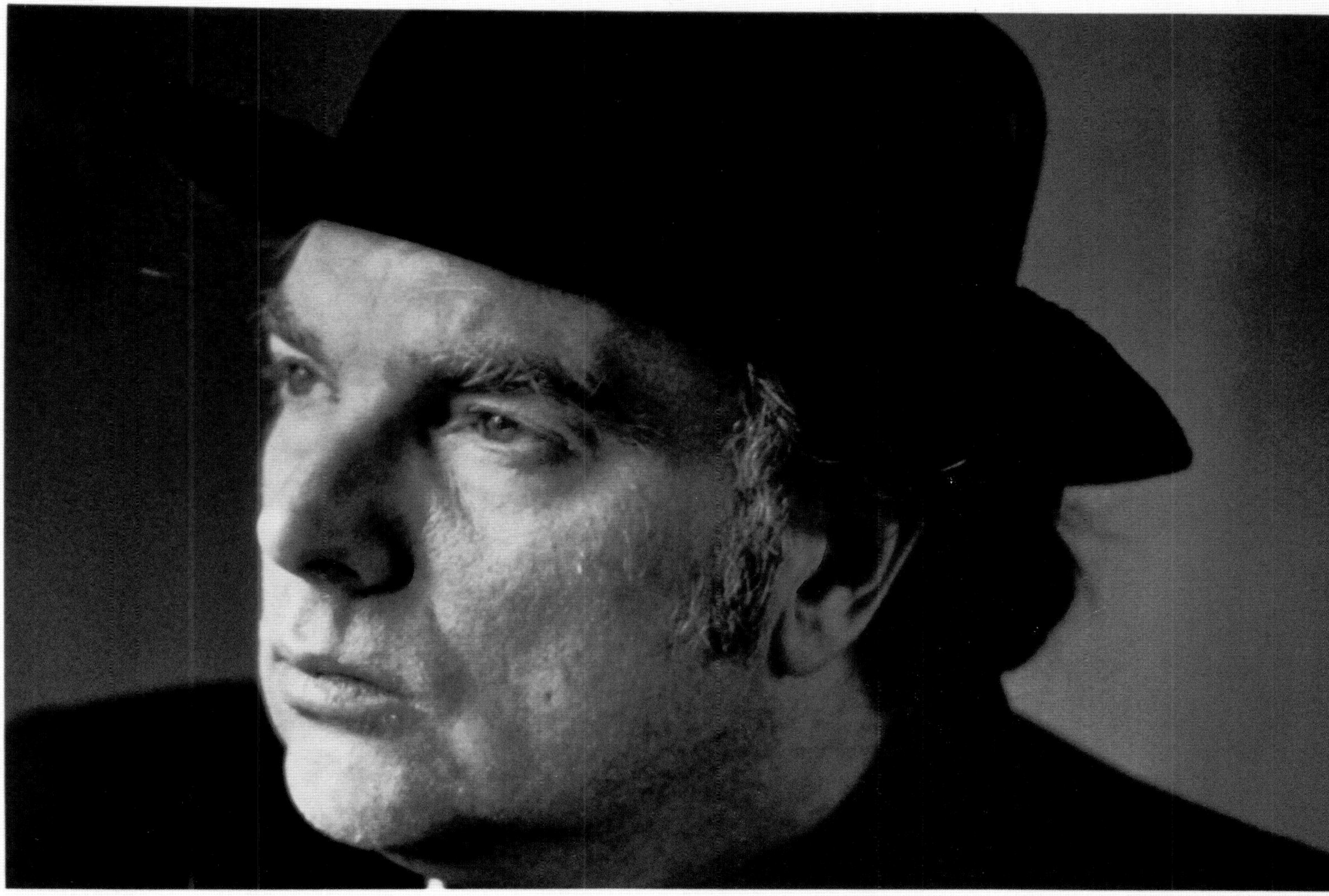

© PolyGram 1989

V A N   M O R R I S O N

A V A L O N   S U N S E T

mercury

PolyGram

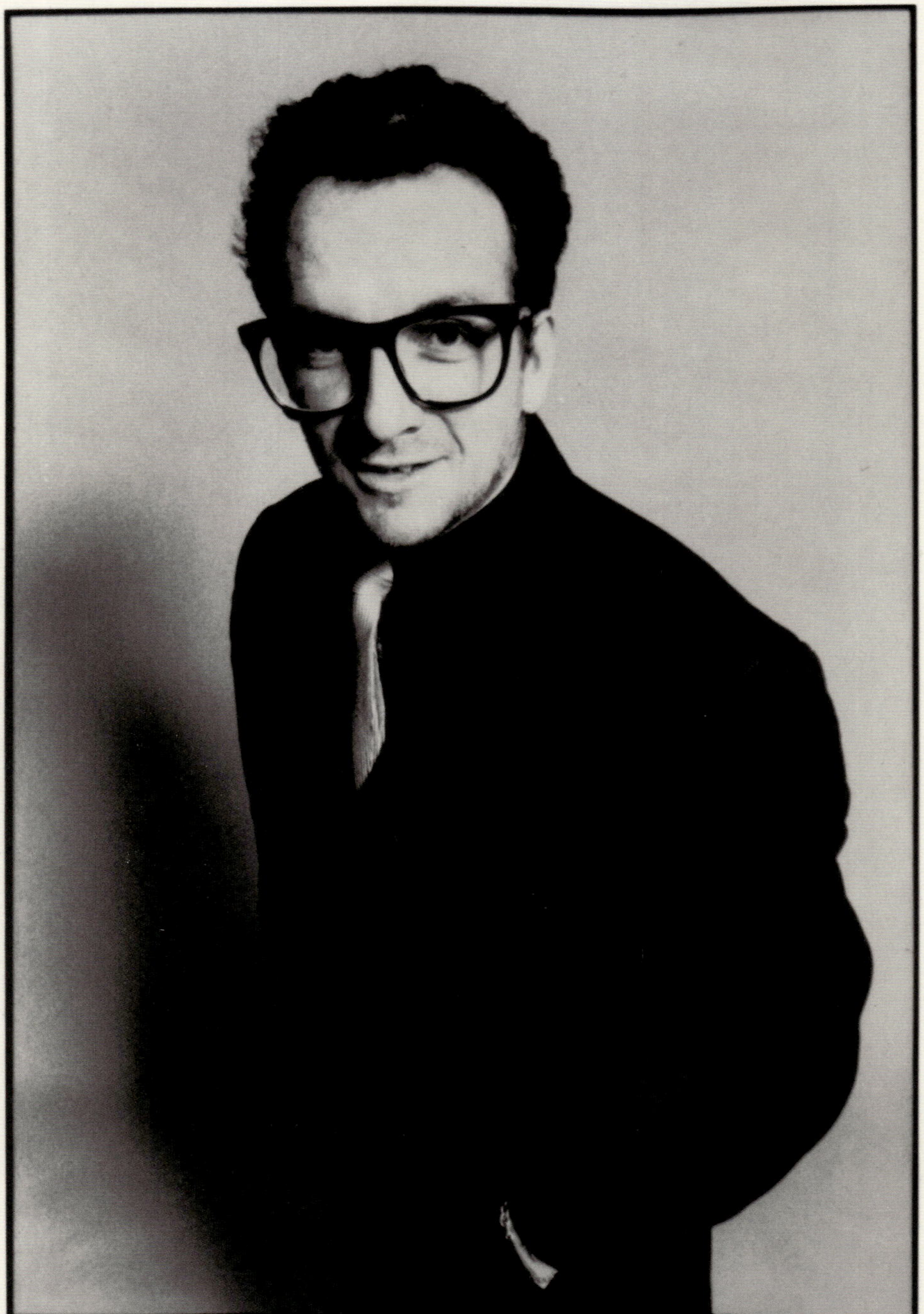

Photo Credit: Keith Morris

ELVIS COSTELLO

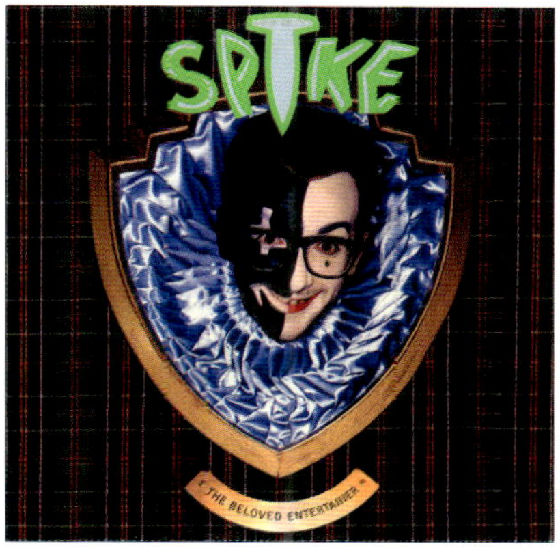

Parting from the Attractions, **Elvis Costello** came out with the diverse *Spike*, which spawned the Top 20 single "Veronica," co-written with Paul McCartney.

Billboard 200: *Spike* (#32)
Billboard Hot 100: "Veronica" (#19)

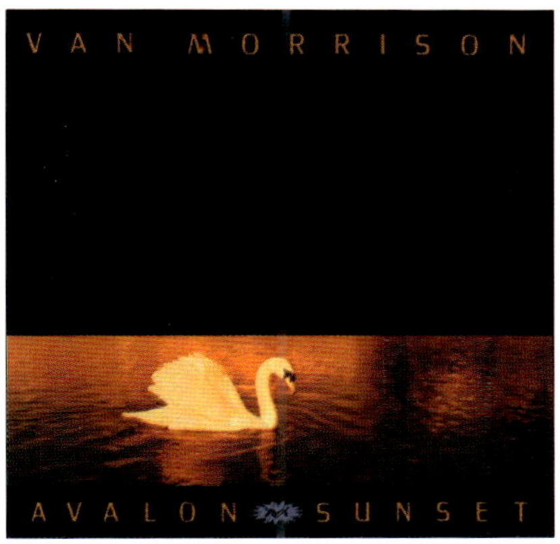

Van Morrison's *Avalon Sunset* played up "Have I Told You Lately," a bonny ballad, and "Whenever God Shines His Light," a stellar duet with Cliff Richard.

Billboard 200: *Avalon Sunset* (#91)

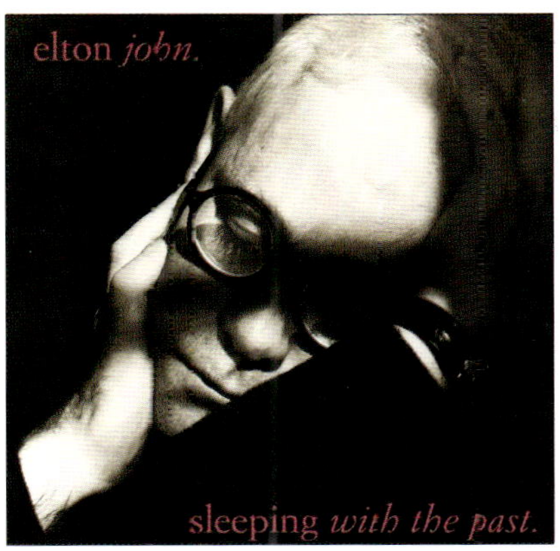

Written with lyricist Bernie Taupin, "Sacrifice" brought **Elton John** his first solo No. 1 hit on the UK charts, a desiderated attainment in his native country.

Billboard 200: *Sleeping with the Past* (#23)
Billboard Hot 100: "Healing Hands" (#13); "Sacrifice" (#18); "Club at the End of the Street" (#28)

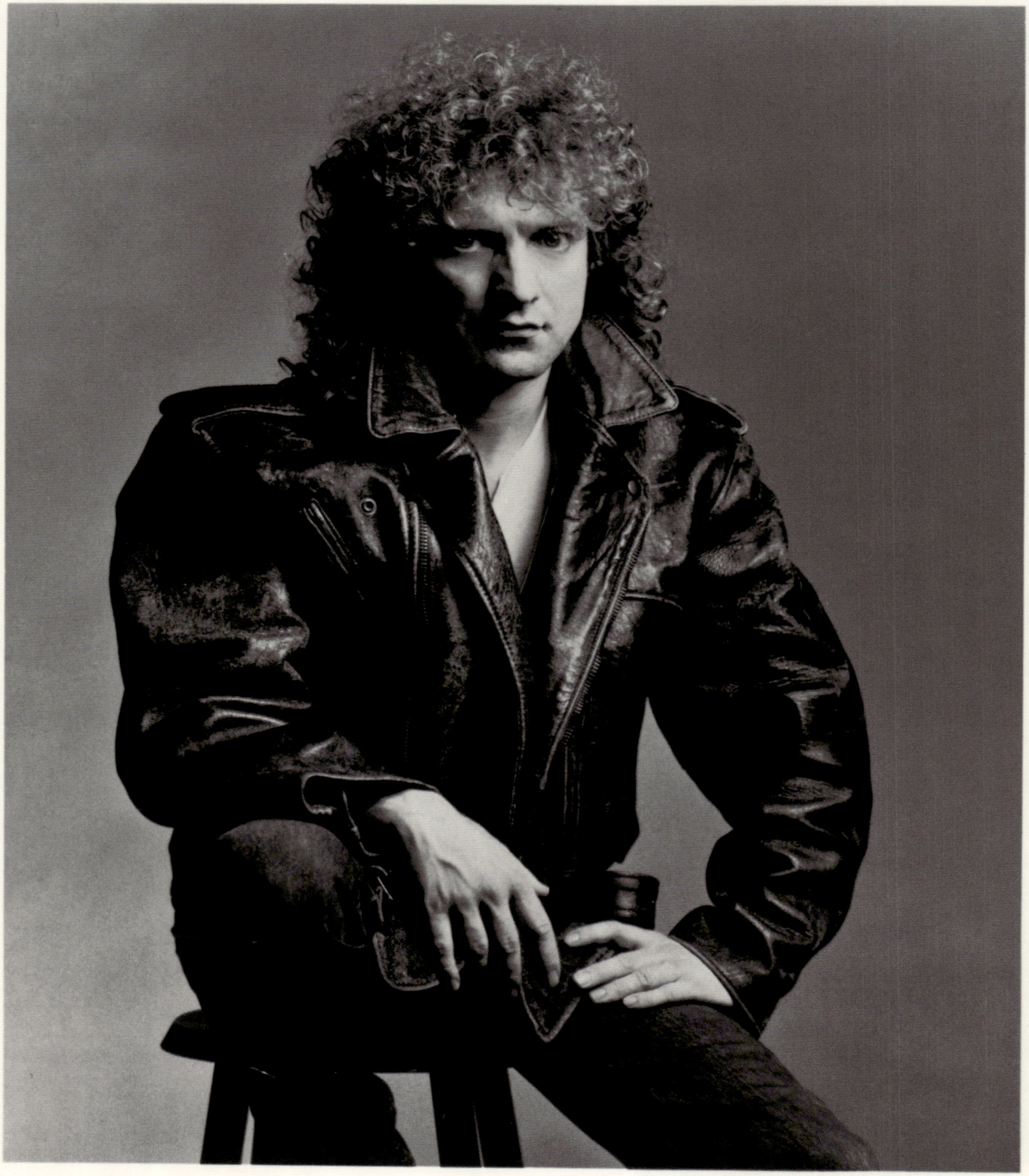

LOU GRAMM

ATLANTIC

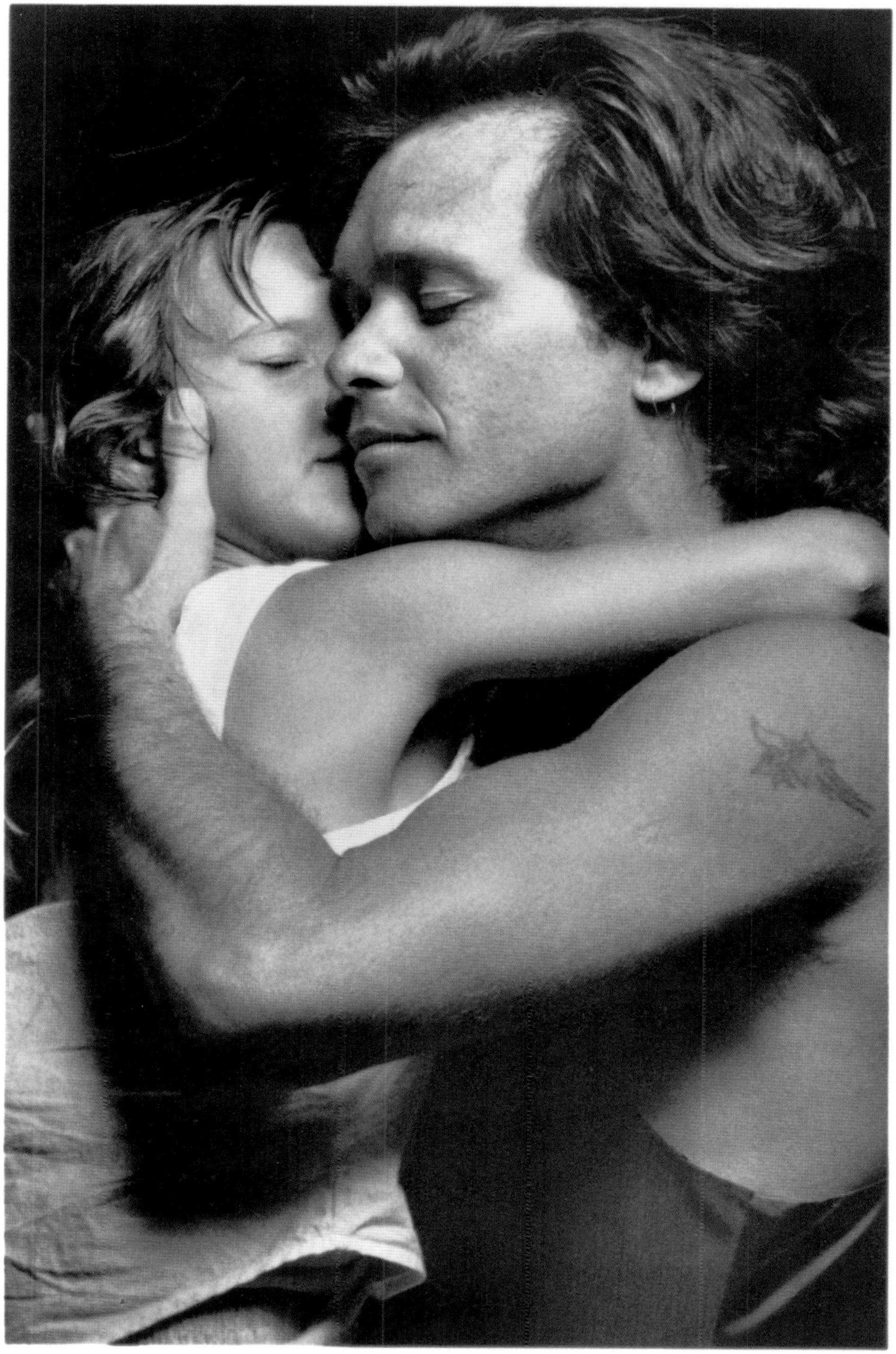

mercury

BIG DADDY

John Cougar Mellencamp

PolyGram™

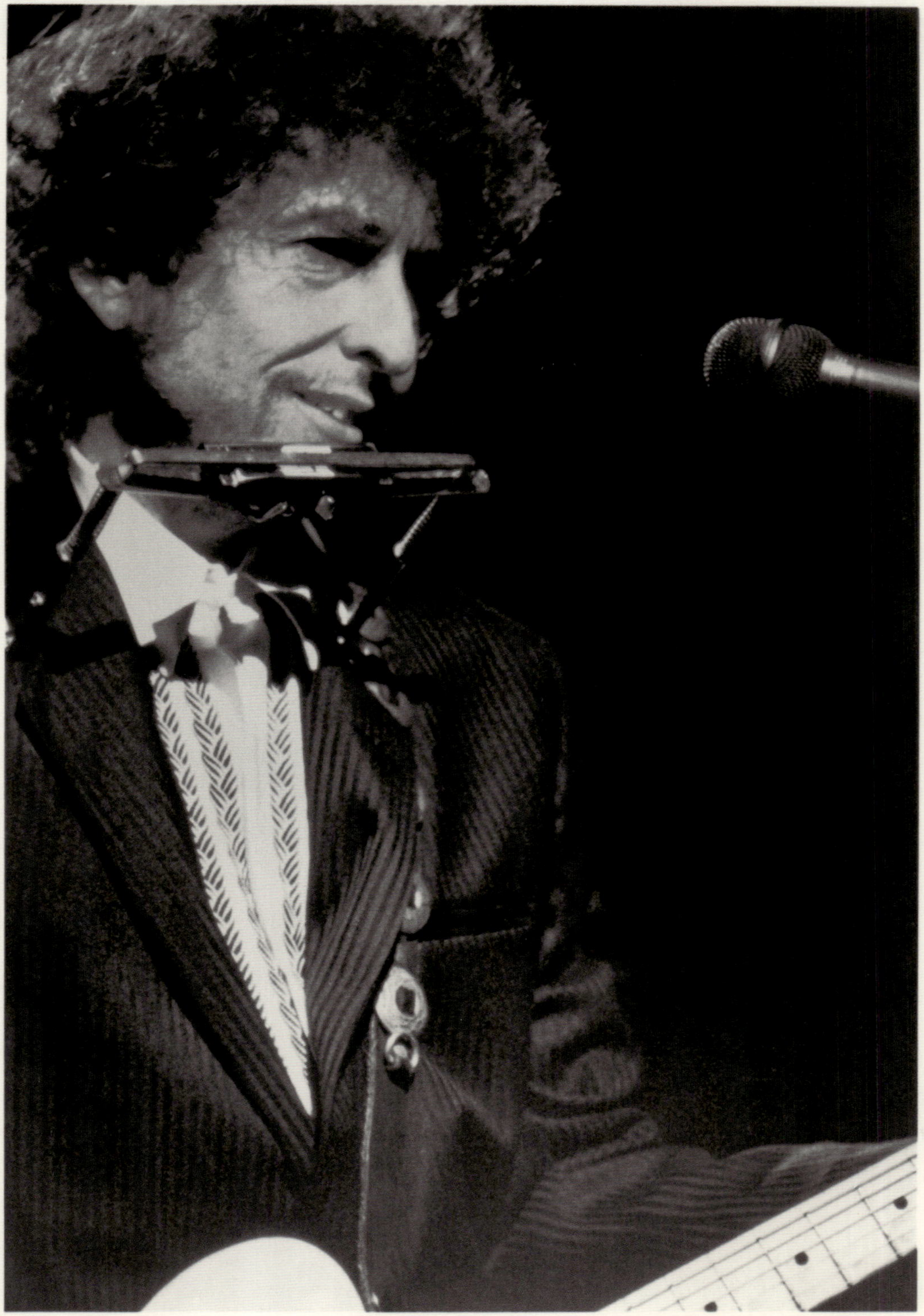

PHOTOGRAPH: © 1989 KEN REGAN/CAMERA 5

Permission to reproduce this photography is limited to editorial uses in regular issues of newspapers and other regularly published periodicals and television news programming.

BOB DYLAN

Columbia
8909

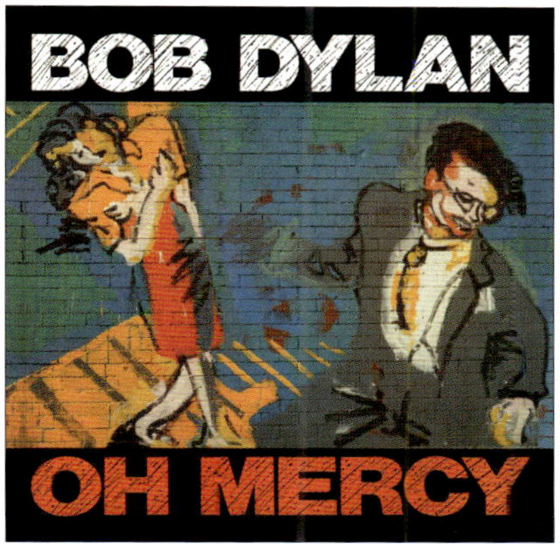

After a succession of poorly received albums, **Bob Dylan** closed out the decade on a high note with *Oh Mercy*, organized by producer Daniel Lanois.

Billboard 200: *Oh Mercy* (#30)

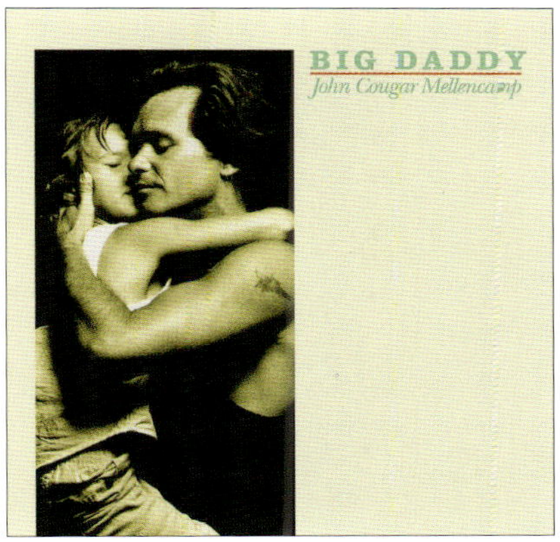

Big Daddy, heartland rocker **John Cougar Mellencamp**'s most contemplative album, yielded the self-obsessed "Pop Singer" and the kind "Jackie Brown."

Billboard 200: *Big Daddy* (#7)
Billboard Hot 100: "Pop Singer" (#15); "Jackie Brown" (#48)

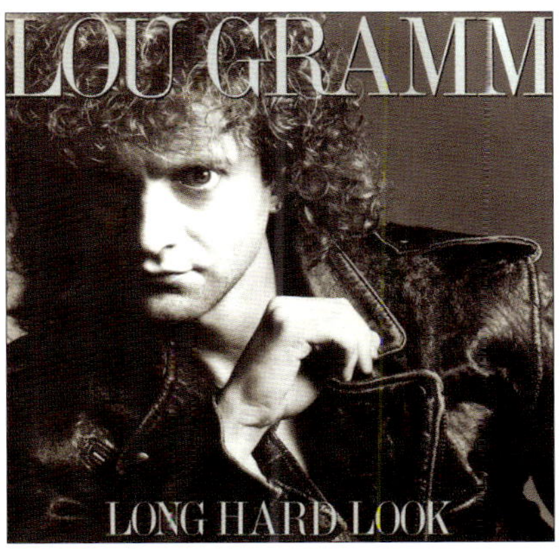

Foreigner lead vocalist **Lou Gramm** unleashed *Long Hard Look*, his second solo album, which spun off a Top 10 single, "Just Between You and Me."

Billboard 200: *Long Hard Look* (#85)
Billboard Hot 100: "Just Between You and Me" (#6);
"True Blue Love" (#40)

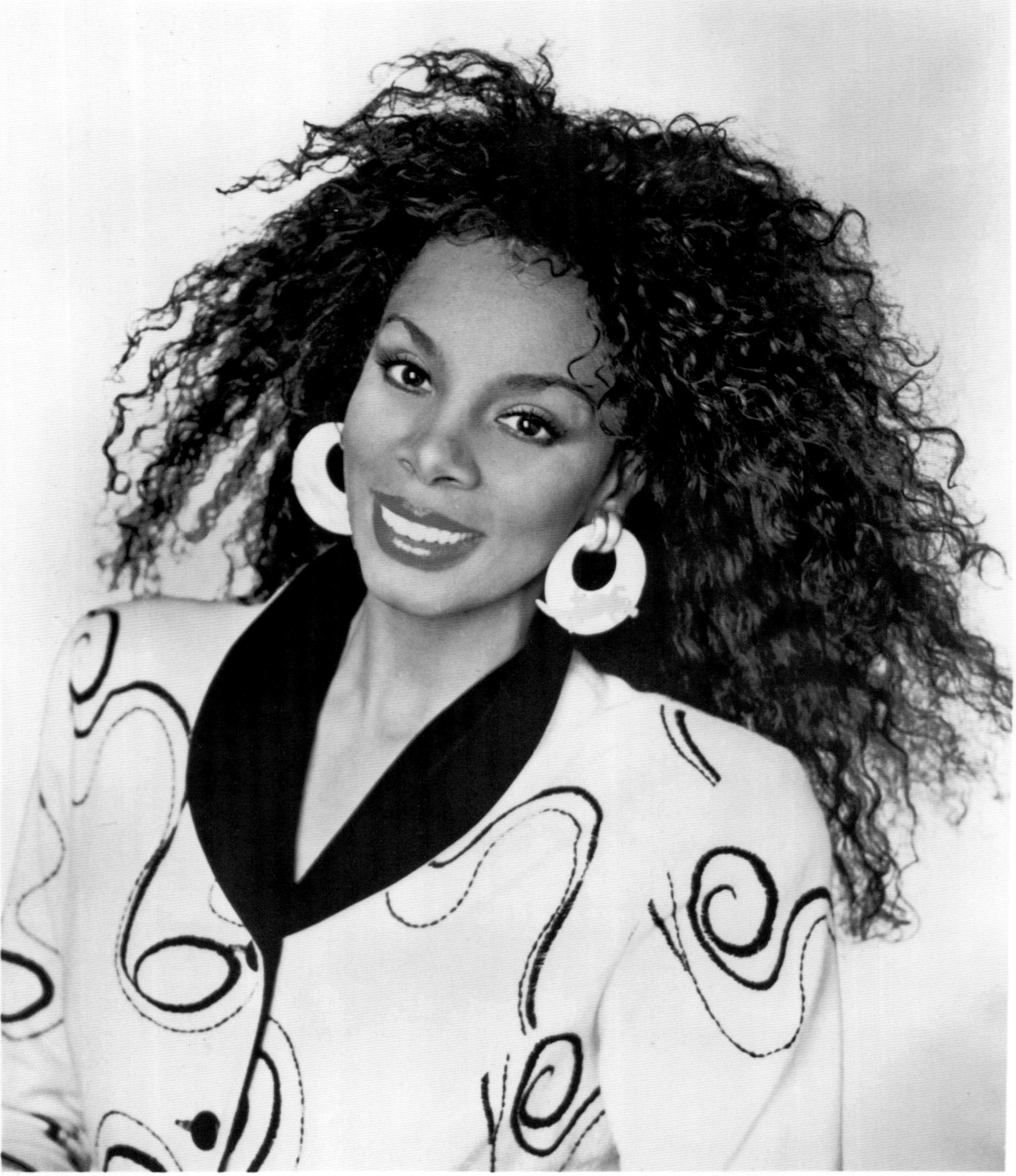

DONNA SUMMER

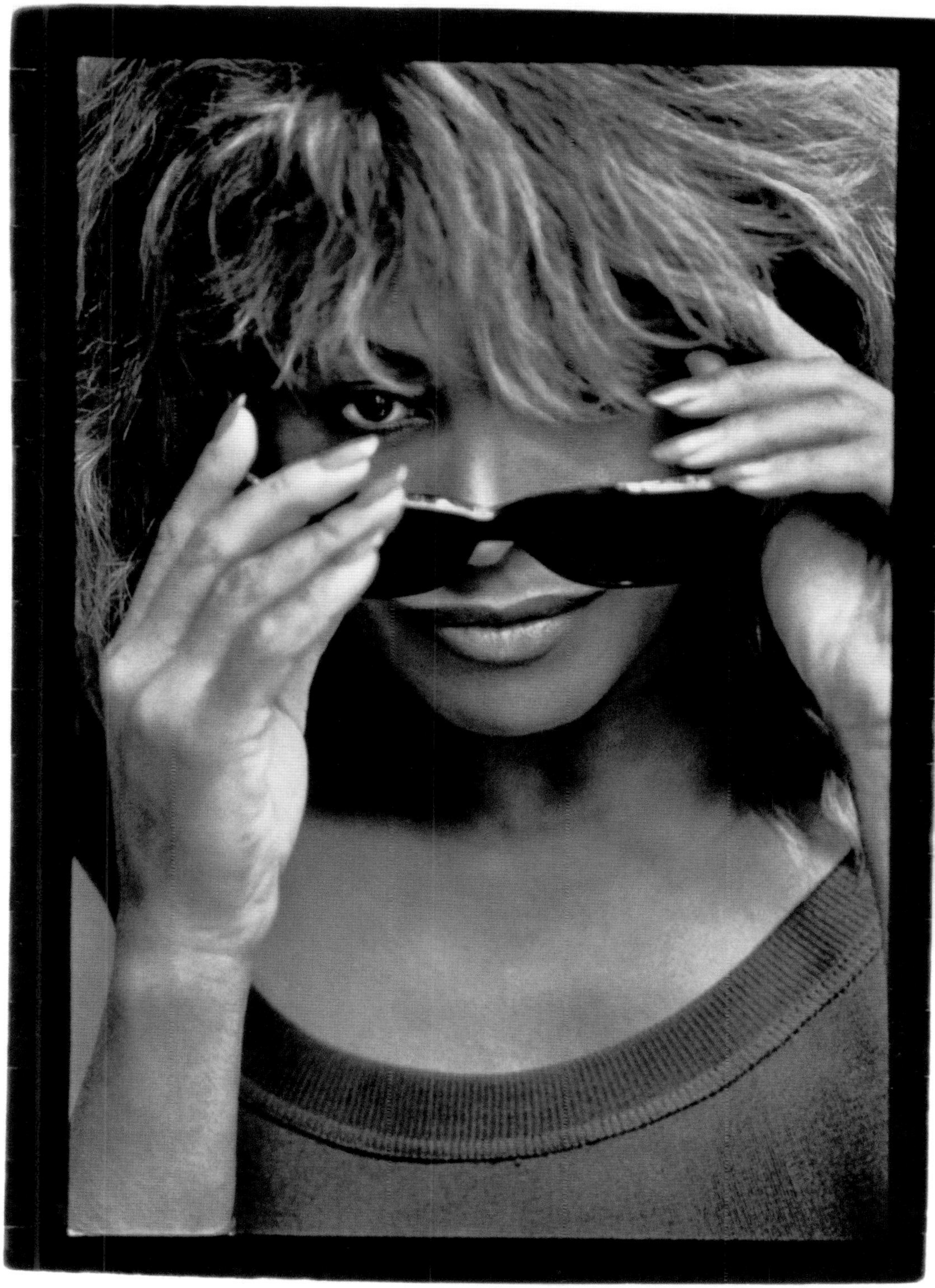

photography: Herb Ritts

tina turner

management: Roger Davies for Roger Davies Management Inc

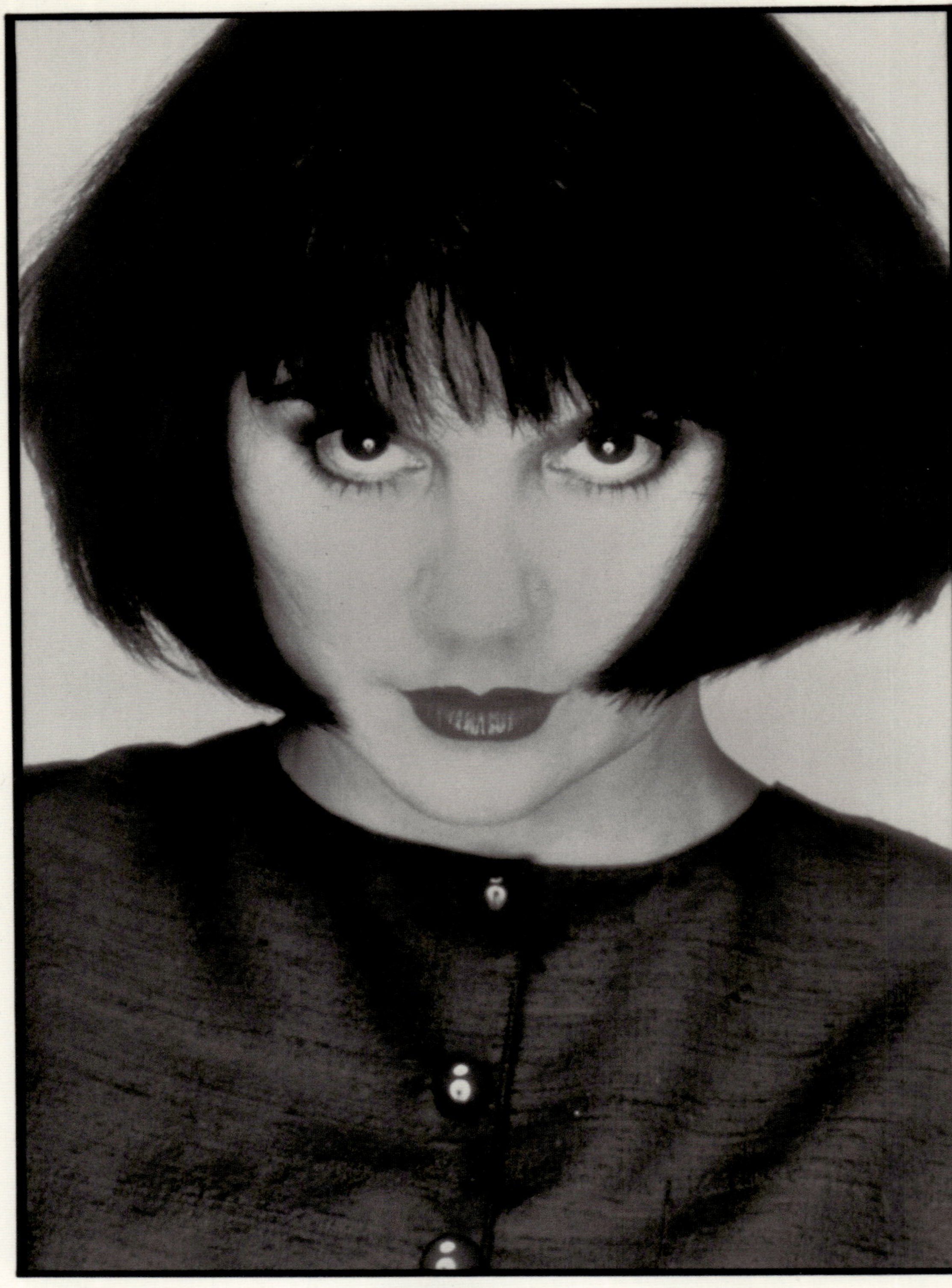

PHOTO CREDIT: ROBERT BLAKEMAN/1989

Linda Ronstadt

Elektra Entertainment

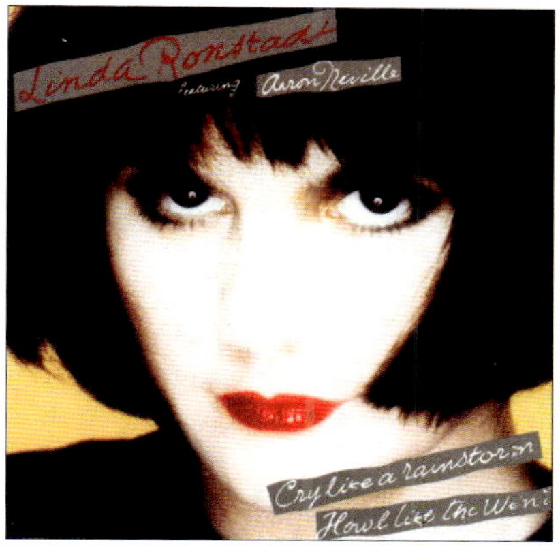

Linda Ronstadt's *Cry Like a Rainstorm, Howl Like the Wind* featured four duets with silky-voiced Aaron Neville, notably the pop smash "Don't Know Much."

Billboard 200: *Cry Like a Rainstorm, Howl Like the Wind* (#7)
Billboard Hot 100: "Don't Know Much" (#2); "All My Life" (#11); "When Something Is Wrong with My Baby" (#78)

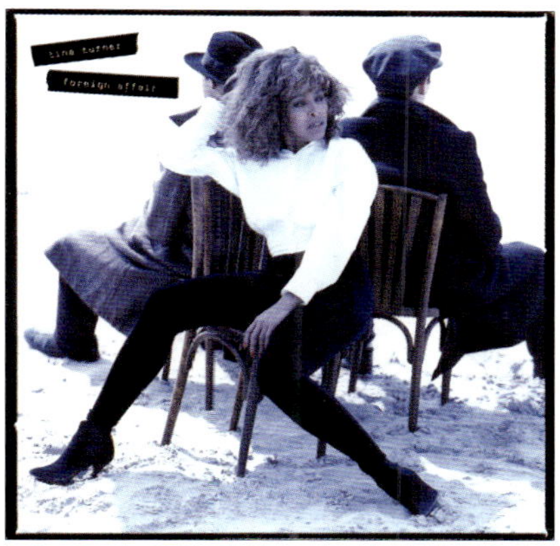

The resurgence of **Tina Turner** as a solo artist continued with the album *Foreign Affair*, which reached No. 1 in numerous countries and included "The Best."

Billboard 200: *Foreign Affair* (#31)
Billboard Hot 100: "The Best" (#15); "Steamy Windows" (#39)

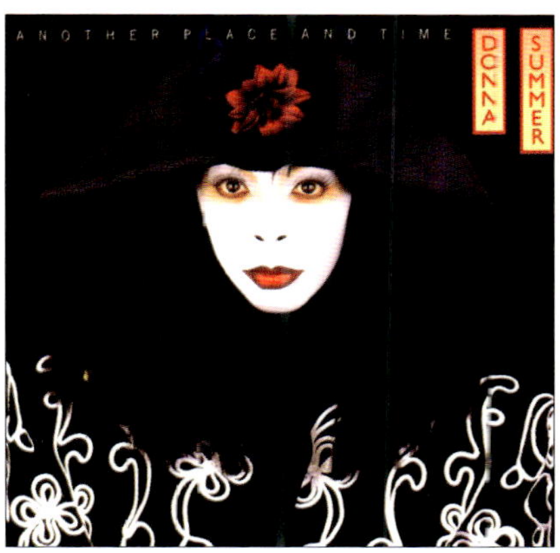

Aided by the UK production trio Stock Aitken Waterman, **Donna Summer** claimed her last Top 10 hit with the exuberant "This Time I Know It's for Real."

Billboard 200: *Another Place and Time* (#53)
Billboard Hot 100: "This Time I Know It's for Real" (#7); "Love's About to Change My Heart" (#85)

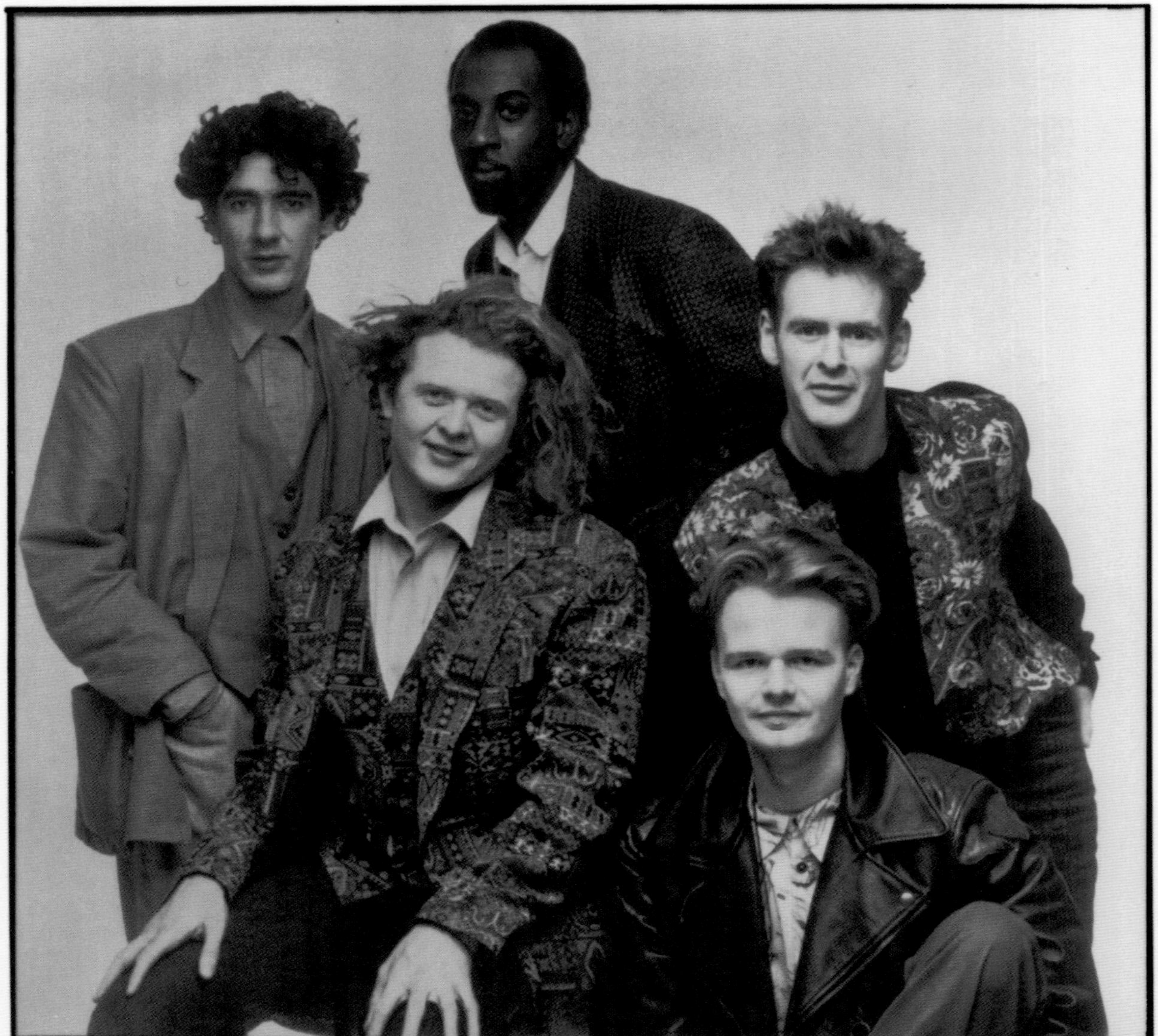

PHOTO CREDIT: SHEILA ROCK/1989

CHRIS JOYCE MICK HUCKNALL FRITZ MCINTYRE TIM KELLETT TONY BOWERS

SIMPLY RED

ELEKTRA

Fine Young Cannibals

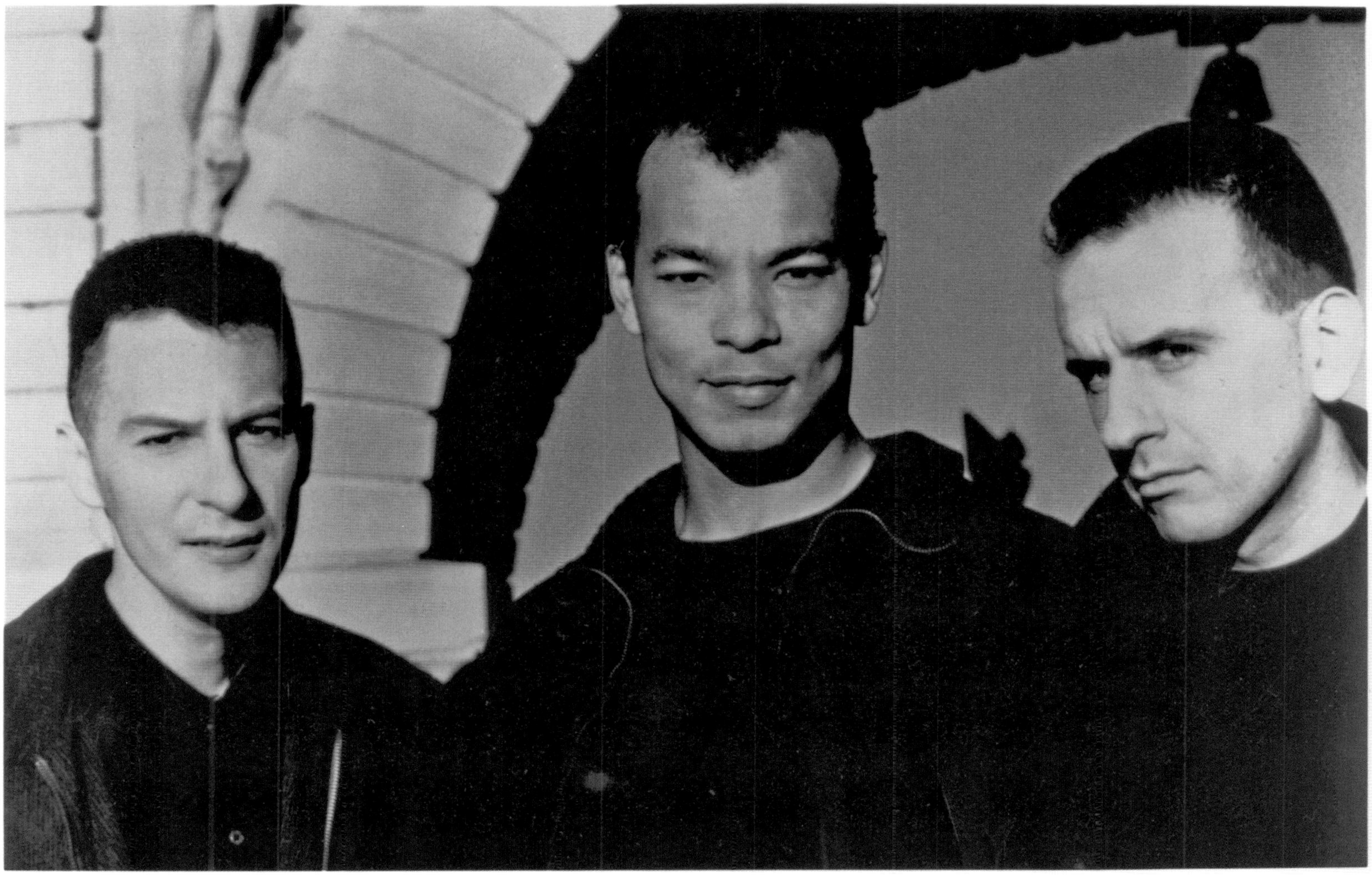

(L-R): David Steele, Roland Gift, Andy Cox

MCA RECORDS I.R.S.

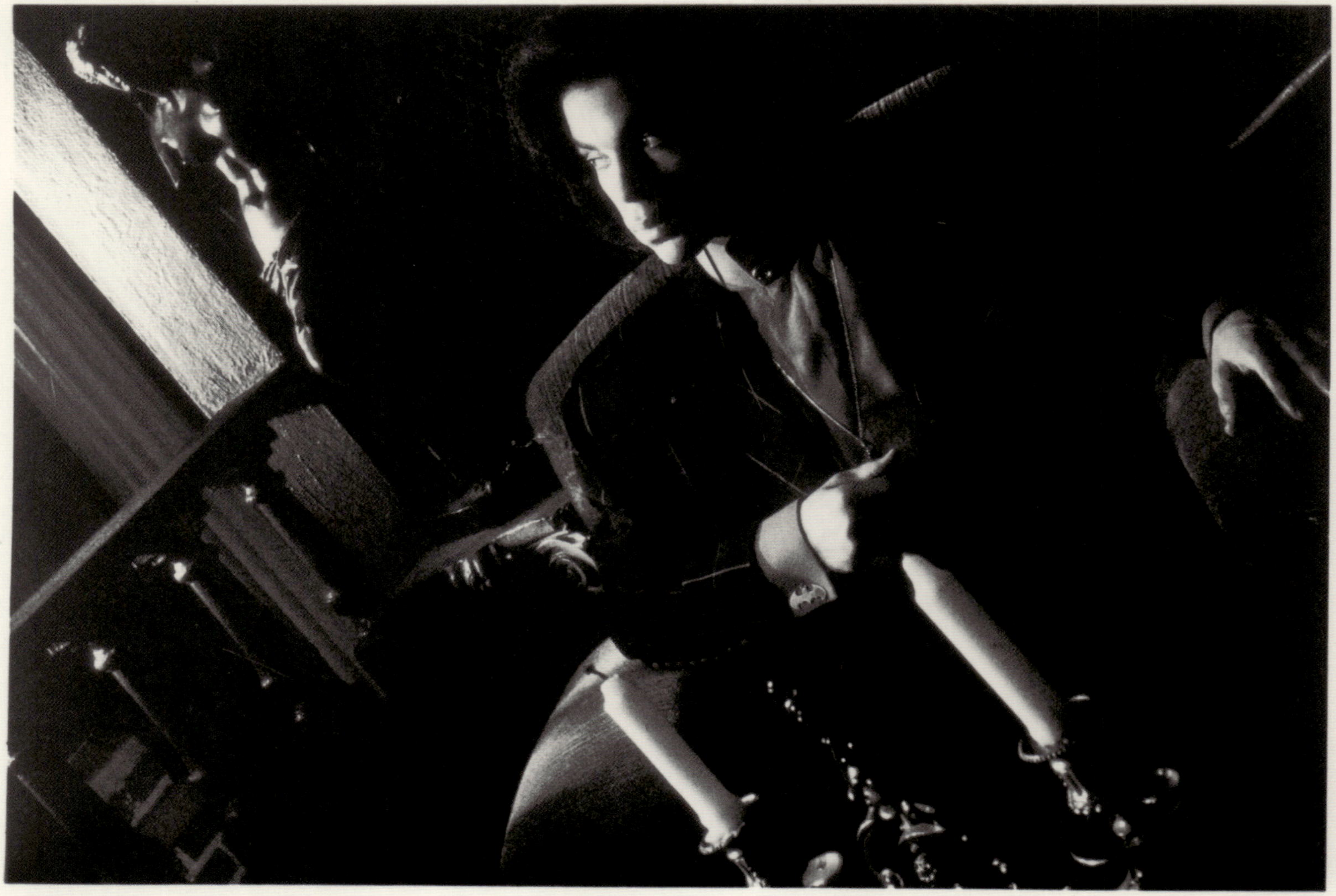

Photo Credit: Jeff Katz

Prince

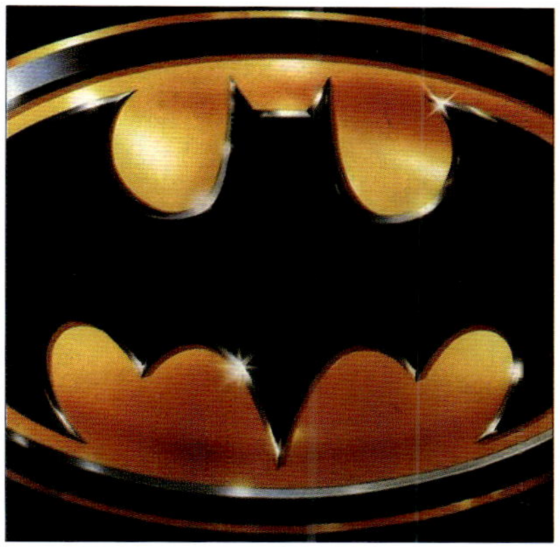

Prince wrote and produced an album inspired by the live-action movie adaptation of *Batman*, and "Batdance" topped the pop and R&B singles charts.

Billboard 200: *Batman* (No. 1)
Billboard Hot 100: "Batdance" (No. 1);
"Partyman" (#18); "The Arms of Orion" (#36)

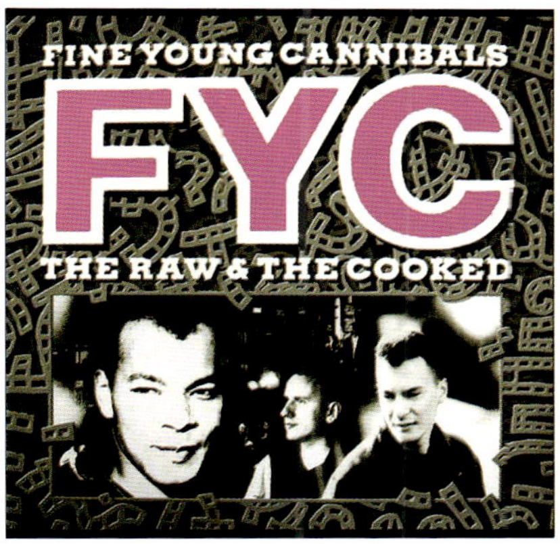

England's **Fine Young Cannibals** peaked at No. 1 on the US pop charts with the hits "She Drives Me Crazy" and "Good Thing," from *The Raw & the Cooked*.

Billboard 200: *The Raw & the Cooked* (No. 1)
Billboard Hot 100: "She Drives Me Crazy" (No. 1);
"Good Thing" (No. 1); "Don't Look Back" (#11);
"I'm Not the Man I Used to Be" (#54); "I'm Not Satisfied" (#90)

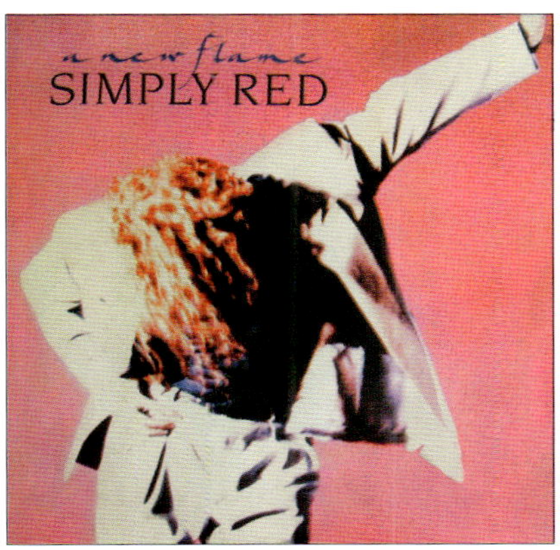

A cover of Harold Melvin & the Blue Notes' "If You Don't Know Me by Now" gave British soul band **Simply Red**, led by singer Mick Hucknall, a US smash.

Billboard 200: *A New Flame* (#22)
Billboard Hot 100: "It's Only Love" (#57);
"If You Don't Know Me by Now" (No. 1)

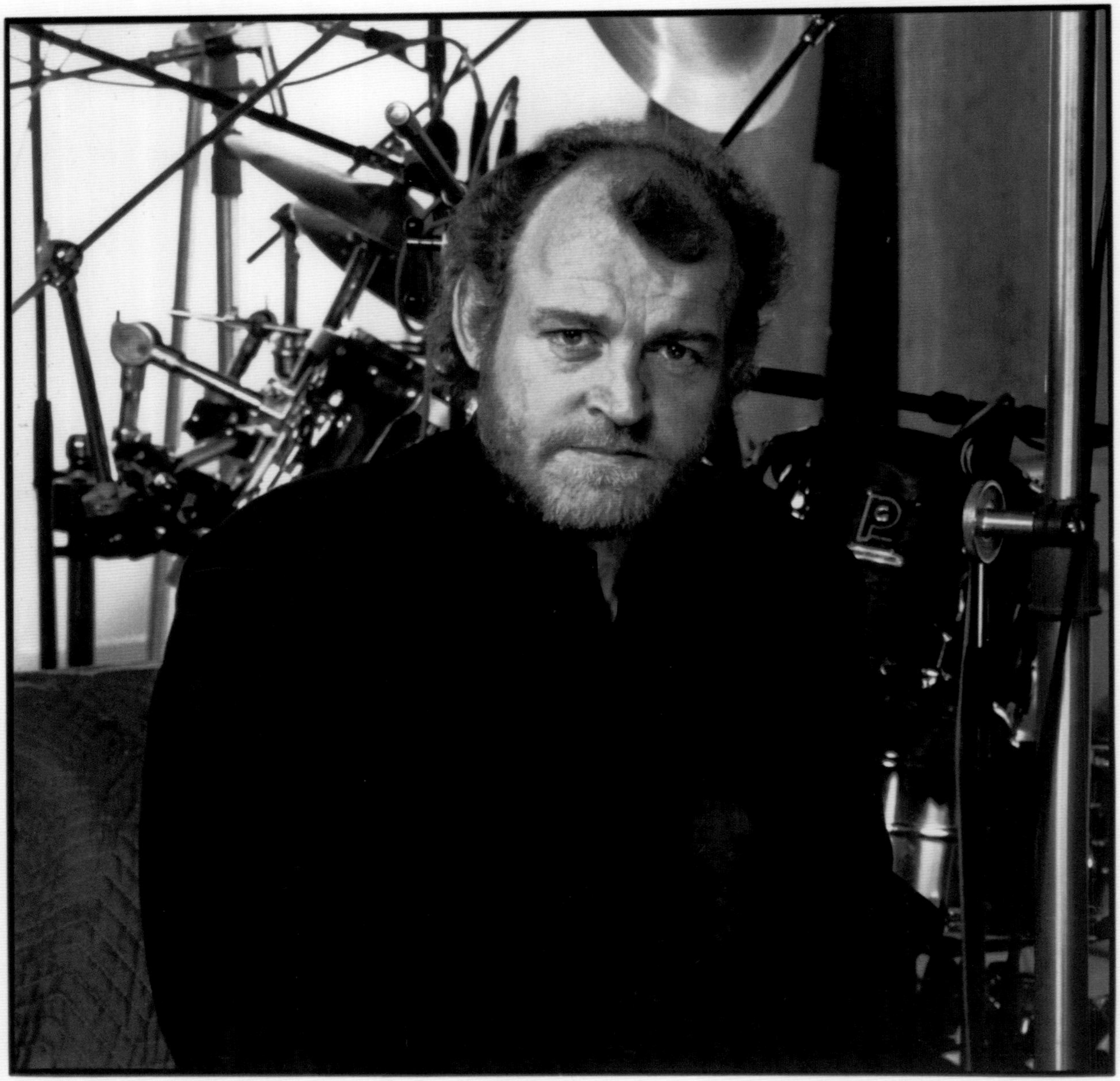

JOE COCKER

Capitol RECORDS

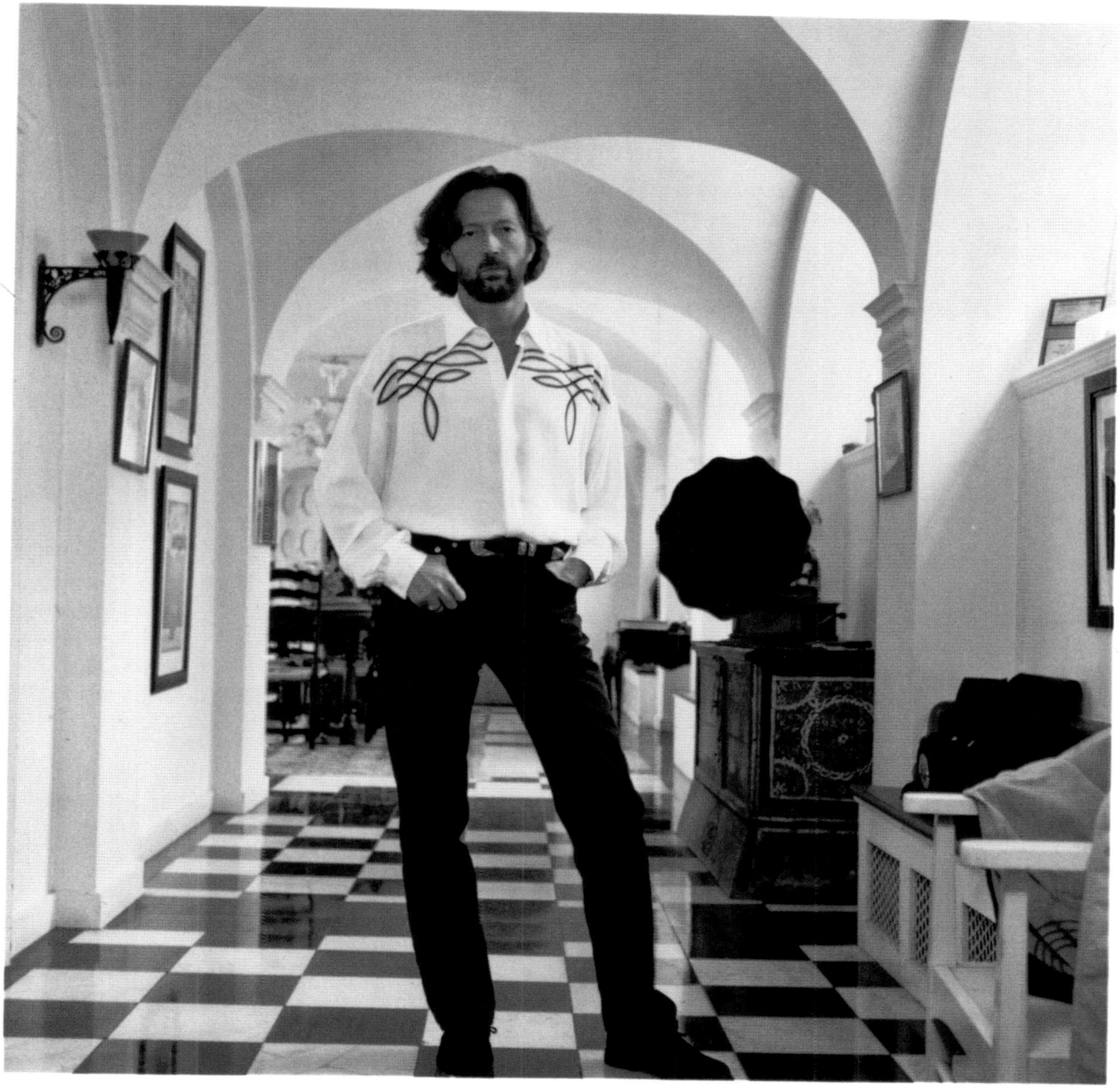

Photo Credit: Terry O'Neil

ERIC CLAPTON

DUCK RECORDS

reprise

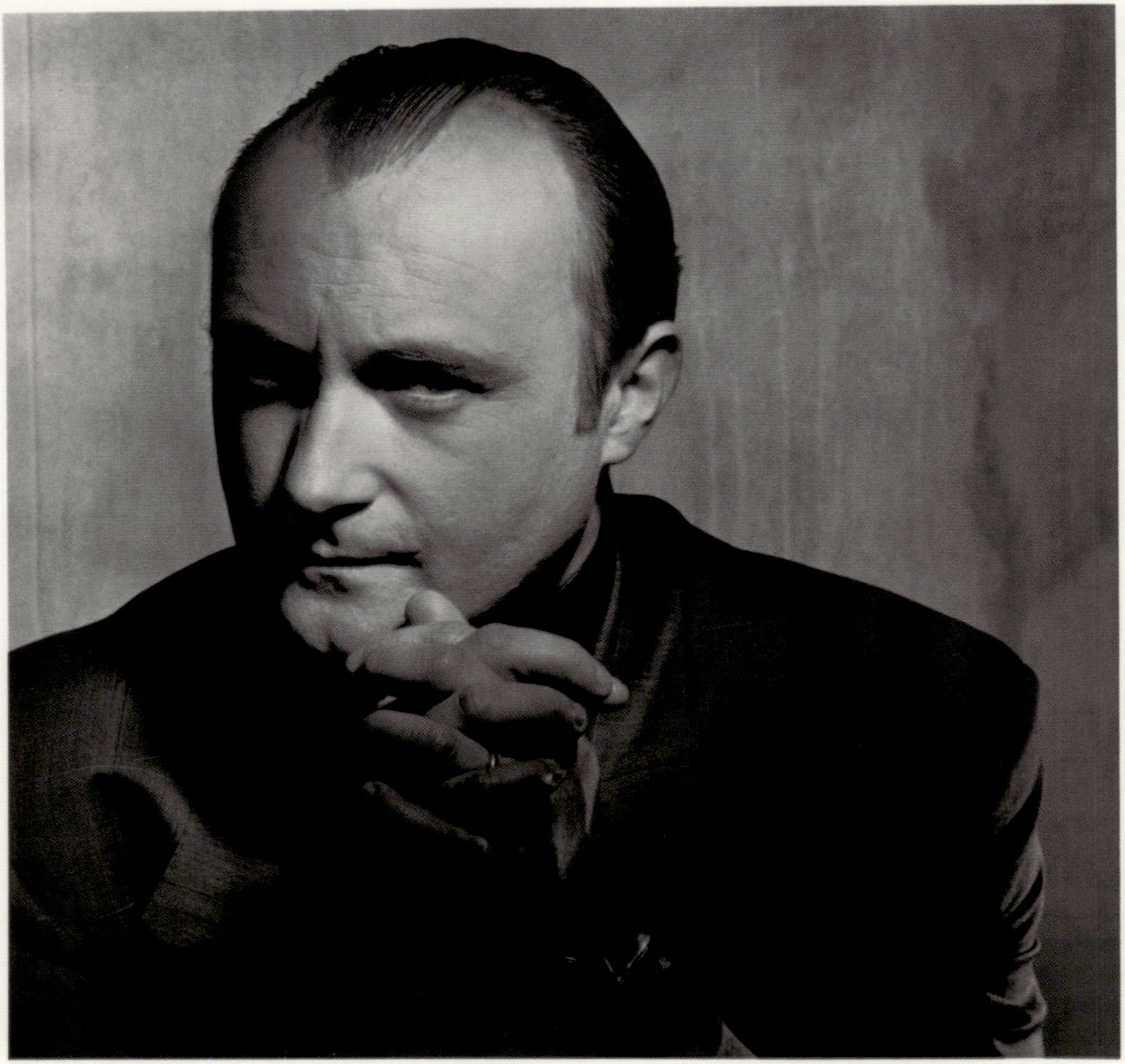

PHOTO CREDIT: SHEILA ROCK

Phil Collins

ATLANTIC

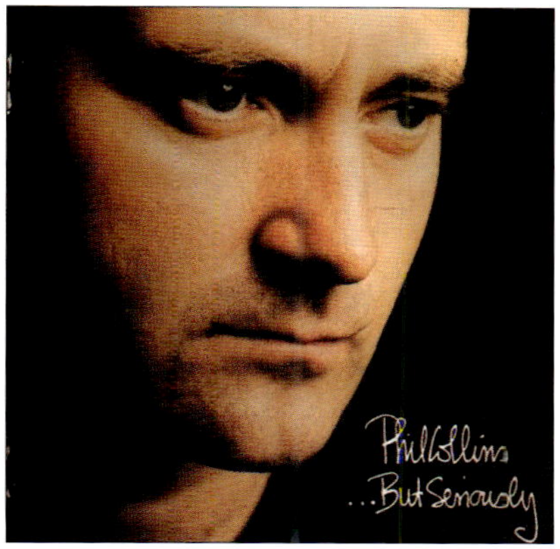

Phil Collins' solo success continued as four singles from *...But Seriously* reached the Top 5, including "Another Day in Paradise," an anti-homelessness song.

Billboard 200: *...But Seriously* (No. 1)
Billboard Hot 100: "Another Day in Paradise" (No. 1); "I Wish It Would Rain Down" (#3); "Something Happened on the Way to Heaven" (#4); "Hang in Long Enough" (#23); "Do You Remember?" (#4)

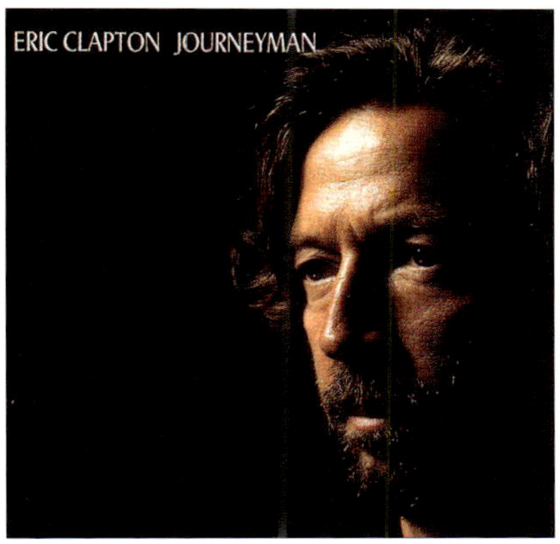

From guitar icon **Eric Clapton**'s album *Journeyman*, the No. 1 mainstream-rock song "Bad Love" won the Grammy for Best Rock Vocal Performance, Male.

Billboard 200: *Journeyman* (#16)
Billboard Hot 100: "Pretending" (#55); "Bad Love" (#88); "Run So Far" (#88)

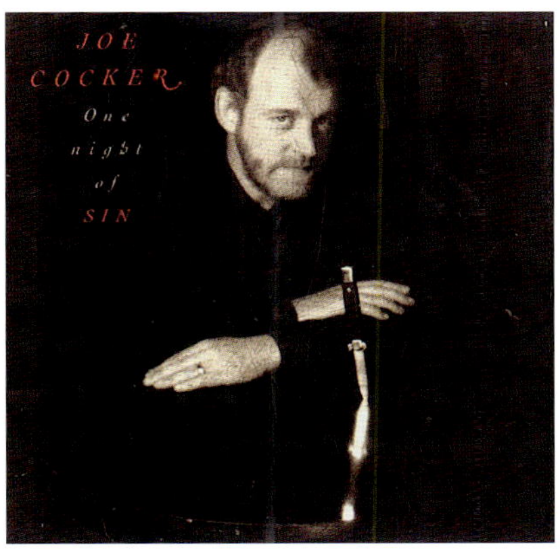

Gravel-voiced singer **Joe Cocker**'s *One Night of Sin* met with considerable global success, yielding a Top 20 smash in the US, "When the Night Comes."

Billboard 200: *One Night of Sin* (#52)
Billboard Hot 100: "When the Night Comes" (#11)

QUINCY JONES BACK ON THE BLOCK

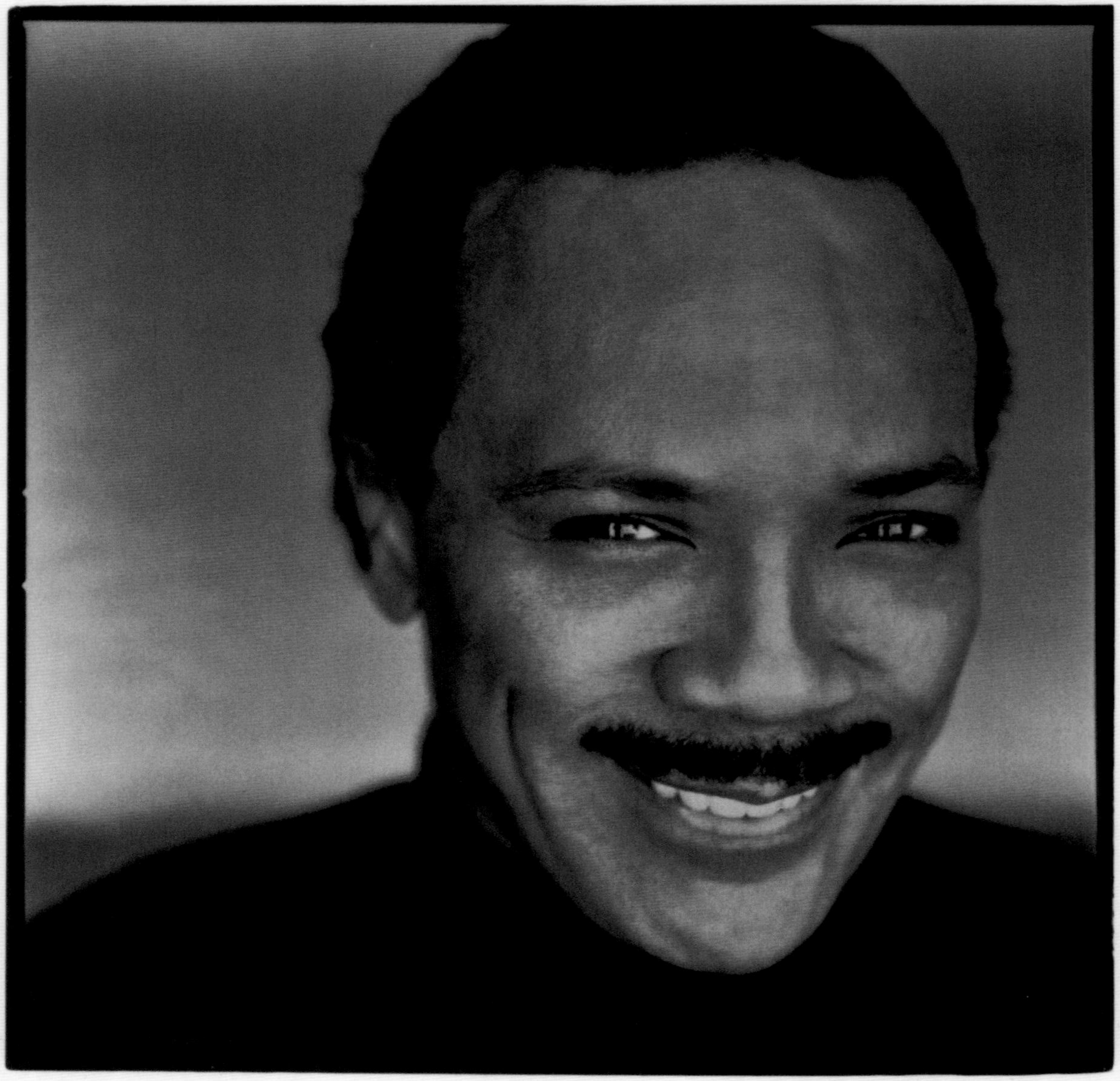

Photo Credit: Matthew Rolston

QWEST

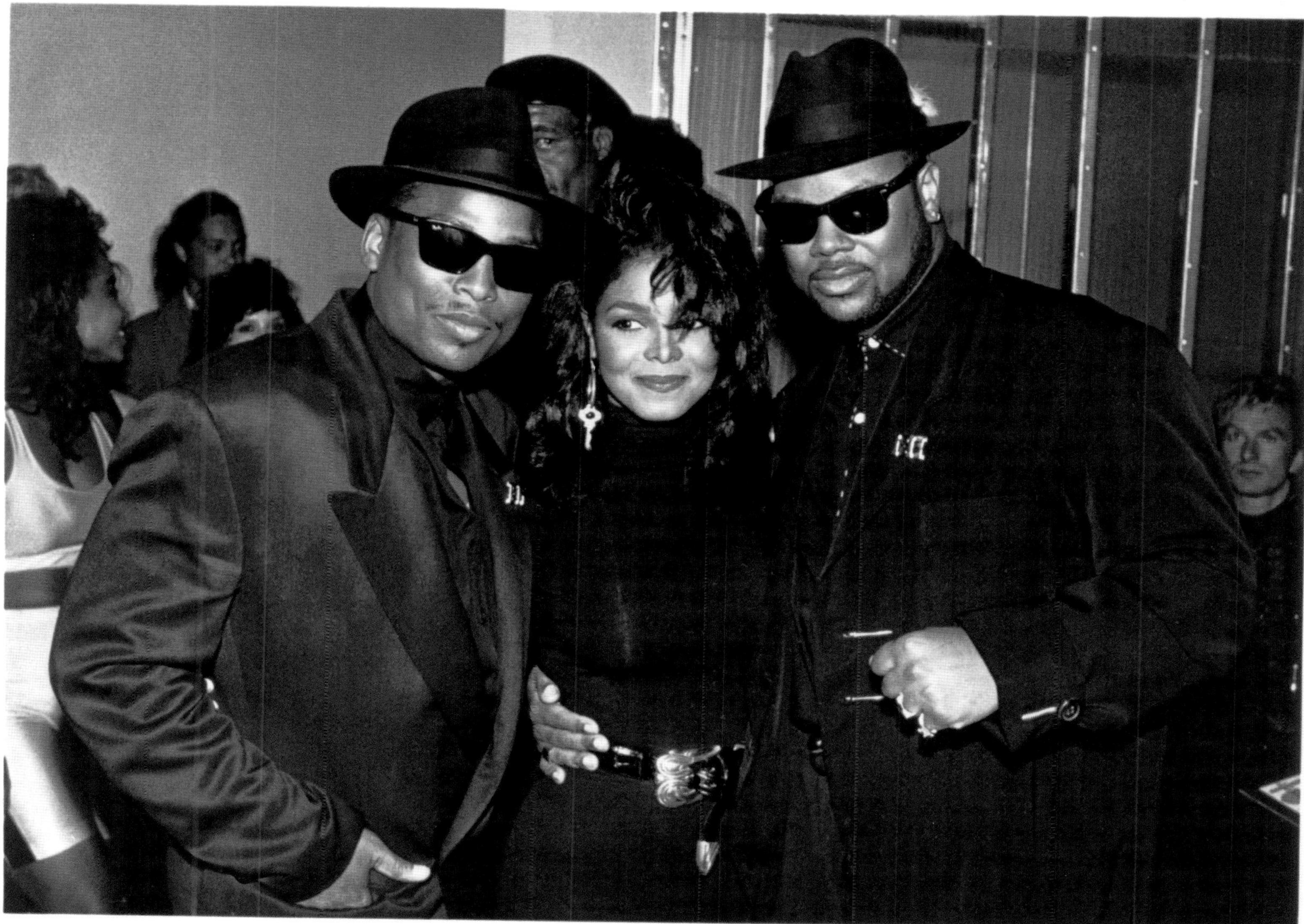

Photo Credit: Eddie Wolfl

TERRY LEWIS JANET JACKSON JIMMY JAM

A&M RECORDS

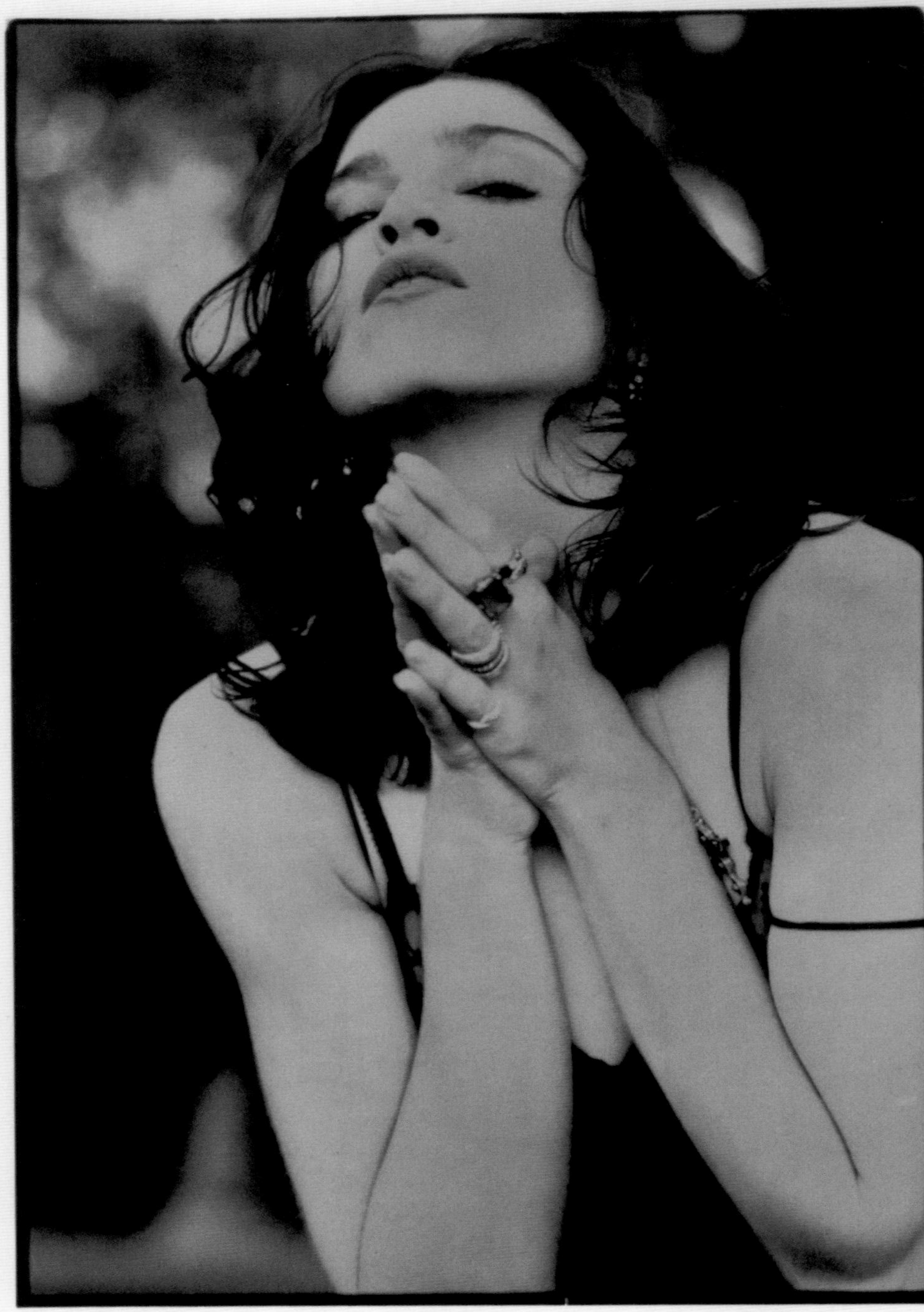

Photo Credit: Herb Ritts

MADONNA

SIRE®

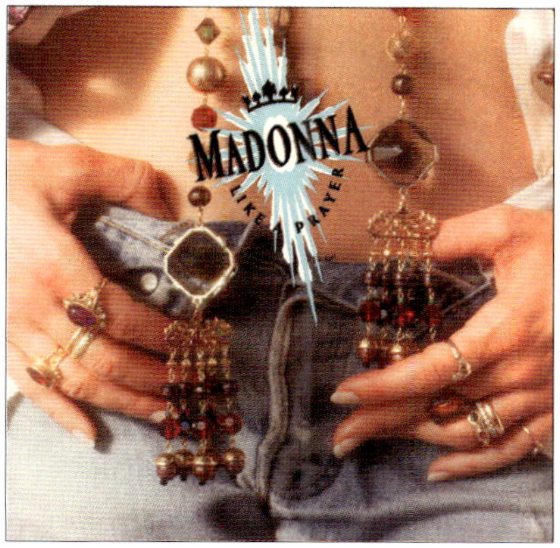

Madonna co-wrote and co-produced the chart-topping *Like a Prayer*, and the title track's video instantly became a lightning rod for religious controversy.

Billboard 200: *Like a Prayer* (No. 1)
Billboard Hot 100: "Like a Prayer" (No. 1); "Express Yourself" (#2); "Cherish" (#2); "Oh Father" (#20); "Keep It Together" (#8)

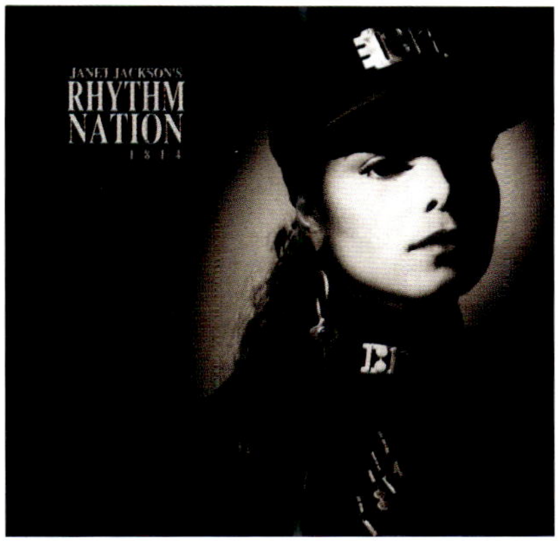

The visionary *Rhythm Nation 1814*, pop queen **Janet Jackson**'s fourth album, gave rise to a record-breaking seven Top 5 hit singles, including four No. 1s.

Billboard 200: *Rhythm Nation 1814* (No. 1)
Billboard Hot 100: "Miss You Much" (No. 1); "Rhythm Nation" (#2); "Escapade" (No. 1); "Alright" (#4); "Come Back to Me" (#2); "Black Cat" (No. 1); "Love Will Never Do (Without You)" (No. 1)

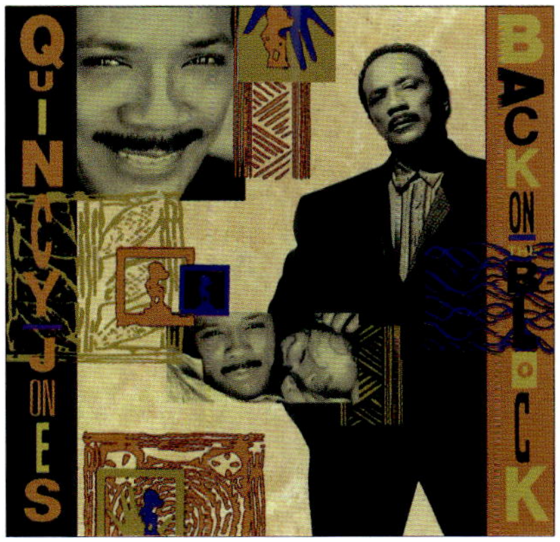

Quincy Jones' *Back on the Block* featured legendary musicians and singers across three generations and won seven Grammys, notably Album of the Year.

Billboard 200: *Back on the Block* (#9)
Billboard Hot 100: "I'll Be Good to You" (#18); "The Secret Garden (Sweet Seduction Suite)" (#31); "Tomorrow (A Better You, Better Me)" (#75)

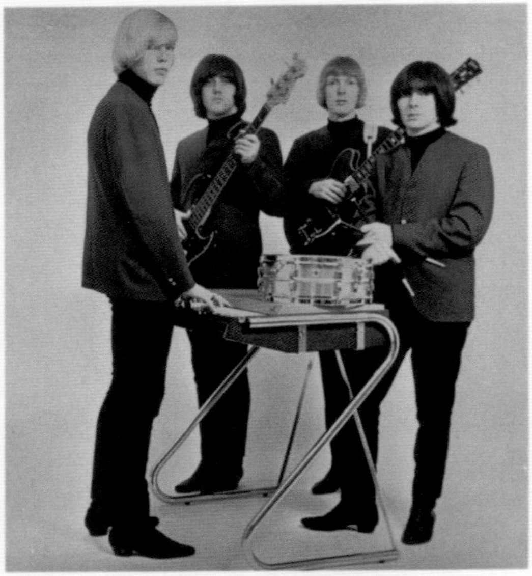

THE ALLMAN JOYS, 1966

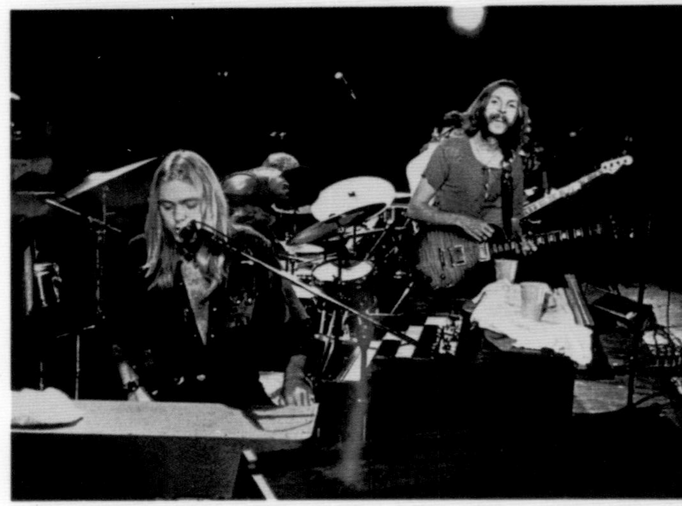

ALLMAN BROTHERS BAND LIVE AT FILLMORE EAST, 1971

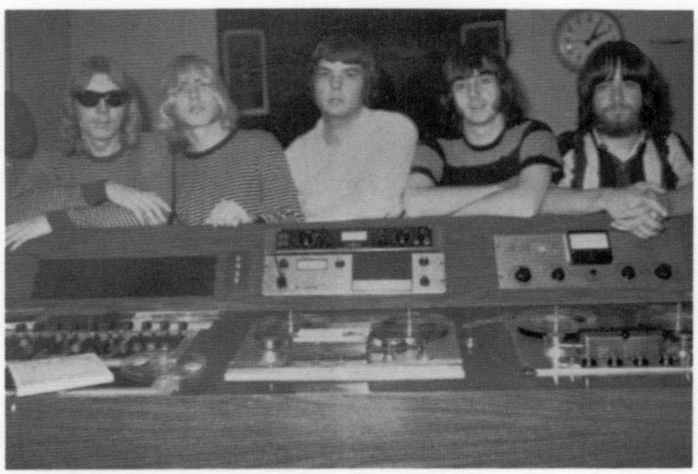

THE HOUR GLASS, 1967

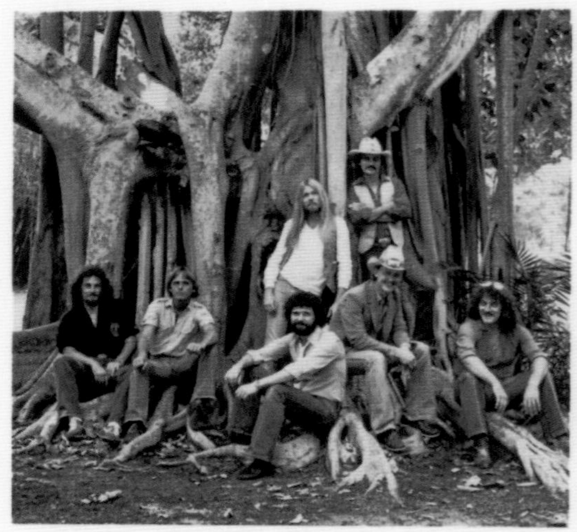

ALLMAN BROTHERS BAND, 1982

polydor

PolyGram™

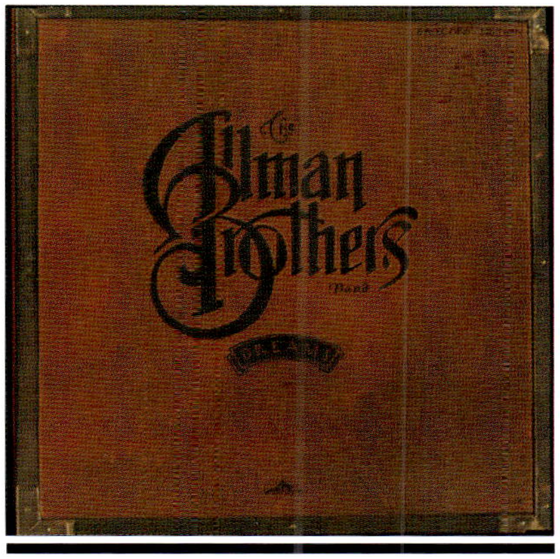

Billboard 200: *Dreams* (#103)

The Allman Brothers Band forged a distinctive style before treachery and tragedy brimmed within their ranks.

CELEBRATING A twentieth anniversary in 1989, four charter members of the Allman Brothers Band—Gregg Allman, guitarist Dickey Betts and drummers Butch Trucks and Jaimoe—reunited for a summer tour. In addition, they featured Warren Haynes and pianist Johnny Neel, both from the Dickey Betts Band, and bassist Allen Woody. There was no shortage of the ABB's fabled improvisations in the sets, with soaring solos and instrumental authority powering the hybrid of blues, rock and country.

The classic-rock radio format had given the band's catalog new relevance. A 55-track retrospective box set, *Dreams,* offered some five hours of vintage selections to observe the ABB's anniversary. "I put it on and listened to it from start to finish, and I was exhausted from the memories by the end," Allman exclaimed. "Some of that stuff was found in my mother's closet!"

Dreams began with the first recordings made by Gregg and Duane Allman as members of the Allman Joys and Hourglass. Duane, one year older than brother Gregg, already was in demand as a session guitarist based on his work with Wilson Pickett and Aretha Franklin, among others. But Duane wanted to front his own group, which led to the 1969 formation of the Allman Brothers Band in Macon, Georgia.

The ABB went to the top with a rumbling rhythm section, Gregg's gritty, world-weary vocals and gospel organ, and unusual interplay between Dickey Betts on lead and Duane on slide guitar—thereby pioneering the Southern rock genre. At their peak, they took the blues farther into rock than any other group had done. "The sound just evolved out of where each of us came from," Allman said. "Duane and I came from strong R&B roots, Butch had played with a folk-rock band, Jaimoe played jazz—if someone was ordering it on paper, they'd be told they had the wrong file."

The band's reign was short-lived—Duane died in a motorcycle smash near Macon in October 1971; 13 months later, bassist Berry Oakley was killed in a carbon-copy accident in the same vicinity. "It was just pandemonium—we were almost catatonic, frozen, devoid of emotion," Allman said. "We decided that if we didn't get back together and play, we were gonna dry up and blow away. So we buried ourselves in our work."

The Allmans kept packing arenas. Duane's death put Betts in the spotlight, and he fulfilled his duty by notching hits with "Ramblin' Man" and the instrumental "Jessica." But the creative momentum Duane had inspired was never regained. By 1975, the attention was centered on personal and legal problems. Gregg testified before a grand jury in a narcotics trial against his own road manager in exchange for immunity from prosecution for his own drug abuse. Allman's cohorts vowed not to work with him again. Gregg sought the band's forgiveness at Jimmy Carter's 1977 inauguration.

Yet a third edition of the Allmans was well out of fashion among emerging Eighties trends. *Dreams* ended with solo efforts of recent years by Allman and Betts. ■

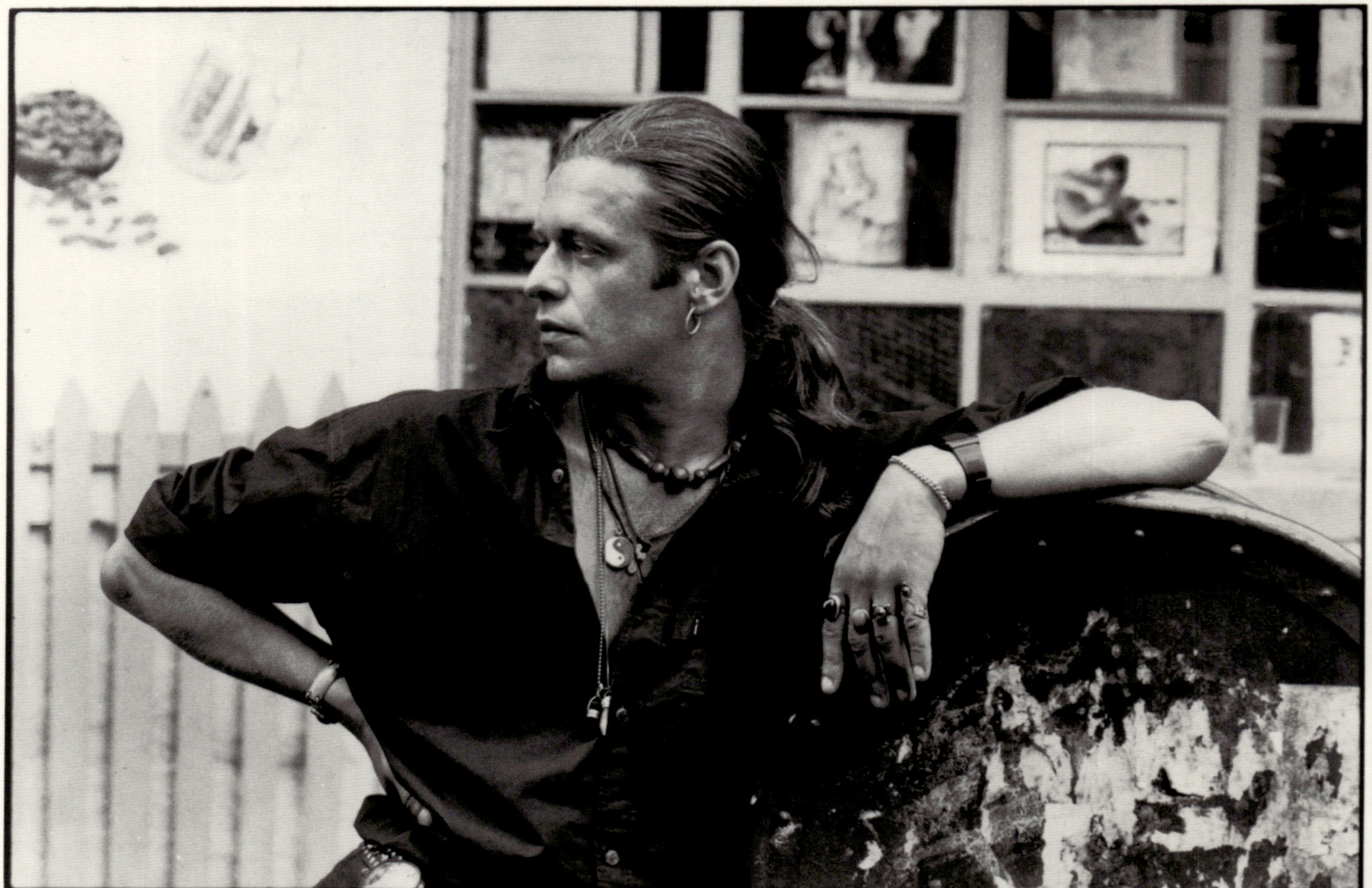

PHOTOGRAPH: DAVID GAHR

Representation:
BELKA International Incorporated
New York

BORIS GREBENSHIKOV

Columbia
8903

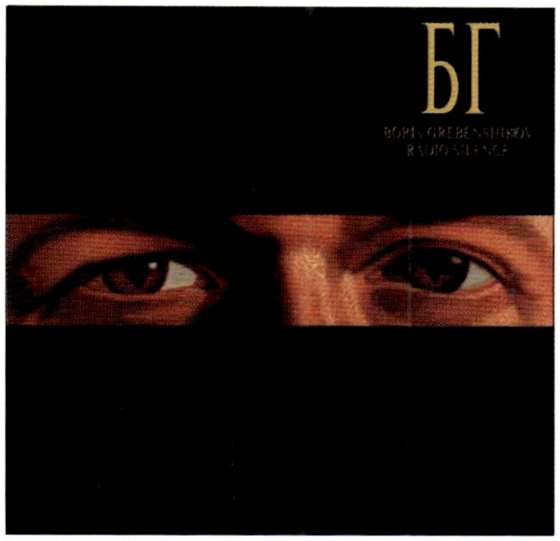

Billboard 200: *Radio Silence* (#198)

Boris Grebenshikov's *Radio Silence* was touted as the first American recording released by a Russian artist.

WIDELY REGARDED as the poet laureate of his generation, Boris Grebenshikov—the Soviet Union's foremost rock artist—grew up on the same classic English-language rock 'n' roll as his peers in the West did. The Leningrad-bred performer cited the Beatles, Led Zeppelin and T. Rex among those who had impacted his music, but in his case, the sounds had to be smuggled into a closed society.

"You must understand that for the past 70-plus years, we've had to live in a totally artificial world with an artificial culture and behavior, where you don't feel like a human being because you are taught to think of yourself as just a participant in a historic event," Grebenshikov explained. "When you're 16 years old and all you see around you is bullshit and you don't want to live your life like this, you seek out something that is real to you, to answer the basic question of love and life and death. This is the role that rock 'n' roll played for me."

Grebenshikov had been the guiding force in Soviet rock for a decade—his pioneering Russian band Aquarium's recordings were duplicated extensively throughout his country's vast underground music cassette network. His work had only been made available above ground by the state-run Melodiya label in 1987, and the initial copies of Aquarium's first officially released album sold out within hours.

Grebenshikov's reputation spread beyond Russian borders, and he became the first "unofficial" rock musician to be allowed to visit the West after the efforts of a New York firm formed to facilitate contact with Soviet entities. Produced by Dave Stewart of Eurythmics fame, *Radio Silence* was hailed as the first contract of a Soviet rock musician with a Western label. Working with such rock stars as Annie Lennox and Chrissie Hynde, Grebenshikov composed directly in English for the first time. The album brought the singularity of the English-fluent songwriter's experience to the forefront.

"Because we don't have much informational stimuli in Russia, people tend to take fewer things in, but deeper—they sit at home and listen for hours like it's a sacrament or an evening sermon," he noted. "But here, it's a completely different idiom—people are bombarded by tons of information, and to keep their brains intact they have to limit their attention span. It's familiar to me from 25 years of listening to and reading about rock 'n' roll, but the first time dealing with it face-to-face is an interesting challenge."

The single "Radio Silence" became a hit outside of Russia, reaching #7 on the modern-rock chart in *Billboard*. But exporting the Russian songwriting tradition, which valued lyrical elaboration over melodic hooks and verve, proved disillusioning to Grebenshikov.

"Because I recorded in the West for release in the West, I'm competing with artists whom I've never competed against back home. So I have to think twice about doing something in a Lou Reed vein, for example, because I'm competing with Lou himself. Whereas in Russia, all similarities with Lou would vanish because of language and cultural differences." ■

Laura

LAURA NYRO

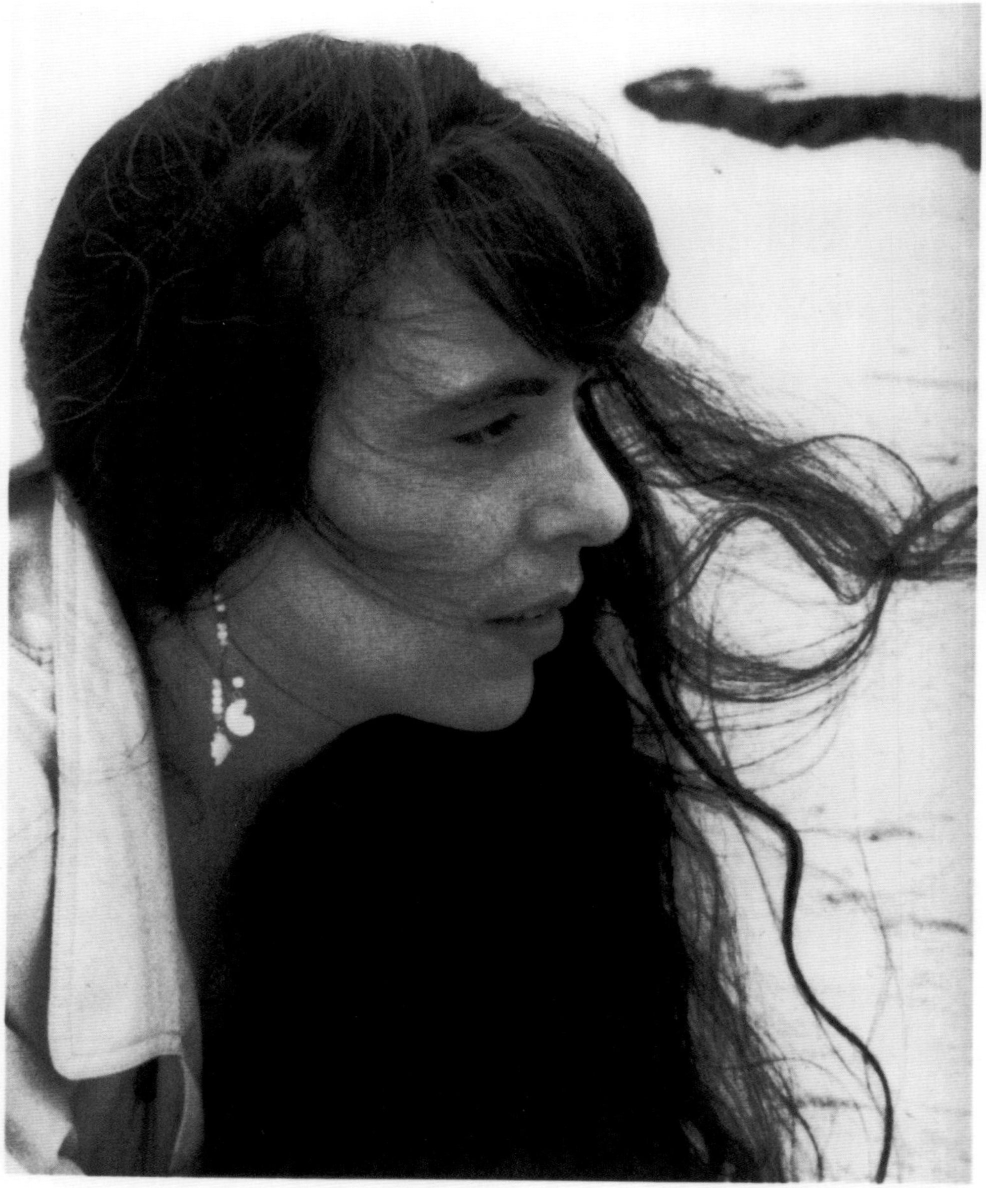

Photo Credit: Nancy LeVine

CYPRESS RECORDS

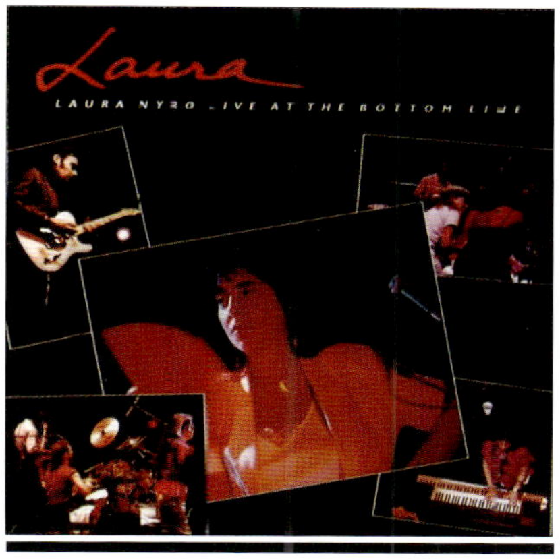

In the aftermath of her first national tour in ten years, Laura Nyro released *Laura: Live at the Bottom Line*.

FOR A period in the late Sixties and early Seventies, Laura Nyro rated as one of pop music's most evocative songwriters. Her unprecedented hybrid of soul and jazz tunes possessed an intensity of uncommon wordplay and melodies that left listeners impressed, if occasionally bewildered.

"When I was young, there was a strong radical energy in music that had its influence on me," the New York City native noted. "I got to listen to the early rock 'n' roll that was coming off the streets—lush and melodic with great signers. And there was jazz appreciation among street kids, particularly for John Coltrane. He introduced me to music as art, to having a creative vision."

Throughout her career, Nyro had been an enigmatic, sheltered figure sustained only by a cult audience. Her youthful, jubilant songs became hits for Three Dog Night ("Eli's Coming") and Barbra Streisand ("Stoney End"), and artists from Linda Ronstadt to Carmen McRae to Mongo Santamaria had recorded her work.

The renowned singer-songwriter decided to return to the concert stage—*Laura: Live at the Bottom Line*, her first album in five years, was recorded at the famed New York club. It contained such early Nyro classics as "And When I Die" (popularized by Blood, Sweat & Tears) and "Stoned Soul Picnic" and "Wedding Bell Blues" (hits for the Fifth Dimension).

But there were six new tunes as well, which were placed in flattering settings by a small, sharp band led by guitarist Jimmy Vivano. "Broken Rainbow" was featured in the 1985 Academy Award-winning documentary of the same name about the plight of the Native Americans. And "The Wild World" pointedly addressed animal rights—Nyro dedicated her album and tour to the movement, as her grandfather, who died in 1986, imparted his respect for animals to her.

"I'm finally at a point where I'm enjoying my life—I have to follow my heart and pursue a career that I can relate to," she said. "I just wanted that same feeling I had when I was a kid, when my friends and I would meet out on the streets and sing. But making a record in a studio isn't that lifestyle. So I decided to play some small clubs with a soulful band, and it really fit me. The music is natural and uncomplicated, although there's years of training behind it. This is where my art is right now. I'm into the art of singing. I'm no longer a writer who happens to sing." ■

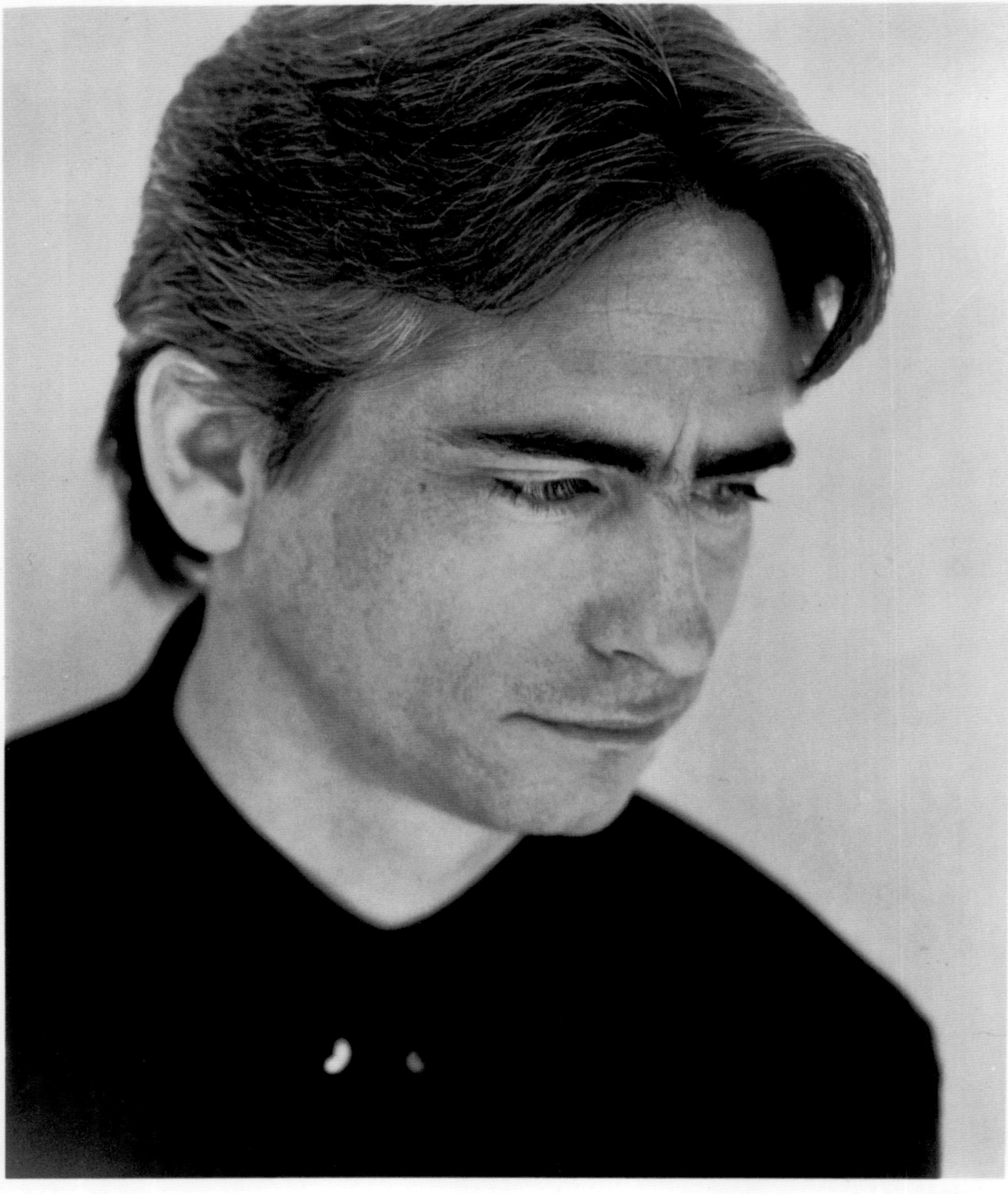

DAVID BENOIT

GRP Records

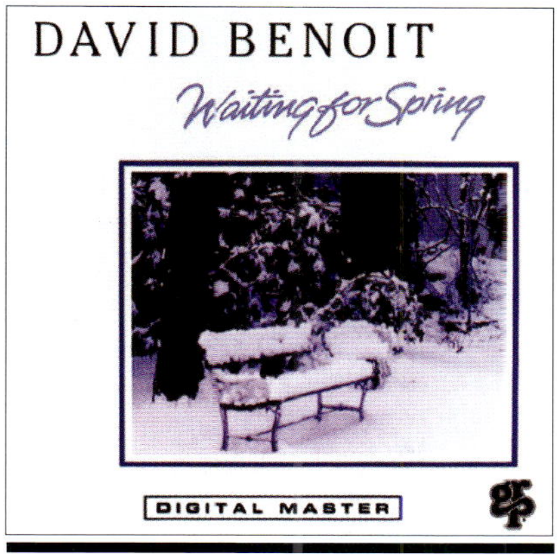

Waiting for Spring by popular keyboardist David Benoit reached the top of the traditional jazz album charts.

CUTTING HIS teeth in the music business in the late Seventies, Los Angeles native David Benoit gained experience as a player, arranger, composer and conductor on the studio scene. After recording several albums for the tiny AVI label, he broke into the upper reaches of the jazz charts in 1985 with a Spindletop release, *This Side Up*. Shortly thereafter Benoit signed with GRP, the jazz label founded by Dave Grusin and Larry Rosen, and his artistry and commercial appeal soared.

His first releases achieved success in the contemporary jazz field, but on *Waiting for Spring*, the pianist decided on a change of pace from his characteristic smooth, lyrical approach, veering instead towards straight-ahead acoustic jazz. He cut the record in a classic jazz trio/quartet setting with guitarist Emily Remler, drummer Peter Erskine (known for his work with Weather Report) and bassists Luther Hughes and John Patitucci.

Remler, in particular, was a sympathetic and appealing soloist. "I have a lot of Emily's recordings and am a big fan," Benoit explained. "When I got in touch with her, she was quite friendly and aware of my music. I went to the Vine Street Bar & Grill in Hollywood to hear her play and asked her to be on my record while she was in town."

The album showed great reverence for one of Benoit's main influences, Bill Evans, the late piano legend. The title track employed altered chord changes reminiscent of those that Evans played, and "Turn Out the Stars" was a Benoit-Remler duet rendition of the Evans composition. Benoit played "My Romance" in the Evans tradition and followed it up with Evans' "Funkallero."

"I was fortunate enough to meet Bill Evans a couple of times," Benoit noted. "He had a primary effect on me, not so much from the notes he played but spiritually, his feeling when he touched the piano. I wrote (the closing) 'I Remember Bill Evans' on the day that he died."

Waiting for Spring sold surprisingly well, making it to the No. 1 spot on *Billboard*'s Top Jazz Albums chart. Benoit enjoyed his newfound acclaim as a melodic mainstream jazzer, but he hoped to make a vocal-oriented contemporary jazz recording. "*Waiting for Spring* is a concept album—a jazz record and a wintertime record—but I want to explore as many things as possible. People are asking me, 'Are you going to do another jazz record?' Well, I might, but not right away—I don't think there's any point. That's like *Back to the Future Part II*—it's not as good as the original." ■

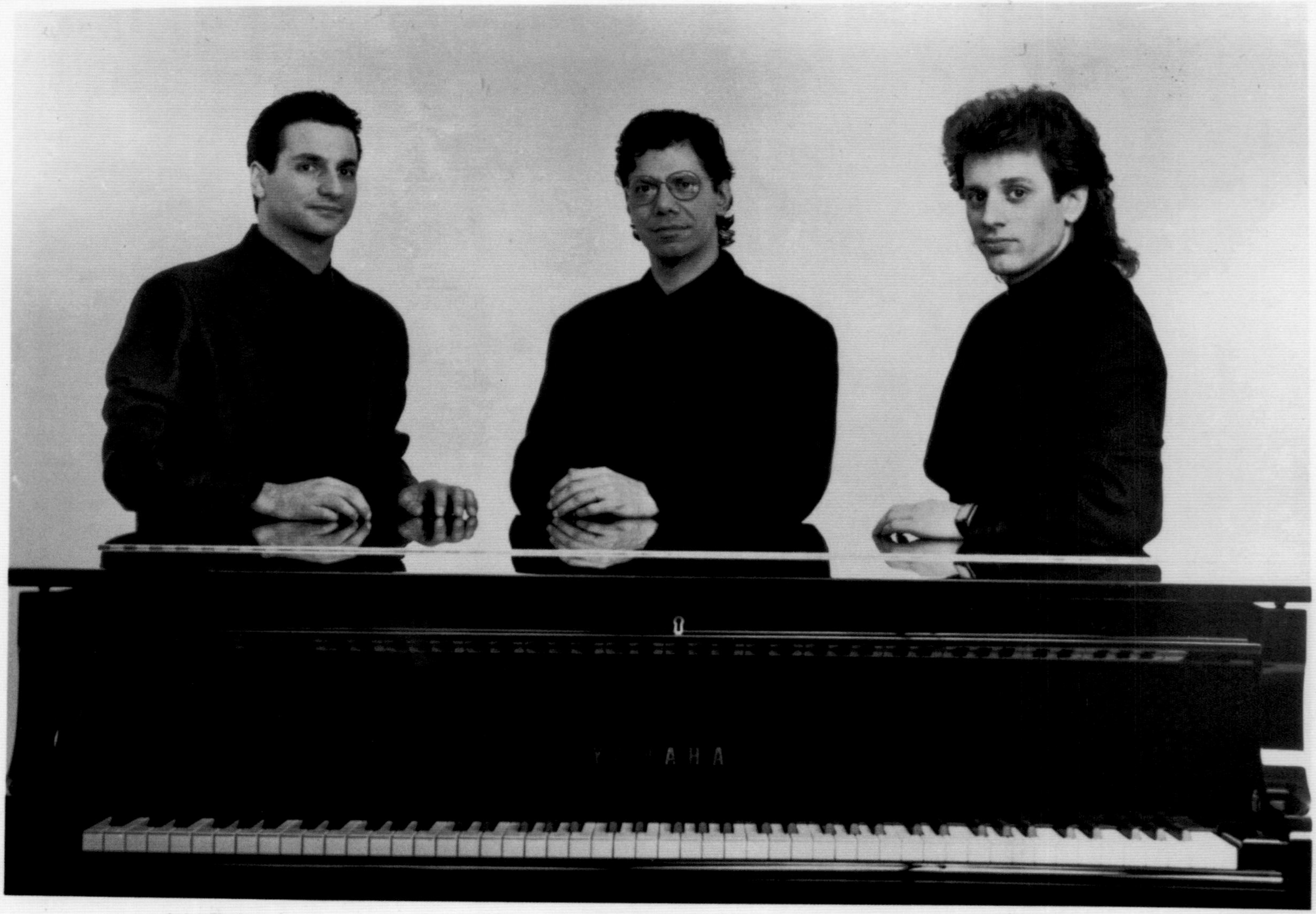

John Patitucci Chick Corea Dave Weckl

Chick Corea Akoustic Band

GRP Records

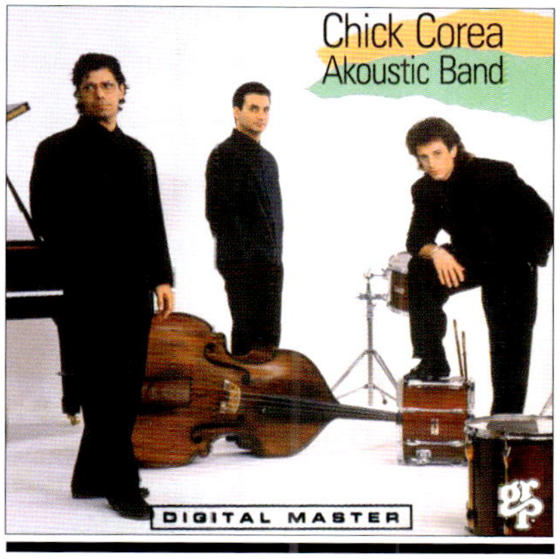

The first record by Chick Corea Akoustic Band won a Grammy Award for Best Jazz Instrumental Performance.

AN ACCOMPLISHED and creatively far-reaching jazz pianist, Chick Corea arrived on the jazz scene in the Sixties with solo albums and sideman work. He joined Miles Davis' initial electric group and founded his own innovative ensemble, Return to Forever. He carried on a continuous course of lauded albums investigating modern post-bop, electric fusion, classical and Latin traditions.

The prolific performer led the Chick Corea Akoustic Band, which had its beginnings in 1985 with his Elektric Band, featuring John Patitucci on bass and Dave Weckl on drums.

"I've always tended to start new groups as a trio," Corea explained. "Even Return to Forever was originally a trio with Stanley Clarke and Horacee Arnold. And when I got around to forming the Elektric Band, I wanted to start out as a trio to solidify the rapport and form a nucleus for the band. So Patitucci, Weckl and I played a season of concerts as a trio before guitar and eventually saxophone were added to the group."

After two years of touring and recording with the Elektric Band, Corea began getting requests to do trio performances in Europe. He worked up a repertoire with Patitucci and Weckl and began doing Akoustic Band gigs in between Elektric Band travel dates.

Corea returned to his roots with the release of *Chick Corea Akoustic Band,* leaving all the electronics in the closet and performing acoustic jazz standards and originals in the setting of his grand piano, Patitucci's upright bass and Weckl's drums. The swinging set reached No. 1 on the *Billboard* Top Jazz Albums chart.

"The way I came up as a musician, this combination was always the basic jazz-making unit," he said. "With solo piano, it can really go in any direction. Duo music is the ultimate intimacy between two people, but it can also go in lots of directions. But you add the drums to bass and piano and I seem to groove in this tradition that filters back through Thelonious Monk, Bill Evans, Horace Silver, Bud Powell, Earl Hines and Duke Ellington, to name a few." ■

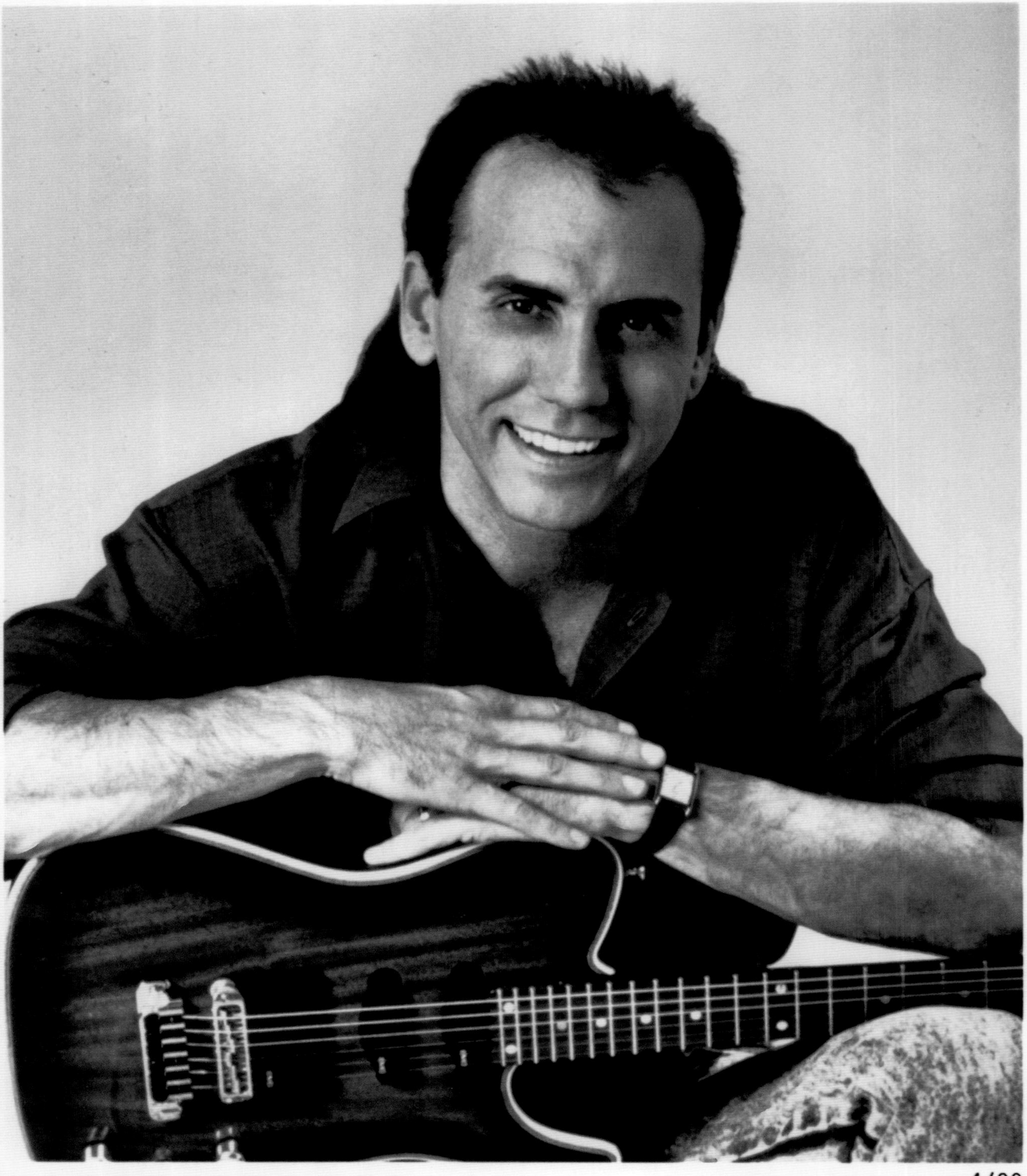

LARRY CARLTON

4/89

MCA RECORDS

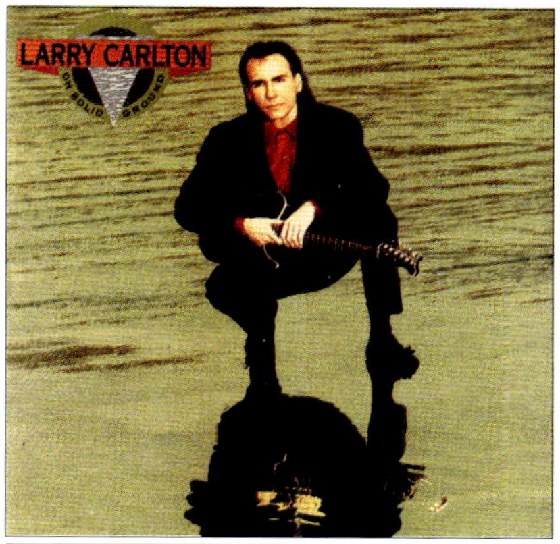

Billboard 200: *On Solid Ground* (#126)

Larry Carlton returned to music, releasing the *On Solid Ground* album one year after a close brush with death.

ON APRIL 6, 1988, Larry Carlton walked out of his Hollywood Hills studio and was shot and brutally wounded by an unknown gunman for unknown reasons. One of the hottest guitarists, composers, producers, arrangers and session players in the music industry, Carlton came within minutes of bleeding to death as a single bullet shattered his left vocal cord and rendered his left arm lifeless.

But Carlton survived the tragic ordeal. Surgeons grafted arteries from his leg to repair damage to his severed carotid artery. After seven months of rigorous therapy and medical attention, feeling slowly returned to his left side, and he found that he could handle the guitar. His album *On Solid Ground* went to #3 on the jazz charts.

"I'm 100 percent back, playing-wise," Carlton said with a voice still raspy from the shooting. "And emotionally, I feel great for the tour. People in the crowd are always yelling out, 'We're glad you made it, welcome back,' but they're curious if my attitude toward music is different now. I'm not sure it is. I try to put them at ease at the beginning of my set and move forward."

On Solid Ground returned to what Carlton called "the electric side" after two acoustic releases. His solo career had progressed steadily since the early part of the Eighties, but the guitarist first made his mark in the early Seventies as one of Los Angeles' busiest studio musicians, notably for his legendary work on Steely Dan's albums. *On Solid Ground* opened with a Carlton first—a cover of a Steely Dan tune, "Josie." Carlton had played all of the guitar parts (with the exception of the solo) on the original version.

"I tried to find one Dan cut that I could make my own and that I could enjoy playing the rest of my career," he laughed, citing the 1987 Grammy Award for Best Pop Instrumental Performance he collected for his cover of Michael McDonald's hit "Minute by Minute."

Carlton included some of his most moving playing to date on an aggressive instrumental version of the Eric Clapton/Derek & the Dominoes classic 'Layla." "It's a song I've been considering for years, knowing it would make a great comeback someday. Everyone says it took a lot of moxie to do a classic, but I wasn't intimidated—it just sounded like fun. I first cut a polite version of the song before the accident, but after the shooting, I went back in and erased everything. The end result that's on the album is one complete take, all the way through." ■

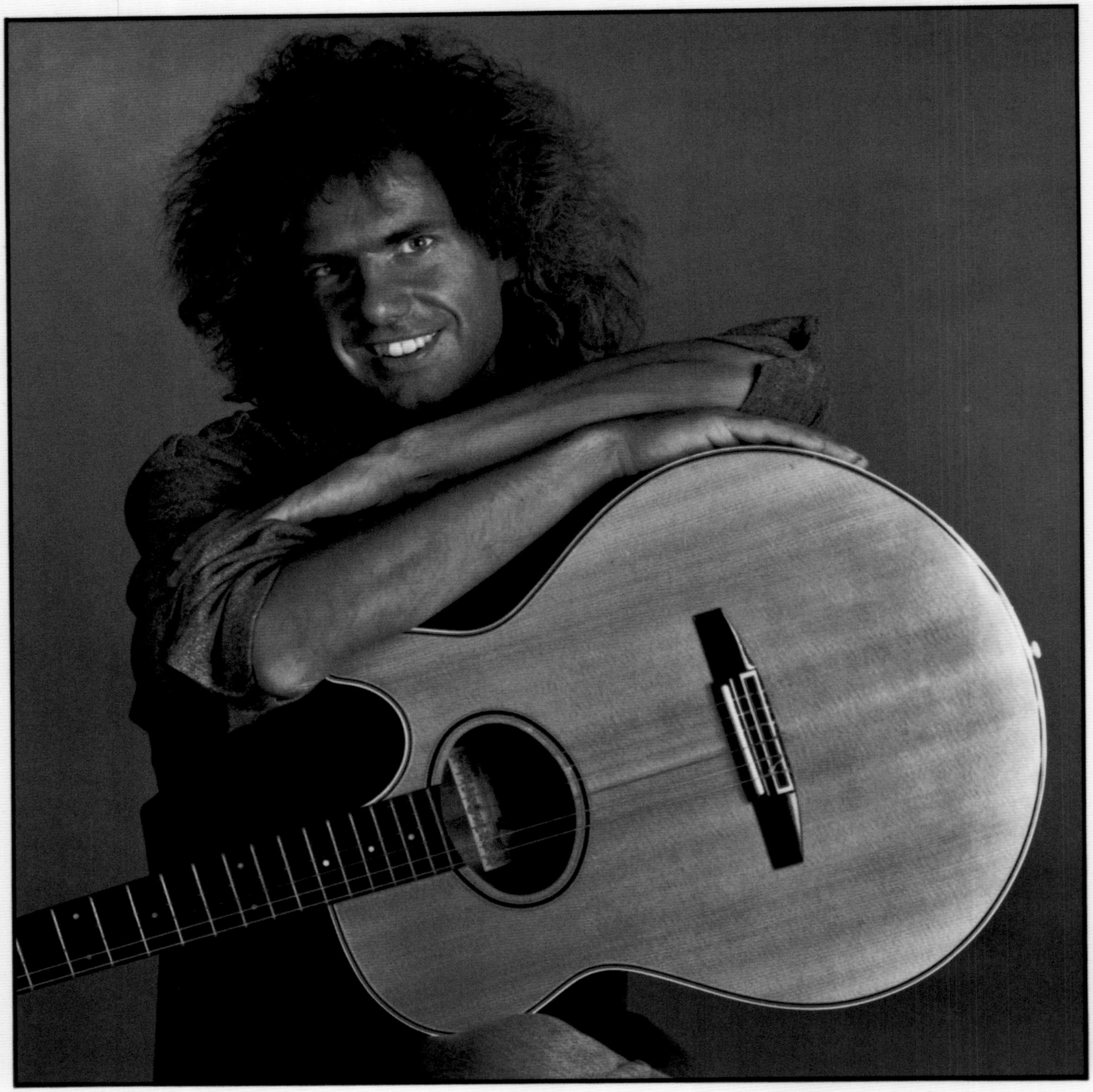

Photo Credit: Jesse Frohman

PAT METHENY GROUP

GEFFEN RECORDS

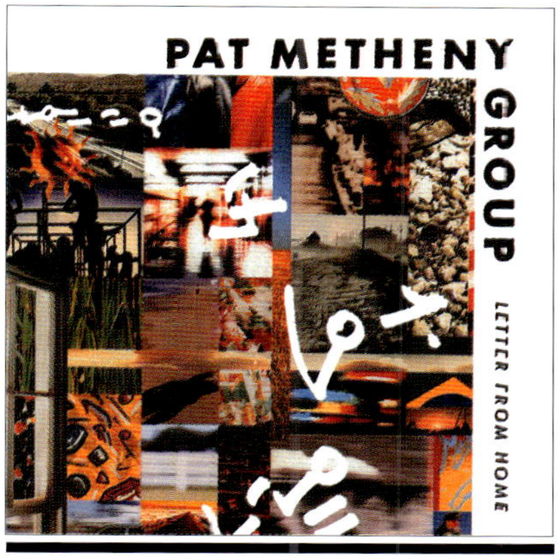

Billboard 200: *Letter from Home* (#66)

Letter from Home earned Pat Metheny Group a fourth Grammy, the award for Best Jazz Fusion Performance.

TWO YEARS removed from the biggest-selling album of his group's career, *Still Life (Talking),* virtuoso guitarist Pat Metheny was back with *Letter from Home*, which he arranged and produced with orchestration help from co-writer and fellow Pat Metheny Group member Lyle Mays.

"It's not a radical departure from our last few records—instead of expanding into wider stylistic zones, we've gone deeper into the jazz/rock concepts we'd already established, putting electric and acoustic instruments together," the understated Metheny said. "There's still a pronounced Brazilian influence since a third of the band is from South America (multi-instrumentalist Pedro Aznar and percussionist Armando Marçal)."

With some wordless vocalizing ("Slip Away") complementing the group's extempore pieces, *Letter from Home* sounded like Metheny was aiming for broad acceptance. "But I haven't sat down and said, 'Okay, what's gonna be the strategy to get them this time?'" Metheny said. "In fact, there have been times in my career when I've gone against conventional wisdom. I've seen a lot of people with the same opportunities get lost in the business of wanting more hits—they start trying to guess what people are going to like. As soon as you cross that line, it's hard to come back. You have to play music that you feel strongly about. I play for the listener inside of me."

Metheny remained the rare improvising artist who had reached a wide audience without diluting his art. "When I did my first album, I had been playing for just six or seven years. Now I've been playing for 20, and the music has evolved naturally, without me having to change my philosophy to accommodate anyone else," he said. "There's been a large degree of luck involved—I was lucky to be born into a family where music was encouraged, and I was really lucky to meet Gary Burton when I was a kid (Metheny first came to international attention when, at age 19, he joined the vibist's band for three years).

"All of those factors combined to make things happen for me, but it boils down to keeping an eye on the music. As long as it's the main priority, everything else has a way of falling into place." ■

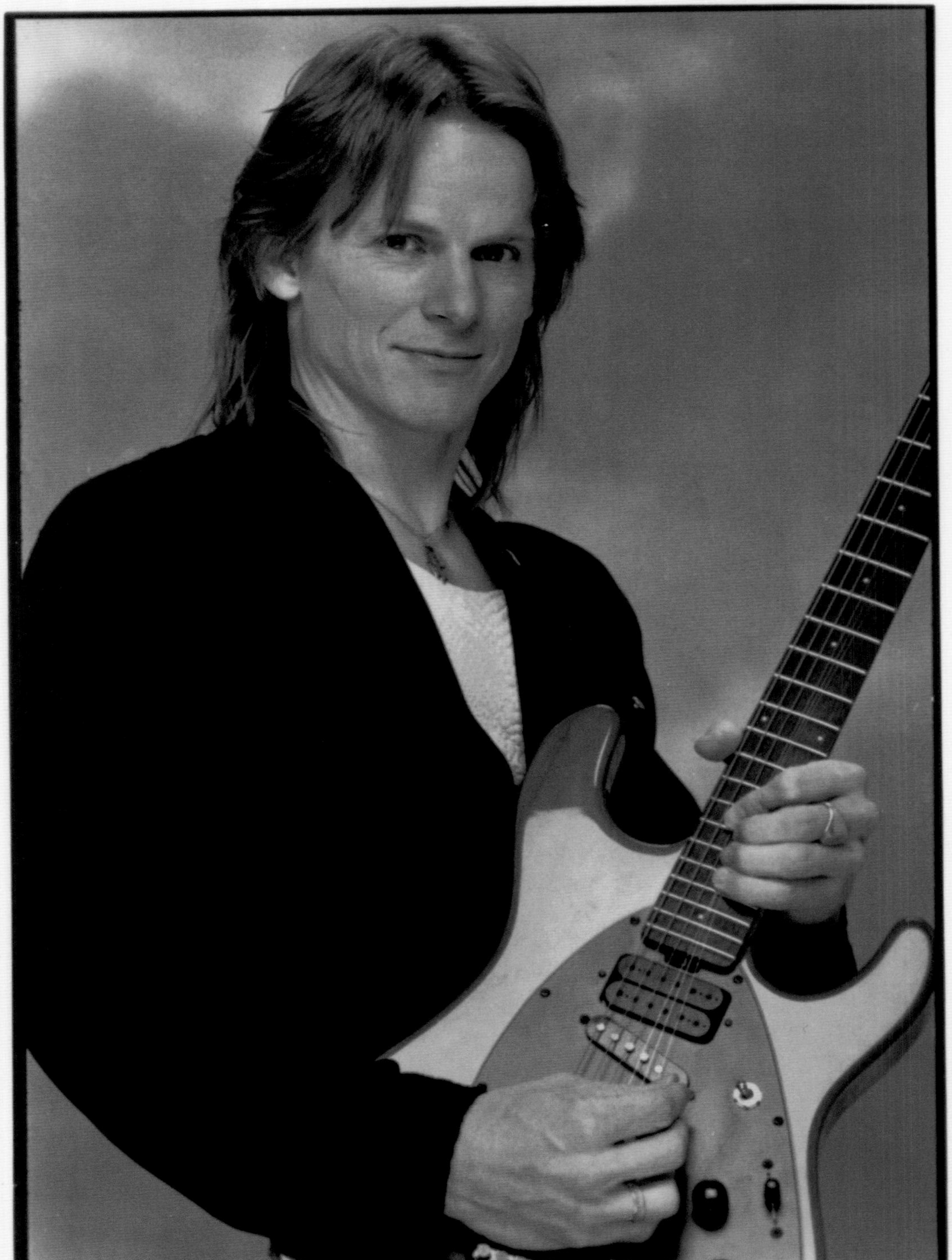

Photo Credit: Larry DiMarzio

STEVE MORSE

5/89

MCA RECORDS

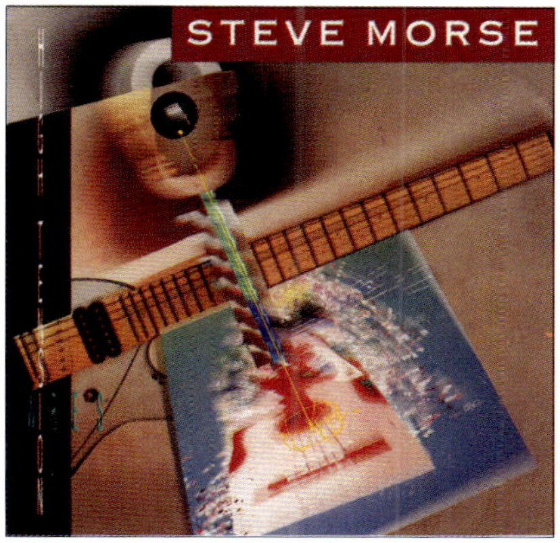

Billboard 200: *High Tension Wires* (#182)

Playing in a less structured environment, gifted guitarist Steve Morse was free to roam on *High Tension Wires*.

EARNING ACCOLADES as a solo artist, bandleader and band member, Steve Morse had been named the Best Overall winner of *Guitar Player* magazine's readers poll for five years running. He was equally at home with progressive rock or classical traditions, as evidenced by the six albums he made with the Dregs (originally the Dixie Dregs) as well as recordings with his own group and, for two albums and tours, with the band Kansas.

"I really wanted to be in the band because Steve Walsh, the original lead singer, was coming back," Morse said. "It was such a pleasure to work with a singer of his talents, and I enjoyed helping revive that big Kansas instrumental sound with my guitar parts. But I'm not going to plan my career around Kansas anymore—they can call me when the time comes, but right now I'm simply more interested in my own projects."

High Tension Wires, an album of typically dizzying fretwork, earned Morse a Grammy nomination for Instrumental of the Year. "I consider it my first solo work," he said. "When you create music with other musicians, there's always an outside element because of the nature of collaboration. With this record, I called all the shots instrumentally for the first time—I used familiar forms with band instruments and certain synthesizer things I knew really well. It's the most unrestrained collection of songs I've ever done."

Morse was a sought-after leader of guitar clinics and also a pilot who had briefly flown a commercial airliner between his musical projects. "When I was a pilot, I never meant to give up music—I just thought it would be great to make a real dependable living for a while," he admitted. "I've risen to a certain status, but that's not how I look at my career. I just like to spread out my interests. I'm not really worried about what to do next. I just want to maintain free rein with my music and see what unfolds." ■

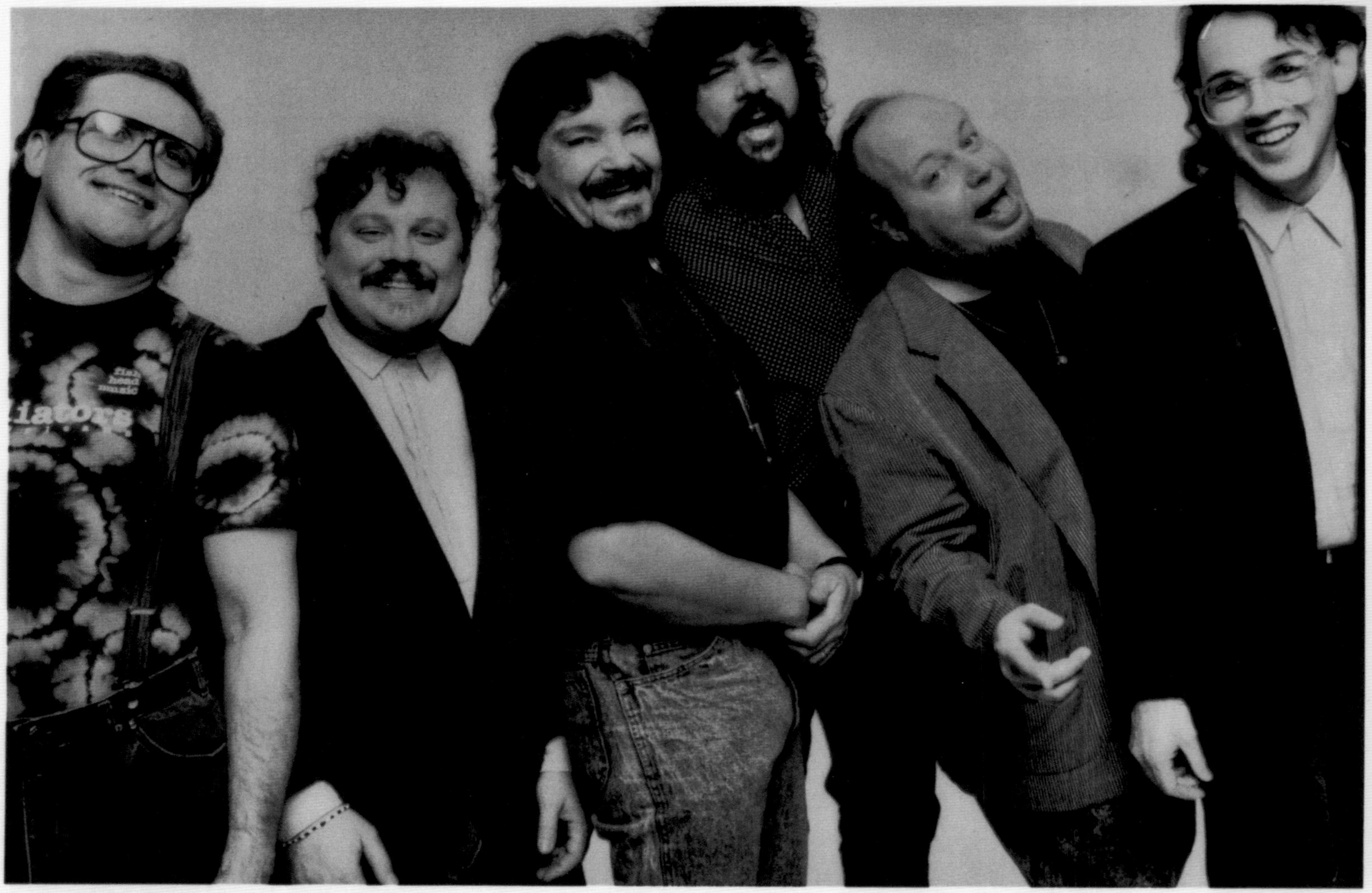

PHOTO: CAROLINE GREYSHOCK

CAMILLE BAUDOIN GLENN SEARS FRANK BUA DAVE MALONE ED VOLKER REGGIE SCANLAN

THE RADIATORS
NEW ORLEANS

Epic
8903

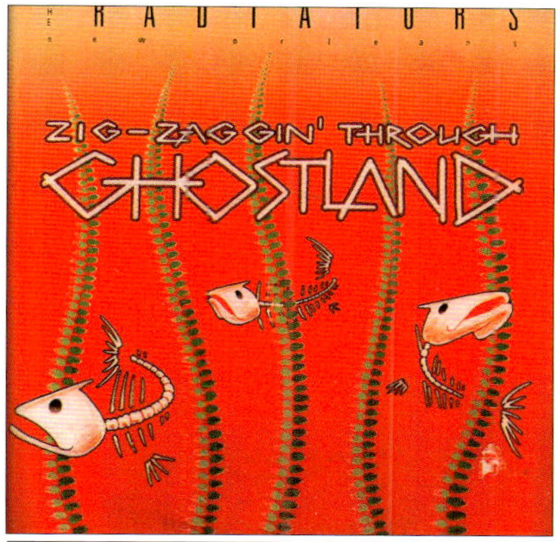

Billboard 200: *Zig-Zaggin' Through Ghostland* (#122)

The Radiators added another chapter to their rich musical story with the funky *Zig-Zaggin' Through Ghostland.*

IN THEIR hometown of New Orleans, the Radiators had achieved legendary status, though they were not a Crescent City revivalist R&B group. "We live there, but it's not like we're the Neville Brothers," bassist Reggie Scanlan said. "Everybody in the group has wide-ranging tastes, from country to Cajun, and it all comes into play."

An American rock band compared with the Allman Brothers and Little Feat, the Radiators' amalgam of influences combined Sixties soul and twin-guitar harmonies with the undulating rhythms of New Orleans R&B. The members' affiliations spanned nearly three decades. Scanlan, a veteran bluesman with an almost Ivy League appearance, was nicknamed "Mr. Sophisticate"—he spent many years propelling the likes of New Orleans piano legend Professor Longhair, Charles Brown and others.

They formed officially into the Radiators in 1978, and throughout most of their career they had remained out of the music industry mainstream. "When we got together, bands like us were cut the door in the industry," Scanlon noted. "Disco and new wave and punk were going on, and we didn't see any place for us."

So the Radiators released privately made albums, and marathon live performances earned the group a hardcore following everywhere it played, notably on the East Coast and the Minneapolis and Chicago areas. 1988's *Law of the Fish* album introduced the band's "fish head music" nationally, and an instructional ode on the proper consumption of crawfish titled "Suck the Head" deserved to be an album-rock hit. "But most radio stations were not amused by it," Scanlon lamented.

Zig-Zaggin' Through Ghostland inserted more commercial instincts to the band's powerhouse grooves. "Confidential" landed at #8 on the mainstream rock charts. A nifty update of "But It's Alright," the 1966 hit from J.J. Jackson, represented a departure for the Radiators, with a soulful vocal from guitarist Dave Malone (brother of the Subdudes' Tommy Malone). "Ed has literally written thousands and thousands of songs, but our record company suggested that we consider a cover," Scanlan said. "There wasn't much to the original. It was simple, but we got a handle on it in the studio, and now it's fun to play."

The title track was based on a nightmarish memory from Vietnam. "Ed (Volker, the keyboardist, vocalist and principal songwriter) was watching a documentary, and they interviewed a guy who used to be the point man on patrol. He said 'zigzaggin through ghostland' was what they called going through an unsecured section of land—if you moved in a straight line, you'd get knocked off." ■

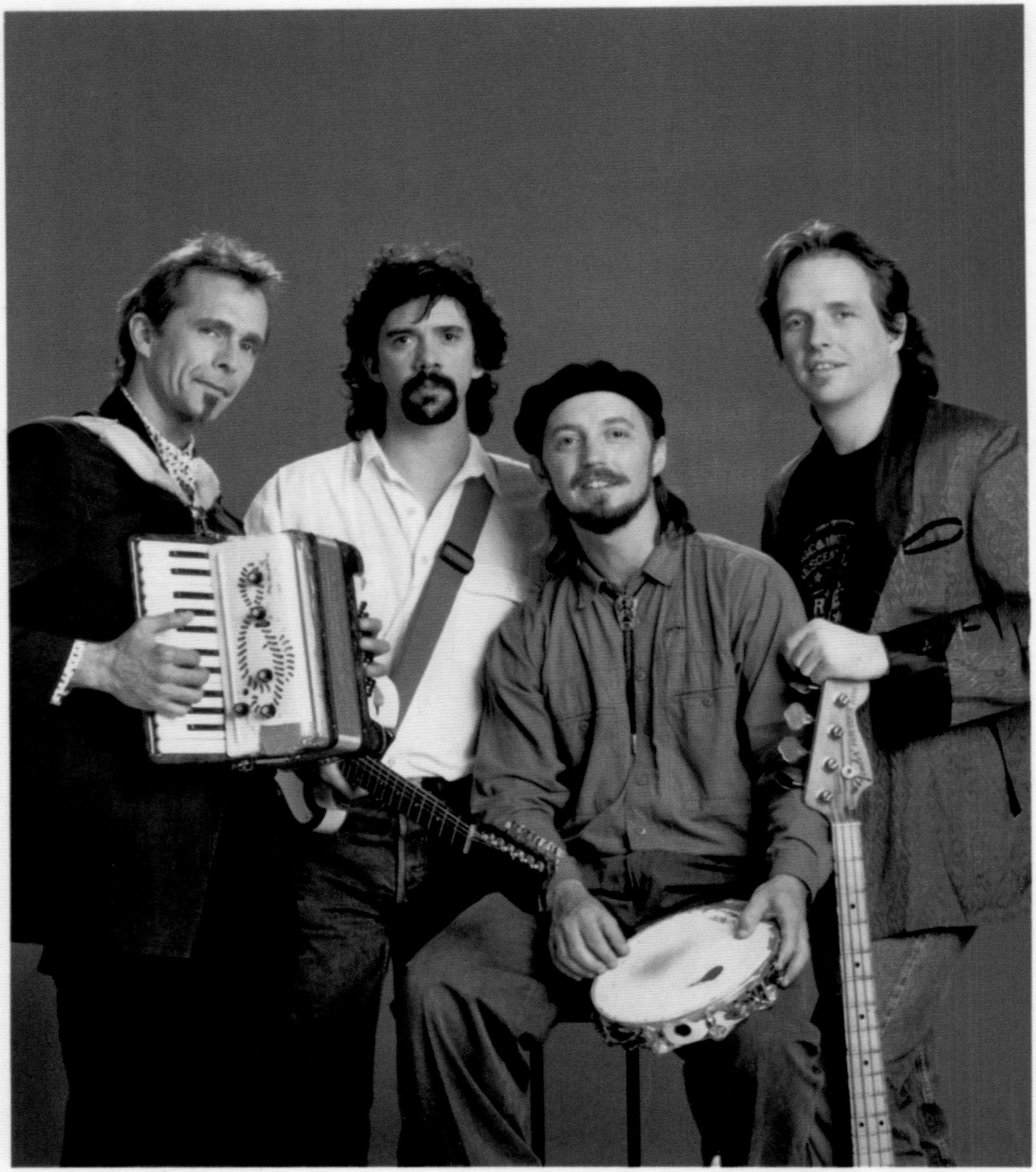

JOHN MAGNIE TOMMY MALONE STEVE AMEDEE JOHNNY RAY ALLEN

the
subdudes

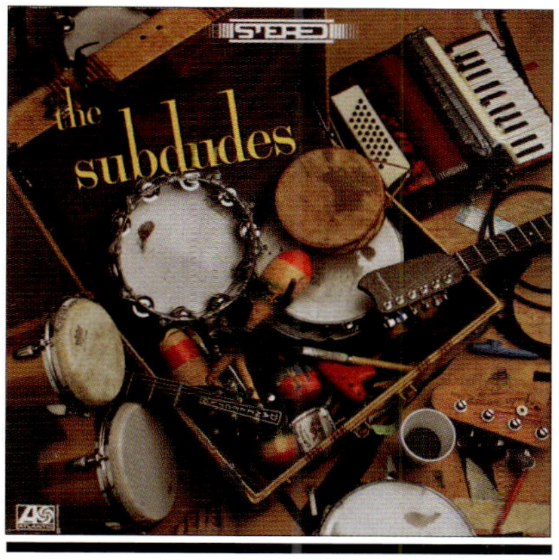

The Subdudes' soulful harmonies, insightful lyrics and rootsy grooves inspired a niche in the Americana genre.

THE LINEAGE of the Subdudes went back to Edgard, Louisiana, where frontman Tommy Malone, bassist Johnny Ray Allen and percussionist Steve Amadee grew up together. They formed their first band in high school, inspired by Malone's older brother, guitarist Dave Malone of the celebrated Radiators. The trio welcomed Colorado native John Magnie as the keyboardist in 1984.

The friends performed in various combinations with other local musicians for several years. But as players came and went, frustration grew. "Tommy and I were in one of those bands around town, the Continental Drifters," Magnie said. "We had some good songs, but they didn't seem to be in the right format. My wife complained one night about how damn loud we were, so Tommy and I said, 'Let's do a night where we play in a subdued way.'"

One spontaneous evening in April 1987, the Subdudes were born at Tipitina's bar in Uptown New Orleans. The four musicians showed up and started jamming, and Amadee, a drummer who liked to travel light, used a tambourine—"It was ripped off from my landlady"—working it as if it were a full drum kit. The scaled-down acoustic sound worked. Later that year, the Subdudes relocated with their families, en masse, to the quiet and inexpensive town of Fort Collins, Colorado.

"I'd had a little time in Fort Collins going to college and I just loved it," Magnie said. "I thought that we'd be able to work there doing our original material. We got to Colorado, and dang if it didn't go just as good as it could, because we were the only band around with that sound."

Amadee's percussion and Magnie's wheezing accordion began imbuing Malone and Allen's concise songs. The band's funky, danceable performances garnered rave reviews from the local media, and a demo of the song "Got You on His Mind" finished #2 in *Musician* magazine's Best Unsigned Band contest. By the fall of 1988, the Subdudes had landed a recording deal with Atlantic Records.

The Subdudes delivered both charm and first-rate chops, mixing elements of New Orleans R&B, roots rock, gospel and country on "Need Somebody" and "Any Cure." The album didn't light up the charts, but the national music community loved the band's mastery of American music styles. They had good word-of-mouth from peers who were zealous fans—Bonnie Raitt, Linda Ronstadt, Huey Lewis, John Hiatt and especially Bruce Hornsby.

"We've been able to meet a lot of people—the music community really loves our record," Allen said. "You can't buy that kind of endorsement, or get it through promotion. The album may not have done as well as we'd like, but when you consider that 80 percent of the records that come out don't even sell 5,000 copies, I'm grateful it did anything." ■

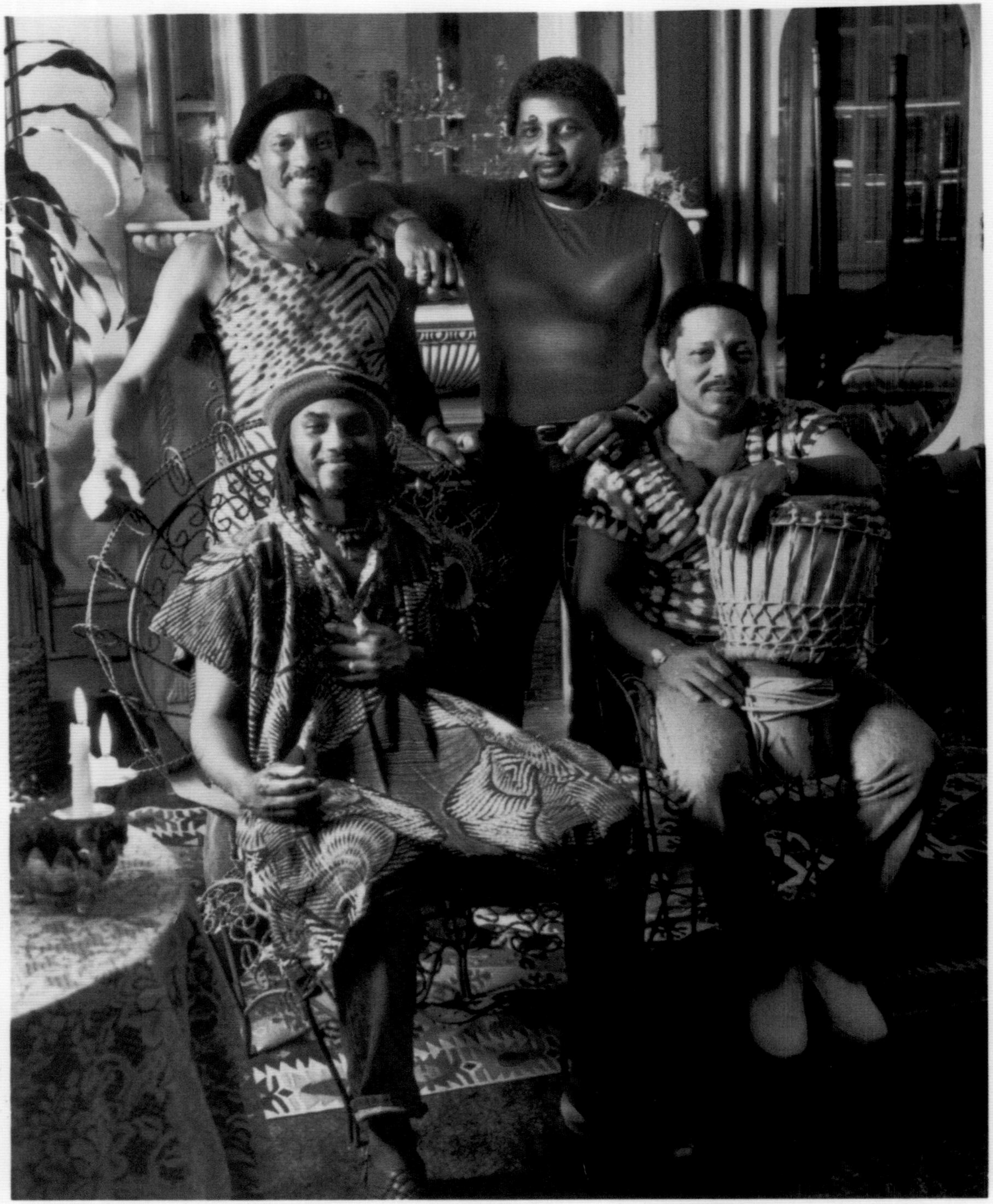

Photo Credit: Christine Alicino

CHARLES NEVILLE
CYRIL NEVILLE

AARON NEVILLE
ART NEVILLE

BGP
BILL GRAHAM MANAGEMENT
415/541-4900

NEVILLE brothers

A&M RECORDS

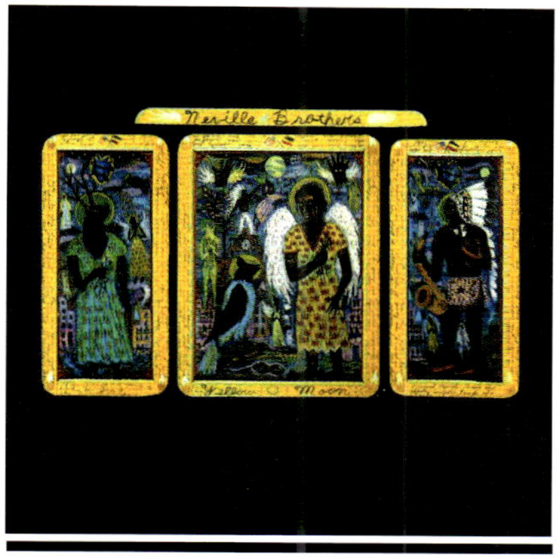

After 12 years of regional gigs, New Orleans' Neville Brothers seduced the rest of the world with *Yellow Moon*.

MUSIC FANS in their New Orleans hometown had long expected the Neville Brothers to become superstars. No other group better embodied the sound of the Crescent City. Despite massive acclaim from fellow musicians and a cult following, the Nevilles' history had been cluttered with bad business deals and commercially disappointing albums.

"We're blessed to still be around—at one point, we were totally naïve about the business side to the music," Art, the eldest brother, said. "For years, we were told we were the hottest act in the industry not to have a record deal. Everybody knew about the buzz, but no one knew how to handle us. We couldn't get out of New Orleans—no promoter was willing to take a chance. It just took time."

The Neville Brothers emerged as a band in 1977, but the Neville name had been synonymous with New Orleans music for more than four decades. Art had solo hits in the Fifties before forming the Meters, who rapidly became New Orleans' equivalent of Memphis' Booker T. & the M.G.'s in the Sixties, playing as the house band behind many productions and recording as an R&B instrumental group in their own right. In 1966, singer Aaron scored a million-selling pop hit with "Tell It Like It Is."

The brothers—Art, Aaron, Charles (sax) and Cyril (percussion)—merged their talents in 1977 and opened shows for the Rolling Stones, the Grateful Dead and Huey Lewis & the News, as well as the first Amnesty International tour in 1986. But the Nevilles never had a truly successful record that captured the cathartic energy and spirit of their live shows, as their New Orleans background—Indian chants, Afro-Caribbean rhythms, Mardi Gras parade music—didn't mix well with mainstream pop.

But the Nevilles finally enjoyed national recognition thanks to *Yellow Moon*, a moving, impassioned display of their talent which outsold all their previous albums. The brothers recruited the services of producer Daniel Lanois (Peter Gabriel, U2), who captured the uniquely funky R&B traditions they played onstage. The album drove home social and personal messages, including Aaron's tremulous vocal on "A Change Is Gonna Come" and a Bob Dylan protest song ("With God on Our Side").

The centerpiece was Cyril's anthemic "Sister Rosa"—set to a rap beat, the song was equal parts history lesson and thank-you note to Rosa Parks, the diminutive black woman who sparked the nascent civil rights movement back in 1955 when she refused to give up her "whites only" seat on an Alabama public bus. The track "Healing Chant" brought the brood a Grammy Award for Best Pop Instrumental Performance.

"We had the patience to want to continue, recognizing that we had something good enough to stand the test of time," Art said. "We beat the bushes for a long time, playing tiny clubs, but we wanted to see what could happen around the world. And it's worked." ■

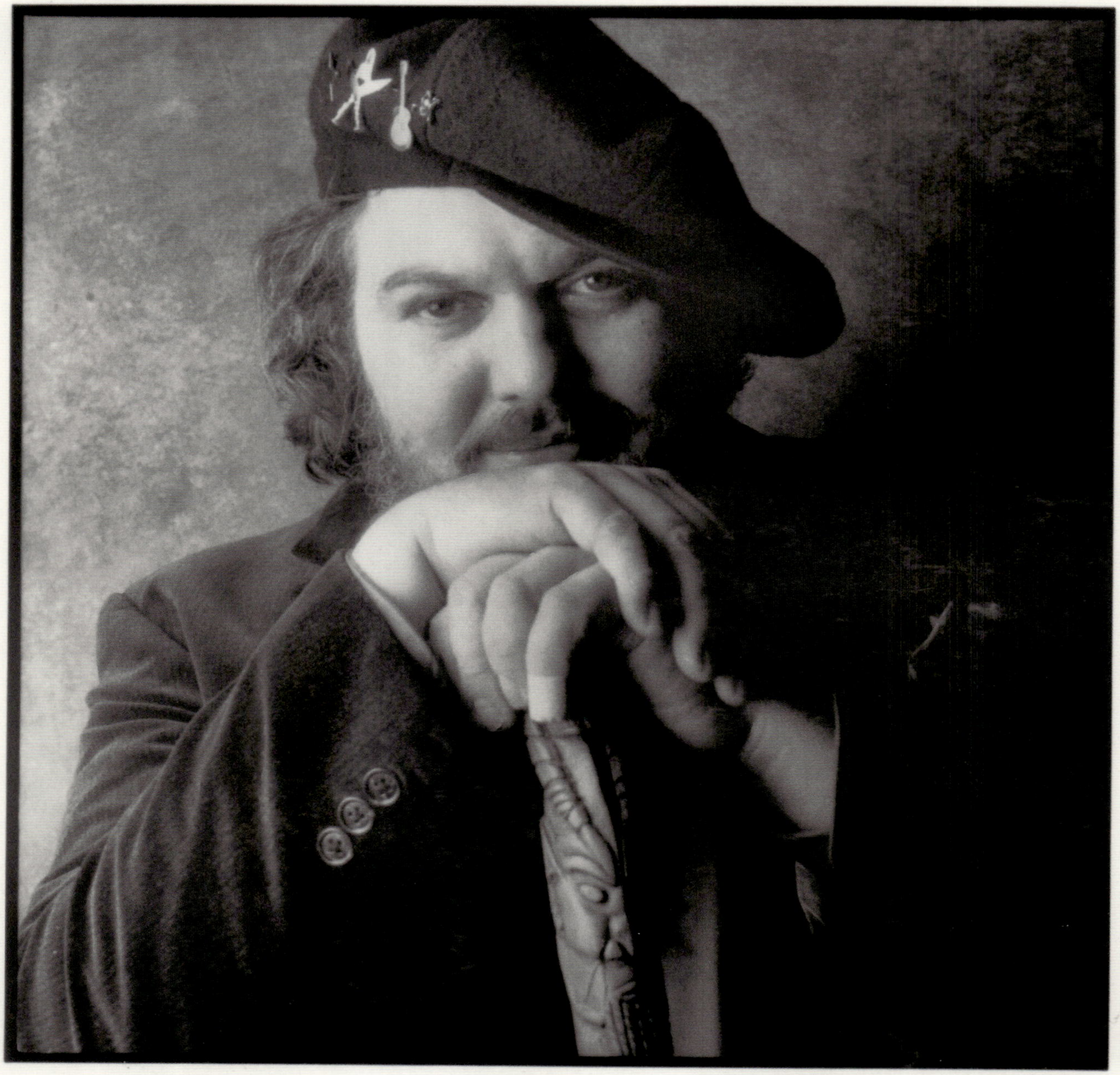

Photo Credit: William Coupon

DR. JOHN

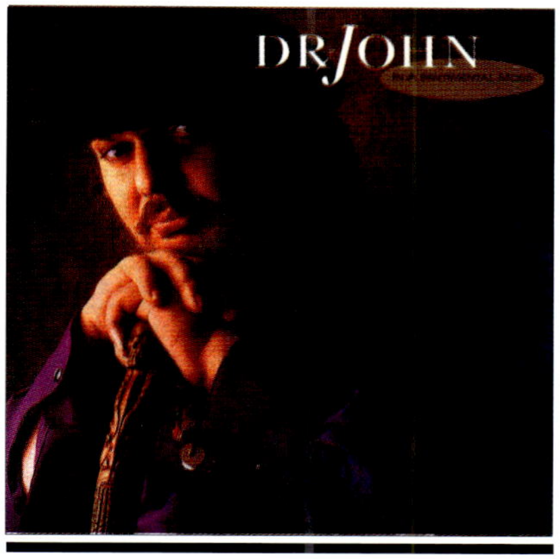

Billboard 200: *In a Sentimental Mood* (#142)

In a Sentimental Mood found Dr. John bringing home a Grammy Award for an extraordinary kind of roots music.

THANKS TO the popularity of zydeco music and films like *The Big Easy* that portrayed the Crescent City as a vast, all-night honky-tonk party, the Eighties saw a flood of renewed interest in New Orleans music. And as a result, Dr. John found himself in demand.

"People get into different things at different times," he drawled. "What I find strange is that people have credited (celebrity chef) Paul Prudhomme in the last few years, that he has made people aware of New Orleans and Louisiana music. That cracks me up."

Dr. John had been immersed in music for nigh on four decades. Born Malcolm John 'Mac' Rebennack, the son of a record store owner in New Orleans, he was already a seasoned session hand and production prodigy by the time he was a teenager. He became part of the bustling Hollywood session scene and eventually transmuted into an enduring character creation—Dr. John, the Night Tripper, a mythic, mystical gris-gris man.

With his flamboyant bayou sorcerer attire and smoky evocations of backwoods magic, Dr. John was catapulted into the international spotlight, hitting the top of the charts with a pair of classics, "Right Place, Wrong Time" and "Such a Night." He took a long-delayed and much deserved sabbatical, then returned in 1978 with *City Lights,* an album that marked the beginning of his long association with the multiple Grammy-winning producer Tommy LiPuma.

His latest career phase included producing (jazz great Bernie Wallace), writing songs (his soundtrack contributions were heard in *Cannery Row, St. Elmo's Fire, Bull Durham, Angel Heart* and *Colors*), studio sessions (guest vocalizing on the Dirty Dozen Brass Band waxing) and commercial jingles (his voice graced musical pitches for everyone from Popeyes chicken to Thomas' English muffins).

In a Sentimental Mood, his first major label effort in a decade, was a look back to the golden age of Tin Pan Alley tunesmiths—compositions including "My Buddy," "Don't Let the Sun Catch You Crying" and "Love for Sale"—produced by LiPuma. "Tommy pulled out a bunch of old sheet music and we started fooling around with songs, and I dug it from Jump City," Dr. John explained. "Originally, we were just going to cut Louis Jordan tunes, but we shifted gears. The Cole Porter song ('Love for Sale') is real close to me."

Rickie Lee Jones shared vocals on "Making Woopie," and the easygoing duet earned a Grammy Award for Best Jazz Vocal Performance, Duo or Group. "I've been around Rickie since she first started in music," Dr. John reminded. "I worked on her first record, and we've stayed friends. That's the nice thing—I've made a lot of friends through the years." ■

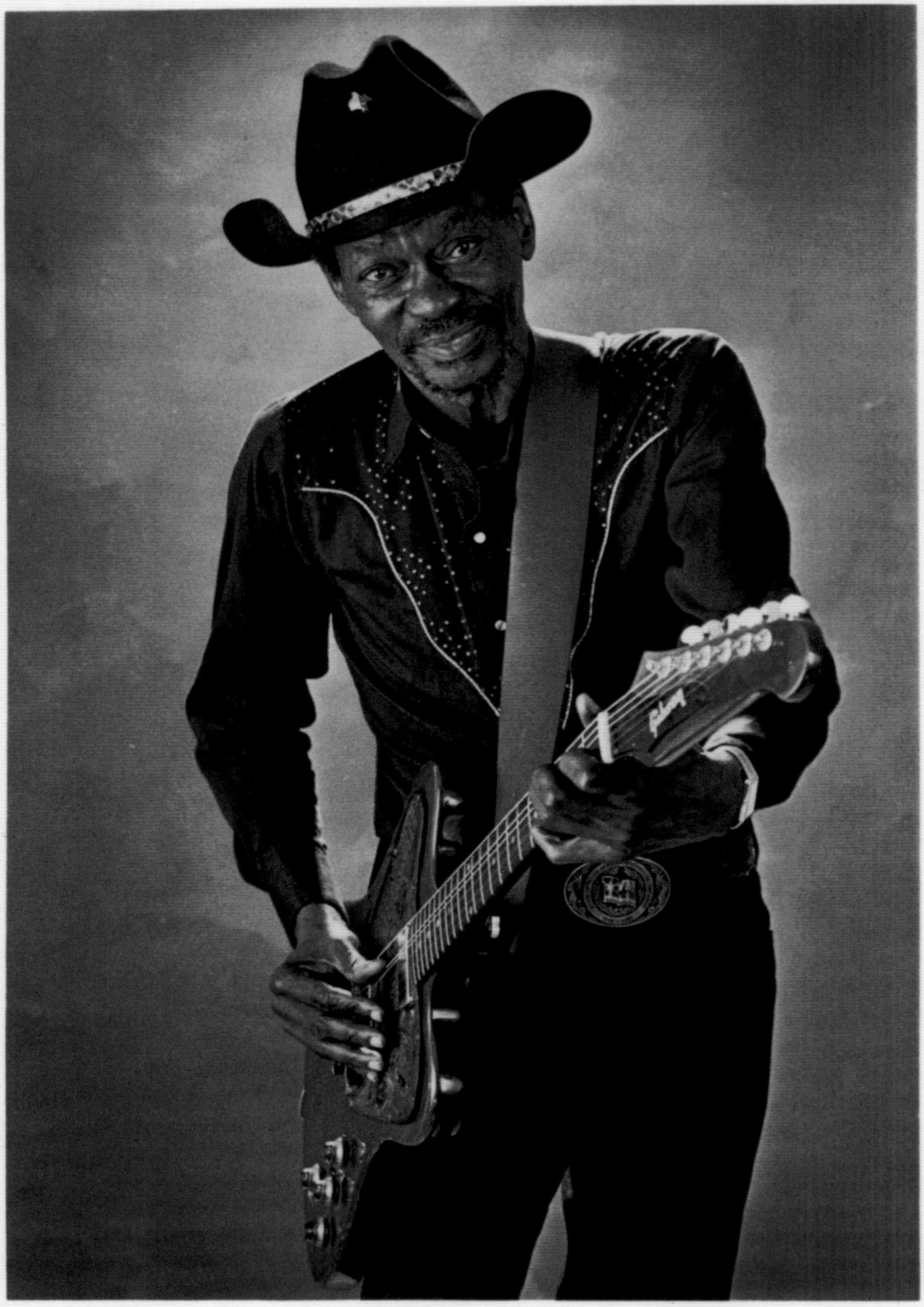

Booking:
CONCERTED EFFORTS
110 Madison Ave.
Newtonville, MA 02160
(617) 969-0810

CLARENCE "GATEMOUTH" BROWN

Photo: Robert Barclay

ALLIGATOR RECORDS
Box 60234
Chicago, IL 60660
(312) 973-7736

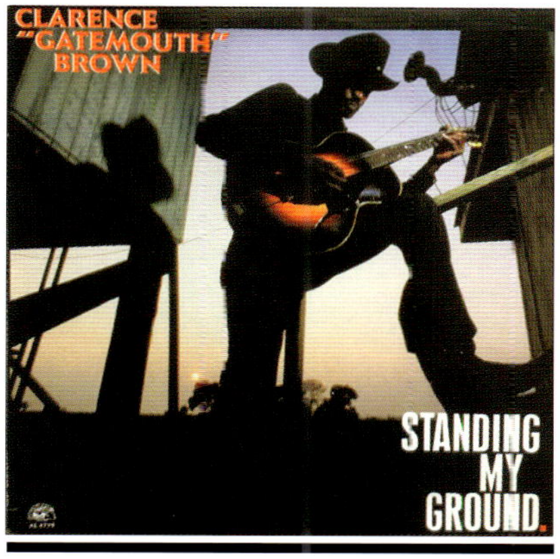

Well into his sixties, the distinguished Clarence "Gatemouth" Brown maintained his hectic touring schedule.

THE WELL-PUBLICIZED musical acts who had performed in far-flung corners of the world had nothing on Clarence "Gatemouth" Brown. "Hey, I've still got good health, a lot of speed at 64," the venerable guitarist said. "I'm still a goodwill ambassador for the US State Department. They sent me to Nicaragua and Honduras. I've been to Russia and parts of Africa, too, and I stayed six weeks in each country."

Explaining his tours to such politically tense areas, Brown replied, "People can't come to me, so I go to them. See, most of these young rock bands go behind the Iron Curtain for ten days or so and make a big deal out of it to get attention. I just go to remote places and play music. That's how I get my recognition."

Brown had remained engaging and persuasive while bringing his "American World Music, Texas Swing"—blending big band swing, downhome blues, funk, jazz and zydeco—to global audiences. In support of his *Standing My Ground* album, he endured subzero temperatures in Alaska to perform a series of sold-out shows. "That's because no one can copy what I do," he explained. "Yet that's made my career much harder."

Standing My Ground gave promience to Brown's acclaimed multi-instrumental abilities—he played guitar, fiddle, piano and drums—and the impressive variety of his musical leanings. Although widely perceived as a Texas bluesman, in the Eighties he'd weaved in the R&B, country, jazz and Cajun influences he heard while growing up in Louisiana and Texas.

Brown had no plans to decrease his workload. "I'm fine," he assured. "Heck, I still do a lot of the driving between gigs—I did 285 miles by myself the other night. I'm not gonna quit playing. I don't see why a person should retire unless he has to." ■

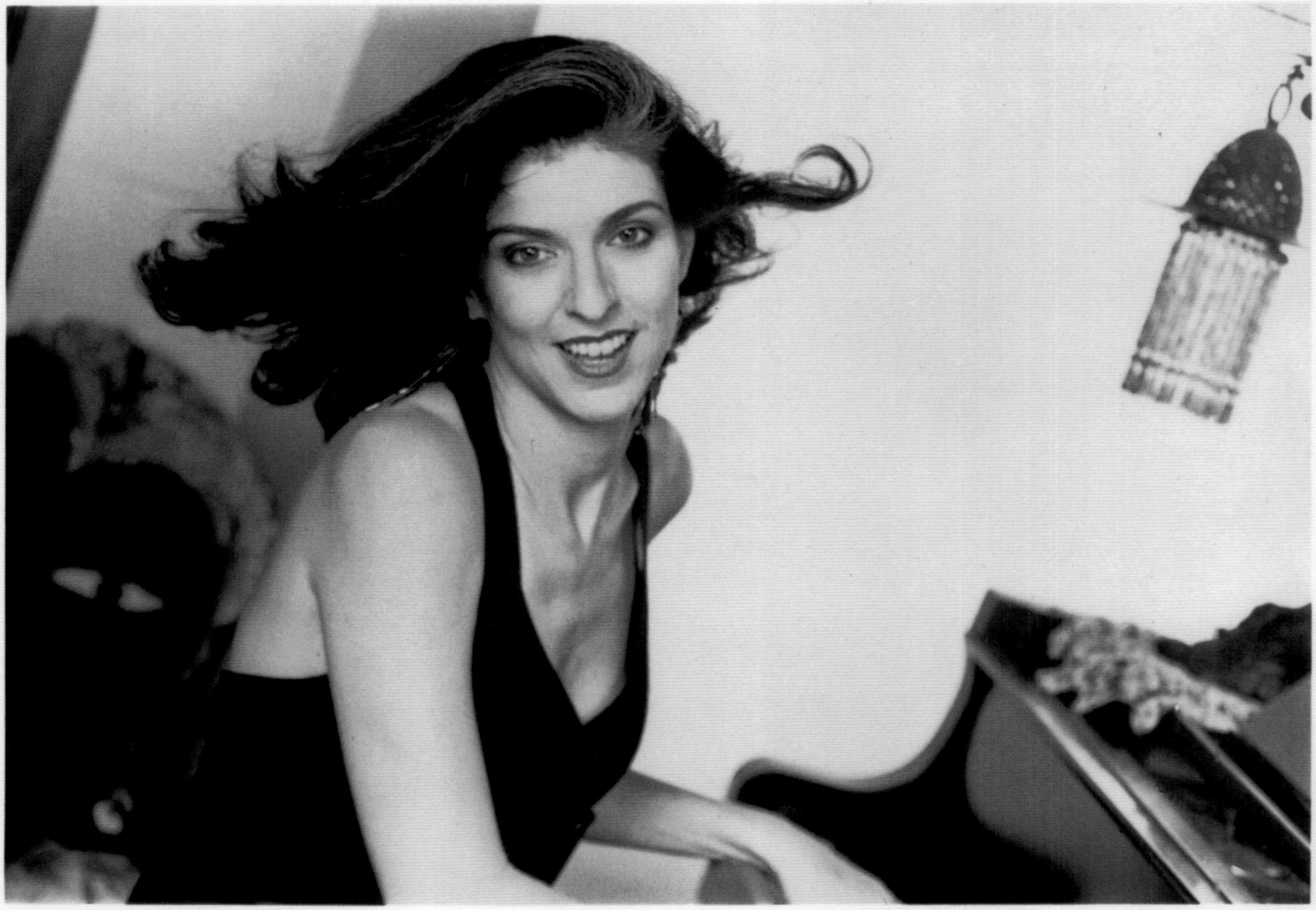

Photography © 1989 Mark A. Guerra

ATS Management
Carlyne Majer
8306 Appalachian Dr.
Austin, Texas 78759
(512) 338 – 1991

MarciaBall
gatorhythms

ROUNDER
Rounder Records
One Camp Street
Cambridge, MA 0214
617–354–0700

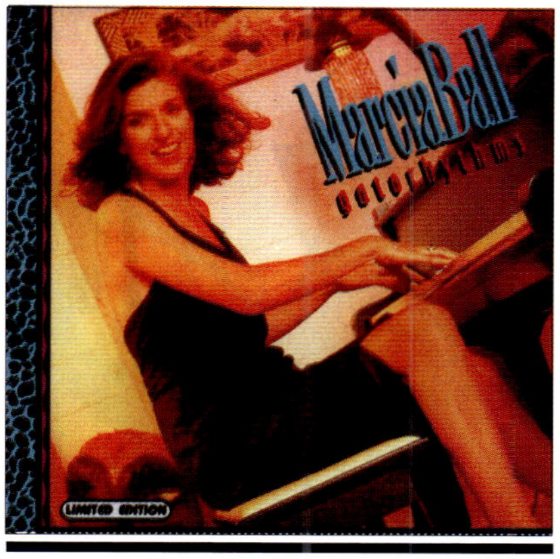

As Marcia Ball won a loyal audience through her energetic live shows, *Gatorhythms* connected with blues buffs.

A RESIDENT of the Lone Star state for many years, Marcia Ball was billed as the "Queen of the Texas Blues." But she grew up in southern Louisiana, banging out ragtime tunes and absorbing the piano wizardry of New Orleans masters like Professor Longhair and Fats Domino. She didn't discover the blues until she moved to Texas. The influences of both locales ran through her music.

"Having grown up being exposed to a lot of R&B and soul, they're old and familiar to me," Ball said. "I didn't discover Clifton Chenier in the Eighties, I discovered his music when I was eight. So I'm not particularly contemporary. Guitars are rock 'n' roll instruments. My music is piano-based and leans so much toward R&B."

The long-legged songstress had refined her easy onstage charm in honky-tonks, juke joints and roadhouses all over the South, her regular "crawfish circuit" where she was still primarily a regional performer. "There have been reasons for that, having to do with raising kids and not being in the musical mainstream," Ball said. "But now the mainstream seems to be moving toward interest in R&B, soul and zydeco music."

Gatorhythms, Ball's third album, featured seven original songs produced by her, ranging from the Cajun sass of "Daddy Said" to the bluesy strut of "The Power of Love." It was her best work—and her most personal.

"I never had the confidence to put those songs together," she said. "I finally told myself it was time to do it, and it took several years and a lot of encouragement to get them done. I didn't know what I was going to end up with. But I'd like to go as far as I can with it. I've never turned my back on my profession. There's always someplace new to play, and I'm glad to go there. The work doesn't get any harder if you're more successful. I just want more quality work." ■

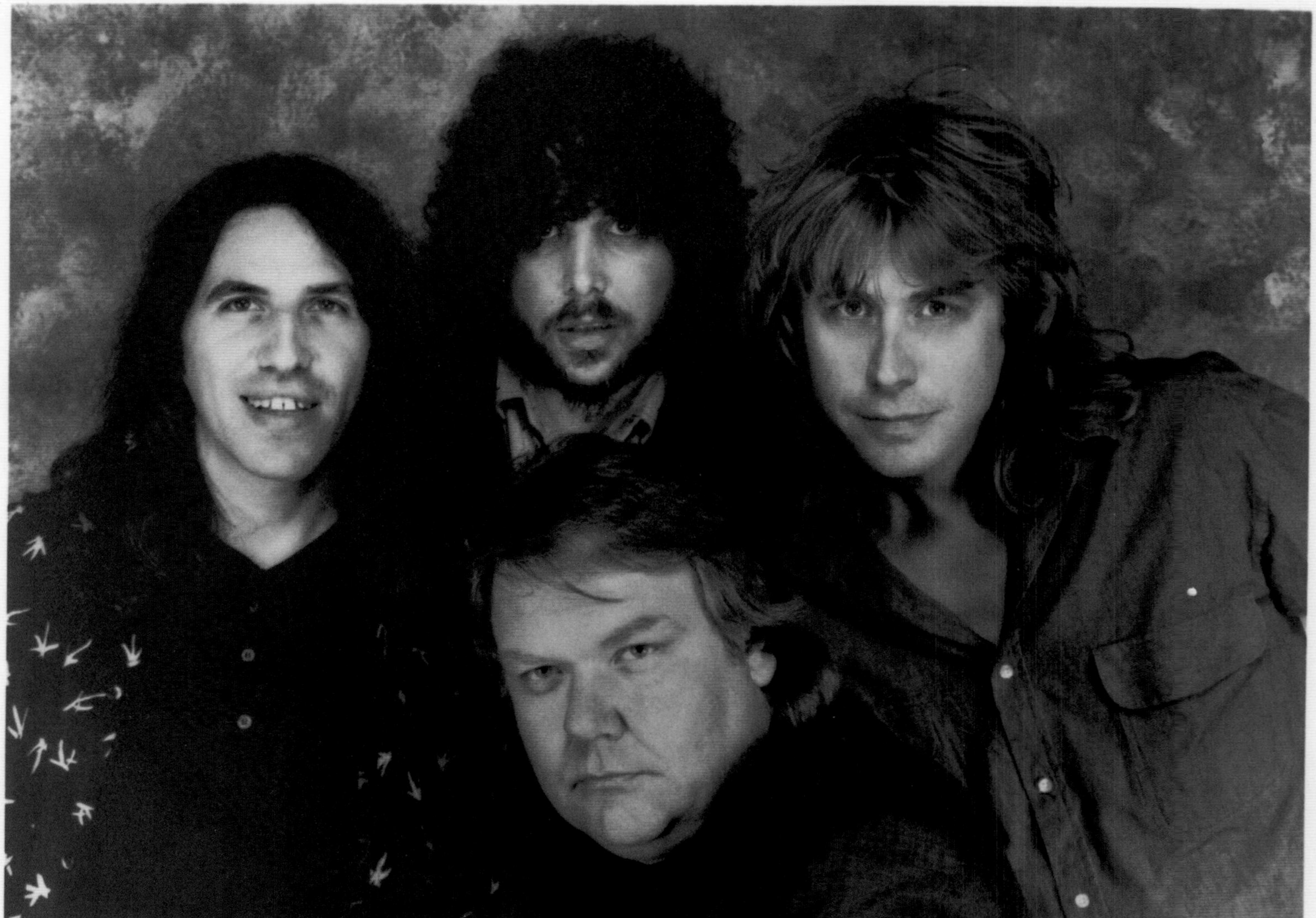

Photo Credit: Waring Abbott

NRBQ

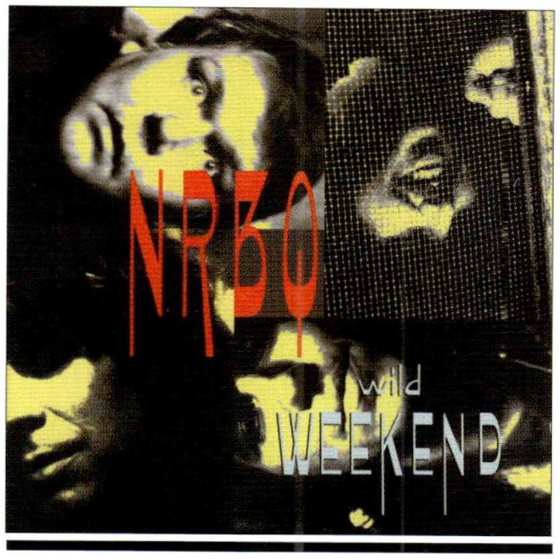

Billboard 200: *Wild Weekend* (#198)

Having a last hurrah with a major record label, the members of NRBQ released the idiosyncratic *Wild Weekend*.

WHILE MANY new bands went for a mix-and-match style of music, NRBQ had jumbled virtually every American pop idiom for over two decades. Standing for New Rhythm and Blues Quartet, NRBQ had been called the best-kept secret in rock 'n' roll, playing wacky sets in hundreds of clubs.

"The first time I heard the phrase 'roots rock' a few years ago, I wanted to throw up," keyboardist Terry Adams said. "People keep bringing it up, and I don't know what it means—if it doesn't have roots in it, it can't be rock. And we object to being called 'the world's greatest bar band.' It insinuates that we drink beer and play old R&B tunes—that's definitely not what we are. I just think we've been given some kind of talent, and we enjoy playing. As long as people deal with the music, that's all I care about."

The band's artistry was combined with a goofy eclecticism—songs drawn from rock and swing, Sixties schlock and children's music. NRBQ was at its explosive, comic best live. "We can't predict how a certain night will go," Adams said. "We know zillions of songs."

Past shows had seen bouts with professional wrestler Captain Lou Albano, an exploding Cabbage Patch Doll skit and a request-a-song-any-song Magic Box. The record industry suspected that musicians with a sense of humor somehow lacked purpose. The pop market thrived on new faces and established formulas, and NRBQ had neither. Since Adams founded the band in the late Sixties, NRBQ had released nearly a dozen records on independent labels, and they'd fallen through the cracks.

"Maybe at one time people were more open-minded—a band could have different sounds," Adams mused. "I don't think the Lovin' Spoonful or the Beatles or the Rolling Stones had two hits in a row that sounded the same. Nowadays everybody sounds like everybody else to fit in. If you have a little bit of imagination, some people have trouble with it. But the public has never refused our music when they've heard it."

Isolation from the mainstream had kept NRBQ true to its own style. The *Wild Weekend* album was clean, fast and loud, a mix of snappy chops (chiming harmonies and Al Anderson's nasty guitar licks) and lyrical celebrations of familiar rock 'n' roll landscape (cars and girls). The set wandered from a romantic ballad ("If I Don't Have You") to an obscure cover (adding lyrics and a nine-bar bridge to the title track, a Sixties instrumental hit by the Rockin' Rebels) to a zydeco stomp ("Boozoo, That's Who!").

"Success? 'Ain't no hoss that can't be rode, ain't no man that can't be throwed'—I say that every time I get a chance," Adams laughed. "We stay together because we're stuck—we don't know how to do anything else." ■

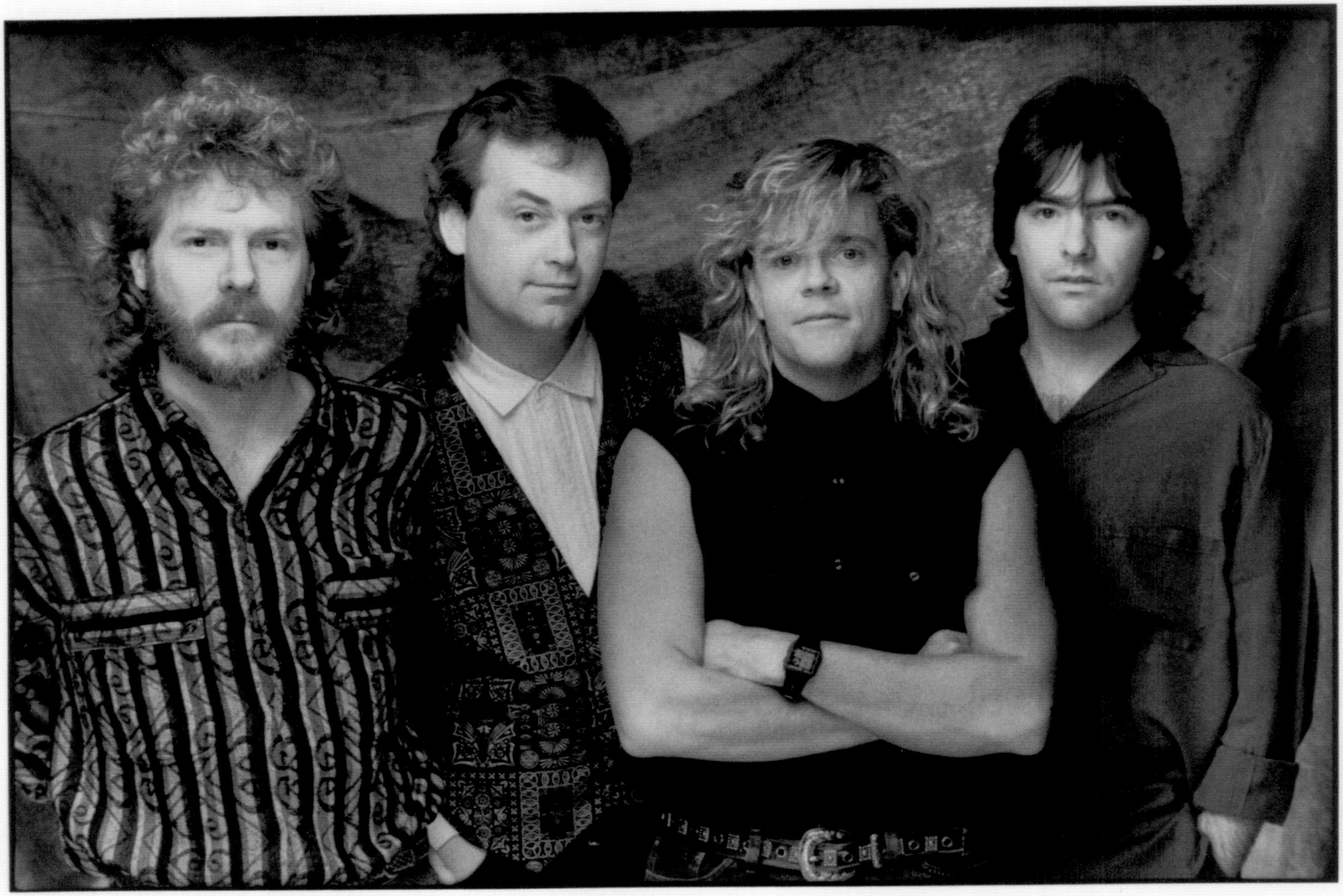

credit: Peter Nash 5/89

Capitol REG. U.S. PAT. OFF. RECORDS

NEW GRASS REVIVAL

Jeff Wagner
Levine/Schneider P.R.
213/659-6400

Vector Management
P.O. BOX 121684 NASHVILLE, TN 37212 615-386-9090

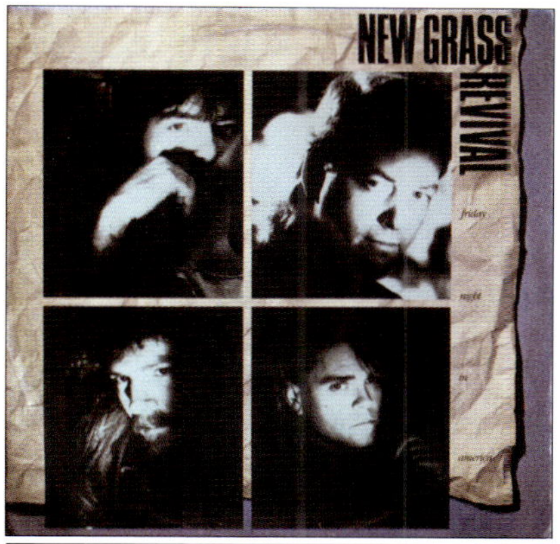

Friday Night in America demonstrated New Grass Revival's confident mastery of progressive bluegrass music.

LIKE BLUEGRASS music itself, Sam Bush was born and raised in Kentucky, where his interest in the music genre blossomed in the Sixties. At age 11, he'd saved enough money to buy a mandolin, and he soon took up fiddling and finished first in a national contest. In the Seventies, Bush was a charter member of New Grass Revival, a band that sparked renewed attention to bluegrass by blending the old-time form with more modern influences.

The first album included songs like Jerry Lee Lewis' "Great Balls of Fire" and Leon Russell's "Prince of Peace." The rhythms of rock had not been done with banjo and mandolin before. "The music was called bluegrass by name, but it wasn't bluegrass by the strict standards set by the traditional community," Bush said. "We were vilified for straying so far from the fold. So we were forced to establish our own circuit."

New Grass Revival appeared at consequential Telluride Bluegrass Festivals, winning enthusiastic approval in the summer of 1977, both for its own set and for supporting John Hartford and Byron Berline. As the Eighties began, New Grass Revival established itself as the most talented—and hardworking—band of the progressive bluegrass movement, on the road 42 weeks a year. The group teamed with Russell for an extensive concert tour, opening with its own program and then backing the rocker for a rousing second half.

"It was a new day—it felt like the gates were breaking open," Bush enthused. "Now the new acoustic music movement that stemmed from bluegrass had gone farther than anyone expected."

New Grass Revival went through numerous personnel changes, with Bush remaining as the sole remaining member. The lineup of Bush, guitarist Pat Flynn, banjoist Béla Fleck and bassist/lead vocalist John Cowan recorded *Friday Night in America*, the band's third major-label album. The Cajun-spiced "Callin' Baton Rouge" became the band's first Top 40 hit on the country charts, followed by another single, the stately "You Plant Your Fields." An epic jam, "Big Foot," was a convocation of astounding string licks.

But Bush had also kept a high profile among acoustic music devotees, making frequent appearances as a session player with artists like Doc Watson, Vassar Clements, Tony Rice, Mark O'Connor and John Prine. After the release of *Friday Night in America*, even though New Grass Revival was more popular than ever, a mutual decision was made to disband. Bush formed the Sam Bush Band and joined Emmylou Harris' Nash Ramblers. ■

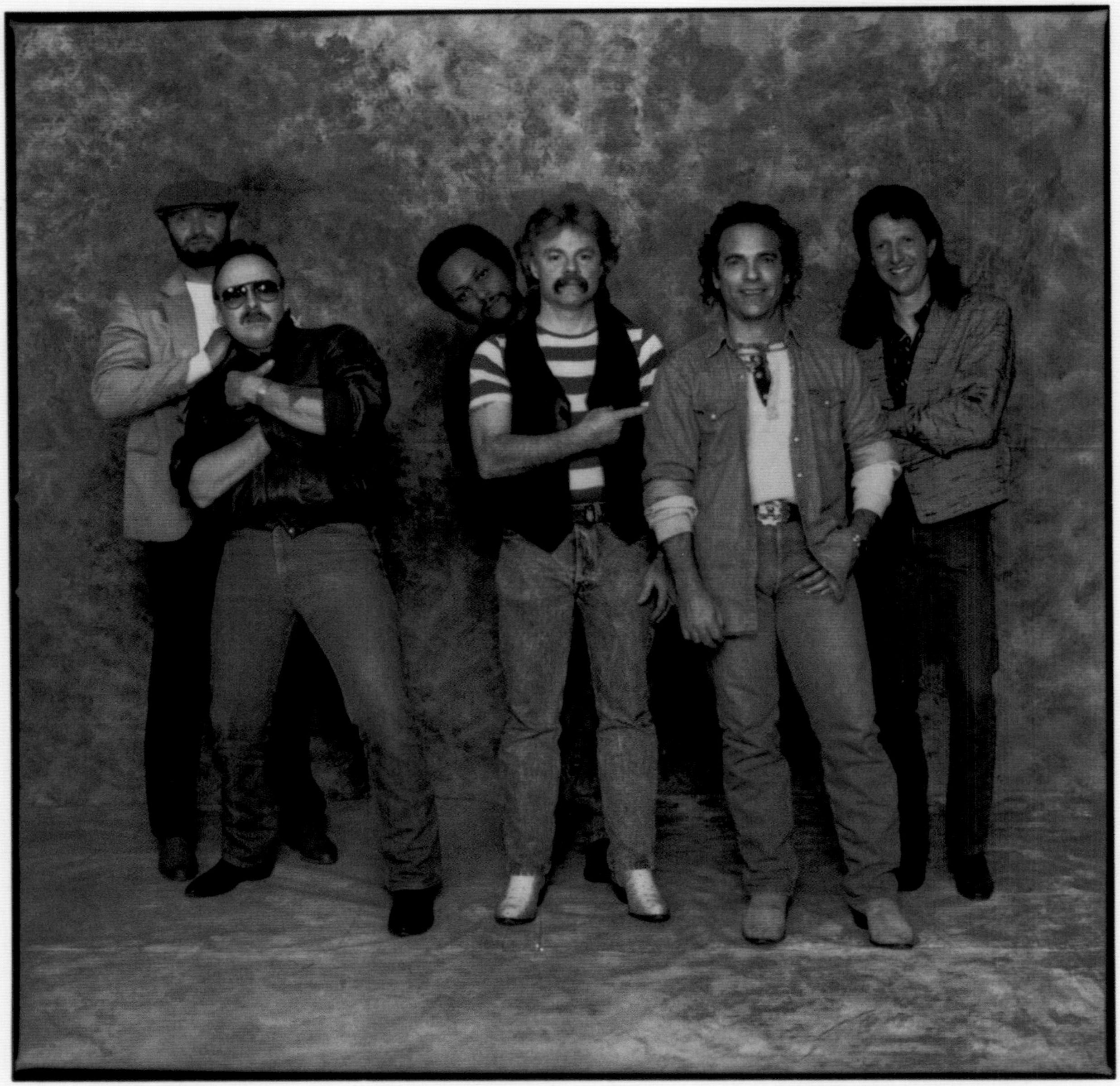

Photo: Joyce Ravid / 1989

L-R: Michael Hossack, John Hartman, Tiran Porter, Tom Johnston, Bobby LaKind, Patrick Simmons

THE DOOBIE BROTHERS

Capitol Records

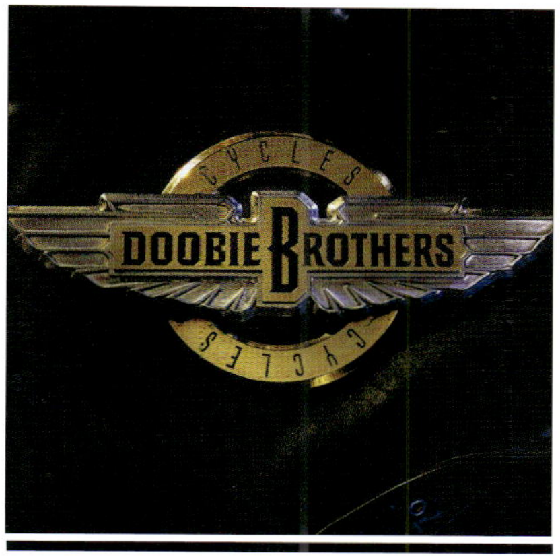

Billboard 200: *Cycles* (#17)
Billboard Hot 100: "The Doctor" (#9);
"Need a Little Taste of Love" (#45)

The Doobie Brothers sparked their reunion with the album *Cycles* and "The Doctor," which stormed the charts.

THEY NEVER had any direct kinship to each other, yet the Doobie Brothers did relate well to a large share of the rock music audience in the Seventies. The band's personnel started to change in 1975, and for the first time since then, guitarist Tom Johnston and the original lineup—essentially the same one that recorded the classics *Toulouse Street* (1972) and *The Captain and Me* (1973)—was back with a new album, entitled *Cycles* because of the act's life cycle and its roots.

Originally known as a hard-rocking biker band, the Doobies (named after California slang for a marijuana joint) started out in San Jose in the late Sixties. The group never thought all that much about a little number Johnston had written called "Listen to the Music"—until it established them as one of rock's most promising groups in 1972. A year later, the Doobies were back with the whooping-it-up hits "China Grove" and "Long Train Running."

While on a US tour in 1975, Johnston became ill with a stomach disorder and had to drop out. He rejoined the Doobies after his recuperation but officially left the band for a solo career in 1977—"I needed to distance myself for a while, to go at a little lower speed and get heathy," he said. The group had brought in Michael McDonald as a substitute, and his vocal and songwriting style eventually came to dominate the Doobies' sound, changing it dramatically from Johnston's hard-rocking tunes to sleek R&B ("What a Fool Believes").

Many people assumed that Johnston resented McDonald's role in the spotlight—a notion that he quickly put to rest. "The original configuration of the Doobies was very much a group, and later on it was more like Michael and the rest of the band, but that wasn't Michael's doing," Johnston said. "It was the public's choice as much as anything—he has such an original sound that it culled him away from the band, but he's a sweetheart of a guy."

In 1987, five years after the Doobies' farewell tour, 12 alumni got together for an 11-city tour that resulted in raising nearly $1 million for a variety of charities. Ted Templeman, who helped sign the Doobies in 1970 and produced all of their albums, suggested after those shows that the original band members—Johnston, guitarist Patrick Simmons, drummers Michael Hossack and John Hartman, bassist Tiran Porter and percussionist (and more recent member) Bobby LaKind—might want to reform in earnest.

The result was *Cycles*, a work that reproduced the classic high-spirited, good-time Doobie Brothers sound. The most popular example of that sound, "The Doctor," reached the Top 10. "When certain people play together, a certain chemistry is going to happen," Johnston said. "We wanted a single that wouldn't lose what we had in the old days but would bring us up to date at the same time, one where people wouldn't have to do a lot of guesswork." ■

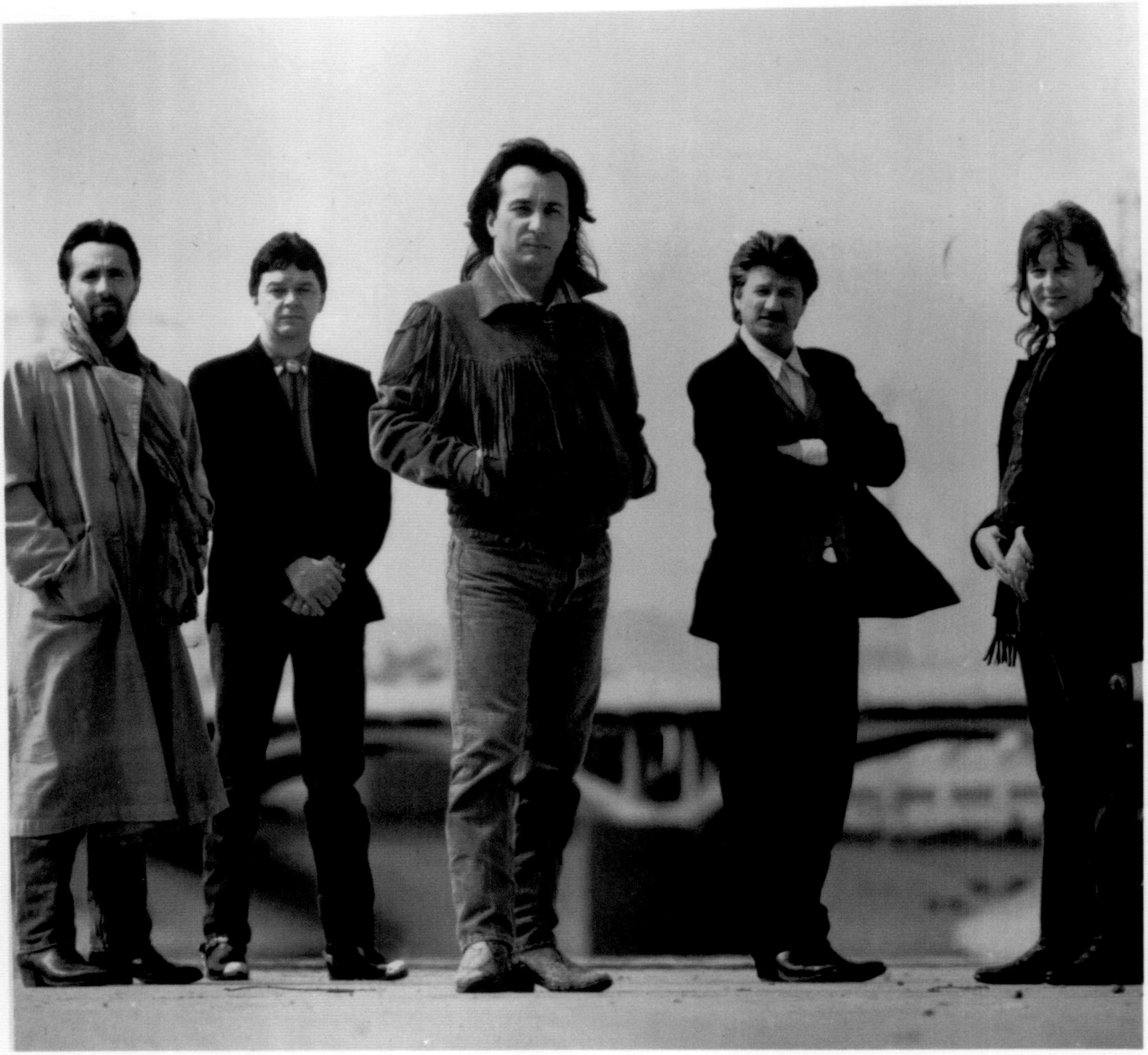

POCO

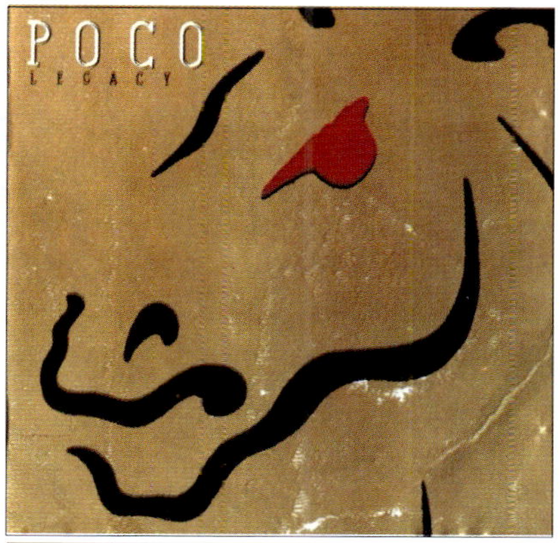

Billboard 200: *Legacy* (#40)
Billboard Hot 100: "Call It Love" (#18); "Nothin' to Hide" (#39)

Twenty years after their debut record was released, the five original members of Poco remerged with *Legacy*.

AS THE first band to combine country music's then-untapped rock possibilities, Poco had assured its place in rock history. Guitarists Richie Furay and Jim Messina, former members of Buffalo Springfield, formed the group in 1968 along with multi-instrumentalist Rusty Young, drummer George Grantham and bassist Randy Meisner. Poco had no agenda or message—the band stood for goodwill and good feelings.

"It's what we consciously wanted to to—take our country roots and incorporate those with popular music," Furay explained. "The nation was going through the struggle of Vietnam, and I thought our music would touch people whose lives were weighted down with that crisis. We wanted to lighten things up, and country music takes on that direction when it's not syrupy with scenarios—'I'm drinking beer because she left me.'"

Furay's gorgeous, engaging tenor and Young's rockified pedal steel guitar were imaginatively mixed with acoustic and electric instrumentation. Yet the group spent years on the verge of making it big, only to watch other country-rock outfits enjoy much greater success. The band changed personnel almost as often as it put out albums. Meisner took off after recording the first album and wound up with the Eagles. Messina departed to form Loggins & Messina.

In the fall of 1970, Furay provided Poco's most distinctive composition, "A Good Feelin' to Know." Frustrated by the record's failure to generate the expected commercial success, he left to form the Souther-Hillman-Furay Band, a would-be supergroup. Acclaim—at least as measured by hit records—eluded Poco until the 14th album, 1979's *Legend*. By that point, the only charter member left was Young, who, fittingly, wrote and sang the smash "Crazy Love."

Poco lost its recording contract five years later, but Young, the one who stuck it through, orchestrated the reunion album *Legacy*. "We had such a tremendous influence," he said. "I thought it would be interesting to put it back together, and I missed my original partners—it was never as exciting as that first 1968-69 period."

Furay had abandoned his music in 1983, becoming a pastor in Boulder, Colorado. At the urging of Young, he decided to give the rock world one more try, and his "When It All Began," a Poco history lesson, led off *Legacy*. A return to the sweet harmonies, bright melodies and boisterous playing that characterized the original outfit, the album produced the Top 40 hits "Call It Love" and "Nothin' to Hide" and earned a gold record.

But back on the road, Furay stated he could no longer participate. Without proselytizing, he had concluded that the rock-star life simply clashed with his religious beliefs. "It's been tough—my life's been scrutinized," he said. "But when I'm in the rock 'n' roll world, I'm not of it. I've got a new direction, a desire to share the Lord."

"A minister can't be in a rock 'n' roll band," Young allowed. "It's too tense." ■

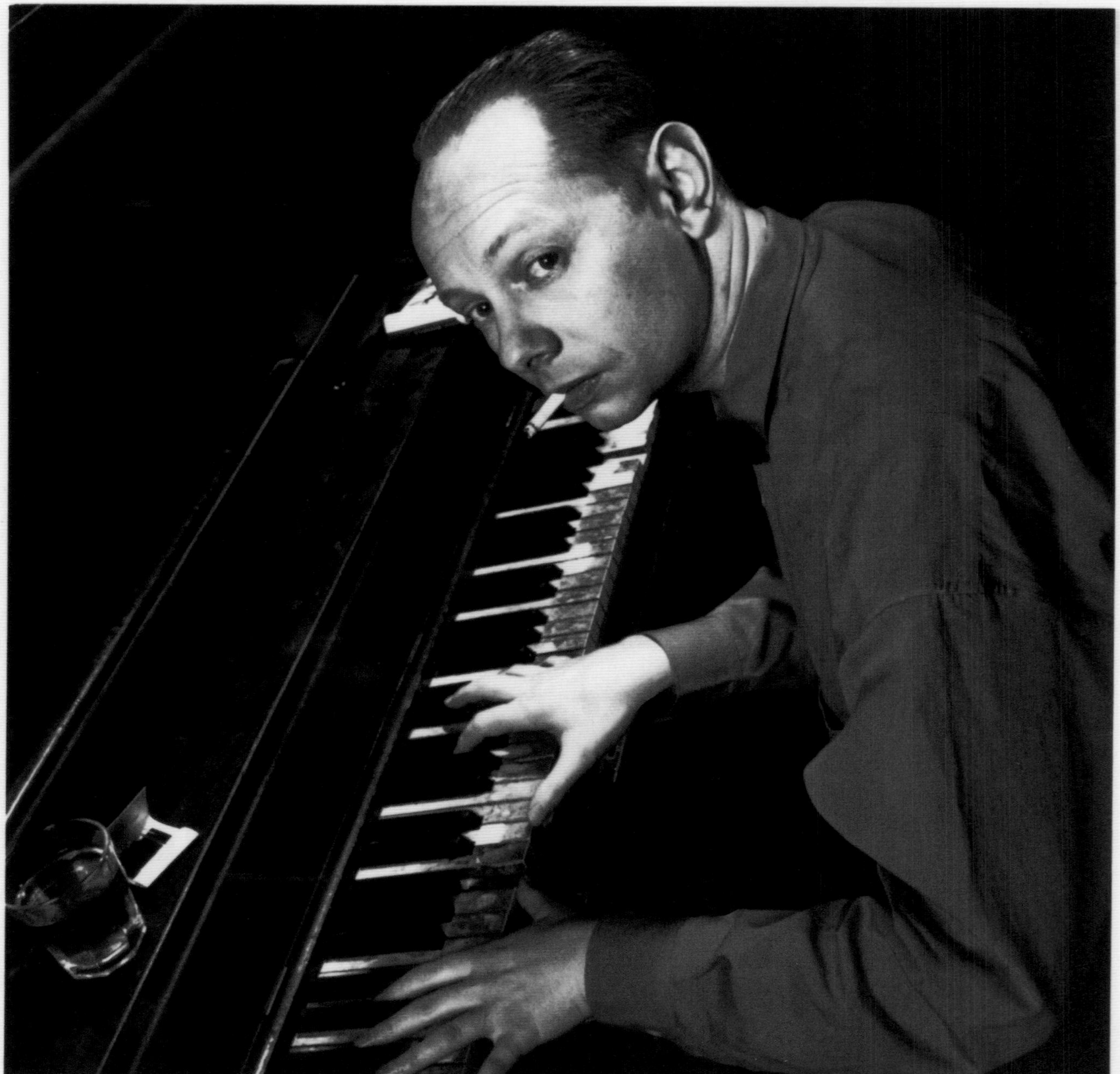

JOE JACKSON

A&M RECORDS

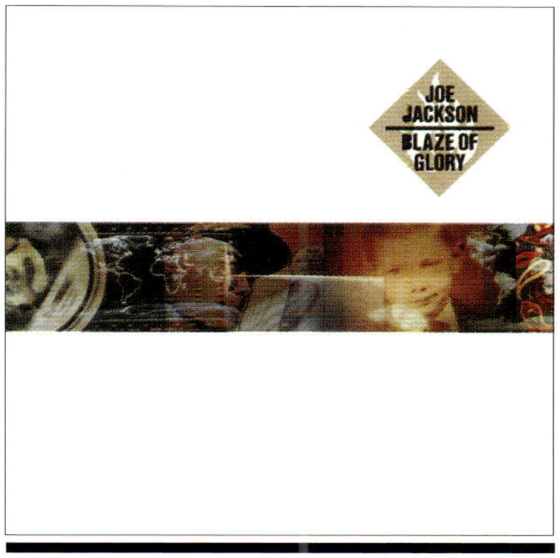

Billboard 200: *Blaze of Glory* (#61)

Despite his well-publicized aversion to the configuration, Joe Jackson promoted "Nineteen Forever" with a video.

FASHIONING A decade-long career out of musical mood swings—from brash angry-young-man rock to jump blues to symphonic instrumentals—Joe Jackson had unashamedly straddled genres. Not all of the efforts had proved equally successful on the charts, but Jackson had come to realize that his goals for art and commerce didn't necessarily align.

Jackson, a crafty arranger who knew how to generate musical excitement, never failed to assemble a crack band to put across his ideas. *Blaze of Glory* was his strongest album since *Night and Day* met with Top 10 success in 1982. With its blend of arcane pop styles, the 12-song cycle was autobiographical but not introverted or confessional, speaking to fans well past their teens.

"It's not a fucking concept album, but it chronicles things that my generation has been through," he said. "The first half is about what it was like growing up in the Sixties and Seventies, and the second half is about the Eighties."

Jackson cited the get-rich-quick mentality and phoniness of late Eighties "instant MTV pop stars." Back in 1984, he had announced his intention to abstain from the making of videos for his music, citing "the devaluation of musicians and the unreasonable pressure to make them." But Jackson decided to produce a video for the song "Nineteen Forever," appearing with a wig, make-up, prosthetic belly and lame jacket.

"I really hate dumb videos," he mused. "But it gets lonely—I got tired of being the only guy who wasn't doing them." On tour, his trademark surly demeanor remained intact, dedicating "Nineteen Forever" to "all those rock bands on tour this summer after having retired several times." ■

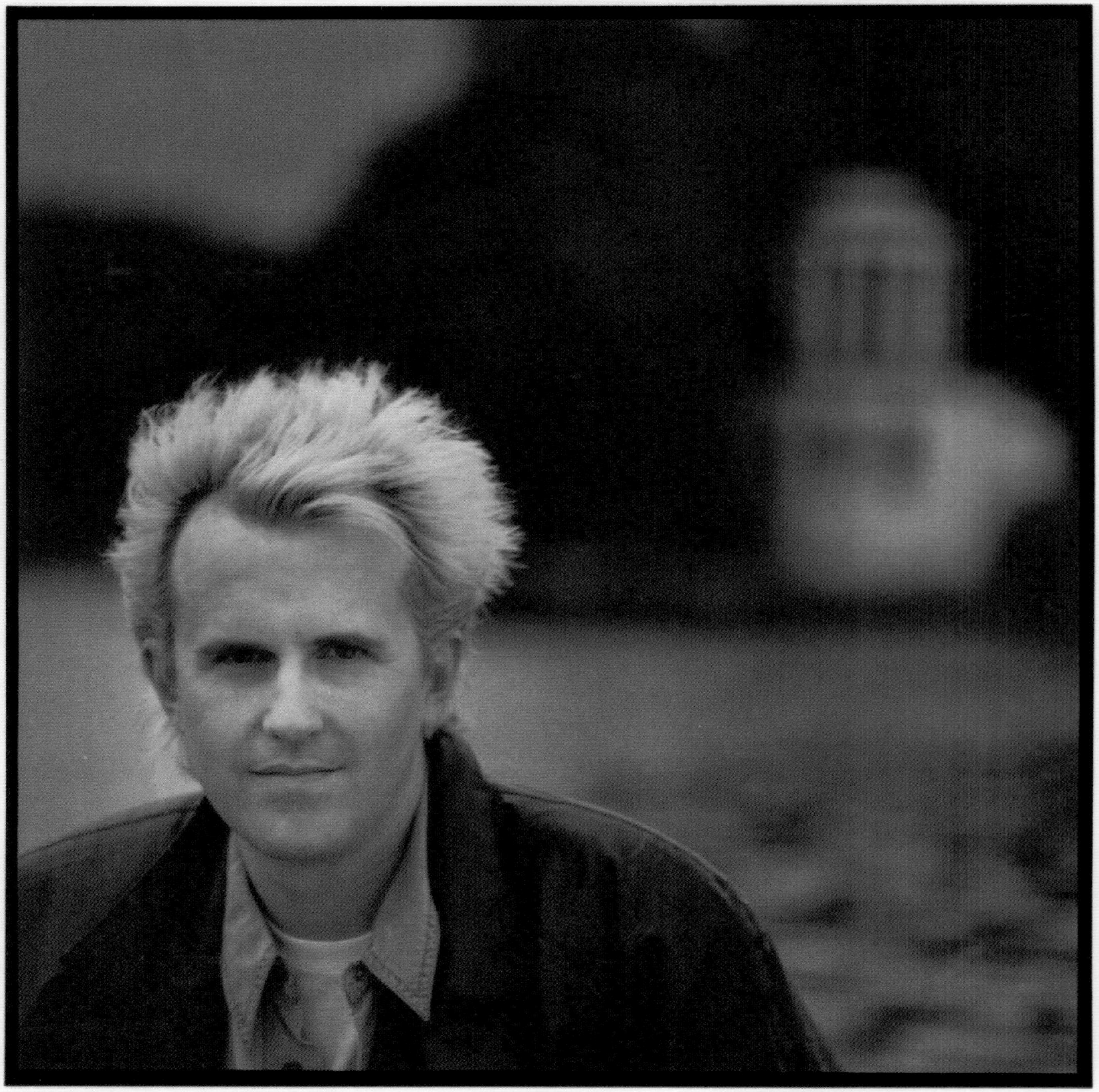

PHOTO CREDIT: SIMON FOWLER /

Howard Jones

ELEKTRA

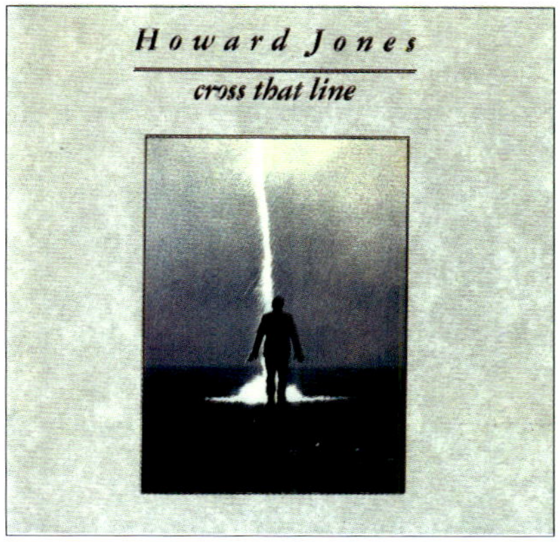

Billboard 200: *Cross That Line* (#65)
Billboard Hot 100: "Everlasting Love" (#12); "The Prisoner" (#30)

Howard Jones returned with "Everlasting Love," which emerged at No. 1 on the adult-contemporary charts.

SINCE DEBUTING in 1984, Howard Jones had scored several standout techno-pop hits—"New Song," "Things Can Only Get Better" and "No One Is to Blame" among them. Yet nearly three years had passed since the British singer, songwriter and keyboardist released an album of his lofty synthesizer music and earnest lyrics.

Jones returned with the self-produced *Cross That Line*. "Actually, I didn't take any time off," he said. "I finished my last tour and went straight into my studio. But I gave myself plenty of time to record the album. I made sure I could step back from what I was doing and take stock of myself, because it had been a mad circus since I first started out."

While *Cross That Line* sported less of a techno edge than his early work, pop still wasn't a dirty word to Jones, as evidenced by the classic hook of "Everlasting Love," a Top 20 single. "It's a three-chord wonder, but those are the hardest things to write," he noted. "When you get them right, it's so satisfying." "The Prisoner" was also hit-bound. "That song is the best thing I've ever done," Jones said. "I'm proud of it because it has such an interesting sound, a lot of surprises in the track—it drops down to piano and cello—but it's still fairly commercial."

The *Cross That Line* material that never got played on the radio—an unaccompanied piano improvisation ("Cut of Thin Air") and more extended pieces—was showcased on Jones' tour of North America. In the mid-Eighties he'd taken the concept of the one-man-band to the limit, with audiences enduring an onstage mime. Now HoJo was on the road with a bassist and drummer.

"When I started out with my first record, I made a conscious attempt to write music that was dressed in the musical clothes of the day," he said. "This album is an experiment to get to what I really should be doing." ■

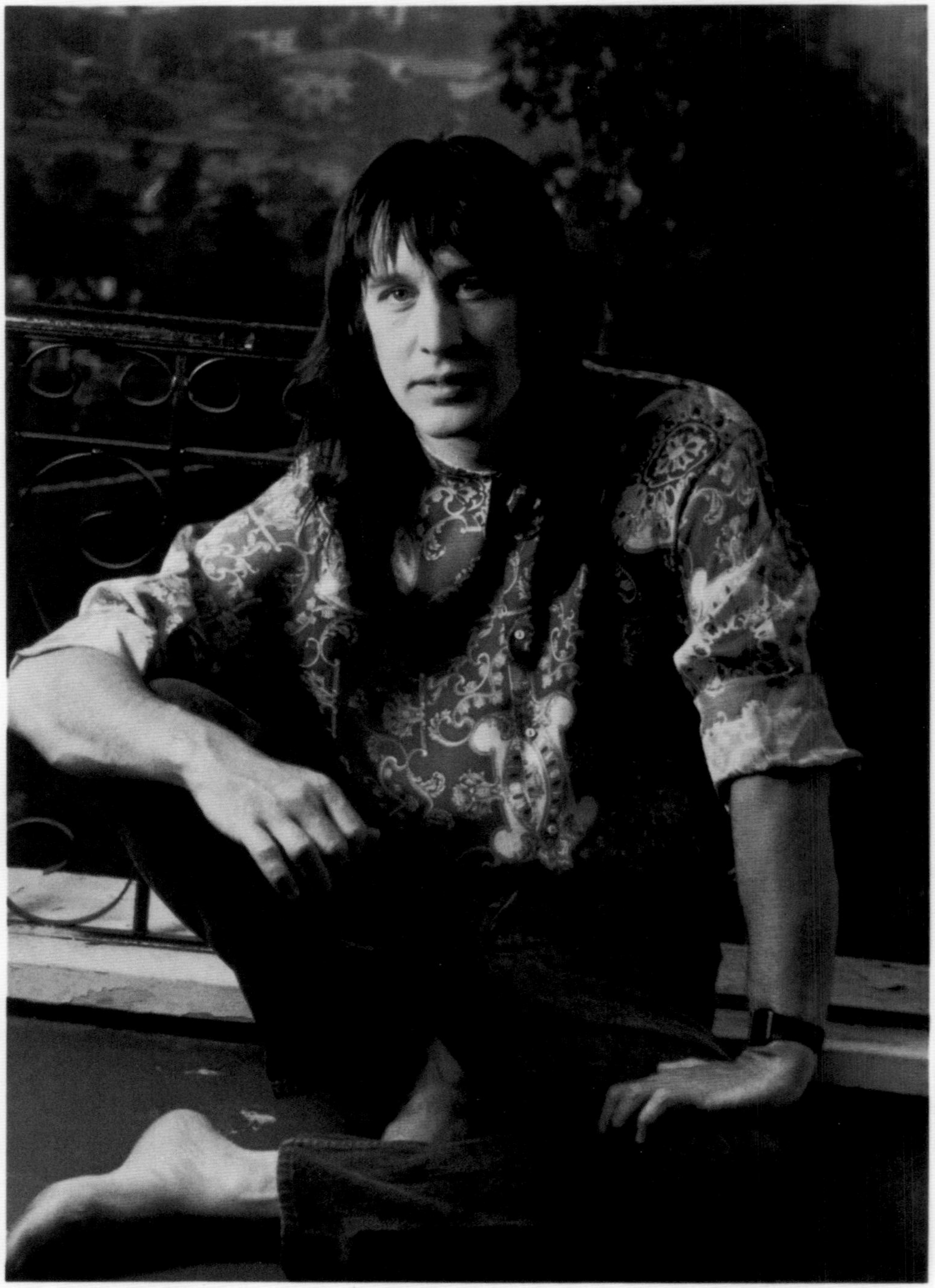

Photo Credit: Lynn Goldsmith/LGI

todd rundgren

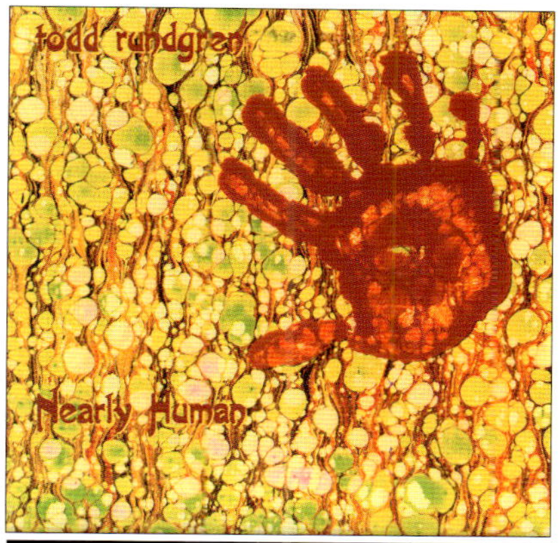

Billboard 200: *Nearly Human* (#102)

Todd Rundgren's uncommon *Nearly Human* album was noteworthy for its spontaneous recording techniques.

LONG REVERED by critics and music-industry insiders as a songwriter, producer, recording artist and conceptualist, native Philadelphian Todd Rundgren had been using computers and synthesizers long before they became fashionable. He became a rock video pioneer by building himself a $2 million digital-effects studio two years before MTV.

But for all his accomplishments, the public still tended to take Rundgren for granted, save for "Todd is Godd" loyalists. He'd never had a platinum record, and his performing and recording career had largely retreated into cult status during the past decade as he delved into intriguing musical premises. His *A Cappella* in 1985 featured just Rundgren's voice and a keyboard emulator to make a variety of vocal-based sounds.

"The only reason I'm still around after 22 years is because there are particular fans who are determined to get whatever message or benefit is buried on my records," he laughed. "Our relationship isn't based on the latest trend. Fortunately, they're a large enough group—I think that's the only reason I'm still signed to a record company. I don't sell a million copies, but it's a solid 100,000 every time out."

Much of Rundgren's work was caught between two worlds—he was a student of modern technology as well as an incurable romantic with a penchant for soulful ballads. *Nearly Human* rediscovered spontaneity, an element he felt was missing from modern music. Wanting audiences to become more aware of the performance and less mindful of the transcription aspect, he took between eight and 30 musicians into the studio and recorded live with no overdubs immediately after teaching them the material.

The record melded gospel-flavored vocal arrangements with high-tech, synth-pop settings, and Rundgren delivered some of his most emotional, edgy performances—his outpouring of inspiration was contagious, imparting his philosophy of mind and heart working together. "The Want of a Nail," (featuring the soul legend Bobby Womack), was a churchy raver. "I have concerns in my forebrain about the meaning of life. It's valid as long as nobody tries to ascribe some kind of dogma to it. No, I'm not born again—as the comedian Dennis Miller says, 'Excuse me for getting it right the first time.'"

Having scored TV shows (*Pee-Wee's Playhouse*, *Crime Story)*, Rundgren turned to writing for the musical theater. He composed music and lyrics for the play *Up Against It*, based on Joe Orton's script for the Beatles' third, unproduced movie. "Parallel Lines," the best song from the show, was featured on *Nearly Human.*

"I never said, 'Please make me Mr. Broadway,' but I've always had an interest in show music," Rundgren said. "*Play Up Against It* closed after seven weeks, but it was a great experience. TV and film scoring is more of an exercise—you're low man on the totem pole, an indentured servant, and the only reward is that you're paid so much. In theater, you're relatively high in the pecking order—you get some control. The writing doesn't have the same restrictions—a song doesn't have to have a drumbeat all the way through." ■

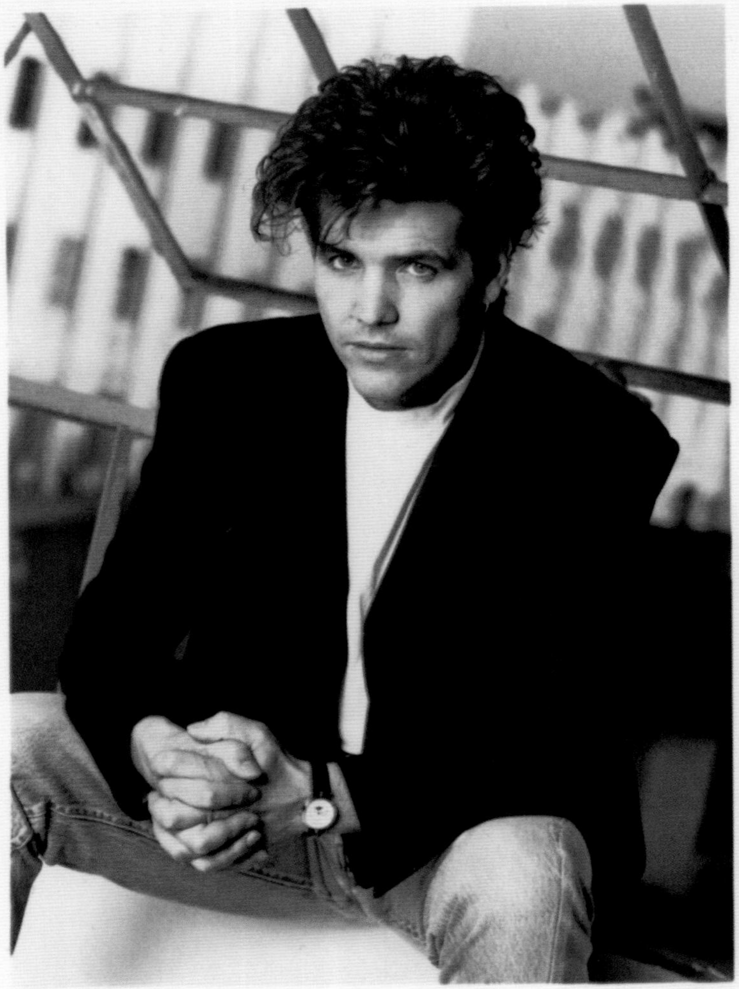

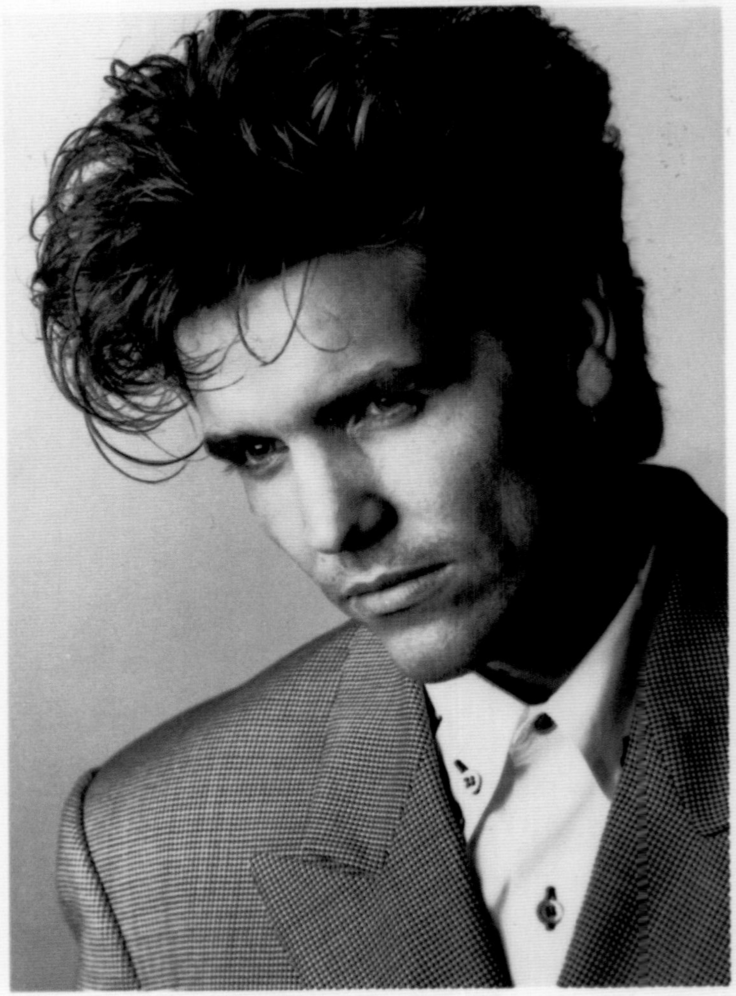

PHOTOGRAPHY: CHRIS CUFFARO/VISAGES

Michael Damian

CYPRESS RECORDS

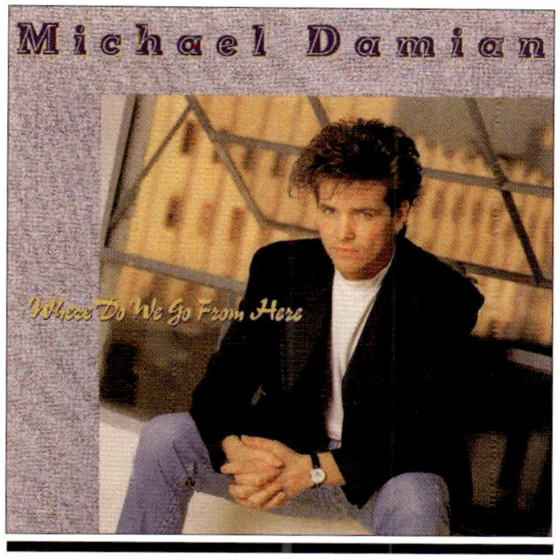

Billboard 200: *Where Do We Go from Here* (#61)
Billboard Hot 100: "Rock On" (No. 1);
"Cover of Love" (#31); "Was It Nothing at All" (#24)

Known for acting on TV's *The Young and the Restless*, Michael Damian recorded a No. 1 hit single, "Rock On."

SEVERAL DAYTIME soap-opera stars doubled as singers in the Eighties. Jack Wagner of ABC-TV's *General Hospital* notched a Top 10 single with "All I Need" in 1984, and Gloria Loring of NBC soap *Days of Our Lives* scored a hit in 1986 with "Friends and Lovers" (with Carl Anderson). Most soap singers wound up perceived as merely handsome faces with limited vocal talent, and that worked against their credibility.

Michael Damian was the latest soap star to have a hit single. For the last eight years, he had portrayed Danny Romalotti on TV's top daytime drama, *The Young and the Restless*. His remake of David Essex's 1974 classic "Rock On" went to No. 1, but his relationship with pop music was more believable—like Rick Springfield, Damian was a musician long before he became a TV personality.

He released three albums as a member of the Weirz, a new-wave group featuring his brothers and sisters (the family name was Weir). In 1981, at age 17, he recorded a remake of Eric Carmen's "She Did It," and the single landed on the *Billboard* Hot 100 chart and led to an appearance on Dick Clark's *American Bandstand*.

He was spotted by the producers of *The Young and the Restless*, who were looking to add the character of a struggling young rock 'n' roll musician to the cast. Danny Romalotti was created after they saw Damian perform.

"I had no acting experience at the time, so I just played myself," Damian explained. "Danny was a struggling musician and waiter, and that's exactly what I was doing in real life. So, in a way, Danny Romalotti is Michael Damian."

Damian made two albums for Canadian release and recorded "Rock On" while working on *Where Do We Go from Here*, his first US solo album. The single, which was subsequently picked up for inclusion on the soundtrack of the teen film *Dream a Little Dream*, earned him his first gold record.

"'Rock On' was my favorite song when I was 11," he said. "I wasn't doing too well in school at the time, and I wasn't really fitting in the social scene because I played clarinet in the school band, which wasn't the coolest instrument. 'Rock On' was my anthem—it had a rebellious edge to it. Recently, I was driving along and had a flashback to that time in my life. I thought the song would be a new experience for younger audiences." ■

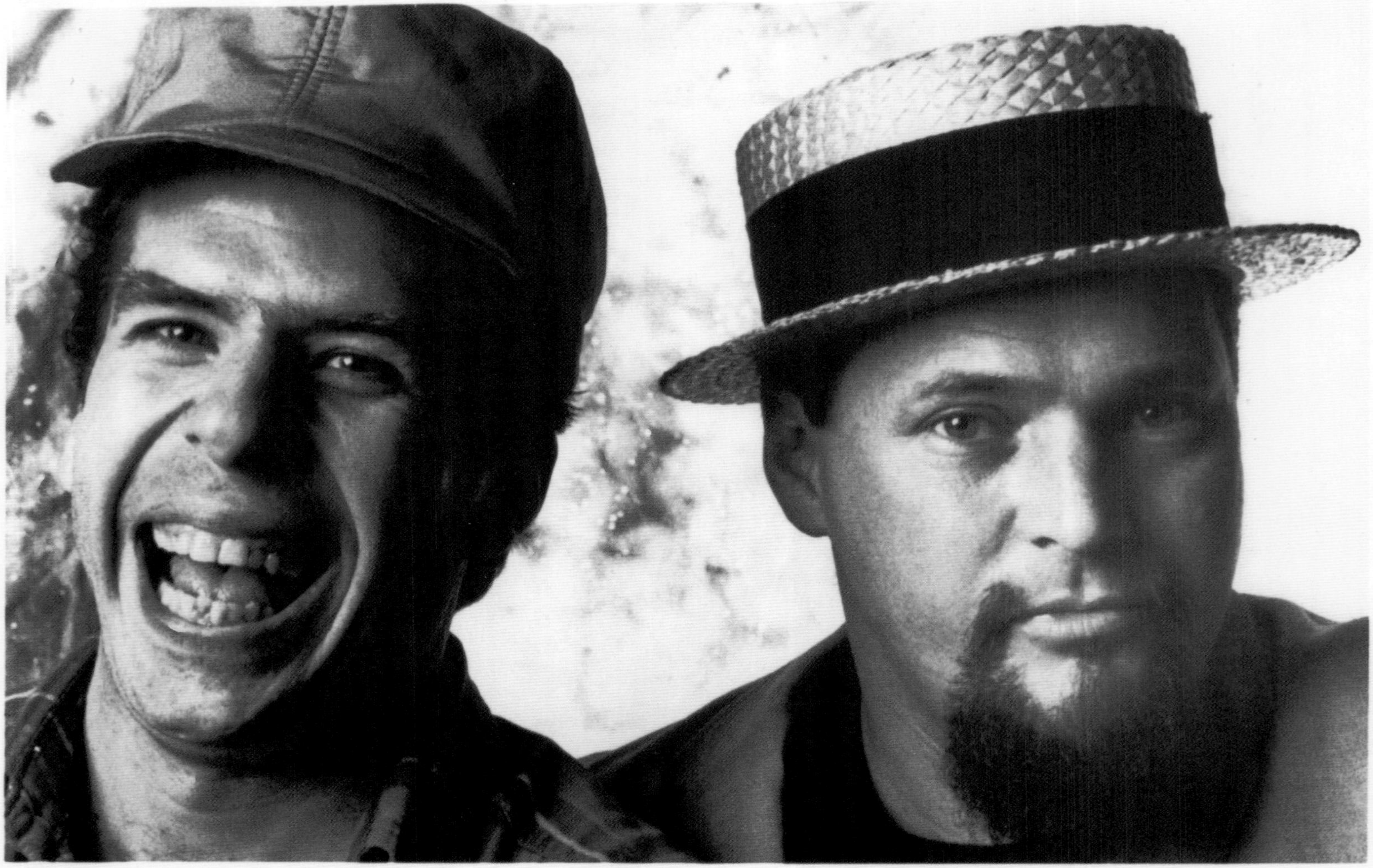

PHOTOGRAPH © 1989 ALEX REMLIN

MOJO NIXON & SKID ROPER

ENIGMA. ENIGMA RECORDS CULVER CITY, CALIFORNIA 90231-3628 213/390-9969 ENIGMA CANADA 2183 DUNWIN DRIVE MISSISSAGUA, ONTARIO L5L 3S3 416/828-6121

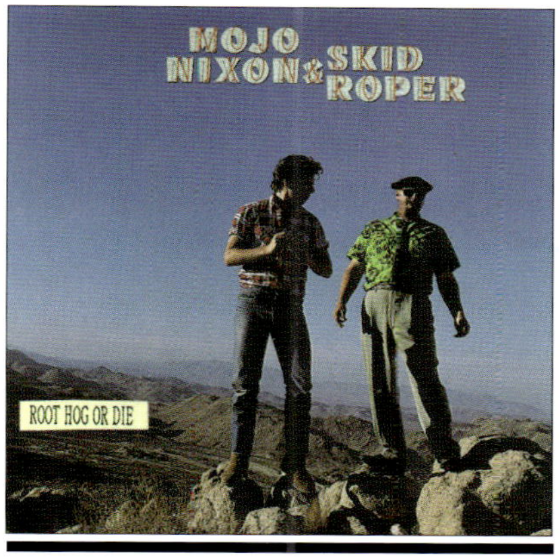

Psychobilly lampoon specialists Mojo Nixon & Skid Roper returned to the recording fray with *Root Hog or Die*.

RELEASED 10 years after Elvis Presley's death, 1987's epic "Elvis Is Everywhere" revealed that Mojo Nixon and his semi-silent sidekick Skid Roper had a severe case of Presley-itis. Two years later, a cut off their *Root Hog or Die* album indicated their condition had only intensified. "619-239-KING" was not only a single, but an honest-to-goodness phone number tied to an answering machine with a plea for Elvis to phone home and for callers to leave messages about Elvis sightings.

"It was in my house, but now it's set up where paid professionals are monitoring it," Nixon crowed. "It's always busy, but a lot of people aren't leaving messages—the weak, the puny, the pusillanimous just giggle and hang up. But one in 10 calls is a certified raving nut/lunatic/psychopath who should probably be locked up. That makes me feel good."

Nixon insisted Elvis was a point of reference for his satire, not a fixation. "Some guys write about their girlfriends on their records—I just write about the king of rock 'n' roll sometimes," he said. "The song is a comment on the 'Is Elvis alive?' BS, but it also has to do with those 900 numbers you see on TV late at night." Nixon's raucous social commentary was also featured on "Debbie Gibson Is Pregnant with My Two Headed Love Child." "We made love 14 hours straight," he insisted. "But she's denying that she's incubating the incubus."

Nixon was seen on the big screen co-starring with Dennis Quaid in the feature film *Great Balls of Fire*, playing Jimmy Van Eaton, the drummer in Jerry Lee Lewis' band. "Jerry Lee can't separate when he's a nut and not a nut—shooting his wife or talking to God, it's the same thing."

Nixon's jabbering bumpkin persona made him a pillar on college radio. "It's almost like I have a career now," he allowed. "Before, I was in the bleachers, and now I'm in left field. But I'm still not running the basepaths like Poison—I'm in the corner taking bets from Pete Rose." ■

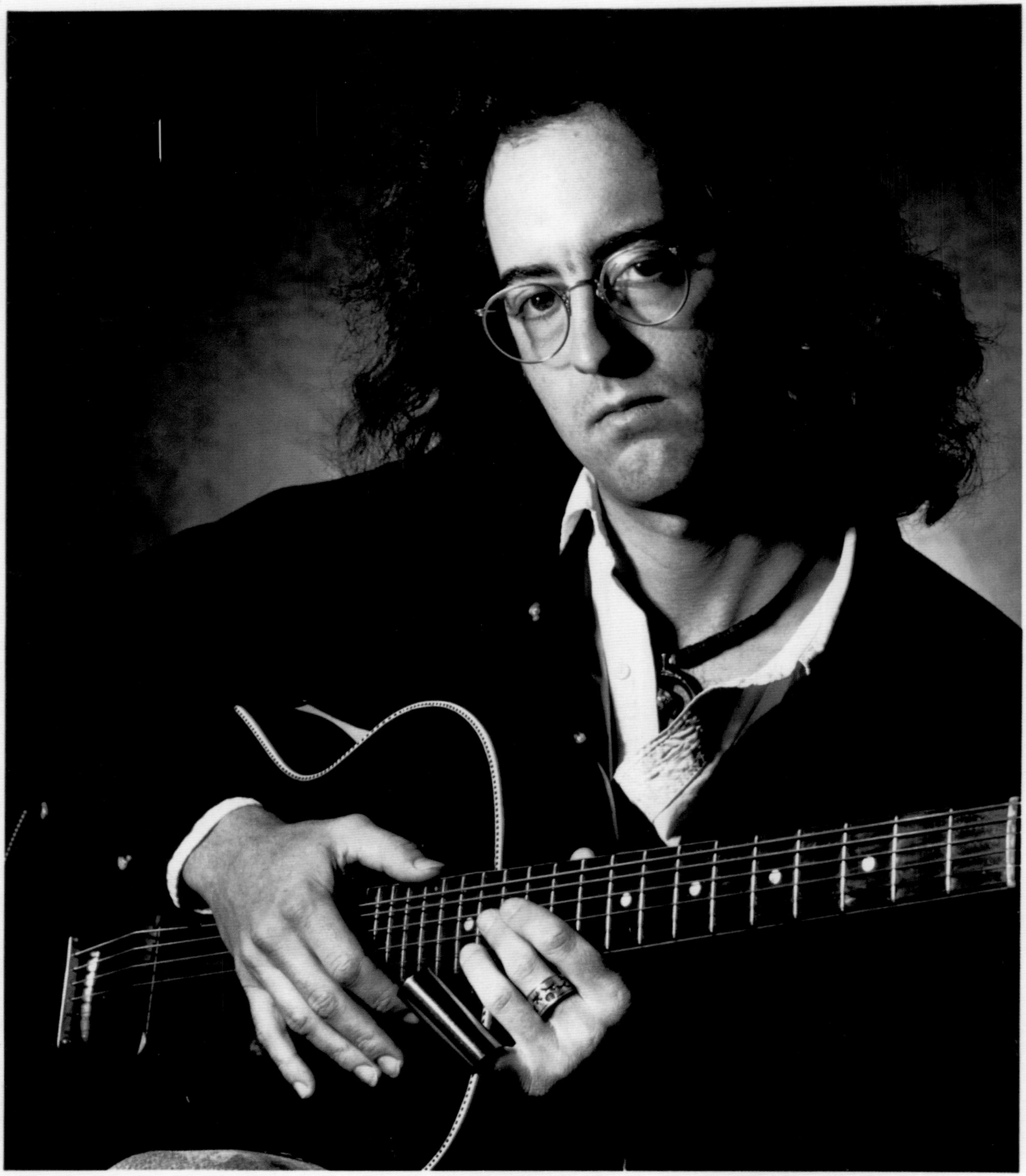

PHOTOGRAPH: KEITH McDONALD

CHAMPION ENTERTAINMENT

JAMES McMURTRY

Columbia
8907

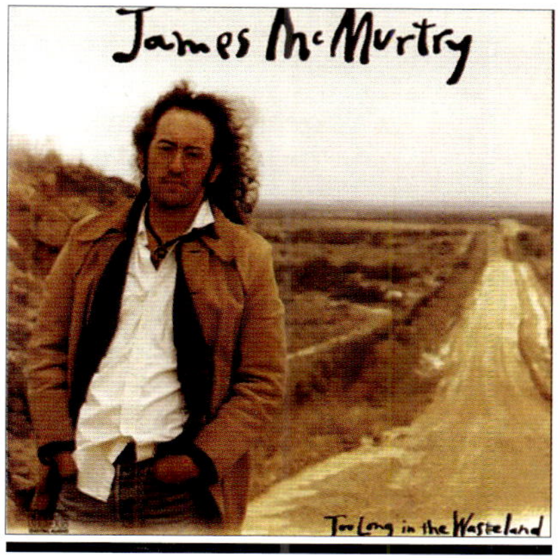

Billboard 200: *Too Long in the Wasteland* (#125)

The capacity to come up with a short story within the framework of a song came naturally to James McMurtry.

IT ELUDED many singer-songwriters, but James McMurtry's facility with language was practically genetic. He was the son of novelist and screenwriter Larry McMurtry, author of *The Last Picture Show* and *Lonesome Dove*, who gave him his first guitar at age seven. "My mother taught me three chords," James said, "and the rest I just stole as I went along."

McMurtry started writing in 1985, inspired by such fellow Texans as Guy Clark and Townes Van Zandt. He first notoriety came at the Kerrville Festival in Texas, where he won the New Folk competition and the admiration of such songwriters as Ian Tyson, John Hiatt and Fred Koller. His plainspoken stance helped to bring his music to the attention of John Mellencamp who'd received a tape of James' songs from the elder McMurtry. "It was the best door that was open," McMurtry said. "I was about to go to Nashville and spend years trying to be a country songwriter."

Mellencamp served as producer of McMurtry's debut album, *Too Long in the Wasteland*, flavoring rural folk and rock styles with his crisp and direct sound. McMurtry sang about small-town values with a laconic delivery, striking a nerve with his compressed vignettes of life on the song "Painting by Numbers." He portrayed his subjects with the same blend of romance and despair often found in the work of his father.

"You do it just like you write a book," he advised. "You make up a character, then you make up a story—something for the character to do. And hopefully you've got a melody to go with it. So there it is." ■

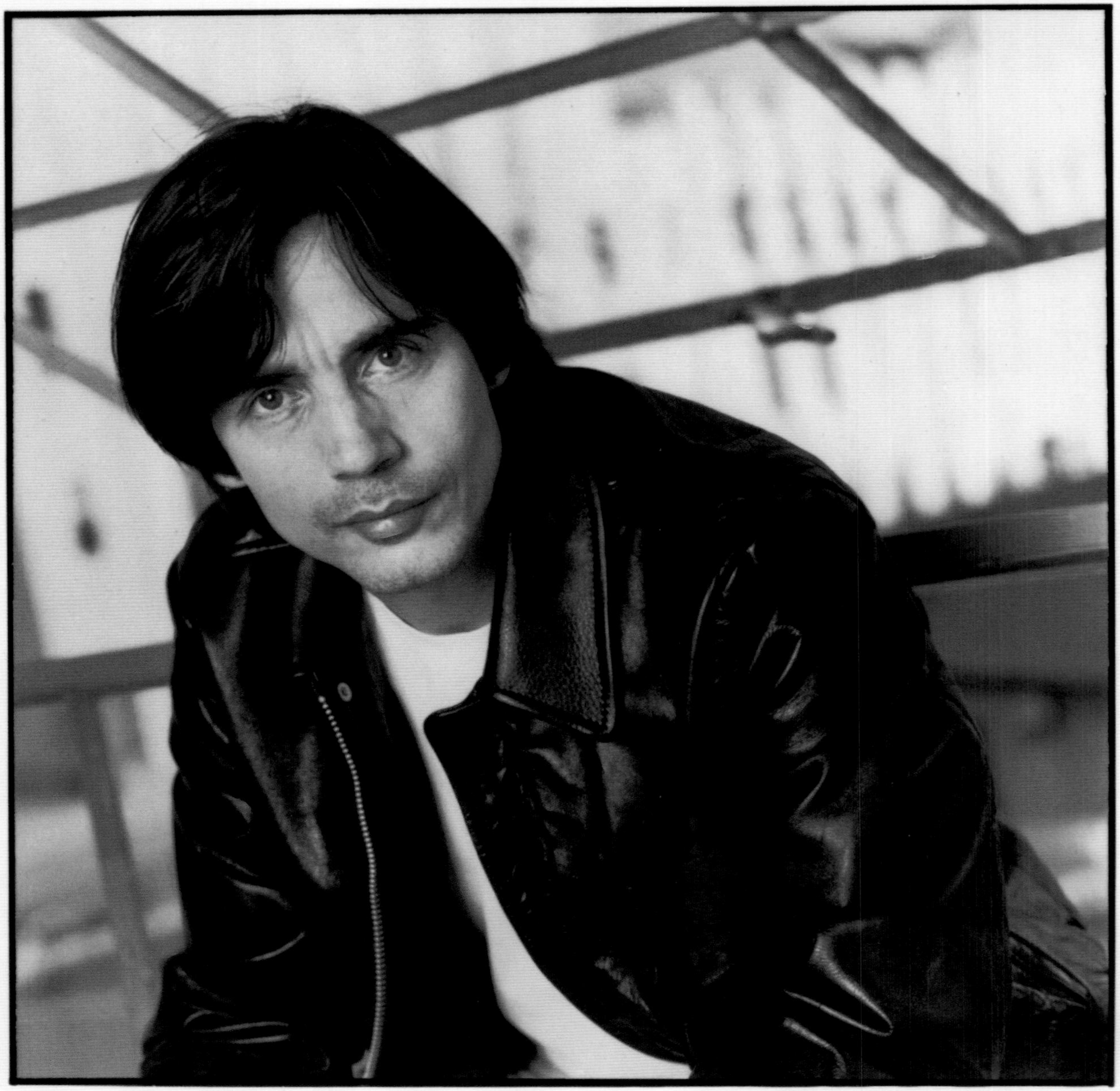

PHOTO CREDIT: CHRIS CUFFARO / 1989

JACKSON BROWNE

ELEKTRA

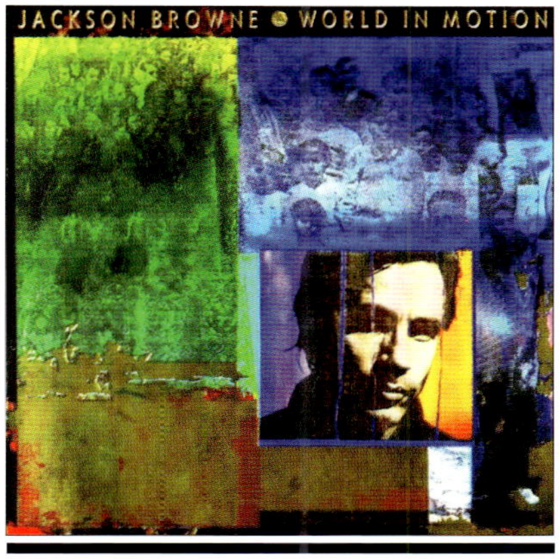

Billboard 200: *World in Motion* (#45)

His sales declined, yet Jackson Browne set his finely observed songs on a new trajectory of political protest.

IN THE late Seventies, Jackson Browne and other musician organized the No Nukes movement, and his arrest in the early Eighties for civil-disobedience demonstrations in front of California's Diablo Canyon nuclear plant left no doubt to his sincerity. As an outspoken critic of US foreign policy and a strong supporter of Amnesty International, the singer-songwriter bared his conscience with 1986's *Lives in the Balance*, an ardently political album far removed from his earlier romanticism.

Browne had hoped *Lives in the Balance* would have an impact beyond record sales, but it didn't do as well as his other albums. He nevertheless retained the courage of his convictions. He toured the US in the fall of 1988 in support of the Christic Institute, a Washington, DC organization investigating the alleged involvement of government officials in drug and gun smuggling. After that tour, Browne put his energy into *World in Motion*, an album also dealing with economic, social and political injustice. "On this album, I've tried to examine the questions that occur to me about peace," he said.

"How Long," written around the time of "We Are the World," Live Aid and Band Aid, made the connection between hunger and military spending. "The arms race is the biggest robber of freedom in the world," Browne said. "The global economy is based on war, and somehow that's going to have to change." He covered Steven Van Zandt's "I Am a Patriot," which he had performed at many concerts.

The most incisive track was "The Word Justice," about the Iran-Contra hearings. "In a jaded, cynical way, people don't wonder if the allegations are true, they wonder if they can be proven and made to stick," Browne said. "It's such a stupid way to conduct our world affairs. We tend to believe that somebody's got to have the license to kill, and that we have to be as bad as our enemies—not only to be as tough, but to fight evil with evil.

"And it's coming home to roost—there's a karmic tab that we're running up. We've found that we don't hold the moral high ground in terms of terrorism. The things we excuse in our own behavior happen to be things that we condemn in others. There's only one word for that—hypocrisy. So I'm making a rousing appeal to people's common sense, their better judgment and decency, to put two and two together, and make the connections of where the drugs come from and were the covert wars are being waged. It's time to admit what kind of people we are—and to think about what kind of people we want to be."

With co-producer Scott Thurston providing a "sense of groove," *World in Motion* included a few songs about the perils of romance, and Browne still dealt with personal emotions more honestly than most other singers. "I'm earnest to a fault," he laughed. "'Ernie' would be a suitable *nom de plume* for me." ■

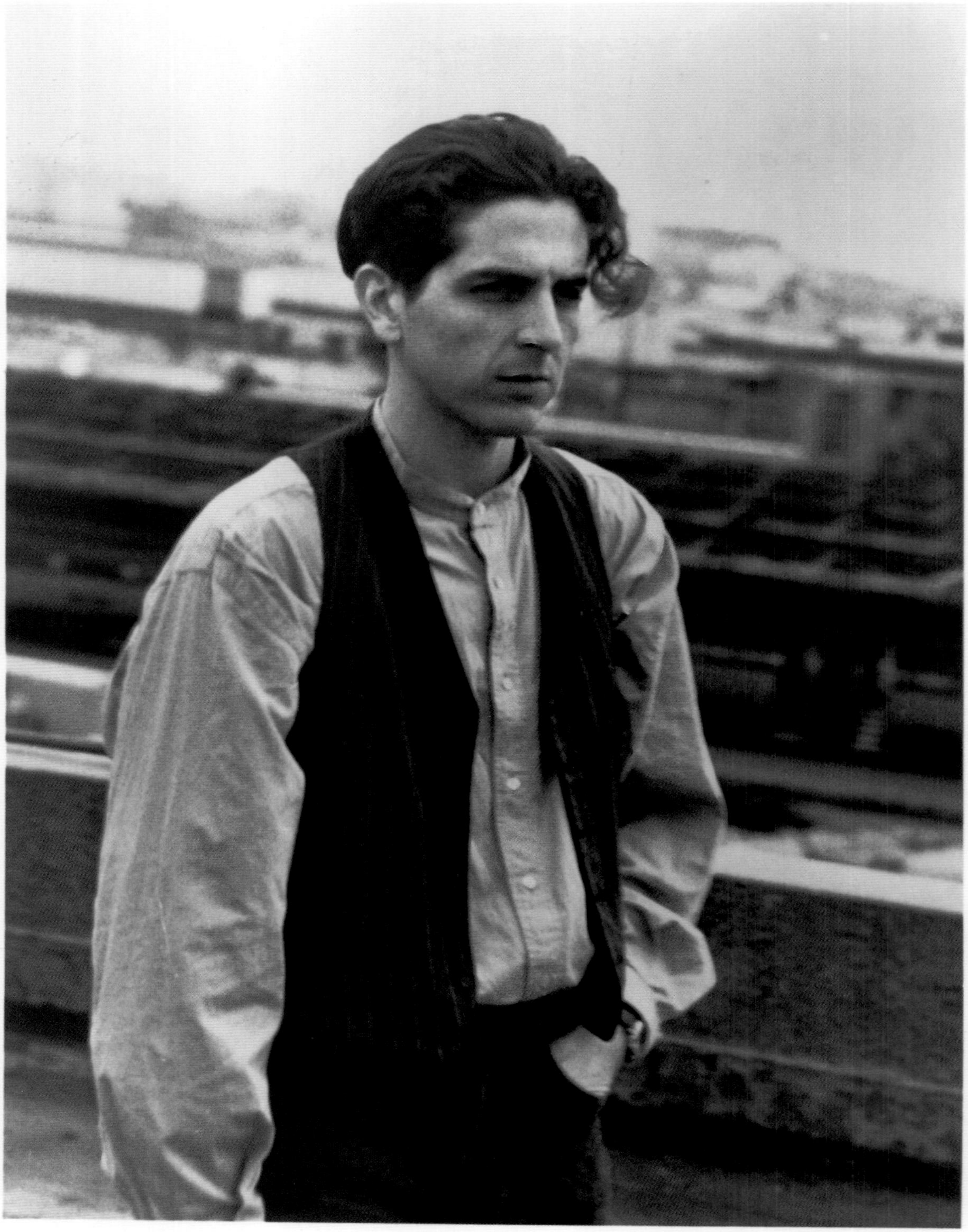

Photo Credit: Glenn Urler

Michael Penn

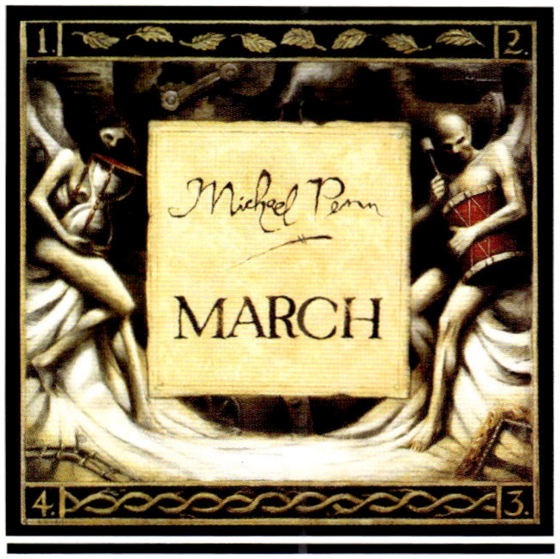

Billboard 200: *March* (#31)
Billboard Hot 100: "No Myth" (#13); "This & That" (#53)

After years on the fringes, Michael Penn scored MTV's Best New Artist award on the strength of "No Myth."

A SEAMLESSLY crafted piece that balanced rhythmic pop and sensitive folk, Michael Penn's impressive debut album *March* warranted attention. But because Penn was the older brother of both Sean Penn, a leading actor of his generation, and character actor Chris Penn, he had to grin and bear comments about his famous siblings as he went about the difficult process of establishing his own name.

"I never tried acting and I don't think I will—it never really appealed to me," he said. "Songwriting is a natural thing for me, as I'm sure acting is for actors."

Penn spent much of the early Eighties in Doll Congress, a band that included keyboardist Patrick Warren. By 1986, he realized the group wasn't going anywhere and departed, taking Warren with him. Penn busied himself with a four-track recorder and wrote a new batch of songs, many of which appeared on *March*. Most of the sounds were acoustic—even if sampled—and the album had a demo-ish flavor that Penn said was intentional. "I wasn't trying to make a record that sounded like demos, I was trying to make a record with an edge to it that I liked. The four-track arrangements had that quality."

One of the tunes was "No Myth," which climbed steadily up the charts. Some of Penn's lyrics had a pessimistic slant, and "No Myth" started "with the idea of writing something desperately sarcastic." The catchy chorus: "What if I were Romeo in black jeans/What if I was Heathcliff/It's no myth/Maybe she's just looking for/Someone to dance with."

Penn admitted he didn't expect "No Myth" to do so well. "I was thrilled to be signed to a company to pay for a record, and it's gone far past my expectations. I thought it might do a little something on alternative or college radio, maybe sell enough that I'd be able to make another album." Yet he wished "No Myth" hadn't been the lead track. The song was the most Beatlesesque on *March*, and it established a mindset. "It worked well to open the album, but too much has been made of that comparison."

But the Beatles were definitely Penn's biggest influence, given his smart, pleasing sense of song structure and folk-tinged melody. Penn recorded *March* with an impressive assembly of musicians, including drummers Kenny Aronoff and Jim Keltner and Prince's former sidewomen Wendy & Lisa. Warren provided intriguing moments with his Chamberlin, a primitive proto-synthesizer instrument.

"If this record does well enough for me to survive for the next couple of years, Patrick and I will have the luxury of exploring how to expand this vocabulary," he said. "It's kind of like inventing, where you work for a long time, and your work is based on other people's patents, and then at some point, maybe you come upon a patent of your own." ■

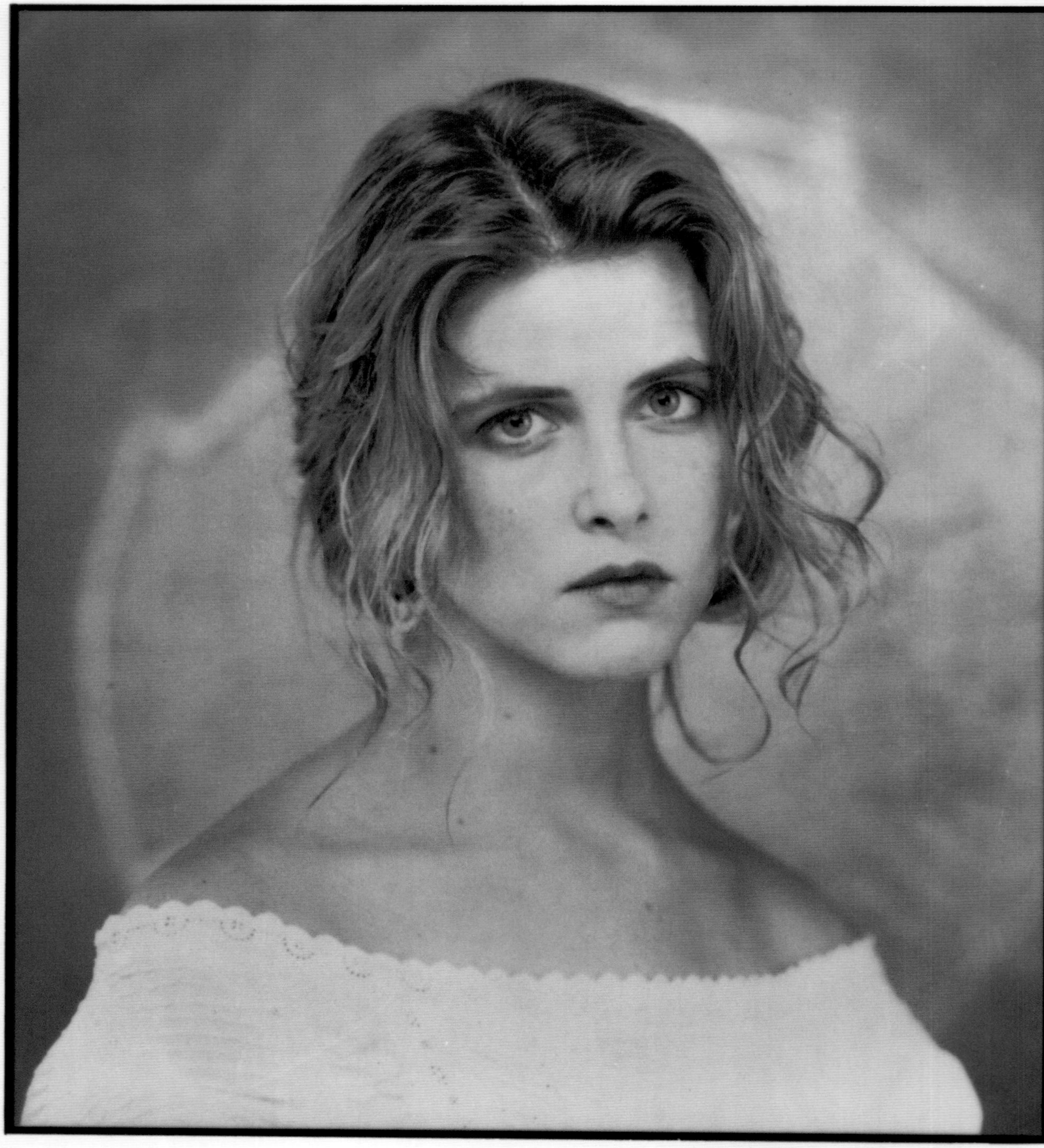

Photo Credit: Deborah Frankel

MARIA McKEE

GEFFEN RECORDS

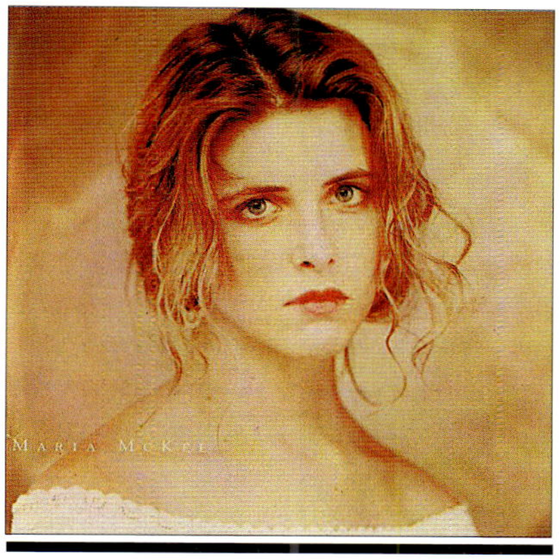

Billboard 200: *Maria McKee* (#120)

After a fast but ill-fated stint with the act Lone Justice, Maria McKee celebrated a no-nonsense solo album.

MAKING HER recording debut in 1985 with the ballyhooed band Lone Justice, singer Maria McKee was marketed as the little Los Angeles girl with the huge voice and rootsy spirit leading the band's frisky country-rock tunes—akin to, say, Dolly Parton backed by the Blasters.

"I had worked my way up from the street, hanging out at underground clubs, singing wherever I could—onstage or in a parking lot with friends," McKee, a fourth-generation Californian, said. "Then I got exposed to traditional country music, and Lone Justice was our version of that—a young garage-rock band playing hard country."

Lone Justice released two albums and toured with the likes of U2 and Tom Petty, but when the members went their separate ways, McKee was liberated from the guitar-drenched rock 'n' roll wall-of-sound that was imposed by the band.

On *Maria McKee*, her newly defined sound was more downbeat and melancholy, largely influenced by the gospel music she'd heard and sang in church. Her sharp-edged, resonant voice burned with intensity on the quietest songs, and her eclectic songwriting—"Breathe," "I've Forgotten What It Was in You (That Put the Need in Me)"—was more personal than her previous work. "It was a bit daring to break up that band and then come out with a very feminine stance," she said, "but it was important for me to do."

McKee toured with Neil Young in support of her album. Aided by Lone Justice holdover Bruce Brody on keyboards, she performed an acoustic set.

"My solo musical vision developed when the band was still together," McKee explained. "The other members were totally understanding, and a lot of them played on the album. Lone Justice never had any charting albums, so people have no preconceptions—I'm starting over. I used to feel if I didn't bust a gut or have a nervous breakdown onstage, I wasn't giving a good show. Now I just want to have fun, whether that means turning a backflip or just standing there with my guitar and singing." ■

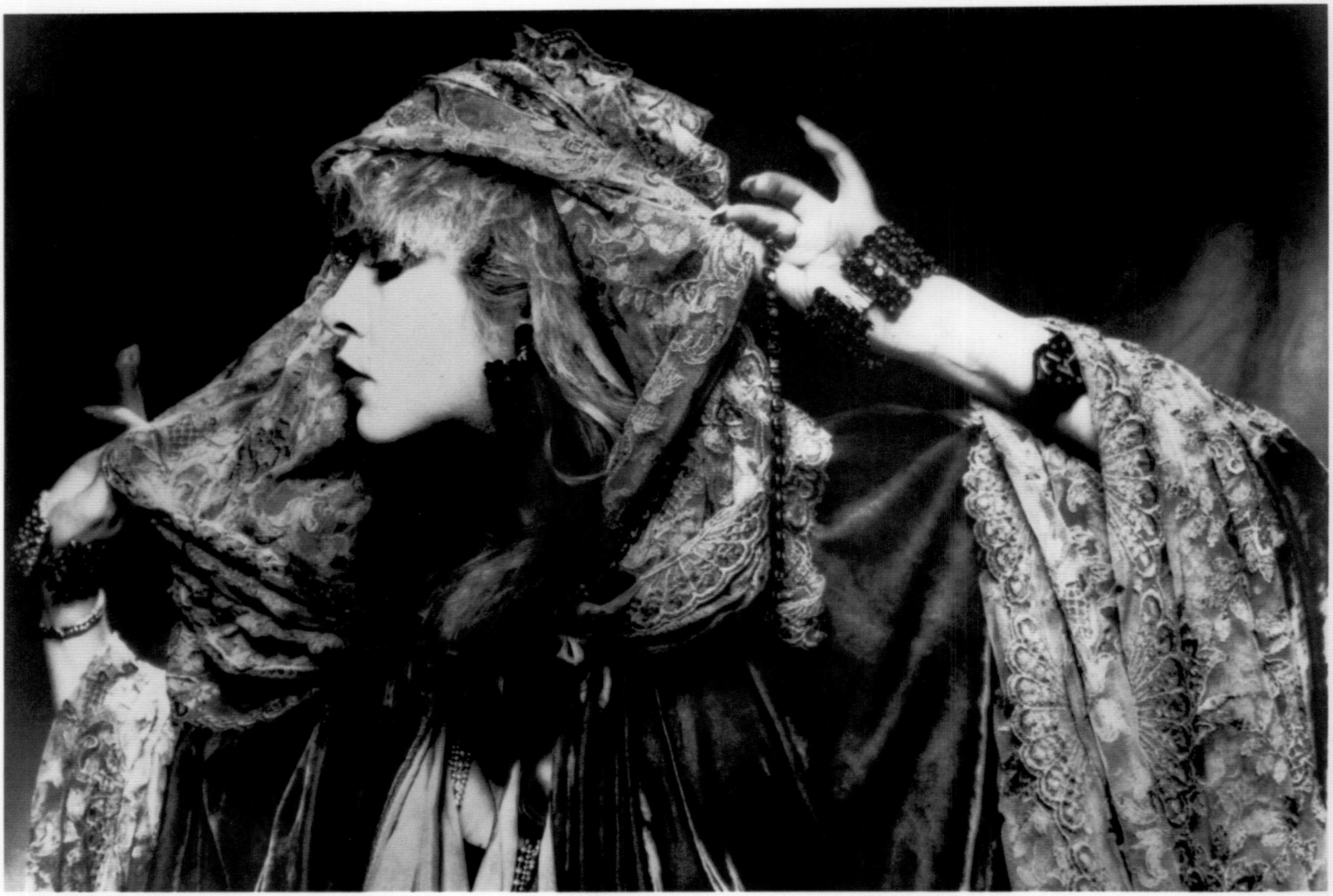

STEVIE NICKS

Modern Records

Distributed by Atlantic Records

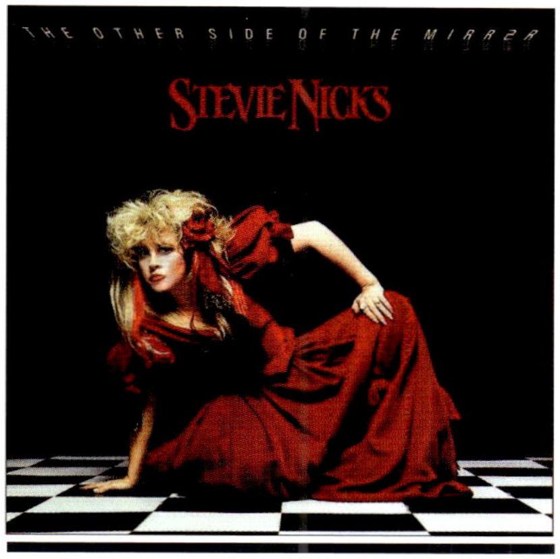

Billboard 200: *The Other Side of the Mirror* (#10)
Billboard Hot 100: "Rooms on Fire" (#16)

On the album *The Other Side of the Mirror*, Stevie Nicks delved into her own personal and spiritual quests.

EVER SINCE joining the legendary band Fleetwood Mac in 1975, Stevie Nicks had reigned as one of rock's most distinctive female voices. Her hip but glamorous couture, her bewitching, spellbinding presence (the "nix Nicks" contingent cited her space-cadet/heartthrob presence)—Nicks communicated in her own special language and imagery, and such nominal profundity had earned her a remarkably dedicated group of fans

Her ability to reach people with songs crafted from experiences remained unique on *The Other Side of the Mirror,* her first solo album in three years. Nicks joined forces with producer Rupert Hine, noted for his work with Tina Turner, the Fixx and Howard Jones, among others. He captured the immediacy of her trademark rasping—Nicks, it was said, recorded her voice in the middle of the night in a studio lit by candles, an evocative image that fit the songs' allusions to the shadows cast by hard living and loving.

"When I record, I pretend that I'm onstage, and it goes on the record pretty much how I know it will come out onstage," the singer explained. "It's important for a connection to exist between albums and live performances."

"Rooms on Fire" was another pop hit for Nicks, and "Long Way to Go" got ample rock radio airplay. Bruce Hornsby duetted with her on the moving "Two Kinds of Love"—"I didn't even consider anyone else," she stated. Guitarist Mike Campbell of Tom Petty & the Heartbreakers co-wrote "Whole Lotta Trouble" with Nicks. "Writing with Michael is one of the great loves of my life," she said. "He sends me these incredible guitar tracks and I write lyrics to them, and everything grows from there."

Nicks managed to balance her solo career and her role in Fleetwood Mac. "I work constantly," she said. "I also paint and draw, but that's very tied to the music, too. I don't go to parties—I don't go out much at all." She paused. "I love being surrounded by my really true friends." ■

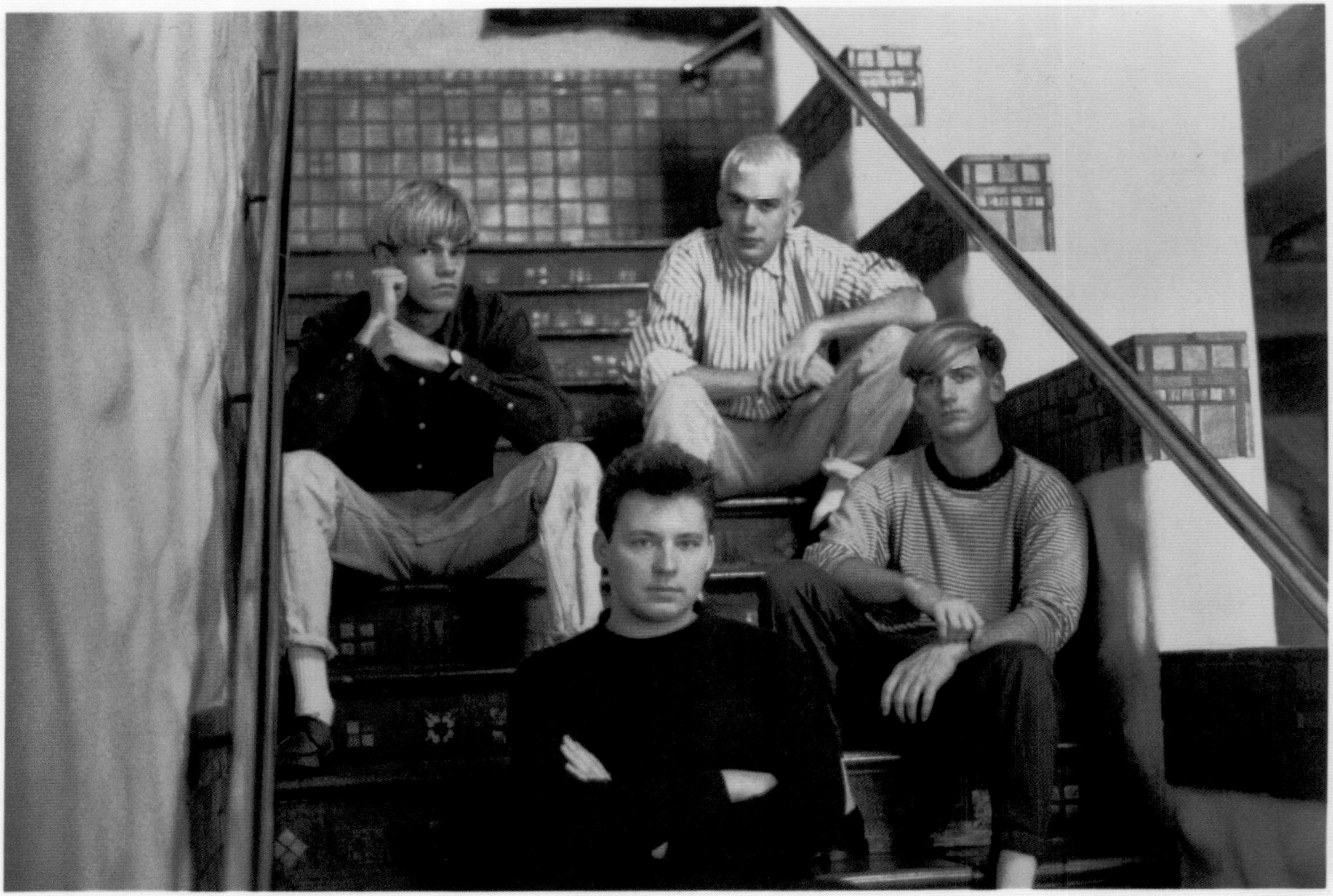

Photo Credit: William Lau

THE OCEAN BLUE

reprise SIRE

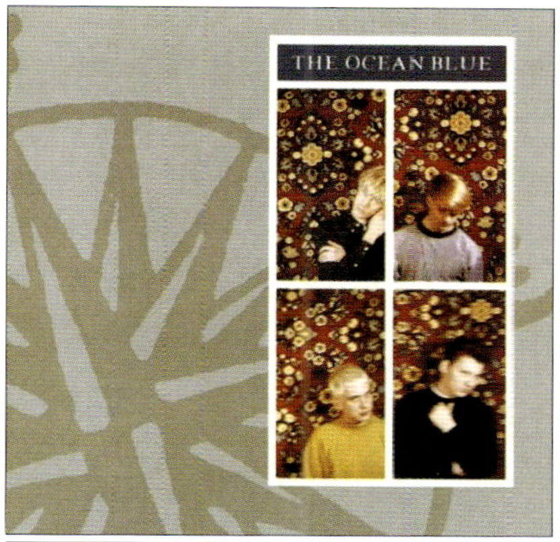

Billboard 200: *The Ocean Blue* (#155)

The Ocean Blue passed muster on alternative and college-rock radio with a gentle, jangly self-titled debut.

MASTERS OF richly textured pop in the British vein, the Ocean Blue emerged from an unlikely spawning ground—landlocked Hershey, Pennsylvania. "A lot of music from the early Eighties post-punk era was English, and we listened to a lot of that," guitarist David Schelzel said. "People hear it in our music. Three of us have been friends since junior high school, but there was no music scene when we were growing up—we didn't even play a club until 1987. We did a lot in our basements and bedrooms."

All the members came from musical families, with various teachers, professionals and aficionados in their collective backgrounds. Initially going under challenging monikers (Molecules of the Master Element for two parties, then The Next Big Thing for six months), the four-piece band established a local reputation for live shows and bid for a recording contract with an eight-song, self-produced demo. They were rewarded with a multi-album deal.

The members flew to London for a three-month recording stint with producers Mark Opitz (INXS, Divinyls) and John Porter (the Smiths, the Alarm). *The Ocean Blue*, their debut album, featured a pair of hook-laden singles, "Between Something and Nothing" and "Drifting, Falling," that reached #2 and #10 on the modern-rock charts, respectively.

"I'm amazed at how well it's doing," Schelzel marveled. "We were just hoping to get on the charts, and now we're there with bands we grew up with." ■

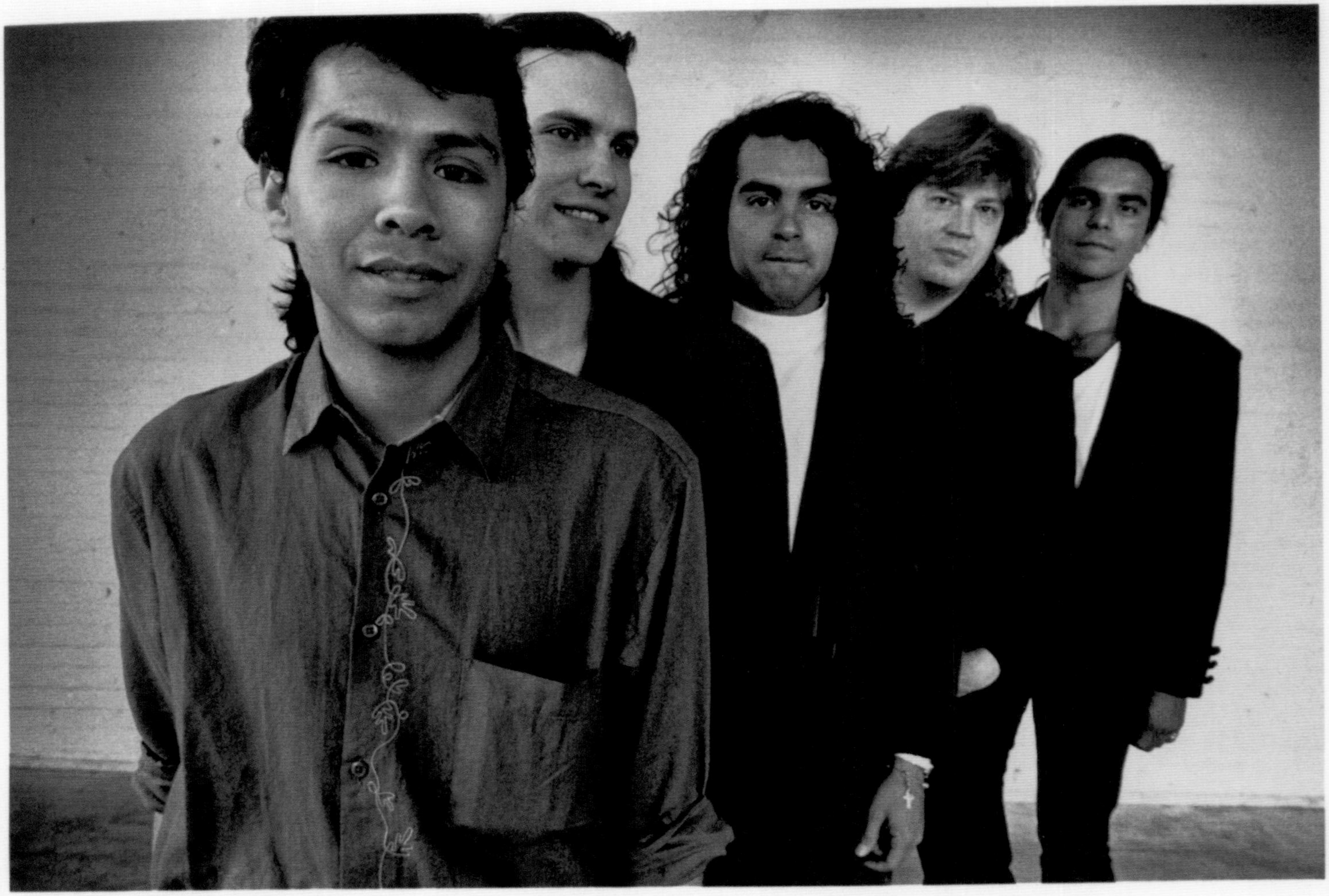

Photo Credit: Gary Porter

Sammy Llanas Kurt Neumann Michael Ramos Bob Griffin Danny Gayol

BO DEANS

Slash™ reprise

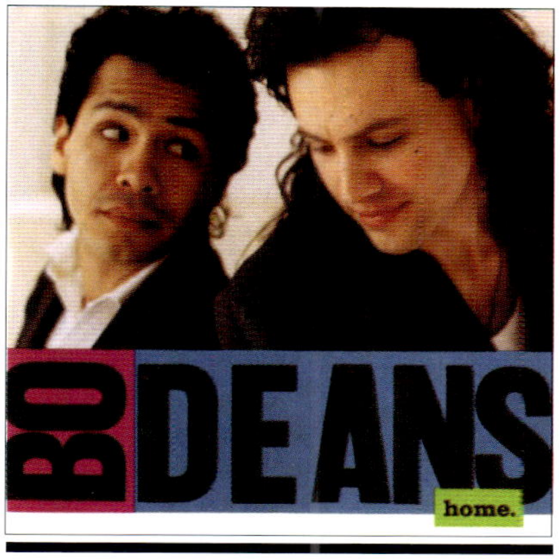

Billboard 200: *Home* (#94)

Calling the creative shots, BoDeans formulated a range of fresh ideas and applied them to the songs of *Home*.

A GRITTY "roots-rock" production was provided by T Bone Burnett on *Love & Hope & Sex & Dreams*, BoDeans' 1986 debut, but the shot for "the big sound" came on 1987's *Outside Looking In*. Jerry Harrison, keyboardist with Talking Heads, did the radio-ready production, smoothing out rough edges and leaving BoDeans sounding like the arena-rock competition. U2 hired the critically acclaimed band as opening act on the six-week "Joshua Tree" tour.

BoDeans laid down *Home*, their third album, in a mobile studio located in an old warehouse near the group's hometown of Milwaukee. As always, both Sammy Llanas and Kurt Neumann recorded vocals and played guitar, and production was handled by Jim Scott and "He & He." "This band is very much the vision of Kurt and myself—we are 'He & He,'" Llanas said. "We started the band, we write the songs, we sing the songs. It makes us come across as a team."

An inspired variation of styles emerged, including blue-collar rock (Neumann's witty "Good Work") and U2-inspired ambient guitar handiwork (the dramatic "You Don't Get Much" made the modern-rock charts). Llanas' urgent voice shined on "Beautiful Rain," a song about the drought that gripped the Midwest in the summer of 1988. Kenny Aronoff of John Cougar Mellencamp's band sat in on drums, providing a drive not found on the first two BoDeans albums.

"All of a sudden we were a great band," Llanas noted. "There's a magic that only happens when everybody plays together in the same room at the same time, bleeding into each other's mikes. It also has to do with not trying to filter out all of the imperfections that give a band its sound." ■

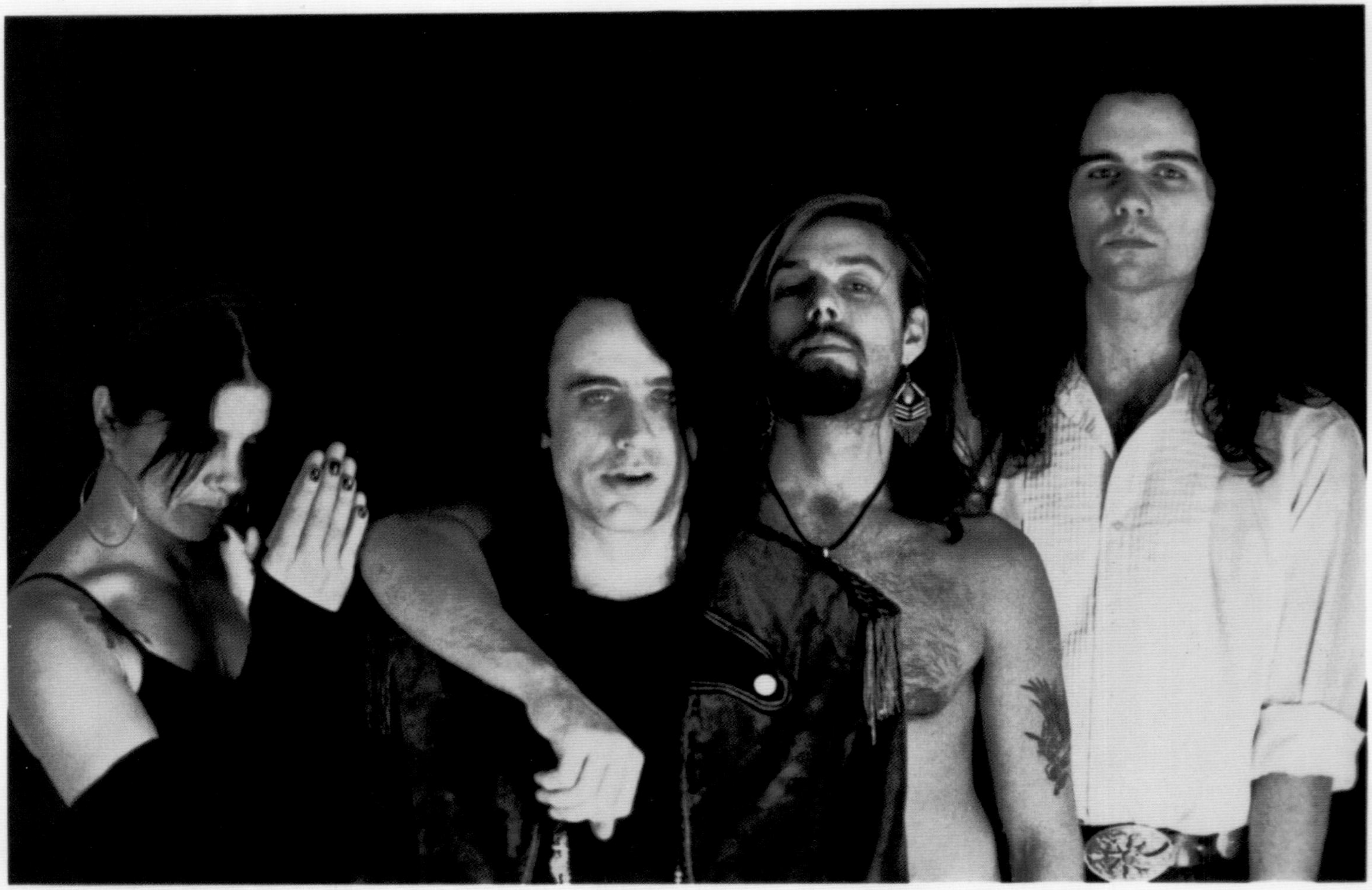

Photo: Anne Sperling

Concrete Blonde

MANAGEMENT:
Frank Volpe
L.A. (213) 661.8637

I.R.S.

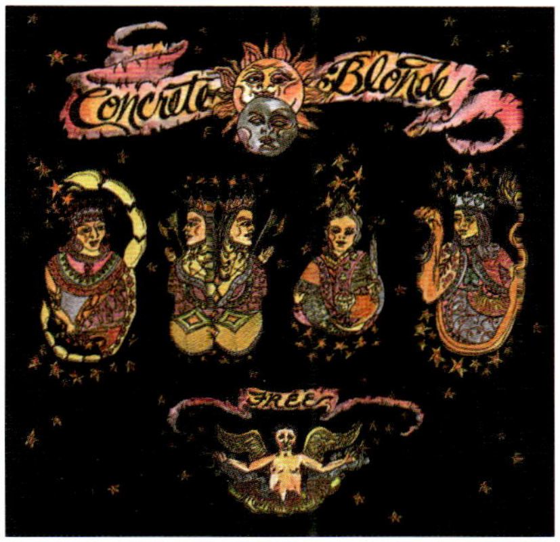

Billboard 200: *Free* (#148)

Concrete Blonde's album *Free* produced the fierce "God Is a Bullet," a big favorite on college radio stations.

ONE OF the most populist Los Angeles bands, Concrete Blonde rocked with authority and conviction. A 1986 self-titled debut drew comparisons to X and the Pretenders and cracked the Top 100 album chart. Johnette Napolitano, the frontperson for Concrete Blonde, defied leather-clad bad-girl stereotypes—tough but casual, she was smart, aggressive and a hell of a musician.

But the original members were shortly mired in some complex financial and legal problems. The resulting distrust of music business establishment ethics largely accounted for Concrete Blonde's heavy reputation in the underground scene. "We're not out for control—I think of it more as freedom of expression," Napolitano said of the band's sense of conviction. "Personal and business hassles have nothing to do with music, but they do reinforce why you want to do this for a living."

Following two stormy years, Concrete Blonde released *Free*. The album was electrified by the literate urgency of Napolitano's lyrics. Her passionate vocal powered "God Is a Bullet," a trenchant observation on urban violence.

"I've had that phrase for several years, and even after all the delays, it's still timely," she allowed. "I wish it wasn't. It expresses my fear of firearms and the people licensed to carry them or not. Strange that the issue seems hotter now more than ever. Maybe if the song reaches people, it'll support the campaign against semi-automatic weapons in some way." ■

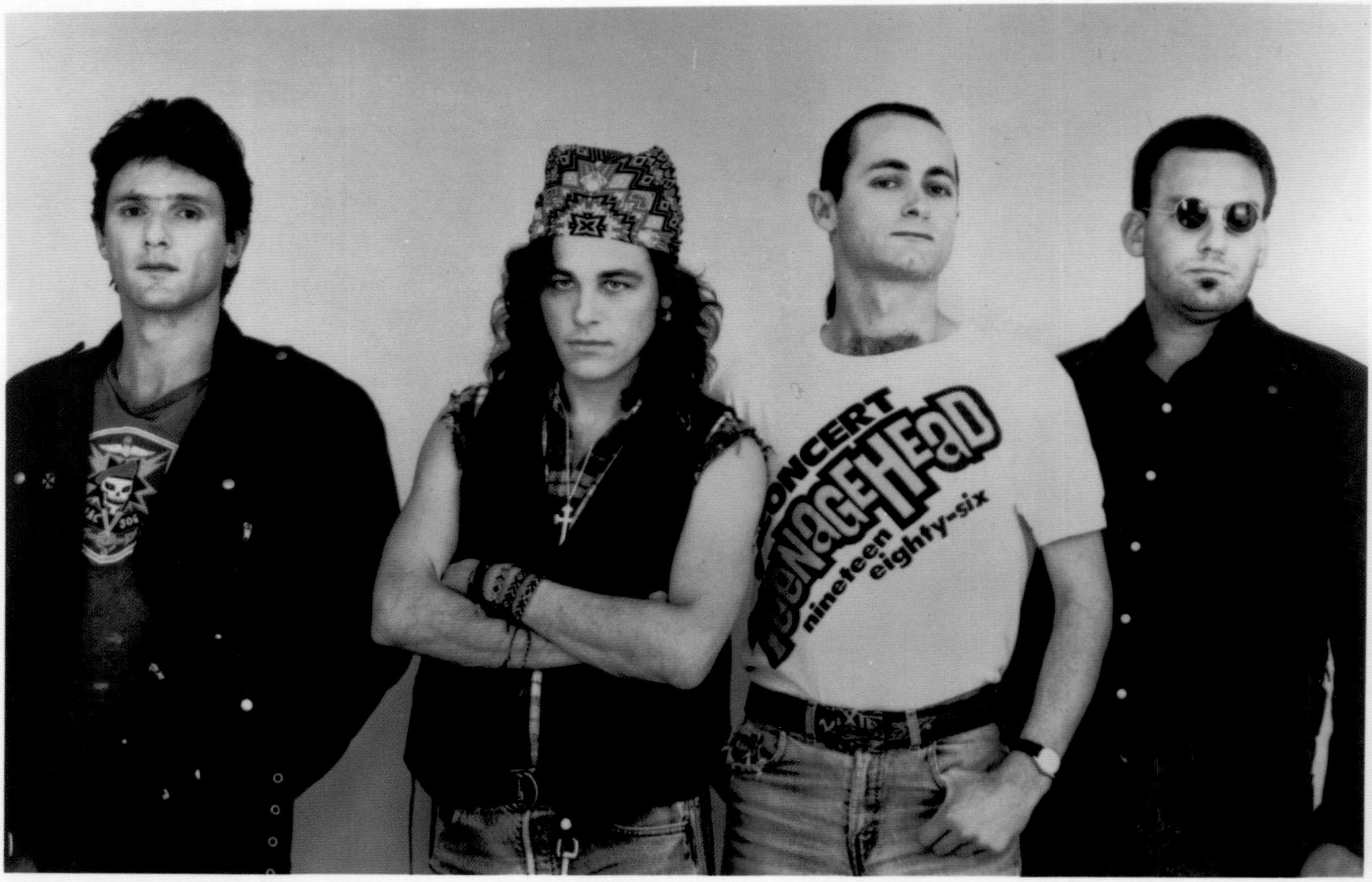

Photo. Philip. Le Masurier

RICK GROSSMAN, BRAD SHEPHERD, DAVE FAULKNER, MARK KINGSMILL

HOODOO GURUS

RCA

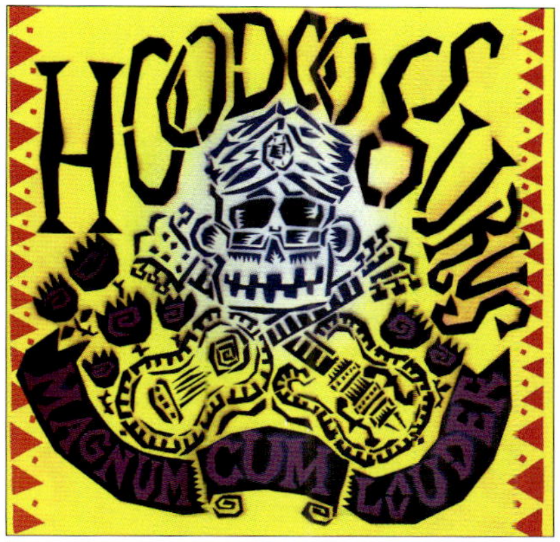

Billboard 200: *Magnum Cum Louder* (#101)

Australia's Hoodoo Gurus channeled their inspiration from American pop culture on *Magnum Cum Louder*.

HOODOO GURUS' backstory was equal parts randomness and impudent creativity. The Australian band's first job, an appearance on a children's show, came about after they convinced the producers that their $10 demo would top the charts. Their next televised gig, as backing band for an act called Phil Lattery & His Singing Dog, earned them a recording contract "and a chance to work without the dog."

"We're a rock 'n' roll band, but now we're pop stars in Australia," guitarist Brad Shephard said. "We feel uncomfortable being projected that way, because we're really just a bunch of buffoons. I can't deal with being a poster pinup. Down there we have hit singles, so we have teenage girls following us. It's nice, but in the States, maybe they think it's funny like we do."

In the US, the band's repute peaked with *Magnum Cum Louder*, the fourth consecutive album to top college radio charts, and the exemplary single "Come Anytime" reached No. 1 on the modern-rock charts. The icons mentioned in the lyrics ran the gamut from Barbie dolls (the satirical "Glamourpuss") to the New York Mets (the levity of "Where's That Hit?"). On the inner sleeve, the members divulged their "Semi-Annual Hall of Fame"—and their pop heroes were Americans like Rod Serling and Mary Tyler Moore.

"*The Brady Bunch*, *Get Smart*, *Gilligan's Island*—a lot of American junk culture makes its way to Australia," Shephard said. "We're all in our late 20s, the first generation of television watchers, so it made its mark on us. When I watch *Remote Control* (MTV's trivia show), I win with the best of them!" ■

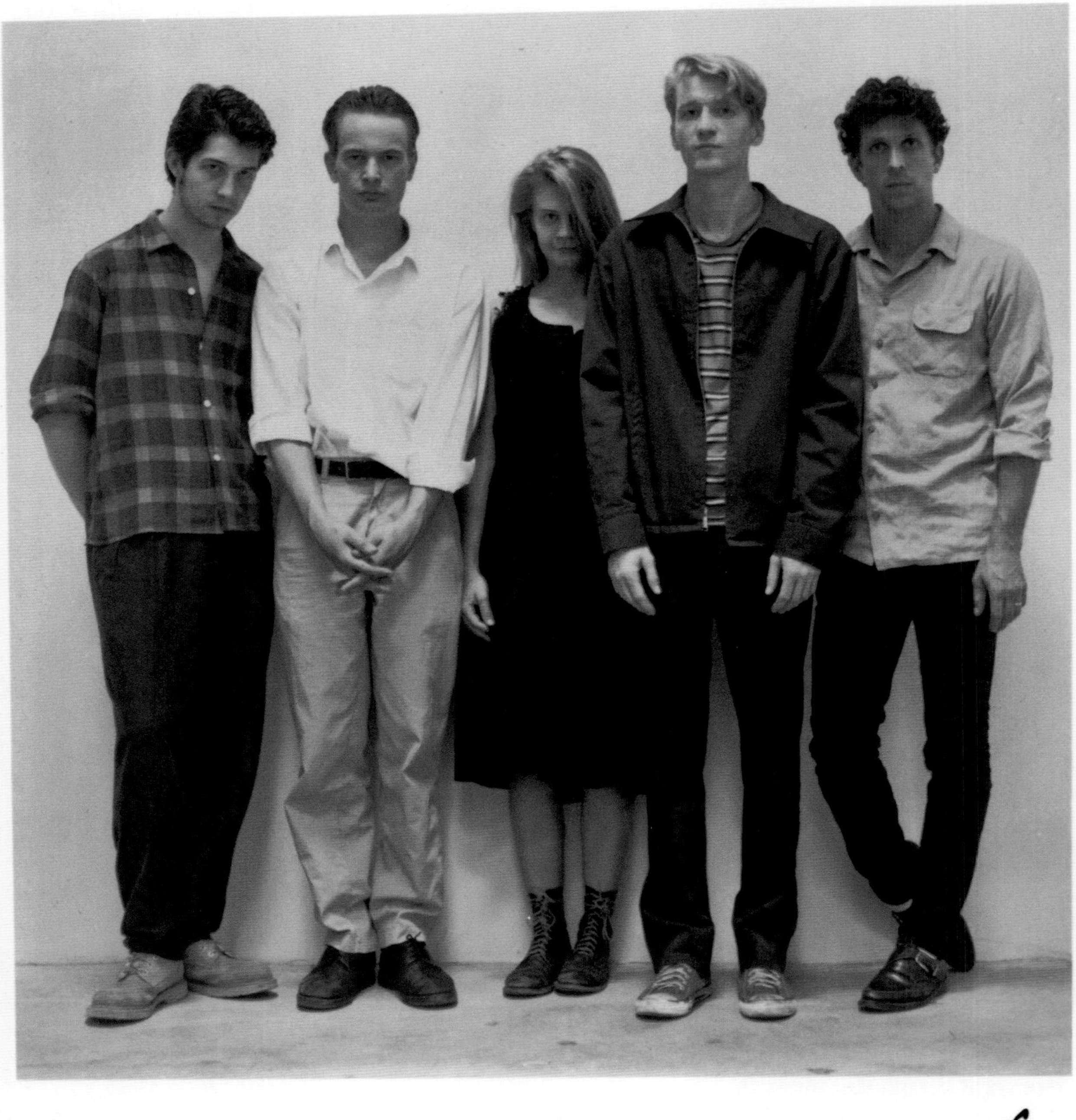

Photo Credit: Andre Lansel

CAMPER VAN BEETHOVEN

Virgin

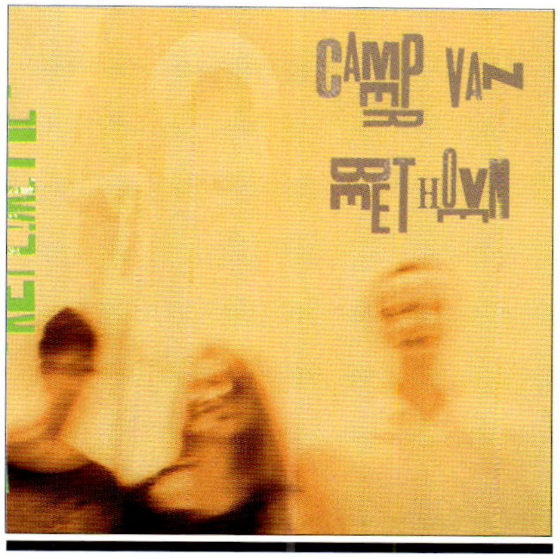

Billboard 200: *Key Lime Pie* (#141)

Camper Van Beethoven picked up steam with a cover of Status Quo's evergreen "Pictures of Matchstick Men."

KNOWN AS a college party band offering quasi-ethnic lunacy, Camper Van Beethoven had established a reputation for eclectic but fun music with numerous independent releases (including the classic "Take the Skinheads Bowling"). Yet *Key Lime Pie*, the California-based quintet's second album since signing with a major label, had a somber tone.

"That doesn't mean my life has taken a turn for the worse," lead singer David Lowery said. "We're an experimental band playing with mood and attitudes. I just didn't want to make your typical 'twentysomething' record—appreciating the richness of life, the ripening, the humor, the ironies, but also seeing the decay that goes right along with it. Playing music is such an anti-intellectual process for me."

Not to say that Camper Van Beethoven had abandoned their revered sense of humor. Songs like "(I Was Born in a) Laundromat" and "When I Win the Lottery" had humorous aspects, and a gleeful version of Status Quo's 1968 psychedelic hit "Pictures of Matchstick Men" emerged as a No. 1 hit on *Billboard*'s Modern Rock Tracks chart.

"It's a really stupid song—that's why I like it," Lowery said. "We've enjoyed playing it live for a couple of years. The violin plays the original guitar part. The record company wanted us to record the song for our last album, but we wanted them to deal with our own material first. Now they're happy, and we're glad it worked."

Amid creative and personal strife, Camper Van Beethoven called it a day following the tour for *Key Lime Pie*. ■

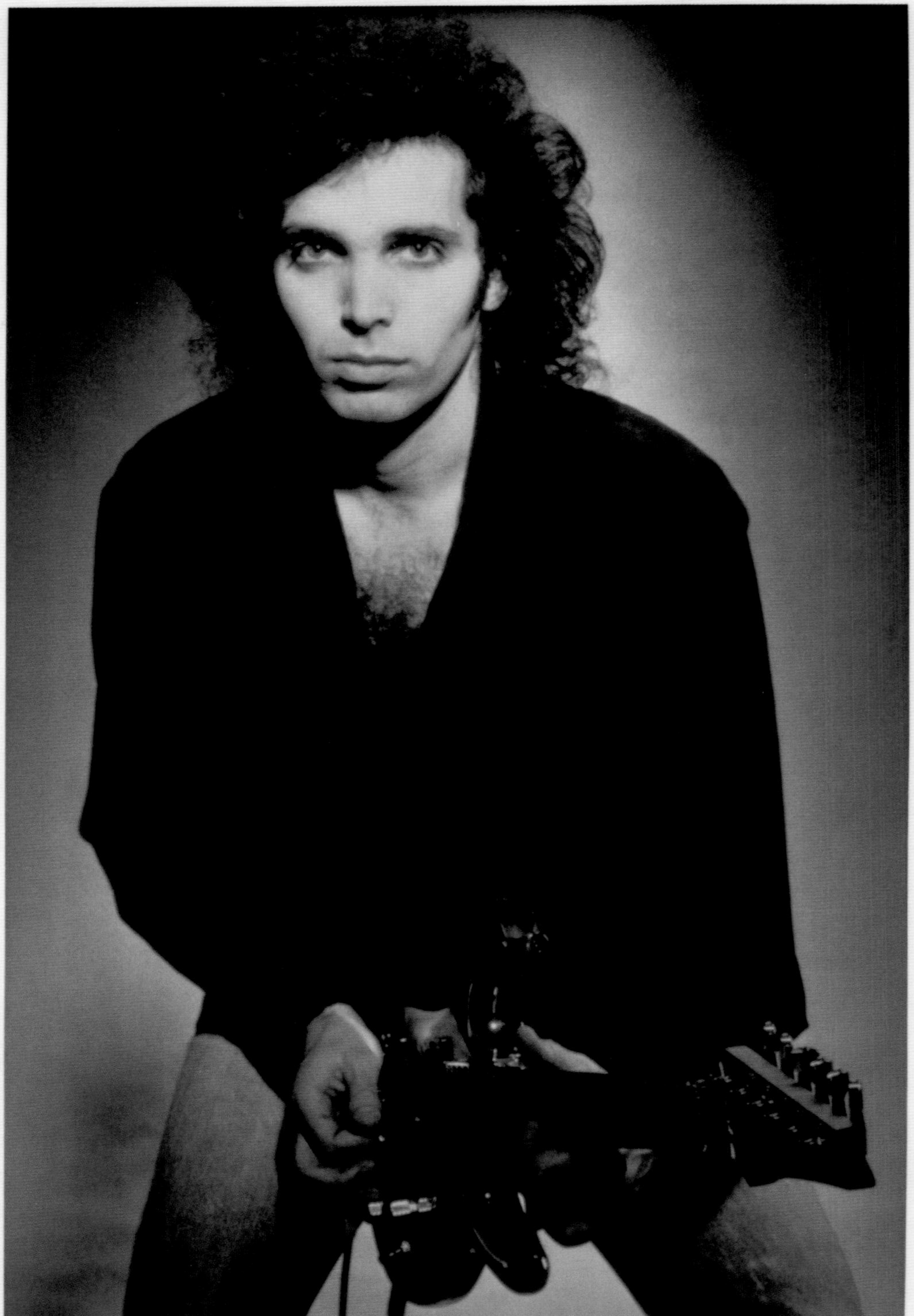

DIRECTION BY BILL GRAHAM MANAGEMENT

PHOTO BY LARRY DIMARZIO

JOE SATRIANI
FLYING IN A BLUE DREAM

RELATIVITY

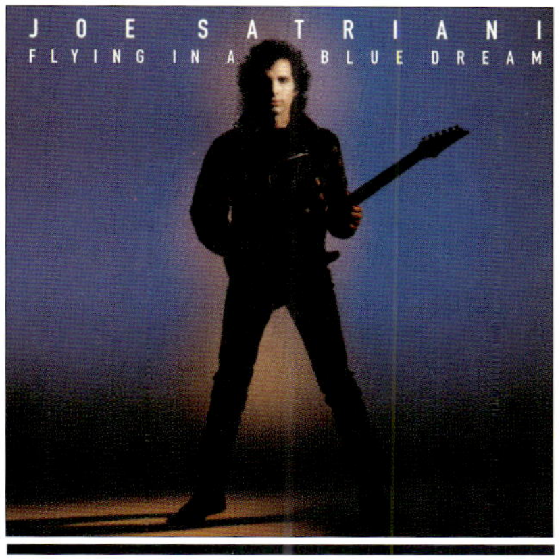

Billboard 200: *Flying in a Blue Dream* (#23)

With virtuosity, popularity and peer respect, Joe Satriani spearheaded a revival of the guitar-hero observance.

ALTHOUGH HE wore the mantle humbly, Joe Satriani had upped the ante as a guitar god. His albums were the highest-charting rock instrumental records since Jeff Beck's *Blow by Blow* in 1976, and the three leading guitar magazines rolled out the red carpet to salute him with "Best Guitarist" honors.

"Sitting in my apartment, there's nothing that makes me feel like a guitar hero," Satriani said. "I know there's a reason for the tag being applied. When I was a kid, my exposure to guitar heroes was possible because the media lifted them up on a pedestal and allowed me to see them. But I won't let it go to my head now. I'm really a nobody, just a guy who plays guitar."

The *Flying in a Blue Dream* album picked up where 1987's *Surfing with the Alien* left off, and Satriani exhibited artistic growth by singing for the first time on not one, but six cuts. Satriani's rarefied gift was apparent in the album's dozen instrumentals. He received acclaim for his dazzling array of tricks—whammy-bar theatrics, precision speed picking, double-handed hammer-ons.

But Satriani exhibited none of the ego-fed narrowness generally associated with his line of work. Offstage, instead of talking guitar shop, he explained the influence of the Silver Surfer, the comic book character who appeared on the cover of *Surfing with the Alien*. The single from *Flying in a Blue Dream* was the fire-breathing "Return to Shalla-Bal," Shalla-Bal being the queen of the Silver Surfer.

"My parents never allowed me to read comics—they thought I should be reading James Baldwin or Sartre," Satriani recalled. "When the title 'Surfing with the Alien' just popped into my head, I wrote a song around that little mind-movie. The day I delivered the record to my label, I learned the Silver Surfer used to be the production manager's nickname. He sent me some comic books, and I was surprised at this character, a metaphysical good guy who had missed growing up. That's something I identify with.

"So I got involved in comics very late in life, and now I've written a lot of songs around the series. The Surfer is still in love with Shalla-Bal, but they can't consummate the relationship in the comic book because of who they are now. It's part of the poor guy's angst as he rides his surfboard around the universe protecting planets—he's conquering all of these ridiculous forces of evil, and he keeps thinking, 'I've got to get back to Shalla-Bal.' The guy lives a pretty sad life, actually."

Satriani was attracting a following beyond drooling guitar fanatics obsessed with technique. While he'd long been accustomed to fans hopping onstage to play air guitar with him, adamant female fans were jumping stage barriers to hug and kiss him. "I've seen a change," he laughed. "You still see guys up front banging their heads, but now you see couples, less-energetic folks who have come to listen. Either way, I like it. I haven't yet met an audience I haven't enjoyed." ■

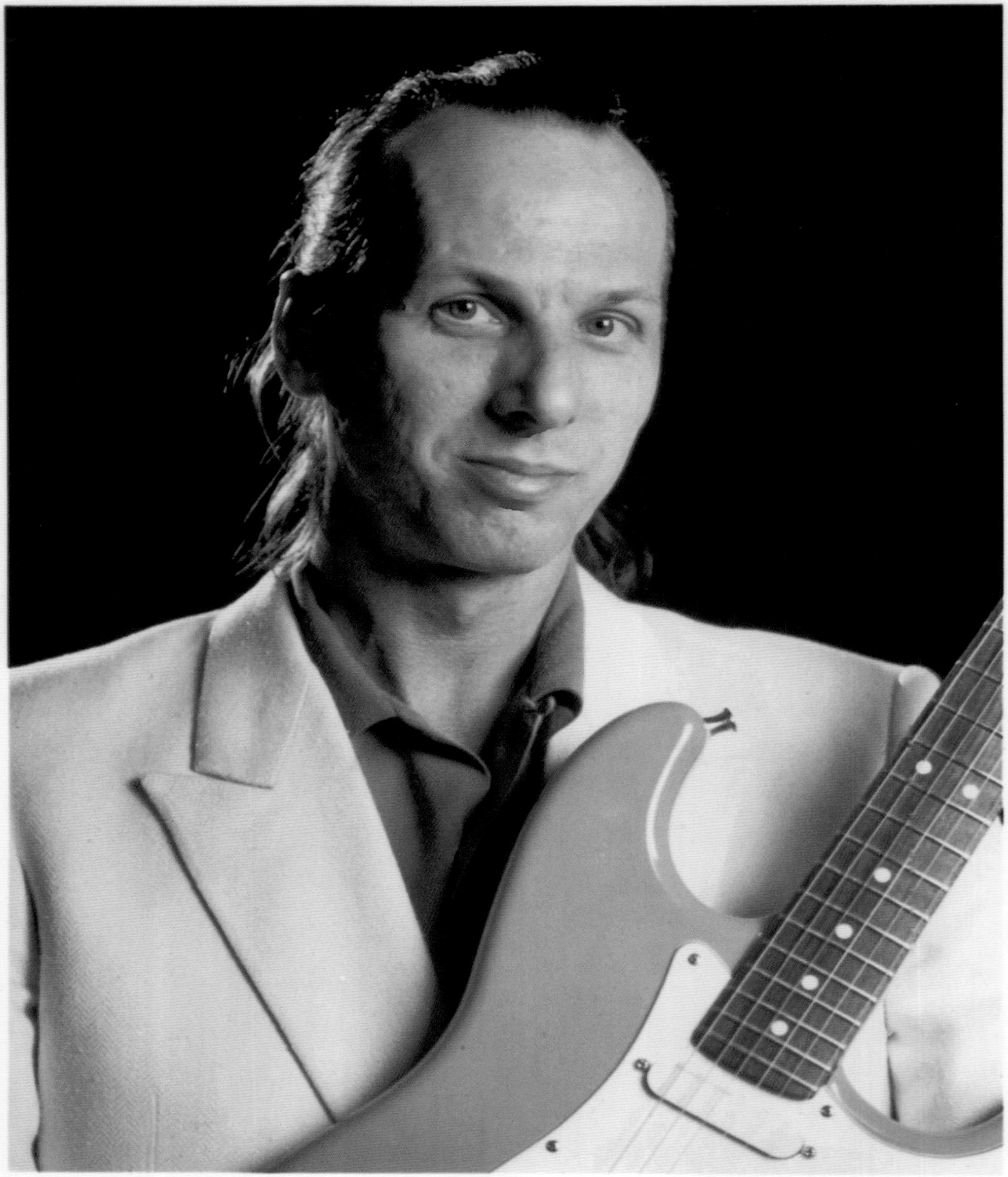

Adrian Belew

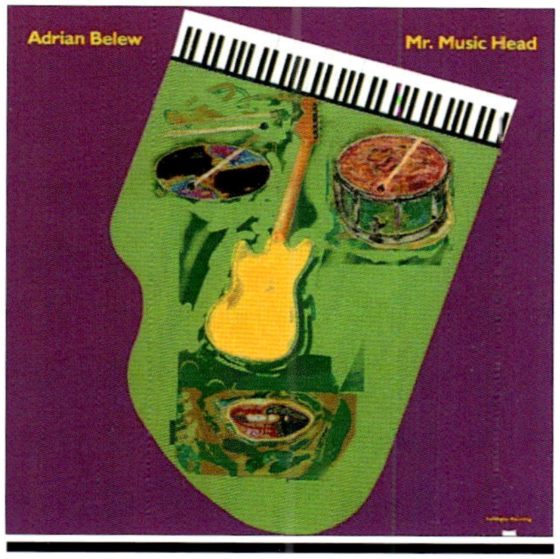

Billboard 200: *Mr. Music Head* (#114)
Billboard Hot 100: "Oh Daddy" (#58)

Adrian Belew's "Oh Daddy," a hit on the modern-rock charts, began with questions his children posed to him.

EVER SINCE Frank Zappa discovered him in a Nashville club circa 1977, guitarist Adrian Belew had served as a hired gun with such notables as David Bowie, Talking Heads, Tom Tom Club, Laurie Anderson and Paul Simon. When Robert Fripp, another virtuoso guitarist, decided to reform King Crimson, he hired Belew.

But that résumé hadn't been enough to impress Belew's kids. "My 10-year-old son is a literal-minded, straightforward little boy—he's always saying stuff like, 'Hey, Dad, when you die, do I get all your stuff?'" the Kentucky native laughed. "One day he said, 'Hey, I thought you were supposed to be a rock star—how come you're not on MTV?' So I put that question and my answers into a tongue-in-cheek song."

The outcome was "Oh Daddy," a light-hearted duet between Belew and his 11-year-old daughter Audie about the music industry's star-making machinery. Ironically, the radio/video fave single allowed Belew to reach a new audience in a major way.

Belew considered himself fortunate to have started as a sideman, but he felt strongly about striking out as an artist in his own right. "Oh Daddy" opened *Mr. Music Head*, his fourth solo album. It featured Belew not only playing guitars and singing but also handling all other instruments (except for bass on two tracks). The result? A work laced with humor, overt references to *Revolver*-era Beatles and an array of calculatedly weird guitar noises.

"I'm trying to craft a form of pop music that's a little left of center," Belew mused. "The combination of something slightly avant-garde and pop at the same time intrigues me. My favorite period was when you were able to hear (the Beatles' classic) 'Strawberry Fields' on the radio—the idea that thousands of housewives all over the world were grooving on that song was fascinating to me. I'm still trying to wave that flag. And people are waking up to the idea that music on the radio can be a little unusual and still memorable and accessible."

Long-time friend Bowie greeted *Mr. Music Head* with enthusiasm, approaching Belew about joining him as musical director for the "Sound + Vision" world tour. ■

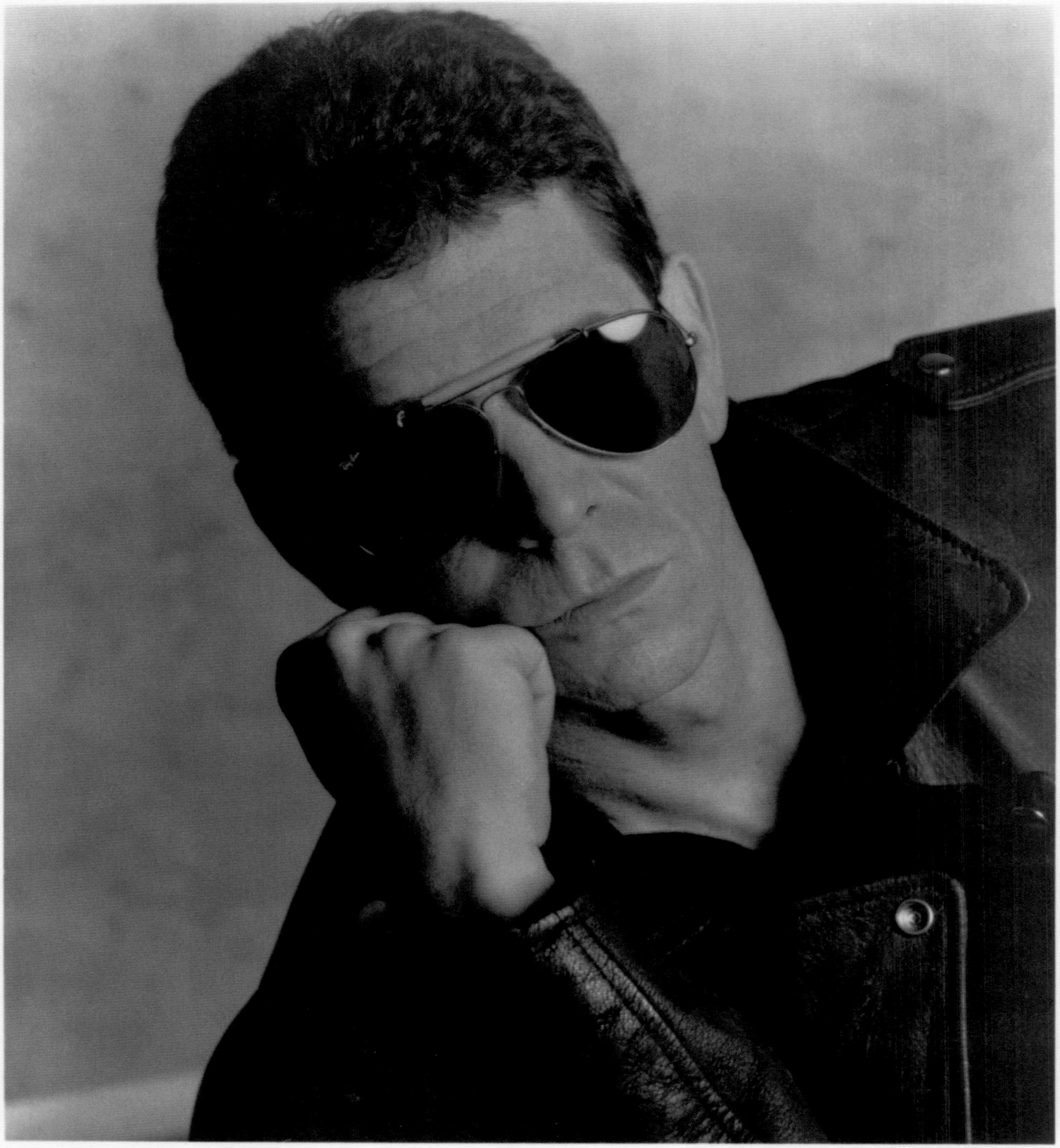

PHOTO CREDIT: WARING ABBOTT

LOU REED

SIRE™

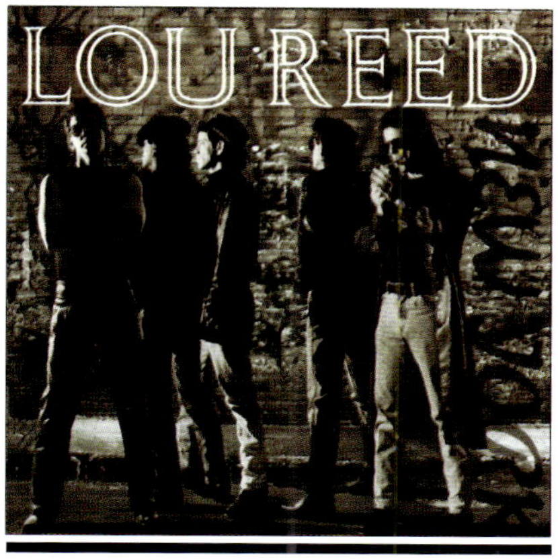

Billboard 200: *New York* (#40)

Lou Reed examined and exposed the horrors and slight joys of urban existence with his vivid *New York* album.

TWO-PLUS decades into a remarkable career—founder of the Velvet Underground, solo artist behind "Walk on the Wild Side" and "Perfect Day," protégé of Andy Warhol and an enduring figure on the art and music scene—Lou Reed remained the master of chronicling slices of life in the Big Apple. *New York* was his strongest performance in years, a typically uncompromising vision of urban angst filled with streetwise references to AIDS, poverty, family violence, pollution, drugs and race relations.

"I had three years to think about it," Reed said. "As I was writing the songs, I saw a certain direction, an edge. My guitar player heard them and said, 'That's what eight years of Reagan does to you.' I knew then I wasn't the only one feeling that way."

The infectious collection of riffs Reed created for *New York* belied the naked truth of the lyrics. The old-fashioned crackle of Reed's Fender guitar propelled "Dirty Blvd.," a contrast of the city's haves and the have-nots that topped the modern rock charts.

"I wasn't worried about the 'topicality' of the record," Reed said, "because from my point of view, things didn't look like they were getting better, they looked like they were getting worse. I figured that by the time the record hit, there would be a whole slew of circumstances similar to what I was writing about in the first place—like Exxon (the *Exxon Valdez* oil spill). It's a sad comment on things, but we've been joking—every catastrophe makes *New York* more timely."

In the album's liner notes, Reed advised that the 14-song *New York* was "meant to be listened to once, in one 58-minute sitting, as though it were a book or a movie." In performance, he presented *New York* in its entirety, with the same clarity and directness found on the record.

"Some of the songs were just based on particular instances in New York City that shouldn't be forgotten. You see the effects of our mutual inhumanity first in New York, but in every city, you just change the name, and the incidents are the same. I called the album *New York*, but there's a 'Dirty Blvd.' in every city. We haven't rolled into a town yet that doesn't have a problem or a little secret." ■

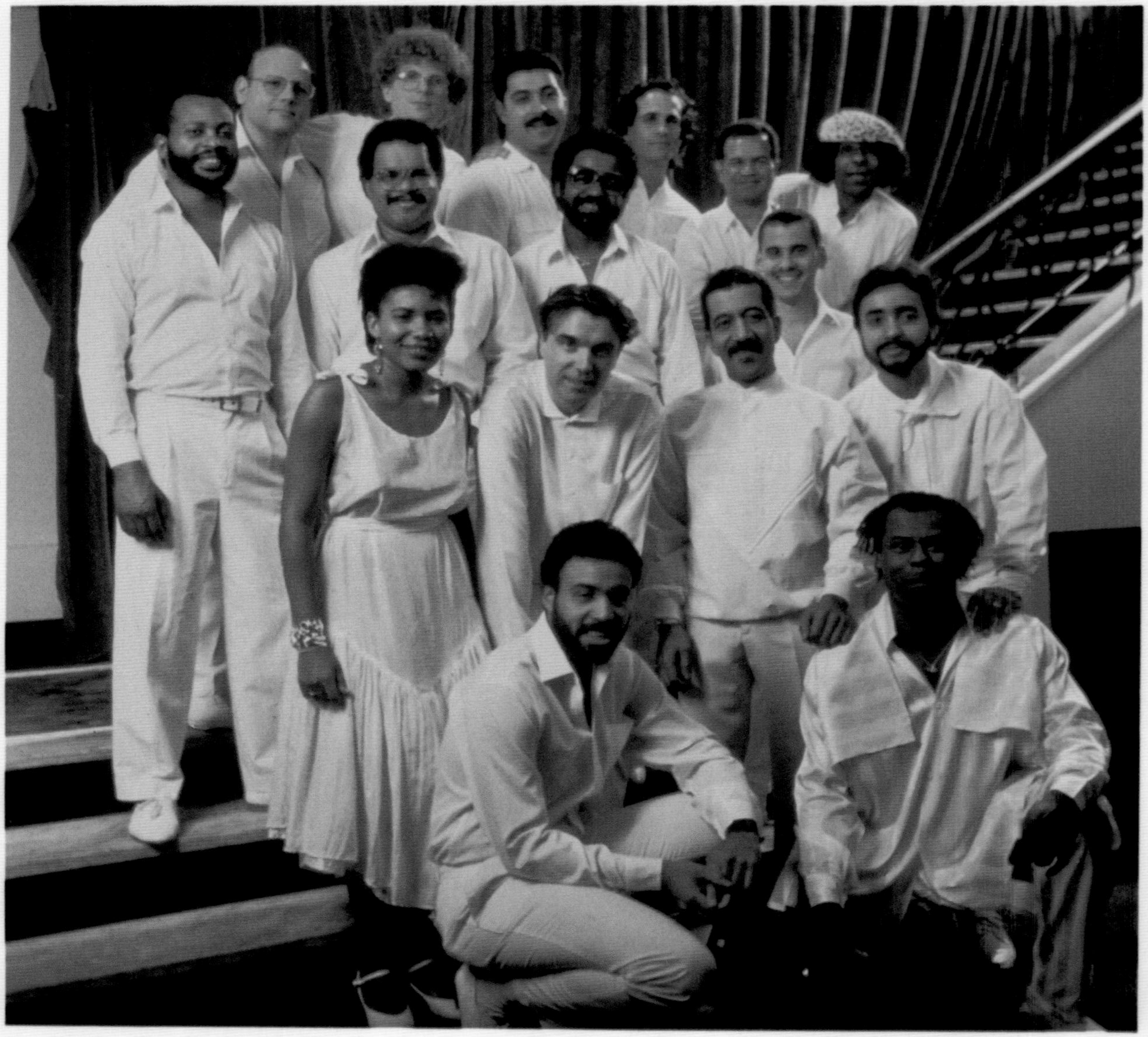

Photo Credit: F. Stop Fitzgerald

David Byrne Rei Momo Tour

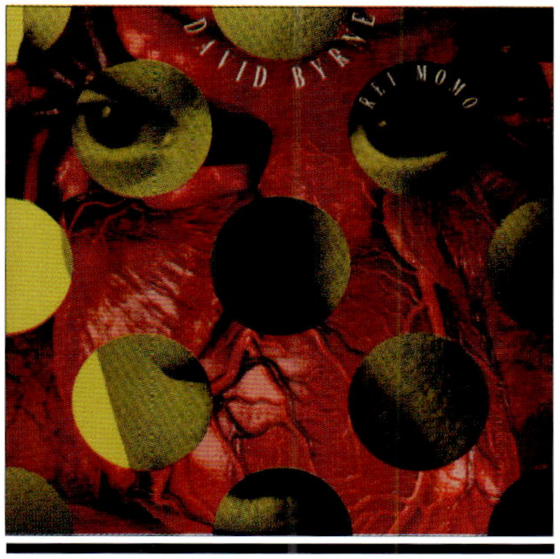

Billboard 200: *Rei Momo* (#71)

David Byrne's obsession with world music inspired *Rei Momo*, his first solo album after leaving Talking Heads.

AFTER PIONEERING new-wave performances circa 1978, Talking Heads took on overt African influences, and frontman David Byrne continued to draw on global civilization for his work in music, film and theater. While the band was on "a long sabbatical," Byrne's interest turned to the brassy, vigorously percussive style of Brazilian and Latin American pop music. "The rhythms are more sensual—I found it more enjoyable to go out dancing at the Latin clubs than the discos," he explained.

Byrne's first project exploring Latin sounds materialized with the 1987 single "Loco De Amore," a song he wrote and produced for Celia Cruz (known as "the queen of Latin music") and recorded with several salsa stars; it was included on the soundtrack of Jonathan Demme's movie *Something Wild*. He also compiled two anthologies of Brazilian music.

Byrne's passion blossomed into *Rei Momo* (translated to "Carnival King"), a solo album of original songs combining Latin influence (salsa, merengue, charanga) and pop styles. A progressive juxtaposition, it melded Byrne's off-kilter narrative sense (the lyrics were in English) with his band's energy and involvement. Byrne collaborated with the finest New York-based salsa musicians in the studio and on the accompanying tour, his first stage foray since the 1983 shows filmed for Talking Heads' *Stop Making Sense* movie, which Demme also directed.

The tour stopped in major cities through the US, Europe and Japan—and South America, where Byrne said he felt "a lot of trepidation, but I thought I needed to 'do the right thing,' to show those people what I was doing with their music.

"The local musicians articulated a good feeling—we were contributing to a sense of national pride. They see a lot of their culture being swallowed up by rock 'n' roll—the people who succeed are the people who sell out and don't play their native music. They were totally excited to see that other people love it and consider it part of the fabric of music in the new world. And what a relief. They could have hated it and said, 'Hey, he doesn't know how to dance or play the samba, so get him out of here.'"

Cynics cast Byrne as a musical dilettante who had raided non-Western cultures for his own devices, but his players convinced him he wasn't mutilating the music. "I was aware that those kinds of accusations were going to come up, so I was careful," he said. "But cultural meetings are already happening. For instance, the African musicians I know who live in Paris are already working with samplers and rhythm machines. It's not like going into the bush. So I just keep doing something different and having a good time with it. I've always felt I could go back and write regular songs, or as close to regular as I can get. But I'm trying to mix things together in my own way." ■

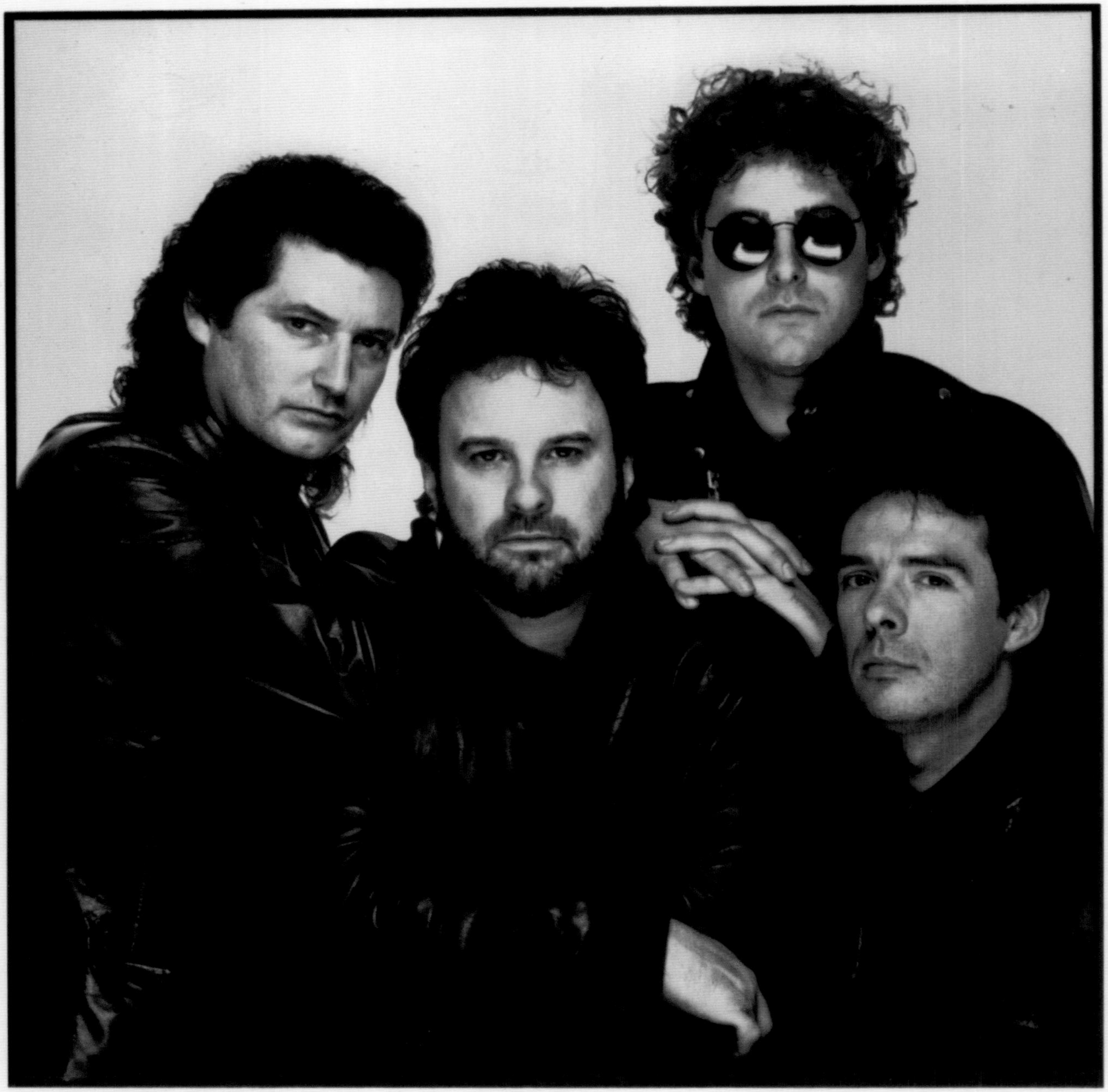

THE CALL

5/89

MCA RECORDS

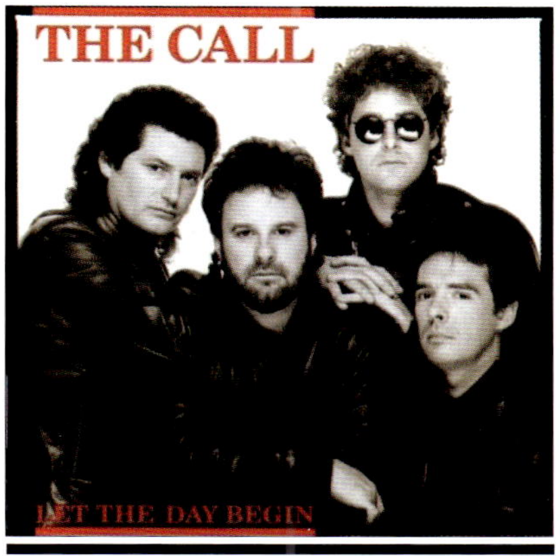

Billboard 200: *Let the Day Begin* (#64)
Billboard Hot 100: "Let the Day Begin" (#51)

The Call had a real shot at gaining widespread radio acceptance with the anthemic song "Let the Day Begin."

AFTER NEARLY a decade of work, the Call's fiery and literate rock had led to acclaim by critics and peers. "We never asked for music to give us a free ride or make us big shots," singer-songwriter-bassist Michael Been said. "All we ever asked was to be working musicians."

The Call's social awareness, musical passion, anthemic sound and even spirituality had resulted in partnerships with such movers and shakers as Peter Gabriel, Simple Minds singer Jim Kerr and former Band members Garth Hudson and Robbie Robertson. Been, one of rock's most literate lyricists, made his acting debut when director Martin Scorsese cast him as the apostle John in 1988's controversial *Last Temptation of Christ.* He also contributed to the soundtrack for Scorsese's Paul Newman/Tom Cruise film *The Color of Money.*

"We all had offers to do other things, to play with other people," Been said. "But when the four of us play together, it's better than any one of us and more than the sum of the parts. That's why we do it."

The Call made a breakthrough with *Let the Day Begin*, providing the compassionate "Uncovered" and the title track, which became a No. 1 hit on album-oriented rock radio. "And it got on Top 40 formats before the hammer fell," Been said. "We'd love to have a big smash, but we have this reputation as a political/spiritual/message/alternative band, and we still carry that around. If Paul McCartney had put out 'Let the Day Begin,' it would have been Top 10, but people don't think of the Call that way." ■

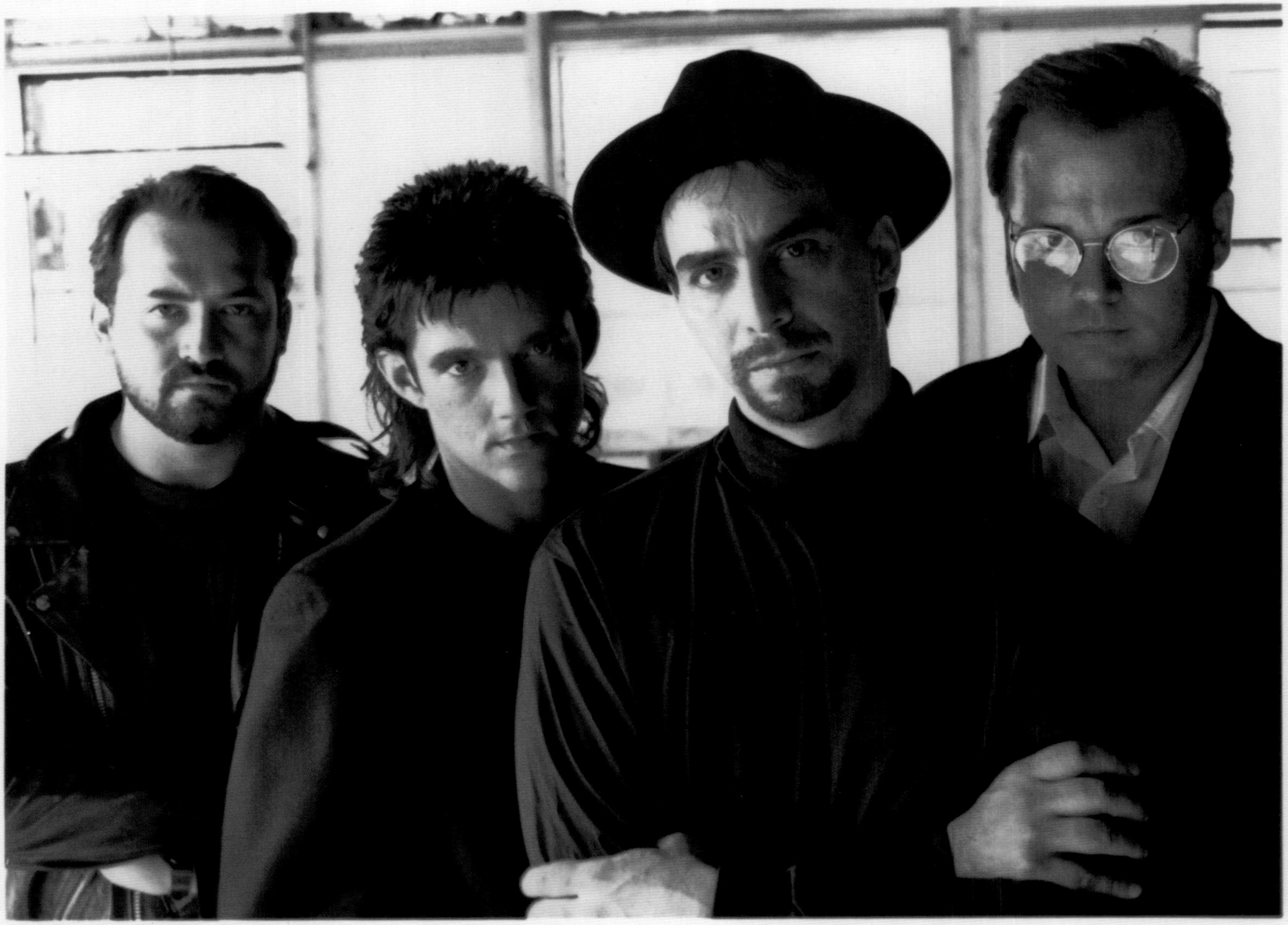

Photo: Dewey Nicks / 1989

THE SMITHEREENS

L-R: Jim Babjak, Mike Mesaros, Pat DiNizio, Dennis Diken

ENIGMA. Capitol RECORDS

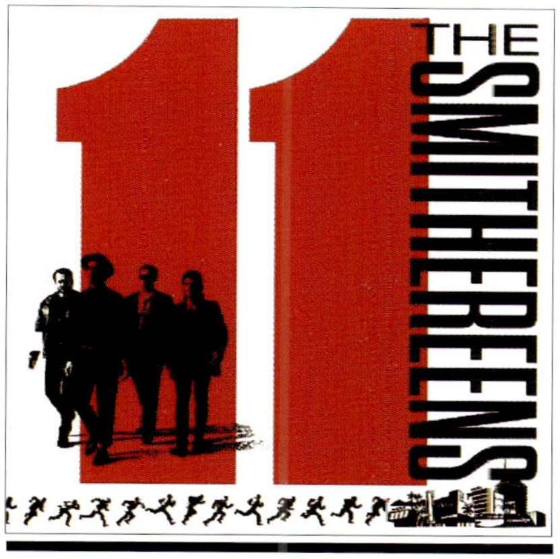

Billboard 200: *11* (#41)
Billboard Hot 100: "A Girl Like You" (#38);
"Blues Before and After" (#94)

The Smithereens' *11* featured "A Girl Like You," an urgent pop-rock classic and the group's first Top 40 hit.

IN JUST a few years, the Smithereens had brought an intelligent, passionate approach to guitar-drenched power-pop, delivering some terrific hook-laden songs—"Blood and Roses," "Behind the Wall of Sleep," "Only a Memory" and "House We Used to Live In."

And *11*, the New Jersey band's third album, was even more aggressive and focused than its predecessors, signaled by the pulverizing opening chords of "A Girl Like You"—the guitars punched, the drums snapped and the pretty harmonies kept the sound edgy but nonabrasive. "It's nice that we're having some success with that song, considering how heavy the guitars are," vocalist and guitarist Pat DiNizio said. "Maybe it'll change something for the better on the radio."

DiNizio and Jim Babjak played Rickenbacker guitars (which produced a ringing chiming sound associated with the Byrds) through Marshall amplifiers (like those used by heavy-metal bands such as Black Sabbath). DiNizio's songs on *11* were Sixties-going-on-Nineties—a fuzzed-out solo on "Blues Before and After" paid tribute to Jeff Beck's Yardbirds days, and his moody, winsome voice drove the Beatlesesque ballad "Blue Period" (with harmonies from Belinda Carlisle).

DiNizio collected movie posters, and the title of the Smithereens' *11* was a sly sendup of the 1960 film *Ocean's 11*, a comedy starring the Rat Pack—Frank Sinatra played the kingpin of a gang scheming to heist millions for a few Las Vegas casinos.

"When I'm home, I don't listen to much music," he said. "I'm visually oriented, and I try to exploit whatever hobbies I have for my work. I get a lot of imagery that winds up as musical ideas and lyrics in songs. So when Dennis and I walked into a used bookstore and found a paperback book tie-in for *Ocean's 11*, that sparked our imagination to re-create the image of the paperback cover on our album. And part of the point was to mislead people. Now a lot of fans are looking for albums four through ten." ■

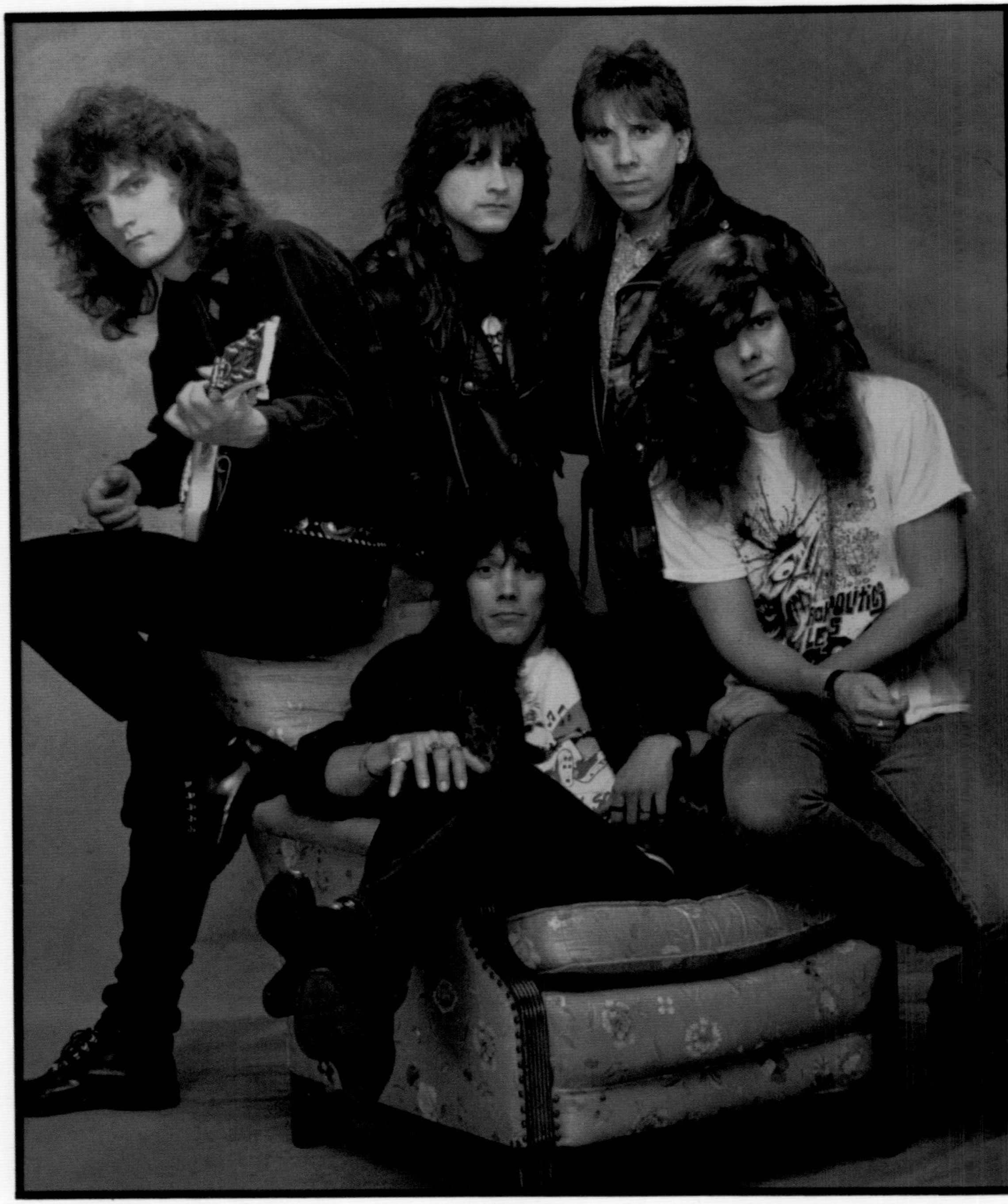

Photo Credit: Gene Kirkland

Frank Hannon Brian Wheat Jeff Keith Troy Luccketta Tommy Skeoch

TESLA

GEFFEN RECORDS

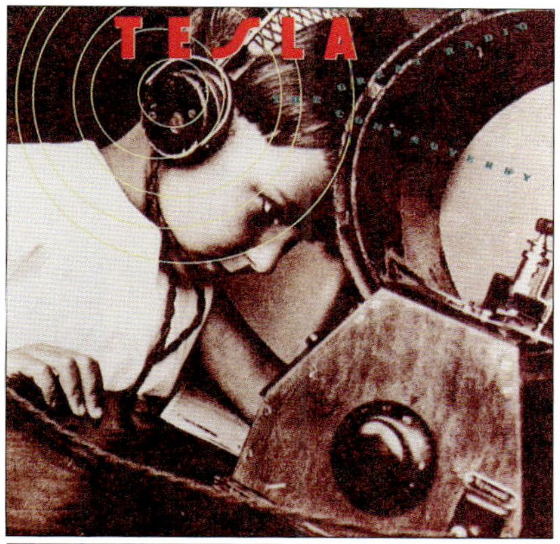

Billboard 200: *The Great Radio Controversy* (#18)
Billboard Hot 100: "Love Song" (#10)

Tesla's *The Great Radio Controversy* reached the Top 20 and spawned a gold single, the graceful "Love Song."

FOR A group hailing from decidedly unglamorous Sacramento, California, and had purposefully tried not to contrive an image for itself, Tesla may have surprised a few people with its rise to stardom. The band's 1986 debut album, *Mechanical Resonance*, went gold as the members toured for 14 months opening for David Lee Roth, Alice Cooper and Def Leppard. "We're out there grindin' and workin'," bassist Brian Wheat said. "Maybe if we had quick success, we might've been weirded out, but it's been step-by-step."

It was management and label executives who had suggested the band name. Eccentric and compulsive, Nikola Tesla was an innovative genius who discovered rotating magnetic fields, the basis of all alternating current machines. At first working for Thomas Edison, and later becoming his greatest rival, he invented the Tesla coil which powered the transformers in many radio sets. "He never got the credit he deserved," Wheat said. "Tesla was the underdog, and so were we when we were starting out in Sacramento. We could relate to the name."

The Great Radio Controversy was named for the legal struggle in the Forties when, five months after Tesla's death, the US Supreme Court upheld his patent for the invention of radio, long attributed to Guglielmo Marconi. Two songs from the album, "Hang Tough" and "Heaven's Trail (No Way You)" received considerable airplay, while "Love Song," a power ballad, rocketed the band into the Top 10. "You can destroy your life looking for it, but there's a love out there for everybody," singer and lyricist Jeff Keith said. "Maybe it's not here now, but you'll know it when you find it."

Despite the success, the musicians in Tesla remained as grounded as a coil invented by the man whose name they took. "In rock 'n' roll, people get all excited about you and would love to fill your shoes," Keith said. "But there's reality, too. Seeing a bum on the street is enough to pop my balloon. Or when you're at a party and some asshole screws it up. Or at a concert and everyone's having a great time and some guy gets hit over the head with a bottle. There's no way out but to walk heaven's trail—if it even exists."

Tesla shined at gritty, blues-based hard rock, but the band's commercial acme coincided with the "hairspray and makeup" movement. The members refused to conform to a premeditated "look" and remained gimmick-free, choosing instead to tour relentlessly. "We never think about being lumped in with the hair bands," Keith said. "We're a hair band—we're right 'hair' right now!" ■

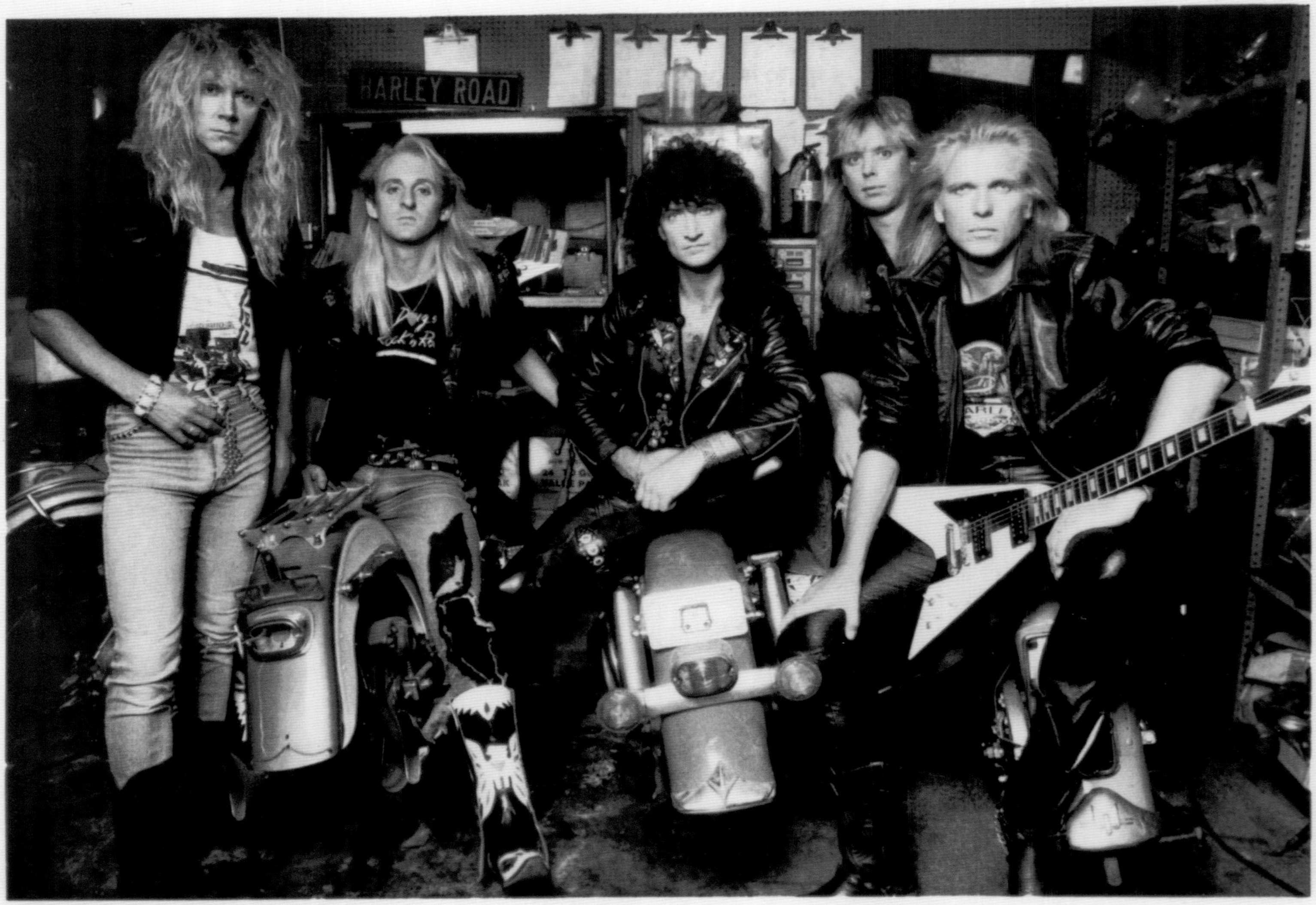

Photo: Robert John / 1989

Steve Mann Rocky Newton Robin McAuley Bodo Schopf Michael Schenker

McAULEY SCHENKER GROUP

Capitol Records

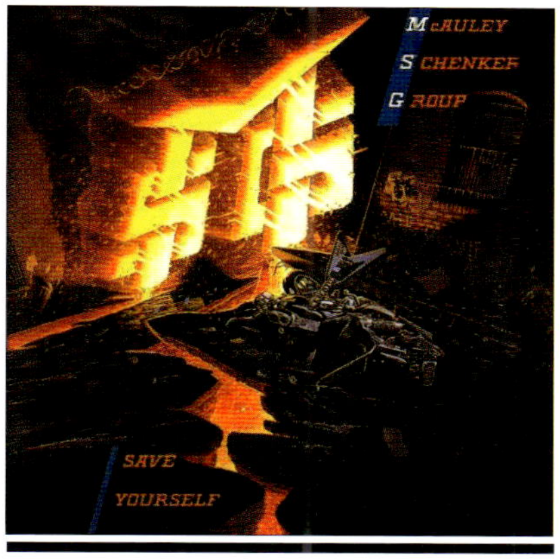

Billboard 200: *Save Yourself* (#92)
Billboard Hot 100: "Anytime" (#69)

A new incarnation of the hard-rocking McAuley Schenker Group had its highest-charting hit with "Anytime."

BECAUSE THE music demanded aggression and energy, most hard-rock bands subscribed to a faster-is-better approach. But even the metal crowd wasn't immune to the commercial value associated with a power ballad, an emotional song with a slow tempo and dramatic vocals.

The McAuley Schenker Group (also known as M.S.G. and originally as the Michael Schenker Group) was led by Michael Schenker, the influential ex-Scorpions and UFO guitarist who had earned a reputation among musicians and fans as one of rock's top players. A master of the Gibson Flying V, the German native not only played at a hundred miles an hour, but he also could craft powerful melodies.

"We are two different temperaments entirely," the Irish vocalist Robin McAuley said. "Michael plays from his heart, whatever a song calls for, but there's always a place for him to hook into. Few guitarists of his stature would listen to a singer."

Schenker's in-your-face heavy riffing marked the *Save Yourself* album, though he confined his guitar gymnastics to a well-executed part on the hit power ballad "Anytime," with passionate singing by McAuley. "Whatever kind of song it takes to 'make it' is okay with me," Schenker said, "as long as something makes it." ■

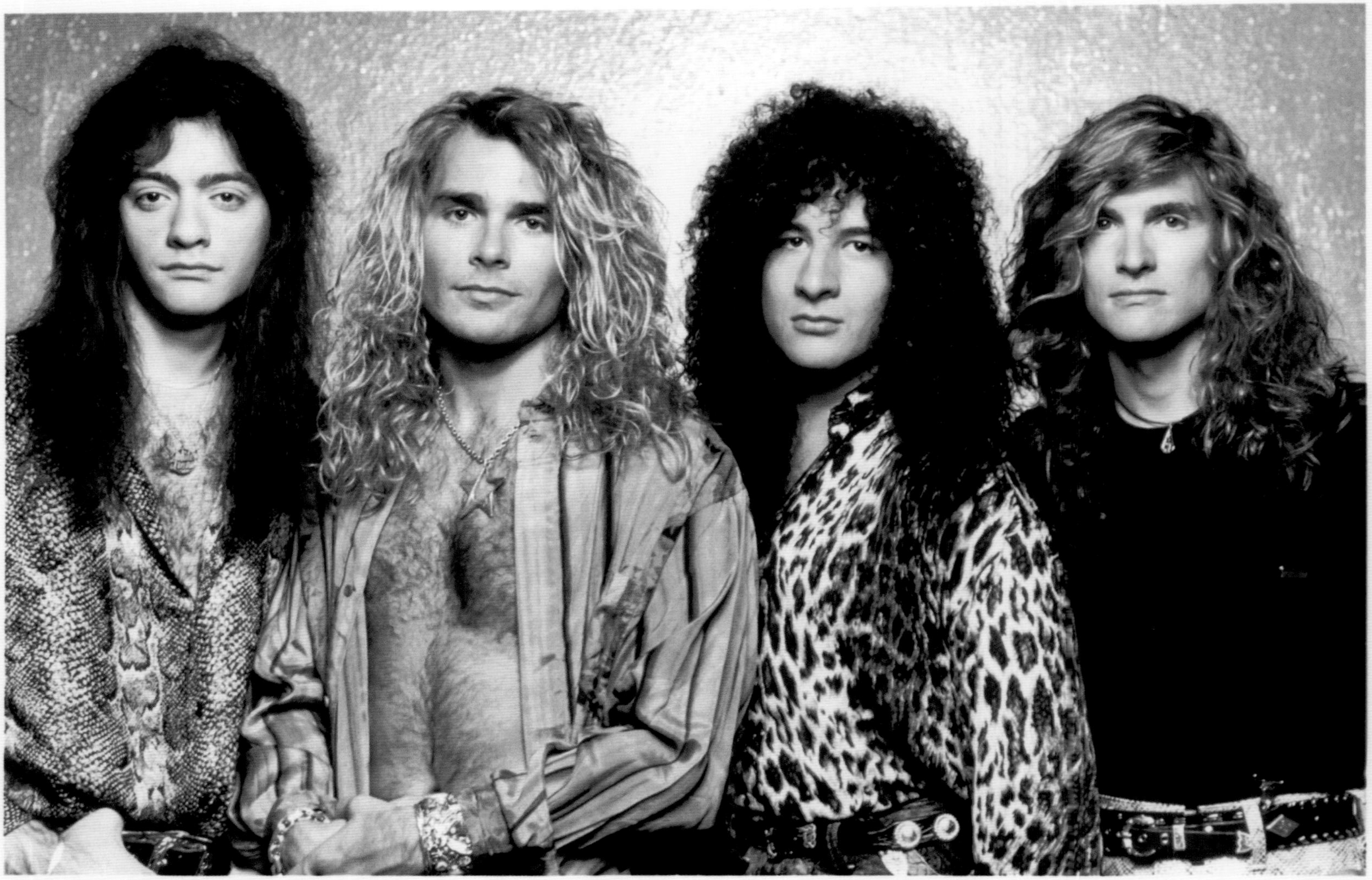

VITO BRATTA MIKE TRAMP GREG D'ANGELO JAMES LOMENZO

White Lion

ATLANTIC

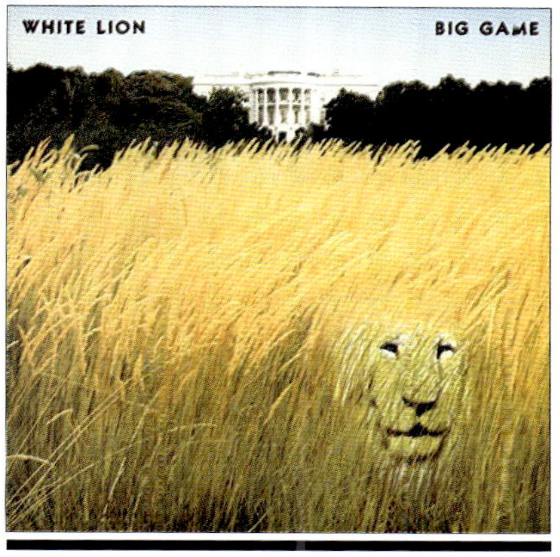

Billboard 200: *Big Game* (#19)
Billboard Hot 100: "Little Fighter" (#52); "Radar Love" (#59)

With the glam-metal genre reaching a mainstream peak, White Lion delivered another solid effort, *Big Game*.

THE 2-MILLION-SELLING *Pride* and the Top 10 hits "Wait" and "When the Children Cry" had propelled White Lion to stardom. On *Big Game*, the follow-up album, the hard-rock guys based lyrical themes on environmental issues. The scorching "Little Fighter," subtitled "In Memory of the Rainbow Warrior," was an anthem about the efforts of Greenpeace, the environmental group whose ship—the *Rainbow Warrior*—had been bombed and sunk in a New Zealand harbor by French intelligence operatives in 1985.

Mike Tramp, the band's Danish-born lead singer, donated a share of the song's proceeds to the Greenpeace organization. "If I can throw in a message while giving people a good time, I do it," Tramp said. "It's not that I'm gung-ho, but I would really prefer to see the grass very green and the sky very blue." "We made the video on a beach, and our clothes got destroyed from all the oil and tar," guitarist and co-founder Vito Bratta added. "People might say, 'Ah, they're rock stars, what do they care?' But we understand what's going on. We don't want to preach, but we want to do what we can."

Big Game also featured a hit cover of Golden Earring's classic "Radar Love," but Bratta wasn't convinced that the album would have an easier time commercially than *Pride*, which was out for eight months before it took off. "This business is horribly unpredictable," he said. "So I'm realistic. I'm not walking around with a big head. The music is the pride of it, and as long as people hear it…am I sounding like John Denver again?" ■

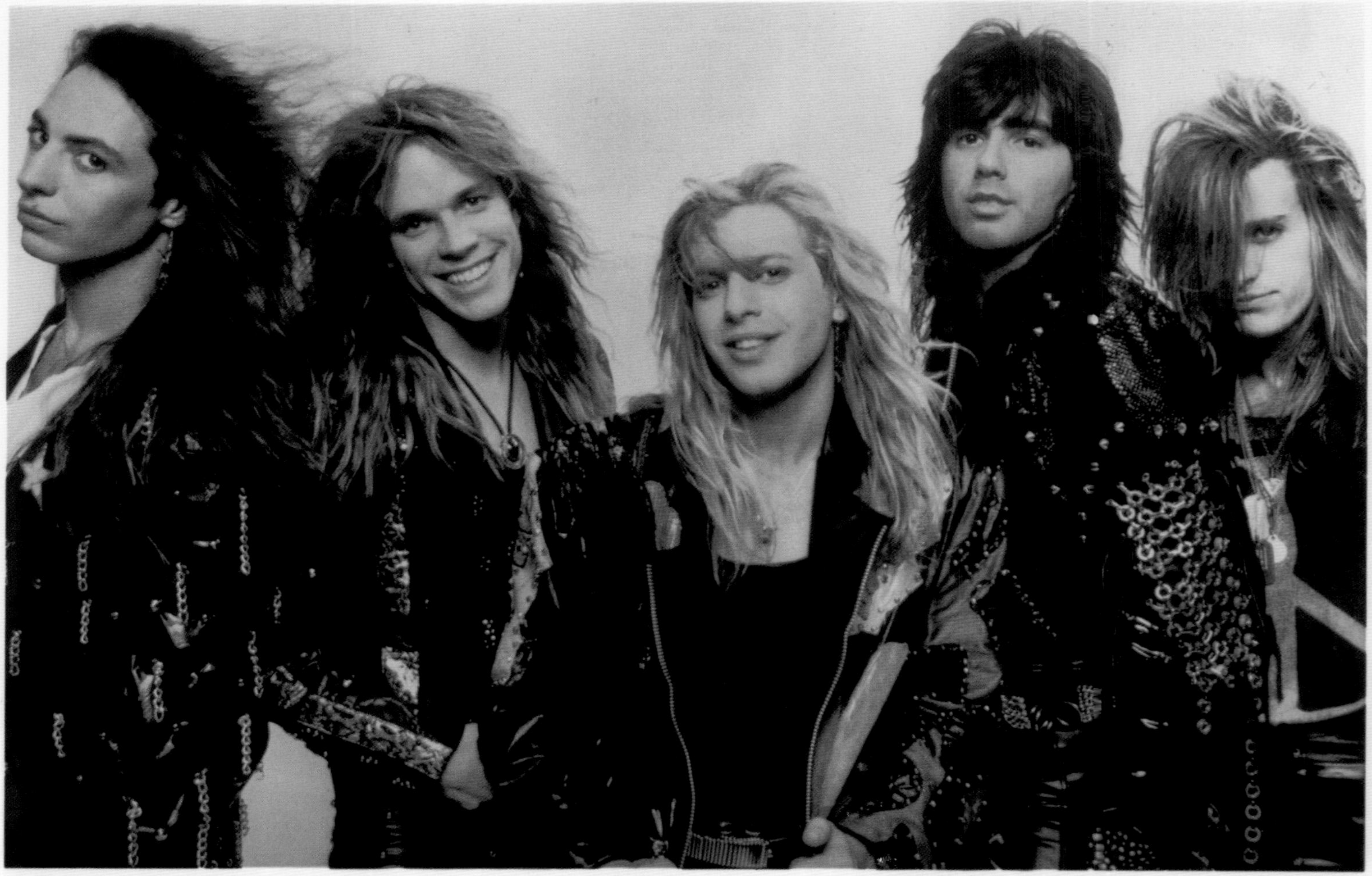

PHOTO: CAROLINE GREYSHOCK

L to R: KASEY SMITH, Keyboards: ANDY TIMMONS, Guitar: TED POLEY, Lead Vocals: BRUNO RAVEL, Bass: STEVE WEST Drums

IMAGINE RECORDS

CARBINE MANAGEMENT, INC.

Danger DANGER

EPA
EPIC PORTRAIT ASSOCIATED
8906

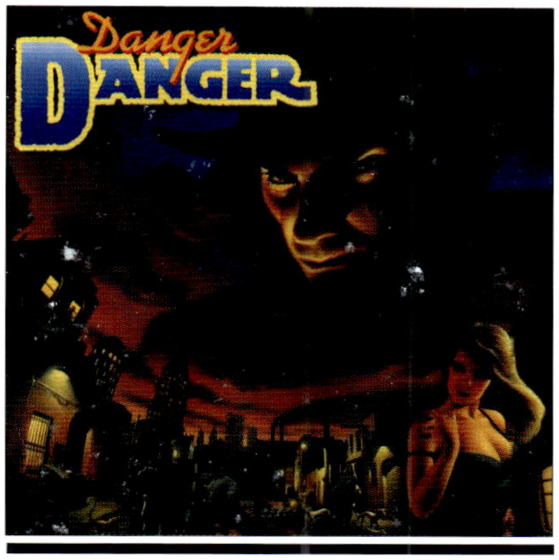

Billboard 200: *Danger Danger* (#88)
Billboard Hot 100: "Bang Bang" (#49)

MTV's exposure of the "Naughty Naughty" and "Bang Bang" videos galvanized Danger Danger's fan base.

IN MOST glam-rock bands, the guitar player wrote the music and the singer wrote the lyrics. But the visionaries in Danger Danger played in the rhythm section—drummer Steve West and bassist Bruno Ravel co-founded the band in New York during the fall of 1987.

"Bruno is a classically trained cellist, and I've been into music ever since I was six," West explained. "We wanted to play a certain kind of music that no one in New York was playing, and we didn't want to wait around. So we wrote songs and determined our own fate."

The two friends grew up in the New York borough of Queens, powerfully influenced by flamboyant stage styles. "We're into American rock 'n' roll, heartland radio songs—Night Ranger, 38 Special, Loverboy, Kiss, Aerosmith, Eddie Money, Bryan Adams," West enthused. "Cheap Trick is my favorite band." They found the perfect lineup for their own group, and *Danger Danger* interspersed salacious rockers such as "Naughty Naughty" with right-to-rock anthems like "Bang Bang."

"Nobody in New York is into that stuff, but they're not setting any trends—they follow everything that comes out of Los Angeles," West said. "When L.A. started the new-wave "skinny-tie" thing, every New York band did that. Then the Quiet Riot/Mötley Crüe heavy-metal thing started happening, and everybody in New York wanted to do that. The latest is the Guns N' Roses 'street gypsy' thing, and now everybody is doing that. Danger Danger isn't." ■

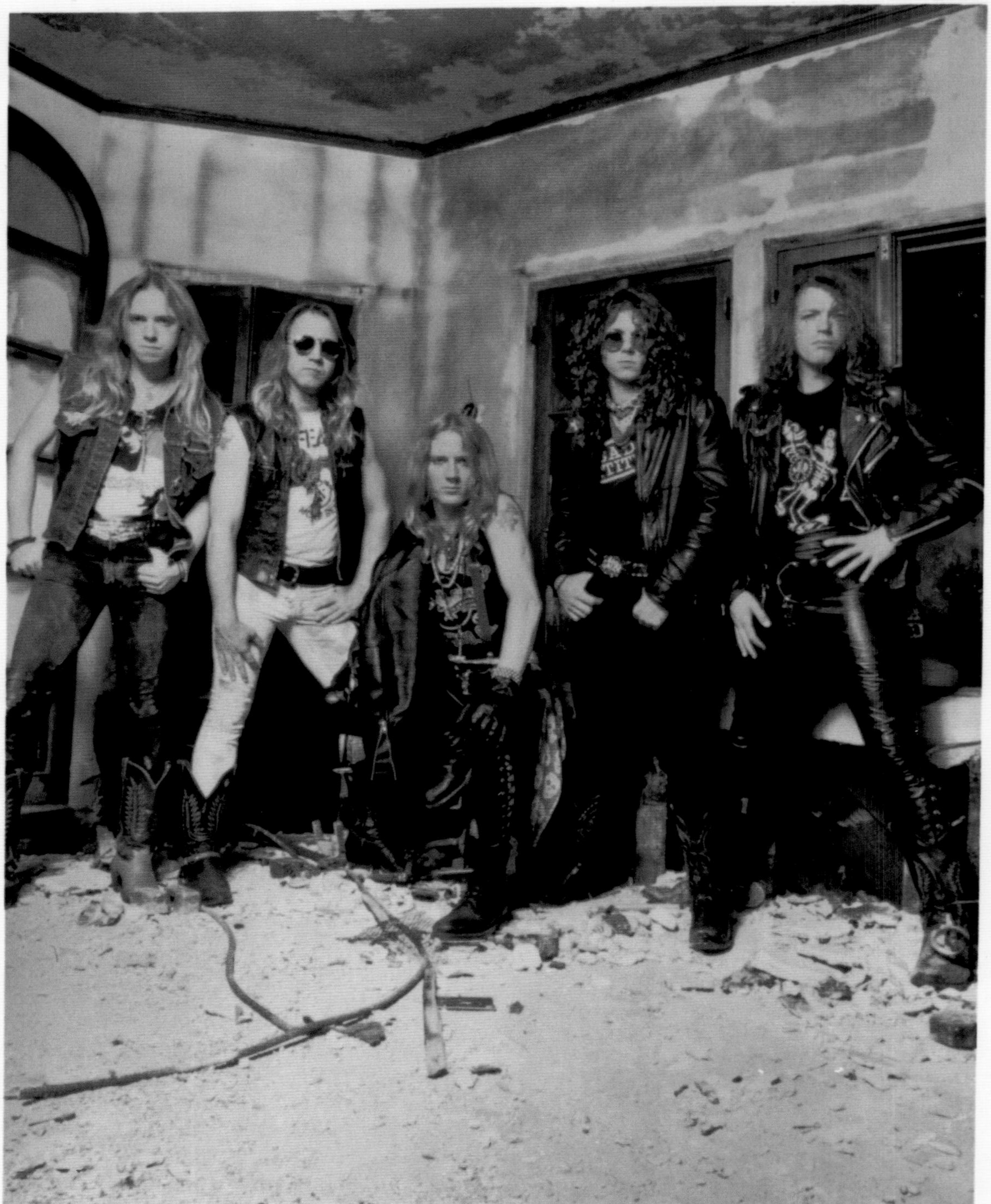

PHOTOGRAPH: NEIL ZLOZOWER

From left: MIKE WATSON, MARK GEARY, JASON McMASTER, DANNY AARON, SCOTT DALHOVER.

DANGEROUS TOYS

Columbia

8911

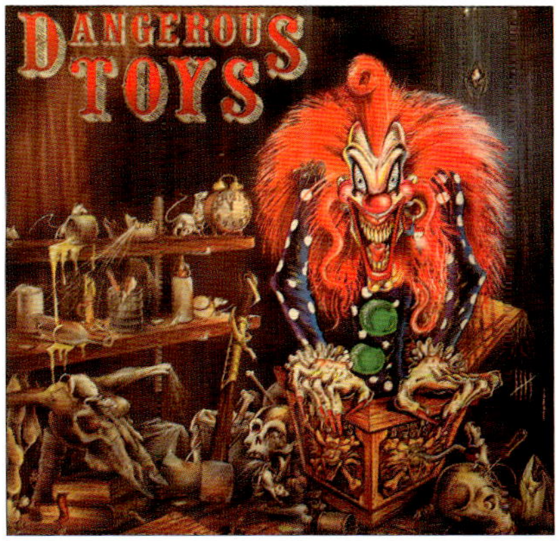

Billboard 200: *Dangerous Toys* (#65)

Dangerous Toys consolidated its rough-and-tumble blues-rock sound within an eponymous debut recording.

THE FIVE youthful members of the Austin, Texas-based quintet DangerousToys backed up their songs with a playfully brazen attitude. "We're street kids—I haven't had a job in the last six years, and one of our guitarists lived in his old screwed-up Mazda for a while," singer Jason McMaster recalled. "We never intended to get signed, we never made a demo tape. We just played clubs twice a week so we could make 40 bucks and eat. But when you don't have intentions, good things happen."

On the strength of an early performance at the South by Southwest festival in 1988, before the band had even been together six months, Dangerous Toys signed with Columbia Records. Produced by Max Norman, who had worked with Ozzy Osbourne, *Dangerous Toys* was true to the band's fiery brand of rock.

The driving rhythms of "Teas'n, Pleas'n" and the tuneful "Scared" received scattered radio airplay, and the frivolously brazen "Sport'n a Woody" was also released as a single to promote the album. Dangerous Toys' raw blend of metal with "chicken-fried-steak-Texas-style-blues," as McMaster put it, differed greatly from the glam fare reigning on MTV's *Headbanger's Ball*.

"For me, Dangerous Toys is back-to-basics roots-rock, even though the structuring of our songs gets a little funked out," McMaster said. "You can't just get a tattoo and shave your head, or grow your hair and wear Spandex, or poof your hair and put eyeliner on. You have to grow up around it, have some kind of heart for it." ■

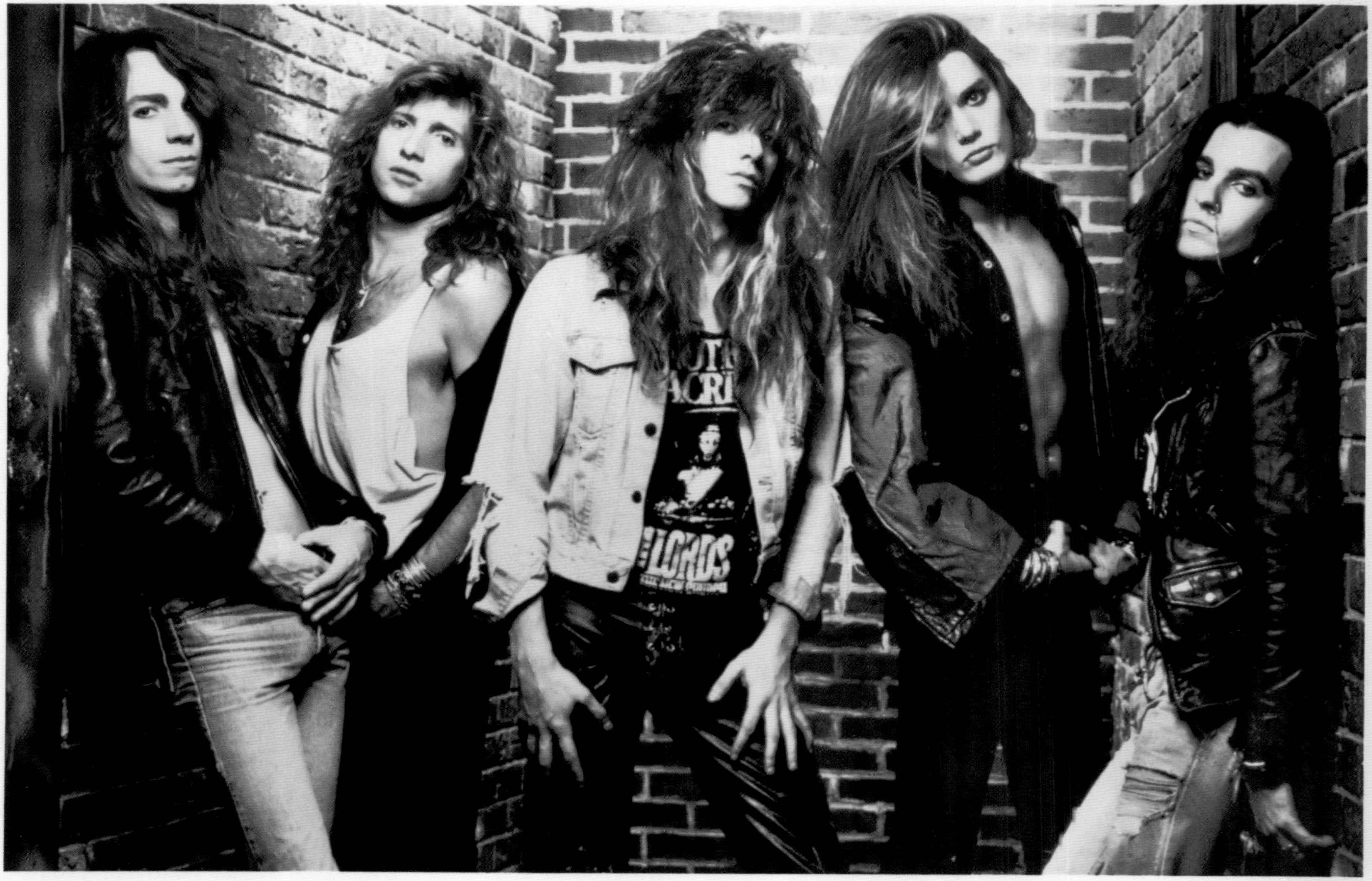

SCOTTI HILL ROB AFFUSO DAVE "THE SNAKE" SABO SEBASTIAN BACH RACHEL BOLAN

SKID ROW

ATLANTIC

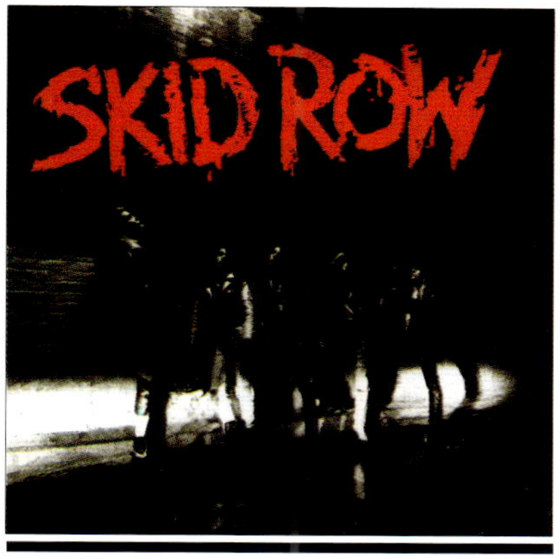

Billboard 200: *Skid Row* (#6)
Billboard Hot 100: "Youth Gone Wild" (#99);
"18 and Life" (#4); "I Remember You" (#6)

Skid Row's self-titled first album yielded a couple of accessible metal hits, "18 & Life" and "I Remember You."

HARD ROCK'S hottest new act was a rude 'n' rowdy band from the New York tri-state area. *Skid Row*, a Top 10 album, featured the radio-friendly anthems "Youth Gone Wild," "I Remember You" and "18 & Life" (a No. 1 video on *Dial MTV*). But Skid Row received more attention for the rebel-without-a-clue posturing of Sebastian Bach, the band's fast-talking, good-looking frontman.

The untamed vocalist was arrested after a Massachusetts concert when a bottle he threw back at an audience member who'd struck and bloodied him accidently hit an innocent woman. He outraged non-homophobes when he appeared in a photograph wearing a T-shirt bearing the slogan "AIDS Kills Fags Dead." And Bach was charged on numerous occasions by assorted law-enforcement officials with onstage obscenity—he screamed the f-word at least four times per sentence fragment.

The four members of Skid Row had enlisted the 20-year-old Bach for the lead singer job in the fall of 1988, after they already had the songs that ended up on their debut album. "We wanted someone perfect, a brat," drummer Rob Affuso laughed. "He's got that reckless, don't-give-a-damn attitude. We call him 'Marshall Mouth.'"

Skid Row's chief songwriter, bassist Rachel Bolan—the guy with the nose chain (his last name was a tribute to Marc Bolan of T. Rex, an early hero)—was a founding member with guitarist Dave "the Snake" Sabo (so nicknamed for the Frank Zappa song "Baby Snakes," "but he gets tired of telling that story and says it's because of his nipple hair"). Bolan insisted he had no problem with Bach's prominence.

"That kind of stuff is so trivial to me—it really doesn't mean all that much," Bolan said. "Bas' uses the f-word like punctuation. We don't all agree with each other all the time—in this band, you get five different opinions on the same subject, that's the way it is. Everyone's responsible for his own actions. But sometimes if Bas does something, it comes down on all of us. That's a lot of shit, but hey—things could be worse."

Another catalyst for Skid Row's success was its tour opening for Bon Jovi. "That exposure has helped," Affuso said. "People see our 'here we are, take it for what it's worth' attitude. Our appearance is real—we don't have to go out of our way to put on makeup every night or buy special clothes to look bad or nasty. It's easy—and cheap, too!" "It's been our dream all our lives," Sabo added. "Make a record, go on tour, eat junk food until we're sick." ■

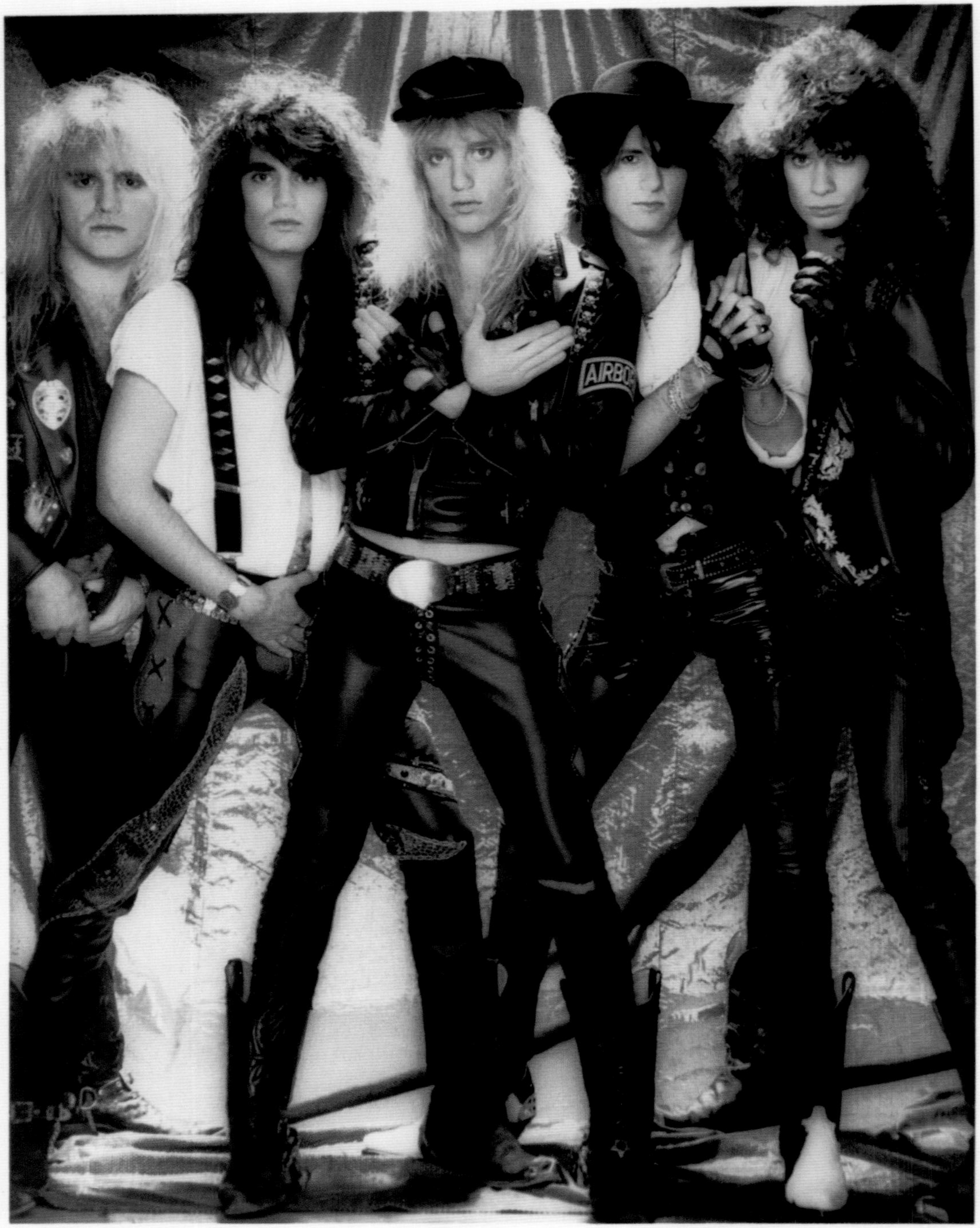

PHOTO CREDIT: NEIL ZLOWZOWER

JOEY ALLEN JERRY DIXON JANI LANE ERIC TURNER STEVEN SWEET

WARRANT

WEINTRAUB ENTERTAINMENT GROUP

Direction Tom Hulett
213-477-8900

Columbia
8904

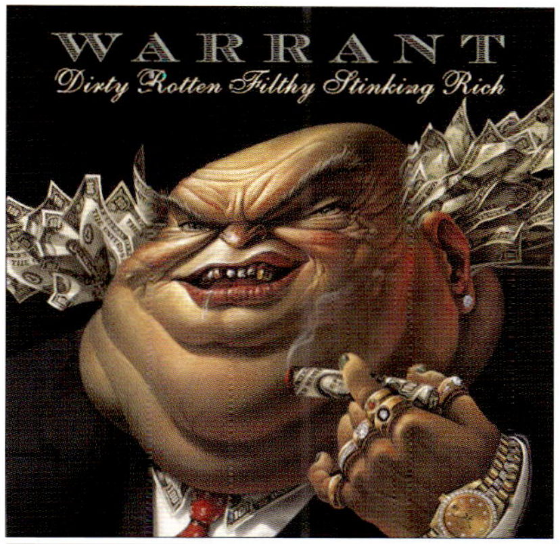

Billboard 200: *Dirty Rotten Filthy Stinking Rich* (#10)
Billboard Hot 100: "Down Boys" (#27); "Heaven" (#2); "Big Talk" (#93); "Sometimes She Cries" (#20)

With an arresting debut album and the pop-metal ballad "Heaven," Warrant came into the national spotlight.

FOUNDED IN 1984, Warrant morphed into one of the top-drawing acts on the Los Angeles club scene with the addition of singer Jani Lane. "Jani's cool—he's got an attitude, but most singers do," bassist Jerry Dixon chuckled. "The band's sound changed a lot when we got him. 'Down Boys' was the first song we played together, and we still do it the same way."

The quintet worked its way to the top of the competitive local scene with a party-down image. "L.A. crowds are one of the toughest in the world to play for—they've seen everything," Lane advised. "People are so desensitized to anything you can do onstage that to get a reaction, you have to be pretty damned good. We kick down the barriers between ourselves in the audience. I spend half my time at the shows in the crowd, tasting their drinks, making sure they're having fun."

Skeptics portrayed Warrant as vapid rock 'n' roll extroverts, but the band built a sturdy fan base. "Down Boys," an accessible teen anthem, set the stage, and the second single, "Heaven," scaled the charts, bound to heavy metal's "ballad scene." Multiplatinum sales of the band's debut album, *Dirty Rotten Filthy Stinking Rich,* got pushed by the hit singles, power play on MTV and massive touring with a variety of bands, including Mötley Crüe, Ratt, Poison and Queensrÿche. "It's like driving a big bus through an X-rated Disneyland," Lane enthused. "Every city is a new ride." ■

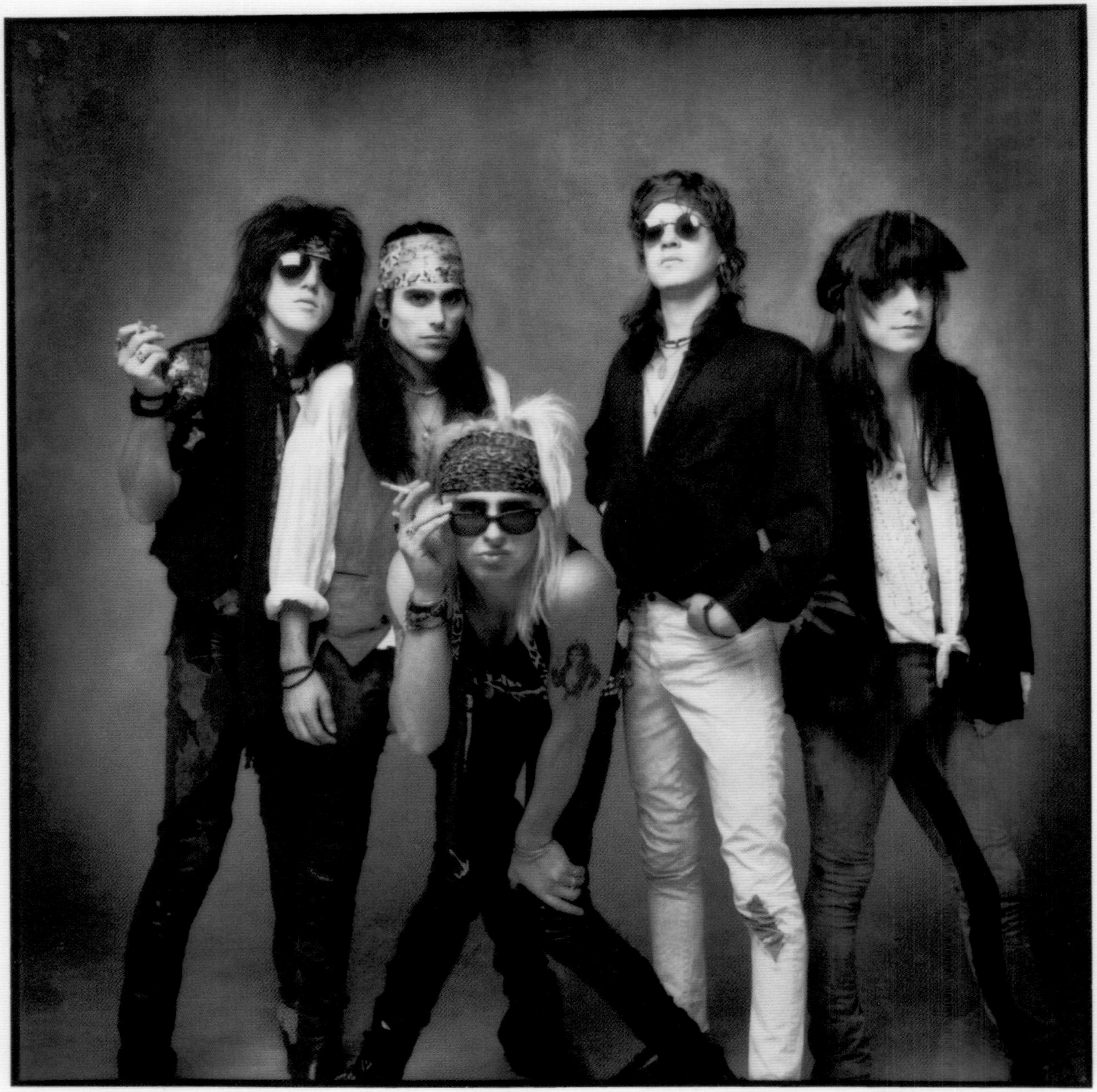

PHOTO CREDIT: GLEN LA FERMAN / 1989

ERIC STACY GREG STEELE TAIME DOWNE MARK MICHALS BRENT MUSCAT

FASTER PUSSYCAT

ELEKTRA

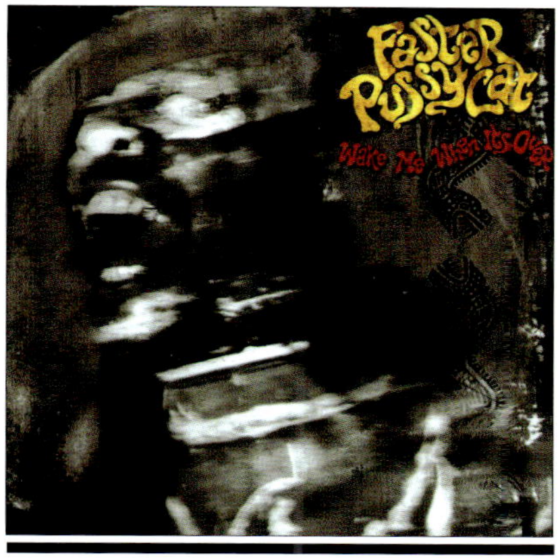

Billboard 200: *Wake Me When It's Over* (#48)
Billboard Hot 100: "House of Pain" (#28)

Kings of Sunset Strip sleazy metal, Faster Pussycat hit a commercial plateau with the ballad "House of Pain."

A GLAM-METAL sound and "gypsy trash" image had gained Faster Pussycat as many detractors as it had fans of the band's fun/degeneration business. The group was either one of the seminal Hollywood bad-boy rock combos or another leatherette act in search of a hairstylist. But the members had always taken pride in being themselves.

"We've gotten so much flak and resistance for what we do," guitarist Greg Steele said. "People in a crowd will flip us off or throw something at us—they're trying to see what they can get away with. But we retaliate, and nine times out of ten, they love us after that. We're going to do what we want to do."

Faster Pussycat came together amid the hard-rock fervor that gripped Los Angeles in the mid-Eighties. Singer Taime Downe was known as a co-founder of the Cathouse, a famous steamy dive. Billed as the ultimate party band, Faster Pussycat created its own scene.

"There were a lot of places to go see bands at the time—Guns N' Roses and L.A. Guns were playing—but there weren't any places to hang out," Steele recalled. "So Taime and his roommate decided to start a rock club. For the first few months, it was underground, but when the scene exploded, the Cathouse became really popular."

The band's name was lifted from the title of an early Sixties murder movie called *Faster, Pussycat! Kill! Kill!,* a sleazy soft-core effort from perennial dirty old man Russ Meyer. When a self-titled debut album was released in 1987, Faster Pussycat was known for loose playing.

But in two years of nonstop touring, the songwriting and playing had matured. On the *Wake Me When It's Over* album, Faster Pussycat was a tight, blues-oriented, groove-based band. The sleazeball songs—"Little Dove" (about a porn actress) and "Where There's a Whip There's a Way"—weren't exactly examples of subtle musicianship, but they kicked.

And there was a turn toward substantive lyrics on "House of Pain," a surprisingly mature power ballad. According to Downe, the band's principal lyricist, the song, which built to a climax from an acoustic guitar base and guest Jimmy Z's plaintive harmonica, concerned his dad, who wasn't around much when he was a kid.

"My music was sad," Steele added, "and Taime wanted words that meant something. He finally hit on one-parent families. In the Fifties, if that song come out, I don't think that many people could have related to it. Nowadays, there's divorce in three out of five families. Ward Cleaver is gone—he's probably off with his secretary now!" ■

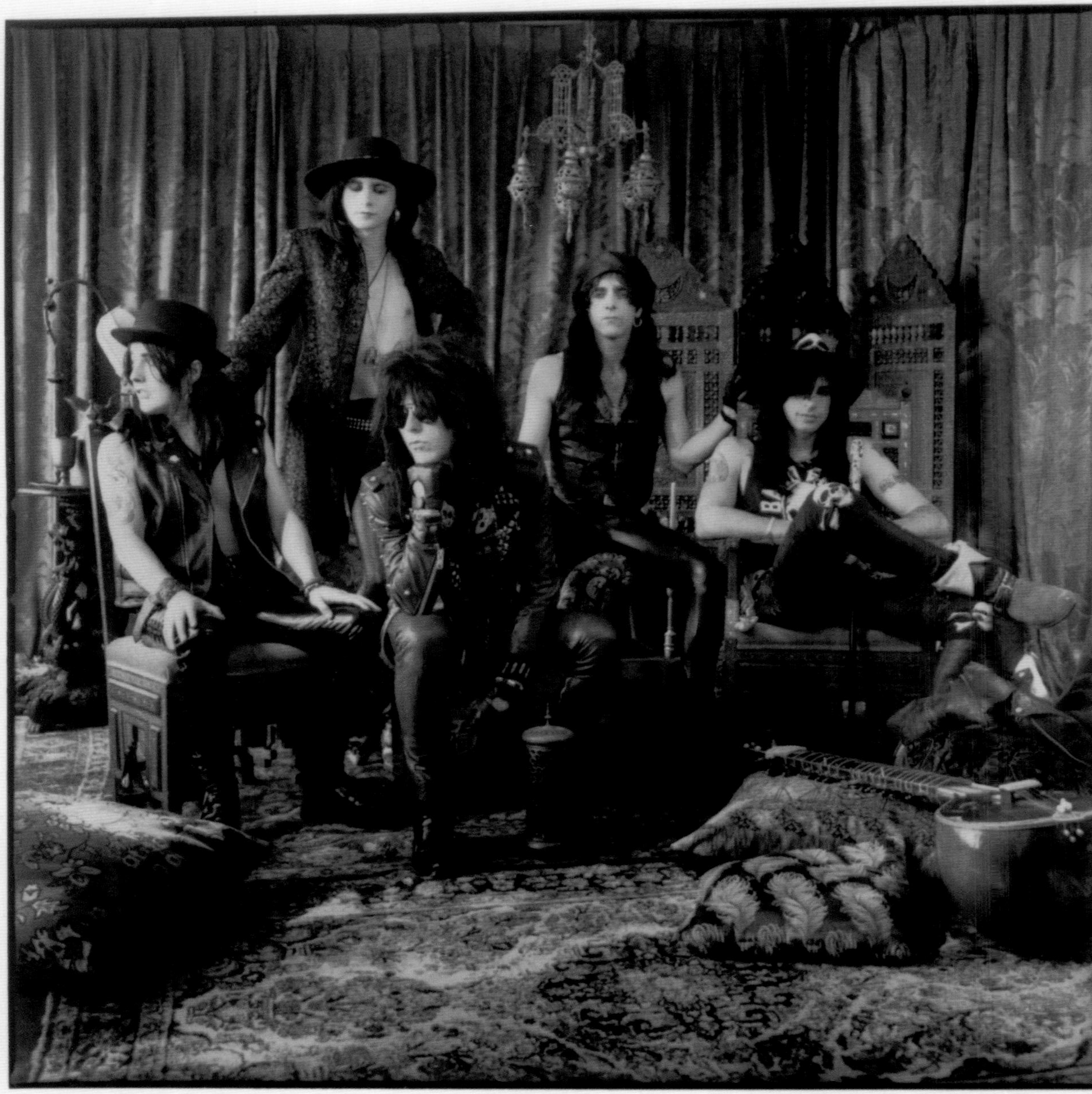

Photo Credit: J. Katz

Mick Cripps Philip Lewis Tracii Guns Steve Riley Kelly Nickels

L.A. GUNS

VERTIGO

PolyGram™

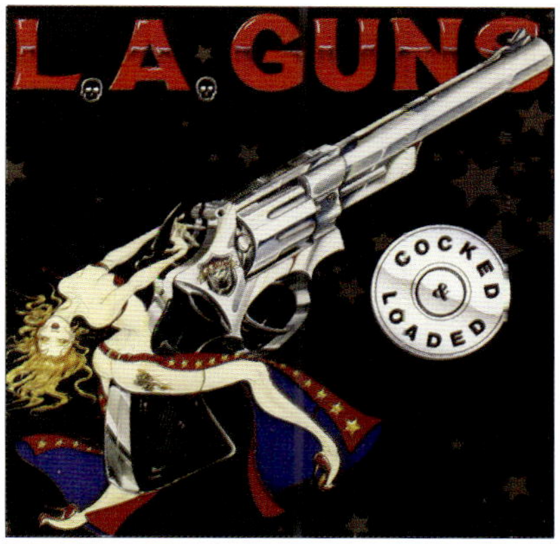

Billboard 200: *Cocked & Loaded* (#38)
Billboard Hot 100: "The Ballad of Jayne" (#33)

L.A. Guns' "The Ballad of Jayne" delivered the glam-metal band from Hollywood debauchery to the masses.

VETERANS OF the hair-metal explosion—guitarist and founder Tracii Guns was included in Guns N' Roses first lineup—L.A. Guns' formula of bad attitude and volume wasn't that different from the next band on the streets of Hollywood. But while the group's 1988 self-titled debut album was abrasive, *Cocked & Loaded* was slicker and more accessible—relentless touring had made them much better players.

"We're not trying to set the world on fire with some unusual form of commercial hard rock," Guns said. "We just try to touch on the stuff that we grew up listening to—Van Halen, Aerosmith, AC/DC. Rock 'n' roll doesn't go that much further—it's white-boy blues."

The tunes on *Cocked & Loaded* reflected the band's lifestyle. The single "Rip and Tear" detailed one too many nights prowling the infamous Sunset Strip. "It's sex, booze and tattoos, part two," Guns laughed. "Going for it with reckless abandon, that's our inspiration." The sentimental yearning of "The Ballad of Jayne" put L.A. Guns in the mainstream when it went on to become a Top 40 single.

"Sex and rock 'n' roll don't work for everyone," lead singer Philip Lewis surmised, "but they've worked out great for us." Bassist Kelly Nickels was more philosophical. "It's still shit," he said, "but I like walking in it." ■

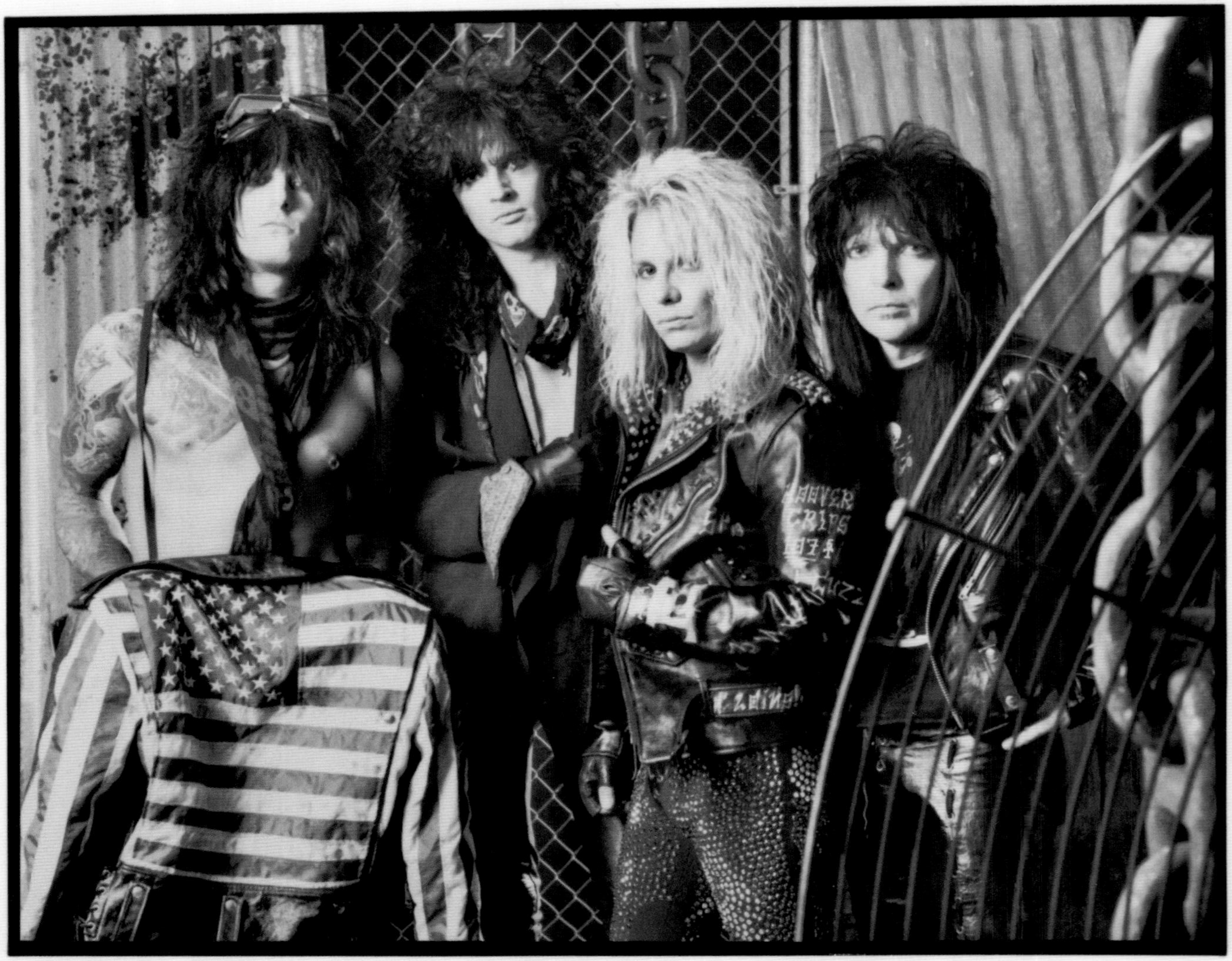

PHOTO CREDIT: RANDEE ST. NICHOLAS

NIKKI SIXX TOMMY LEE VINCE NEIL MICK MARS

Mötley Crüe

ELEKTRA

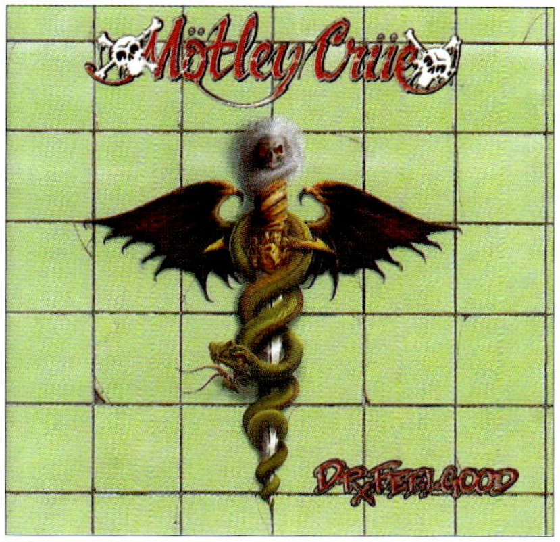

Billboard 200: *Dr. Feelgood* (No. 1)
Billboard Hot 100: "Dr. Feelgood" (#6); "Kickstart My Heart" (#27); "Without You" (#8); "Don't Go Away Mad (Just Go Away)" (#19); "Same Ol' Situation (S.O.S.)" (#78)

Playing it straight, Mötley Crüe regained popularity with *Dr. Feelgood*, the hair-metal band's first No. 1 album.

FOR YEARS, detractors lambasted Mötley Crüe as an execrable excuse for a rock band. It wasn't because the members were sexist, lewd, juvenile or unethical—playing up to a young, hell-raising audience's worst impulses earned high praise in heavy-metal circles. The Crüe was just painfully untalented musically. And it turned out that bassist Nikki Sixx agreed.

"When we did our first album, we really weren't that good," Sixx said. "But we had that trashy street magic, that against-the-grain attitude. We loved to shock the shit out of people."

Sixx made his peace with the faultfinders because Mötley Crüe delivered a satisfying albeit derivative work with *Dr. Feelgood*, a No. 1 album that eventually sold more than 5 million copies. The band worked with Bob Rock, the latest career-saving hit producer, but the big news was that the guys in the Crüe learned to play their instruments sans the use of illicit drugs.

A transformation was necessary. Ever since 1980, when Frank Feranna began calling himself Nikki Sixx and formed Mötley Crüe in Los Angeles, the members of the madeup-and-moussed quartet began playing increasingly outrageous gigs. They chainsawed mannequins and set their pants on fire, and by 1984, the Crüe's hedonistic, reckless ways had made them America's most notorious group.

Not even singer Vince Neil's 1984 involvement in a drunken-driving accident that killed passenger Nicholas Dingley of Hanoi Rocks, nor Sixx's stint in a rehab clinic for heroin addiction, could temper Mötley Crüe's heedless behavior. By 1988, things were seriously out of control.

"We were having a lot of fun in the beginning, but as the years went on, the partying became an everyday event," Sixx mused. "When our *Too Fast for Love* album came out, I was mainlining heroin, guzzling tons of Jack Daniel's, snorting blow all night and having two or three Hustler Honeys in my bedroom. And it was exciting—we were doing the things the Rolling Stones did.

"But the glamour is only true for a split second, when you've come up through the ranks and you've peaked. And then you've gotta pay—you're addicted to drugs, you're a complete alcoholic, your career starts to fall apart because nobody wants to be around you. That's not being glamorous."

So the band cleaned up. And even though its wild reputation had faded, Sixx opined that Mötley Crüe was louder, nastier and more aggressive than ever. The high point of *Dr. Feelgood* was the title track, propelled by Mick Mars' squalling guitar work, and the sexually charged "Kickstart My Heart" epitomized the group's collective personality. "It's a snarl at a few people who say, 'Oh, so now Mötley Crüe are clean—can they still do it?' Nine years later, we're still burnin'—that's hunger, and you can't fake it." ■

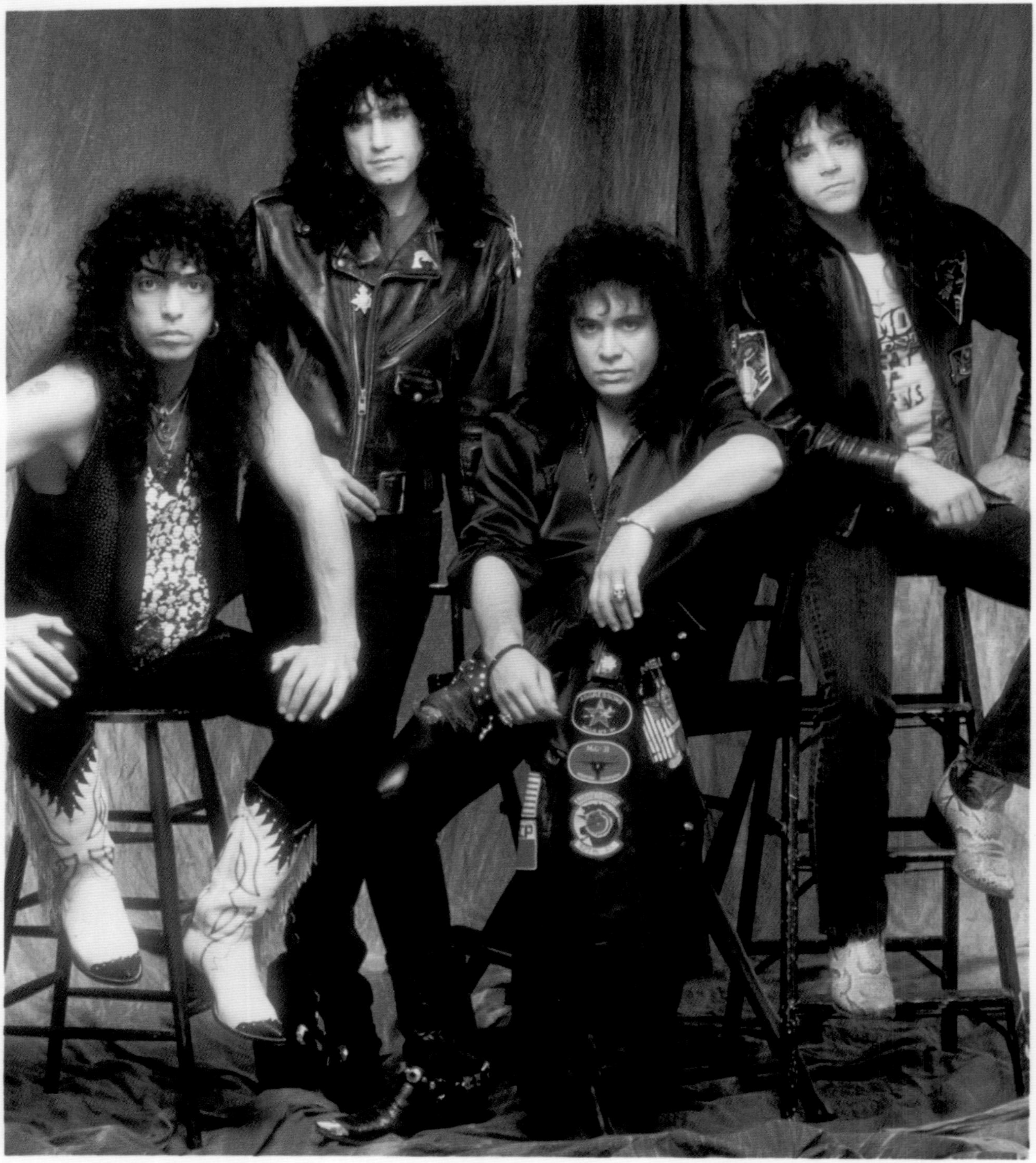

PAUL STANLEY BRUCE KULIICK GENE SIMMONS ERIC CARR

mercury

KISS®

PolyGram™

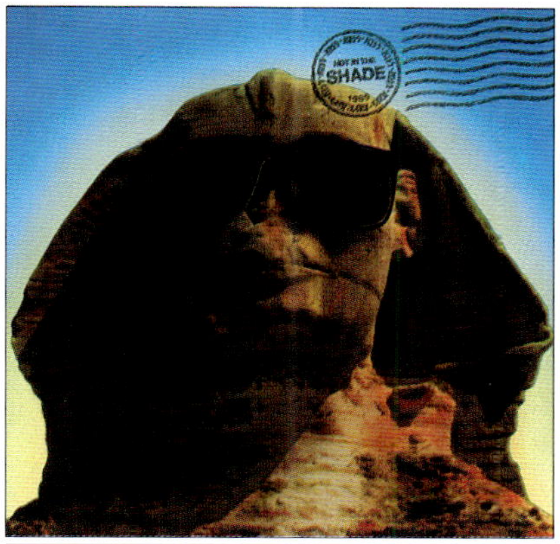

Billboard 200: *Hot in the Shade* (#29)
Billboard Hot 100: "Hide Your Heart" (#66);
"Forever" (#8); 'Rise to It" (#81)

Kiss ended the decade with the power ballad "Forever," the biggest hit of the group's makeup-free chapter.

THE HISTORY of Kiss was laden with gimmicks, hype and excess—and undeniable commercial success. Detractors considered the band a fluke, but in 16 years of overkill, leaders Paul Stanley and Gene Simmons had never parted ways or taken time off.

"We started as a very basic rock 'n' roll band," Stanley said. "When you take a trip that's lasted as long as our career has, you accumulate excess baggage. It was time to throw away stuff we didn't need and head for home, our roots."

Hot in the Shade, the band's 23rd release, featured a lineup including drummer Eric Carr and guitarist Bruce Kulick. The album contained some blustery heavy metal, but the obvious intent of "Rise to It" and "Hide Your Heart" was getting on the radio. MTV success made a hit of "Forever," co-written by Michael Bolton—the saccharine ballad became the band's highest-charting single since "Beth," 13 years earlier.

"It's funny—Michael started as a rocker, but now people think of him doing a whole different thing," Stanley noted. "We'd always talked about writing together, and I knew after two lines that there was magic. I told the band that I wrote a ballad and they said, 'Oh, no!' But when I played it, they beamed—'Well, that's a smash.' When something's good, there's no getting around it."

Kiss took to the road, and the two-year tour that followed featured an outrageous show—the centerpiece was a 40-foot sphinx that spoke and shot lasers from its eyes. It proved to be Carr's last outing with Kiss before he died due to complications from open-heart surgery. ■

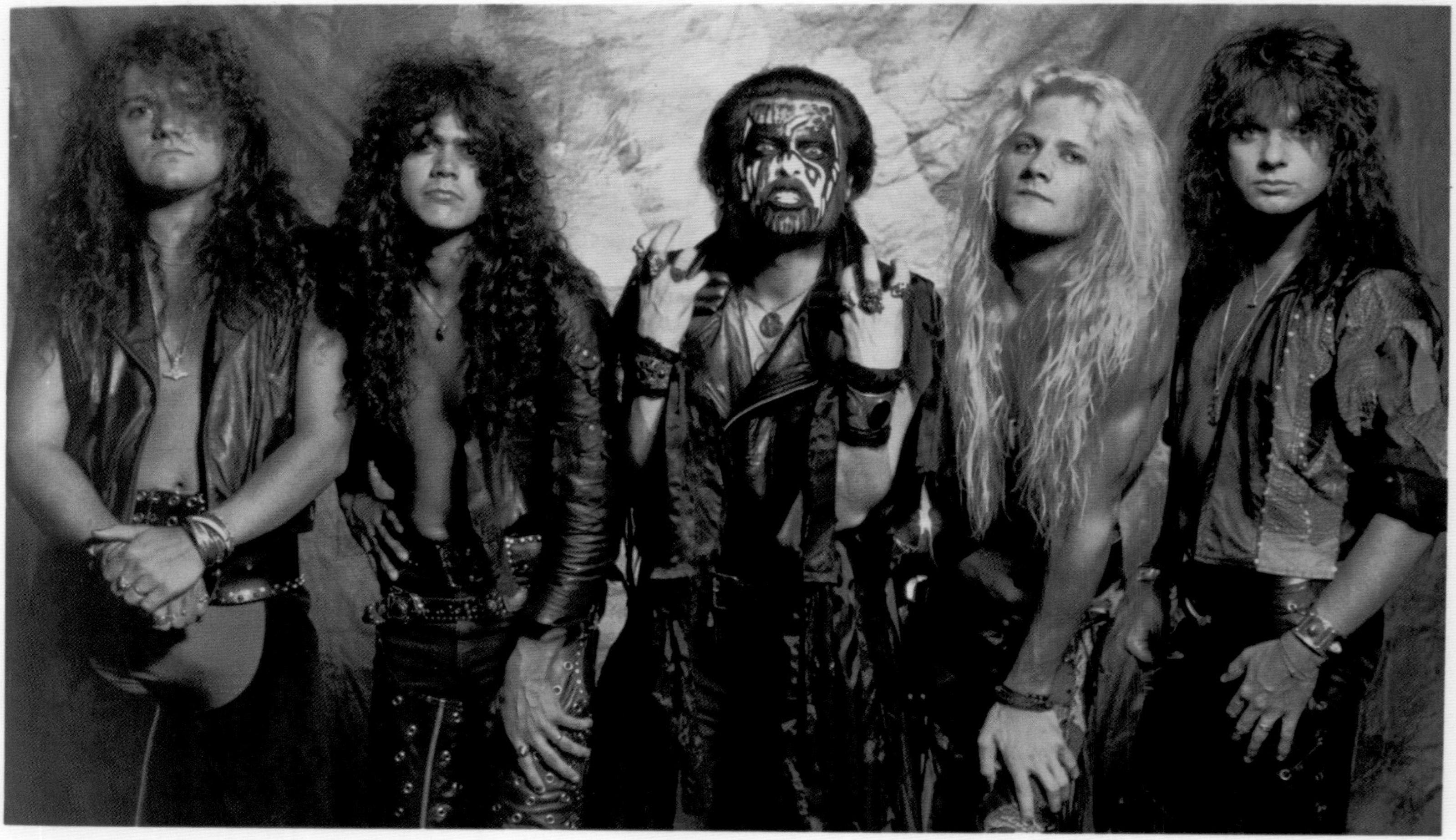

Pete Blakk
Guitars

Hal Patino
Bass

King Diamond
Vocals

Snowy Shaw
Drums

Andy La Rocque
Guitars

ROADRACER RECORDS

225 LAFAYETTE STREET,
SUITE 709
NEW YORK, N.Y. 10012
TELEPHONE: (212)219-0077
FAX: (212) 219-0301

Photo By: Alex Solca

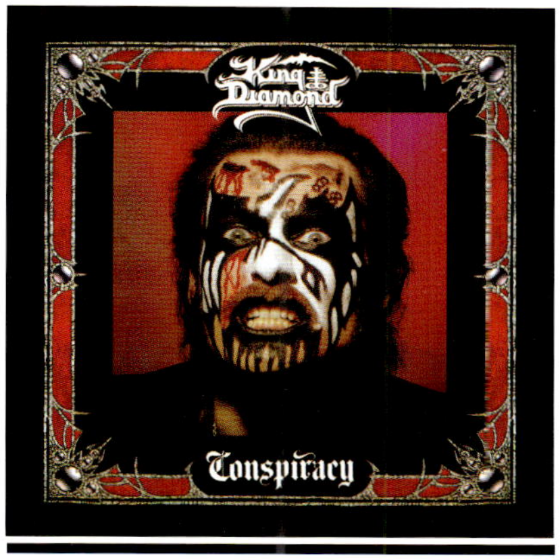

Billboard 200: *Conspiracy* (#111)

Turning albums into protracted gothic tales, King Diamond called his theatrical brand of music "horror metal."

THE DOOM-LADEN sound of King Diamond the band was in the tradition of Mercyful Fate, Denmark's defunct black-metal group that King Diamond the vocalist debuted in the early Eighties. "Occult stuff gives me the creeps—that's why I like it," the Danish singer said. "When we play a show, it's an atmosphere like Halloween."

Diamond, who always appeared in public in his trademark necromantic makeup, had released several ambitious concept albums, including 1988's *Them* and *Conspiracy*, a continuation and conclusion of a fright-filled storyline. Electric guitar symphonies supported Diamond's groaning, growling and shrieking in the voices of different demonic characters.

Ascribing his creativity to his immersion in the literary and cinematic forms of horror, Diamond defended his subject matter and refuted charges that the violent content could be harmful. "I don't believe that the heavy-metal audience is that stupid, that they can't divide between what's real and what's fantasy."

Diamond was a self-professed practicing Satanist, but he'd found that discussing his beliefs only created puzzlement and malice in the American public. He wanted to be an entertainer, not an advocate of any religion.

"I'm into the powers of the unknown—I prefer to describe it that way rather than Satanism," he said. "When most people hear the word *Satanism*, they have the negative idea of drinking blood and human slaughter, but nothing could be further from the truth. You could almost call it 'humanism' instead. It has to do with accepting the way you were born, your feelings, the way you live your life."

In the underground world of heavy metal, King Diamond's record sales were impressive, cracking the US album charts. Tours drew inspiration from the extravaganzas that Alice Cooper had put on, and Diamond stalked the stage using a microphone stand said to be made of two human bones. A professional illusionist designed the sets by involving such effects as levitation. The spectacle illustrated the demise of Diamond's character at the end of the opus.

"It's very extreme, and fun to watch," Diamond promised. "Some people might say that you shouldn't fool around with death, but that's what I'm here for—doing what others won't." ■

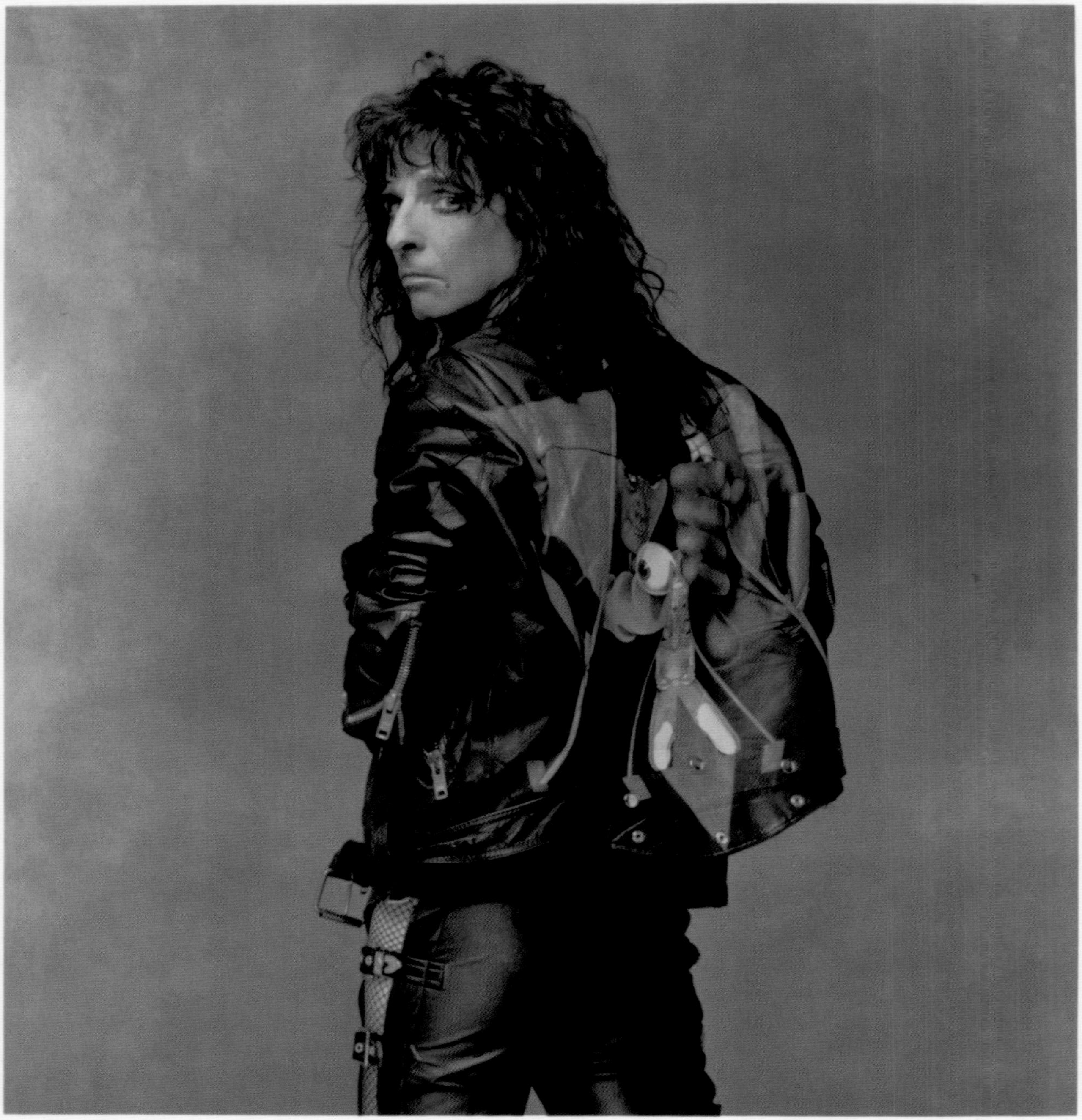

Photo Credit: Glen LaFerman

ALIVE

ALICE COOPER

Epic
E907

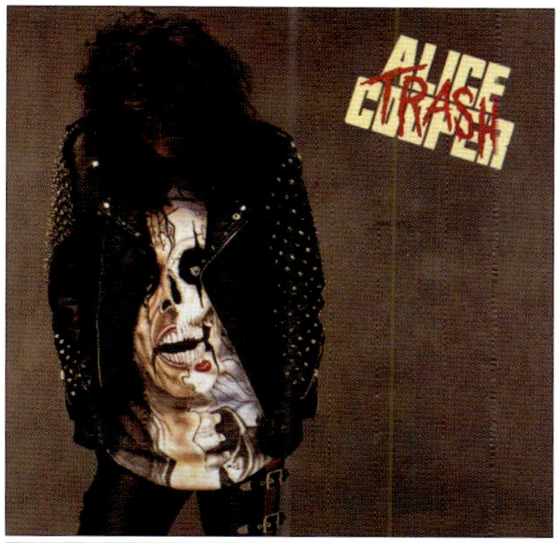

Billboard 200: *Trash* (#20)
Billboard Hot 100: "Poison" (#7);
"House of Fire" (#56); "Only My Heart Talkin'" (#89)

Once rock's greatest showman, Alice Cooper regained his relevance in the Eighties with the smash "Poison."

HIS APPEAL had started abating during the late Seventies, but at the ripe old age of 42, Alice Cooper enjoyed the multiplatinum success of *Trash*, his 20th album and his biggest-selling record ever.

"A lot of people forget that Alice was never really an underground act. Alice Cooper was a hit band—'I'm Eighteen,' 'School's Out,' 'No More Mr. Nice Guy,'" he said. "I was just looking for an opening to get back in, and *Trash* was perfect timing. I saw what Aerosmith and Bon Jovi were doing—putting out rock songs that appealed to a lot of people but actually had guitars in them. And they cracked prime radio for rock 'n' roll again, and that's where Alice used to live at his peak."

The master of "shock rock" first came lunging out at America in 1968 as the most perverse and subversive teen idol in the history of popular music—a dark-haired, spider-eyed, cross-dressed menace with a black sense of humor. He soon established himself as America's top box-office attraction with his stage show, chopping up dolls and employing props such as electric chairs, boa constrictors and gallows. "Now you can't shock audiences anymore, but you can amaze them," Cooper said.

Although he had moved away from the gore of his previous albums, *Trash* was still controversial. "This was the first time I made a record with my alcoholism and my big heavy image off my back," he mused. "I felt secure in doing an album that was going to be fun, rather than Alice's next doomsday project. I like to make fun of death, but at the same time, I've always been known to have a certain sexual image, too."

Thus, *Trash* explored the good, the absurd and the scary sides of love and sex. "The key phrase in the studio was 'more bed, less red'—'Poison' is a song about S&M if you listen to it," he said. "You just can't stop a good song. What I needed to do on *Trash* was get together with a good writer and apply the songs more than the theatrics."

Cooper hooked up with hitmaker Desmond Child as both co-writer and producer to unleash some rocking but highly commercial songs. "Poison" was a Top 10 hit worldwide. "House of Fire" was supported by an anthemic chorus, and "Only My Heart Talkin'" featured a harmony vocal by Aerosmith's Steven Tyler.

"But I didn't give that much up," he said of the blatant attempt at radio exposure. "I might have put a couple of extra hooks in the choruses, but I don't think it was any travesty to Alice Cooper, because the attitude was still there. On tour, I haven't lost the hardcore audience—they're still there. But now I'm getting an entirely new audience that's 15-17 years old, and they walk in like lambs to the slaughter. They've only heard about the legend—now they want to see the guillotine." ■

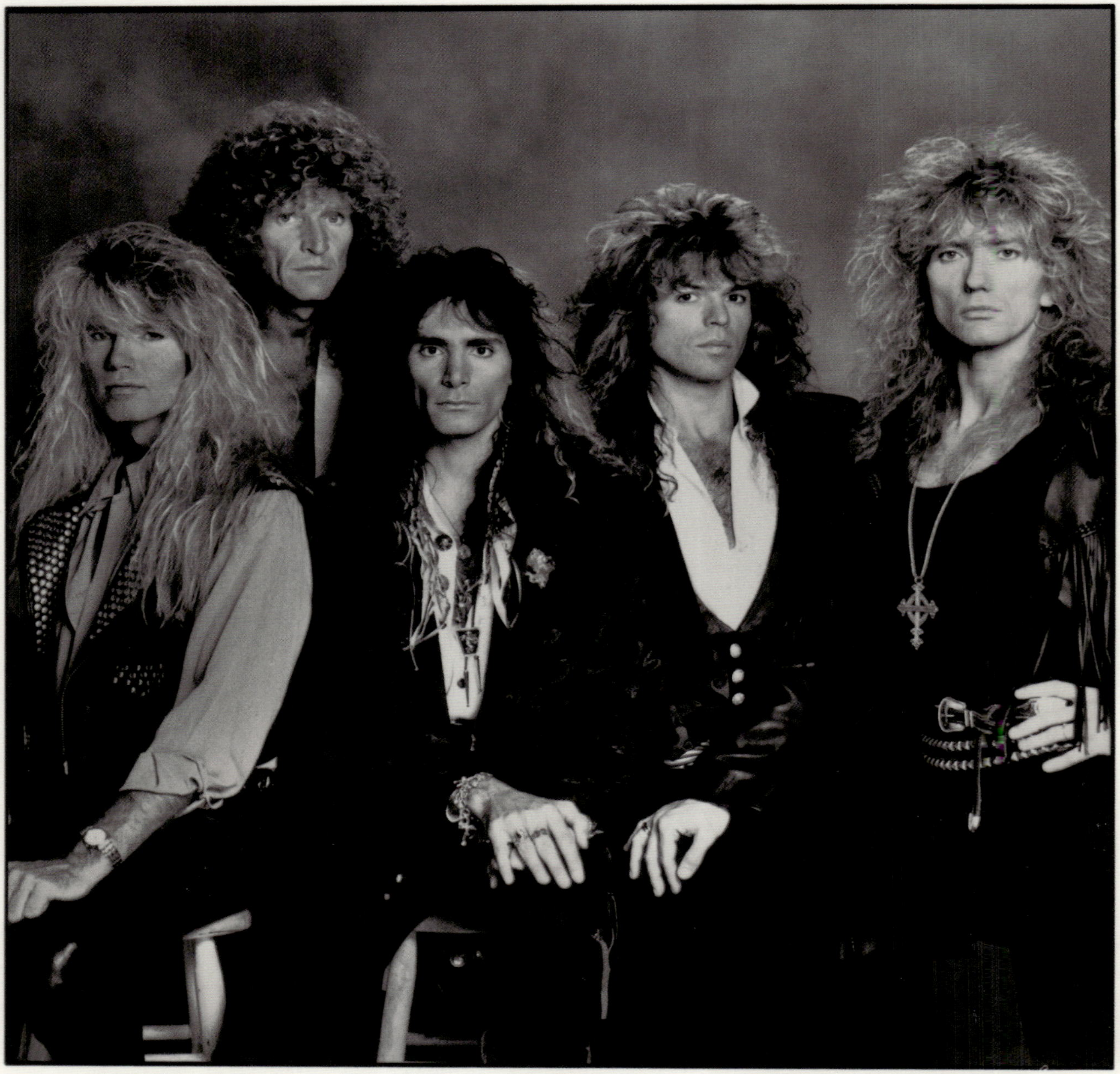

Photo Credit: Greg Gorman

Adrian Vandenberg Tommy Aldridge Steve Vai Rudy Sarzo David Coverdale

WHITESNAKE

GEFFEN® RECORDS

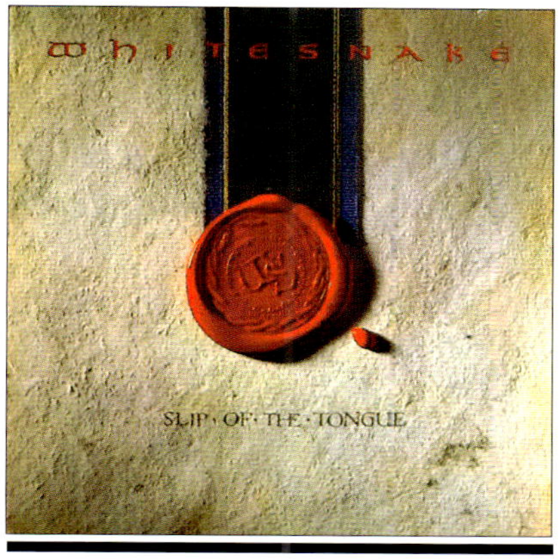

Billboard 200: *Slip of the Tongue* (#10)
Billboard Hot 100: "Fool for Your Loving" (#37); "The Deeper the Love" (#28); "Now You're Gone" (#96)

A freak injury sidelined guitarist Adrian Vandenberg for the recording of Whitesnake's *Slip of the Tongue* album.

THE PHENOMENAL success of Whitesnake's 1987 self-titled album, which sold 10 million copies worldwide and boasted the No. 1 single "Here I Go Again" and the #2 "Is This Love," challenged guitarist Adrian Vandenberg physically as well as musically. "These days, everybody knows somebody who has suffered a job-related injury, a problem that occurs as a result of poor body position while working," Vandenberg said. "But it doesn't happen only in the office. And when it happens to a musician, he can't perform."

On Whitesnake's supporting tour, Vandenberg co-wrote the songs for the next album, *Slip of the Tongue*, with David Coverdale, the dictatorial leader of the English hard-rock band. But Vandenberg, described by vocalist Coverdale as "a blond Viking from Hell," was unable to record them because of an arm and hand problem.

"The cause only became clear a few months before the tour," he said. "I tend to hunch my right shoulder a bit because my arms are so long—I'm six foot six. When I sit down with a guitar on my lap and rest my arm on the body, it blocks the blood flow and affects the functioning in my picking hand. I was overplaying—we were recording and rehearsing in the studio for nine hours, then I'd go back to the hotel and play again to prepare my guitar parts for the next day.

"The tightness in my muscles moved down my arm, but I didn't notice it until it got to the wrist area. Nobody knew what it was. I went to every nerve doctor and acupuncturist I could find. I flew back to my native Holland when my dad found a doctor who specializes in musicians' injuries. There's nothing to do for my condition but rest. I had my hands in a cast for four weeks, and I've had to work on relaxing my shoulders when I play. It's been a pretty hectic year of struggling."

Vanderberg's absence on *Slip of the Tongue* highlighted the talents of Steve Vai, who had replaced guitarist Vivian Campbell early in 1989. Voted by *Guitar Magazine* as "Best Rock Guitarist" in 1987 and 1988, Vai pulled off the intense guitar leads on the album, and a re-recorded version of "Fool for Your Loving" and "The Deeper the Love" fared well on the album rock charts. Vandenberg recovered to join Whitesnake on a worldwide concert tour.

"It's an interesting guitar lineup now because our styles are miles apart," Vandenberg said. "I try to be as melodic as I can, because I try to play as an extension of my emotions, like a voice. Steve likes to get into fast, weird-sounding runs."

Because of the lyrics to songs like "Cheap an' Nasty" and "Kitten's Got Claws," Coverdale got called a sexist. "It surprises me when David is attacked," Vandenberg noted. "Rock 'n' roll has always been sexually oriented, going all the way back to Chuck Berry. David's probably a little more explicit, but he's also very intelligent about it, not just 'Hey, babe, let's party.' And it's better than death-and-violence lyrics." ■

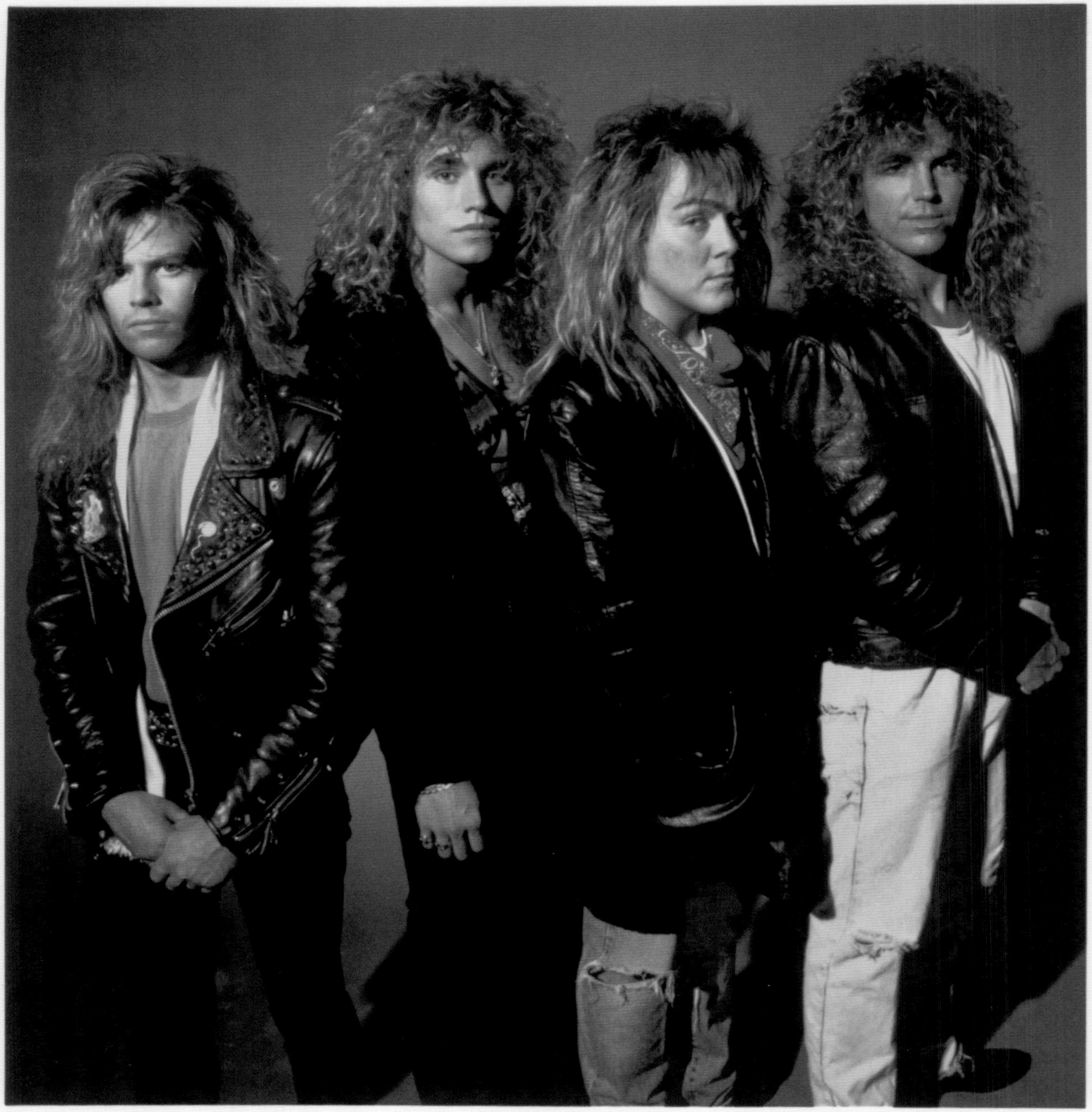

Photo Credit: Jeff Katz

Bonham

WTG RECORDS
8907

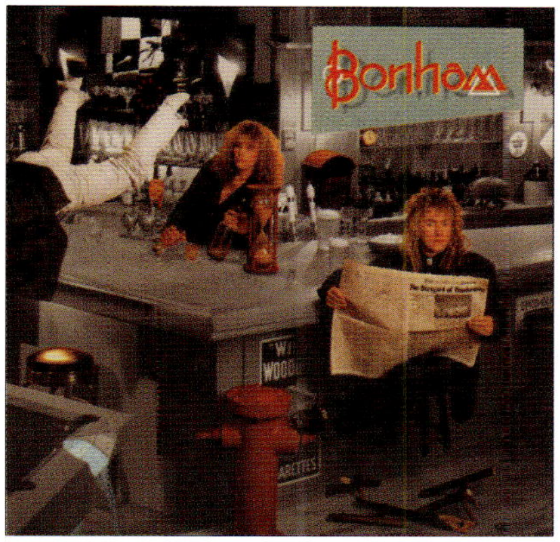

Billboard 200: *The Disregard of Timekeeping* (#38)
Billboard Hot 100: "Wait for You" (#55)

Led by the son of Led Zeppelin's legendary drummer, the band Bonham put together a gold-selling debut album.

MORE THAN most imitators, Jason Bonham had claim to the Led Zeppelin sound—his father was the Zep's drummer, the late John "Bonzo" Bonham. "Most dads give their four-year-old children train sets or tricycles," Jason recalled. "Mine gave me a scaled-down Ludwig drum kit," he said.

After apprenticeships in two bands, the young scion went on to drum with a reunited Led Zeppelin at the Atlantic Records 40th anniversary bash. "It was always my dream to play with them," he said. "When that goal was over, I wanted to put my own group on top."

So Bonham tapped two longtime friends, John Smithson (keyboards, bass) and Ian Hatton (guitar), and brought in vocalist Daniel MacMaster from Canada. The collaboration resulted in the band Bonham. The title of *The Disregard of Timekeeping* referred to the presence of sequencers in modern recording. "I hate the method of turning on a drum machine, putting a vocal over it and having a hit," Bonham said. "My father threw things around for an element of surprise."

Bonham, 23, knew that people couldn't help drawing comparisons, and he seemed happily at ease with his father's legacy. The hit single "Wait for You" didn't downplay his musical relationship to his dad. He shared the same aggressive style, and there was a Middle Eastern mystique that strongly suggested Zeppelin.

"What my father did with his right foot and his left hand was amazing," Bonham said regarding the Zep's loping powerhouse backbeat. "I have a similar approach. I try to make things explosive. If I wasn't influenced by Led Zeppelin, then I must have been deaf as a child. We're not trying to disguise a riff and call it our own. But some of our songs don't sound anything like Led Zeppelin."

Bonham's invocation of his late father's legacy thrilled young kids who never saw Led Zeppelin. Yet if the Zep ruled as the "hammer of the gods," his band simply rated as the gods' "rubber mallet." "But we're still getting a lot of young girls at concerts for the way we look," he enthused. ■

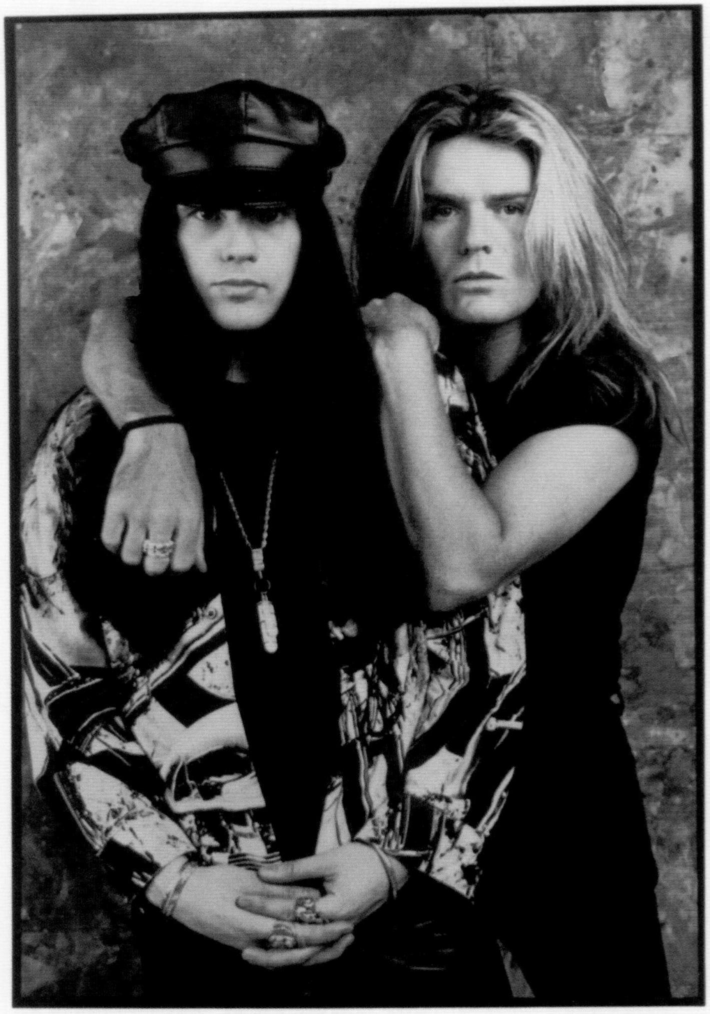 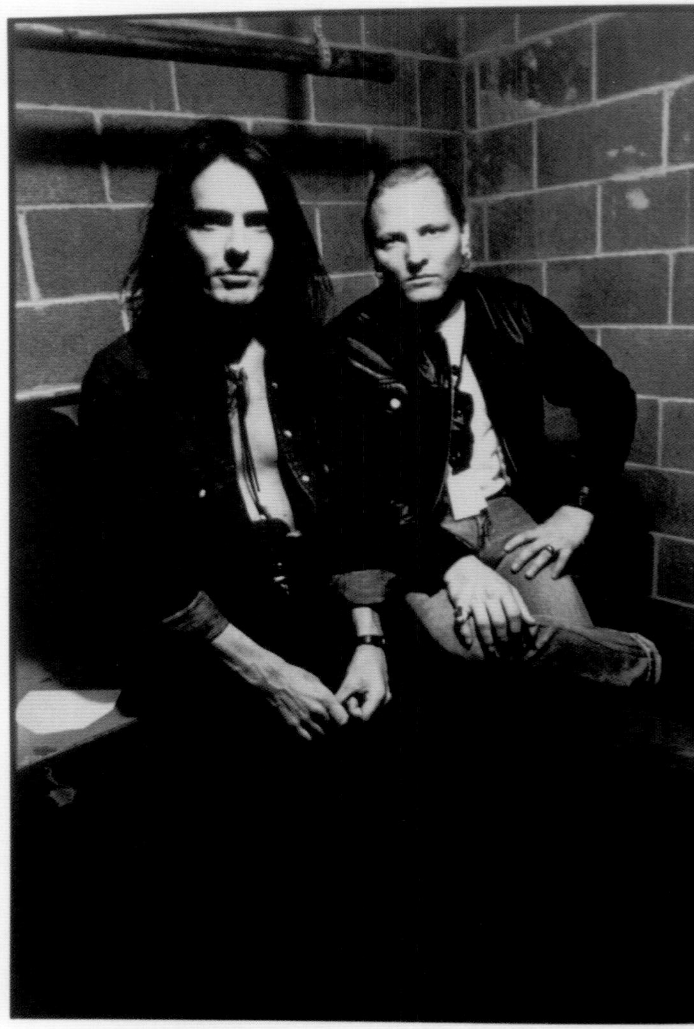

Photo Credit: Jim Marshall

THE CULT

SIRE® reprise®

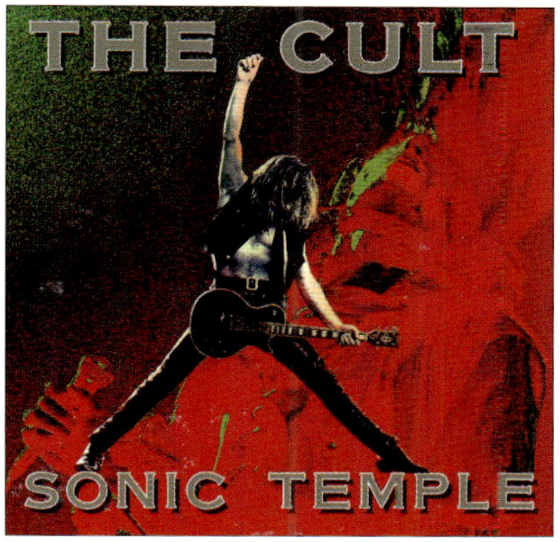

Billboard 200: *Sonic Temple* (#10)
Billboard Hot 100: "Fire Woman" (#46); "Edie (Ciao Baby)" (#93)

The Cult commanded arena-headlining prominence with *Sonic Temple*, which hurtled to platinum-plus status.

WITH THE album *Sonic Temple*, a sensually gratifying guitar maelstrom, the Cult set itself apart from its peers. Or did it make the British band's contribution to modern music seem marginal?

"It's occurring to us that we're one of a dying species—we're dodos," guitarist Billy Duffy laughed. "Heavy metal has turned into a bunch of bullshit solos. Traditional rockers like a more exciting, dirty, simpler approach, so people are looking back to where heavy rock started, getting off on that feel. *Sonic Temple* will be as good in three years as when it came out because it's an investment in our career, not an attempt to make a quick buck with a power ballad."

A controversial buzz had surrounded the Cult since the band's early days. 1985's *Rain* invoked the Sixties hard-rock and psychedelic era, particularly the atmospherically powerful and catchy "She Sells Sanctuary," a college radio smash. But with 1987's *Electric*, the Cult's hip heavy metal metamorphosed into AC/DC-inflected rock, as heralded by the opening guitar riff on the hit "Love Removal Machine."

The expansiveness of *Sonic Temple* was all about style—exciting, and sometimes moronic. The latter quality was usually traced to drama-drenched lead singer Ian Astbury, whose mannered killing-cockroaches-on-a-hardwood-floor dance steps in concert were, in fact, engaging. He performed in Europe with his arm in a cast after a backstage "altercation" in Berlin. In England, he allegedly dismantled his hotel room to the tune of $6,000 after one drink too many.

But Duffy just chuckled at his songwriting partner's exploits. "We try and be reasonable, but there is an understated tension with us. We may not verbalize what we're thinking, but it's communicated through vibes. It's almost like boxers psyching themselves out."

Duffy's guitar work, a blend of thick chording and hard-bitten guitar runs on the tracks "Fire Woman" and "Edie (Ciao Baby)," was equally important in creating the dark atmospheres in the Cult's songs. "I've spent my past studying the art of the riff," he explained. "I'm an ex-punk rocker—I never had a music lesson in my life. I get off on songs that have good guitar licks to them. That's why I dug Led Zeppelin so much. I'm trying to keep it interesting and not churn out the same drudging chords."

Sonic Temple united alternative and hard-rock camps, blending the cerebral part of the Cult with the electric side. "We get a very broad spectrum of fans—gothic-alternative types, collegiate-basketball types, psychedelic-skateboarder types," Duffy noted. Yet the Cult looked and sounded completely different from what was happening in England.

"I don't know what's going on in my own country," Duffy admitted. "It's gone full swing back to the Sixties, with producers writing pop factory hits for the charts. Bands like us sell hundreds of thousands of albums, but it's all underground. We're not banner-waving, but we're trying to do our bit." ■

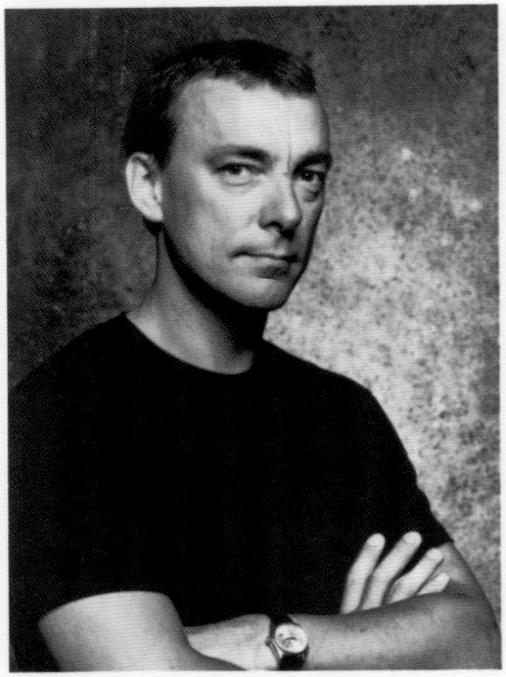

NEIL PEART

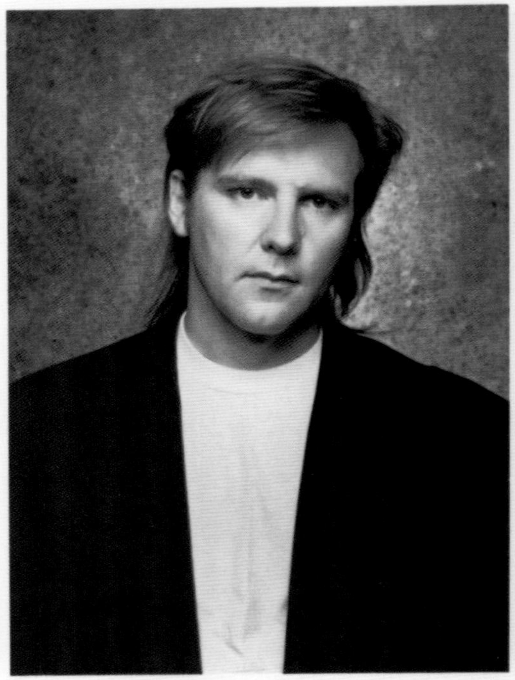

ALEX LIFESON

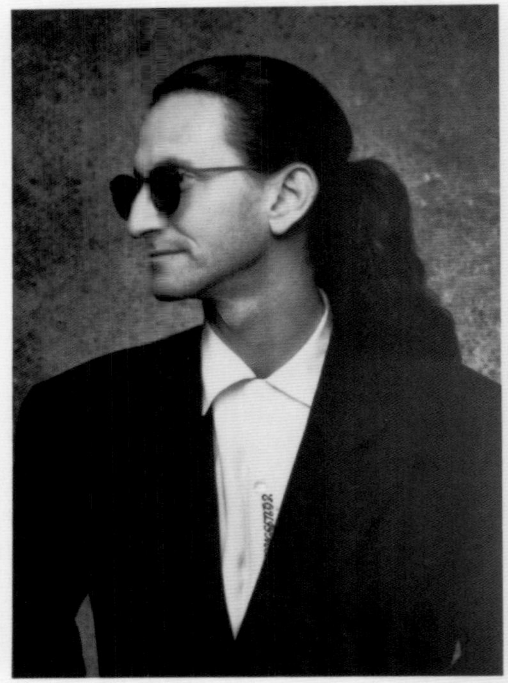

GEDDY LEE

RUSH

ATLANTIC

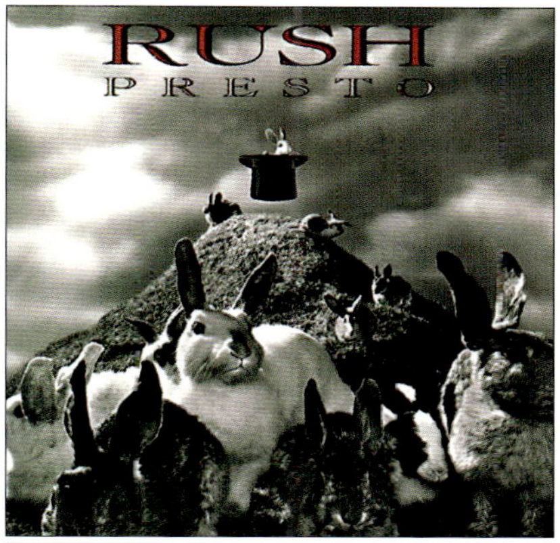

Billboard 200: *Presto* (#16)

Deviating from its synthesizer-driven efforts, Rush returned to heavier guitar-centric arrangements with *Presto*.

BEGINNING IN 1974 as a poor man's Led Zeppelin, the members of the Canadian trio Rush—bassist Geddy Lee, guitarist Alex Lifeson and drummer Neil Peart—had since proven their instrumental chops and incrementally improved their songwriting. By expanding the reach and range of their music, Rush kept progressive rock alive and well, becoming Canada's answer to Pink Floyd, one of the top arena attractions around.

"We've always established our next goal and then directed all our energies toward that," Peart said. "We've never thought too far ahead."

Presto was Rush's 17th album, filled with varied tempos and ambitious arrangements. The band cut back on its sequencer and synth-saturated undertakings, placing a renewed emphasis on Lifeson's guitar work. "I like the two meanings," Peart said. "As a musical word, *presto* means quick and exciting, and then there's its use in magic."

As usual, Peart's literate lyrics were meditations on technology, media and the modern world. "I'm influenced by a lot of writing, but it's difficult to quantify," he said. "It's a parallel of drumming. When you first start playing, there are certain people you tend to emulate, but the longer you go on playing, the broader your influences become. The same with lyrics. I'm drawing from a lot wider range."

The song "Show Don't Tell" was a hit on album-rock radio. "I've been studying prose writing over the last few years," Peart divulged. "A good friend of mine is a professional editor, and I've sent my efforts along to him for suggestions and criticisms. One of his constant pieces of advice has been that little editor's shorthand, 'SDT'—'show don't tell.' You can't say something was beautiful or interesting or amusing, you have to show how it was those things.

"It was a joke that I was wrestling with it, so it became a metaphor for a way of looking at life. I adopted an attitude in the song that isn't necessarily mine. It's a little more cynical and factual than I actually am. But I like the elements of human nature in the verses. You see people going around acting like they know everything—until things go wrong. Then it's, 'Oh, yeah? Well, it wasn't my fault!'"

After 15 years, touring remained part of Rush's vitality. A third live album, *A Show of Hands*, had been released before *Presto*. "It's an increasingly difficult decision to go on the road," Peart admitted. "In the early days, we became better musicians by the end of tours, and we had that reward to reflect on. At this point, however, it doesn't really work that way. In a sense, we spend five months just re-creating something, and that can feel a little futile—you start to wonder, 'Why bother?'" ■

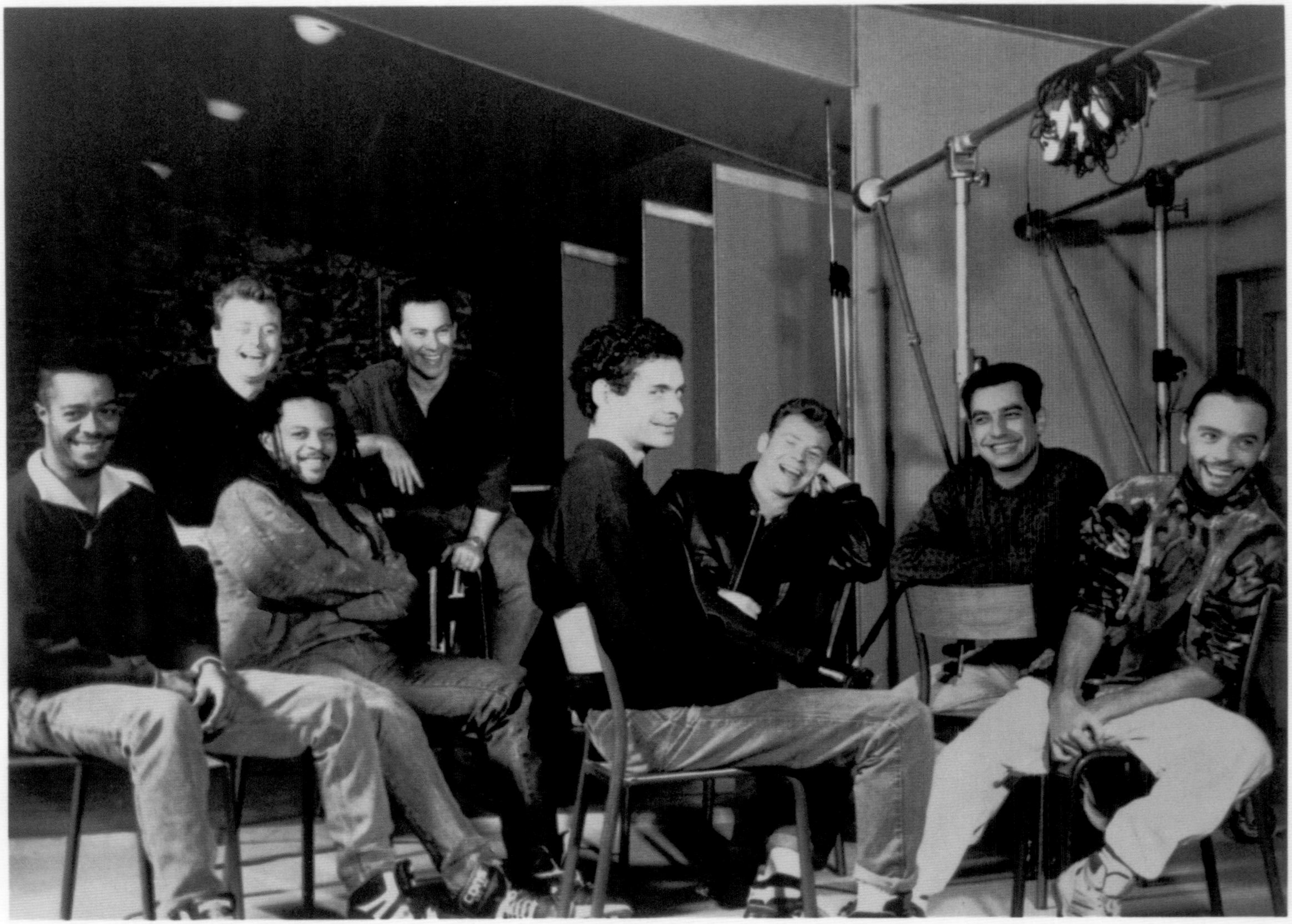

PHOTO CREDIT : ANDY EARLE

UB40

Virgin

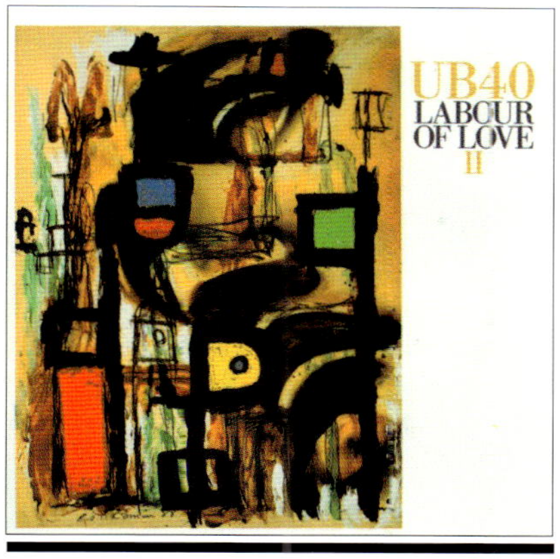

Billboard 200: *Labour of Love II* (#30)
Billboard Hot 100: "Here I Am (Come and Take Me)" (#7); "The Way You Do the Things You Do" (#6); "Groovin'" (#90)

Labour of Love II, UB40's second go-round with an all-cover versions album, contained a pair of Top 10 hits.

IN THE early Eighties, the members of UB40 compiled a list of their favorite reggae songs with a plan to eventually record them. But between 1983's *Labour of Love*, a set of covers, and *Labour of Love II*, UB40 made three albums. The reason the second *Labour* appeared to be a closely matched sequel was a reissue of Neil Diamond's "Red Red Wine" from the first album. Including a toasted/rapped verse, it had become a smash almost four years after it was originally recorded.

But in America, things had always worked strangely for the group named after a British unemployment benefits form. UB40 was Europe's most popular reggae act, but US radio had resisted the band's music. "'Red Red Wine' confirmed everything we'd been saying—that if we could get on the radio, people would like what they heard," singer Robin Campbell said during the band's stateside tour. "But now it comes down to the fact that radio is so conservative over here—people don't know where to put you."

Labour of Love II was another swipe at covers of Jamaican versions of what were originally American R&B singles. The Temptations' "The Way You Do the Things You Do" and Al Green's "Here I Am (Come and Take Me)" gave the veteran British group additional charting singles in the US. Supplementing its tradition of applying layered percussion and simmering horns to songs, the band also made creative use of electronic dance hall stylings. "We listen to modern reggae," Campbell explained, "but our versions are fairly close to the reggae versions we knew as kids." ■

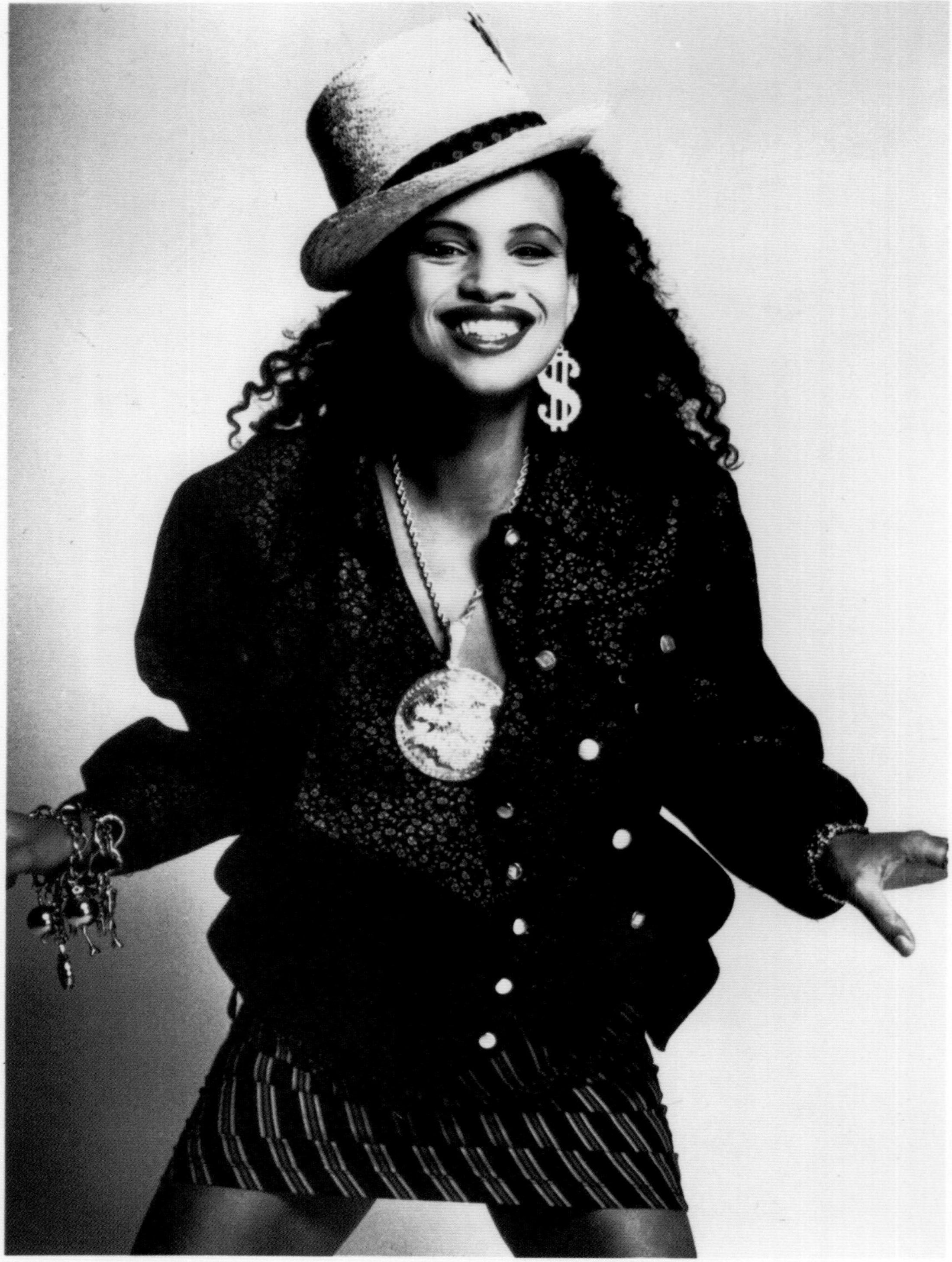

Photo Credit: Enrique

NENEH CHERRY

Virgin

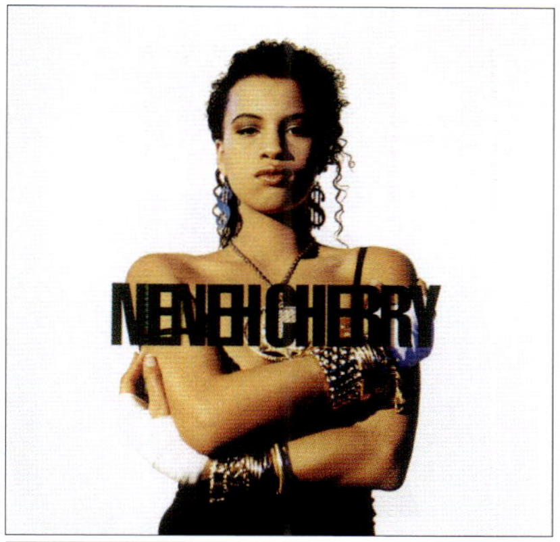

Billboard 200: *Raw Like Sushi* (#40)
Billboard Hot 100: "Buffalo Stance" (#3); "Kisses on the Wind" (#8); "Heart" (#73)

Neneh Cherry made her solo debut with *Raw Like Sushi* and spawned a worldwide smash with "Buffalo Stance."

BORN TO a West African father and Swedish mother, Neneh Cherry's surname came from her stepfather, renowned jazz trumpeter Don Cherry. Her childhood was filled with extensive travel, accompanying Cherry and his band on tour. Most of her school years were spent commuting between a country school in the south of Sweden and a state school in New York City.

At 16, she relocated to London. "I worked for a couple of years looking after kids, in a couple of offices, cleaning whatever I could get my hands on," she explained. "Then the music thing started." Cherry worked with underground cult faves such as the Slits and fronted Rip Rig + Panic, an eccentric punk outfit of "nouveau jazz iconoclasts" which later evolved into Float Up CP. In 1987, she duetted with Matt Johnson on "Slow Train to Dawn," a single drawn from The The's *Infected* album.

"It left me with a fairly open mind," Cherry said. "Everything I take in doesn't necessarily come out having to be something particular. Rip Rig + Panic taught me how to be spontaneous yet disciplined—you had to learn how to reach for things you didn't necessarily know or understand without being scared. It's given me a chance to develop my own sound and find my own voice without having to be perfect each time I open my mouth. It's quite the reverse, actually."

A proud mother of two, Cherry wrote *Raw Like Sushi* in collaboration with her beau, co-producer Booga Bear. The album stretched the conventional boundaries of popular dance music. Cherry drew from an eclectic mix of genres, singing and rapping in a self-assured manner. Her debut solo single, "Buffalo Stance," went gold in the US, and *Raw Like Sushi* sold over 2 million copies worldwide.

"I'm in one of those periods where I can feel everything that I've learned," Cherry said. "That's exciting—it gives me the confidence to move on. A few years ago, I had a lot of insecurities about what I did, and wasn't able to sit in a room with musicians and express my ideas. Now I'm pretty much in control of what's going on around me—I'm not scared. When I think of something, I'm going to say it. If there's something I don't like, I'll fight it." ■

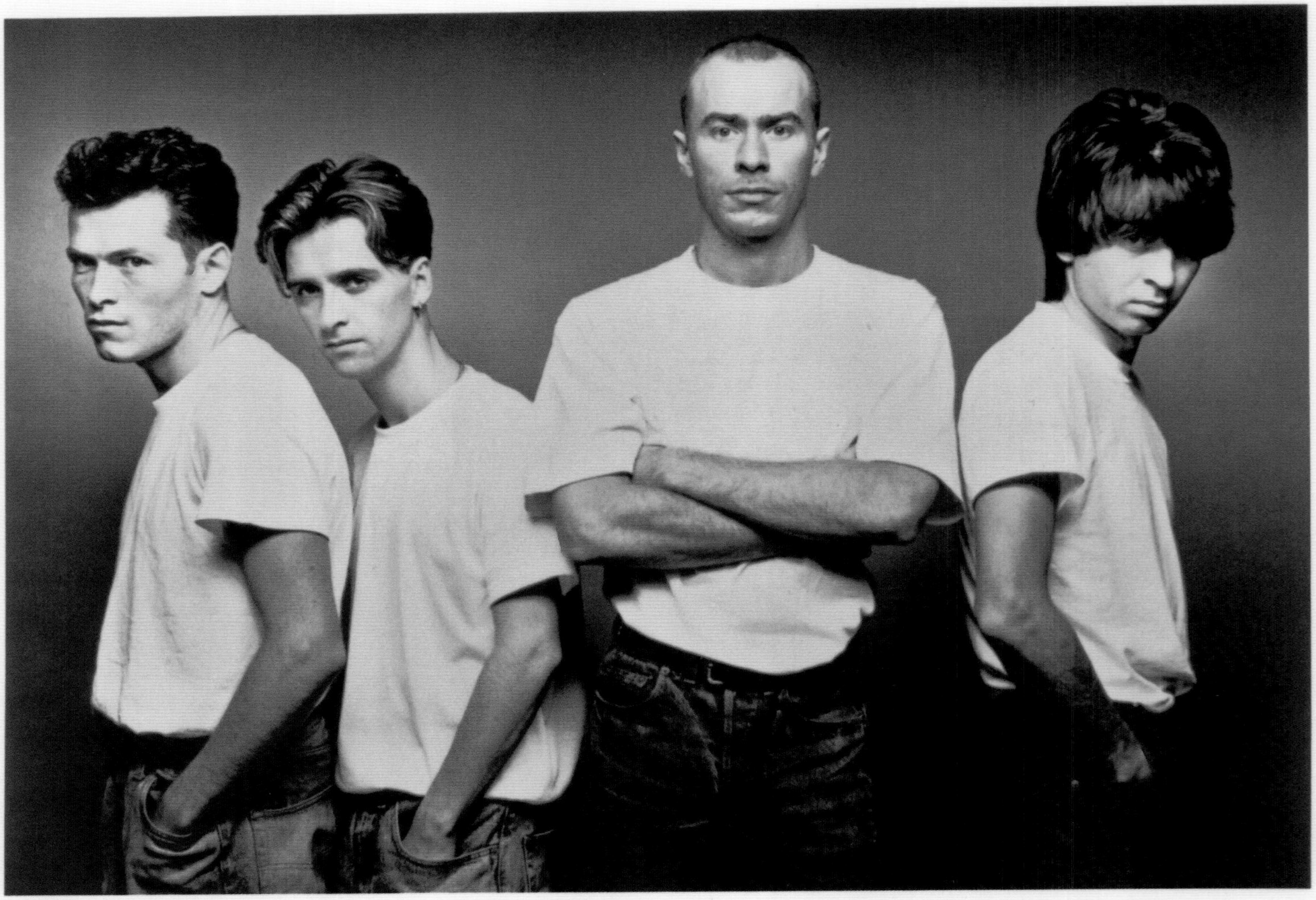

DAVE PALMER JOHNNY MARR MATT JOHNSON JAMES ELLER

the The

Epic

8905

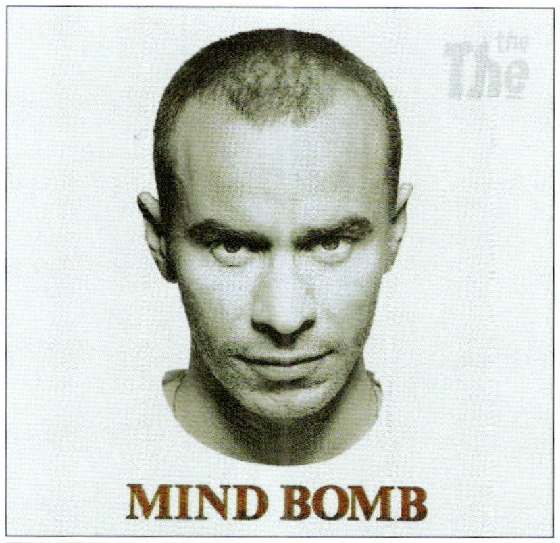

Billboard 200: *Mind Bomb* (#138)

With Matt Johnson at the center, a simpatico band version of The The returned to recording with *Mind Bomb*.

OVER THE span of seven years, England's enigmatic Matt Johnson had released three albums under the moniker The The. Since most British acts had used "the" as a prefix to their names, he thought The The would be the definitive name for his definitive British group.

Johnson described himself as a producer and writer rather than a musician, and as a creative device for each successive project, he'd surrounded himself with a new talent roster. His cast of characters had included David Johansen, Neneh Cherry and Jools Holland. In his guise as The The, Johnson had commanded respect in a highly fickle industry. His low profile belied the intensity he put into his uniquely personal and consistently excellent work.

"I've come to terms with who my audience is," he said. "If reaching everyone in the world is one of your motivations, you have to prostitute or dilute your work. The pressures are hard to resist—success isn't equated with quality, it's how many units you sell, chart position, rotation on radio."

But Johnson had taken long breaks between The The releases. In 1986, the ambitious and sophisticated *Infected* displayed his dark, existential lyrics in metaphorical songs addressing sexual, political and social issues. The album was a hard act to follow, and Johnson decided to form a group with guitarist Johnny Marr, who had brought the Smiths to the top of the British charts during a period dominated by the synthesizer sound and people who thought nothing remained to be said with the electric guitar.

"I've always wanted to work with Johnny, because melodically we are like twins," Johnson said. He also assembled Dave Palmer on drums and James Eller on bass. "I chose people who were in love with their own instruments. Dave has played with me before, and he's considered one of the best drummers in the world. James is the coolest man on four strings."

The *Mind Bomb* album reflected Johnson's optimism, with his passionate, emotional vocals and a muscular, apocalyptic sound on "Armageddon Days Are Here (Again)" and "Gravitate to Me." The The then embarked on its first-ever tour.

"Before, my attitude wasn't 100 percent—it takes so much money and time to tour, and it wasn't my idea of fun," Johnson said. "But when I'm writing and recording in the studio, everything else gets in the way—not sleeping and eating properly runs you down to the breaking point. Ironically, I've found that being on the road is far healthier for me—everything is a disciplined routine geared to the hour-and-a-half onstage. Now I want to get touring out of my system and see if my voice will stand up." ■

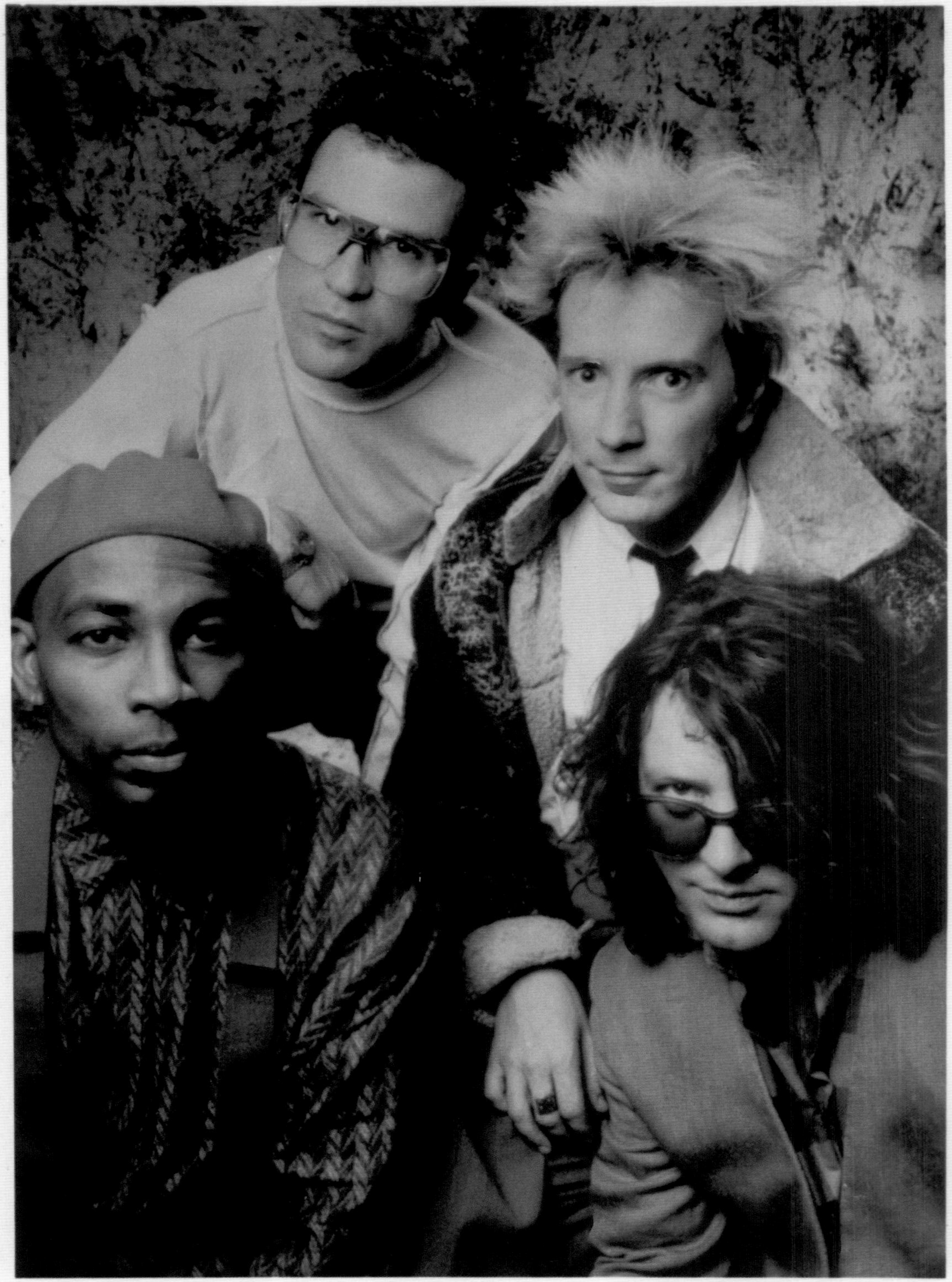

Photo Credit: Bonnie Schiffman

PUBLIC IMAGE LIMITED

Virgin

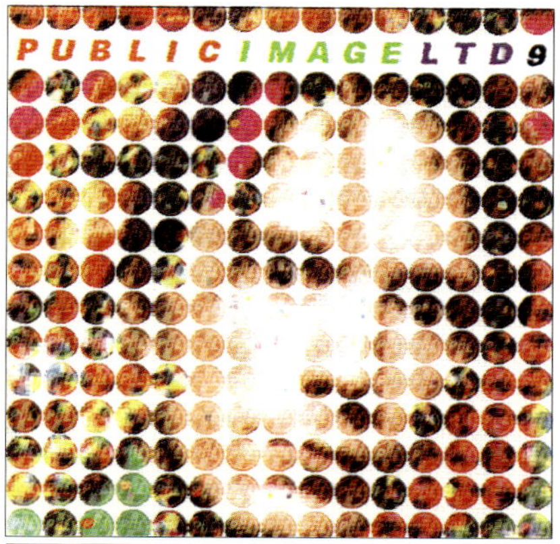

Billboard 200: *9* (#106)

Formed by provocateur John Lydon, Public Image Ltd still carried the flag for post-punk rock with the album *9*.

ALSO KNOWN as Johnny Rotten, John Lydon crashed onto the rock music scene in 1977 as the lead singer and symbolic presence of the infamous Sex Pistols. With his spiky hair, ragamuffin togs, a fiery gleam in his eyes and the most recognizable sneering yowl around, the confrontational and nihilistic Rotten spoke for the angry generation that first cut its teeth on punk.

The Sex Pistols' lone studio album, *Never Mind the Bollocks, Here's the Sex Pistols,* captured a unique moment in rock history. The brash, rude Pistols had an explosive guitar sound that took aggression to previously unheard-of limits. But the Pistols logically self-destructed rather than fall prey to conventions, and Lydon launched the group Public Image Ltd in 1979 to redefine the rock avant-garde, supposedly as a way of life more than a mere rock band.

Lydon's presence had been the only constant in the group's flow of innovative music. PiL played its first New York appearance hidden behind a video screen while music played from tapes. The band released its second album inside a metal box. For much of the Eighties, Lydon had worked with a variety of nonpermanent members and tried to annoy everybody. He remained an icon of the punk movement, and his music and messages were reaching more than the commercial fringes.

"Anyone who doesn't threaten the status quo in the music business is guaranteed success, but let other people be happy with that—I can live without mass acceptance, thank you very much," Lydon said. "It would just be nice if I was understood properly before I was judged."

The album *9* was the closest thing to a group effort that Public Image Ltd had done. Lydon assembled a wonderfully tight band—the refined but jagged dance-pop was the product of interplay among core musicians John McGeoch (guitar), Bruce Smith (drums) and Allan Dias (bass). The haunting single "Disappointed" gave the PiL its biggest US triumph, with much modern-rock radio airplay and moderate rotation on MTV.

But Lydon still had to wait out his past. He couldn't tour with Public Image Ltd in his native England because he had been banned from so many venues during Pistols days. "I could perform if I signed ridiculous insurance policies that would bankrupt me in minutes," he said. "The members of the media over there really have it in for me. They seem to throw everything bad at me as if I was the devil personified. It's sad and stupid. But in America, people are much more open to new ideas." ■

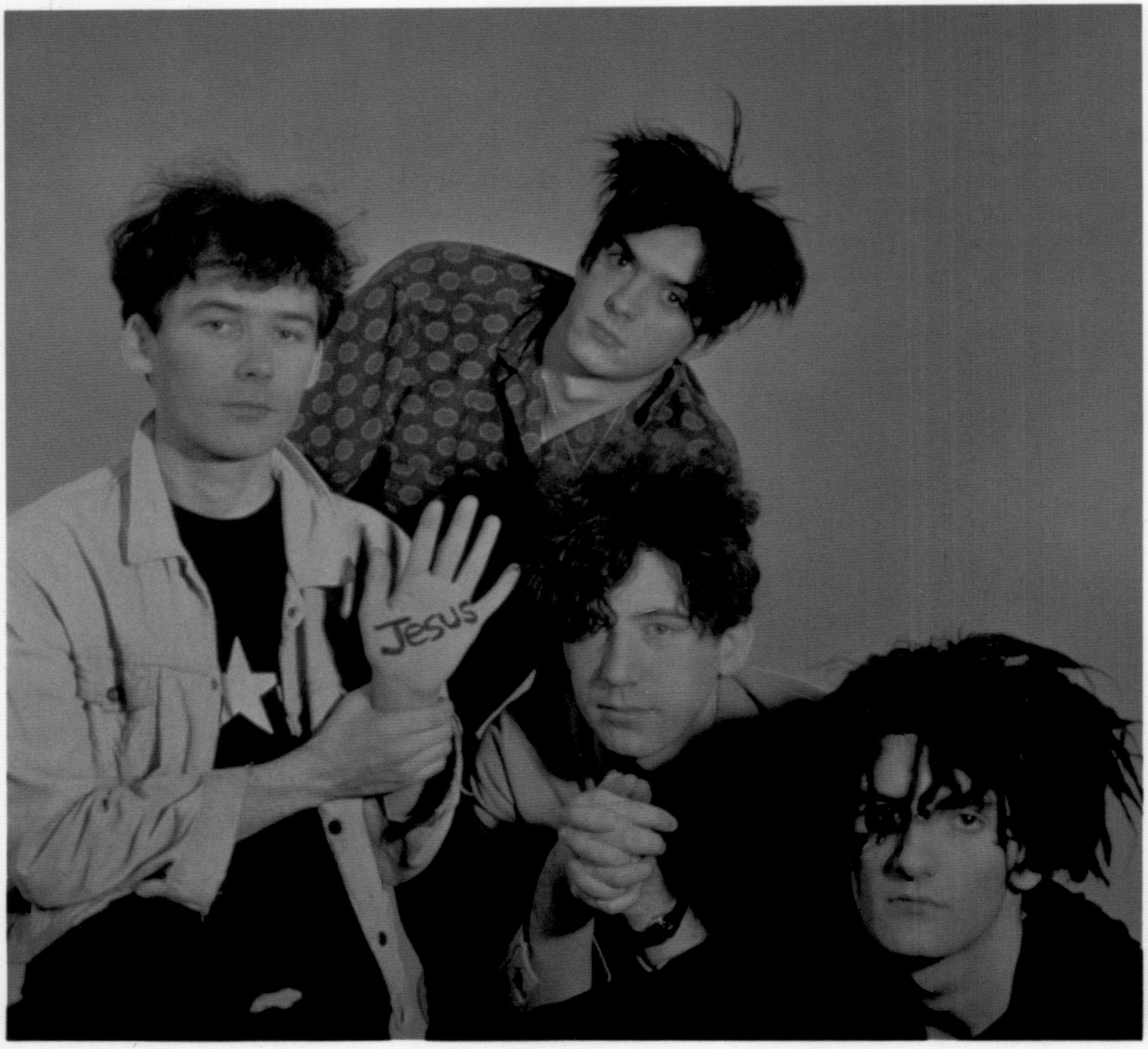

Photo Credit: Andy Catlin

Jim Reid, Richard Thomas, William Reid, Douglas Hart

THE JESUS AND MARY CHAIN *Automatic*

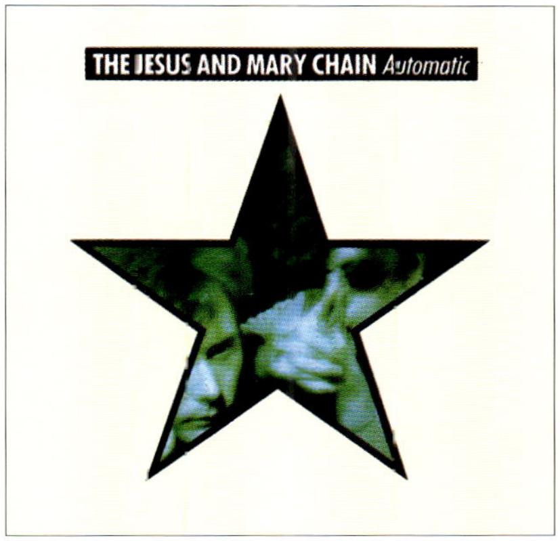

Billboard 200: *Automatic* (#105)

The Jesus and Mary Chain slid into the mainstream with the alternative hits "Head On" and "Blues from a Gun."

EVERY YEAR, a few British bands proved there was a sizable American audience eager for something new and exciting. The Cure and the Cult had crossed the barrier in a big way, and it was time for the Jesus and Mary Chain. The single "Blues from a Gun" and "Head On" topped alternative airplay charts, and the videos were in "Buzz Bin" rotation on MTV.

Such exposure came as a shock, albeit a pleasant one, given the band's determined nonconformist attitudes. In 1985, the Jesus and Mary Chain debuted with *Psychocandy*, an outrage on convention that generated a storm of discussion. The album mixed hooky power-pop and dark wit with ferocious feedback and industrial-strength noise—"We did it just to say we did it," singer Jim Reid said.

Most pop fans found the shrill chainsaw guitars as unsettling as a dentist's drill, and *Psychocandy* struggled on the charts. Yet it rated high in the alternative rock market, which considered bands pioneers for the ability to infuriate and confuse the musical establishment. But even people who found *Psychocandy* absorbing and compelling started saying that all the band could do was make noise with guitars and that they'd never be able to come up with another record near as good.

"I don't see why people expect us to do *Psychocandy II*—what's the point in making it again?" Reid said. "Imagine a movie director making a film about Vietnam, and then making another film about Vietnam, and another. People wouldn't stand for it. Too many people who make music get away with repeating themselves. We're not interested. We simply make the records we want to hear."

Various ancillary members had come and gone, and the Jesus and Mary Chain lineup had been honed down to Jim and William Reid. The Scottish-born brothers produced, wrote and performed the album *Automatic*, which all but eliminated the band's characteristic crazed salvos. On "Head On," the Reids combined a pop song structure with a series of menacing chord changes while submerging the tonal quality of the grinding-gears with a melodic hook.

"Head On" was high-energy, mass-appeal rock, and the raucous "Blues from a Gun" was a No. 1 modern-rock hit in the US. Yet the Reids weren't exactly basking in their popularity—the brothers still had that spirit of staring off dejectedly into space.

"I'd like to be successful in America," Jim, the younger of the two, intoned."What comes with it is the power to do what you want to when you want to. We've done that anyway, but it's always held us back. If you go away for two years, it damages your career, people forget about you. Whereas if you sell 50 million albums, people sit around waiting for your next record. But I really don't care." ■

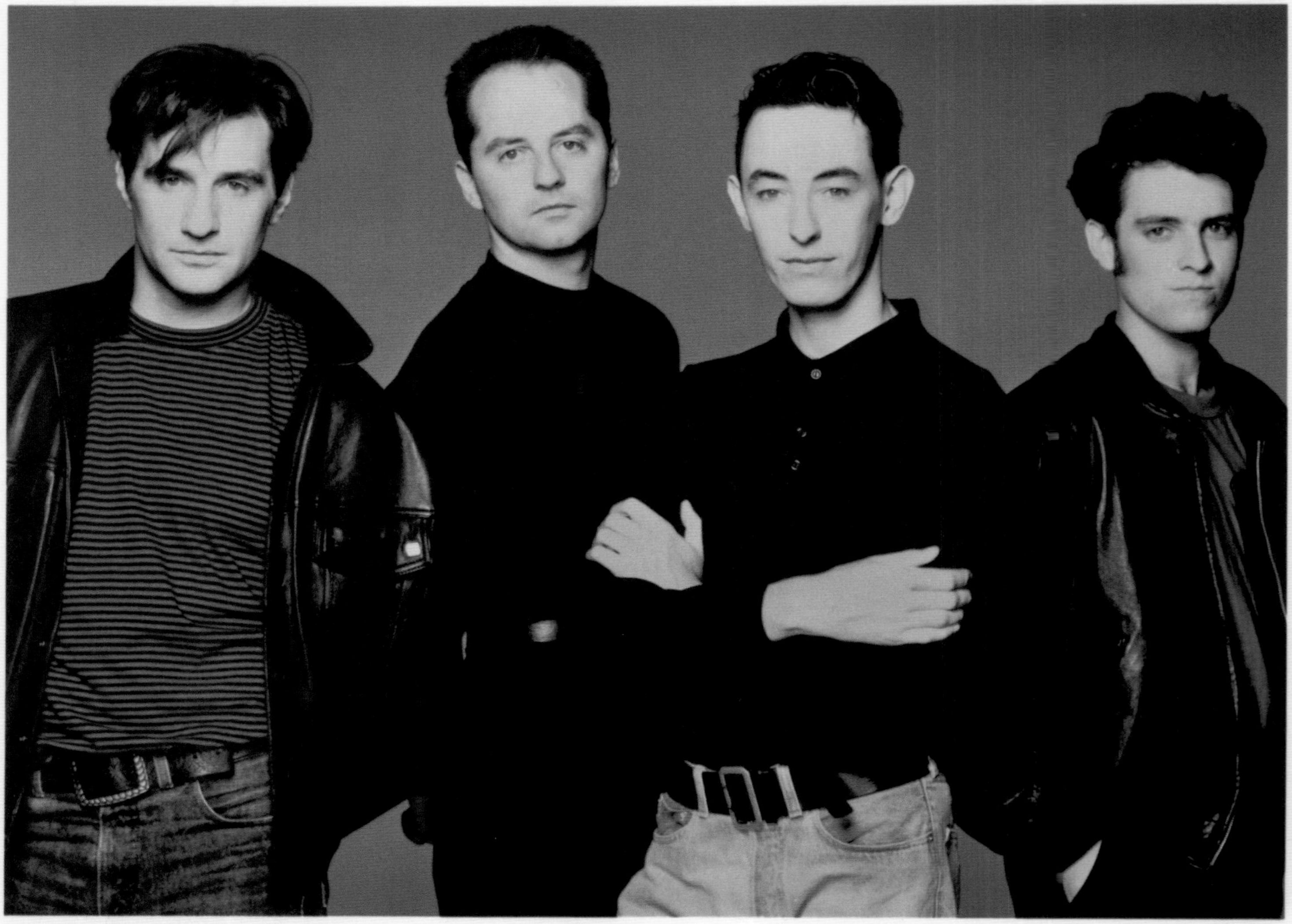

Photo Credit: Simon Fowler

the mighty lemon drops

reprise SIRE

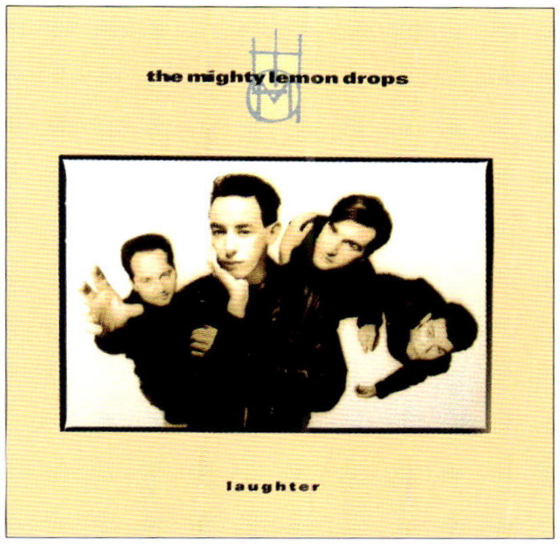

Billboard 200: *Laughter* (#195)

The Mighty Lemon Drops rejected peer comparisons on *Laughter* with a discriminating approach to alt-pop.

A DEPARTURE from two earlier records, the Mighty Lemon Drops' *Laughter* album switched to spicy pop songs from the "mope-rock" for which the English band had become known. The elegant melody of the song "Where Do We Go from Heaven" was pushed along by some tasteful acoustic guitar. That single and "Into the Heart of Love" were both popular in the modern-rock scene.

"We're seen by a lot of people as being a doom-and-gloom band," singer Paul Marsh said. "That's why the album is called *Laughter*—we want people to be happy. We wanted to lose the dark stuff we've done."

The success of *Laughter*, which debuted at No. 1 on the college charts and managed to crack the lower regions of the pop album charts, contrasted markedly with the lack of press attention the band got in its native Britain.

"We can't get arrested over there," Marsh fumed. "They would lead you to believe that the only reason we exist is because of Echo and the Bunnymen. That's totally unjust. There were similar touches in early songs—they listened to a lot of late Sixties psychedelic music and so did we—but I don't even like them." ■

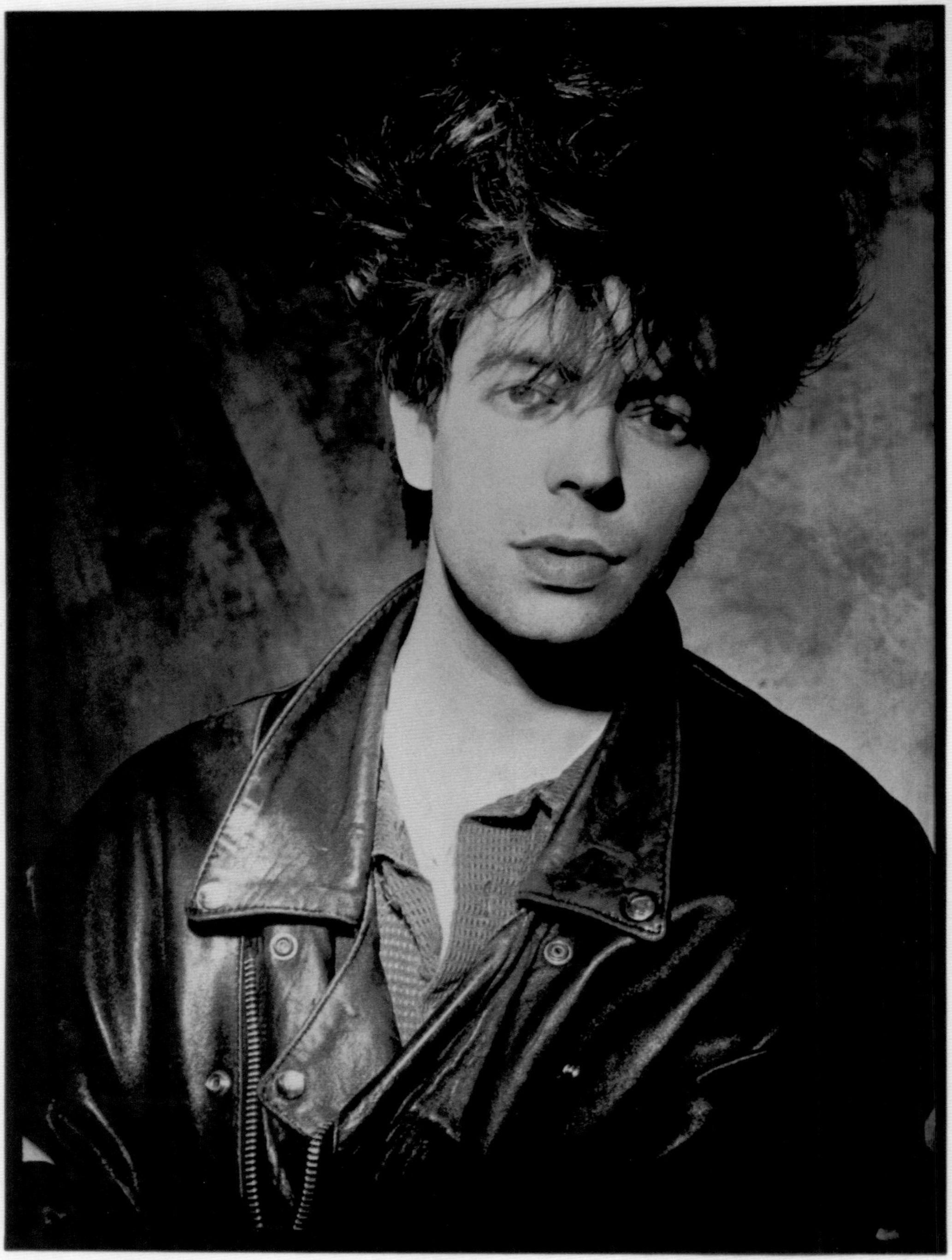

Photo Credit: Andy Catlin

IAN McCULLOCH

SIRE®

reprise®

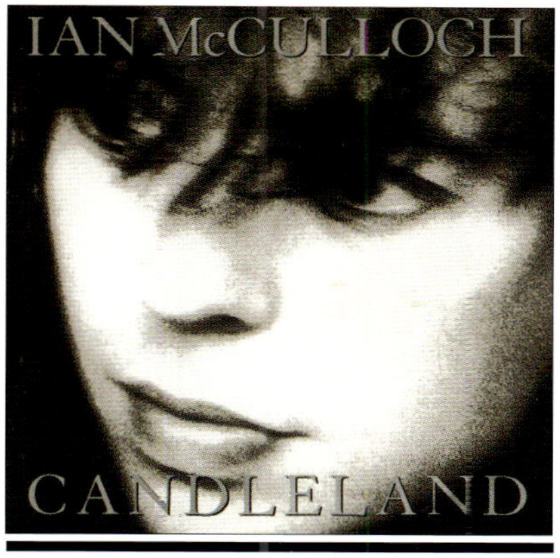

Billboard 200: *Candleland* (#179)

Taking his leave from Echo & the Bunnymen, frontman Ian McCulloch made a solo gesture with *Candleland*.

FORMED IN Liverpool, Echo & the Bunnymen emerged in the Eighties as a forerunner of the new-wave musical renaissance. The foursome's pivotal creative force was lead singer Ian McCulloch, whose strong vocal presence wed pop with drama. But in November 1988, after five albums, McCulloch announced his decision to pursue a solo career.

"Echo was built on this mystical chemistry that people said we had, and I know it was gone for good," he said. "I found writing and singing on the last album difficult—I was drunk because I didn't want to be in the studio. We could have written okay rock songs, but they wouldn't have meant anything. We didn't have the magic."

So McCulloch started over as a solo performer. "I feel much happier, although it's a case of building it up again," he said. "In America, people know the Echo name more than mine. But I've got more stagecraft now!"

Echo had a debt to the Doors that was acknowledged by prominently featuring Ray Manzarek, that band's former keyboardist, on a version of the Doors' "People Are Strange" for the soundtrack of *The Lost Boys*. "That Doors-y thing was so easy to use in America, and for a while it was good," McCulloch mused. "But I never aimed to be Jim Morrison. He was an out-and-out rocker, and I don't think he had much nuance vocally. I always had more in common with David Bowie."

Candleland, McCulloch's debut release, carried on the Echo tradition with a leaner but still lush distillation of the band's post-punk sound. It was a true solo album on which McCulloch played most of the instruments himself, with a somber array of mood swings—the result of personal upheaval (the recent deaths of his father and Bunnymen drummer Pete DeFreitas) and the aftermath of his decision to quit Echo. The ethereal "Proud to Fall," a No. 1 modern rock track, featured the Cure's Boris Williams on drums.

"*Candleland* is specific and literal," he said. "It fulfills me because it's related to a chain of events beyond my control." ■

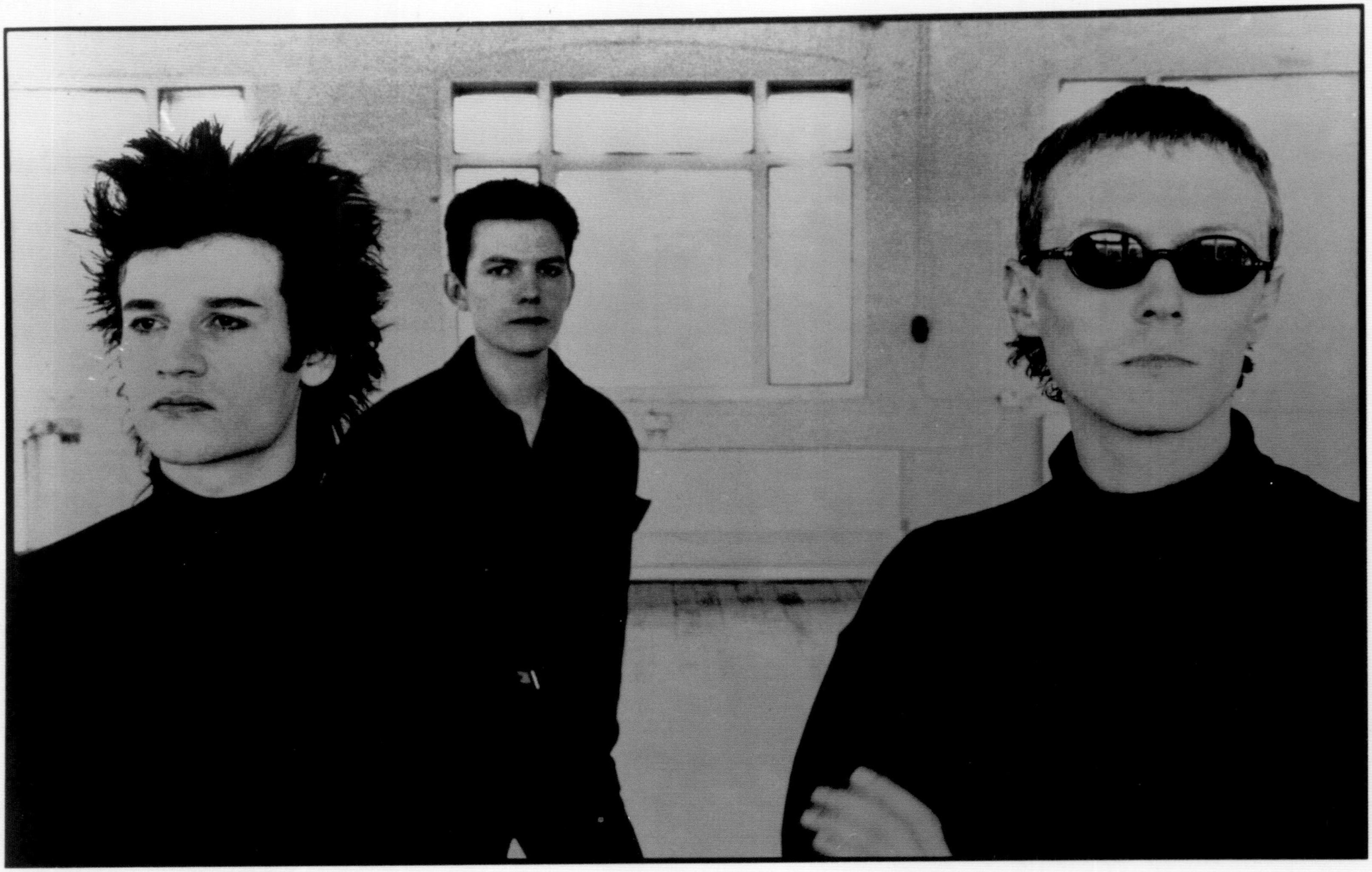

PHOTOCREDIT: DEREK RIDGERS

LOVE AND ROCKETS

bigtime

BEGGARS BANQUET

RCA

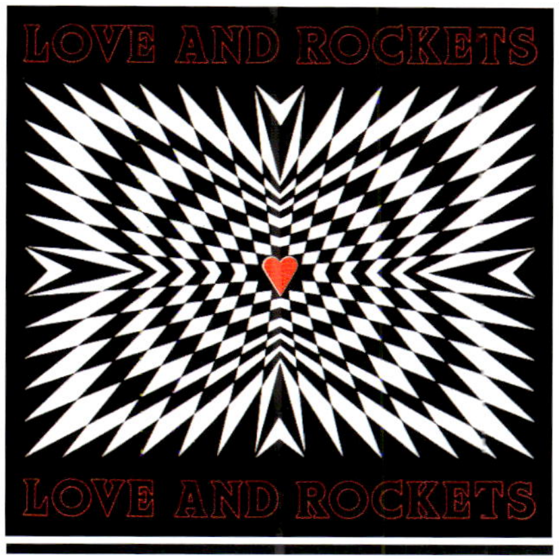

Billboard 200: *Love and Rockets* (#14)
Billboard Hot 100: "So Alive" (#3); "No Big Deal" (#82)

Love and Rockets helped contour the alternative rock of the Eighties, scoring big with the sensuous "So Alive."

A TORTURED, gloomy band, Bauhaus spearheaded Britain's gothic-rock movement before breaking up in 1983. Who thought that three former members would be gracing the US Top 10? But Love and Rockets reunited guitarist and vocalist Daniel Ash, bassist and vocalist David J. and drummer Kevin Haskins, and the trio landed a surprise hit on American hit radio with "So Alive," an Ash-penned single with a T. Rex feel.

Ash had formed Bauhaus when he met up with schoolmate Peter Murphy in 1979. "Somebody in the press coined the phrase 'goth-rock,' and it just stuck," Ash said. "We never thought, 'Right, we're gonna wear black clothes and makeup and plan on playing this music.' It was completely off instinct, but it had to be put in a pigeonhole."

After nearly five years of recording and performing with Bauhaus, Ash put together a group with Haskins, mutating into Love and Rockets when David J. came around. Unnerving variety had been a hallmark of Love and Rockets over the course of four albums. The band debuted with a dance-floor single, a remake of the Temptations' classic "Ball of Confusion," and followed it up with the harmonic structure of "All in My Mind." "The three of us have very different musical styles," Ash said. "It almost sounds like three different bands on the same record, which I find appealing. When you're rehearsing and not concentrating, you make mistakes—and we pick up on those things."

The finely honed pop single "So Alive" brought Love and Rockets' nonconforming ideas into the US mainstream. "I've always hated the phrase 'alternative music,'" Ash said. "I don't think that barrier should exist. It's either good or it isn't. The ideal situation is to make music that appeals to a majority of people but is also challenging. Then you've got the best of both worlds." ■

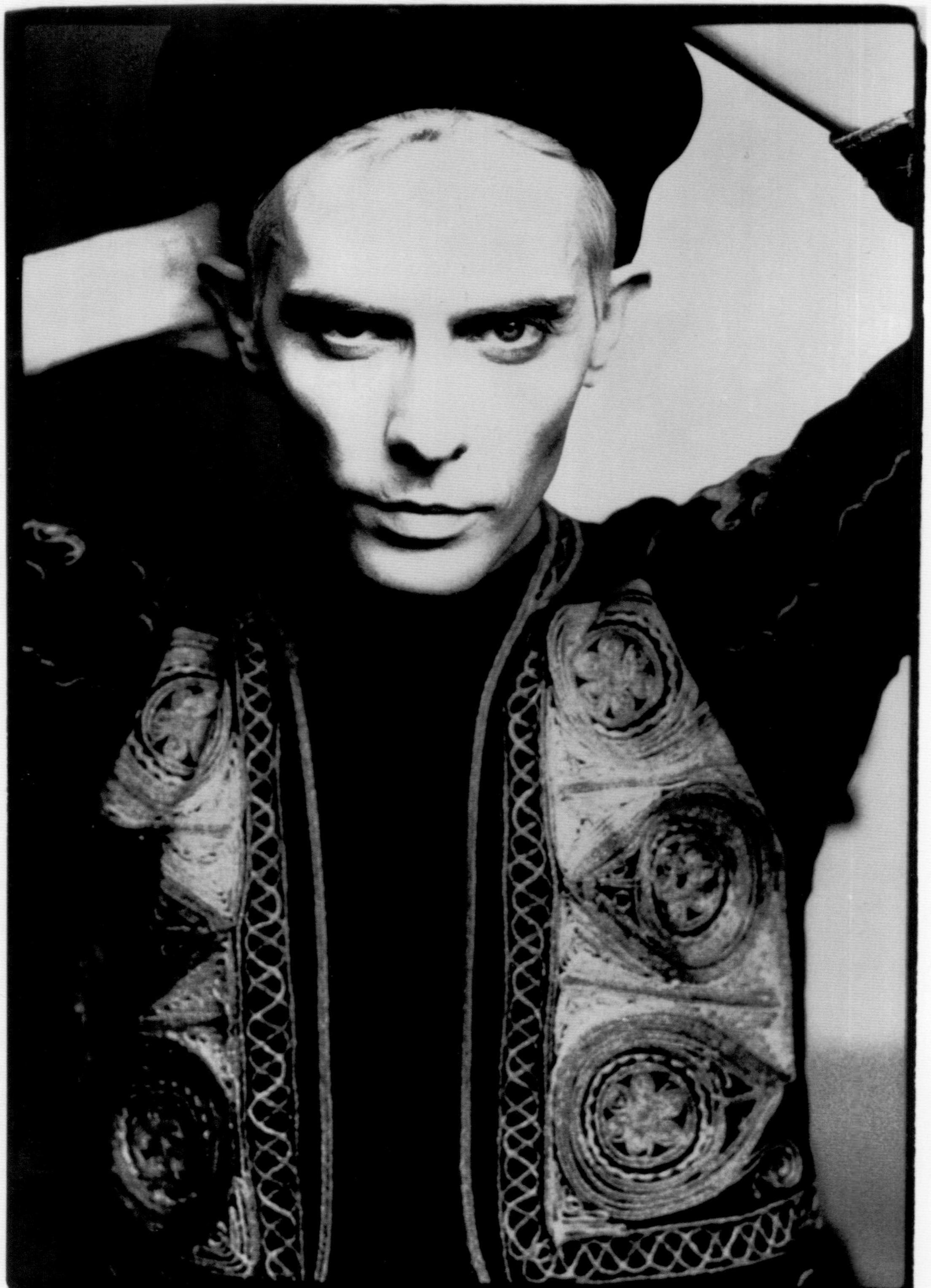

P E T E R M U R P H Y

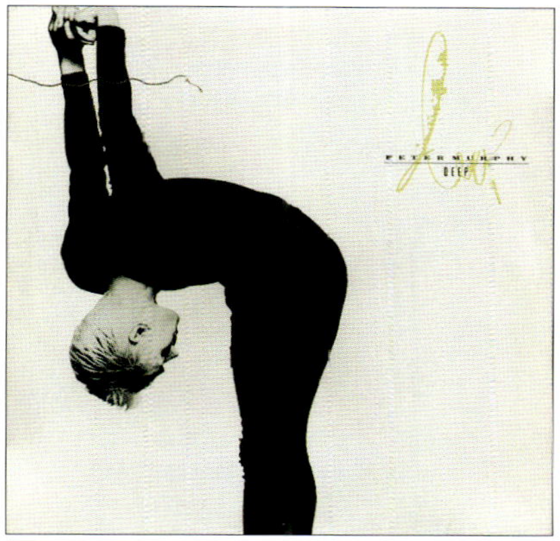

Billboard 200: *Deep* (#44)
Billboard Hot 100: "Cuts You Up" (#55)

Peter Murphy's commanding "Cuts You Up" eventually turned into the modern-rock hit of the year in America.

AS THE brooding, spectral singer with Bauhaus, Peter Murphy first caught the attention of the rock world in 1978. The British band's doom-and-gloom look and sound came to be called "gothic-rock," an influential post-punk musical movement. The group disbanded in 1983, when Murphy pursued a solo career and the remaining three musicians formed Love and Rockets "It was difficult to imagine working without this amazing creative center," Murphy said. "I'm starting to write real quickly and alone now, to feel that confidence, for want of a better word, that there's a creative well there."

Deep, Murphy's third album, was his most accessible venture to date. It became the No. 1 alternative album two weeks after its release because he'd withheld some of his dark excesses and incantations. People were always asking him about the mystique of his lyrics. "It seems as if I'm a philosopher—that's the audience's perception of my work," he said. "So the title *Deep* reflects that element, a mirroring of the image I have. I write more from a prose standpoint than songwriting. I feel that has a place in rock music."

The song "Cuts You Up" became his vehicle to commercial acceptance, with a moody surrealism and infectious chorus giving it a tempting edge. Murphy had a hit on his own terms, layering a weeping fiddle line and a shimmering acoustic angle in a modern production.

"It's a love song, but it's obviously not written that way," Murphy said. "It's a blend between being very romantic and very spacey in the chorus. Some simple things affected that song as well as the entire album. I wanted to involve my band more rather than using individual contributions in the studio."

Vocally, Murphy continued to be accused of parroting David Bowie's forcefully seductive crooning. His stage theatrics also were comparable, when he moved his sinuous, sexless body in and out of lighting settings.

"The lighting in my shows isn't that complex or expensive, it just helps me keep an anything-can-happen edge out there," he noted. "It's exciting to have a certain amount of time to communicate a song, to draw people into a mood. You can take them through doors that they don't expect you to take them through." ■

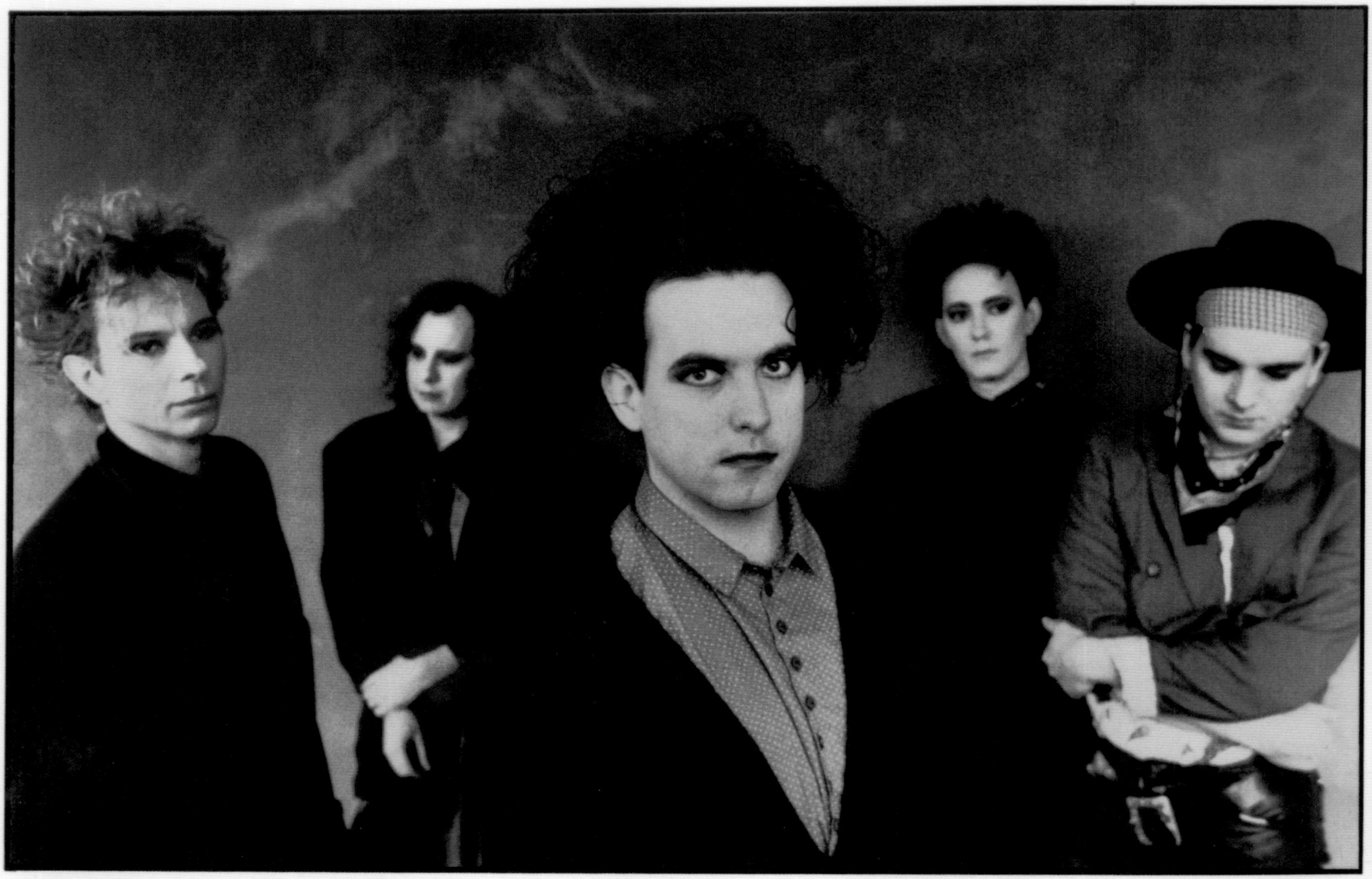

PHOTO CREDIT: DEREK RIDGERS / 1989

BORIS WILLIAMS PORL THOMPSON ROBERT SMITH ROGER O'DONNELL SIMON GALLUP

THE CURE

ELEKTRA FICTION

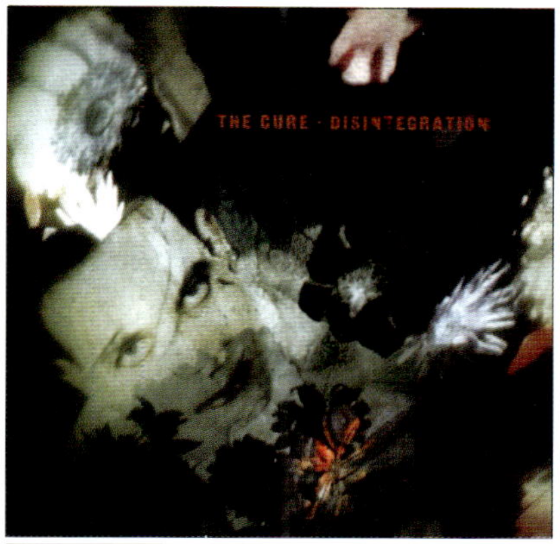

Billboard 200: *Disintegration* (#12)
Billboard Hot 100: "Lullaby" (#74); "Fascination Street" (#46); "Lovesong" (#2); "Pictures of You" (#71)

The Cure's *Disintegration* album announced an unanticipated return to the darker side of the band's psyche.

APPARENTLY, MISERY loved company. That explained the success of the Cure, the masters of mope-rock. Over the course of 11 albums, the British band had specialized in the presentation of a phobic, morbid worldview, a minor-key pop atmosphere for the depression-prone.

And in the process, the Cure emerged as one of the decade's most enduring and successful bands. Millions of fans found a kindred spirit in singer Robert Smith, a guru of gloom with his trademark mane of dark tangled hair, slash of red lipstick and deliberately porcelain complexion. His audience—the majority were in their teens, sullen, pale, somberly attired in black-on-black and guilty of mousse abuse.

Smith added to their depression with the news that "The Prayer Tour," the concert swing in support of the *Disintegration* album, would be the Cure's last. Of course, Smith, ever the tortured soul had said the same thing about the previous two Cure tours, but many things about his band remained unclear. "I lie a lot," he said. "I bore myself if I don't make things up."

Perhaps this explained why Smith made derogatory comments about Americans. "People are so obsessive to the point of being scary in America," he said. "My intention on the tour is not to meet an American." But he also insisted that *Disintegration* was the band's last album. It was a bleak record that hearkened back to the 1982 masterpiece *Pornography*—a musical catharsis, for Smith's obsession with loneliness. Original member Lol Tolhurst departed just before *Disintegration* was released.

Naturally, the album became the band's commercial peak in the US. "Fascination Street" reached No. 1 on the modern-rock chart, and "Lovesong" was the first Cure single to crack the Top 10 on the pop chart. "Robert's not really happy within himself at the moment," bassist Simon Gallup, who was as genial as Smith was traumatized, admitted. "But he can exorcise his thoughts in his lyrics, and that does make him happy." ■

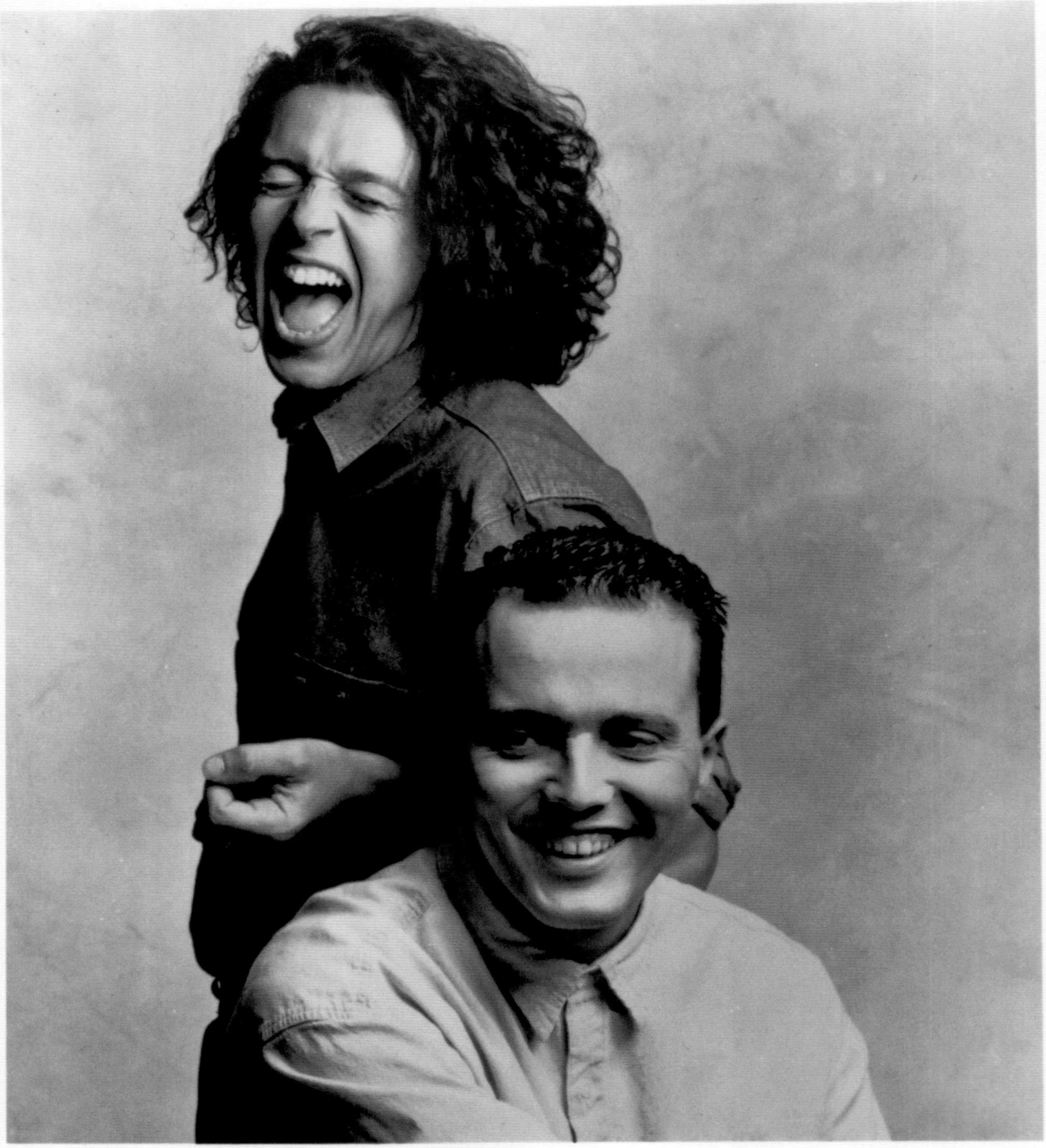

ROLAND ORZABAL

Tears for Fears

CURT SMITH

fontana

PolyGram

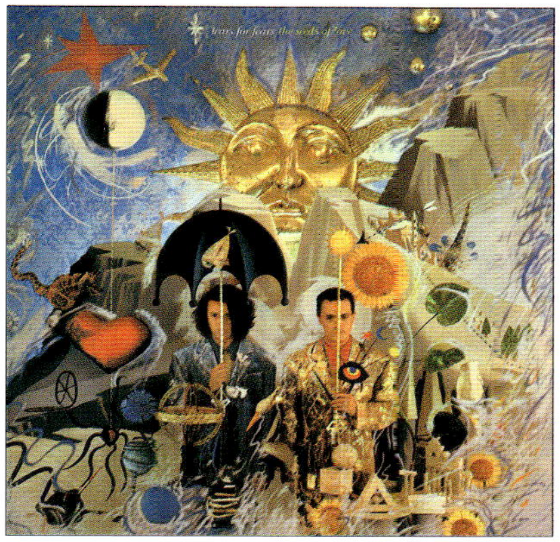

Billboard 200: *The Seeds of Love* (#8)
Billboard Hot 100: "Sowing the Seeds of Love" (#2); "Woman in Chains" (#36); "Advice for the Young at Heart" (#89)

A bout with widespread stardom so upset Tears for Fears that it took four years to develop *The Seeds of Love*.

CONCERNED WITH primal scream theory—confronting fears to eliminate them (or shedding "tears for fears")—Roland Orzabal and Curt Smith took a name from Arthur Janov's book *Prisoners of Pain*. The Britsh pop duo's dour world view was introduced on 1983's *The Hurting*, with songs largely derived from Janovian therapy and other aspects of modern psychology.

1985's *Songs from the Big Chair* topped the US chart for five weeks and established that Tears for Fears wasn't as depressingly serious as some assumed. An ambitious, sophisticated techno-pop album with thought-provoking lyrics about alienation and romance, it sold 5 million copies and gave the band two No. 1 singles, "Everybody Wants to Rule the World" and "Shout."

"When we first started out, it was very fashionable to be against rock 'n' roll cliches—we wouldn't use guitar solos, we would avoid normal beats," Orzabal explained. "With *Songs*, we relaxed and did some things because they worked on an instinctive level. It happened a couple of songs were very catchy—right time, right place."

Caught unaware, Orzabal and Smith struggled to handle the attention and live up to the multiplatinum standards. "The American culture prepares you for that—it's the goal, the dream, and generally, when people get there, they dance to stay there," Orzabal explained. "English culture doesn't prepare you at all—it's about working hard all your life, very anti-overnight success. I was very much a victim of it."

Tears for Fears was reborn with *The Seeds of Love*. Key was Oleta Adams, whom the band discovered in 1985 playing piano and singing in a Kansas City hotel bar.

"We had just played in front of thousands of people with lots of sequencers and emulators, and it was quite vacuous—we came away with a slightly empty feeling," Orzabal explained. "But we ran into something simpler but far more powerful, soulful and expressive. Oleta had us in tears—she was in tears, too, but she had hay fever! I couldn't believe the difference between what we were doing and what she was doing to pay the rent."

Orzabal and Smith invited Adams to England to help make *The Seeds of Love*, vowing that the album would be more alive than their tried-and-trusted programming techniques. A series of live takes, spliced together digitally, produced a feel of "crafted spontaneity." Hits included "Woman in Chains," a stirring duet with Adams, and "Sowing the Seeds of Love," complete with deliberate Beatle-isms, advocating love as the first step in solving everything from the crumbling environment to the "politics of greed."

"It was written around the time of the last general elections in Britain," Orzabal said. "I wanted to write a protest song against the government, but I wanted to evoke the time when the Utopian urge was high, when people weren't afraid to talk about love and creativity. I used the Beatles' sound because people have already bought that message once—it's in the collective consciousness, so I just jerked people's memories." ■

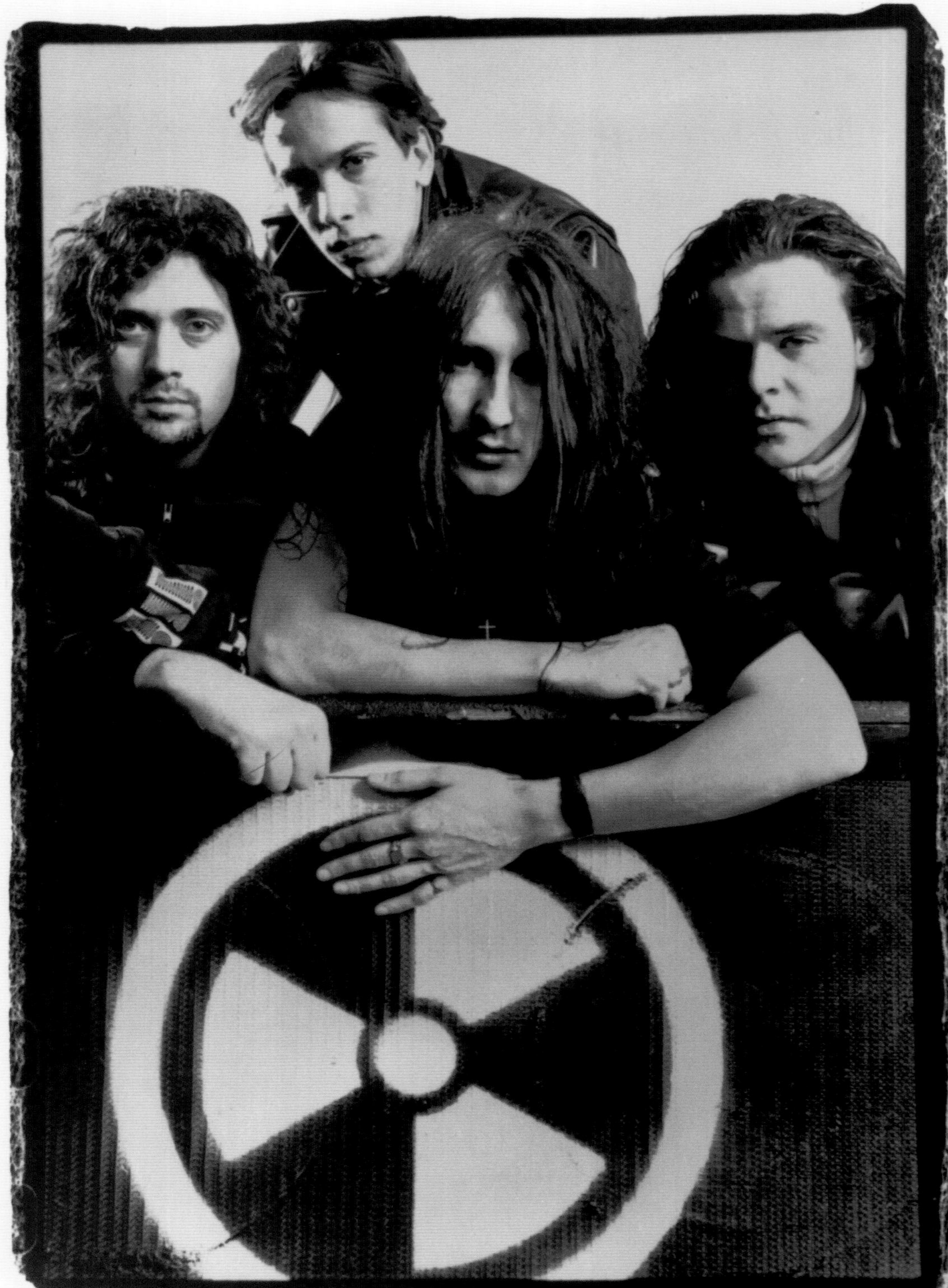

PHOTO CREDIT : Ian TILTON/1989

POP WILL EAT ITSELF

RCA

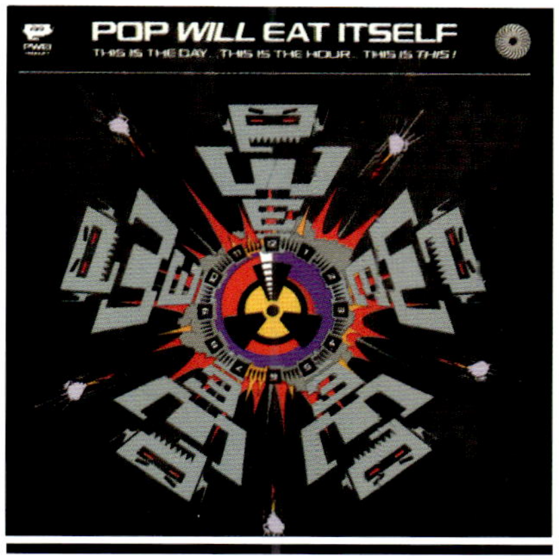

Billboard 200: *This Is the Day...This Is the Hour...This Is This!* (#169)

Pop Will Eat Itself churned out a few of Britain's most preposterous demonstrations in music and poor taste.

BY MAKING records with the punk attitude in mind and a sampler in hand, Pop Will Eat Itself had earned a notorious reputation in England. *This Is the Day...This Is the Hour...This Is This!,* a trashy, beat-crazy assault on the media, had so many "in" jokes and cross-cultural references that the album sounded as if it were mixed in a blender.

"The recording process was quite painstaking, sorting through all of it—like cooking a big stew in a pot, and then deciding that you don't want the carrots and you try to take them out," bassist Richard March laughed.

When Pop Will Eat Itself first emerged on the UK music scene, the members of the group played grinding Buzzcocks-inspired pop and became the greasy, long-haired, leather-jacketed champions of a short-lived movement called "grebo." "Actually, it was more of a look than a movement," March explained. "We were a third-rate punk-thrash band like so many others, except we looked more like the Grateful Dead."

But while visiting European discos, the young British quartet discovered technology. Instead of learning how to play songs, they began experimenting with sampling—borrowing bits of other people's songs, videos, movies, radio or whatever and using them in their music.

The band—March, Adam Mole (guitar) and vocalists Clint Mansell and Graham Crabb—fused loud, wicked electric guitars with samples of everything from Rod Serling to Sid Vicious. *This Is the Day...*, according to March, "does for music what the remote control did for television, bombarding a listener with loads of information."

The album included the UK hits "Wise Up! Sucker" (a propulsive look at love's confusion) and the tumultuous dance mix of "Can U Dig It?" An exploration of international relationships titled "Def. Con. One" (an abbreviation for the final military phase before nuclear war) dented the US alternative charts.

But Pop Will Eat Itself's humor was best displayed on "Not Now James, We're Busy," which mocked the current rage of sampling James Brown while musically re-enacting Brown's recent arrest. The group endured some tenuous comparisons to America's Beastie Boys, as very few white bands were playing a hybrid of rock 'n' roll and hip-hop.

"But we're not into talking about how much beer we can drink," March noted. "And we don't read more comic books or watch more television than the average person. We just store more information for our music." ■

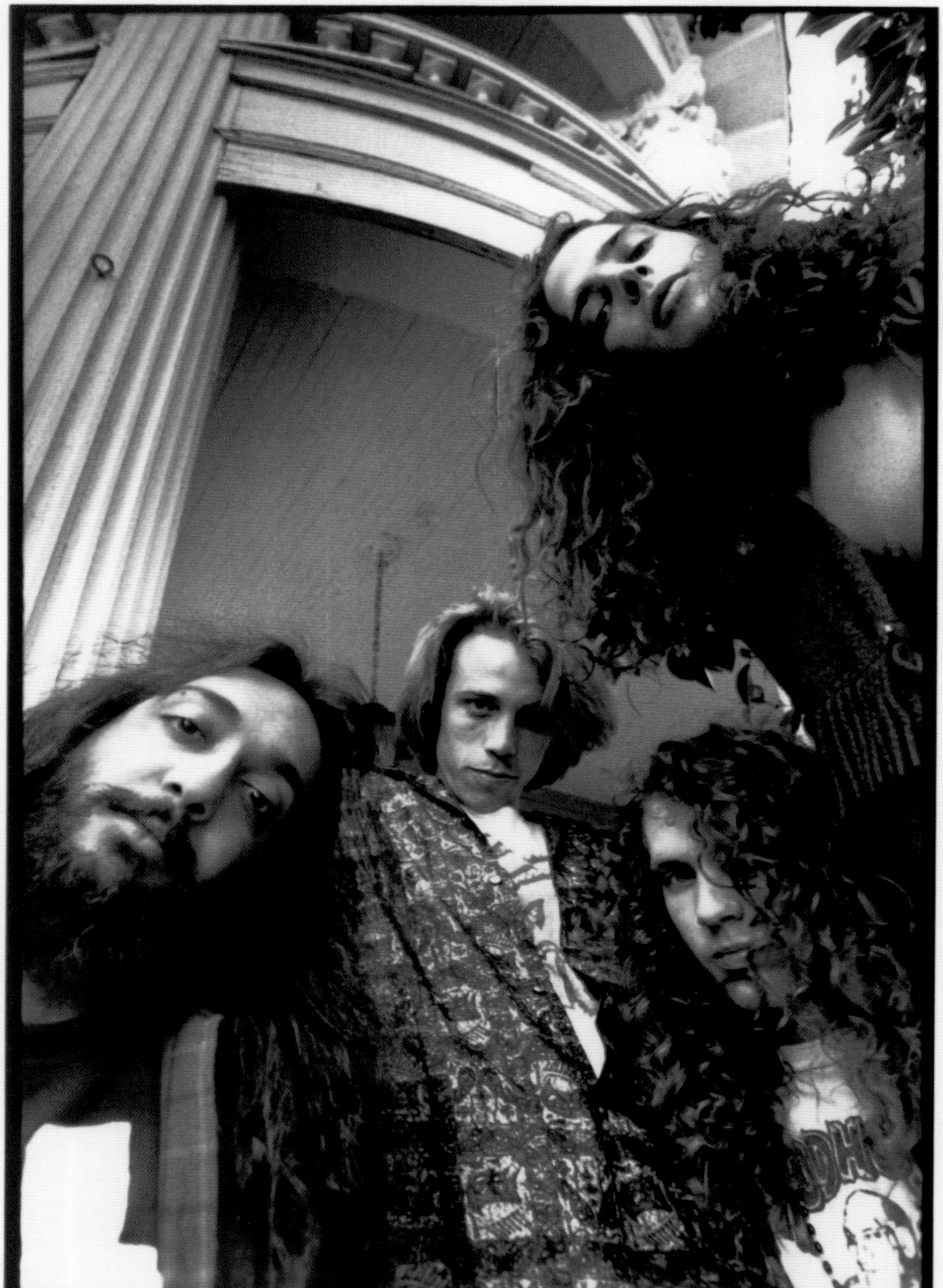

KIM THAYIL MATT CAMERON JASON EVERMAN CHRIS CORNELL

SOUNDGARDEN

A&M RECORDS

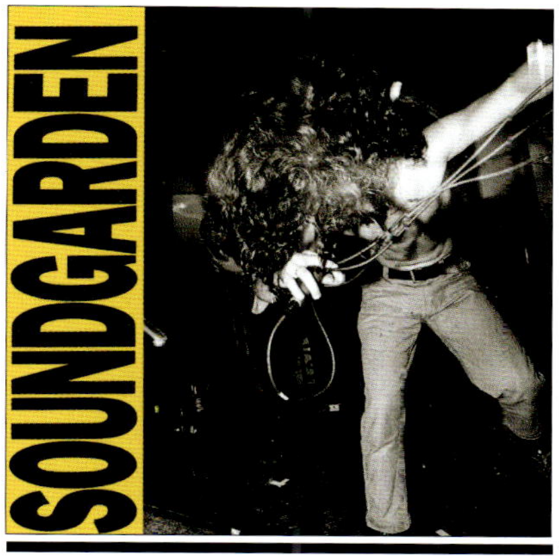

Billboard 200: *Louder Than Love* (#108)

Louder Than Love, the major-label debut by Seattle band Soundgarden, depended on word-of-mouth for success.

IN A *Rolling Stone* interview, Guns N' Roses singer Axl Rose was asked what bands he enjoyed. He named Soundgarden, noting that Chris Cornell "buries me, the guy sings so great." For that kind of heady praise, most unknown acts would have given up a charge account at Herschel's House of Spandex. But according to Soundgarden guitarist Kim Thayil, Rose's testimonial was unsolicited.

"He came to see us a year ago in Los Angeles," Thayil recalled. "He was helping another band carry equipment like he was a roadie. And he stayed and liked us, came backstage and started talking. I didn't believe it was Axl Rose at first. He put us in his Top 10 albums of 1988 list and made that quote. Of course, the publicity department of our record company wanted to use it, and they did. We thought it was pretentious and not very nice to take advantage of him, but we saw him again a few weeks ago, and once again he was very friendly and supportive."

Soundgarden had formed six years earlier in Seattle, and several independent recording ventures had received praise from critics and college radio programmers as well as from Rose. *Louder Than Love* was the band's debut on a major label. "A lot of times, alternative music fans feel alienated if you're signed to a big company, but that didn't seem to hurt Metallica, Hüsker Dü or the Replacements," Thayil noted. "We've got a decent crossover between the punk rockers, heavy metal people, artistes and college students."

Thayil, who referred to the guitar grunge of "Get on the Snake" and "Hands All Over" as "Zen metal" or "acid punk," didn't mind comparisons to contemporary bands like Guns N' Roses and the Cult, but Soundgarden also was being likened to Black Sabbath, AC/DC and especially Led Zeppelin—which left him feeling far from flattered. "Zeppelin wrote about mysticism too much," he said. "It's a little frustrating to be regarded in a class with them." ■

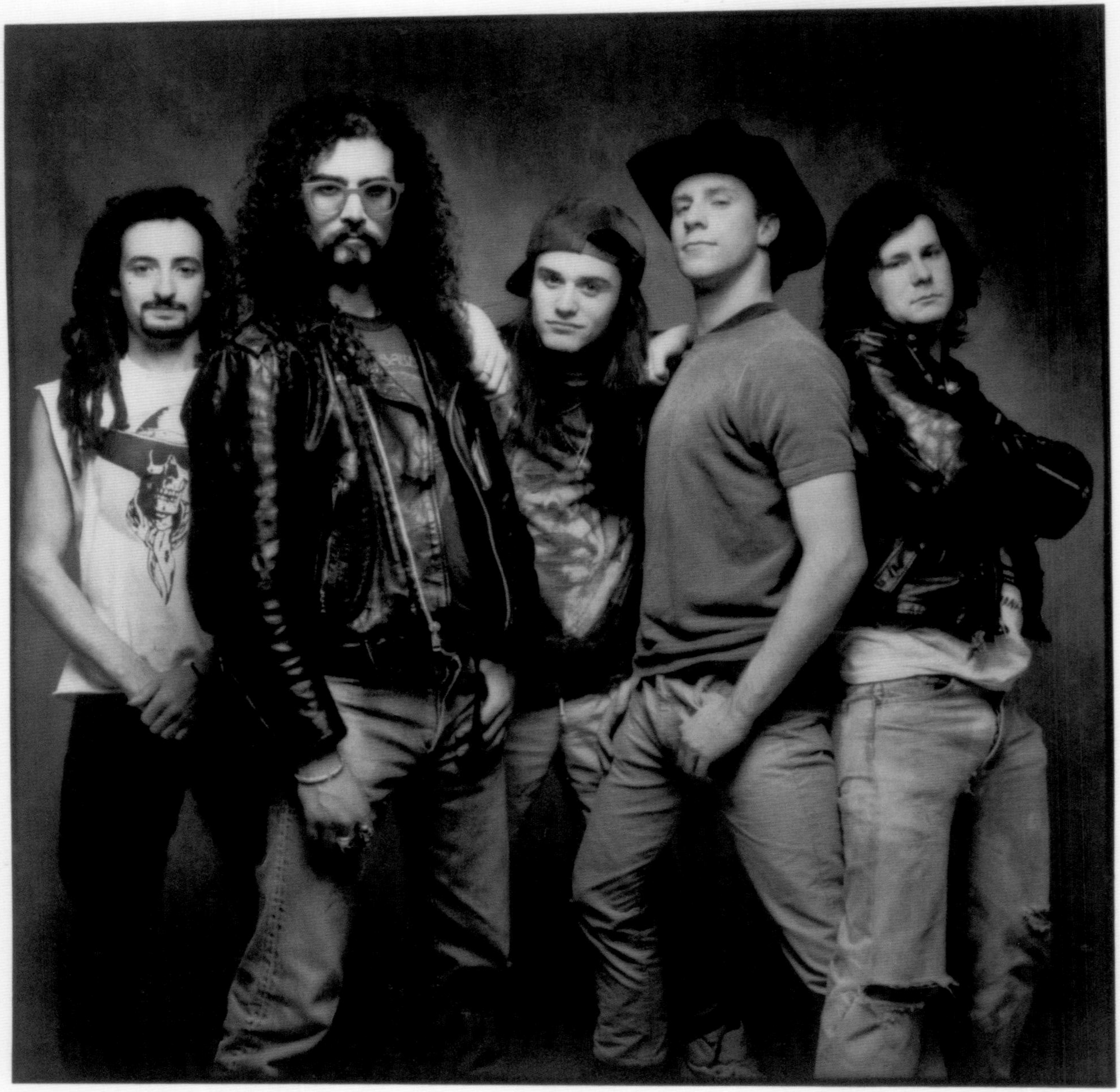

Photo Credit: Glen LaFerman

FAITH NO MORE

Slash™

reprise

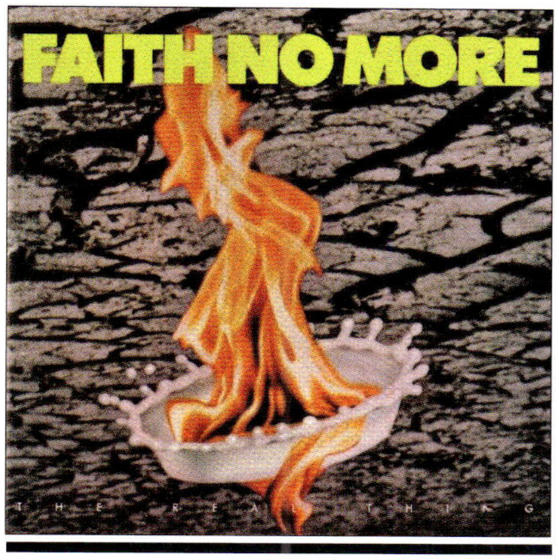

Billboard 200: *The Real Thing* (#11)
Billboard Hot 100: "Epic" (#9); "Falling to Pieces" (#92)

After years of struggle, Faith No More broke out of cult status with a smart, sprawling brand of genre-busting.

COMPARED TO the mainstream, Faith No More's upstart metal was weird—an original meltdown of chainsaw guitar riffs, unexpectedly melodic progressions and tasteful rap vocals. The album *The Real Thing* disappeared from the charts after its release, but the Bay Area quintet started gaining pop acceptance after an attention-getting Grammy nomination for Best Heavy Metal Performance. *The Real Thing* re-entered the charts, and then MTV began airing the arty, breathtaking video for "Epic."

"We called the song 'Epic' because the feel of it was overwhelming, monumental," bassist Billy Gould said. "We wanted elements in our video that would reflect that feeling visually. That's why we went for very big images—natural phenomena like lightning and rain. And the fish."

Ah, the fish. "Epic" concluded with footage of a fish flailing around helplessly out of water, which reportedly drew some fire from animal rights activist groups. The band insisted that the scene was filmed very quickly and the fish was not harmed. The following video for "Falling to Pieces" also offered fish to the viewing masses, but they hung from cables as the band played, then exploded on cue.

Thanks to MTV's massive boost, "Epic" sat in the Top 10 and *The Real Thing* was certified platinum, and Faith No More had crossed over to a different audience. "We're picking up new fans, and that's pleasurable, yet there's this misconception that 'commercial' means 'stupid,'" Gould said. "But you can do a lot of damage by being exposed to a majority. Just because something is accepted by a lot of people doesn't mean there isn't some interesting thought behind it."

The Real Thing was Faith No More's third album. But it marked the first with singer Mike Patton, a classic California skateboarding type who replaced original vocalist Chuck Mosely, whose unpredictable behavior took its toll on the band's collective sanity. The soulful Patton, who still lived with his parents and had never flown in an airplane, suddenly found himself opening for Metallica in filled arenas. But he emerged as a theater-of-the-absurd pro—mugging, leaping, flexing and whipping his chest-length hair around.

"He's five years younger than the rest of us, and we had to get to know each other personally the hardest way possible—on tour," Gould said. "He's got a big mouth, but musically, he fit in right away. He wrote the lyrics for *The Real Thing* within a week and a half of hearing the music." ■

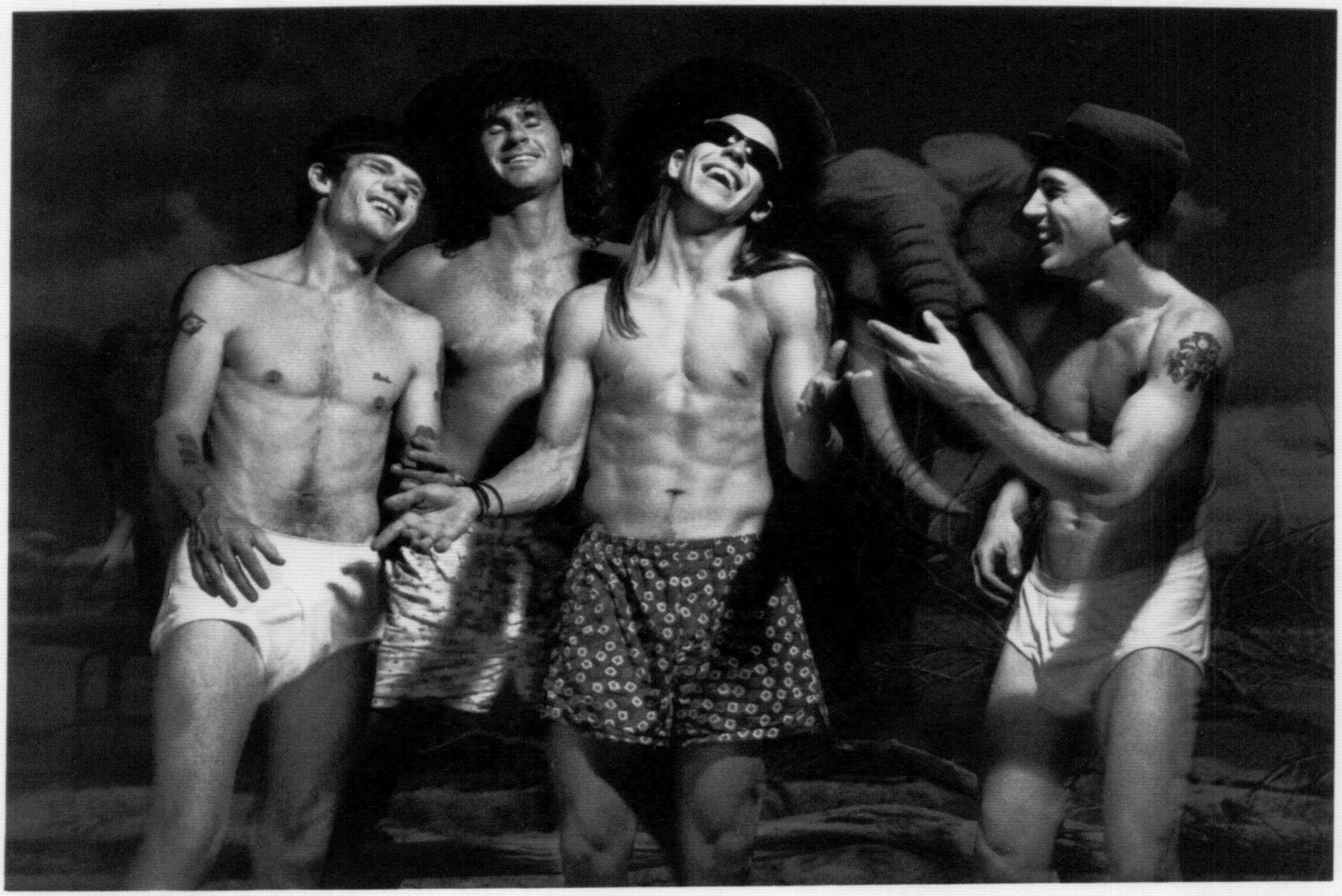

Photography: Nels Israelson

EMI

RED HOT CHILI PEPPERS

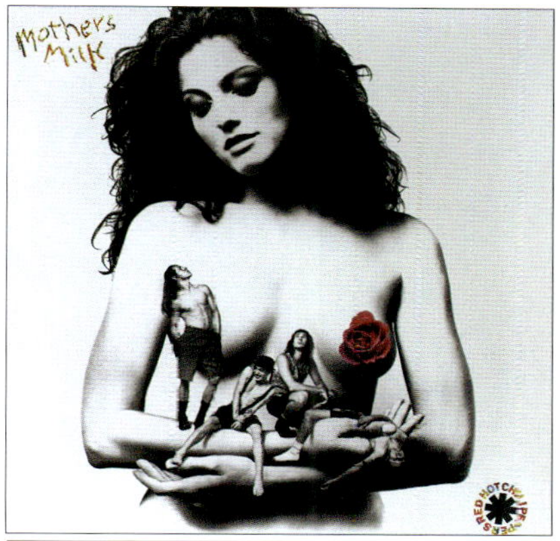

Billboard 200: *Mother's Milk* (#52)

Landing on radio and MTV, the riotous Red Hot Chili Peppers reveled in their first gold record, *Mother's Milk*.

SELF-DESCRIBED AS one of the most untamed bands of the Eighties, the Red Hot Chili Peppers were infamous for their anarchic live shows. But while members of the California punk-funk band had never given a second thought about their wild image, circumstances had steered them toward commercial success. *Mother's Milk,* the band's fourth album, sold more than any of the previous records.

It represented an exciting new start for bassist Flea and singer Anthony Kiedis—the cofounders of the Peppers—following the death of their guitar player and best friend Hillel Slovak in June 1988 and the subsequent exit of devastated drummer Jack Irons. The addition of John Frusciante and Chad Smith to replace them broke the band out of cult status.

"We're still known as 'that hyperkinetic quartet that's been known to perform wearing nothing but strategically placed socks,'" Kiedis said. "So when a band as underground as we are can get through to more people who know what we're all about, it's nice. The elements on the record combined into something profound. For six years we've laid down a formidable foundation. Now we've matured—we've tried to grow and improve."

Mother's Milk was a furious funk/rock/thrash celebration—the Peppers remained a party band—but a number of songs had spiritual depth. "To me, that's not a conflict," Kiedis said. "Our music reflects life. Sex is a valid element of what we experience, and so is the death of a very close friend that we miss very much."

The cautionary anthem "Knock You Down" warned "If you see me getting mighty, if you see me getting high/Knock me down." "The concept came to me four months before Hillel died," Kiedis said. "I could see it coming—his whole attitude was unhealthy. I knew he had to change or lead a dismal life. Unfortunately, he didn't get a chance to turn it around."

A warp-speed remake of Stevie Wonder's classic "Higher Ground" was "a song that Flea wanted to do for a long time, but the band was never really in a position to take on a challenge like that," Kiedis said. "Now we can stand behind the lyrical content of that tune honesty." ■

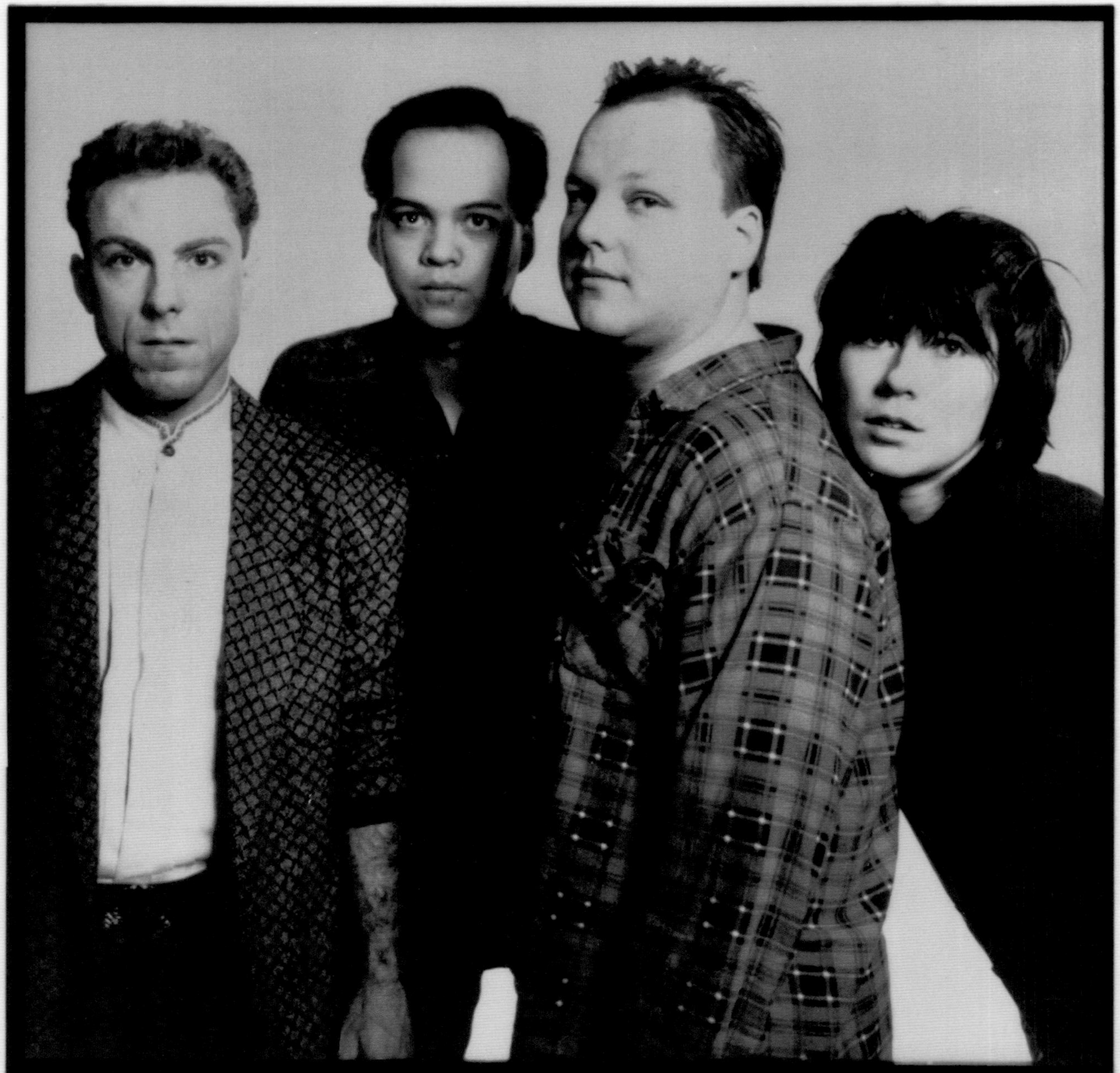

PHOTOCREDIT : ANDREW CATLIN

DAVID LOVERING JOEY SANTIAGO BLACK FRANCIS KIM DEAL

PIXIES

4AD

ELEKTRA

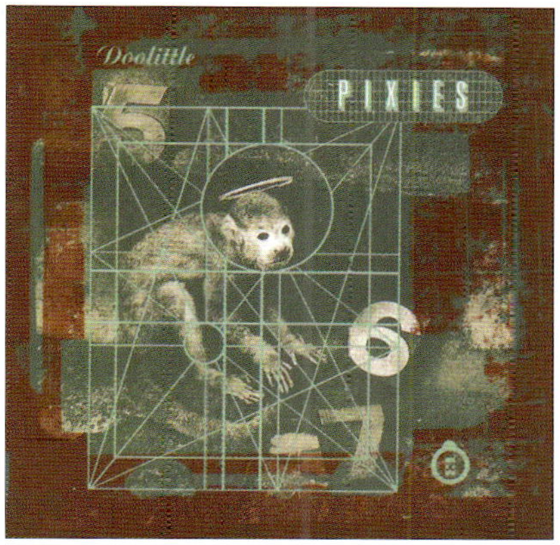

Billboard 200: *Doolittle* (#98)

With the watershed album *Doolittle*, Boston's obscure Pixies became known as trailblazers of alternative rock.

WHEN LEAD singer Black Francis (a.k.a. Charles Michael Kitteridge Thompson IV) met guitarist Joey Santiago at the University of Massachusetts Amherst, the Pixies saga began. In his sophomore year, Francis embarked on a student exchange trip to Puerto Rico and, after six months, returned and dropped out of school, convincing Santiago to ditch higher education to form a band.

They ran a classified ad in a local paper reading "Band seeks bassist into Hüsker Dü and Peter, Paul & Mary" and Kim Deal answered, thinking it was "cute." She arrived without a bass, but she got the job. Her drummer friend, David Lovering, was drafted to complete the lineup of a band in search of a name.

"Joey was in the Philippines until he was seven or something, and with English not his first language, he has a fascination for new words," Francis explained. "He'll say, 'Oh, I like that word,' then look it up and see what it means. He actually wanted to call us 'Pixies in Panoply,' but we shortened it a little."

Pixies avoided the grind of the Boston club circuit and jumped right into recording a rough demo. Issued as a mini-album titled *Come On Pilgrim*, the elliptical lyrics and bizarre splicing of salsa rhythms with distorted guitar riffs quickly made the band a favorite with hipsters. A full-length album, *Surfer Rosa*, shot to #2 on the UK indie charts.

Doolittle, the band's next release, was the first to be licensed to a major label, and producer Gil Norton achieved a sharper studio recording without sacrificing the ferociousness of the sound. With "Monkey Gone to Heaven" and the indelible male-female harmony of their breakthrough, "Here Comes Your Man," the Pixies embodied a balance of the punchy and the profound, the beginnings of alternative rock. "I want to command some faith from an audience," Francis said. "That's what makes music attractive to me, that hole you get sucked into when you really get into a song."

Francis' lyrical fixation with evocatory theological themes on "Gouge Away" and many subsequent Pixies tracks reflected his upbringing in the Pentecostal Church. "I was 12 and religion came over my entire family," he said. "I grew up exposed to a lot of preaching and righteous rage, and although I've rejected the content of all that, the style has left an impression on me. It certainly left me fucked up." ■

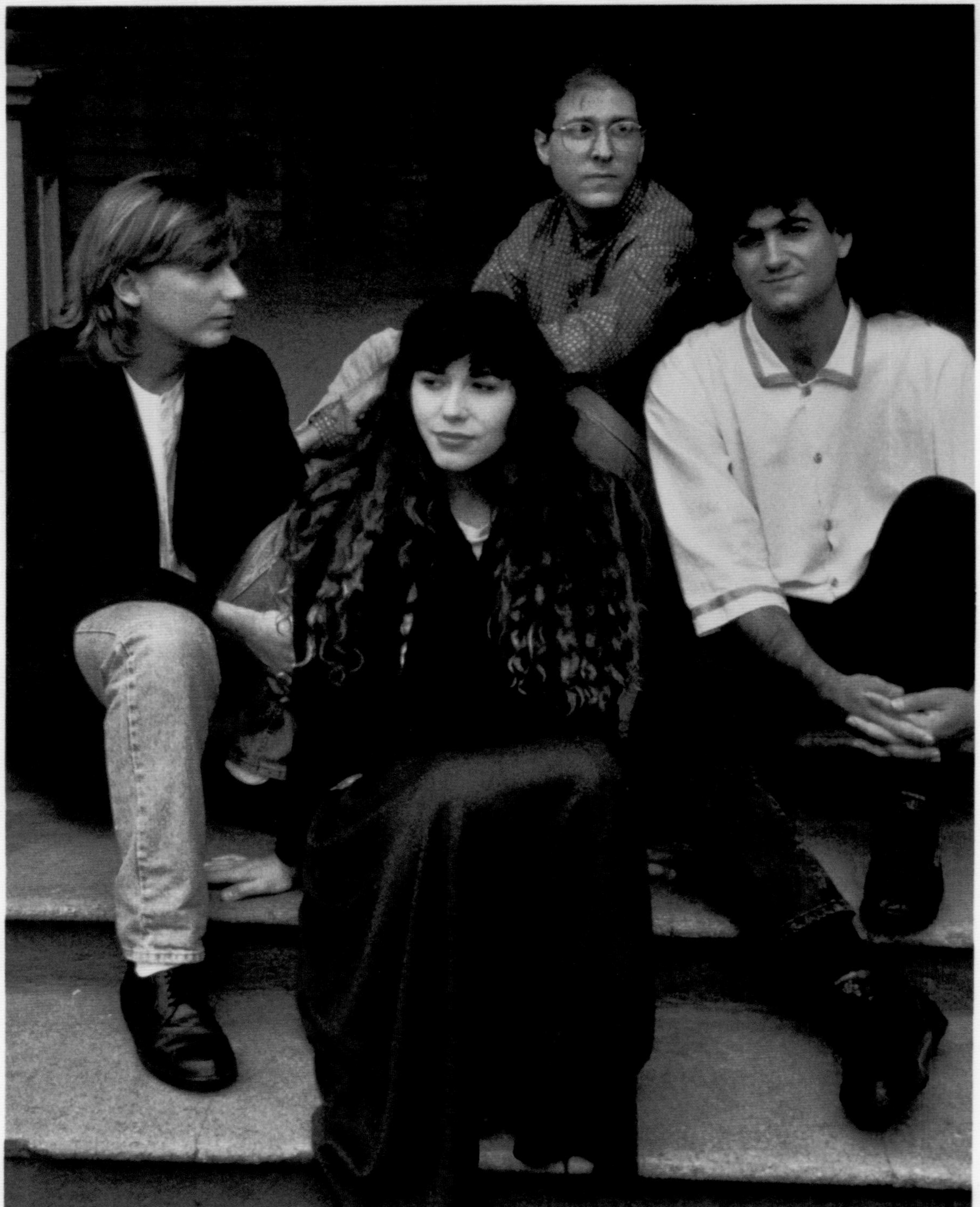

Photo Credit: Ann Cutting

DON PERIS KAREN PERIS MIKE BITTS STEVE BROWN

Asher/Krost Management
213-273-9437

THE INNOCENCE MISSION

A&M RECORDS

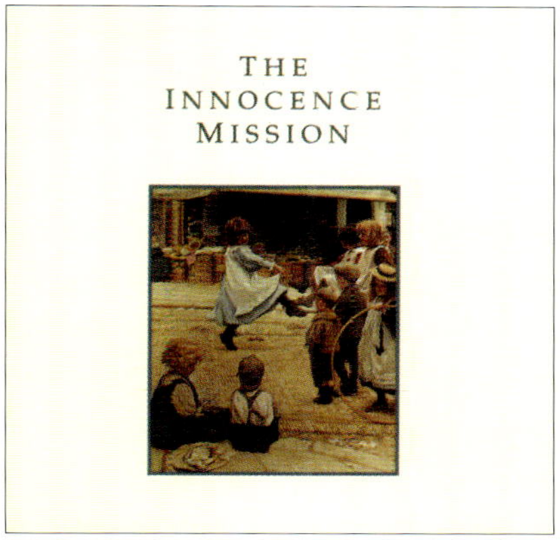

Billboard 200: *The Innocence Mission* (#167)

The Innocence Mission translated the bonds of life's constant concerns into a sage, ruminative debut recording.

THE MEMBERS of the Innocence Mission attended Catholic high school in rural Pennsylvania, and the young, modest band's self-titled debut album captured a relaxing, evocative sound—delicate, ethereal melodies with chiming acoustic guitars and airy synthesizers.

Lead singer Karen Peris scripted poetic lyrics that were beguilingly accurate at describing quiet moments. Her languid meditations of longing, wonder and romance alternated between economical and oblique, more precious than audacious. "I like to read a lot, but I don't know that there's a direct line between our environment and our music—my earlier memories are simply of writing melodies and then making words fit them," she said.

The Innocence Mission, a tight, precise recording, was produced by Larry Klein, the bassist who was married to Joni Mitchell. "He appreciated our lyrics and made sure the instrumentation fit the songs," Peris enthused. "I guess a lot of the songs don't have choruses—the lyrics start with my own frailties, something I want to express for myself, but I hope they touch on people's unique strengths a number of common feelings."

"I Remember Me" was the lament of a confused woman who claimed to be Anastasia, the last Russian czarina. "Black Sheep Wall," a love song to a wayward brother, garnered alternative radio airplay.

"I'd like people to get a sense of encouragement and wonder from the record—issues of family and faith are definite strong points in our music," Peris said. "I'm always surprised when people like the band's name. I just thought of it and liked it—I don't have a definition for it. I always think of the Innocence Mission as a place, a haven, rather than being on a mission."

The quartet's most striking element was Peris' gorgeous, breathy voice. Comparisons abounded, from Kate Bush and 10,000 Maniacs' Natalie Merchant to Rickie Lee Jones and Stevie Nicks.

"You have to expect comparisons when you're new—when I hear something for the first time, I say, 'Oh, that sounds like so-and-so,'" Peris said. "If people make comparisons to people we like, that's flattering, but everyone wants to be recognized for themselves. It occasionally worries me that people make so strong of a connection. I don't hear any, but I admire a lot of women with strong voices." ■

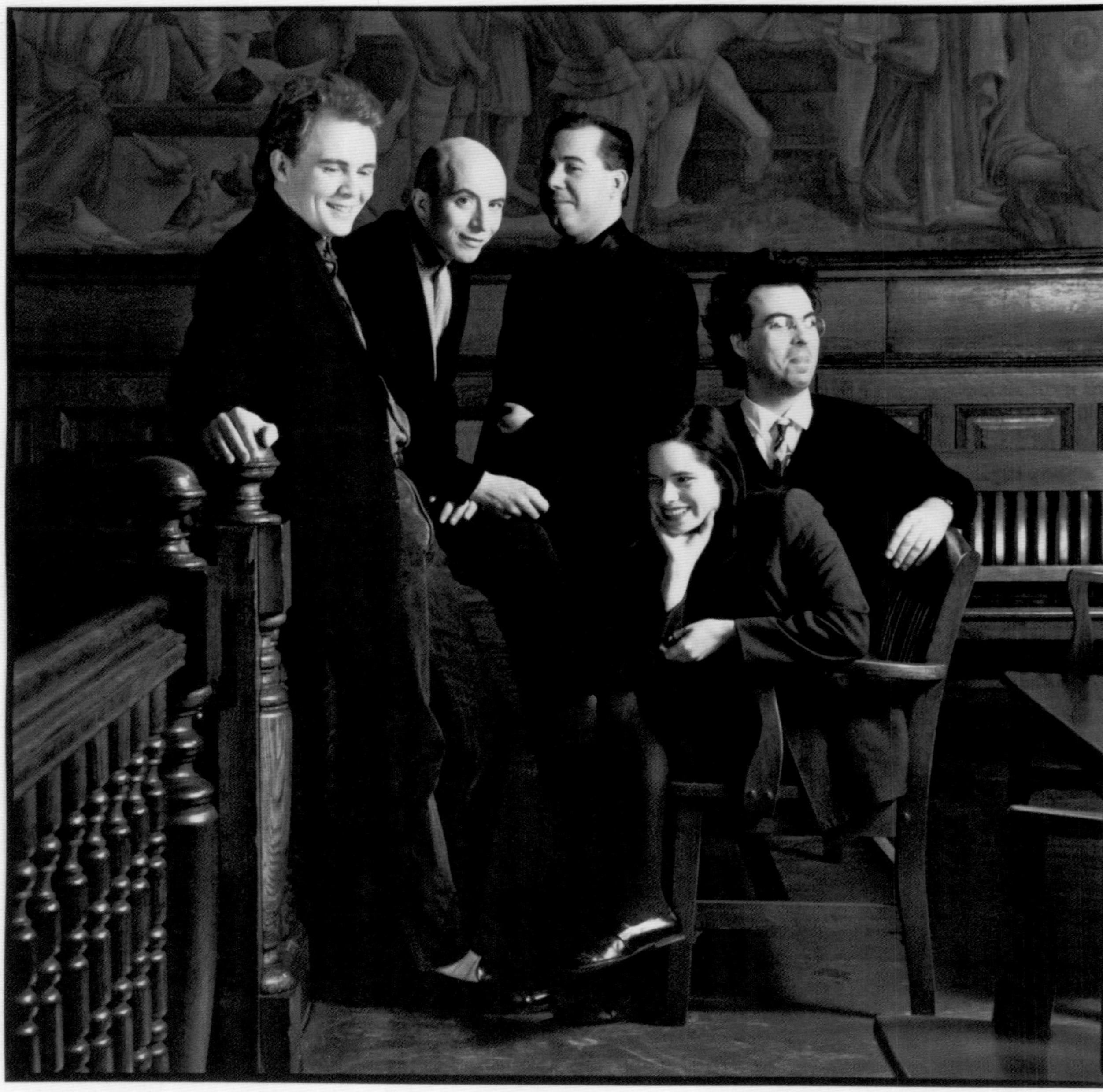

PHOTO CREDIT: TIMOTHY WHITE / 1989

STEVEN GUSTAFSON JEROME AUGUSTYNIAK ROB BUCK DENNIS DREW NATALIE MERCHANT (SITTING)

10,000 MANIACS

ELEKTRA

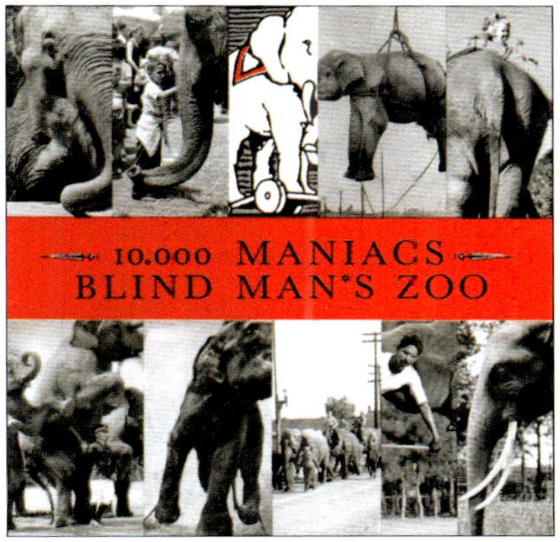

Billboard 200: *Blind Man's Zoo* (#13)
Billboard Hot 100: "Trouble Me" (#44)

Fronted by Natalie Merchant, 10,000 Maniacs gave a pointed account of the world's woes on *Blind Man's Zoo*.

BASED ON the poetic spirituality of singer Natalie Merchant, the folk-rock sound of 10,000 Maniacs had never fit into familiar categories. But 1987's *In My Tribe* broke the intriguing American band with an international audience, propelled by the near-hit single "Like the Weather." After many months of touring, the album cracked the Top 30 and neared the platinum sales mark.

Blind Man's Zoo better captured the feel and emotion of the group's live shows, with a stronger emphasis on instrumentation. The soothing single "Trouble Me" was "the first love song we've had on any of our records," guitarist Robert Buck said.

For the rest of the album, Merchant treated many societal evils, from the Iran-Contra scandal to the political legacy of the Vietnam War. "Poison in the Well" concerned pollution, and "Eat for Two" and "You Happy Puppet" were also released as singles. The boys in the band provided a deceptively pretty and elegant pop setting, although their own views were far more conservative that Merchant's. The members hailed from the isolation of Jamestown, New York, a small city about seven hours west of Manhattan.

"In Jamestown, there was never any music scene for us to become a part of or be influenced by," Buck recalled. "New York City bands have a definite vibe, but we sat around in the vacuum of our hometown and came out sounding like nobody but ourselves."

Their quaint hometown served as the location for the "Trouble Me" video. The "love song" showed a clear friendship between a young woman and a much older one. "The song is universal, all inclusive," Merchant explained. "Local women from the ages of 68 to 83 participated. The criteria for those who auditioned was that they simply agreed that to age is not to die, but to live even more fully." ■

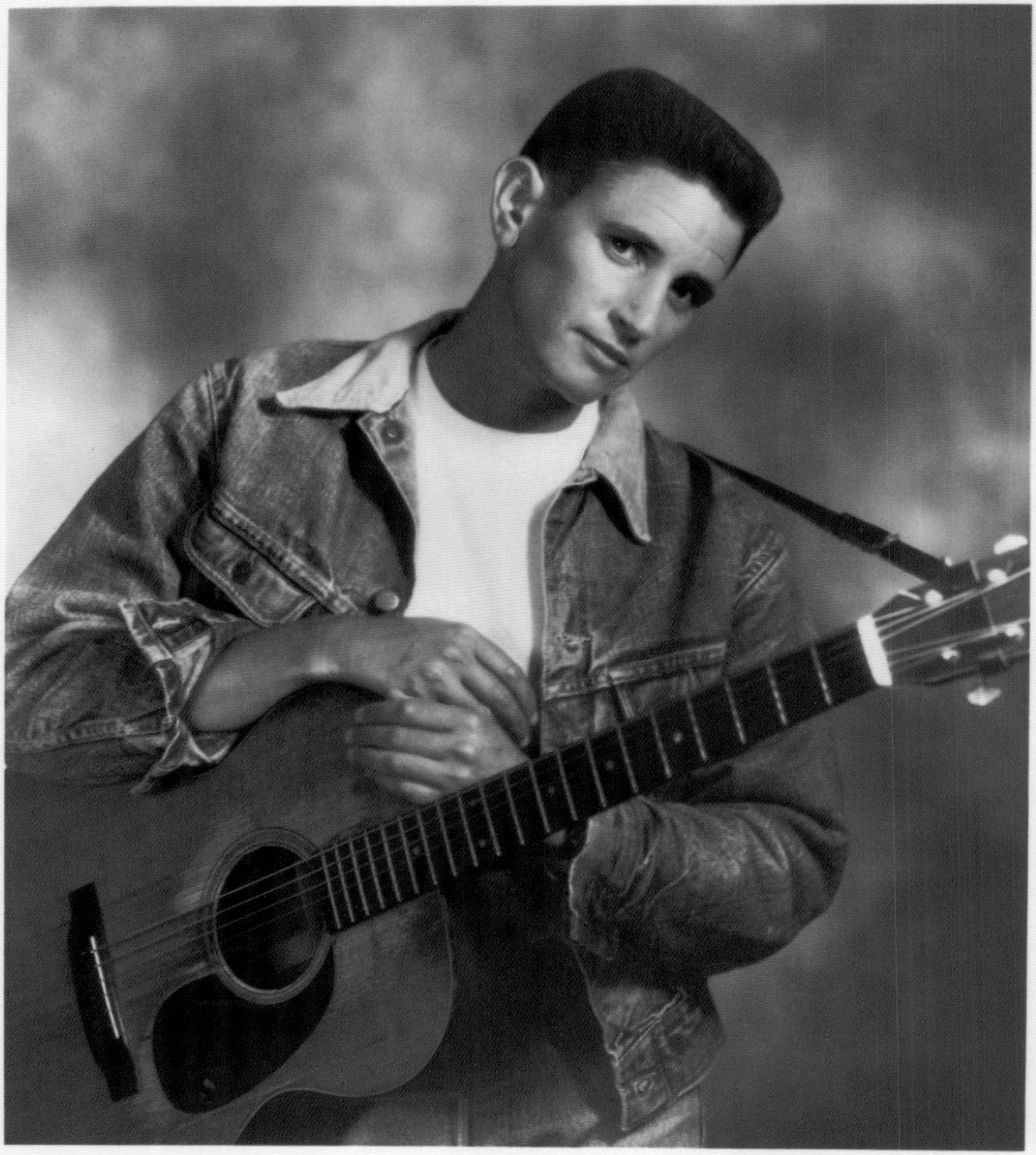

Photo Credit: Rocky Schenck

phranc

ISLAND™

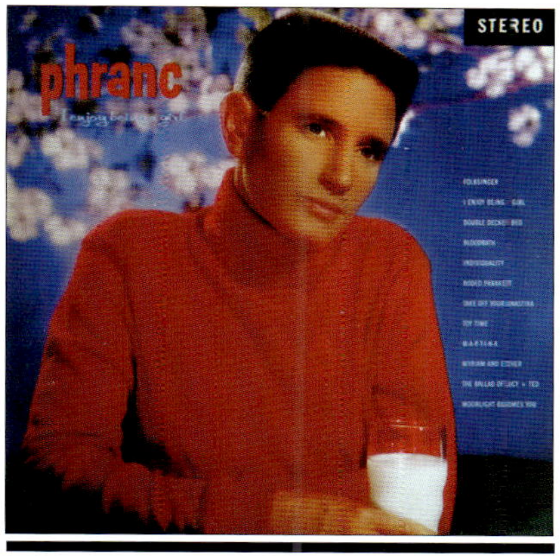

On her notable second album, folk singer Phranc leavened punk anger with diverting, self-deprecating humor.

A SELF-STYLED "average, all-American Jewish lesbian folk singer," Phranc didn't consider herself a "women's musician." Known for scathing political tunes, she also brought wit and irony to the glut of guitar-strumming female singer-songwriter types, proudly including comedians Allan Sherman and Lily Tomlin among her major influences.

"I want to be myself in the big world, to cultivate as diverse an audience as possible," the tough-looking feminist said. "I haven't been supported by the women's community. When I was in a punk band, they considered that to be violence against women. I love folk music and I love folk style. I love songs that tell stories. It's very exciting that there seems to be a return to the solo acoustic performer."

On her album *I Enjoy Being a Girl*, produced by Victor DeLorenzo of Violent Femmes, Phranc took the title track (from the 1958 Rodgers & Hammerstein musical *Flower Drum Song*) and playfully mocked the boy-crazy stereotype. The sexual topics made the album an unlikely prospect for mass appeal, but other subject matter ranged from anger about South African apartheid to her pet parakeet and tennis ace Martina Navratilova. She also sang a nice-Jewish-girl tribute to grandmothers ("Myriam and Esther").

"I don't think it's unusual to be ecstatically silly one day and then respond to something serious and intense the next," she said. "It would be unnatural for me to make a record that would be continuously serious. Humor is a very important tool in my life and in my work. I feel that with humor I can communicate just about anything."

The cover photo was another example of lesbian camp—the flat-topped songstress looked dreamily into the distance, holding a glass of milk.

"It's the best of both worlds," she laughed. "You take a little Pat Boone and Fabian and you mix it with a little Pat Suzuki and Alice Faye and you get Phranc." ■

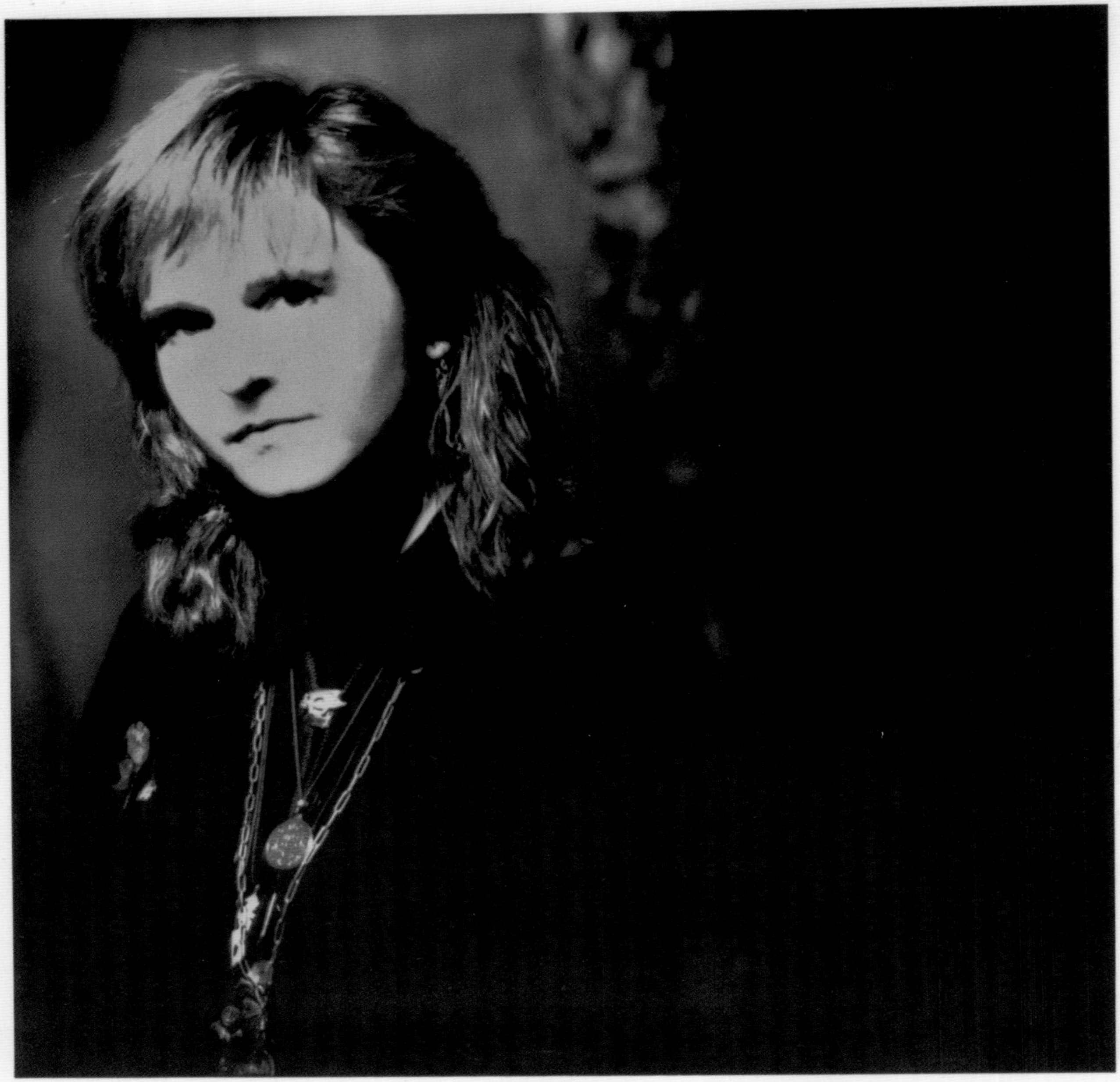

PHOTO CREDIT: DENNIS KEELEY

MELISSA ETHERIDGE

MONTEREY PENINSULA ARTISTS

ISLAND™

W.F. LEOPOLD MANAGEMENT

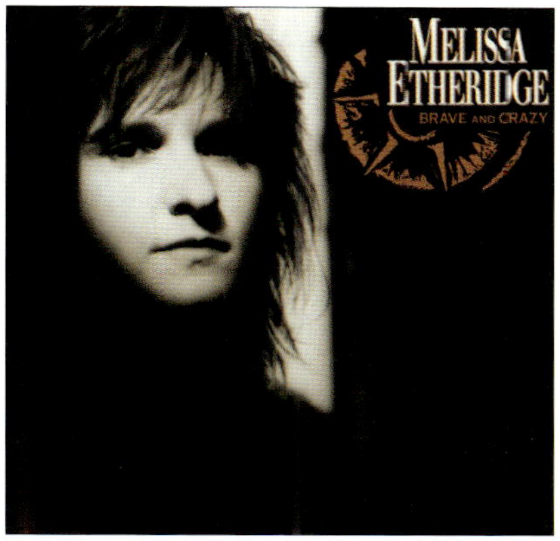

Billboard 200: *Brave and Crazy* (#22)
Billboard Hot 100: "No Souvenirs" (#95)

Following the same precepts with *Brave and Crazy*, Melissa Etheridge showed that her first album was no fluke.

IN YEARS of constant touring, Melissa Etheridge gained seasoning and acceptance, prompting Island Records founder Chris Blackwell to sign her on the spot when he first heard her perform at a Los Angeles area bar in 1987. Later that year, she delivered a jaw-dropping Hollywood debut in front of industry insiders at the famed Roxy Theatre.

"I learned from the artists I respected, things like not to be afraid of intensity in performance," Etheridge said. "It grew from all the years I spent playing in clubs night after night and singing every kind of music imaginable, from pop and rock to country and dance cover tunes to, of course, my own songs. I looked at everything I did as a step forward to where I was going. I was thrilled to be singing and playing and having people listen. I was doing what I wanted to do, and I never looked back."

Melissa Etheridge, her debut album, encompassed an alluring degree of emotion and drive. When it came to tangible rewards, the raspy-voiced singer earned a gold record certification in the US as well as a Grammy nomination for her single "Bring Me Some Water." She went on the road for well over a year, and her concerts amassed an ardent and devoted following, leading to Springsteen and Mellencamp comparisons.

"I've always realized the importance of the discipline and craft that goes into creating music," she said. "I work hard for that element of truth in my writing that gives people something they can relate to. There are only a few who can do it—poets, songwriters, playwrights, screenwriters, authors—and I admire those few tremendously."

More experienced and confident, Etheridge doubled down on her success with *Brave and Crazy*, her second album. "No Souvenirs," about a romantic relationship on a fast timeline that left behind "no souvenirs," gained international exposure. The Kansas native had fully bloomed as a performer.

"We're all a product of where our society is going, technology and achievement-oriented," she mused. "Things are so fast and processed for us, There's less room for emotion these days, and I think that's what draws people to my music. A good performance gives the audience something they can use to release those feelings. That's what I work for, to share. Isn't that a part of what music is about?" ■

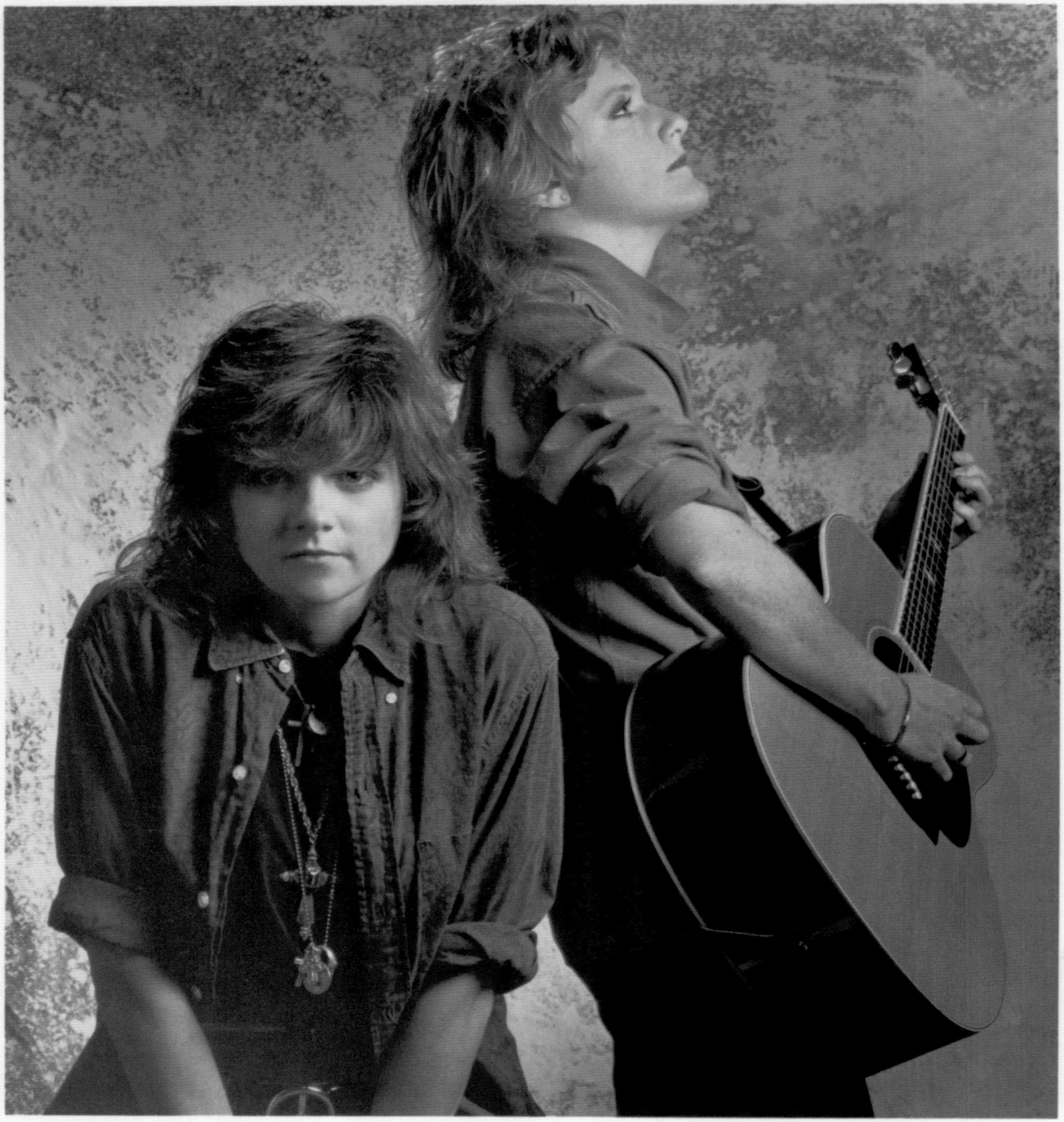

AMY RAY EMILY SALIERS

i n d i g o g i r l s

Epic

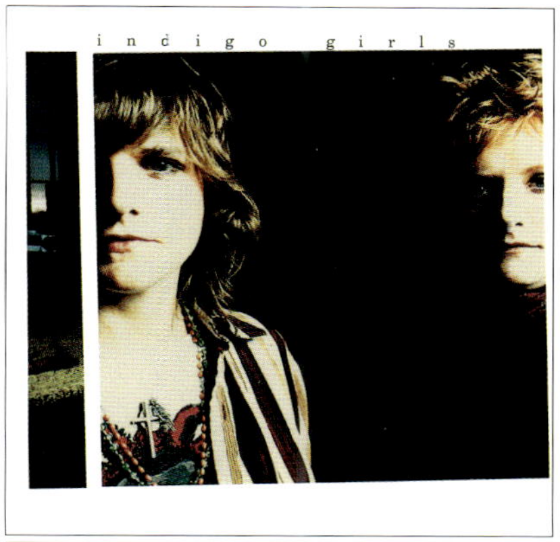

Billboard 200: *Indigo Girls* (#22)
Billboard Hot 100: "Closer to Fine" (#52)

Breakout stars on radio and MTV, Indigo Girls won a Grammy Award for Best Contemporary Folk Recording.

THE FOLK-ROCK revival had swept women like Tracy Chapman, Suzanne Vega and Michelle Shocked to prominence. The new beneficiaries were Indigo Girls, an earnest Atlanta-based duo whose self-titled debut album climbed the charts on the merit of the passionate, winningly personal "Closer to Fine." For singer-songwriters Emily Saliers and Amy Ray, the song's sudden success happily reaffirmed the appeal of intelligent acoustic-based music.

"When we feel strongly about something, we write about it—maybe it comes out as didactic, but it's not intended to be," Saliers said. "We write about the battles between the darkness and the light, all that archetypal stuff. We just can't get away from it—that's what we think about. There's a lot of pain and suffering in the world, but there's also a certain beauty in that pain and suffering."

"A lot of people call us 'grim,' but we think our songs are uplifting, especially live," Ray added. "We can be heavy and dramatic, but people treat each other badly in the world, and we wrote the material at a time when we were recognizing that. As we mature as writers, we'll learn to lighten up."

Saliers and Ray first met as sixth graders and began singing together in high school. They decided to make a career of music at Georgia's Emory University. "We've always had a vocal blend that feels special—I've never wanted to sing with anyone else," Ray said. "The turning point was the year Emily graduated. She wanted to be a teacher, but we got serious about our commitment to Indigo Girls and started doing all original music."

Saliers and Ray filled up their heartfelt songs with pounding acoustic guitars and sturdy, headstrong voices. *Indigo Girls* featured supporting contributions from fellow Georgians R.E.M. and members of Hothouse Flowers. Alternately raucous and soothing, with roots in the message music of the early Sixties, the record climbed the charts and eventually was certified platinum.

"We find hope in the humanness of things when we write about alienation, or the struggles in a relationship, or the way human life has become less sacred," Saliers said. "People go through those experiences themselves, but not everybody writes about it. We're not afraid to, so we get personal letters singling out songs. Our music seems therapeutic, and that's very rewarding to me. There's not a separation between artist and audience." ■

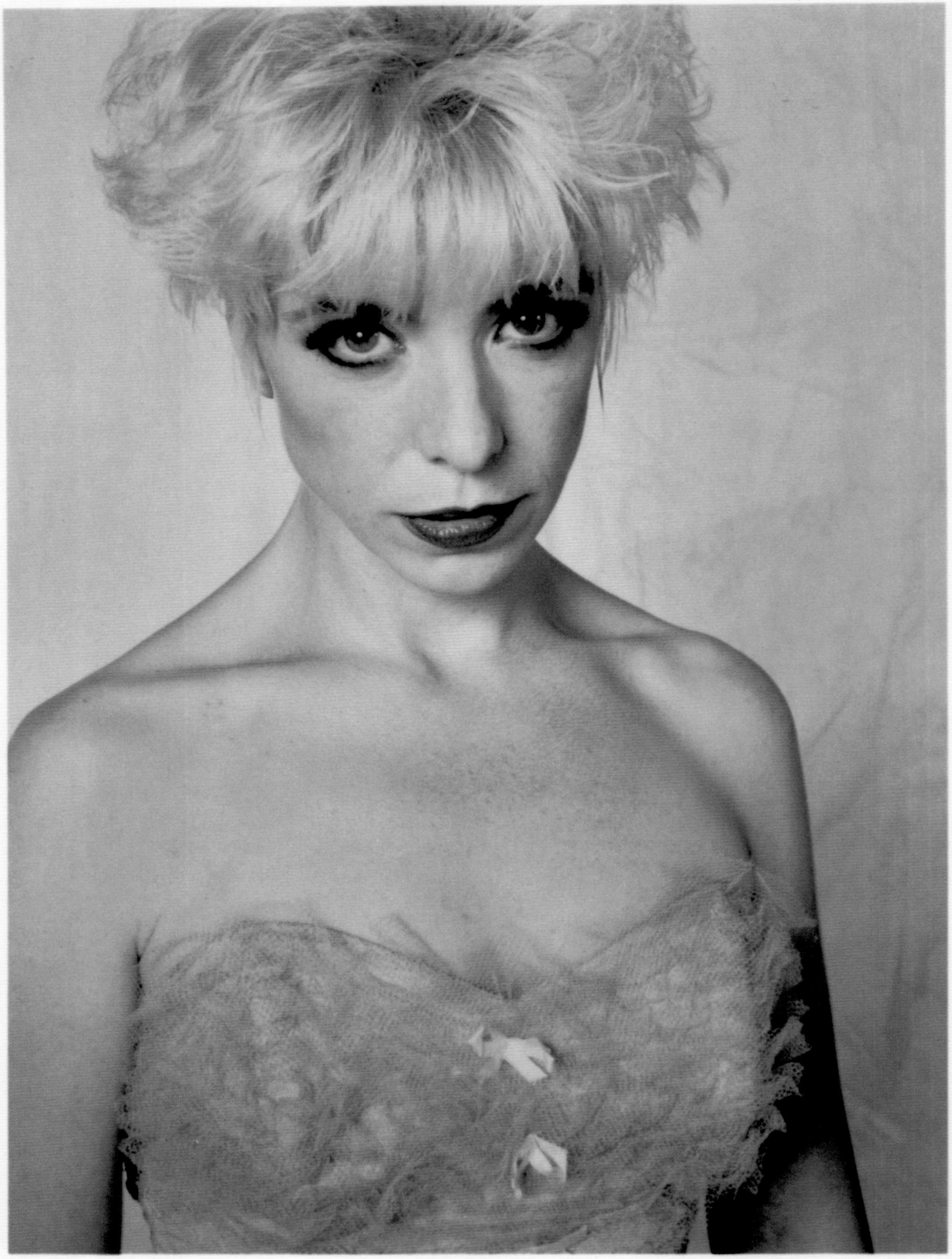

Photo Credit: David Lynch

J U L E E   C R U I S E

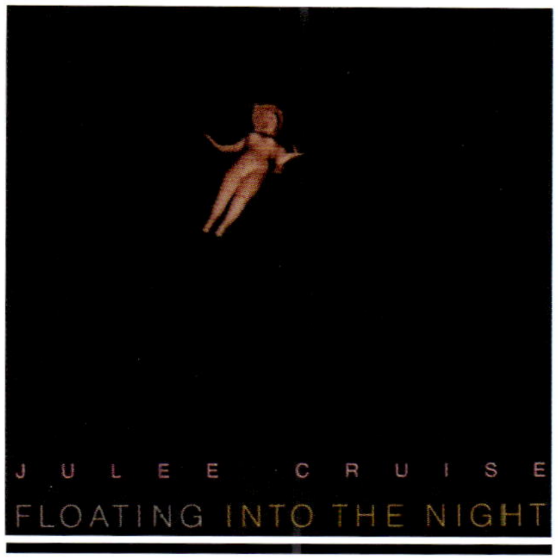

Billboard 200: *Floating into the Night* (#74)

Julee Cruise's "Falling" became the most widely known number from from David Lynch's TV series *Twin Peaks.*

FIRST COLLABORATING with film director David Lynch and veteran movie scorer Angelo Badalamenti in the notorious 1986 movie *Blue Velvet,* singer and actress Julee Cruise gave a compelling performance of the song "Mysteries of Love." She had sung in the chorus in a New York theater where Badalamenti was the musical director.

"I thought of myself mostly as a 'Broadway belter,' an actress who sings," Cruise said. "Angelo met David and got involved in *Blue Velvet,* for which he wrote all the music. He asked me if I could help him find someone to sing 'Mysteries of Love' for the soundtrack. It was a very unusual tune, so I brought him all these friends of mine, and none of them worked out, so I said, 'Let me try.' This was such a precise, pure sound. I wasn't really sure I could do it at first."

It proved a stepping stone to bigger things. Cruise joined up with Lynch and Badalamenti for her debut album, *Floating into the Night.* The music was prominently integrated into Lynch's groundbreaking TV series *Twin Peaks,* in which Cruise had a recurring role. "Falling," the show's arresting and ethereal theme song, enjoyed worldwide success.

"David and Angelo write music together, with Angelo composing and David sort of describing what he hears in his head," Cruise explained. "Even though David's not a musician and doesn't speak in musical terms, Angelo knows what he wants. David wrote all the lyrics, and I'd contribute the occasional vocal harmony. It's an unusual way to write music, but it works. David's a great guy and a lot of fun. Mel Brooks describes him as 'Jimmy Stewart from Mars,' and I think that fits."

The haunting, ethereal texture of Cruise's voice reverberated throughout *Floating into the Night.* Cruise had to quit a three-pack-a-day cigarette habit before recording the tracks. "I started running. I changed everything and I'm a much better singer as a result. Singing as clear as you can is a real challenge, as opposed to 'loud is better.' I had to come up with a whole new style of singing that was really apart from my other work."

Cruise followed up with a concert tour and a controversial musical guest appearance on *Saturday Night Live*—she stepped in when Sinead O'Connor refused to appear with host Andrew Dice Clay. Cruise lived in Manhattan with her husband, Edward Grinnan, the editor of *Guideposts,* founded by author and motivational speaker Norman Vincent Peale.

"I go back to Iowa quite a bit—I've got to have an Orange Julius in a shopping mall in Des Moines every once in a while," she said. "I have friends that are really great singers who are desperate for an album contract, and I felt a little embarrassed to tell them how easy this was for me. It's very hard to describe this music to people. It's somewhere between the Fifties and the Nineties, and it's such a white, white sound—a white-angel sound." ■

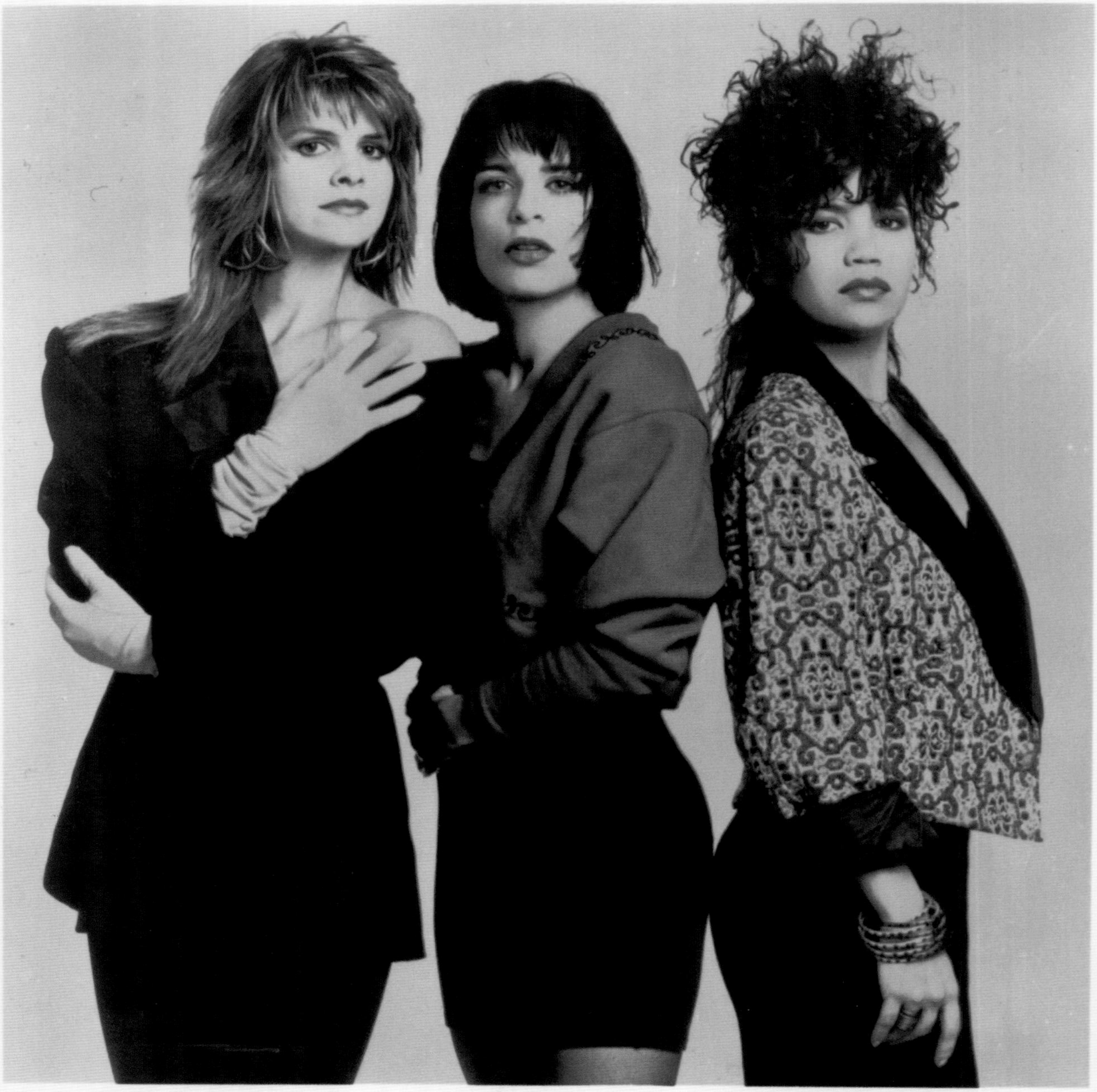

Deborah Feingold

Ann Curless Gioia Jeanette Jurado

Exposé

Management:

Pantera Group Enterprises

Francisco J Diaz
13644 S.W 142nd Avenue
Suite D
Miami, FL. 33186

ARISTA™

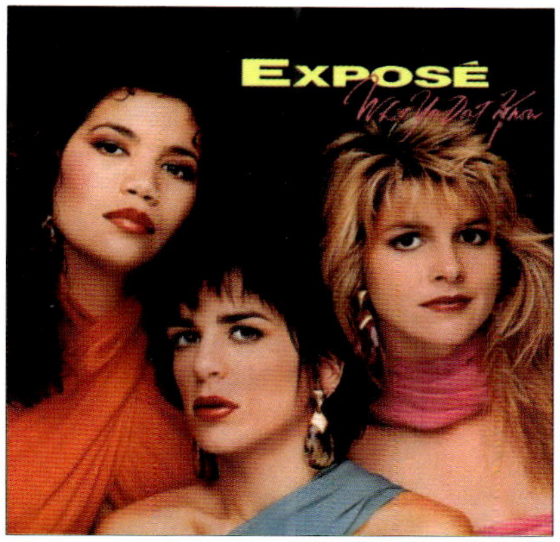

Billboard 200: *What You Don't Know* (#33)
Billboard Hot 100: "What You Don't Know" (#8);
"When I Looked at Him" (#10); "Tell Me Why" (#9);
"Your Baby Never Looked Good in Blue" (#17)

Exposé made a remarkable transition from the Miami club and dance music scene to national pop prestige.

WITH 1987's double-platinum *Exposure*, Exposé became the first group to have four Top 10 hits from a debut album. The female trio of Ann Curless, Jeanette Jurado and Giola then continued their ascent, as three singles from their follow-up album, *What You Don't Know*, also cracked the Top 10—bringing the total to seven successive Top 10 singles.

Exposé's songs were mostly by Lewis A. Martineé, a Miami-based Cuban producer who originated the group as an attractive outlet for his catchy dance music. "Obviously, he has a wonderful knack for memorable hooks that people like," Curless said. "And we have a nice visual appeal. We're all lead vocalists, so there's always one singer to keep your attention. And our record company does a phenomenal job in choosing the songs and working with the radio industry. We feel incredibly lucky—and successful."

In 1985, Martineé wrote "Point of No Return," recorded under the Exposé name but performed by a different trio. The song was a huge hit, but only in clubs, so Martineé aimed for a wider audience. The current version of Exposé emerged from a national search. Martineé conceived a melting pot—Giola was Italian, Jurado Hispanic and Curless "the blond all-American girl." They could have come straight from central casting—nice-looking in a non-threatening way, good role models who could carry a song and dance.

The new threesome redid "Point of No Return" in 1987 and it shot straight to #3 on the Top 40 charts. Expose then made music history with three more Top 10 singles in a matter of six months. But the super-hot trio wasn't taken seriously and had to battle the image of prefab breezy-looking disco divas. Curless, Jurado and Giola had done some dates singing to backing tracks, and they knew that they had to have a band if they wanted to be taken seriously and not as a flash in the pan.

"People thought it was a gimmick," Curless mused. "We knew it was more than that. "We got attached to that dance music stigma of using backing tapes in concert, but all of our vocals are done live. We were trained singers working on our own material in cover bands before Exposé. It was just a matter of getting a successful second album out."

And in three years, what started out as a faceless promotion developed into a genuinely charming chemistry. Instead of being viewed as Martineé's girls, the members of Exposé were recognized as three distinctive personalities and talents working onstage. The unit that began as a dance trio driven by Latin-based percussive music had definitely become a pop group, offering mid-tempo numbers ("Tell Me Why") and ballads ("When I Looked at Him").

"The unique thing about this group is that we got along instantaneously," Curless said. "We've watched a lot of other three-girl groups pop up after us, and already they're replacing members. One girl gets into a fight, or wants to have a baby, or can't sing." ■

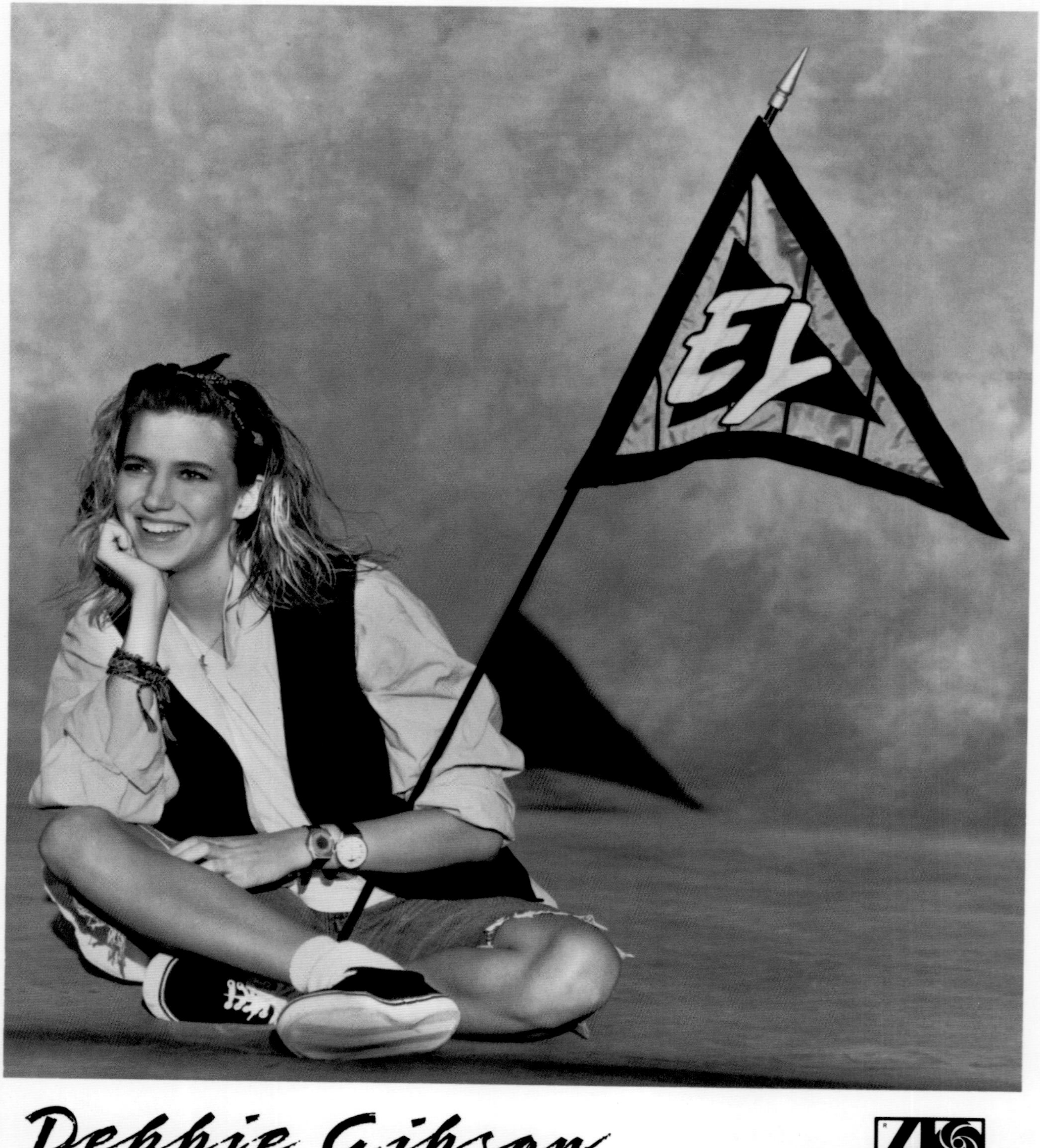

Debbie Gibson

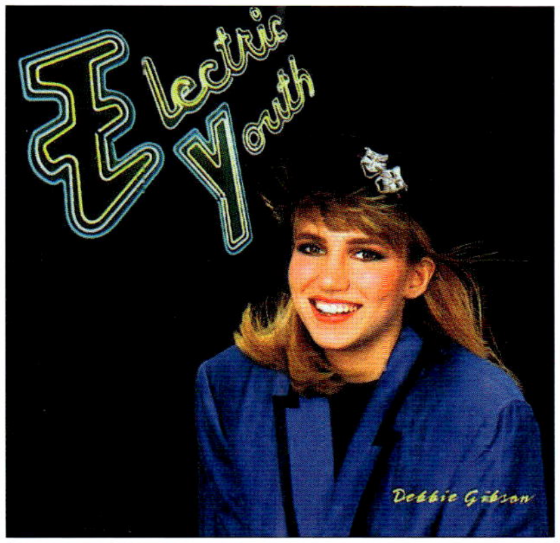

Billboard 200: *Electric Youth* (No. 1)
Billboard Hot 100: "Lost in Your Eyes" (No. 1); "Electric Youth" (#11); "No More Rhyme" (#17); "We Could Be Together" (#71)

Teen-queen Debbie Gibson saw the title track of *Electric Youth* bottled and sold as a drugstore perfume brand.

AT 19, Debbie Gibson reigned as a teen-star role model, but not in the tradition of a puppet being manipulated by a record company and manager. Her two self-composed albums made it abundantly clear that she was the most versatile and gifted of the recent crop of post-pubescent female singers, with success based on talent, not image.

Gibson grew up on Long Island, New York. Gifted with perfect pitch, she started writing tunes and playing piano when she entered kindergarten. "I always knew I would be a performer, but early on, I wasn't sure what type of music was for me," she said. "When I was eight, I got my first pop album, Billy Joel's *52nd Street*. About a year later, I saw him in concert at the Nassau Coliseum, and ever since that day I knew exactly what I wanted to do."

Her parents, recognizing her skills after she won $1,000 in a songwriting contest, invited an entertainment lawyer/manager to guide her career. While still a 16-year-old high schooler, she signed a worldwide recording contract and began laying down tracks for her debut album, *Out of the Blue*—which spawned four Top 5 singles and received triple-platinum certification.

As with *Out of the Blue*, the precocious phenomenon wrote all songs on her second album, *Electric Youth*. The ballads "No More Rhyme" and the No. 1 hit "Lost in Your Eyes," and the perky pop of "Electric Youth."

"If you have children or simply remember what it's like to be a child, you realize how much energy a young person has and how many off-the-wall ideas only a child can come up with," Gibson said. "'Electric Youth' is about not dismissing a young person's ideas because he/she 'is just a kid.' I owe a lot to my family and teachers for helping to develop my creative side and for teaching me and many other children how to channel energy and ideas into worthwhile and creative projects."

One of Gibson's projects, a pink perfume she developed with Revlon called Electric Youth, proved exceedingly worthwhile, generating $15 million in sales that year. Gibson proved to be in command of every aspect of performing as well as her music. Onstage, she was a natural—poised and self-assured, with moves that seemed second nature to her. She bounded around relentlessly in a series of elaborately choreographed dance routines, her puppy-dog energy commanding the stage. Parents appreciated her clean, wholesome persona—only when she swung her hips did she invite thoughts of Lolita-pop.

"Performing is a lot different than record-making, but I got that kind of experience doing community theater when I was a kid," Gibson explained. "Theater teaches you how to cope with any situation—no matter what happens unexpectedly, you learn to deal with it. And that confidence carries over to my concerts." ■

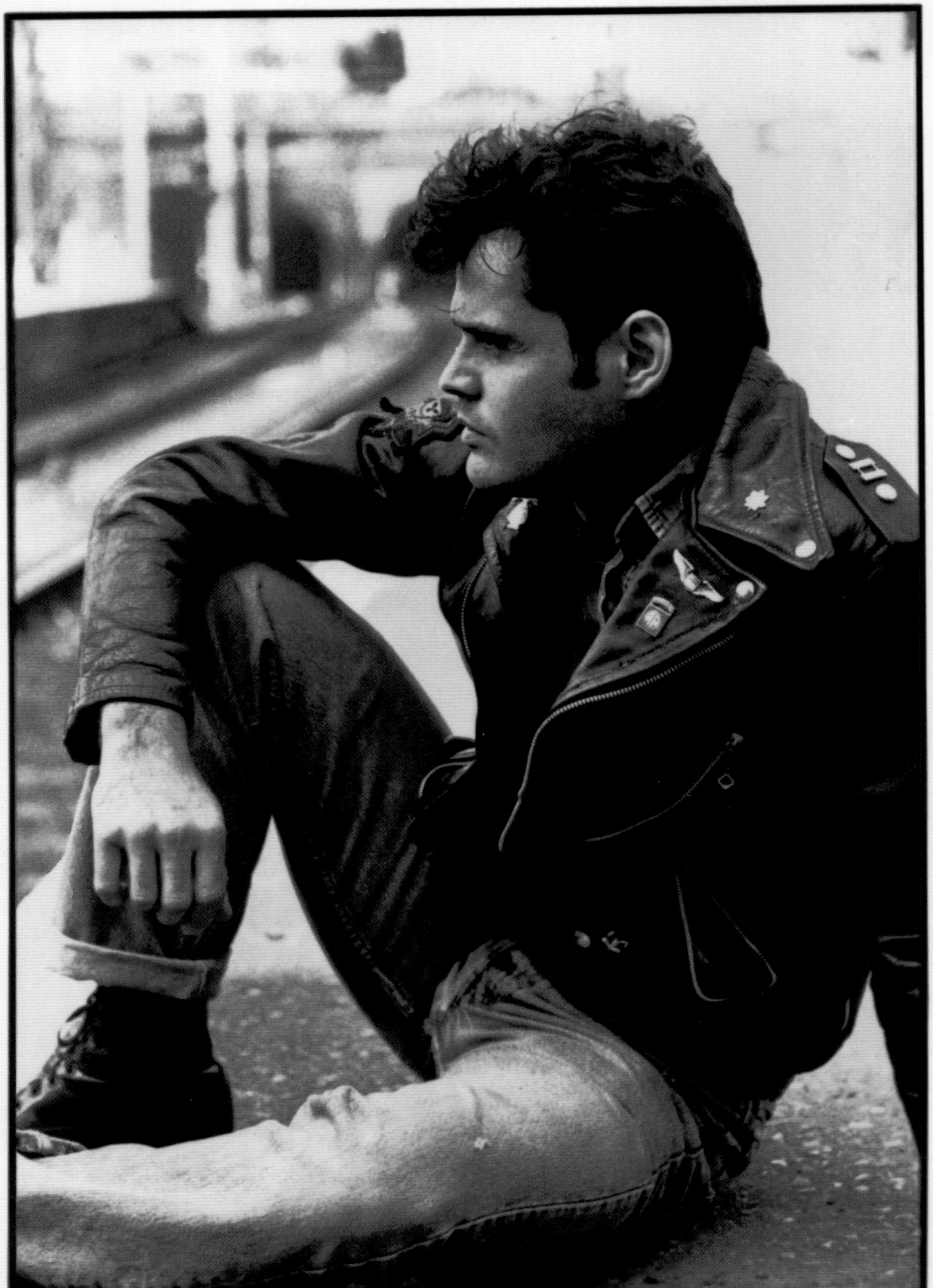
Photo: Dean Freeman / 1989

DONNY OSMOND

Capitol Records

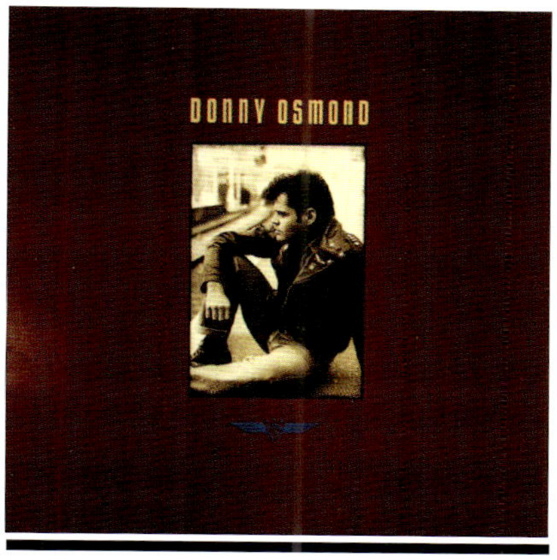

Billboard 200: *Donny Osmond* (#54)
Billboard Hot 100: "Soldier of Love" (#2); "Sacred Emotion" (#13); "Hold On" (#73)

Wending from former child star to career reinvention, Donny Osmond returned with the hit "Soldier of Love."

FOR MORE than 25 years, Donny Osmond had spent a career in the spotlight. At five, he followed in his brothers' footsteps and made his debut on *The Andy Williams Show* in 1963. By 13 he was America's squeaky-clean teen idol—he earned 23 gold records crooning such singles as "Puppy Love" and "Go Away Little Girl." He and his sister, Marie, charmed late-Seventies audiences with *The Donny and Marie Show*, a wholesome weekly prime-time variety series on ABC.

But Osmond wasn't the hippest kid to come out of the Seventies. "As a teenybopper, you go through that period of time where everybody kind of laughs and scoffs at the name Donny Osmond," he admitted.

Osmond attempted a rock 'n' roll return. In 1987, he met Peter Gabriel while they were both participating in a UNICEF show in New York City. Gabriel mentioned that he had flown over to see Osmond at Madison Square Garden during the height of Donnymania and asked him what he'd been up to. Talking about musical vision versus public perception, Gabriel convinced Osmond to visit his Real World studio in Bath, England.

Hooking up with producer George Acogny, a native of Senegal who had remixed Gabriel's "Sledgehammer," Osmond began cutting tracks. One of the songs was "Soldier of Love," which became a hit in the UK. Import copies of the record began showing up in record stores stateside. WPLJ in New York City gave the dance-friendly record a spin—without revealing who was singing it. It became a top-requested song at the station, and from there the song spread to other markets.

"Soldier of Love" climbed up the pop charts and became Osmond's comeback smash, and "Sacred Emotion" was another big radio success. "I'm a singer—I love touring and recording," he enthused. What did his tenor need to put songs across? "Peanuts! I think it's a placebo. I talk to vocal coaches and doctors, and they say, 'You're out of your mind!' But it works for me—unsalted, dry-roasted peanuts." ■

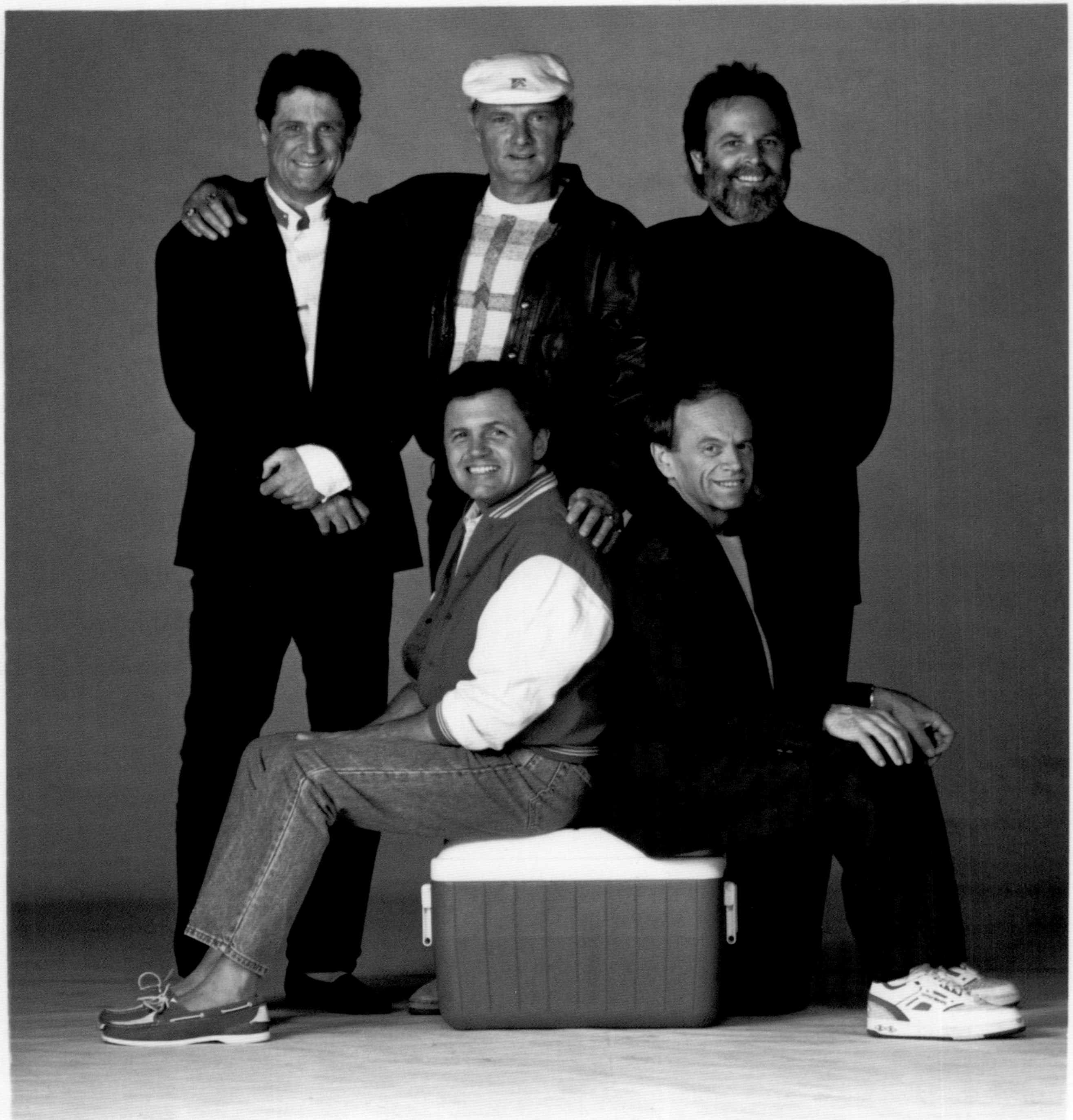

Brian Wilson, Mike Love, Carl Wilson
Bruce Johnston, Al Jardine

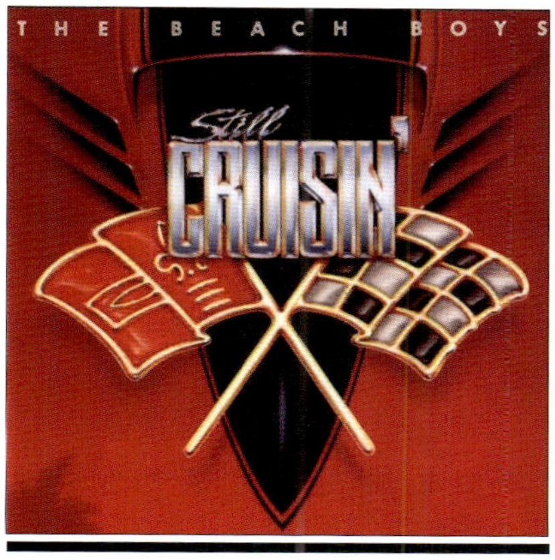

Billboard 200: *Still Cruisin'* (#46)
Billboard Hot 100: "Kokomo" (No. 1); "Still Cruisin'" (#93)

The Beach Boys, criticized for coasting on past glories, paired recent studio cuts with oldies on *Still Cruisin'*.

DURING MUCH of the Seventies and Eighties, the Beach Boys remained the embodiment of the all-American singing group, promoting California girls, little deuce coupes and surfin' USA. The band often seemed stuck in a previous lifestyle and time, selling fewer and fewer records but content to play endless concerts recreating those early hits.

But with the No. 1 single "Kokomo," from the movie soundtrack *Cocktail*, the Beach Boys scored their biggest hit since 1966's "Good Vibrations." For a moment, they were no longer just a live oldies act providing painless nostalgia.

So the Beach Boyos seized that moment and released a new album, *Still Cruisin'*, which haphazardly repackaged all of their tunes that had been featured in recent soundtracks—*Troop Beverly Hills*, *Platoon* and *Good Morning Vietnam*, as well as *Cocktail*. "I like the word 'royalties' better than 'vindicated,'" vocalist Mike Love smirked.

Keyboardist Bruce Johnston took a less mercenary stance for four new songs recorded by the touring Beach Boys band and studio musicians. "We've always been in the Top 10 for box office on the road, knocking 'em dead. It's just nice to be on the radio with something new. Our demographics are very cool."

"Still Cruisin'"—"a real good summer tune," Johnston said—was featured in *Lethal Weapon 2*. The song "Somewhere Near Japan"—"reminiscent of Fleetwood-Mac-meet-the-Byrds-meet-the-Dream-Academy-meet-the-Beach-Boys"—was rejected for the Michael Douglas movie *Black Rain*.

In the band's shows, Brian Wilson, the nominal bandleader during the mid-Sixties, had been hauled out only as a symbolic presence. The confused genius' lone contribution to *Still Cruisin'* was "In My Car." The song was credited as being co-written by Eugene Landy, the controversial therapist-turned-collaborator responsible for Wilson's recent comeback.

"It's really hard to ascertain anything about Brian when Landy is around," Johnston said "But when Landy's not around, which is happening more and more, Brian's his own man doing what Brian wants to do. Right now, Brian wants to participate, but it's a day-to-day thing." Within months, Landy agreed to an ethics-charge settlement after admitting he unlawfully administered drugs to Wilson; he surrendered his license for two years. ■

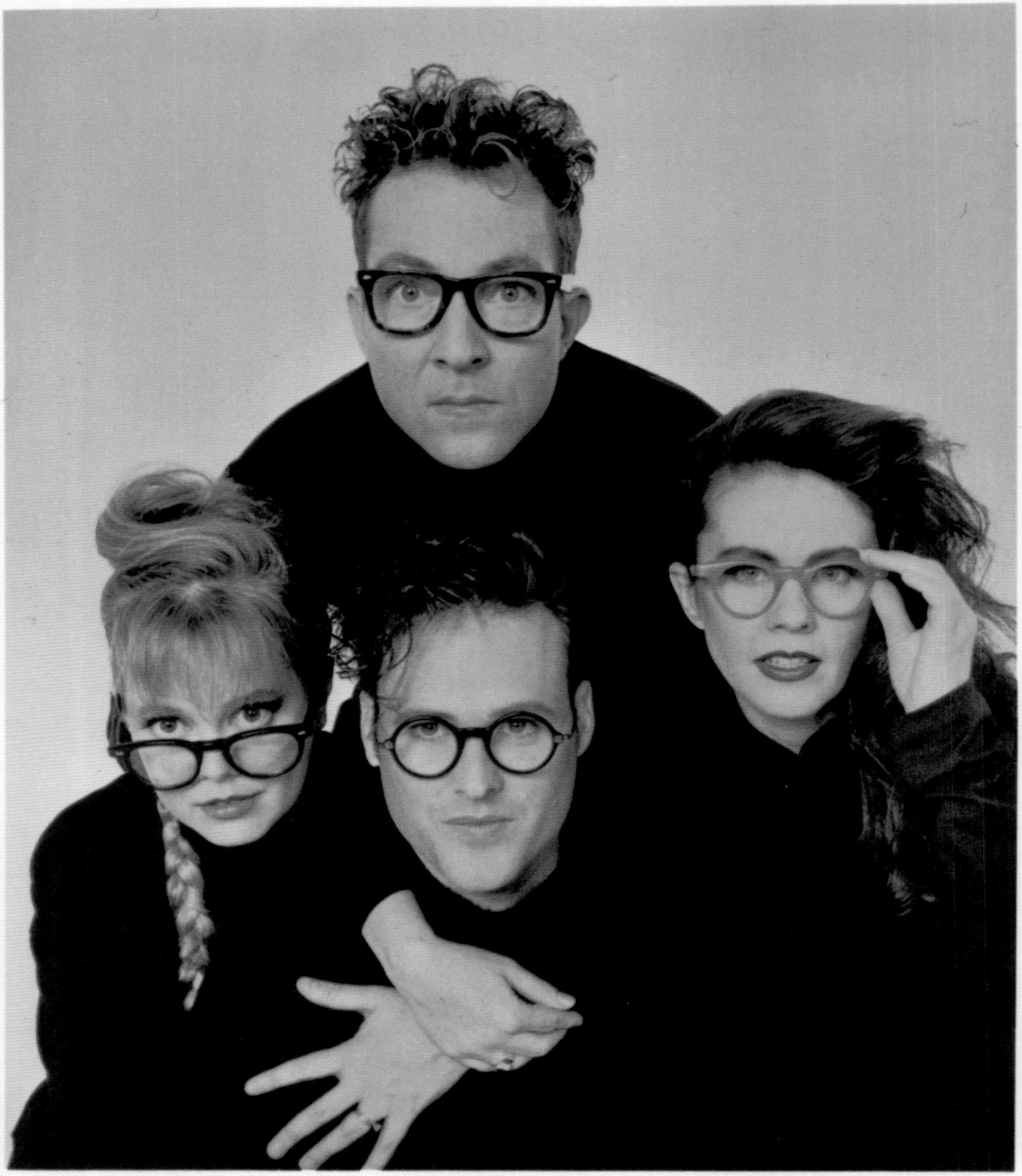

Photo Credit: Janette Beckman

Fred Schneider
Cindy Wilson, Keith Strickland, Kate Pierson

the B-52's

reprise

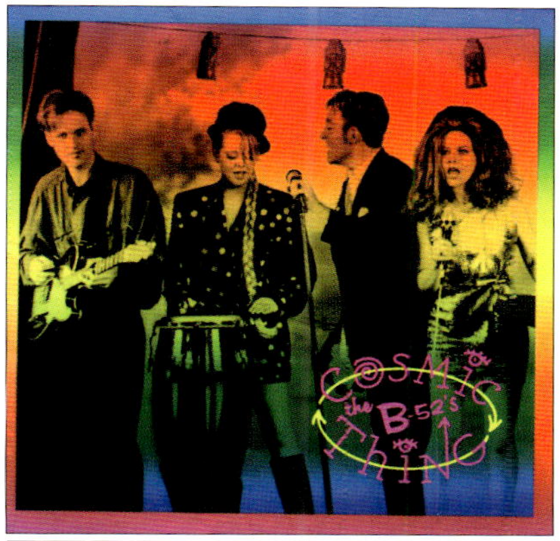

Billboard 200: *Cosmic Thing* (#4)
Billboard Hot 100: "Love Shack" (#3); "Roam" (#3); "Deadbeat Club" (#30)

The B-52's tasted big-scale success with "Love Shack" and "Roam," the party combo's first-ever Top 10 hits.

FROM THEIR late Seventies beginnings, the B-52's immersed themselves in an eccentric musical style that only the rock underground truly appreciated. The band from Athens, Georgia, mixed futuristic electronic effects with echoey guitar and retro melodies, becoming known for the dance hits "Rock Lobster" and "Private Idaho."

Cindy Wilson and Kate Pierson provided surreal, upper-register vocals, decked out in gaudy cut-rate attire and the bomb-shaped wigs that provided the group's name (a B-52 was a bouffant in Georgia slang). With their encyclopedic knowledge of junk culture and kitsch, the members described themselves as tacky and silly.

But the B-52's were also lasting. Always popular on college radio stations, they remained a novelty compared with the early Eighties mainstream. *Cosmic Thing*, the band's seventh album, finally moved it beyond cult status without substantially revamping their freewheeling, wacky sound.

"There's a whole new generation of Top 40 deejays," singer Fred Schneider explained. "They're from the early Eighties when new wave was in full stride—that's what influenced their taste. Now they jump at the chance to promote the music they liked. But we haven't done anything differently—our inspirations are pretty much the same."

"Love Shack," a carefree romp with Sixties-style harmonies and a libidinous beat, was based on actual sites. "We used to have parties where everyone would get together and play rock, soul, funk, mambo—anything you could dance to," Schneider said. "And there were soul clubs on the outskirts of town that didn't look like much on the outside, but when you got in you realized they were really wild and fun. So 'Love Shack' is sort of an idealized place we would like to go to."

The cool creativity of the track "Channel Z," which hit No. 1 on the modern rock charts, was part of a healing process. *Cosmic Thing* was the B-52's first recording since guitarist and principal songwriter Ricky Wilson died at 32 of an AIDS-related illness in late 1985. His death ultimately drew the band closer together.

"We stopped doing music, but we didn't talk of breaking up," Schneider said. "We had time to reassess ourselves and our feelings for each other, and after a while we realized we wanted to keep going. We jammed, took turns writing and arranging, and gradually we got enough music for a new album. It was a three-year period, but we weren't getting any attention anyway. It's not like we disappeared—we were ignored."

Cosmic Thing was the most topical of the B-52's albums. "People dwell on the party aspect of our music, but writing positive songs is also an important part of us," Schneider said. "This album is a little more focused—the songs with a Southern nostalgia ambience are gathered on one side, and on the other side are those that look forward—get on your inner tube, float down the river of life and see the snappers and gators and the amazing things. Just take your life in your own hands and do it." ■

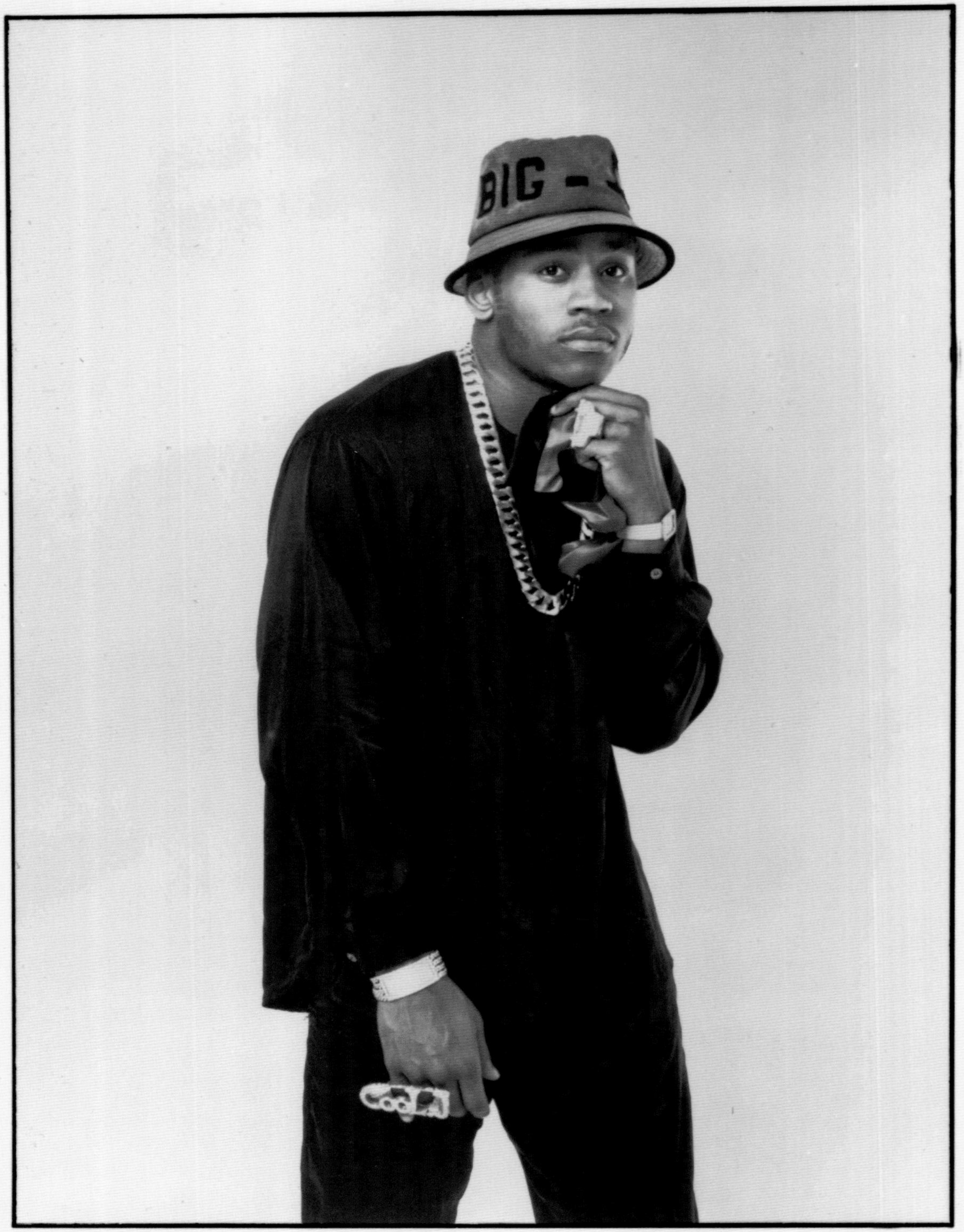

PHOTOGRAPH: ROBERTO RABANNE

Def Jam recordings RUSH ARTIST MANAGEMENT

LL Cool J

Columbia
8906

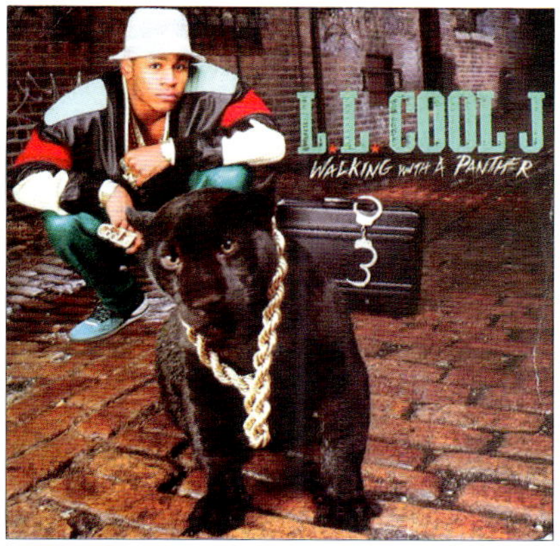

Billboard 200: *Walking with a Panther* (#6)
Billboard Hot 100: "Going Back to Cali" (#31);
"I'm That Type of Guy" (#15)

Already an enthusiastic show business pro, LL Cool J boasted to his own bad beat on *Walkin' with a Panther*.

AT THE age of 13, James Todd Smith was recording demos in his basement, thanks to the generosity and wisdom of his grandfather who bought him DJ gear rather than the dirt bike he really wanted. "I had gotten hit by a car on my friend's minibike," the rapper said. "So instead of getting me a bike, he got me the equipment."

By the time he was 16, LL Cool J (short for Ladies Love Cool James) began his ascent to stardom. "I Need a Beat," his first 12", led to a recording contract with Def Jam and the release of a debut album, *Radio*. The follow-up, *Bigger and Deffer*, lived up to its title, selling 3 million copies, and with "I Need Love," his first Top 40 hit, he became the first rap artist to reach No. 1 on the R&B charts.

At 21, LL Cool J was a seasoned street-smart b-boy with matinee-idol looks and a suave demeanor, rocking an exaggerated gold chain with his prized Kangol bucket hat. Doors had opened to him that few rappers had passed through. He performed on *Saturday Night Live*, headlined an antidrug concert at Radio City Music Hall at the request of First Lady Nancy Reagan's "Just Say No" program and was named one of the 10 sexiest men in rock by *Playgirl* magazine, an honor he didn't dispute.

He released his third album, titled *Walking with a Panther*. "Nobody will mess with a guy who's walking with a panther," he explained. "Gun or no gun, you're gonna leave him alone. Aside from that, if I was an animal, that's the one I would be. I feel like a panther in my heart."

The beguiling "Going Back to Cali" had been featured on the *Less Than Zero* soundtrack, and "I'm That Type of Guy" offered a tip from the Casanova. "No matter how much you think your girl is loyal, and how much you try to lock her away, and how much you think she's God's gift to you and that no other man can touch her—if her price comes walking along, she can always be got. It's unfortunate, but it's true. Everybody has a price, be it clothes, looks, a body—it doesn't have to be money."

Walking with a Panther appealed to a pop audience, but sectors of the hip-hop community accused LL Cool J of selling out. He saw a whole different animal. "I'm not worried about who came before or after me," he said. "I'm a tortoise—all these rabbits running back and forth, but I'm just chillin'. I gotta be like a goat—I'm a Capricorn and I gotta climb a mountain ahead of me. There's a golden microphone on top of it, and I'm just doin' my thing, straight to my goal. If it takes 20 years, I'm a keep strivin'." ■

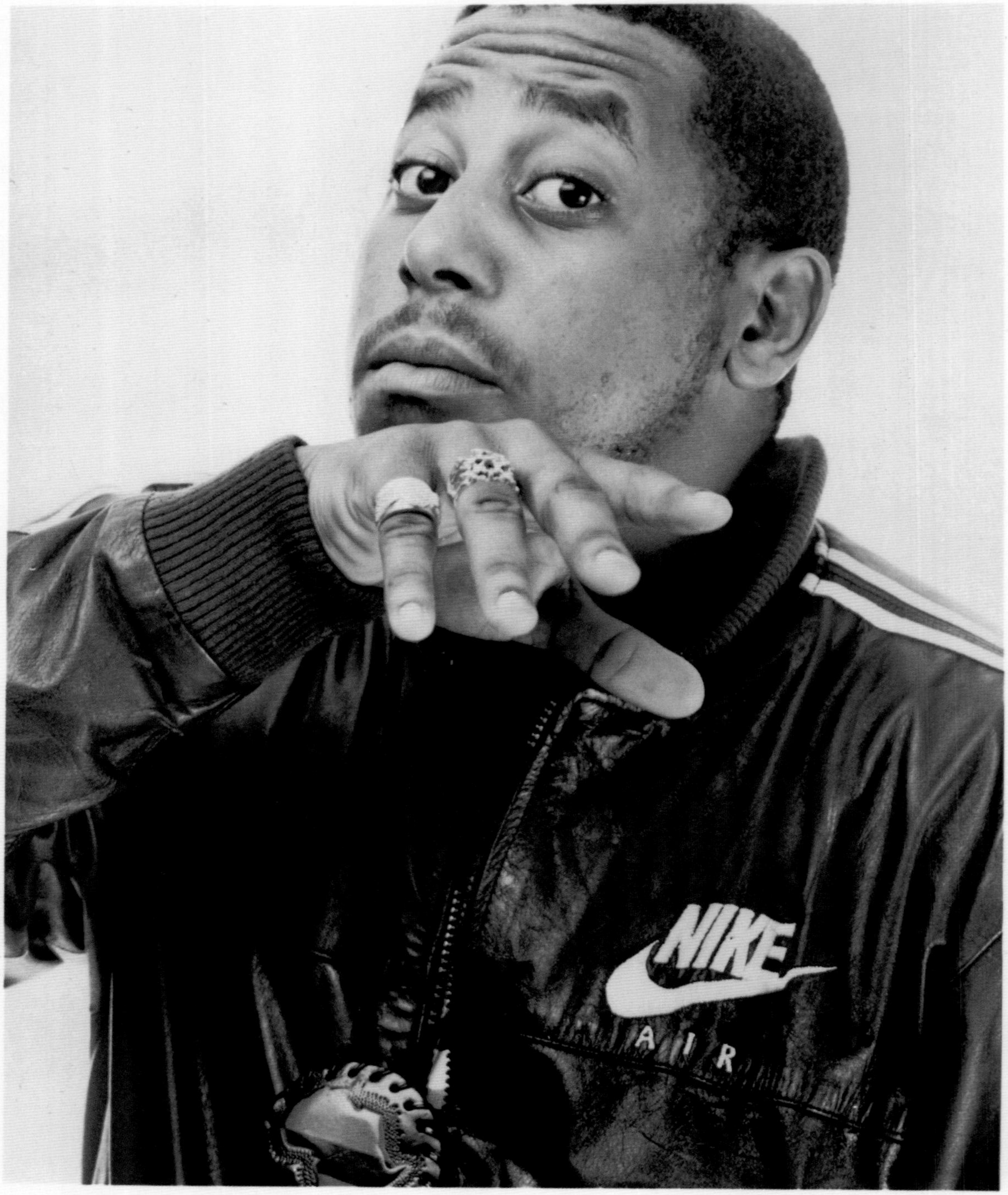

Photo Credit: Chris Carroll

Delicious Vinyl

TONE LŌC

DISTRIBUTED BY THE ISLAND TRADING CO.

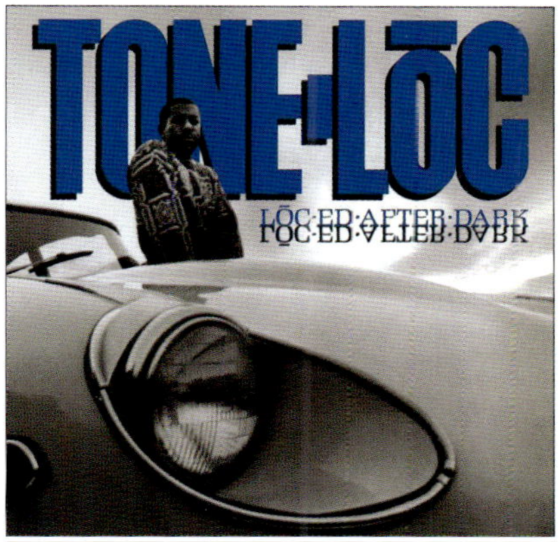

Billboard 200: *Lōc-ed After Dark* (No. 1)
Billboard Hot 100: "Wild Thing" (#2);
"Funky Cold Medina (#3)

Tone Lōc's impertinent, grinding "Wild Thing" qualified as the year's most preposterous music success story.

BESIDES BEING the highest-charting (#2) rap song ever on *Billboard's* pop chart, Tone Lōc's "Wild Thing" was the most successful single of any genre since "We Are the World" in 1985. The platinum success of the follow-up "Funky Cold Medina" made Lōc the first rapper to hit the Top 5 twice and helped *Lōc-ed After Dark* become the first album by a Black rapper to hit No. 1 on the pop charts.

His rise from obscurity into unexpected stardom was nine years in the making. Born and raised on the west side of Los Angeles, Tony Smith was renamed Tone Lōc by his boyhood buddies around the time of his 13th birthday. "I used to do a lot of crazy things, mostly fighting—Lōc is short for 'loco,'" the modest and friendly hitmaker said. "I used to be in a gang, but I quit." After donning his new moniker, Lōc started rapping over instrumental passages of records, hooking up with friends in a short-lived trio called Triple A. After high school, he hit the streets and party scenes, bustin' rhymes.

Los Angeles hadn't produced any significant rap records when Lōc signed to an independent record company, which was headquartered in a room in the back of a Thai restaurant. Producers Matt Dike and Mike Ross, two local DJs, were looking for someone with a unique sound. And Loc's croaky, jolly voice fit the bill. "When I was a kid, I had strep throat, and my mom gave me her throat serum of tea and brandy," Lōc acknowledged. "It scorched my throat, but it gave me a career. My voice used to be a lot deeper. Now it's just funny."

That's was Lōc's path for domination of the rap field. "Wild Thing" melded his salacious lyrics—in a loosely woven narrative, he told how he spelled relief—with a familiar guitar riff atop a hard-pumping beat. The unexpected popularity of the song could be traced to its low budget video ("It only cost $350"), a savvy parody of Robert Palmer's coldly erotic clips. After that triumph, "Funky Cold Medina" ("a wine drink that gets you in the mood for the Wild Thing") broke through.

The runaway hits helped add credibility to L.A.-based rap acts. Those who didn't give Lōc his respect wrote off his good-time music as lightweight, hardly at the cutting edge. But he was a clever writer and had that unique voice. "Everybody in New York thought everybody from Los Angeles was soft," Lōc said. "Now we've gotten so much more airplay—they fell asleep and we jumped in and took over. A lot of people might say, 'It's not rap, it's a sellout.' But my records were made to dance to. I'm a hip-hop artist."

Lōc's easygoing demeanor wasn't a trait characteristic of other rappers. "Lightnin's strikin', thunder's rollin' and I'm livin' large" was his self-described lifestyle. "This business is very demanding, but if you worry about things, you get an ulcer," he concluded. "The fact that I don't take it seriously keeps my head level, like the average Joe Schmo you see on the streets." ■

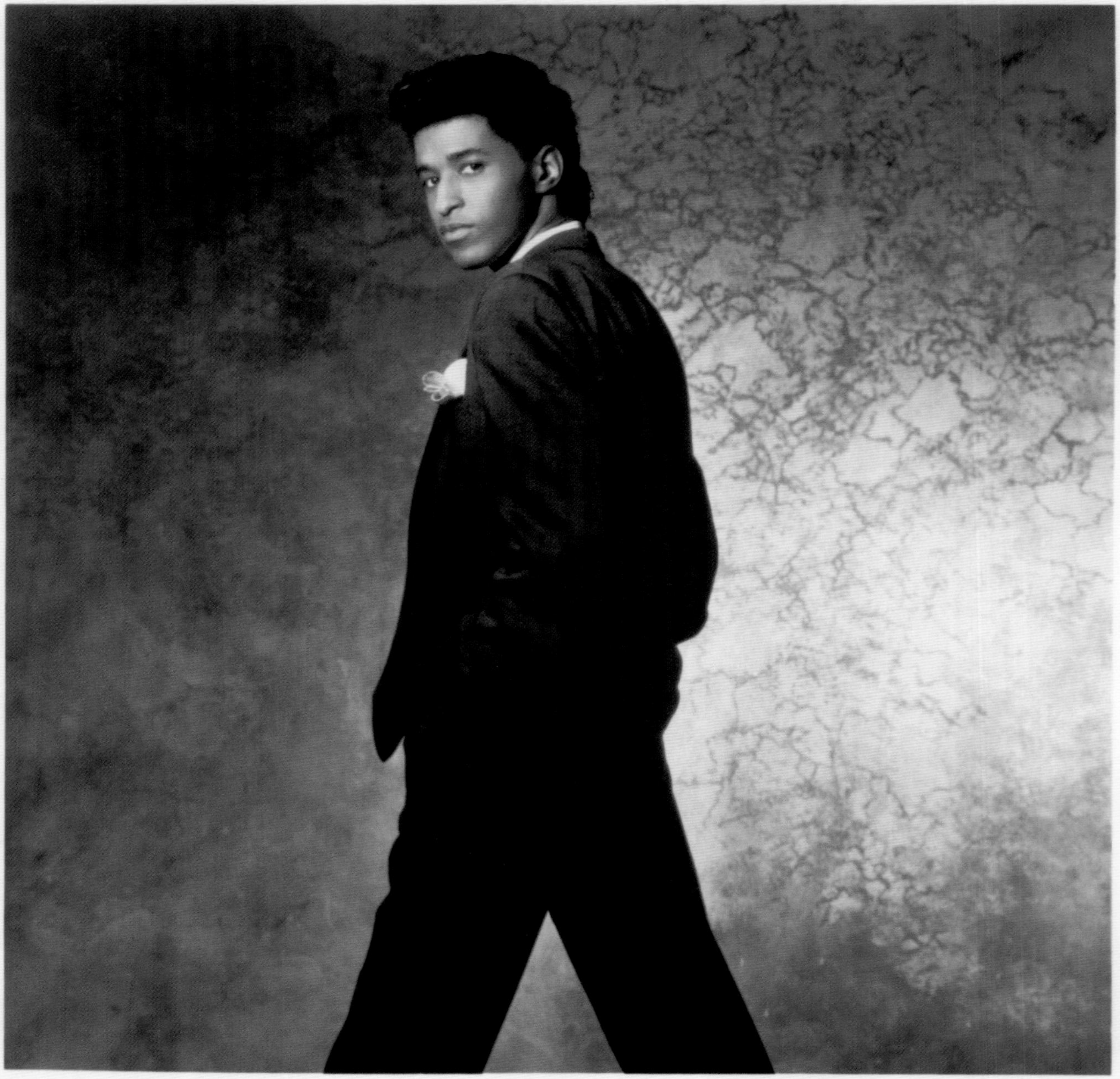

Photo: Randee St. Nicholas

SOLAR SOUND OF LOS ANGELES RECORDS

*baby***face**

Epic
8907

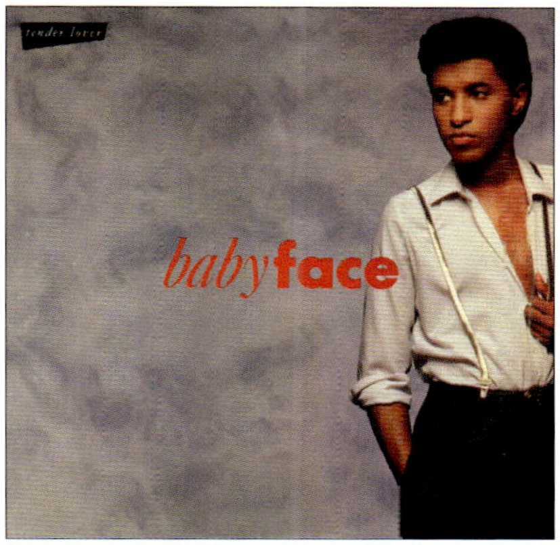

Billboard 200: *Tender Lover* (#14)
Billboard Hot 100: "It's No Crime" (#7); "Tender Lover" (#14); "Whip Appeal" (#6); "My Kinda Girl" (#30)

Having written and produced radio-ready smashes, Babyface stepped into solo artistry by dint of *Tender Lover*.

AN INDIANAPOLIS native Kenny Edmonds got his break in 1981 when he joined the Deele, a Cincinnati-based R&B group which also included drummer Antonio "L.A." Reid. During that time, fellow Ohio musician and funkateer Bootsy Collins noticed his youthful appearance and tagged him "Babyface." The moniker stuck.

Babyface played keyboards in the Deele, and he and Reid formed a successful partnership. "From the beginning, we were a good balance of personalities, me being the quiet one and L.A. being the go-getter," Babyface recalled. "Together we made demos and just sort of started shaping the Deele's musical directions. We were producing back then, but we didn't know it!"

The pair began molding tracks for the Deele and Midnight Star, and Babyface released *Lovers*, a little-noticed debut album, in 1986. The following year, the team put the Whispers back on top with the anthemic "Rock Steady," and the floodgates opened up.

"Two Occasions," the Deele's 1988 breakthrough ballad, was written by Babyface and featured his delicate lead vocal on the bridge. He and Reid began writing and producing major pop/R&B hits for other artists on the side—Pebbles' "Girlfriend," the title hit from Bobby Brown's *Don't Be Cruel*, the Grammy-nominated "The Way You Love Me" from Karyn White's self-titled debut and Paula Abdul's smash "Knocked Out." The newest hit-bound sound from the pair was the Jacksons' "Nothin' (That Compares 2 U)."

The burgeoning activity forced the duo to relinquish membership in the Deele. *Tender Lover*, Babyface's second album, spawned his first Top 10 pop hits as a solo artist—the sexy, rollicking "It's No Crime" and the sultry "Whip Appeal," which also reached No. 1 and #2 on the R&B chart, respectively.

"The objective was to set Babyface the artist apart from Babyface the producer—I think I've accomplished that," the soft-spoken soul crooner said. "I know that being an artist means being stopped in the mall for autographs—but I'm ready for that, too."

The success achieved by *Tender Lover* didn't mean the end of the L.A./'Face team. He and partner Reid relocated from Los Angeles to Atlanta, where they oversaw a growing music empire that included their own label, LaFace. "I'm interested in the creative and financial freedom that goes with being a successful songwriter and producer —and you have the advantage of having a smash but still keeping your privacy," he reasoned. "Now Babyface the solo persona is one thing, and Babyface who writes and produces with L.A. is something else still. Why fix something that isn't broke? I've got the best of both worlds—it's the perfect situation." ■

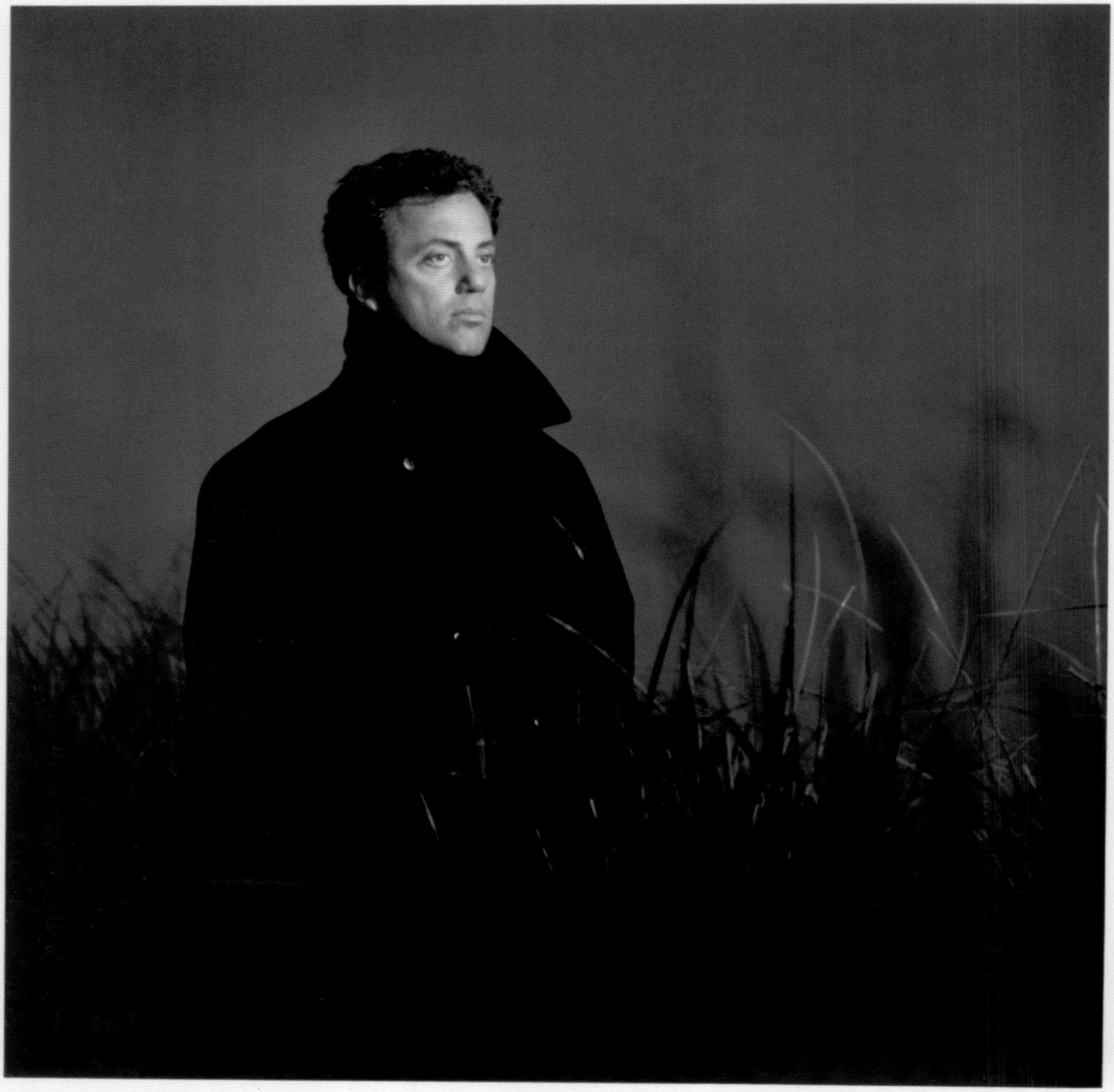

PHOTOGRAPH: TIMOTHY WHITE

BILLY JOEL

Columbia
8910

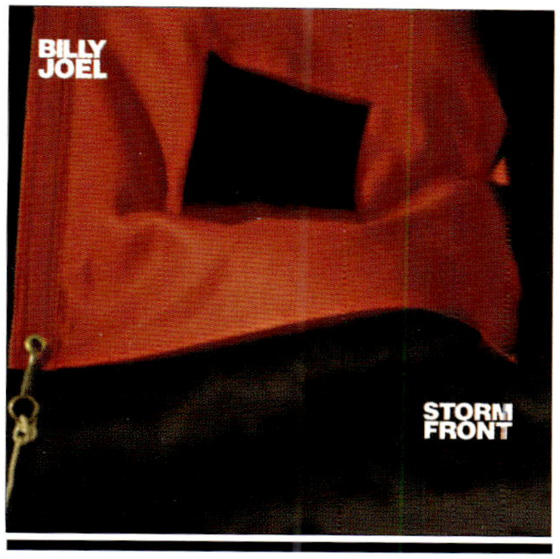

Billboard 200: *Storm Front* (No. 1)
Billboard Hot 100: "We Didn't Start the Fire" (No. 1); "I Go to Extremes" (#6); "The Downeaster 'Alexa'" (#57); "That's Not Her Style" (#77); "And So It Goes" (#37)

Billy Joel's *Storm Front* and "We Didn't Start the Fire" hit No. 1 on the albums and singles charts simultaneously.

FOR GOSSIPS looking for cracks in his marriage with model Christie Brinkley, Billy Joel had become a tabloid target. Fortunately, family life hadn't mellowed him on *Storm Front*, his first new studio recording in three years. He'd fired half his band and taken up with a new producer, Mick Jones of Foreigner, after ten years with Phil Ramone.

"It's not to be timely or more commercial—that stuff is up to the fates," he said. "I just get bored real easily. I want to challenge myself, and with music, you can do that. So I'll continue to make changes. Whenever I hit a wall, I'll experiment a little more."

With two Top 40 hits from *Storm Front*, Joel's commercial success continued unabated. In "I Go to Extremes," Joel unraveled his preoccupation with his craft, the psychic wrestling he endured as a songwriter. "I tend to become pretty difficult when I'm not coming up with something—I become Cro-Magnon, actually," he said.

In rapid-fire style, the chart-topping "We Didn't Start the Fire" catalogued 40 years of headline events, covering dozens of milestones—Harry Truman, the McCarthy years, Korea, Eisenhower, Elvis, Hula Hoops, Dylan, the Bay of Pigs, Beatlemania, Woodstock, Reagan, AIDS, Bernie Goetz and even the "rock and roller cola wars." "Turning 40 is supposed to be some kind of watershed year," Joel explained. "So I was taking inventory, and I started listing things that had happened year by year since I was born. It was there all the time. It was just a matter of somebody saying it."

But "We Didn't Start the Fire" was criticized as a "history-in-flash-cards," a "newsery rhyme" and "Cliff Notes for the MTV generation"—that is, a laundry list of historical buzzwords that failed to draw a conclusion. "Hey, I only had four minutes," Joel said. "I wasn't trying to teach anybody anything. I was trying to pique people's curiosity. Where does it say in my contract with the musical gods that I've gotta explain anything? The whole point is, 'Hey, Jack, look it up!'"

Indeed, the single became a study aid for history teachers—cassettes were mailed to high schools nationwide in 40,000 issues of *Scholastic* magazine. Interestingly, "We Didn't Start the Fire" began as Joel's own exercise in rap music, which he discarded. "The phrase 'rap music' goes unchallenged, and it's really an oxymoron. There is no music in rap—it's rhythm and lyric. There's no melody, chord structure or composition. That doesn't mean I think it's bad—I just don't want to confuse it with music."

Joel said he considered himself a piano player first and foremost. "It's a musician thing as opposed to a singer thing. If you're just a singer, you're not in the club. To me, the term 'singer-songwriter' smacks of that early-Seventies era when we were all supposed to be sensitive, suffering and self-pitying. And singing is basically screaming in key, and anybody can scream—it's not that tough. You're born with it. But to pick up a musical instrument and learn how to use it, that's pretty cool. There's a mystique about it—like watching a plumber work." ■

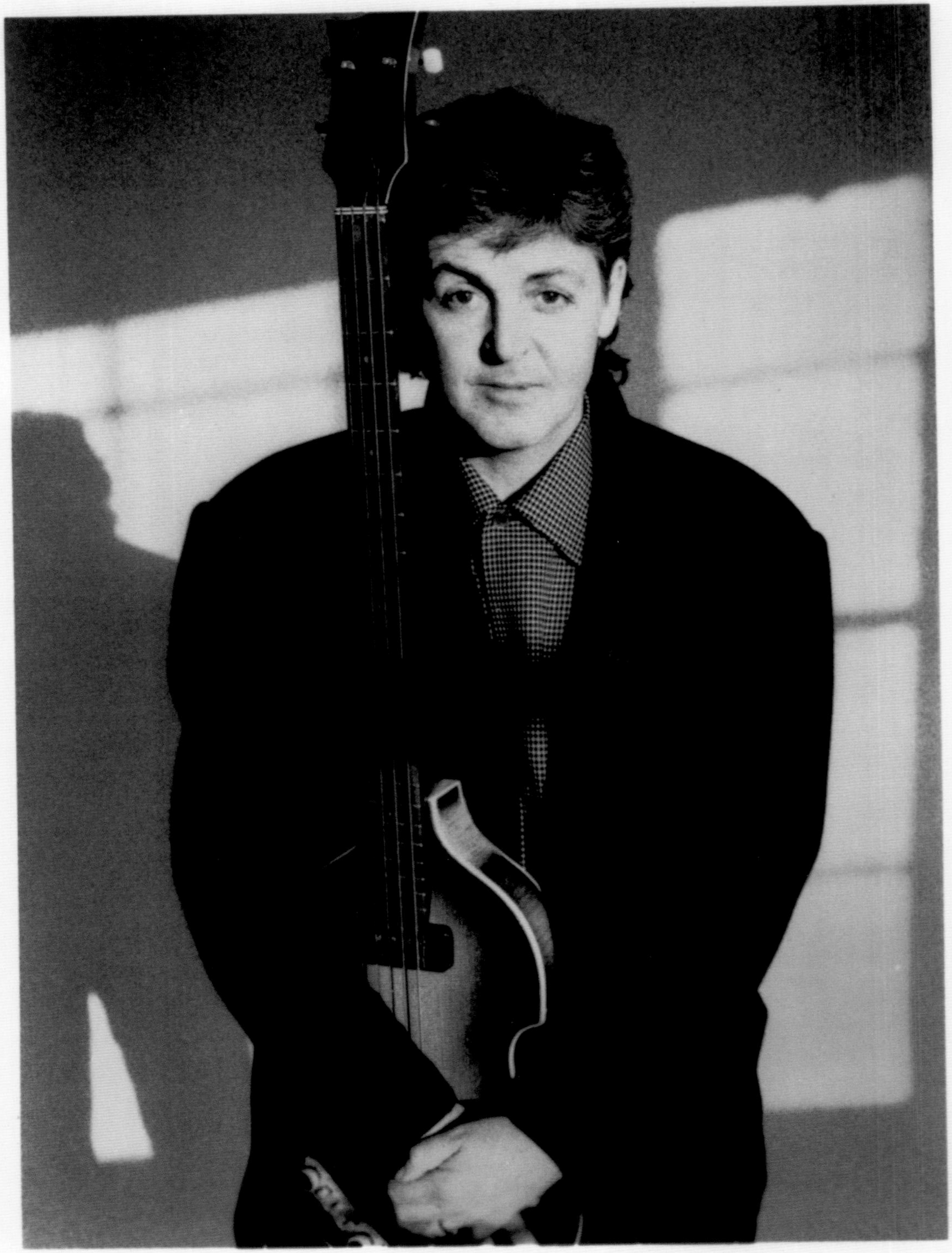

PAUL McCARTNEY

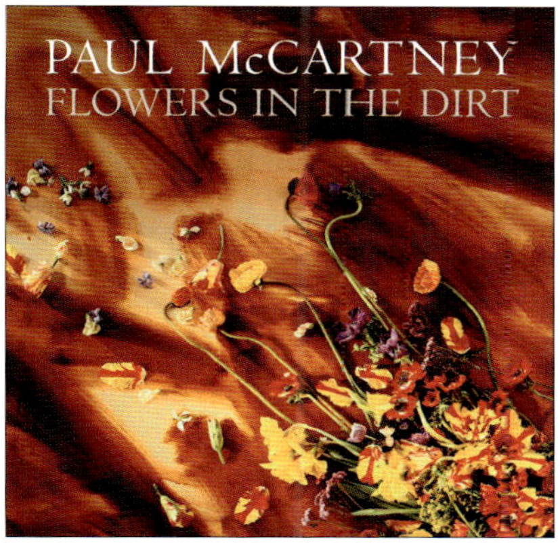

Billboard 200: *Flowers in the Dirt* (#21)
Billboard Hot 100: "My Brave Face" (#25); "This One" (#94); "Figure of Eight" (#92)

To grow his *Flowers in the Dirt* release, Paul McCartney instituted an effective collaboration with Elvis Costello.

A GAP of three years existed since Paul McCartney's last album of new material. While getting to know some of the musicians he hoped to use on *Flowers in the Dirt*, the former Beatle cut 27 classic rock 'n' roll songs in a two-day blast, the choicest of which appeared on the 1988 release *Choba b CCCP* (Back in the USSR)—the first time an album had been available exclusively in the Soviet Union. The impulse factored into the making of *Flowers in the Dirt*, recorded at his home studio in the English countryside.

"I think some of that spontaneity carried over, yeah," McCartney said. "The longer we took on songs, the more time there was to worry and to doubt. The other, old-fashioned recording way—because you didn't have 48 tracks or whatever—you had to make decisions as you went along. I didn't think 'Get Back' (the Beatles' No. 1 hit in 1969) was any kind of single—the other guys had to say, 'No, it's great, man.' I like when things creep up on me. I'm not a great analyzer—I'm a doer."

Considered a full-fledged return to form, *Flowers in the Dirt* contained four songs co-penned by Elvis Costello, one of the UK's most eloquent singer-songwriters and a long-standing fan of McCartney's music. McCartney made a contemporaneous appearance on Costello's *Spike* album and co-wrote two songs, including the sizable hit "Veronica."

"I was looking for a collaborator, I asked around and somebody suggested Elvis Costello," he mused. "I liked the stuff of his I'd heard so he came down here. It seemed to me that he was very good, but occasionally he started to ramble—he's very wordy. I once said to him, 'Have you got any ideas?' I had to laugh—he pulled out three bags, about 50 books full of ideas! He jots down anything he overhears in those books. It reminded me a bit of working with John (Lennon)."

The lighthearted "My Brave Face" enjoyed global success. "Elvis and I did have some laughs, coming to blows and differences of opinion," McCartney allowed. "I'd say, 'Put a bit of echo on the drums.' He'd say, 'No! No echo.' Later I'd say, 'Maybe a bit of chorus effect on that guitar?' 'God, no—no chorus.' 'How about a synth thing then, El?' 'No synthesizers.' Of course, by the time he'd finished his own album, he'd used chorus, echo, synthesizer and the kitchen sink. But it was quite good fun—we rubbed off on each other." ■

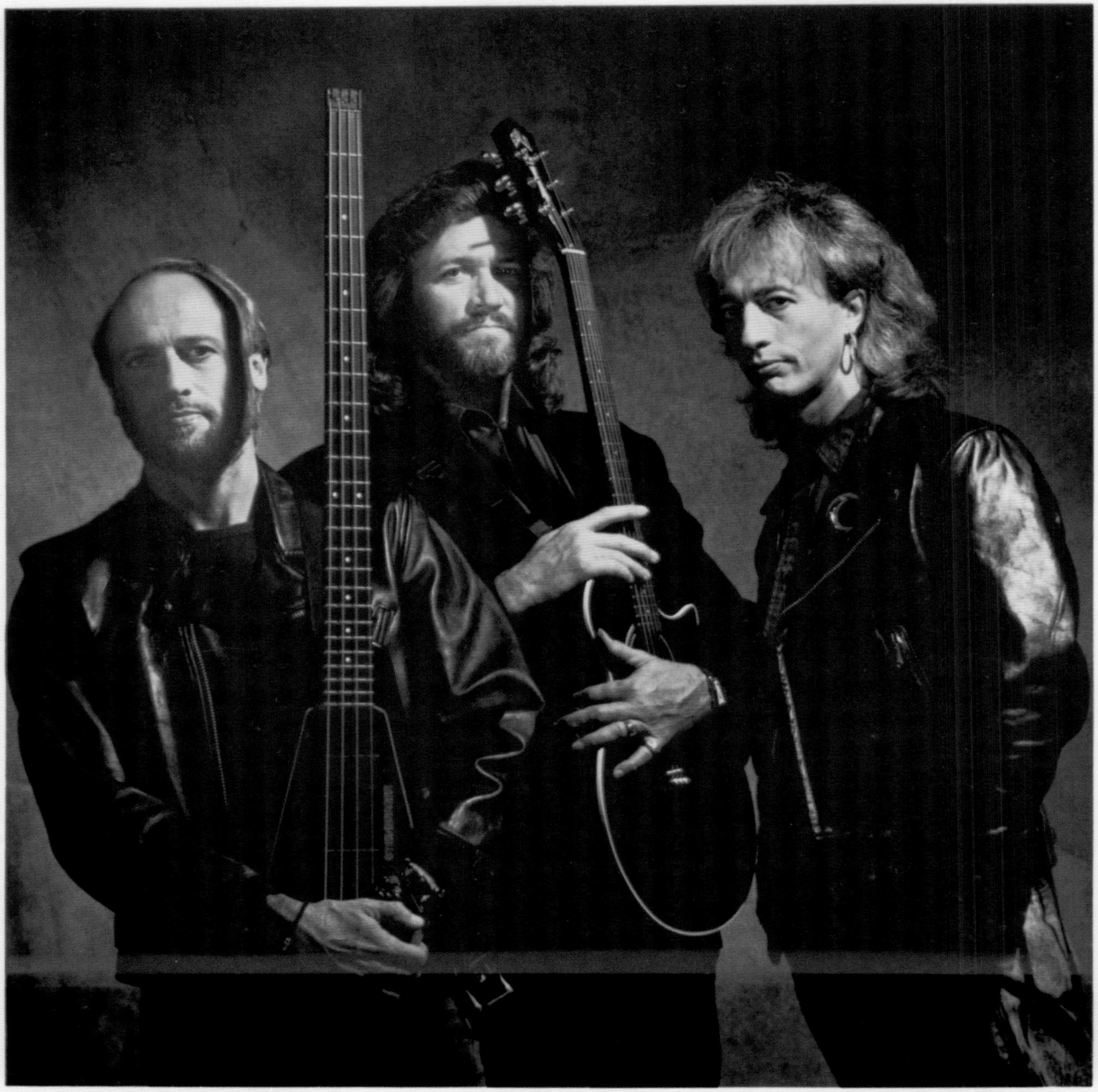

Photo by: E.J CAMP/OUTLINE

MAURICE GIBB BARRY GIBB ROBIN GIBB

BEE GEES

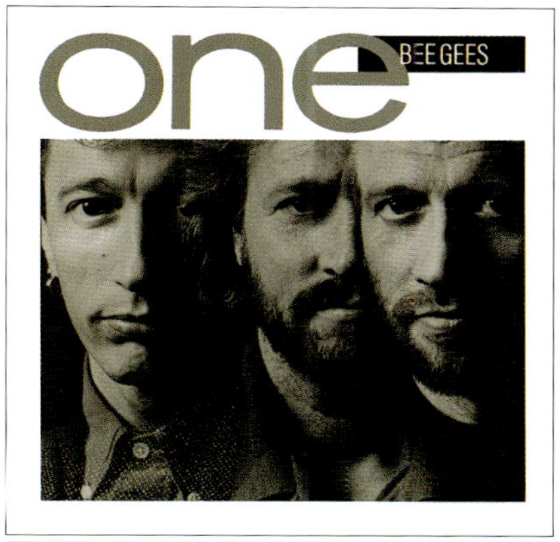

Billboard 200: *One* (#68)
Billboard Hot 100: "One" (#7)

"One," a crack Bee Gees track, returned the trio to the US airwaves and came to be their biggest Eighties hit.

IN THE 22-year saga of the Bee Gees, the legendary musical siblings—Barry Gibb and his fraternal twin brothers, Robin and Maurice—had become a durable and prized musical entity. Their run of British baroque-pop singles in the late Sixties led to American R&B-based dance-pop hits in the early Seventies and then to the defining soundtrack of the disco era. Beyond achieving fame as performers, they also wrote and produced landmark albums for the likes of Barbra Streisand, Dionne Warwick, Diana Ross and Kenny Rogers.

After a six-year absence, the Gibb brothers resumed their own recording career, making a commercial comeback outside the US with 1987's *E.S.P.* and its single, "You Win Again," which reached No. 1 in eight countries. They began work on the *One* album when their younger brother Andy suddenly died of heart failure brought on by long-term abuse of drugs and alcohol. The trio took a break and returned to complete the album, dedicating *One* "to our brother Andy."

The song "Ordinary Lives" was released as a single. "You can find sentences here and there throughout the album that apply to Andy," Barry said. "Losing a member of the family who was that close changes you spiritually. The song is also a reflection about us before we became famous—our way of saying we're just ordinary people. Musically, the song appeals to the European listener."

One contained the Bee Gees' first US hit in a decade, the title track, a No. 1 smash on the adult-contemporary charts in the tradition of their classic tracks. "We're using the concept of one, which is a very important factor in ancient mythology and storytelling—where two people unite and become one," Barry said.

Despite the success of "One" in America, the public still blamed the Bee Gees for the disco aesthetic. The album failed to dent the Top 40. ■

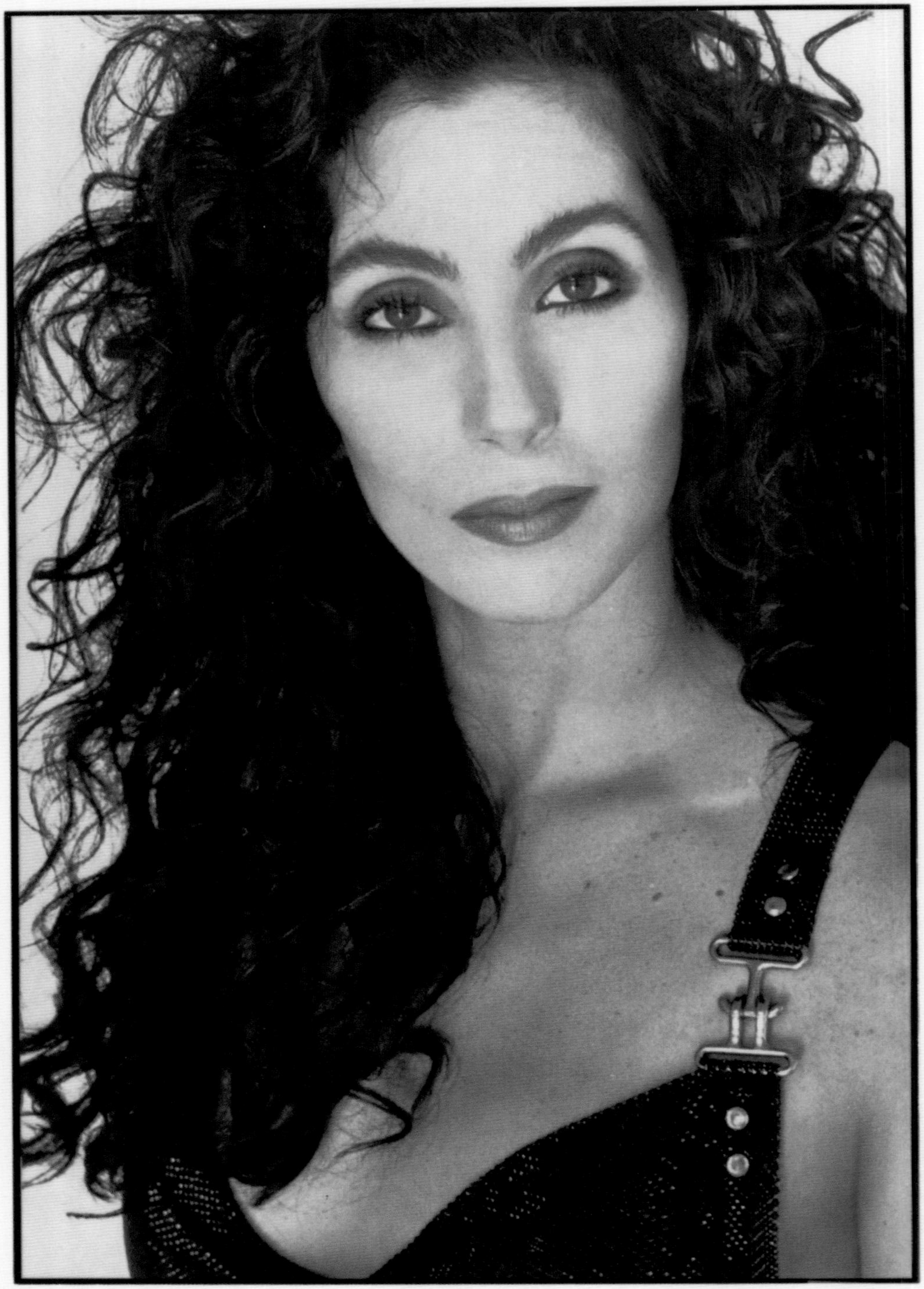

Photo Credit: Herb Ritts

CHER

GEFFEN
RECORDS

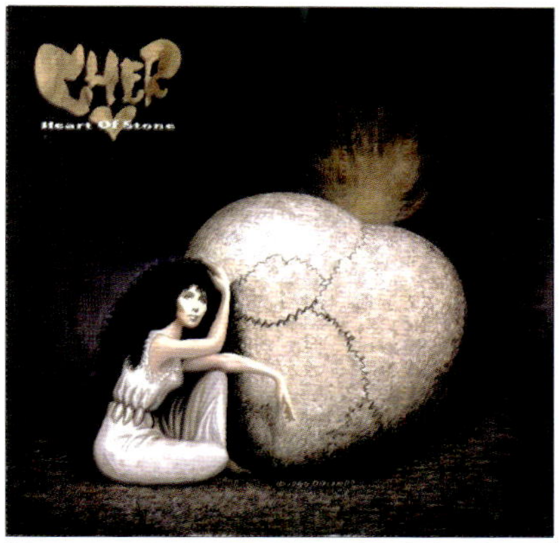

Billboard 200: *Heart of Stone* (#10)
Billboard Hot 100: "After All" (#6); "If I Could Turn Back Time" (#3); "Just Like Jesse James" (#8); "Heart of Stone" (#20)

Heart of Stone cemented Cher's legacy as a thriving recording artist, not an actress who occasionally sang.

THE FIRST record Cher ever sang on was "Be My Baby" for producer Phil Spector. Having met Sonny Bono in the early Sixties while he was working for Spector, the two of them married in 1964 and became Sonny & Cher, and the hits started coming—"Baby Don't Go," "I Got You Babe," "All I Ever Need Is You," "The Beat Goes On."

From 1965 to 1974, Cher (in the duo and as a solo performer) enjoyed 22 Top 40 singles, including four No. 1 hits. There was also success in Las Vegas and, in the summer of 1971, the premier of *The Sonny & Cher Comedy Hour*. The series ended after four years, the marriage after 12.

Then Cher became a movie star in the early Eighties—landing a part in *Come Back to the Five and Dime, Jimmy Dean, Jimmy Dean*, an Oscar nomination as Best Supporting Actress in *Silkwood*, critical acclaim for her performance in *Mask* and, in 1987, an Academy Award as Best Actress for *Moonstruck*.

That same year, she returned to a recording career. Cher included the hits "I Found Someone" and "We All Sleep Alone." "I was 18 the first time I sang," she said. "I loved to sing—it was just fun. But then it becomes a business and you get burnt out to the point where you like it but you don't love it—you just do it. Well, suddenly I've discovered that I love singing even more than I thought I ever did. It's fun again."

For *Heart of Stone*, Cher recruited the top pop songwriters—Diane Warren, Desmond Child, Michael Bolton—and teamed them in various combinations. She claimed four Top 20 singles from the album, including the title track and "Just Like Jesse James." Warren, who wrote the gold-certified "If I Could Turn Back Time," also co-produced it. "She had never produced before, but she was driving me crazy—'Please, please let me'—so I said yes," Cher shared. "She was so excited, and she did a great job. It's my best vocal performance on the album."

Heart of Stone also accommodated "After All," a team-up with Peter Cetera from the soundtrack to the film *Chances Are* (starring Cybill Shepherd and Robert Downey, Jr.). Hearing that the love theme was about to be recorded, Cher asked if she could sing the woman's part on the planned duet.

"They told me, 'We want everyone but you,'" she recalled. "They said my voice wasn't right for it. But I loved the song—I knew it'd be a hit. They promised to at least give me the courtesy of an audition, so I did a demo tape that Peter Asher produced. It was a very traumatic few days, but I must've changed their minds. That demo is what you hear on the album."

"After All" peaked at No. 1 on the adult contemporary charts and was nominated for an Oscar, and *Heart of Stone* became Cher's best-selling album. She thought nothing of it. "This isn't a cure for cancer," she said. "I'm just a singer." ■

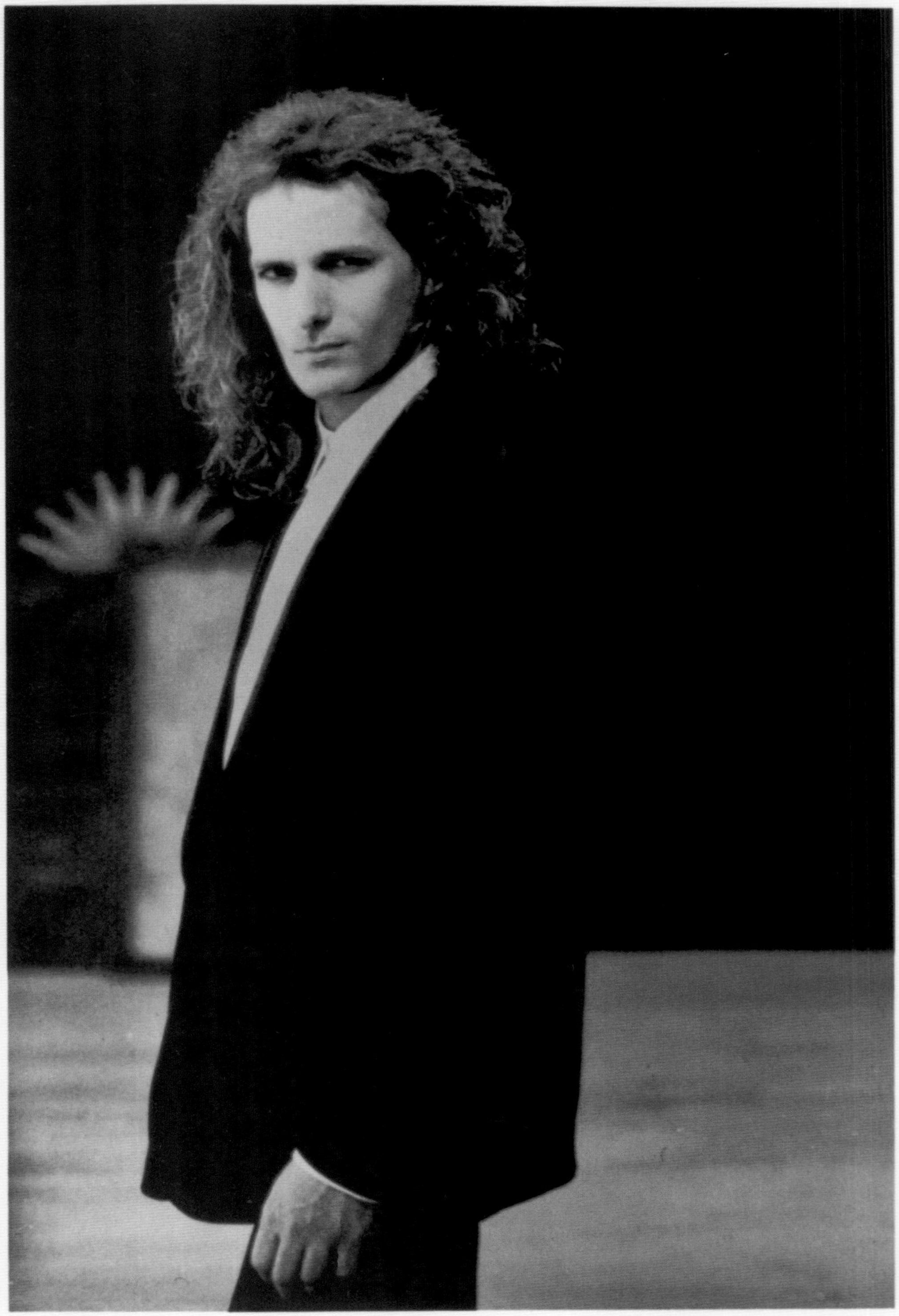

Direction:
Louis Levin Management
360 Central Park West
New York, NY 10025
Phone: 212.932.2429
FAX: 212.932.2529

MICHAEL BOLTON

Columbia
8906

PHOTOGRAPH: GLEN ERLER

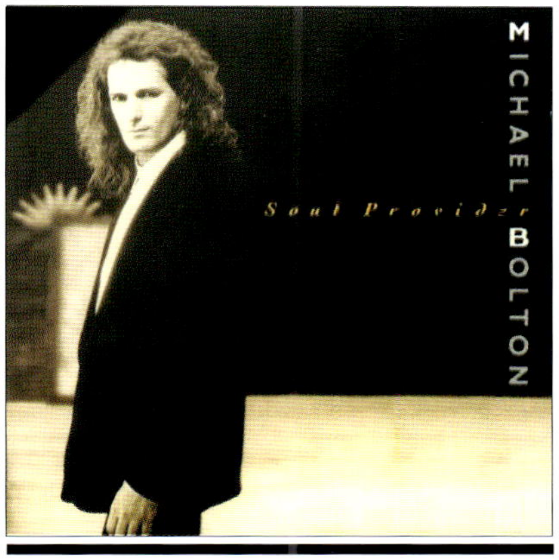

Billboard 200: *Soul Provider* (#3)
Billboard Hot 100: "Soul Provider" (#17);
"How Am I Supposed to Live Without You" (No. 1);
"How Can We Be Lovers?" (#3); "When I'm Back on My Feet Again" (#7);
"Georgia on My Mind" (#36)

Spawning five Top 10 adult contemporary hits, *Soul Provider* turned Michael Bolton into a household name.

ON EARLY solo albums and as the frontman for the group Blackjack, Michael Bolotin performed nondescript hard rock. He then changed his style and his surname, refashioning himself as Michael Bolton, a polished balladeer whose raspy four-octave voice became increasingly familiar as a result of the hit singles "That's What Love Is All About" and an interpretation of Otis Redding's classic "(Sittin' On) The Dock of the Bay."

On *Soul Provider*, Bolton captivated a largely female audience by conveying the intensity of his feelings with an affecting measure of romantic angst. He teamed long-distance with the era's best songwriting partners, Diane Warren and Desmond Child, and the album spawned five smash singles, eventually selling 6 million copies.

A Bolton/Warren/Child collaboration, "How Can We Be Lovers," was co-produced by Bolton and Child. "Sometimes I think it was a brainstorm to put the three of us together, and sometimes I think I just had no idea what I'd be getting myself into," Bolton said. "They knew this would be a great theme, a great title—a song about working it out because of the obvious necessity of being friends, of being able to communicate."

Bolton co-produced the track "When I'm Back on My Feet Again," written by Warren. "She phoned and said, 'I think I just wrote the greatest song I've ever written.' It was somehow connected to her father, who died last year—they were very close—and reminded me of my father, who died quite a while ago. The demo vocal may be technically flawed, but I didn't want to mess with the feeling."

Bolton's new version of "How Am I Supposed to Live Without You," a ballad he co-wrote that became a Top 40 hit for Laura Branigan in 1983, reached No. 1 on the pop charts and netted him his first Grammy Award, for Best Pop Vocal Performance, Male. "It wasn't a close personal experience for me, although writing it was," he noted. "It obviously affected a lot of people."

The title track, featuring saxophonist Kenny G, summed up Bolton's approach to conveying passion in a relationship. The R&B chestnut he revived was Ray Charles' "Georgia on My Mind." "Ray Charles is probably my single strongest vocal influence," Bolton said. "Marvin Gaye, Otis Redding, Wilson Pickett, Stevie Wonder—all the great R&B singers picked up their chops and phrasing from Ray Charles. He wasn't inhibited about expressing emotion." ■

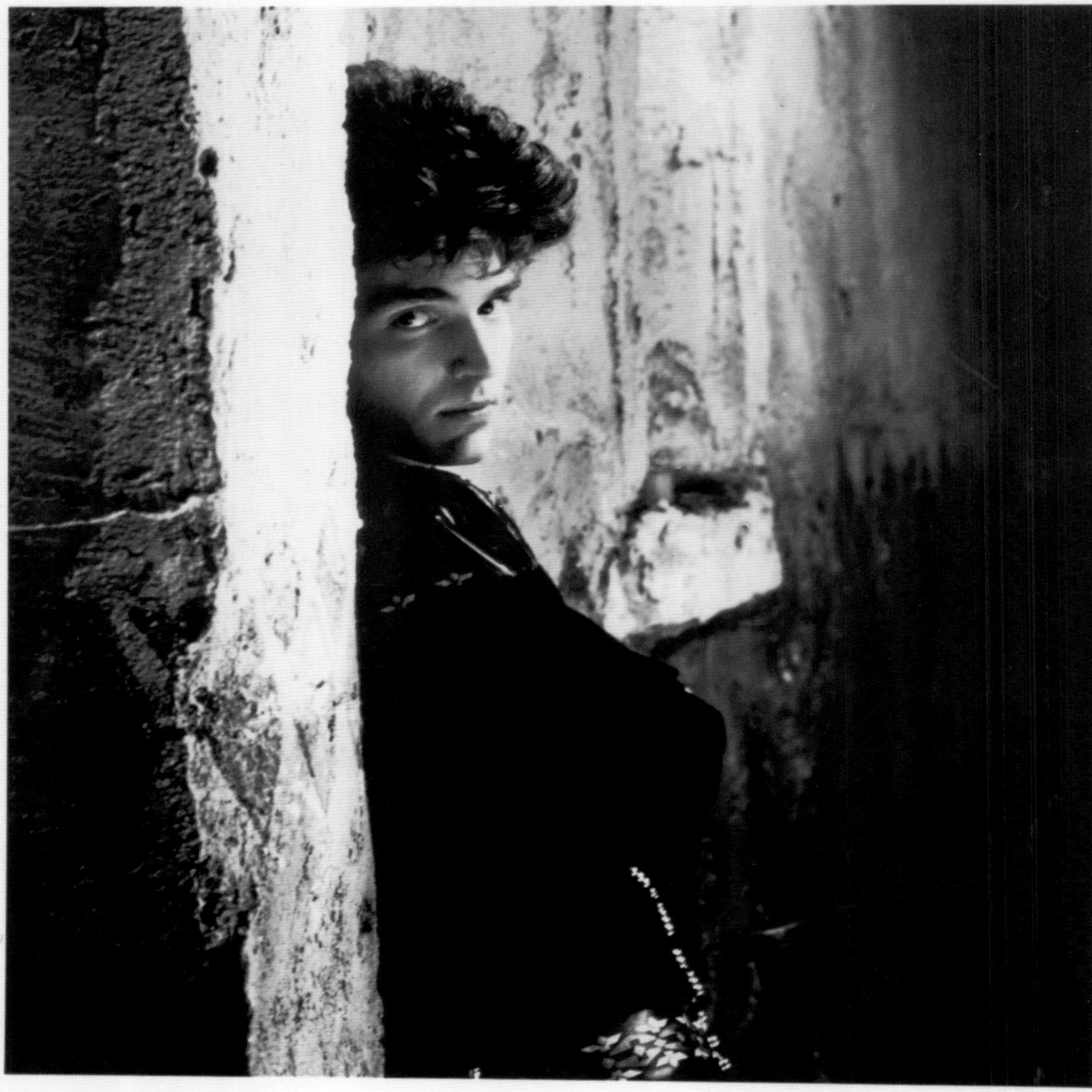

Photography: E.J. Camp

RICHARD MARX

EMI

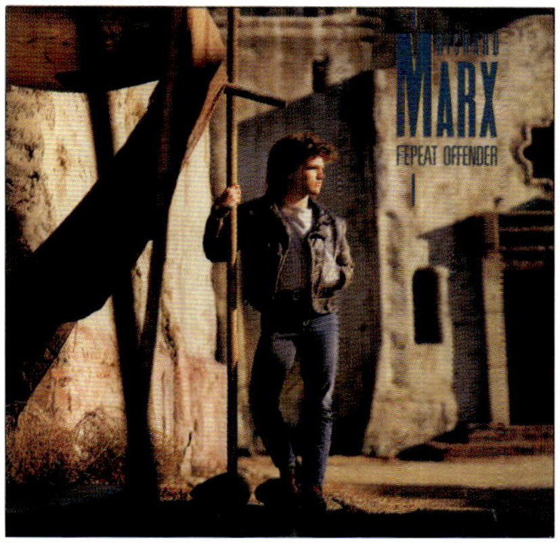

Billboard 200: *Repeat Offender* (No. 1)
Billboard Hot 100: "Satisfied" (No. 1); "Right Here Waiting" (No 1); "Angelia" (#4); "Too Late to Say Goodbye" (#12); "Children of the Night" (#13)

With *Repeat Offender*, Richard Marx duplicated his initiatory success, reigning the charts with five hit singles.

IN THREE years, Richard Marx had graduated to superstar status, the first solo artist to reach the Top 5 with his first seven singles. "Satisfied" and "Right Here Waiting" were two No. 1 smashes from *Repeat Offender*, his second album, which also boasted the hits "Too Late to Say Goodbye" and "Angelia."

Marx released the album's most compelling track as a single. He donated all the proceeds from "Children of the Night" to the suburban Los Angeles teen shelter of the same name; children from the organization sang backup. "I wanted to get the message out there without preaching or being pretentious," he said, "and I figured one way to do that was to put my money where my mouth was."

Marx wanted to address the runaway problem because it was so pronounced in his home base of L.A. "But the problem is nationwide—over a million kids run away from home in America every year. I grew up in a happy family—I played baseball and did my homework, and my term paper was my biggest fear. So I couldn't write about what I thought the plight of runaways and child prostitutes was like. That would have been arrogant."

To authenticate his lyrics, Marx met with runaways from the shelter. "A 19-year-old was very articulate telling me about her whole life," he shared. "She ran away from home when she was five, and by 12 she was a prostitute. At the end of three hours, we were both crying. I got the information I needed, and the rest wasn't anything difficult for me—I just wrote a song, which is what I do. But it's been nice to be involved, because I can see kids getting better. You can't believe that they're involved in hideous things, because they're great kids, real normal. They deserve a better chance."

On his world tour, Marx bridged the spirit of his Bic-lit rockers with earnest ballads. One other stop took him home to Chicago, where he sang the national anthem at baseball's soggy All-Star Game.

"It's exciting, but to be honest, if the game was in New York or Cleveland or Los Angeles this year, I wouldn't be interested. The fact that the game is at Wrigley Field is what made me want to sing the anthem, because I grew up a Cubs fan." ■

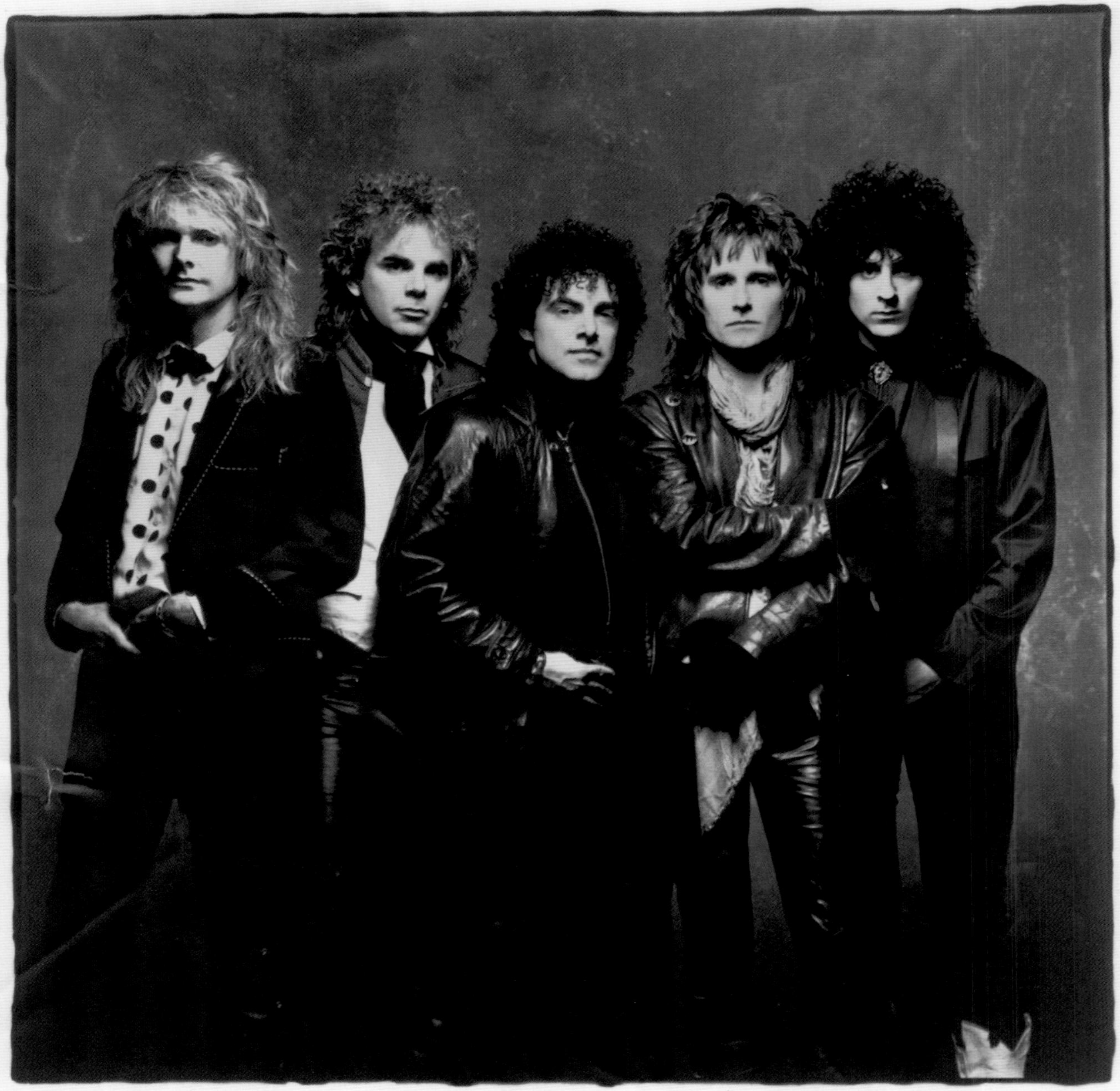

RICKY PHILLIPS
(BASS)

JONATHAN CAIN
(KEYBOARDS)

NEAL SCHON
(GUITAR)

JOHN WAITE
(VOCALS)

DEEN CASTRONOVO
(DRUMS)

BAD ENGLISH

Epic
8905

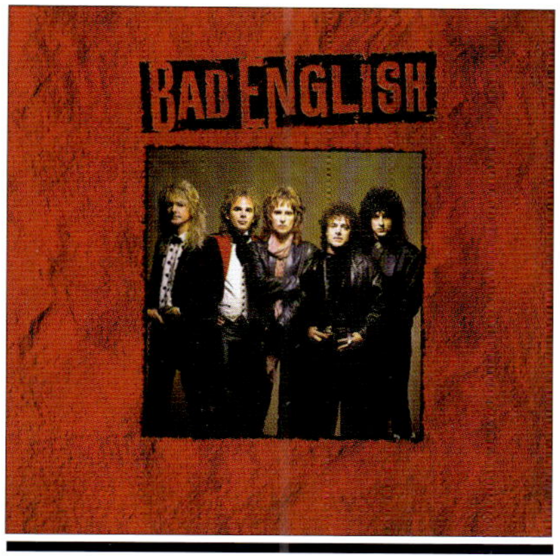

Billboard 200: *Bad English* (#21)
Billboard Hot 100: "Forget Me Not" (#45);
"When I See You Smile" (No. 1); "Price of Love" (#5);
"Heaven is a 4 Letter Word" (#66); "Possession" (#21)

Scoring two huge hits, "When I See You Smile" and "Price of Love," Bad English...well, they wasn't that bad.

BAD ENGLISH was rock's latest reclamation project. Several players who'd had a taste of commercial success—singer John Waite (of "Missing You" fame and the Babys), guitarist Neal Schon and keyboardist Jonathan Cain (both of Journey)—handpicked a bunch of outside songs, and then recruited hit producer Richie Zito to crank up a big recorded sound.

The supergroup was perfectly calculated for exposure on radio playlists, and the Diane Warren-penned power ballad "When I See You Smile" spent two weeks as the No. 1 song in the country. Cynics damned the band's trend-mongering marketing savvy, while fans cited the blistering execution of the well-worn cliches.

Bad English enjoyed instant commercial success, but Schon, who had spent the better part of two decades in Santana and Journey, regretted that his new band's achievement had come at the expense of his own *Late Night* album. When Journey finally called it a day in 1987, Schon was ready to consider a full-time solo career. He began recording his debut album at his own 24-track studio in his hometown of San Francisco.

"I didn't make the record to sell millions of copies," he said. "Journey made some good music, but only 20 percent of that was me. I felt stifled in my situation—there wasn't enough space for guitar. Every time I listen to a new kid, it seems like they play with every finger and toe. How many notes can you cram into a bar? There aren't that many players teaching what Eric Clapton and Jimmy Page taught me when I was learning—to put emotion in it. My album is a more mature statement."

Late Night returned in spirit to the instrumental approach of early Journey albums, although Schon managed as a vocalist on half the tracks. "I'm not the greatest singer in the world—I just wanted to go in the studio, do my vocal thing and get out," he admitted. "But David Gilmour of Pink Floyd is my friend. I went to see the Floyd's show and left saying, 'I can sing.' It was the cinematic concepts of the music that carried it."

While Schon recorded his album, Waite was writing songs with Cain, and Schon eventually wound up on their doorstep. Although he was still skittish about joining a group, Bad English won. "When I'm not playing, I get real stir-crazy. I said, 'I've got my own thing, but I'll see how this band works out.' Now I'm committed to doing two records with Bad English. It's good-time sexy music, not that satanic play-it-backwards stuff." ■

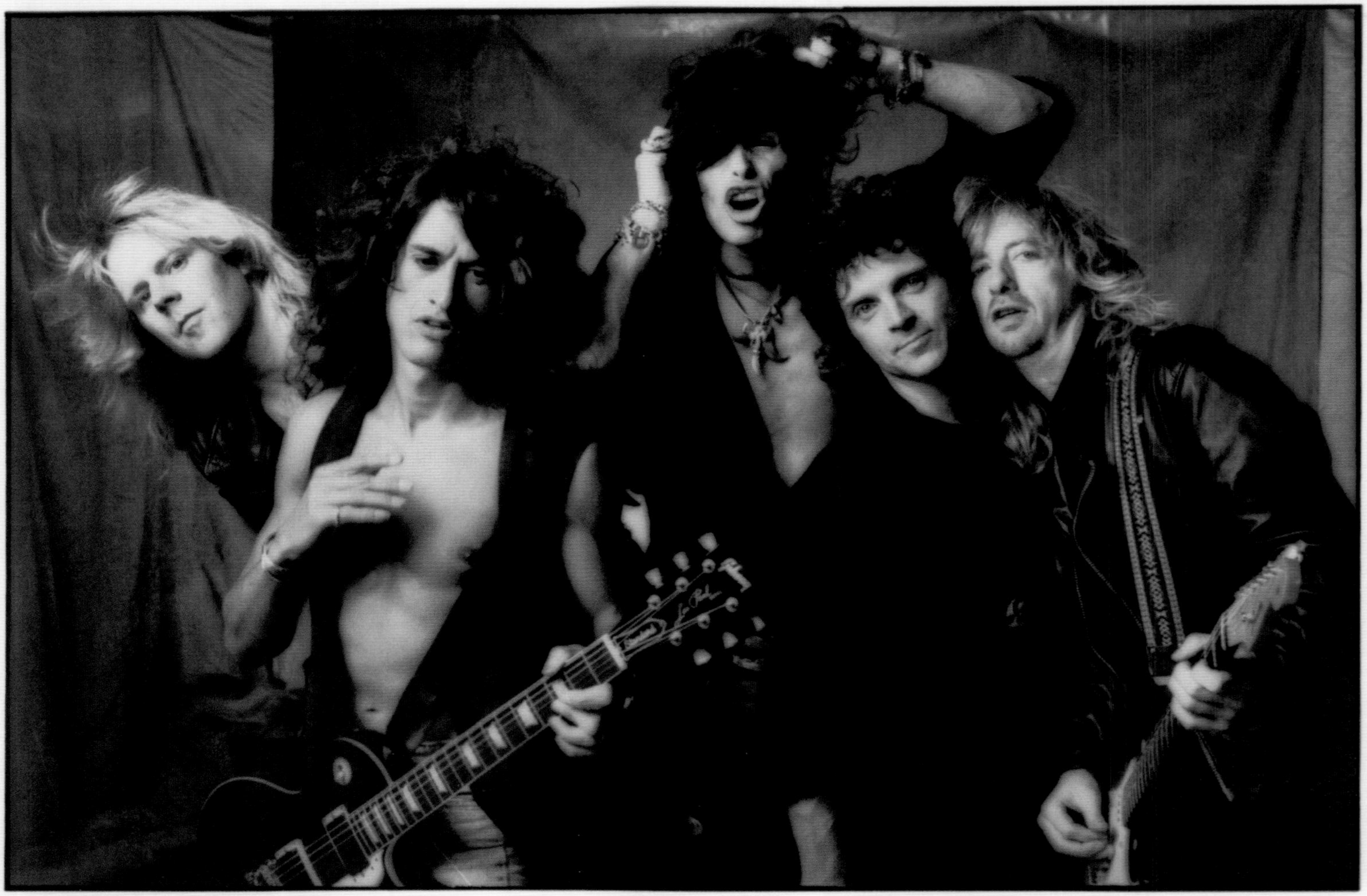

Photo Credit: Norman Seeff

Tom Hamilton Joe Perry Steven Tyler Joey Kramer Brad Whitford

GEFFEN RECORDS

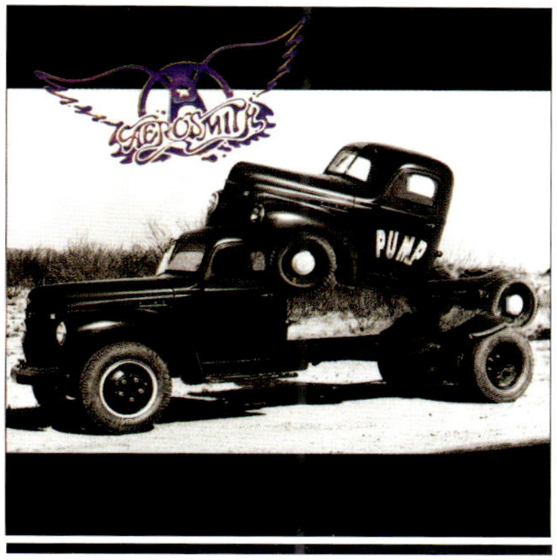

Billboard 200: *Pump* (#5)
Billboard Hot 100: "Love in an Elevator" (#5); "Janie's Got a Gun" (#4); "What It Takes" (#9); "The Other Side" (#22)

Following one of rock's most emotion-charged comebacks, Aerosmith returned to topping the charts with *Pump*.

INFLUENCING A whole generation with a mix of hard rock and R&B, Aerosmith was one of the Seventies' heaviest hitters, elevated to superstardom by "Sweet Emotion," "Dream On," "Walk This Way," "Mama Kin" and "Draw the Line." The band loved the road, but with the notoriety and success of rock's longest party came internal conflicts, substance-abuse problems—flamboyant frontman Steven Tyler and lead guitarist Joe Perry had acquired a nickname, the Toxic Twins—and a messy divorce.

But after years of estrangement, the five members cleaned up their act and came back stronger than ever musically, a tribute to their talent and spirit. 1987's *Permanent Vacation* earned double platinum numbers and three Top 20 hits—"Dude (Looks Like a Lady)," "Angel" and "Rag Doll."

Pump, the band's next album, outdid that performance with contributions from outside songwriters and the production touches of Bruce Fairbairn, who added a horn section and keyboards to tracks, giving substance to what Tyler called the "psycho-acoustic—what's not on the tape but you swear you hear. Aerosmith music has always had that illusion. For this album, I wanted to hear it, so we brought all of these strange instruments, dulcimers and crazy things from all over the world, and jammed."

The dynamics in the music were echoed in the cheekiness and levity of Tyler's words. "Sometimes I wondered what was coming out of my mouth," he allowed with a smile. "A lot of the lyrics are for a 17-year-old—but I'm just going on 20 myself. I figured, don't fight it. When I let the kid out, he stays out—that's why I'm in rock 'n' roll. So I got out of my own way."

Pump generated four hit singles, including "What It Takes" and "The Other Side." The band took home its first Grammy award for "Janie's Got a Gun," a song that surprised some by its social consciousness. "Child abuse is a taboo topic, but I think it should be brought out into the open," Tyler said. "It hurts people, and it's not often given as the cause of someone's troubles. It's like when they say someone died of cancer—no, he didn't. He died of cigarettes."

And Tyler's true-life tale of "Love in an Elevator" weighed in on why getting caught having sex is so exhilarating.

"We were on the road down south, and I had two of Tennessee's finest women escorting me," he revealed. "We got stuck in an elevator somewhere between Nutbush and Lustville discussing the age-old question, 'Who's on first?' While buttons were being pushed, the doors opened, much to my surprise, into the lobby filled with people. Know how a minute can seem like forever? The door was open forever. There was this guy in a tie and jacket waiting to get on—and for me to get off. I did—and he didn't." ■

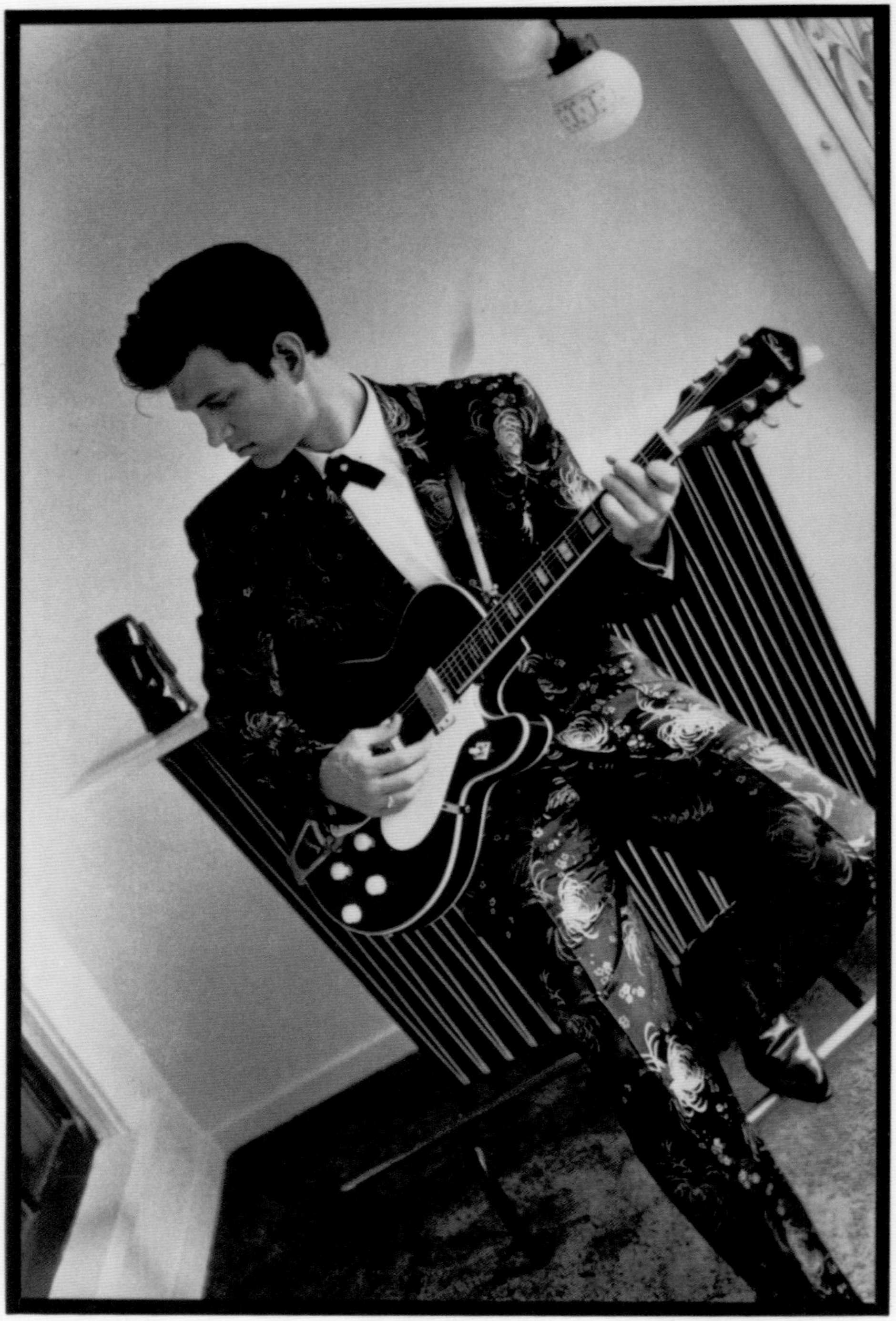

Photo Credit: RICK LOPEZ

Chris Isaak

reprise

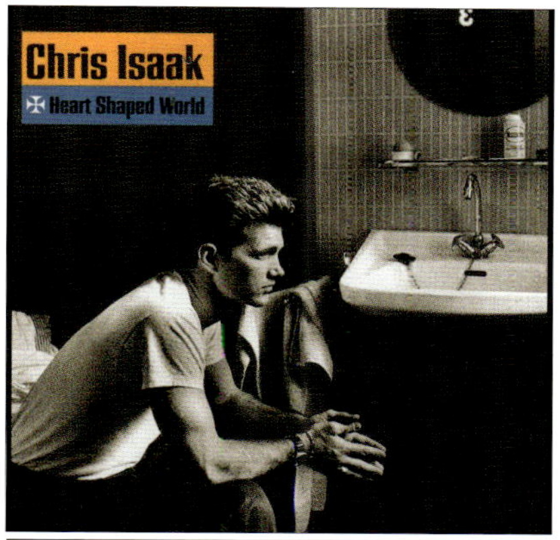

Billboard 200: *Heart Shaped World* (#7)
Billboard Hot 100: "Wicked Game" (#6)

With the belated success of "Wicked Game," Chris Isaak rose rapidly from cult favorite to worldwide phenom.

AN INTENSELY atmospheric collection of love-gone-wrong portraits, *Heart Shaped World*, Chris Isaak's third release, languished on the pop market until the eerily gorgeous "Wicked Game"—possibly the darkest mood piece on the album—gave it a new lease on life. David Lynch would use a hypnotic instrumental version in his 1990 film *Wild at Heart*, exposing the song's otherworldly tremolo-laden guitar riff (played by Isaak's longtime sidekick James Calvin Wilsey) during a car-wreck scene on a desert highway.

An Atlanta radio station found Isaak's vocal on the soundtrack album and began airing "Wicked Game." Besieged by requests, Isaak's record company re-released it as a single. It shot to the top and sold a million copies worldwide, turning Isaak, long a critics' favorite, into a hot property. "I personally loved the song, but I didn't think anybody would be able to play it on the radio because it was so outside of the format," Isaak said. "Once something different gets played, it sounds great. But until it gets played, people act like you handed them a record without a hole in the middle."

Isaak's longing sound drew comparisons to the late Roy Orbison's pure, anguished cry. For most of the six years he had led his ace band Silvertone, Isaak heard about his similarities to Orbison, Elvis Presley, Ricky Nelson and Duane Eddy. Influenced early on by country and western music and crooners, his songs lacked modern production values, but any "roots" identification masked his musical vision, a mix of glossy pop, rock rave-ups and shadowy, introspective ballads.

"Most of the things that I write about aren't stuff I would talk about to my friends—they're deep, important feelings that you don't know what to do with," Isaak mused. "It's not appropriate if you tell people something dark—they say, 'Hey, lighten up, you're bringing me down.' I know I like to be around people that are happy and up. But I also know that people have those feelings of heartache in them. Some tell them to their lover. I tell them to my guitar."

Yet the brooding romantic suggested by his music, his videos (the sensual "Wicked Game" clip set a few fashion trends) and the poses he adopted in photos seemed at odds with the behind-the-scenes Isaak, a bright, silly guy with an off-center wit. He used a string of cheesy plastic tiki patio lights as his sole stage prop. In concert, he preferred donning unconventional attire—he shopped in furniture and auto upholstery outlets for giant floral patterns or metallic satins.

"Offstage, I look like anyone else, but I pick out the material and make all of my onstage clothes," he revealed. "And my mom finds cool stuff. One time she took curtains off the wall to make a suit. I get into it because I know what I want. And if I have somebody else do it, some guy with an accent, he'll charge me $4,000." ■

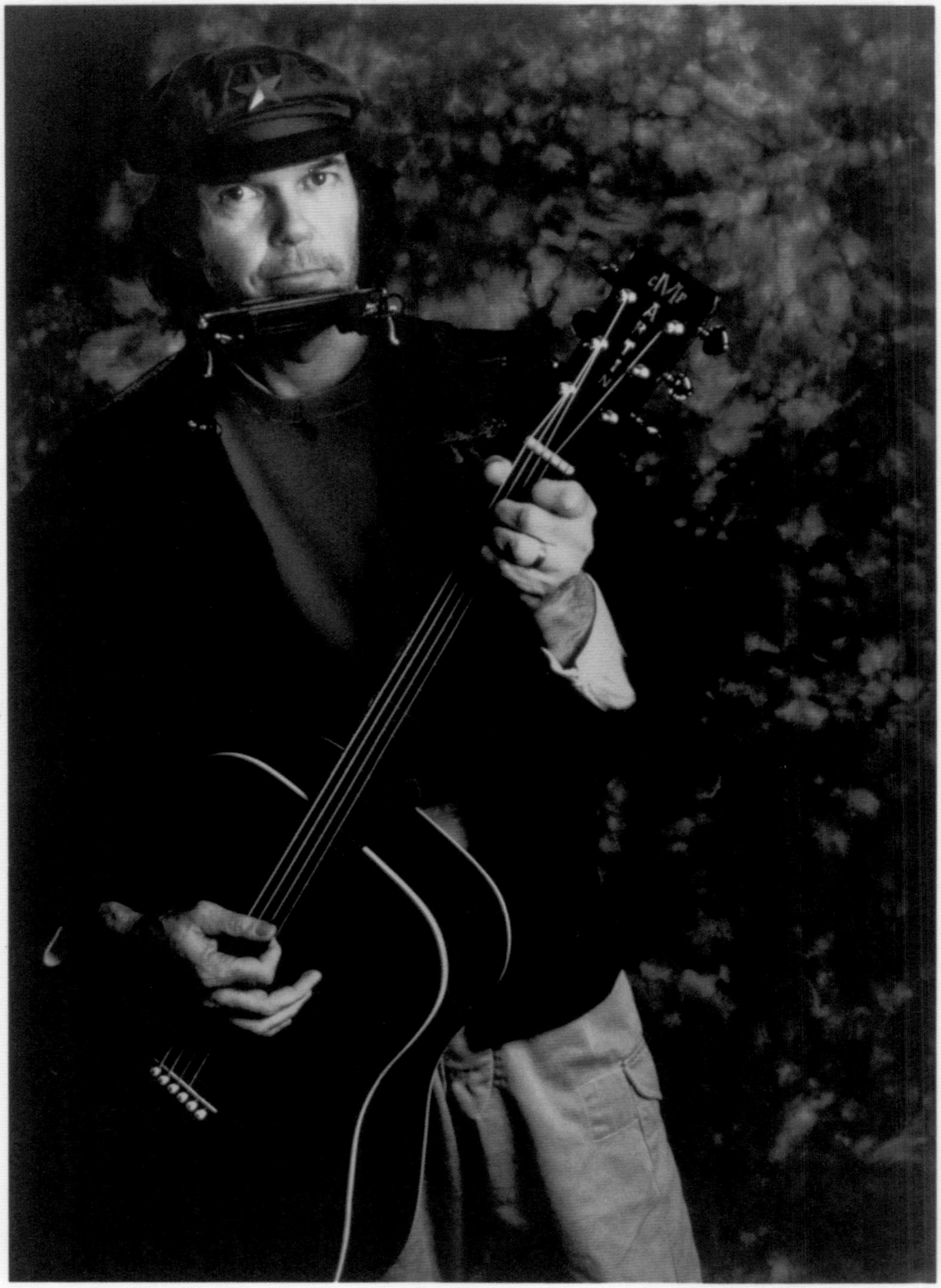

Photo Credit: Ebet Roberts

NEIL YOUNG

reprise

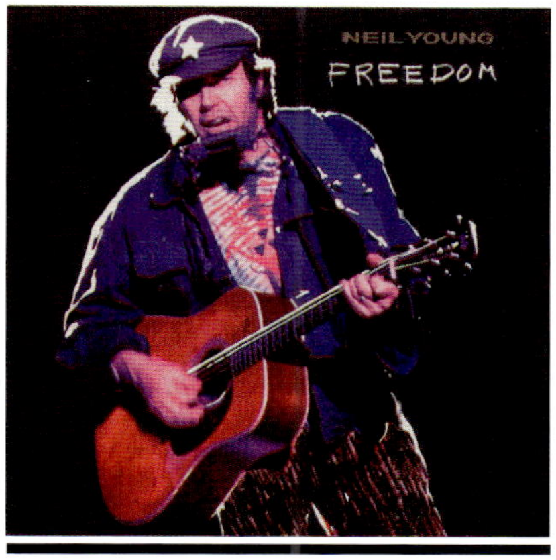

Billboard 200: *Freedom* (#35)

The resonant anthem "Rockin' in the Free World" helped Neil Young figure largely in the public consciousness.

CASTING AROUND with unexpected "experiments," Neil Young frittered away the early part of the Eighties. On *Old Ways* (with the International Harvesters), he took to playing straight country and honky-tonk devoid of irony. On *Everybody's Rockin'* (credited to Neil Young & the Shocking Pinks), he mocked old-fashioned rockabilly.

Those records didn't sell beyond his rapidly shrinking cult. Based on album sales, people preferred Neil Young the rocker.

"The way I like to play it, rock 'n' roll would kill me if I played it all the time—it takes so much out of me, I don't think I could to it 12 months a year for the past 22 years and still be here," Young stated. "So I temper myself by playing other kinds of music, and when I'm just about ready to explode, I go on the road."

His dramatic assessment aside, Young remained a powerfully inventive albeit idiosyncratic figure from the singer-songwriter proliferation of the Seventies. A former label sought punitive and exemplary damages in a suit alleging that Young provided albums that were "musically uncharacteristic of (his) previous records."

But Young's current company was happy—he released *Freedom*, the straight-ahead rock record it had been waiting for him to make. The album was produced by Young and associate Niko Bolas as "the Volume Dealers." The single "Rockin' in the Free World" sported Young's heavily distorted guitar sound.

Part of *Freedom* had been available on an import album, *Eldorado*, which was released in Australia and Japan to coincide with tours. CD copies had been arriving in the US and reportedly selling for $40. Young's American label released portions on *Freedom* to stem the costly import traffic. ■

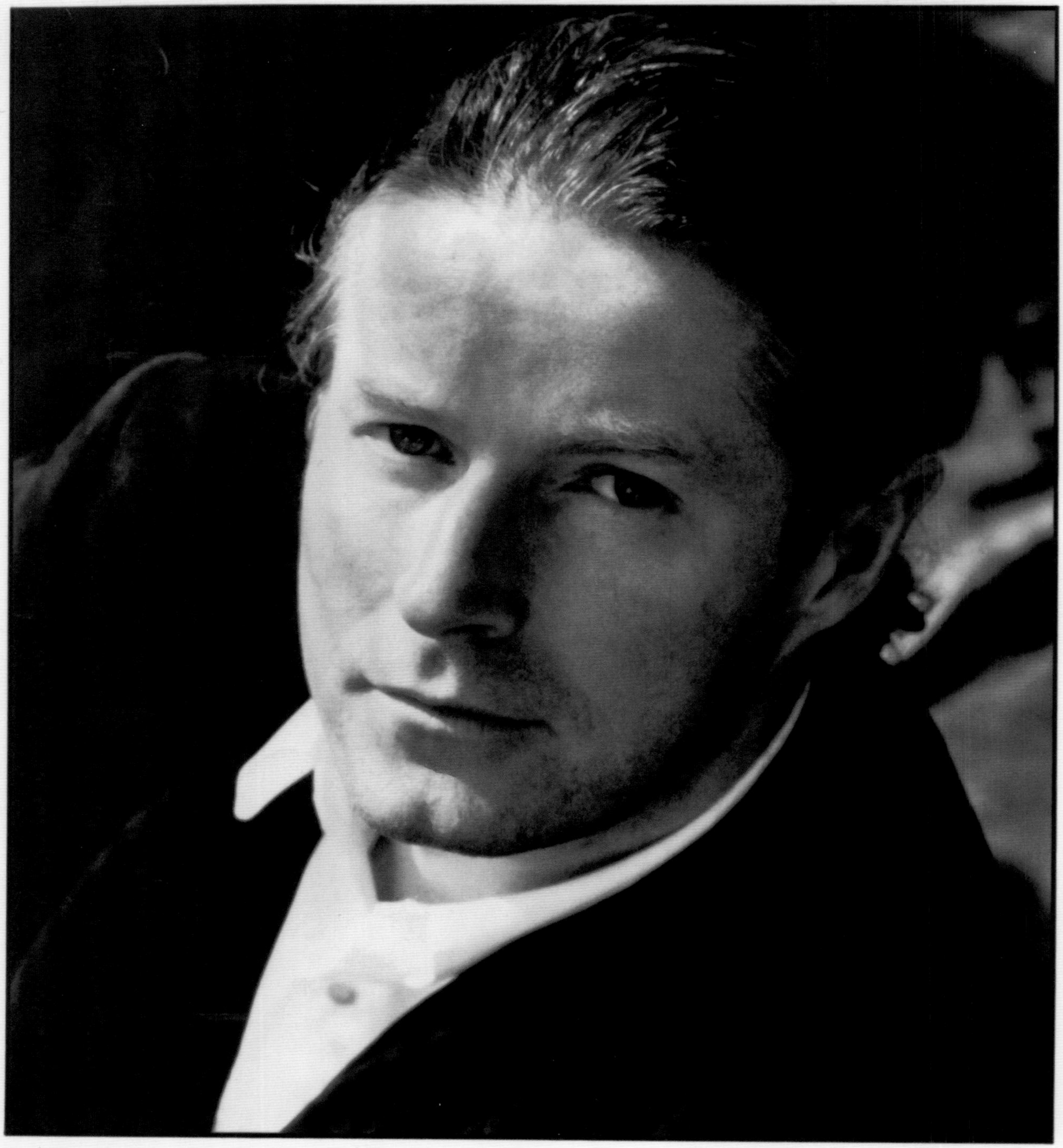

DON HENLEY

GEFFEN RECORDS

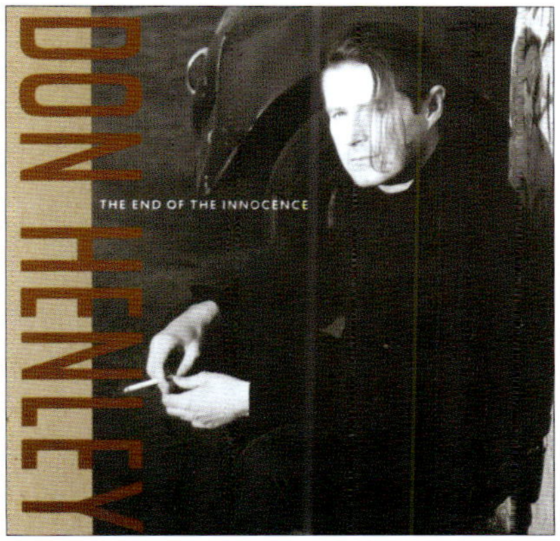

Billboard 200: *The End of the Innocence* (#8)
Billboard Hot 100: "The End of the Innocence" (#8);
"The Last Worthless Evening" (#21); "The Heart of the Matter" (#21);
"How Bad Do You Want It?" (#48); "New York Minute" (#28)

Through his third solo album, *The End of the Innocence*, Don Henley elaborated on his vision of self-reliance.

ACHIEVING A kind of selective anonymity while staking his claim as laid-back observer, Don Henley's name and music were well-known, but his face was not—even though he was a founder of the Eagles, the most successful American music act of the Seventies, with sales of more than 50 million albums worldwide.

Of all the Eagles, who split in 1981, Henley had fared best as a solo act. His 1982 debut, *I Can't Stand Still*, included the #3 hit "Dirty Laundry." His 1984 double-platinum *Building the Perfect Beast* bore three hit singles, "The Boys of Summer" (which earned him a Grammy Award for Best Rock Performance, Male), "All She Wants to Do Is Dance" and "Sunset Grill."

On his first album in five years, *The End of the Innocence*, the self-described iconoclast reflected on embattled relationships and political disenchantment. "The songs have to do with heroes who have feet of clay, who aren't quite what they seem," Henley said. "I am not the answer man, I'm the question man. But I urge people not to be sheep, not to blindly follow leaders—religious, political, what have you. People ought to listen to their own voices more." He laughed. "And the voices of rock stars, I guess."

Henley produced the album with Danny Kortchmar, and there was no overstating the guitarist's importance to his music. "He churns out tracks in the basement studio of his home, and I marry them with ideas I have," Henley explained. "I'm a news junkie—CNN is my MTV. So I write on scraps of paper and spread them all over my house. I have a bad habit of starting three or four songs on one legal pad. When it's time to do a record, I gather that stuff up, try to categorize it and make some sense of it."

A variety of other artists, including Edie Brickell, Melissa Etheridge, Take 6 and members of Tom Petty's and Keith Richards' bands, also lent a hand to the album. "I actively seek out outside writers," Henley said. "I think it's good to bring contrast to a record, so it doesn't get monotonous. Now people say it's either an eclectic album that covers all the bases, or it's disjointed."

The graceful, elegiac title track, which won another Grammy, was co-written by Henley and Bruce Hornsby, while on the defiant "I Will Not Go Quietly," Axl Rose of Guns N' Roses delivered a spectacular background vocal. Much had been made about 1989 being the year of the rock 'n' roll dinosaur, with old guys trotting out their old songs for fun and profit. But for Henley, the issue wasn't whether rock 'n' roll should have a mandatory retirement age, it was whether an artist retained his passion for the music.

"Painters and novelists are supposed to get better with age, and I'm still getting better," he said. "I'm looking forward to doing my best work in my 40s. I'm getting more concise in what I want to say, making it clear so that others can understand. I'm starting to look back and see that I have a nice legacy of tunes, but I'm not done by a long shot." ■

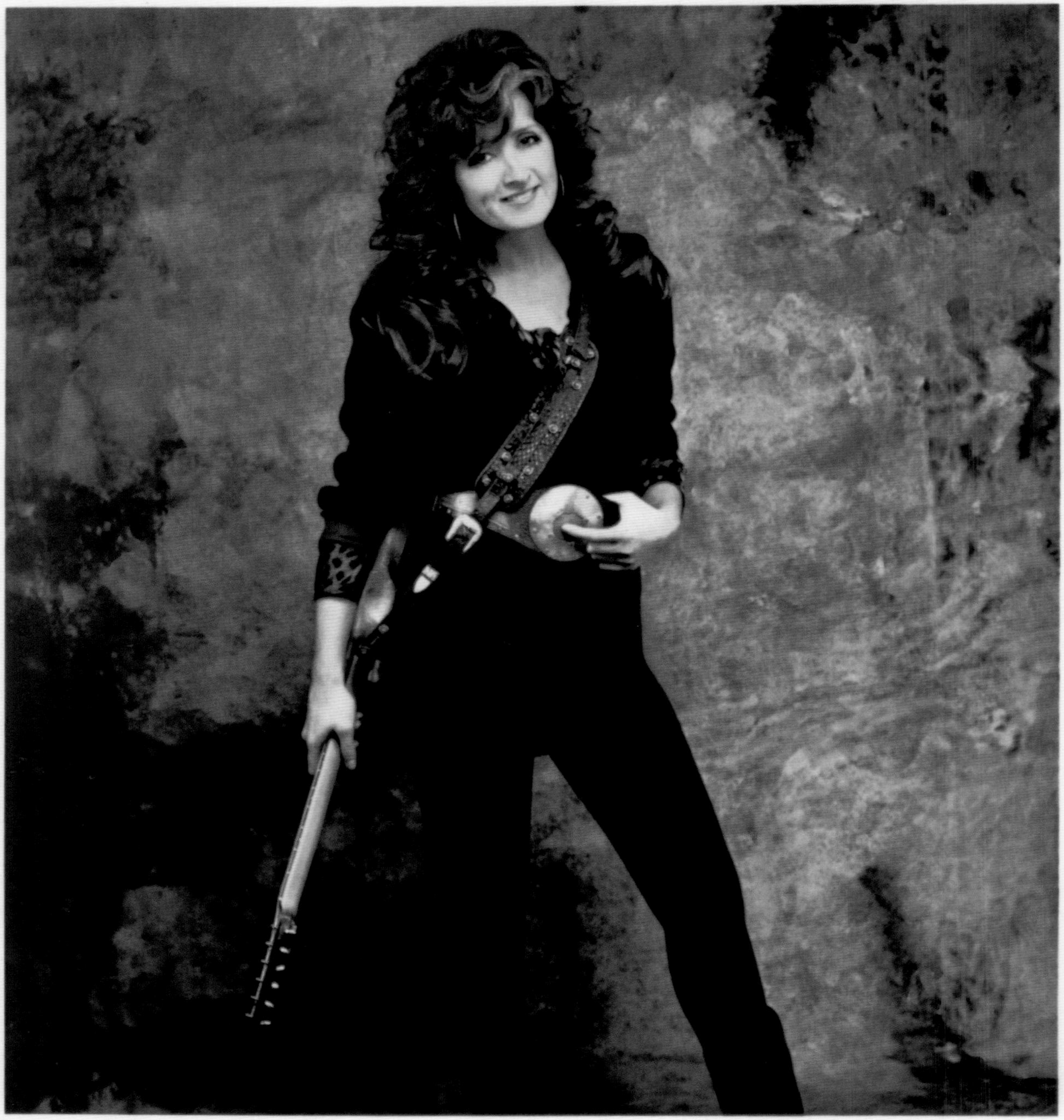

Photo: Deborah Frankel / 1989

BONNIE RAITT

Capitol Records

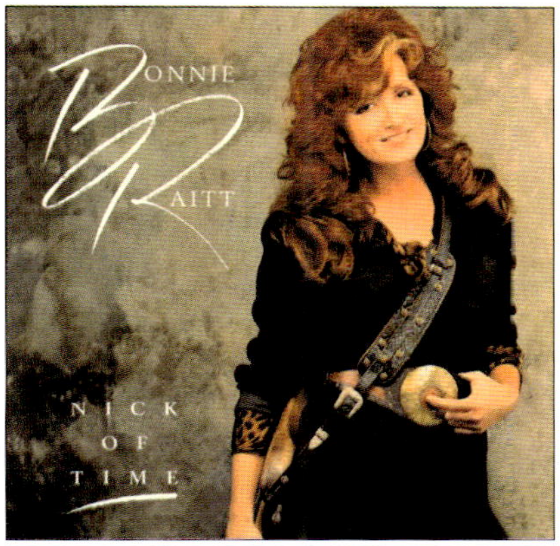

Billboard 200: *Nick of Time* (No. 1)
Billboard Hot 100: "Have a Heart" (#49); "Nick of Time" (#92)

After years of critical approbation, Bonnie Raitt took a quantum leap commercially with her *Nick of Time* album.

IT WAS a gratifying period for Bonnie Raitt, as her *Nick of Time* topped the charts and earned praise as her best album ever. "And it's so convenient, with the buzzwords that are being attached, words like 'comeback,' 'the year of women in rock,' 'clean and sober,' 'where's Prince?' and '*Nick of Time* as harbinger of middle age,'" the feisty blues guitarist laughed.

The "comeback" angle didn't hold up. In 20 years, Raitt had never stopped playing the eclectic blend of folk, soul and R&B that first landed her in the Seventies pop mainstream. She was dropped from her recording contract in 1983, "but it's not like I went away and had a vacation," she said. "For a while my albums got listed in the 'miscellaneous female folk, M to Z' bins. Now I've got my own divider!"

Raitt partly credited *Nick of Time*'s mainstream success to changing times (the "year of women in rock" angle). "People like Tracy Chapman have opened up the musical climate. This record couldn't have gotten played a few years ago."

But Raitt had helped change her rock 'n' roll mama persona as well. She was going to make an album with Prince (the "where's Prince?" angle). "We like the same kind of funky, soulful music," she said. "R&B is R&B—it's just different treatments, drum sequencers or real drums."

The project fell through, but Raitt discovered that hard partying was beating her up too much. So she stopped drinking and drugging (the "clean and sober" angle). Clearheaded, she made *Nick of Time* with producer Don Was of Was (Not Was), who brought Raitt's plaintive/brassy vocals and stellar slide guitar work to center stage. The album marked a return to her roots, and the stripped-down production bolstered a great batch of songs that genuinely reflected her feelings at that point in time.

John Hiatt's "Thing Called Love" and Bonnie Hayes' "Love Letter" set the tone on radio—"I get played on 'greasy listening' formats," Raitt joked—but the centerpiece of *Nick of Time* was her own title track, an unsentimental look at aging and its attendant fears (the "*Nick of Time* as harbinger of middle age" angle).

"It's easier to be an interpreter than to come up with an album of your own brilliant stuff," she admitted. "I've only written 10 songs that have made it to record, when I can't find anything that quite nails a feeling I have. I wanted to write something that wasn't based on being involved with one person, the exhorting-a-no-good-man-to-get-it-together that I always write. So I took a quiet, self-imposed vacation to celebrate that vantage point—being this age, being straight." ■

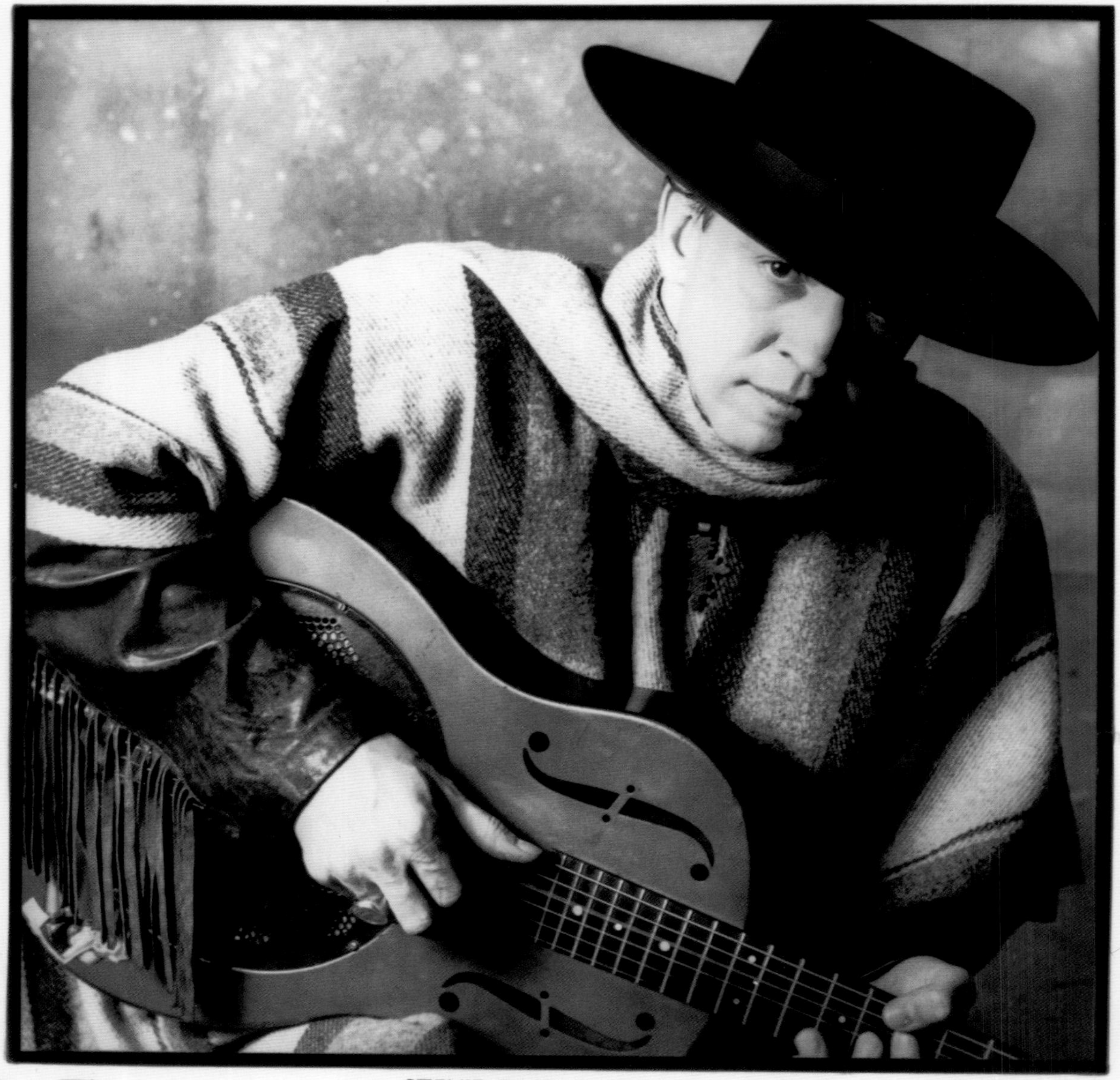

Photo: Alan Messer

STEVIE RAY VAUGHAN

STEVIE RAY VAUGHAN AND DOUBLE TROUBLE

STRIKE FORCE
ARTIST MANAGEMENT

Epic

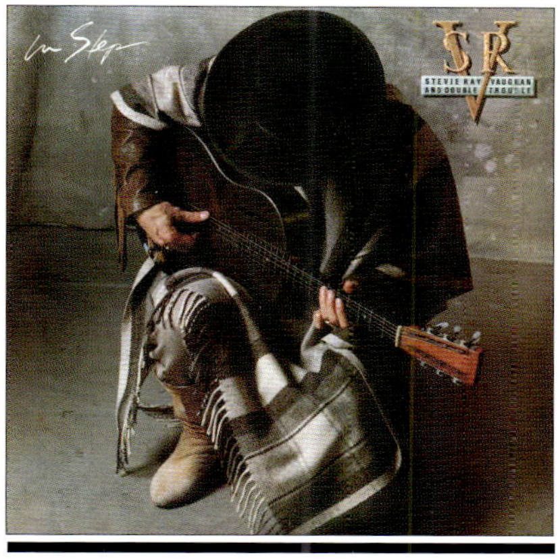

Billboard 200: *In Step* (#33)

Stevie Ray Vaughan's magnificent *In Step* earned the Grammy Award for Best Contemporary Blues Recording.

A BLUES fanatic, Stevie Ray Vaughan remained a genuinely nice person through his ascent to stardom. But while his first four albums were certified gold and created a mass audience for undiluted blues-rock without studio frills, in his mind they were marred by his drinking and drug problem—a situation exacerbated by his 200-plus concerts a year. Vaughan's passion was Seagram's Crown Royal, and he had a bottle in his dressing room for every gig.

His addiction eventually landed him in a rehab center in 1985. A 12-step program provided him with guidelines, and it was no longer Crown Royal backstage, but Royal Crown—as in cola. *In Step*, the best record yet from the Austin guitar whiz, included his No. 1 rock hit "Crossfire" and "The House Is Rockin'," a mighty showcase for Vaughan's aggressive guitar and the strongest singing he'd ever mustered. A few of the songs—the incisive "Tightrope," the weighty "Wall of Denial"—referenced his troubles.

"I'm no saint," he said. "I just want to destroy the myth that rock stars have to do drugs. It's just not true. I think everybody runs into the 'Wall of Denial'—it's one of the hardest things to recognize. I learned about it when I was in treatment, but I'd seen it in people all my life. It's a survival thing in a way. The lyrics talk about all kinds of denials, but for me there were things that kept me from facing up to what was going on."

Vaughan brought his guitar mastery of blues, R&B and roots rock to fans all over the world, but such hard work wasn't a source of burnout, but a big part of his remedy. Never a talkative presence onstage, he started taking the opportunity to point out the differences between his bleary-eyed performing days and his good health.

"There are a lot of party animals at my shows, and I've been one of them," he mused. "That's why I talk about it as much as I can. It's not a preaching deal, I just try to show them where it all got me. Folks come to me all the time who got help and quit because they heard me say something. As long as one person does that, I won't shut up." ■

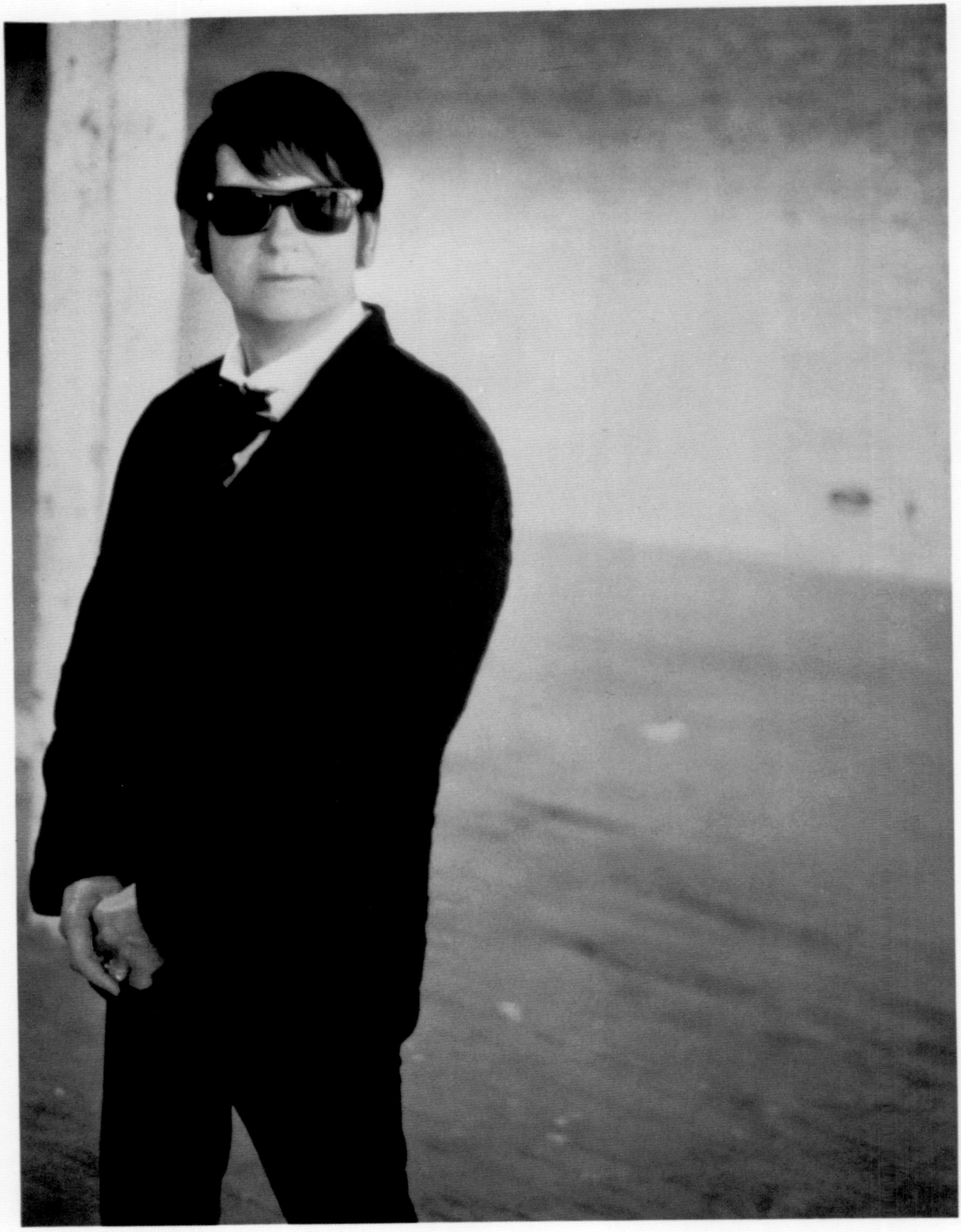

Photo Credit: Glen Erler

ROY ORBISON

Virgin

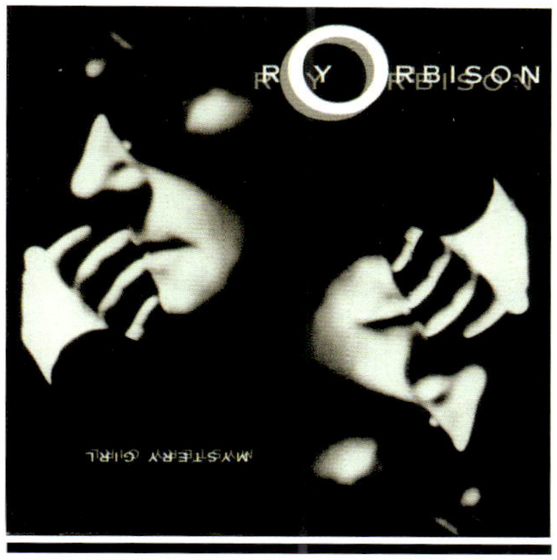

Billboard 200: *Mystery Girl* (#5)
Billboard Hot 100: "You Got It" (#9)

A deeply affirming album of beauty and depth, *Mystery Girl* stood as Roy Orbison's closing musical statement.

THE IMPASSIONED "Only the Lonely," released in 1960, first showcased Roy Orbison's transcendent, expressive, soaring voice. He poured his heart and soul into 21 more Top 40 classics—"Running Scared," "Crying," "Dream Baby (How Long Must I Dream)," "In Dreams," "Mean Woman Blues," "It's Over" and "Oh, Pretty Woman" among them.

But only in later years had his contributions to rock 'n' roll been fully appreciated. Bruce Springsteen inducted the singer into the Rock and Roll Hall of Fame in 1987. The acclaimed Cinemax special *Roy Orbison and Friends - A Black and White Night* featured such stars as Springsteen and Elvis Costello, Jackson Browne, Tom Waits, Bonnie Raitt and k.d. lang playing in his band. The 1963 hit "In Dreams" was used for a memorable scene in the David Lynch film *Blue Velvet*.

Orbison was high on the charts with a hit album and single as a member of the Traveling Wilburys, the supergroup he co-founded with George Harrison, Tom Petty, Jeff Lynne and Bob Dylan, when he died of a heart attack at age 52 on December 6, 1988. Before his untimely death, the gentle legend summed up the attention and belated recognition.

"All of these events have helped me put things in a perspective," he said. "Looking back on the history of rock 'n' roll, most people originally thought it was going to be a fad—I didn't know how long it was going to stay around in years. I thought the things that influenced Elvis and me would probably influence other people. We didn't change that much, we just put a few things together."

Orbison's passing came while he was at another career peak—he had just completed recording *Mystery Girl*, his first album of new material in a decade, produced by Lynne. Orbison had written between his tour dates, collaborating with some of rock's most illustrious names, among them Springsteen, Costello, Petty and Harrison as well as Steve Cropper, T-Bone Burnett and Will Jennings.

Orbison's three-octave voice rang out with the same power that galvanized fans more than it had twenty years earlier. "You Got It," co-written with Lynne and Petty, was released as a single, becoming Orbison's first Top 10 hit in nearly 25 years. The evocative ballad "She's a Mystery to Me," written by U2's Bono and The Edge, was an exquisite setting for Orbison's vocal prowess. Such homage made Orbison realize the benefits of his elder statesman of rock 'n' roll status.

"I thought I was more important than I was acknowledged to be, than I was led to believe, but I didn't know," he said. "But now I know I've taken a path to get to this point, and now there's another path leading from that." ■

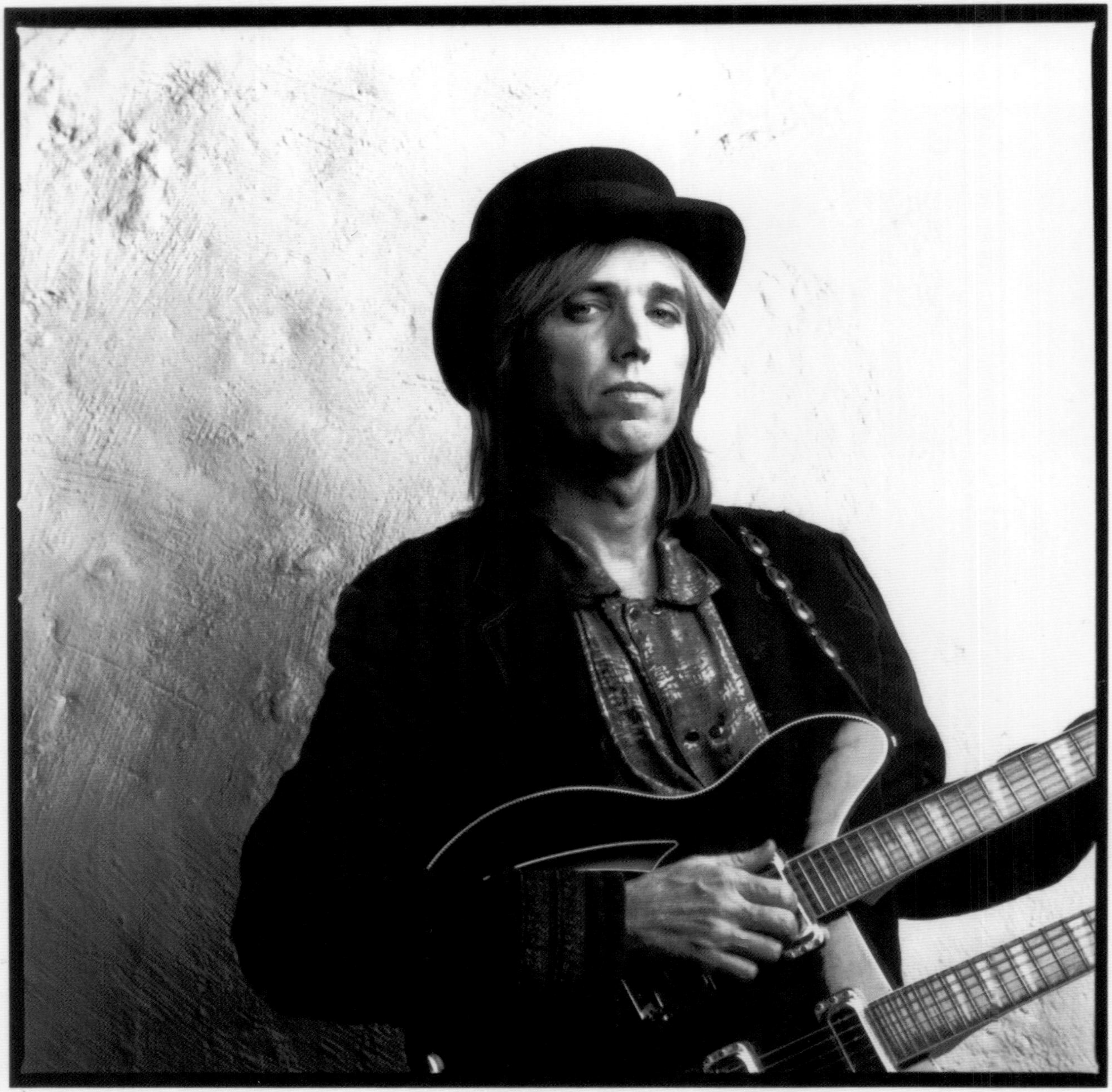

Photo Credit: Aaron Rapoport

FULL MOON FEVER

TOM PETTY

3/89

MCA RECORDS

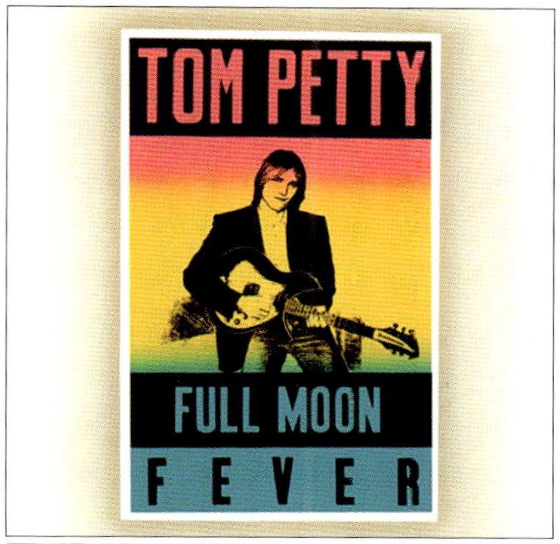

Billboard 200: *Full Moon Fever* (#3)
Billboard Hot 100: "I Won't Back Down" (#12); "Runnin' Down a Dream" (#23); "Free Fallin'" (#7); "A Face in the Crowd" (#46)

Full Moon Fever, a Tom Petty solo album, marked a new creative and commercial zenith for the veteran rocker.

IN FIVE years, Tom Petty's luck had taken some unusual turns. Frustrated at his inability to finish 1985's *Southern Accents* album, he punched a wall and broke his hand. While he was on tour in 1987, a fire destroyed his Los Angeles home. But there had finally been a happy accident in Petty's life—*Full Moon Fever* marked the biggest selling album of his career. He had enjoyed mainstream rock success for a dozen years with his band the Heartbreakers, but his first solo work was smart, witty and thoroughly entertaining.

"And the strangest thing is that it wasn't planned at all," Petty said. "It was a casual project that took months to complete. The way it has been received has given me a wonderful feeling. I'm proud of it because it's something I did sheerly for my own enjoyment. I never dreamed it would be a big hit record."

Full Moon Fever had its beginning in late 1987, when Petty crossed paths with Jeff Lynne of ELO, whom he had met backstage at a Bob Dylan/Tom Petty & the Heartbreakers stadium show in England. "I didn't plan on seeing him again," Petty recalled. "But back in Los Angeles I was at a red light, and there's Jeff in the next car over. It turned out he lived in my neighborhood. We didn't plan on working together musically; we just started playing around at home over the holidays."

Full Moon Fever was mostly recorded before some interesting musical relationships resulted in the Traveling Wilburys, teaming Petty and Lynne with Dylan, George Harrison and Roy Orbison. Because of that commitment, work on the album temporarily came to a halt, and Petty returned to the studio with Lynne in late 1988 to finish.

Harrison played guitar and sang backing vocals on the single "I Won't Back Down." "It's a very honest song," Petty mused. "That one was so much like me that it almost put me off for a minute. But you can't fight things that just pop out of you, either." The album also spawned the classic hits "Free Fallin'" and "Runnin' Down a Dream."

Petty's approach to the acoustic guitar was that it could be "a real rocking thing," he said. "If you're a fan of rhythm guitar the way I am, it's a thrill to hear the acoustic guitar as an anchor and the power instrument in a song, rather than making it folksy and introspective. Jeff and I would write together on acoustic guitars. When we'd go to the studio, we'd try to put it down exactly the way we'd been doing it on the couch."

Full Moon Fever didn't signal the end of Tom Petty & the Heartbreakers—nearly all the members showed up in cameo roles, and Mike Campbell co-wrote, co-produced and engineered the album while firing up songs with his ringing electric guitar. The band toured the country, playing material from *Full Moon Fever* in concert.

"They wanted some new songs to play as badly as I did," Petty laughed. "I keep thinking I'm going to be sick of them, but every time we play, it amazes me how good we are. There wouldn't be any point in going solo, because you can't put together a band like the Heartbreakers." ■

ON RECORD VOL.11 1989

DRIVEN BY a love of music, I've led a blessed existence writing about my passion, interviewing thousands of musicians in hotel lobbies and backstage areas. But I also conducted many phone interviews with acts doing tour publicity. Those conversations could be, well, a different animal than face-to-face encounters.

Two of my more memorable instances came in 1989, when the Who was on tour performing selections from *Quadrophenia* and *Tommy*.

I had the opportunity to speak with guitarist Pete Townshend—journalistic objectivity aside, one of my all-time idols (his early written essays on the cultural and spiritual implications of rock music were more insightful than any critic's). The catch—I was told he would have to call me after a concert in Atlanta, two hours later than in my Mountain time zone. Would that be alright?

Well, duh. I sat in my non-air-conditioned home office on a hot summer night until the phone rang at midnight. It turned out to be the perfect circumstance to chat. The legend was in a quiet, reflective mood—alone in his hotel room after the gig, the adrenaline worn off, nothing scheduled on the back end. We embarked on a remarkably thoughtful conversation, one of the highlights of my career.

Except I kept hearing this *snik-snik-snik* sound behind me. I tried to block it out—what could it be, a paper flapping in the fan?—but after many minutes of trying to focus on my dialogue, I swiveled around in my chair. And there was my beloved black lab, Syd, on the floor…loudly licking herself to beat the band. *Snik-snik-snik.*

For chrissakes. I held the phone tightly to my ear and covered the other ear with my free hand. But I felt akin to the narrator in Edgar Allan Poe's *The Tell-Tale Heart*. *Snik-snik-snik.* I finally turned around again; by now Syd had worked herself into a trance, eyes closed in her own state of bliss. *Snik-snik-snik.*

While listening to Pete's every word, I grabbed a paperback and threw it across the room at Syd. She awoke with a startle, looked up at me, put her head down and passed out. I was free at last to work without the aid of her soundtrack.

Another member of the Brown menagerie got in the act when I spoke with singer Roger Daltrey a few months later. From the moment I picked up the phone, my cockatiel, Flop, kept sounding off. *Chirp-squawk-screech.* "Are you in a zoo?" Roger finally asked. Sheepishly, I explained my circumstance, and he exclaimed, "I have several cockatiels! Aren't they amazing birds?" And our chat took an entertaining turn. When a local radio station played the recorded interview, my phone rang off the hook, with friends exclaiming, "Hey, I just heard Flop on the air!"

More important things happened to humankind in 1989. Paul McCartney released an album exclusively in the USSR; bootlegs of *Choba B CCP* sold for as much as $1,000 in the US. Madonna's "Like a Prayer" music video attracted criticism from religious groups and praise for busting taboos. The Rolling Stones opened their Steel Wheels North American tour. And I got to interview artists, listen to all the records, go to all the concerts and pore over press kits. I was and am a lucky boy. Please allow me to share. — **G. Brown**

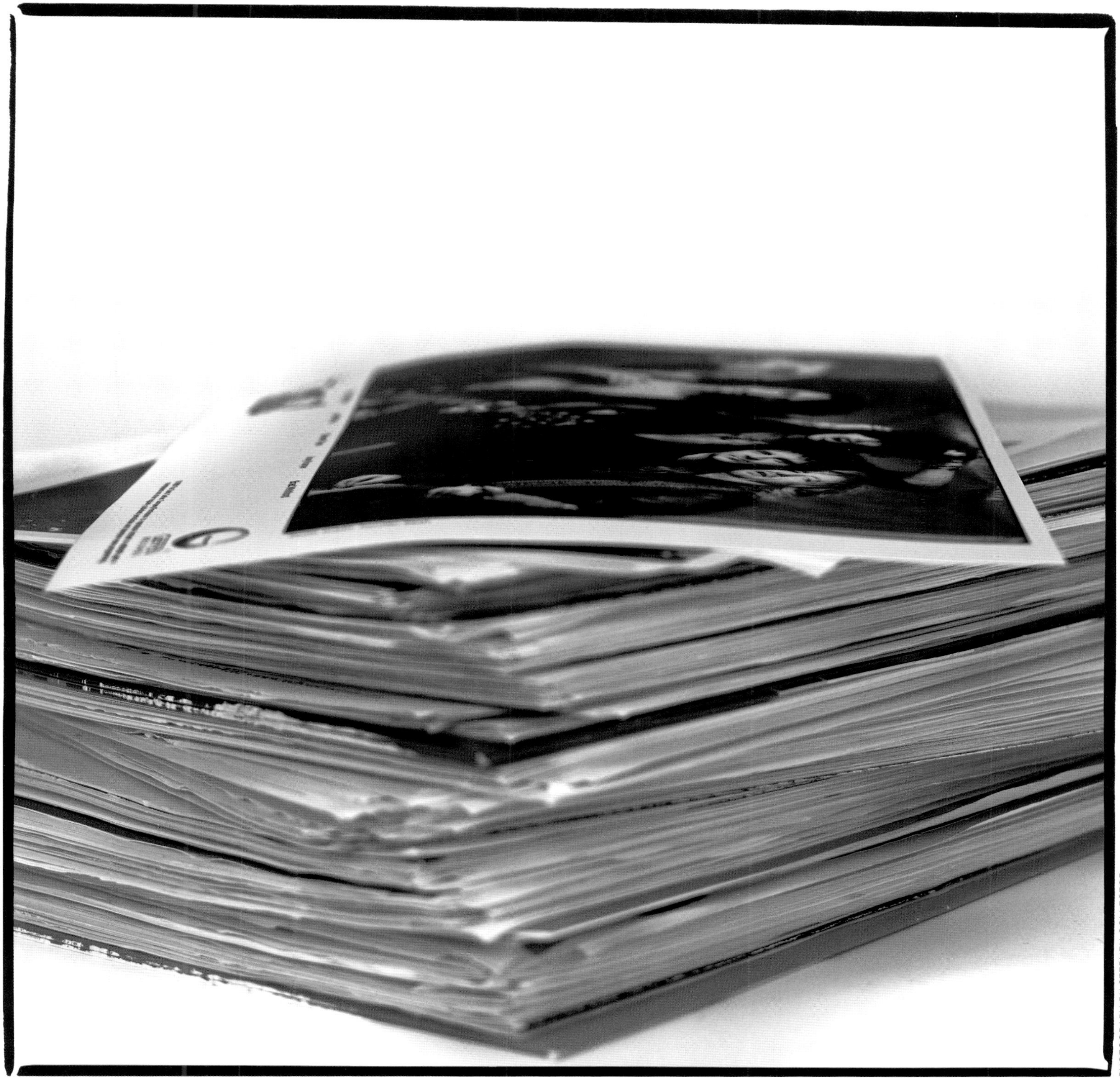

PHOTOGRAPH BY STEPHEN COLLECTOR

CONTENTS

ON RECORD ENTRIES ARE NOT ORDERED ALPHABETICALLY, BUT ORGANIZED INTUITIVELY—A MIXTURE OF SEGUES BY MUSICAL GENRE OR STYLE.